Contents of This Manual

Explanation of the Cost Tables

This manual shows construction or replacement costs for a wide variety of residential, commercial, industrial, public, agricultural and military buildings. For your convenience and to minimize the chance of an error, all the cost and reference information you need for each building type is brought together on two or three pages. After reading pages 4 to 6, you should be able to turn directly to any building type and create an error-free estimate or appraisal of the construction or replacement cost.

The costs are per square foot of floor area for the basic building and additional costs for optional or extra components that differ from building to building. Building shape, floor area, design elements, materials used, and overall quality influence the basic structure cost. These and other cost variables are isolated for the building types. Components included in the basic square foot cost are listed with each building type. Instructions for using the basic building costs are included above the cost tables. These instructions include a list of components that may have to be added to the basic cost to find the total cost for your structure.

The figures in this manual are intended to reflect the amount that would be paid by the first user of a building completed in mid 2012.

Costs in the tables include all construction costs: labor, material, equipment, plans, building permit, supervision, overhead and profit. Cost tables do not include land value, site development costs, government mandated fees (other than the building permit) or the cost of modifying unusual soil conditions or grades. Construction expense may represent as much as 60% or as little as 40% of the cost to the first building owner. Site preparation, utility lines, government fees and mandates, finance cost and marketing are not part of the construction cost and may be as much as 20% of the cost to the first building owner.

Building Quality

Structures vary widely in quality and the quality of construction is the most significant variable in the finished cost. For estimating purposes the structure should be placed in one or more quality classes. These classes are numbered from 1 which is the highest quality generally encountered. Each section of this manual has a page describing typical specifications which define the quality class.

Each number class has been assigned a word description (such as best, good, average or low) for convenience and to help avoid possible errors.

The quality specifications do not reflect some design features and construction details that can make a building both more desirable and more costly. When substantially more than basic design elements are present, and when these elements add significantly to the cost, it is appropriate to classify the quality of the building as higher than would be warranted by the materials used in construction.

Many structures do not fall into a single class and have features of two quality classes. The tables have "half classes" which apply to structures which have some features of one class and some features of a higher or lower class. Classify a building into a "half class" when the quality elements are fairly evenly divided between two classes. Generally, quality elements do not vary widely in a single building. For example, it would be unusual to find a top quality single family residence with minimum quality roof cover. The most weight should be given to quality elements that have the greatest cost. For example, the type of wall and roof framing or the quality of interior finish are more significant than the roof cover or bathroom wall finish. Careful evaluation may determine that certain structures fall into two distinct classes. In this case, the cost of each part of the building should be evaluated separately.

Building Shapes

Shape classification considers any cost differences that arise from variations in building outline. Shape classification considerations vary somewhat with different building types. Where the building shape often varies widely between buildings and shape has a significant effect on the building cost, basic building costs are given for several shapes. Use the table that most closely matches the shape of the building you are evaluating. If the shape falls near the division between two basic building cost tables, it is appropriate to average the square foot cost from those two tables.

$63.00

2012
NATIONAL
BUILDING COST
MANUAL

36th Edition

Edited by
Gary Moselle

Craftsman Book Company
6058 Corte del Cedro / P.O. Box 6500 / Carlsbad, CA 92018

Looking for Other Construction Reference Manuals?

Craftsman has the books to fill your needs. Call 1-800-829-8123 or write to:
Craftsman Book Company, P.O. Box 6500, Carlsbad, CA 92018
for a **Free Catalog** of over 100 books, including how-to manuals,
annual cost books, and estimating software.
Visit our Web site: http://www.craftsman-book.com

Download all of Craftsman's most popular costbooks for one low price with the
Craftsman Site License. http://www.CraftsmanSiteLicense.com

Cover design by Bill Grote
Illustrations by Laura Knight, Devona Quindoy
© 2011 Craftsman Book Company
Portions © 2011 Saylor Publications, Inc.
ISBN 978-1-57218-256-1
Published October 2011 for the year 2012

Explanation of the Cost Tables

Area of Buildings

The basic building cost tables reflect the fact that larger buildings generally cost less per square foot than smaller buildings. The cost tables are based on square foot areas which include the following:

1. All floor area within and including the exterior walls of the main building.

2. Inset areas such as vestibules, entrances or porches outside of the exterior wall but under the main roof.

3. Any enclosed additions, annexes or lean-tos with a square foot cost greater than three-fourths of the square foot cost of the main building.

Select the basic building cost listed below the area which falls closest to the actual area of your building. If the area of your building falls nearly midway between two listed building areas, it is appropriate to average the square foot costs for the listed areas.

Wall Heights

Building costs are based on the wall heights given in the instructions for each building cost table. Wall height for the various floors of a building are computed as follows: The basement is measured from the bottom of floor slab to the bottom of the first floor slab or joist. The main or first floor extends from the bottom of the first floor slab or joist to the top of the roof slab or ceiling joist. Upper floors are measured from the top of the floor slab or floor joist to the top of the roof slab or ceiling joist. These measurements may be illustrated as follows:

Other Adjustments

A common wall exists when two buildings share one wall. Common wall adjustments are made by deducting the in-place cost of the exterior wall finish plus one-half of the in-place cost of the structural portion of the common wall area.

If an owner has no ownership in a wall, the in-place cost of the exterior wall finish plus the in-place cost of the structural portion of the wall should be deducted from the total building costs. Suggested common wall and no wall ownership costs are included for many of the building types.

Some square foot costs include the cost of expensive veneer finishes on the entire perimeter wall. When these buildings butt against other buildings, adjustments should be made for the lack of this finish. Where applicable, linear foot cost deductions are provided.

The square foot costs in this manual are based on composite costs of total buildings including usual work room or storage areas. They are intended to be applied on a 100% basis to the total building area even though certain areas may or may not have interior finish. Only in rare instances will it be necessary to modify the square foot cost of a portion of a building.

Multiple story buildings usually share a common roof structure and cover, a common foundation and common floor or ceiling structures. The costs of these components are included in the various floor levels as follows:

Square foot costs of most building design types must be adjusted if the actual wall height differs from the listed wall height. Wall height adjustment tables are included for buildings requiring this adjustment. Wall height adjustment tables list square foot costs for a foot of difference in perimeter wall height of buildings of various areas. The amount applicable to the actual building area is added or deducted for each foot of difference from the basic wall height.

Buildings such as residences, medical-dental buildings, funeral homes and convalescent hospitals usually have a standard 8-foot ceiling height except in chapels or day room areas. If a significant cost difference exists due to a wall height variation, this factor should be considered in establishing the quality class.

Explanation of the Cost Tables

The first or main floor includes the cost of a floor structure built at ground level, foundation costs for a one-story building, a complete ceiling and roof structure, and a roof cover. The basement includes the basement floor structure and the difference between the cost of the first floor structure built at ground level and its cost built over a basement. The second floor includes the difference between the cost of a foundation for a one-story building and the cost of a foundation for a two-story building and the cost of the second story floor structure.

Location Adjustments

The figures in this manual are intended as national averages for metropolitan areas of the United States. Use the information on page 7 to adapt the basic building costs to any area listed. Frequently building costs outside metropolitan areas are 2% to 6% lower if skilled, productive, lower cost labor is available in the area. The factors on page 7 can be applied to nearly all the square foot costs and some of the "additional" costs in this book.

Temporary working conditions in any community can affect construction and replacement costs. Construction which must be done under deadline pressure or in adverse weather conditions or after a major fire, flood, or hurricane or in a thin labor market can temporarily inflate costs 25% to 50%. Conditions such as these are usually temporary and affect only a limited area. But the higher costs are real and must be considered, no matter how limited the area and how transient the condition.

Depreciation

Depreciation is the loss in value of a structure from all causes and is caused primarily by three forms of obsolescence: (1) physical (2) functional, and (3) economic.

Physical obsolescence is the deterioration of building components such as paint, carpets or roofing. Much of this deterioration is totally curable. The physical life tables on pages 43, 235 and 269 assume normal physical obsolescence. Good judgment is required to evaluate how deferred maintenance or rehabilitation will reduce or extend the anticipated physical life of a building.

Functional obsolescence is due to some deficiency or flaw in the building. For example, too few bathrooms for the number of bedrooms or an exceptionally high ceiling can reduce the life expectancy of a residence. Some functional obsolescence can be cured. The physical life tables do not consider functional obsolescence.

Economic obsolescence is caused by conditions that occur off site and are beyond control of the owner. Examples of economic obsolescence include a store in an area of declining economic activity or obsolescence caused by governmental regulation (such as a change in zoning). Because this kind of obsolescence is particularly difficult to measure, it is not considered in the physical life tables.

"Effective age" considers all forms of depreciation. It may be less than chronological age, if recently remodeled or improved, or more than the actual age, if deterioration is particularly bad. Though effective age is not considered in the physical life tables, it may yield a better picture of a structure's life than the actual physical age. Once the effective age is determined, considering physical, functional and economic deterioration, use the percent good tables on pages 43, 235 or 269 to determine the present value of a depreciated building. Present value is the result of multiplying the replacement cost (found by using the cost tables) by the appropriate percent good.

Limitations

This manual will be a useful reference for anyone who has to develop budget estimates or replacement costs for buildings. Anyone familiar with construction estimating understands that even very competent estimators with complete working drawings, full specifications and precise labor and material costs can disagree on the cost of a building. Frequently exhaustive estimates for even relatively simple structures can vary 10% or more. The range of competitive bids on some building projects is as much as 20%. Estimating costs is not an exact science and there's room for legitimate disagreement on what the "right" cost is. This manual can not help you do in a few minutes what skilled estimators may not be able to do in many hours. This manual will help you determine a reasonable replacement or construction cost for most buildings. It is not intended as a substitute for judgment or as a replacement for sound professional practice, but should prove a valuable aid to developing an informed opinion of value.

Area Modification Factors

Construction costs are higher in some cities than in other cities. Add or deduct the percentage shown on this page or page 8 to adapt the costs in this book to your job site. Adjust your estimated total project cost by the percentage shown for the appropriate city in this table to find your total estimated cost. Where 0% is shown it means no modification is required. Factors for Canada adjust to Canadian dollars.

These percentages were compiled by comparing the construction cost of buildings in nearly 600 communities throughout North America. Because these percentages are based on completed projects, they consider all construction cost variables, including labor, equipment and material cost, labor productivity, climate, job conditions and markup.

Modification factors are listed alphabetically by state and city, followed by the first three digits of the postal zip code.

These percentages are composites of many costs and will not necessarily be accurate when estimating the cost of any particular part of a building. But when used to modify costs for an entire structure, they should improve the accuracy of your estimates.

Alabama Average		-6%
Anniston	362	-10%
Auburn	368	-9%
Bellamy	369	-9%
Birmingham	350-352	2%
Dothan	363	-7%
Evergreen	364	-14%
Gadsden	359	-8%
Huntsville	358	-4%
Jasper	355	-15%
Mobile	365-366	1%
Montgomery	360-361	-5%
Scottsboro	357	-6%
Selma	367	-8%
Sheffield	356	0%
Tuscaloosa	354	-4%

Alaska Average		25%
Anchorage	995	36%
Fairbanks	997	26%
Juneau	998	21%
Ketchikan	999	12%
King Salmon	996	30%

Arizona Average		-6%
Chambers	865	-8%
Douglas	855	-11%
Flagstaff	860	-9%
Kingman	864	0%
Mesa	852-853	1%
Phoenix	850	1%
Prescott	863	-9%
Show Low	859	-10%
Tucson	856-857	-6%

Arkansas Average		-9%
Batesville	725	-14%
Camden	717	-7%
Fayetteville	727	-5%
Fort Smith	729	-8%
Harrison	726	-15%
Hope	718	0%
Hot Springs	719	-15%
Jonesboro	724	-10%
Little Rock	720-722	-5%
Pine Bluff	716	-6%
Russellville	728	-10%
West Memphis	723	-8%

California Average		9%
Alhambra	917-918	9%
Bakersfield	932-933	3%
El Centro	922	2%
Eureka	955	-2%
Fresno	936-938	-1%
Herlong	961	1%
Inglewood	902	10%
Irvine	926	13%
Lompoc	934	5%
Long Beach	907-908	10%
Los Angeles	900-901	9%
Marysville	959	2%
Modesto	953	0%
Mojave	935	6%
Novato	949	16%
Oakland	945	21%
Orange	928	12%
Oxnard	930	6%
Pasadena	910-912	10%
Rancho Cordova	956-957	8%
Redding	960	-2%
Richmond	948	21%
Riverside	925	5%
Sacramento	958	8%

Salinas	939	5%
San Bernardino	923-924	6%
San Diego	919-921	11%
San Francisco	941	28%
San Jose	950-951	20%
San Mateo	943-944	22%
Santa Barbara	931	8%
Santa Rosa	954	8%
Stockton	952	3%
Sunnyvale	940	21%
Van Nuys	913-916	9%
Whittier	906	9%

Colorado Average		0%
Aurora	800-801	5%
Boulder	803-804	2%
Colorado Springs	808-809	0%
Denver	802	6%
Durango	813	-4%
Fort Morgan	807	-2%
Glenwood Springs	816	6%
Grand Junction	814-815	-1%
Greeley	806	4%
Longmont	805	1%
Pagosa Springs	811	-6%
Pueblo	810	0%
Salida	812	-5%

Connecticut Average		13%
Bridgeport	066	11%
Bristol	060	17%
Fairfield	064	15%
Hartford	061	15%
New Haven	065	13%
Norwich	063	9%
Stamford	068-069	16%
Waterbury	067	12%
West Hartford	062	8%

Delaware Average		3%
Dover	199	-4%
Newark	197	7%
Wilmington	198	6%

District of Columbia Average		14%
Washington	200-205	14%

Florida Average		-6%
Altamonte Springs	327	-6%
Bradenton	342	-7%
Brooksville	346	-8%
Daytona Beach	321	-12%
Fort Lauderdale	333	1%
Fort Myers	339	-9%
Fort Pierce	349	-11%
Gainesville	326	-11%
Jacksonville	322	-1%
Lakeland	338	-9%
Melbourne	329	-9%
Miami	330-332	1%
Naples	341	-3%
Ocala	344	-12%
Orlando	328	-2%
Panama City	324	-9%
Pensacola	325	-10%
Saint Augustine	320	-6%
Saint Cloud	347	-5%
St Petersburg	337	-5%
Tallahassee	323	-5%
Tampa	335-336	-1%
West Palm Beach	334	-2%

Georgia Average		-6%
Albany	317	-12%
Athens	306	-7%

Atlanta	303	13%
Augusta	308-309	-6%
Buford	305	-4%
Calhoun	307	-11%
Columbus	318-319	-8%
Dublin/Fort Valley	310	-10%
Hinesville	313	-7%
Kings Bay	315	-12%
Macon	312	-5%
Marietta	300-302	4%
Savannah	314	-4%
Statesboro	304	-14%
Valdosta	316	-9%

Hawaii Average		28%
Aliamanu	968	29%
Ewa	967	27%
Halawa Heights	967	27%
Hilo	967	27%
Honolulu	968	29%
Kailua	968	29%
Lualualei	967	27%
Mililani Town	967	27%
Pearl City	967	27%
Wahiawa	967	27%
Waianae	967	27%
Wailuku (Maui)	967	27%

Idaho Average		-8%
Boise	837	0%
Coeur d'Alene	838	-10%
Idaho Falls	834	-7%
Lewiston	835	-10%
Meridian	836	-8%
Pocatello	832	-9%
Sun Valley	833	-10%

Illinois Average		6%
Arlington Heights	600	18%
Aurora	605	17%
Belleville	622	2%
Bloomington	617	3%
Carbondale	629	-7%
Carol Stream	601	18%
Centralia	628	-4%
Champaign	618	2%
Chicago	606-608	19%
Decatur	623	-9%
Galesburg	614	-5%
Granite City	620	10%
Green River	612	4%
Joliet	604	17%
Kankakee	609	2%
Lawrenceville	624	-6%
Oak Park	603	21%
Peoria	615-616	6%
Peru	613	10%
Quincy	602	21%
Rockford	610-611	7%
Springfield	625-627	2%
Urbana	619	-4%

Indiana Average		-2%
Aurora	470	0%
Bloomington	474	-2%
Columbus	472	-3%
Elkhart	465	-2%
Evansville	476-477	7%
Fort Wayne	467-468	-1%
Gary	464-464	11%
Indianapolis	460-462	1%
Jasper	475	-9%
Jeffersonville	471	-5%
Kokomo	469	-8%
Lafayette	479	-5%
Muncie	473	-11%

South Bend	466	-1%
Terre Haute	478	-2%

Iowa Average		-7%
Burlington	526	-7%
Carroll	514	-15%
Cedar Falls	506	-4%
Cedar Rapids	522-524	1%
Cherokee	510	-8%
Council Bluffs	515	-6%
Creston	508	-6%
Davenport	527-528	-1%
Decorah	521	-7%
Des Moines	500-503	2%
Dubuque	520	-3%
Fort Dodge	505	-8%
Mason City	504	-6%
Ottumwa	525	-7%
Sheldon	512	-11%
Shenandoah	516	-19%
Sioux City	511	-3%
Spencer	513	-10%
Waterloo	507	-7%

Kansas Average		-7%
Colby	677	-13%
Concordia	669	-13%
Dodge City	678	-5%
Emporia	668	-10%
Fort Scott	667	-9%
Hays	676	-15%
Hutchinson	675	-2%
Independence	673	-5%
Kansas City	660-662	6%
Liberal	679	-6%
Salina	674	-10%
Topeka	664-666	-3%
Wichita	670-672	-5%

Kentucky Average		-5%
Ashland	411-412	-3%
Bowling Green	421	-6%
Campton	413-414	-9%
Covington	410	1%
Elizabethtown	427	-11%
Frankfort	406	-2%
Hazard	417-418	-6%
Hopkinsville	422	-8%
Lexington	403-405	1%
London	407-409	-5%
Louisville	400-402	1%
Owensboro	423	-5%
Paducah	420	-4%
Pikeville	415-416	-3%
Somerset	425-426	-9%
White Plains	424	-9%

Louisiana Average		4%
Alexandria	713-714	-4%
Baton Rouge	707-708	12%
Houma	703	15%
Lafayette	705	9%
Lake Charles	706	5%
Mandeville	704	5%
Minden	710	-3%
Monroe	712	-6%
New Orleans	700-701	9%
Shreveport	711	-3%

Maine Average		-8%
Auburn	042	-7%
Augusta	043	-10%
Bangor	044	-8%
Bath	045	-8%
Brunswick	039-040	-3%
Camden	048	-11%

Cutler	046	-11%
Dexter	049	-8%
Northern Area	047	-18%
Portland	041	0%

Maryland Average		4%
Annapolis	214	9%
Baltimore	210-212	8%
Bethesda	208-209	15%
Church Hill	216	-4%
Cumberland	215	-7%
Elkton	219	1%
Frederick	217	4%
Laurel	206-207	11%
Salisbury	218	-4%

Massachusetts Average		14%
Ayer	015-016	9%
Bedford	017	19%
Boston	021-022	37%
Brockton	023-024	23%
Cape Cod	026	4%
Chicopee	010	10%
Dedham	019	19%
Fitchburg	014	14%
Hingham	020	24%
Lawrence	018	17%
Nantucket	025	11%
New Bedford	027	8%
Northfield	013	1%
Pittsfield	012	1%
Springfield	011	11%

Michigan Average		1%
Battle Creek	490-491	0%
Detroit	481-482	12%
Flint	484-485	-1%
Grand Rapids	493-495	-1%
Grayling	497	-10%
Jackson	492	-1%
Lansing	488-489	1%
Marquette	498-499	-3%
Pontiac	483	12%
Royal Oak	480	9%
Saginaw	486-487	-1%
Traverse City	496	-1%

Minnesota Average		1%
Bemidji	566	21%
Brainerd	564	-1%
Duluth	556-558	0%
Fergus Falls	565	-9%
Magnolia	561	-10%
Mankato	560	-4%
Minneapolis	553-555	12%
Rochester	559	-1%
St Cloud	563	1%
St Paul	550-551	13%
Thief River Falls	567	-3%
Willmar	562	-3%

Mississippi Average		-10%
Clarksdale	386	-11%
Columbus	397	-10%
Greenville	387	-17%
Greenwood	389	-13%
Gulfport	395	-4%
Jackson	390-392	-6%
Laurel	394	-6%
McComb	396	-12%
Meridian	393	-8%
Tupelo	388	-10%

Missouri Average		-4%
Cape Girardeau	637	1%

7

Area Modification Factors

City	Zip	Factor
Caruthersville	638	-9%
Chillicothe	646	-10%
Columbia	652	-4%
East Lynne	647	-6%
Farmington	636	-12%
Hannibal	634	-5%
Independence	640	8%
Jefferson City	650-651	-3%
Joplin	648	-12%
Kansas City	641	9%
Kirksville	635	-16%
Knob Noster	653	-7%
Lebanon	654-655	-12%
Poplar Bluff	639	-8%
Saint Charles	633	1%
Saint Joseph	644-645	9%
Springfield	656-658	-7%
St Louis	630-631	6%

Montana Average -5%

City	Zip	Factor
Billings	590-591	-2%
Butte	597	-5%
Fairview	592	-2%
Great Falls	594	-3%
Havre	595	-11%
Helena	596	-6%
Kalispell	599	-7%
Miles City	593	-5%
Missoula	598	-6%

Nebraska Average -11%

City	Zip	Factor
Alliance	693	-13%
Columbus	686	-8%
Grand Island	688	-12%
Hastings	689	-9%
Lincoln	683-685	-5%
McCook	690	-14%
Norfolk	687	-13%
North Platte	691	-11%
Omaha	680-681	-1%
Valentine	692	-19%

New Hampshire Average 0%

City	Zip	Factor
Charlestown	036	-4%
Concord	034	-1%
Dover	038	5%
Lebanon	037	-1%
Littleton	035	-3%
Manchester	032-033	2%
New Boston	030-031	7%

New Jersey Average 15%

City	Zip	Factor
Atlantic City	080-084	11%
Brick	087	7%
Dover	078	15%
Edison	088-089	17%
Hackensack	076	15%
Monmouth	077	22%
Newark	071-073	15%
Passaic	070	16%
Paterson	074-075	12%
Princeton	085	16%
Summit	079	21%
Trenton	086	14%

New Mexico Average -10%

Alamogordo	883	-10%
Albuquerque	870-871	-2%
Clovis	881	-14%
Farmington	874	-1%
Fort Sumner	882	-3%
Gallup	873	-10%
Holman	877	-11%
Las Cruces	880	-13%
Santa Fe	875	-10%
Socorro	878	-15%
Truth or Consequences	879	-15%
Tucumcari	884	-11%

Nevada Average 2%

City	Zip	Factor
Carson City	897	-4%
Elko	898	6%
Ely	893	-10%
Fallon	894	5%
Las Vegas	889-891	12%
Reno	895	4%

New York Average 11%

City	Zip	Factor
Albany	120-123	9%
Amityville	117	15%
Batavia	140	1%
Binghamton	137-139	0%
Bronx	104	19%
Brooklyn	112	14%
Buffalo	142	2%
Elmira	149	1%
Flushing	113	24%
Garden City	115	23%
Hicksville	118	21%
Ithaca	148	-3%
Jamaica	114	21%
Jamestown	147	-5%
Kingston	124	-3%
Long Island	111	47%
Montauk	119	13%
New York (Manhattan)	100-102	46%
New York City	100-102	46%
Newcomb	128	1%
Niagara Falls	143	-7%
Plattsburgh	129	0%
Poughkeepsie	125-126	2%
Queens	110	25%
Rochester	144-146	3%
Rockaway	116	17%
Rome	133-134	-3%
Staten Island	103	14%
Stewart	127	-6%
Syracuse	130-132	3%
Tonawanda	141	-1%
Utica	135	-4%
Watertown	136	3%
West Point	109	14%
White Plains	105-108	19%

North Carolina Average -5%

City	Zip	Factor
Asheville	287-289	-8%
Charlotte	280-282	2%
Durham	277	2%
Elizabeth City	279	-7%
Fayetteville	283	-8%
Goldsboro	275	-2%
Greensboro	274	-3%
Hickory	286	-10%
Kinston	285	-12%
Raleigh	276	1%
Rocky Mount	278	-7%
Wilmington	284	-2%
Winston-Salem	270-273	-5%

North Dakota Average 0%

Bismarck	585	0%
Dickinson	586	4%
Fargo	580-581	-2%
Grand Forks	582	1%
Jamestown	584	-1%
Minot	587	0%
Nekoma	583	-13%
Williston	588	9%

Ohio Average -1%

Akron	442-443	-1%
Canton	446-447	-4%
Chillicothe	456	0%
Cincinnati	450-452	4%
Cleveland	440-441	3%
Columbus	432	6%
Dayton	453-455	-2%
Lima	458	-7%
Marietta	457	-4%
Marion	433	-8%
Newark	430-431	5%
Sandusky	448-449	-1%
Steubenville	439	-3%
Toledo	434-436	6%
Warren	444	-4%
Youngstown	445	-1%
Zanesville	437-438	2%

Oklahoma Average -9%

Adams	739	-12%
Ardmore	734	-7%
Clinton	736	-11%
Durant	747	-10%
Enid	737	-9%
Lawton	735	-11%
McAlester	745	-11%
Muskogee	744	-15%
Norman	730	-5%
Oklahoma City	731	-4%
Ponca City	746	-5%
Poteau	749	-10%
Pryor	743	-13%
Shawnee	748	-14%
Tulsa	740-741	-2%
Woodward	738	-4%

Oregon Average -4%

City	Zip	Factor
Adrian	979	-15%
Bend	977	-5%
Eugene	974	-1%
Grants Pass	975	-6%
Klamath Falls	976	-11%
Pendleton	978	-3%
Portland	970-972	10%
Salem	973	-1%

Pennsylvania Average -1%

Allentown	181	5%
Altoona	166	-6%
Beaver Springs	178	-5%
Bethlehem	180	7%
Bradford	167	-8%
Butler	160	-1%
Chambersburg	172	-5%
Clearfield	168	-1%
DuBois	158	-11%
East Stroudsburg	183	-3%
Erie	164-165	-6%
Genesee	169	-7%
Greensburg	156	-2%
Harrisburg	170-171	3%
Hazleton	182	-4%
Johnstown	159	-8%
Kittanning	162	-6%
Lancaster	175-176	3%
Meadville	163	-13%
Montrose	188	-7%
New Castle	161	-3%
Philadelphia	190-191	15%
Pittsburgh	152	6%
Pottsville	179	-7%
Punxsutawney	157	-5%
Reading	195-196	3%
Scranton	184-185	-2%
Somerset	155	-7%
Southeastern	193	12%
Uniontown	154	-5%
Valley Forge	194	16%
Warminster	189	13%
Warrendale	150-151	6%
Washington	153	6%
Wilkes Barre	186-187	-2%
Williamsport	177	-4%
York	173-174	2%

Rhode Island Average 8%

City	Zip	Factor
Bristol	28	7%
Coventry	028	7%
Cranston	029	9%
Davisville	028	7%
Narragansett	028	7%
Newport	028	7%
Providence	029	9%
Warwick	028	7%

South Carolina Average -5%

City	Zip	Factor
Aiken	298	5%
Beaufort	299	-8%
Charleston	294	-3%
Columbia	290-292	-5%
Greenville	296	-6%
Myrtle Beach	295	-9%
Rock Hill	297	-8%
Spartanburg	293	-7%

South Dakota Average -9%

City	Zip	Factor
Aberdeen	574	-7%
Mitchell	573	-9%
Mobridge	576	-14%
Pierre	575	-14%
Rapid City	577	-8%
Sioux Falls	570-571	-3%
Watertown	572	-9%

Tennessee Average -4%

Chattanooga	374	0%
Clarksville	370	0%
Cleveland	373	-4%
Columbia	384	-10%
Cookeville	385	-6%
Jackson	383	-6%
Kingsport	376	-6%
Knoxville	377-379	-3%
McKenzie	382	-12%
Memphis	380-381	2%
Nashville	371-372	5%

Texas Average -4%

City	Zip	Factor
Abilene	795-796	-6%
Amarillo	790-791	-3%
Arlington	760	-1%
Austin	786-787	1%
Bay City	774	23%
Beaumont	776-777	9%
Brownwood	768	-14%
Bryan	778	-8%
Childress	792	-19%
Corpus Christi	783-784	2%
Dallas	751-753	4%
Del Rio	788	-19%
El Paso	798-799	-13%
Fort Worth	761-762	-1%
Galveston	775	9%
Giddings	789	-3%
Greenville	754	-5%
Houston	770-772	10%
Huntsville	773	10%
Longview	756	-2%
Lubbock	793-794	-9%
Lufkin	759	-7%
McAllen	785	-18%
Midland	797	2%
Palestine	758	-6%
Plano	750	4%
San Angelo	769	-11%
San Antonio	780-782	-3%
Texarkana	755	-11%
Tyler	757	-8%
Victoria	779	-4%
Waco	765-767	-8%
Wichita Falls	763	-12%
Woodson	764	-9%

Utah Average -4%

City	Zip	Factor
Clearfield	840	0%
Green River	845	-3%
Ogden	843-844	-9%
Provo	846-847	-10%
Salt Lake City	841	1%

Virginia Average -6%

City	Zip	Factor
Abingdon	242	-7%
Alexandria	220-223	13%
Charlottesville	229	-6%
Chesapeake	233	-3%
Culpeper	227	-3%
Farmville	239	-15%
Fredericksburg	224-225	-5%
Galax	243	-13%
Harrisonburg	228	-7%
Lynchburg	245	-11%
Norfolk	235-237	-2%
Petersburg	238	-5%
Radford	241	-12%
Richmond	232	3%
Roanoke	240	-12%
Staunton	244	-9%
Tazewell	246	-6%
Virginia Beach	234	-5%
Williamsburg	230-231	-2%
Winchester	226	-6%

Vermont Average -5%

Albany	058	-7%
Battleboro	053	-3%
Beecher Falls	059	-9%
Bennington	052	-8%
Burlington	054	3%
Montpelier	056	-3%
Rutland	057	-7%
Springfield	051	-6%
White River Junction	050	-5%

Washington Average 2%

Clarkston	994	-2%
Everett	982	5%
Olympia	985	-1%
Pasco	993	3%
Seattle	980-981	14%
Spokane	990-992	-3%
Tacoma	983-984	5%
Vancouver	986	4%
Wenatchee	988	-8%
Yakima	989	-4%

West Virginia Average -5%

City	Zip	Factor
Beckley	258-259	-6%
Bluefield	247-248	0%
Charleston	250-253	5%
Clarksburg	263-264	-5%
Fairmont	266	-8%
Huntington	255-257	0%
Lewisburg	249	-15%
Martinsburg	254	-5%
Morgantown	265	-1%
New Martinsville	262	-13%
Parkersburg	261	5%
Romney	267	-7%
Sugar Grove	268	-12%
Wheeling	260	-5%

Wisconsin Average 1%

Amery	540	-1%
Beloit	535	5%
Clam Lake	545	-2%
Eau Claire	547	-2%
Green Bay	541-543	2%
La Crosse	546	-3%
Ladysmith	548	-2%
Madison	537	8%
Milwaukee	530-534	9%
Oshkosh	549	3%
Portage	539	2%
Prairie du Chien	538	-6%
Wausau	544	-1%

Wyoming Average -2%

Casper	826	2%
Cheyenne/Laramie	820	-5%
Gillette	827	8%
Powell	824	-8%
Rawlins	823	0%
Riverton	825	-7%
Rock Springs	829-831	4%
Sheridan	828	-4%
Wheatland	822	-12%

UNITED STATES TERRITORIES

	Factor
Guam	18%
Puerto Rico	-21%

VIRGIN ISLANDS (U.S.)

	Factor
St. Croix	2%
St. John	20%
St. Thomas	5%

CANADIAN AREA MODIFIERS

These figures assume an exchange rate of $0.98 Canadian to $1.00 U.S.

Alberta Average 23%

	Factor
Calgary	23%
Edmonton	24%
Ft. McMurray	22%

British Columbia Average 14%

	Factor
Fraser Valley	13%
Okanagan	14%
Vancouver	16%

Manitoba Average 8%

	Factor
North Manitoba	8%
South Manitoba	9%
Selkirk	8%
Winnipeg	8%

New Brunswick Average -10%

	Factor
Moncton	-10%

Nova Scotia Average -3%

	Factor
Amherst	-4%
Nova Scotia	-4%
Sydney	-3%

Newfoundland/Labrador Average -4%

Ontario Average 16%

	Factor
London	16%
Thunder Bay	14%
Toronto	16%

Quebec Average 4%

	Factor
Montreal	4%
Quebec City	4%

Saskatchewan Average 10%

	Factor
La Ronge	10%
Prince Albert	9%
Saskatoon	12%

Building Cost Historical Index

Use this table to find the approximate current dollar building cost when the actual cost is known for any year since 1945. Multiply the figure listed below for the building type and year of construction by the known cost. The result is the estimated 2012 construction cost.

Year	Masonry Buildings	Concrete Buildings	Steel Buildings	Wood-Frame Buildings	Agricultural Buildings	Year of Construction
1945	21.28	23.58	27.59	19.25	17.47	1945
1946	18.27	20.69	24.53	17.23	15.11	1946
1947	15.58	17.11	21.44	13.83	12.24	1947
1948	13.67	14.65	19.12	12.67	11.20	1948
1949	13.75	14.49	19.03	12.83	11.54	1949
1950	13.09	13.83	18.67	12.26	10.73	1950
1951	12.24	13.06	16.95	11.47	9.96	1951
1952	11.80	12.74	16.58	11.27	9.87	1952
1953	11.65	12.32	15.83	10.99	9.65	1953
1954	11.43	11.88	15.83	10.99	9.65	1954
1955	10.96	11.33	15.00	10.41	9.23	1955
1956	10.39	10.83	13.81	9.97	8.85	1956
1957	10.10	10.42	13.26	9.90	8.64	1957
1958	9.81	10.03	12.62	9.88	10.30	1958
1959	9.50	9.71	12.32	9.46	8.25	1959
1960	9.28	9.53	12.12	9.31	8.09	1960
1961	9.09	9.49	11.92	9.14	8.07	1961
1962	8.89	9.22	11.63	9.04	7.94	1962
1963	8.76	8.98	11.49	8.86	7.21	1963
1964	8.50	8.87	11.33	8.56	7.57	1964
1965	8.23	8.64	10.94	8.38	7.36	1965
1966	7.86	8.39	10.52	8.02	7.16	1966
1967	7.67	7.99	9.84	7.62	6.87	1967
1968	7.36	7.55	9.39	7.20	6.57	1968
1969	6.95	7.22	9.07	6.94	6.20	1969
1970	6.67	6.90	8.62	6.59	5.89	1970
1971	6.26	6.32	8.00	5.68	5.49	1971
1972	5.82	5.85	7.48	5.70	5.10	1972
1973	5.31	5.54	6.64	5.26	4.79	1973
1974	4.73	5.08	6.23	4.91	4.45	1974
1975	4.30	4.49	5.61	4.62	3.96	1975
1976	4.03	4.28	5.32	4.45	3.76	1976
1977	3.75	4.01	5.05	4.13	3.53	1977
1978	3.49	3.75	4.65	3.80	3.20	1978
1979	3.21	3.34	4.17	3.48	3.03	1979
1980	2.91	3.03	3.71	3.12	2.74	1980
1981	2.74	2.86	3.40	2.98	2.56	1981
1982	2.65	2.74	3.30	2.88	2.47	1982
1983	2.53	2.65	3.23	2.75	2.33	1983
1984	2.36	2.49	3.09	2.54	2.26	1984
1985	2.30	2.36	3.00	2.46	2.22	1985
1986	2.24	2.34	2.95	2.42	2.18	1986
1987	2.23	2.30	2.92	2.38	2.16	1987
1988	2.18	2.21	2.86	2.36	2.12	1988
1989	2.13	2.17	2.72	2.31	2.06	1989
1990	2.01	2.09	2.58	2.15	1.96	1990
1991	2.17	2.06	2.46	2.03	1.86	1991
1992	1.94	2.03	2.43	2.02	1.84	1992
1993	1.89	2.01	2.34	1.99	1.81	1993
1994	1.85	1.88	2.25	1.92	1.68	1994
1995	1.75	1.71	2.09	1.80	1.59	1995
1996	1.69	1.68	2.03	1.77	1.56	1996
1997	1.64	1.64	1.95	1.73	1.52	1997
1998	1.56	1.56	1.87	1.65	1.50	1998
1999	1.50	1.50	1.83	1.63	1.48	1999
2000	1.46	1.46	1.76	1.57	1.43	2000
2001	1.42	1.42	1.72	1.52	1.39	2001
2002	1.38	1.38	1.68	1.50	1.36	2002
2003	1.36	1.36	1.64	1.49	1.34	2003
2004	1.30	1.30	1.60	1.45	1.30	2004
2005	1.21	1.21	1.43	1.30	1.27	2005
2006	1.14	1.14	1.32	1.16	1.14	2006
2007	1.10	1.10	1.25	1.08	1.06	2007
2008	1.03	1.03	1.19	1.03	1.00	2008
2009	1.02	1.02	1.15	1.03	1.00	2009
2010	1.00	1.00	1.08	1.02	0.99	2010
2011	1.01	1.01	1.12	1.04	1.02	2011
2012	1.00	1.00	1.00	1.00	1.00	2012

Residential Structures Section

The figures in this section include all costs associated with normal construction:

Foundations as required for normal soil conditions. Excavation for foundations, piers, and other foundation components given a fairly level construction site. Floor, wall, and roof structures. Interior floor, wall, and ceiling finishes. Exterior wall finish and roof cover. Interior partitions as described in the quality class. Finish carpentry, doors, windows, trim, etc. Electric wiring and fixtures. Rough and finish plumbing as described in applicable building specifications. Built-in appliances as described in applicable building specifications. All labor and materials including supervision. All design and engineering fees, if necessary. Permits and fees. Utility hook-ups. Contractors' contingency, overhead and profit.

The square foot costs do not include heating and cooling equipment or the items listed in the section "Additional Costs for Residential Structures" which appear on pages 27 to 31. The costs of the following should be figured separately and added to the basic structure cost: porches, basements, balconies, exterior stairways, built-in equipment beyond that listed in the quality classifications, garages and carports.

Single Family Residences

Single family residences vary widely in quality and the quality of construction is the most significant factor influencing cost. Residences are listed in six quality classes. Class 1 is the most expensive commonly encountered and Class 6 is the minimum required under most building codes. Nearly all homes built from stock plans or offered to the public by residential tract developers will fall into Class 3, 4, 5, or 6. For convenience, these classes are labeled *Best Standard, Good Standard, Average Standard* or *Minimum Standard.* Class 1 residences are labeled *Luxury.* Class 2 residences are labeled *Semi-Luxury.* Class 1 and 2 residences are designed by professional architects, usually to meet preferences of the first owner.

The shape of the outside perimeter also has a significant influence on cost. The more complex the shape, the more expensive the structure per square foot of floor. The shape classification of multiple story or split-level homes should be based on the outline formed by the outer-most exterior walls, including the garage area, regardless of the story level. Most residences that fall into Classes 3, 4, 5 or 6 have 4, 6, 8 or 10 corners, as illustrated below. Small insets that do not require a change in the roof line can be ignored when evaluating the outside perimeter.

Class 1 and 2 (*Luxury* and *Semi-Luxury*) residences have more than ten corners and are best evaluated by counting the "building masses." A building mass is a group of contiguous rooms on one or more levels with access at varying angles from a common point or hallway. The illustration at the right below represents a residence with two building masses. Most Class 1 and Class 2 residences have from one to four building masses, ignoring any attached garage. For convenience, cost tables for Class 1 and 2 single family residences with one, two, three or four building masses have been appended to cost tables for Class 3, 4, 5 and 6 residences with 4, 6, 8 and 10 building corners.

Residences on larger lots often include a separate housekeeping unit, either remote from the main structure (as illustrated below at the right) or joined to the main structure by a hallway (no common wall). Evaluate any separate housekeeping unit as a separate residence. The quality class of separate housekeeping units will usually be the same as the main residence if designed and built at the same time as the main residence.

Residences which have features of two or more quality classes can be placed between two of the six labeled classes. The tables have five half-classes (1 & 2, 2 & 3, etc.) which can be applied to residences with some characteristics of two or more quality classes. If a portion of a residence differs significantly in quality from other portions, evaluate the square footage of each portion separately.

These figures can be applied to nearly all single-family residences built using conventional methods and readily available materials, including the relatively small number of highly decorative, starkly original or exceptionally well-appointed residences.

4 corners

6 corners

8 corners

10 corners

2 building masses and one separate unit

Single Family Residences

Quality Classification

	Class 1 Luxury	Class 2 Semi-Luxury	Class 3 Best Std.	Class 4 Good Std.	Class 5 Average Std.	Class 6 Minimum Std.
Foundation (9% of total cost)	Reinforced concrete.	Reinforced concrete.	Reinforced concrete.	Reinforced concrete or concrete block.	Reinforced concrete or concrete block.	Reinforced concrete.
Floor Structure (12% of total cost)	Engineered wood or steel exceeding code minimums.	Engineered wood or steel or reinforced concrete slab.	Engineered wood or steel or reinforced concrete slab.	Wood frame or slab on grade, changes in shape and elevation.	Standard wood frame or slab on grade with elevation changes.	Slab on grade. No changes in elevation.
Wall Framing and Exterior Finish (14% of total cost)	Wood or steel, very irregular walls, stone veneer, many architectural doors and windows.	Wood or steel, irregular shape, masonry veneer, better grade doors and windows.	Wood or steel, several wall offsets, wood or masonry accents, good grade doors and windows.	Wood or steel, stucco or wood siding, some trim or veneer, average doors and windows.	Wood or steel, stucco or wood siding, few offsets, commodity grade doors and windows.	Wood or steel, stucco or hardboard siding, minimum grade doors and windows.
Roof (10% of total cost)	Complex plan, tile, slate or metal, highly detailed.	Multi-level, slate, tile or flat surface, decorative details.	Multi-pitch, shake, tile or flat surface, large closed soffit.	Wood trusses, tile or good shingles, closed soffit.	Wood frame, shingle or built-up cover, open 24" soffit.	Wood frame, composition shingle cover, open soffit.
Floor Finish (5% of total cost)	Terrazzo, marble, granite, or inlaid hardwood or best carpet throughout.	Marble or granite entry, hardwood, good carpet or sheet vinyl elsewhere.	Simulated marble tile entry, good carpet, hardwood or vinyl elsewhere.	Better sheet vinyl and average carpet, some areas with masonry or tile.	Good sheet vinyl and standard carpet, small area with tile or hardwood.	Composition tile or minimum grade sheet vinyl.
Interior Wall and Ceiling Finish (8% of total cost)	Plaster or gypsum wallboard with artistic finish, many offsets and wall openings, decorative details in nearly all rooms.	Plaster on gypsum or metal lath or 2 layers of 5/8" gypsum wallboard, decorative details, many irregular wall openings.	Gypsum wallboard with putty or texture coat finish, some irregular walls, decorative details in living room, entry and kitchen.	1/2" gypsum wallboard with textured finish, several irregular walls and wall openings, some decorative details.	1/2" gypsum wallboard with textured finish, most walls are rectangular, doors and windows are the only openings.	1/2" gypsum wallboard, smooth or orange peel finish. Nearly all walls are regular, no decorative details.
Interior Detail (5% of total cost)	Exposed beams or decorative ceiling, 12' to 16' ceiling in great room, many sky widows, built-in shelving and alcoves for art.	Great room has 12' to 16' ceiling, most rooms have windows on two sides, formal dining area, several framed openings.	Cathedral ceiling at entry, one or more floor level changes, several wall openings or pass-throughs, formal dining area.	8' or 9' ceiling throughout, walk-in closet in master bedroom, separate dining area, some decorative wood trim.	8' or 9' ceiling throughout, sliding mirrored closet doors, standard grade molding and trim, breakfast bar or nook.	Drop ceiling in kitchen, other rooms have 7'6" to 8' ceiling, minimum grade molding and trim.
Bath Detail (4% of total cost)	Custom large tile showers, separate elevated spa in master bathroom.	Large tile showers, at least one bathtub, glass block or large window by each bath.	Tile or fiberglass shower, at least one built-in bathtub, window in bathroom.	Good plastic tub and shower in at least one bathroom, one small window in each bath.	Average plastic tub and shower in at least one bathroom.	Minimum plastic tub and shower in one bathroom.
Kitchen Detail (8% of total cost)	Over 30 LF of deluxe wall and base cabinets, stone counter top, island work area, breakfast bar.	Over 25 LF of good custom base and wall cabinets, synthetic stone counter top, desk and breakfast bar.	Over 20 LF of good stock wall and base cabinets, tile or acrylic counter top, desk and breakfast bar or nook.	Over 15 LF of stock standard grade wall and base cabinets, low-cost tile or acrylic counter top, breakfast nook.	Over 10 LF of stock standard grade wall and base cabinets, low-cost acrylic or laminated plastic counter top.	Less than 10 LF of low-cost wall and base cabinets, laminated plastic counter top, space for table.
Plumbing (12% of total cost)	4 deluxe fixtures per bathroom, more bathrooms than bedrooms.	4 good fixtures per bathroom, more bathrooms than bedrooms.	3 good fixtures per bathroom, as many bathrooms as bedrooms.	3 standard fixtures per bathroom, less bathrooms than bedrooms.	3 standard fixtures per bathroom, less bathrooms than bedrooms.	3 minimum fixtures per bathroom, 2 bathrooms.
Special Features (3% of total cost)	10 luxury built-in appliances, wet bar, home theater, pantry, wine cellar.	8 good built-in appliances, wet bar, walk-in pantry, central vacuum.	6 good built-in appliances, walk-in pantry, wet bar, central vacuum.	5 standard built-in appliances, sliding glass or French doors, laundry room.	4 standard grade kitchen appliances.	4 minimum grade kitchen. appliances.
Electrical System (10% of total cost)	Over 100 recessed or track lights, security system, computer network.	80 to 100 recessed lighting fixtures, security system, computer network.	Ample recessed lighting on dimmers, computer network, multiple TV outlets.	Limited recessed lighting on dimmers, multiple TV outlets.	12 lighting fixtures, switch-operated duplex plug outlets in bedrooms.	10 or less lighting fixtures, switch-operated plug outlets in most rooms.
If Exterior Walls are Masonry	Reinforced split face concrete block or brick with face brick veneer.	Reinforced block or brick with masonry veneer or stucco coat.	Textured or coated concrete block or good quality detailed brick.	Colored or coated concrete block or good quality brick.	Colored concrete block or painted common brick.	Painted concrete block or common-brick.

Note: Use the percent of total cost to help identify the correct quality classification.

Single Family Residences

4 Corners (Classes 3, 4, 5 and 6) or One Building Mass (Classes 1 and 2 Only)

Estimating Procedure

1. Establish the structure quality class by applying the information on page 11.
2. Multiply the structure floor area (excluding the garage) by the appropriate square foot cost below.
3. Multiply the total from step 2 by the correct location factor listed on page 7 or 8.
4. Add, when appropriate, the cost of a porch, garage, heating and cooling equipment, basement, fireplace, carport, appliances and plumbing fixtures beyond that listed in the quality classification. See the cost of these items on pages 27 to 31.

Single Family Residence, Class 4

Single Family Residence, Class 6

Square Foot Area

Quality Class	700	800	900	1,000	1,100	1,200	1,300	1,400	1,500	1,600	1,700	1,800	2,000
1, Luxury	482.19	462.00	445.34	430.93	419.72	409.71	400.84	392.87	386.90	381.05	375.73	371.20	362.74
1, & 2	419.30	401.74	387.24	374.73	364.99	356.21	348.59	341.61	336.45	331.38	326.65	322.72	315.41
2, Semi-Luxury	293.05	280.78	270.65	261.89	255.08	249.00	243.63	238.79	235.15	231.48	228.33	225.62	220.41
2 & 3	215.10	206.15	198.66	192.28	187.28	182.79	178.83	175.28	172.57	169.96	167.55	165.62	161.80
3, Best Std.	187.70	179.90	173.36	167.80	163.36	159.49	156.05	152.98	150.61	148.34	146.27	144.48	141.19
3 & 4	160.52	153.72	148.20	143.48	139.66	136.34	133.43	130.73	128.78	126.71	125.05	123.51	120.76
4, Good Std.	138.31	132.41	127.71	123.59	120.39	117.52	114.93	112.63	110.88	109.23	107.72	106.31	104.02
4 & 5	124.58	119.34	115.09	111.35	108.42	105.78	103.48	101.51	99.92	98.38	97.05	95.89	93.64
5 Avg. Std.	112.12	107.48	103.59	100.27	97.69	95.32	93.25	91.33	89.95	88.58	87.36	86.32	84.34
5 & 6	97.35	93.27	89.92	87.04	84.73	82.70	80.91	79.26	78.09	76.86	75.93	74.91	73.21
6, Min. Std.	88.50	84.78	81.72	79.09	77.03	75.17	73.57	72.09	70.98	69.87	68.98	68.08	66.51

Square Foot Area

Quality Class	2,200	2,400	2,600	2,800	3,000	3,200	3,400	3,600	4,000	4,200	4,400	4,600	5,000
1, Luxury	356.43	350.45	345.63	341.33	338.28	335.44	332.37	330.14	325.49	322.55	319.97	317.74	314.56
1, & 2	310.01	304.75	300.54	296.81	294.14	291.70	289.03	287.06	283.05	280.48	278.23	276.29	273.54
2, Semi-Luxury	216.75	212.99	210.08	207.44	205.55	203.81	201.96	200.63	197.81	196.02	194.45	193.10	191.17
2 & 3	159.02	156.36	154.20	152.29	150.88	149.57	148.28	147.27	145.22	143.90	142.74	141.75	140.33
3, Best Std.	138.78	136.41	134.51	132.91	131.71	130.59	129.39	128.49	126.69	126.71	125.69	124.82	123.57
3 & 4	118.65	116.65	115.08	113.66	112.58	111.58	110.67	109.91	108.37	107.40	106.53	105.79	104.73
4, Good Std.	102.23	100.48	99.15	97.88	97.05	96.17	95.34	94.61	93.33	92.49	91.73	91.11	90.20
4 & 5	92.07	90.56	89.19	88.18	87.34	86.65	85.78	85.28	84.12	83.35	82.69	82.11	81.30
5 Avg. Std.	82.91	81.56	80.43	79.34	78.70	78.00	77.30	76.77	75.72	74.62	74.45	73.93	73.21
5 & 6	71.97	70.78	69.78	68.90	68.33	67.66	67.04	66.57	65.73	65.05	64.63	64.13	63.54
6, Min. Std.	65.34	64.29	63.44	62.69	62.10	61.53	61.00	60.55	59.74	59.12	58.74	58.29	57.75

Note: Tract work and highly repetitive jobs may reduce the cost 8 to 12%. Add 4% to the square foot cost of floors above the second floor level. Work outside metropolitan areas may cost 2 to 6% less. When the exterior walls are masonry, add 9 to 10% for class 2 and 1 structures and 5 to 8% for class 3, 4, 5 and 6 structures. The building area includes all full story (7'6" to 9' high) areas within and including the exterior walls of all floor areas of the building, including small inset areas such as entrances outside the exterior wall but under the main roof. For areas with a ceiling height of less than 80", see the section on half-story areas on page 30.

Single Family Residences

6 Corners (Classes 3, 4, 5, and 6) or Two Building Masses (Classes 1 and 2 Only)

Estimating Procedure

1. Establish the structure quality class by applying the information on page 11.
2. Multiply the structure floor area (excluding the garage) by the appropriate square foot cost below.
3. Multiply the total from step 2 by the correct location factor listed on page 7 or 8.
4. Add, when appropriate, the cost of a porch, garage, heating and cooling equipment, basement, fireplace, carport, appliances and plumbing fixtures beyond that listed in the quality classification. See the cost of these items on pages 27 to 31.

Single Family Residence, Class 5

Single Family Residence, Class 5

Square Foot Area

Quality Class	700	800	900	1,000	1,100	1,200	1,300	1,400	1,500	1,600	1,700	1,800	2,000
1, Luxury	491.44	470.87	453.89	439.21	427.80	417.88	409.71	401.62	395.26	389.44	384.11	379.36	371.28
1, & 2	427.35	409.46	394.68	381.93	371.98	363.31	356.21	349.26	343.71	338.63	334.07	329.89	322.84
2, Semi-Luxury	298.74	286.24	275.65	267.34	259.97	253.94	249.00	244.08	240.18	236.63	233.48	230.52	225.68
2 & 3	219.26	210.11	202.34	196.25	190.80	186.36	182.79	179.17	176.28	173.71	171.37	169.17	165.64
3, Best Std.	191.34	183.32	176.58	171.20	166.54	162.65	159.49	156.36	153.90	151.58	149.54	147.72	144.54
3 & 4	163.58	156.80	150.90	146.41	142.44	139.01	136.42	133.67	131.63	129.56	127.88	126.22	123.53
4, Good Std.	140.97	135.08	130.03	126.12	122.68	119.80	117.52	115.18	113.28	111.66	110.24	108.79	106.40
4 & 5	127.03	121.70	117.06	113.60	110.48	107.87	105.78	103.71	102.15	100.56	99.26	97.98	95.94
5 Avg. Std.	114.36	109.62	105.46	102.33	99.53	97.13	95.32	93.52	92.03	90.60	89.37	88.25	86.33
5 & 6	99.25	95.06	91.58	88.83	86.32	84.27	82.70	81.09	79.79	78.61	77.56	76.52	74.96
6, Min. Std.	90.26	86.49	83.25	80.71	78.51	76.67	75.17	73.72	72.50	71.41	70.47	69.59	68.11

Square Foot Area

Quality Class	2,200	2,400	2,600	2,800	3,000	3,200	3,400	3,600	4,000	4,200	4,400	4,600	5,000
1, Luxury	365.30	359.68	354.67	350.45	347.03	343.69	340.87	338.28	334.73	331.73	329.06	328.04	324.76
1, & 2	317.64	312.82	308.48	304.75	301.81	298.82	296.42	294.14	291.14	288.49	287.50	285.48	282.62
2, Semi-Luxury	222.09	218.56	215.53	212.99	210.87	208.84	207.15	205.55	203.43	201.60	199.98	198.59	196.59
2 & 3	162.97	160.44	158.24	156.36	154.80	153.29	152.06	150.88	149.30	148.19	146.34	145.23	144.21
3, Best Std.	142.18	140.00	138.02	136.41	135.13	133.78	132.69	131.71	130.30	129.14	128.10	127.21	125.93
3 & 4	121.56	119.70	118.01	116.65	115.47	114.34	113.40	112.58	111.35	110.33	109.46	108.70	107.62
4, Good Std.	104.74	103.07	101.67	100.48	99.50	98.50	97.78	97.05	96.01	95.14	94.40	93.72	92.79
4 & 5	94.36	92.84	91.58	90.56	89.56	88.75	88.04	87.34	86.46	85.69	85.00	84.40	83.55
5 Avg. Std.	84.94	83.63	82.56	81.56	80.68	79.92	79.27	78.70	77.86	77.17	76.54	76.02	75.24
5 & 6	73.72	72.50	71.53	70.78	70.02	69.40	68.83	68.33	67.53	66.92	66.38	65.94	65.26
6, Min. Std.	67.01	66.00	65.08	64.29	63.69	63.06	62.55	62.10	61.41	60.86	60.38	59.96	59.36

Note: Tract work and highly repetitive jobs may reduce the cost 8 to 12%. Add 4% to the square foot cost of floors above the second floor level. Work outside metropolitan areas may cost 2 to 6% less. When the exterior walls are masonry, add 9 to 10% for class 2 and 1 structures and 5 to 8% for class 3, 4, 5 and 6 structures. The building area includes all full story (7'6" to 9' high) areas within and including the exterior walls of all floor areas of the building, including small inset areas such as entrances outside the exterior wall but under the main roof. For areas with a ceiling height of less than 80", see the section on half-story areas on page 30.

Single Family Residences

8 Corners (Classes 3, 4, 5, and 6) or
Three Building Masses (Classes 1 and 2 only)

Estimating Procedure

1. Establish the structure quality class by applying the information on page 11.
2. Multiply the structure floor area (excluding the garage) by the appropriate square foot cost below.
3. Multiply the total from step 2 by the correct location factor listed on page 7 or 8.
4. Add, when appropriate, the cost of a porch, garage, heating and cooling equipment, basement, fireplace, carport, appliances and plumbing fixtures beyond that listed in the quality classification. See the cost of these items on pages 27 to 31.

Single Family Residence, Class 1

Single Family Residence, Class 2 & 3

Square Foot Area

Quality Class	700	800	900	1,000	1,100	1,200	1,300	1,400	1,500	1,600	1,700	1,800	2,000
1, Luxury	501.44	480.76	462.96	448.38	436.49	426.65	417.88	409.99	402.96	397.56	392.40	387.87	379.81
1, & 2	436.01	418.12	402.55	389.93	379.52	371.00	363.31	356.57	350.42	345.72	341.21	337.28	330.31
2, Semi-Luxury	303.62	291.24	280.92	272.30	265.24	259.27	253.91	249.16	244.89	241.61	238.51	235.68	230.83
2 & 3	222.89	213.79	206.18	199.85	194.70	190.32	186.36	182.90	179.78	177.37	175.02	173.04	169.45
3, Best Std.	194.50	186.57	179.97	174.44	169.89	166.10	162.65	159.57	156.87	154.79	152.74	151.05	147.88
3 & 4	166.26	159.47	153.78	149.06	145.23	142.04	139.01	136.49	134.07	132.34	130.59	129.11	126.41
4, Good Std.	143.26	137.38	132.52	128.53	125.05	122.35	119.80	117.61	115.53	114.08	112.50	111.23	108.90
4 & 5	129.07	123.80	119.35	115.77	112.63	110.16	107.87	105.97	104.07	102.70	101.33	100.16	98.05
5 Avg. Std.	116.23	111.48	107.52	104.25	101.46	99.26	97.13	95.41	93.65	92.50	91.24	90.29	88.33
5 & 6	100.87	96.74	93.28	90.44	88.08	86.18	84.27	82.80	81.35	80.27	79.20	78.28	76.67
6, Min. Std.	91.68	87.96	84.80	82.23	80.02	78.28	76.67	75.30	73.92	72.96	72.02	69.45	68.16

Square Foot Area

Quality Class	2,200	2,400	2,600	2,800	3,000	3,200	3,400	3,600	4,000	4,200	4,400	4,600	5,000
1, Luxury	373.41	372.61	362.74	358.99	355.63	352.65	349.11	347.13	342.80	339.72	336.99	334.64	331.29
1, & 2	324.71	317.64	315.41	312.16	309.25	306.68	303.56	301.90	298.18	295.47	293.11	291.05	288.16
2, Semi-Luxury	226.89	222.09	220.41	218.15	216.21	214.32	212.12	210.91	208.36	206.52	204.85	203.43	201.38
2 & 3	166.56	162.97	161.80	160.15	158.65	157.34	155.73	154.86	152.98	151.60	150.39	149.34	147.85
3, Best Std.	145.33	142.18	141.19	139.74	138.43	137.28	135.91	135.14	134.62	133.43	132.39	131.47	130.15
3 & 4	124.14	121.56	120.76	119.44	118.37	117.40	116.24	115.53	114.15	113.11	112.22	111.43	110.30
4, Good Std.	107.06	104.74	104.02	102.95	101.99	101.22	100.16	99.51	98.34	97.43	96.67	95.98	95.04
4 & 5	96.47	94.36	93.64	92.71	91.94	91.12	90.11	89.67	88.58	87.29	86.56	85.96	85.10
5 Avg. Std.	86.85	84.94	84.34	83.52	82.69	82.04	81.23	80.78	79.76	79.06	78.42	77.86	77.10
5 & 6	75.42	73.72	73.21	72.45	71.83	71.19	70.46	70.04	69.26	68.65	68.09	67.61	66.94
6, Min. Std.	67.02	65.63	65.17	64.56	63.97	63.43	62.85	62.44	61.76	61.20	60.72	61.32	59.69

Note: Tract work and highly repetitive jobs may reduce the cost 8 to 12%. Add 4% to the square foot cost of floors above the second floor level. Work outside metropolitan areas may cost 2 to 6% less. When the exterior walls are masonry, add 9 to 10% for class 2 and 1 structures and 5 to 8% for class 3, 4, 5 and 6 structures. The building area includes all full story (7'6" to 9' high) areas within and including the exterior walls of all floor areas of the building, including small inset areas such as entrances outside the exterior wall but under the main roof. For areas with a ceiling height of less than 80", see the section on half-story areas on page 30.

Single Family Residences

10 Corners (Classes 3, 4, 5 and 6) or Four Building Masses (Classes 1 and 2 only)

Estimating Procedure

1. Establish the structure quality class by applying the information on page 11.
2. Multiply the structure floor area (excluding the garage) by the appropriate square foot cost below.
3. Multiply the total from step 2 by the correct location factor listed on page 7 or 8.
4. Add, when appropriate, the cost of a porch, garage, heating and cooling equipment, basement, fireplace, carport, appliances and plumbing fixtures beyond that listed in the quality classification. See the cost of these items on pages 27 to 31.

Single Family Residence, Class 2 & 3

Single Family Residence, Class 1

Square Foot Area

Quality Class	700	800	900	1,000	1,100	1,200	1,300	1,400	1,500	1,600	1,700	1,800	2,000
1, Luxury	511.92	490.51	472.79	458.83	445.63	435.30	426.78	419.56	412.53	406.73	401.62	396.95	388.63
1, & 2	445.17	426.64	411.16	399.00	387.50	378.57	371.10	364.86	358.71	354.11	349.28	345.20	337.95
2, Semi-Luxury	308.44	296.20	286.25	277.49	270.83	264.56	259.37	254.99	250.71	247.18	244.08	241.19	236.16
2 & 3	226.44	217.46	210.13	203.75	198.78	194.19	190.35	187.11	184.03	181.36	179.17	177.04	173.37
3, Best Std.	197.57	189.74	183.36	177.76	173.44	169.49	166.14	163.32	160.62	158.32	156.36	154.55	151.26
3 & 4	168.94	162.10	156.80	151.99	148.34	144.85	142.06	139.60	137.26	135.35	133.67	132.14	129.39
4, Good Std.	145.58	139.77	135.16	130.96	127.72	124.84	122.35	120.36	118.28	116.65	115.18	113.79	111.46
4 & 5	131.11	125.88	121.72	117.98	115.12	112.47	110.24	108.39	106.59	105.11	103.71	102.49	100.42
5 Avg. Std.	118.11	113.29	109.65	106.25	103.67	101.32	99.30	97.60	96.01	94.58	93.52	92.34	90.44
5 & 6	102.43	98.36	95.08	92.20	89.95	87.88	86.21	84.69	83.26	82.09	81.09	80.04	78.51
6, Min. Std.	93.18	89.40	86.50	83.83	81.76	79.88	78.31	77.01	75.67	74.59	73.72	72.80	71.33

Square Foot Area

Quality Class	2,200	2,400	2,600	2,800	3,000	3,200	3,400	3,600	4,000	4,200	4,400	4,600	5,000
1, Luxury	382.36	380.68	371.72	367.26	364.04	361.05	358.11	355.77	351.20	348.04	345.25	342.84	339.36
1, & 2	332.51	327.48	323.28	319.32	316.65	313.96	311.44	309.36	305.49	301.86	299.47	297.40	294.46
2, Semi-Luxury	232.34	228.88	225.88	223.23	221.27	219.40	217.65	216.26	213.45	211.55	209.82	208.36	206.27
2 & 3	170.54	167.96	165.80	163.84	162.39	161.08	159.74	158.69	156.71	150.57	149.38	148.31	146.84
3, Best Std.	148.84	146.64	144.74	142.95	141.70	140.51	139.39	138.50	136.76	135.53	134.44	133.50	132.17
3 & 4	127.21	125.36	123.73	122.25	121.18	120.13	119.23	118.40	116.82	115.79	114.86	114.07	112.91
4, Good Std.	109.65	108.02	106.71	105.27	104.36	103.49	102.70	102.15	100.73	99.83	98.68	97.66	96.68
4 & 5	98.83	97.26	96.03	94.86	94.03	93.25	92.50	91.95	90.68	89.87	89.15	88.54	87.63
5 Avg. Std.	88.87	87.60	86.49	85.43	84.62	84.02	83.31	82.84	81.65	80.91	80.27	79.70	78.92
5 & 6	77.17	76.03	75.00	74.10	73.41	72.89	72.30	71.84	70.91	70.27	69.71	69.21	68.54
6, Min. Std.	70.19	69.07	68.22	67.38	66.79	66.27	65.73	65.31	64.46	63.88	63.37	62.92	62.30

Note: Tract work and highly repetitive jobs may reduce the cost 8 to 12%. Add 4% to the square foot cost of floors above the second floor level. Work outside metropolitan areas may cost 2 to 6% less. When the exterior walls are masonry, add 9 to 10% for class 2 and 1 structures and 5 to 8% for class 3, 4, 5 and 6 structures. The building area includes all full story (7'6" to 9' high) areas within and including the exterior walls of all floor areas of the building, including small inset areas such as entrances outside the exterior wall but under the main roof. For areas with a ceiling height of less than 80", see the section on half-story areas on page 30.

Quality Classification

	Class 1 Best Quality	Class 2 Good Quality	Class 3 Average Quality	Class 4 Low Quality	Class 5 Lowest Quality
Roof (11% of total cost)	Gable accented roof; asphalt shingles; min roof pitch of 3" in 12"; front and rear overhangs	One piece white baked enamel; asphalt shingles, gable accents; front and rear overhangs	One piece white baked enamel metal; asphalt shingles on gable accented roof	One piece fabricated steel; minimum pitch; small overhang in front; or asphalt shingles	Painted lightweight galvanized steel with minimum pitch; or asphalt shingles
Exterior Walls (16% of total cost)	Pre-finished shiplap aluminum siding or 1/2" masonite siding; stone accent; matching skirting; coordinated exterior colors; 6" exterior wall construction	Pre-finished shiplap alum. siding or flush-type masonite with concealed fasteners; coordinated exterior colors; exterior walls 4" thick; aluminum skirting	Pre-finished aluminum siding and/or flush-type masonite panels with concealed fasteners; 4" exterior wall thickness; aluminum skirting	Covering is pre-finished aluminum siding or flush-type masonite panels with some concealed fasteners; exterior wall thickness is 3" to 4"; skirting is lightweight	Pre-finished aluminum panels with exposed hex-heads; panels of modified corrugated pattern; exterior wall thickness 3" to 4"; lightweight skirting
Trim and Sash (8% of total cost)	Painted aluminum and/or imitation stone trim; many sash; picture/bay windows; sliding glass doors; recessed entry; dual glazed vinyl windows	Painted aluminum and/or imitation stone (fiberglass) trim; large amount of good house-type sash; picture windows; sliding glass door; recessed entry	Little or no trim; two-tone exterior coverings; large, good, house-type sash; some picture windows; optional 6' sliding glass door	No trim; exterior decoration two types of color; coordinated exterior covering; tract house windows; optional 6' sliding glass door	No ornamental trim; minimum window area and sash
Interior (5% of total cost)	Expensive hardwood paneling/gypsum board; careful workmanship throughout; coffered/vaulted/beamed ceiling; plank-type acoustical tile; 8' min ceiling; mirrored walls; built-in buffet cabinet; custom drapes; raised panel doors; skylights; window sills	Pre-finished and grooved hardwood paneling or gypsum board; careful workmanship throughout; vaulted/beamed, ceilings; 8' min ceiling height; floor to ceiling drapes over sheer underlays in living room and dining room; raised panel doors; window sills	Pre-finished and grooved hardwood, plywood paneling, or gypsum board; 8' acoustical plank-type ceilings; decorator coordinated drapes in all rooms except kitchen and baths; optional vaulted ceilings with decorative beams	Pre-finished fire rated plywood paneling or partial gypsum board; acoustical tile ceiling, 8' height; drapes in living room, dining room, and bedrooms	Walls are pre-finished 3/16" fire rated paneling; hardboard or firtex ceiling cover with exposed fasteners and/or stapled holding strips; 7' 6" ceiling heights
Floors (7% of total cost)	Hardwood or ceramic tile entry, deluxe carpet; vinyl tile in utility and guest bath. Good tile or hardwood flooring in kitchen.	Carpet with 1/2" thick pads in all rooms except guest bath and utility room; vinyl tile in kitchen, utility, and guest bath	Carpet with 1/2" thick pad in all rooms except baths and kitchen; vinyl in kitchen and baths	Carpet with 1/2" thick pad in living, dining, and bedrooms; vinyl in other areas	Vinyl; lightweight carpet in living room and master bedroom only
Heating (6% of total cost)	110,000 BTU upflow air-condition-ready forced air furnace with exterior access door; ducting to all rooms; optional air conditioning and fireplace; dual-zone heating in larger units	80,000 to 110,000 BTU upflow or downflow air-condition-ready furnace with exterior access door; ducting to all rooms; optional air conditioning and fireplace	80,000 BTU upflow or downflow forced air furnace; ducting to all rooms; optional air conditioning and fireplace	Forced air furnace; ducting in all rooms; perimeter floor return system; optional air conditioning	Forced air furnace; minimum ducting and outlets
Kitchen (21% of total cost)	18± linear foot plastic laminate or ceramic tile counter top; quality wood cabinets and hardware; dropped luminous ceiling; island work space; walk-in pantry; good quality vinyl tile	Circular or elaborate kitchen; walk-in pantry; 16± linear feet of plastic laminate counter; quality wood cabinets; dropped luminous ceiling; island work space; microwave oven	14± linear foot plastic laminate counter; good quality cabinets; built-in range and oven with a hood and fan; optional dishwasher and pantry	12± linear foot plastic laminate counter; average quality plywood cabinets with raised panel doors; built-in range and oven, hood and fan; optional dishwasher	10± linear foot plastic laminate counter; minimum quality plywood cabinets; built-in or drop-in range and oven
Baths and Plumbing (13% of total cost)	2 to 2¾ baths; 8 fixtures; master bath with two basins, sunken tub, fiberglass shower with glass door; quality medicine cabinets; 4± feet of mirror over 8± feet of cultured marble or ceramic tile lavatory top; decorative faucets; 40-gal. water heater; separate commode closet	2 baths; vent fans; master bath will have two basins, sunken tub, and stall shower; quality medicine cabinets and fixtures; cultured marble vanities; good cabinets; fiberglass shower in guest bath; 30- to 40-gallon water heater; separate commode closet	2 baths; vent fans; fiberglass shower with glass or plastic door; fiberglass or enameled steel tub; 6 to 8 linear foot cultured marble vanity, twin basin master bath; good cabinets; 30- to 40-gallon water heater	1¾ baths; fiberglass shower with glass or plastic door; fiberglass or enameled steel tub; 4 to 5 linear foot cultured marble vanity single basin; average quality cabinets; 30-gallon hot water heater	One bath; fiberglass tub or shower with curtain; small 4' plastic marble vanity; minimum quality cabinets
Bedrooms (4% of total cost)	9 to 14 linear foot floor-to-ceiling sliding mirrored wardrobe doors, or large walk-in closets	9 to 14 linear foot floor-to-ceiling mirrored sliding wardrobe doors in master bedroom, or walk-in closets	10± linear foot wardrobe; floor-to-ceiling mirrored sliding doors in master bedroom	8± linear foot wardrobe; pre-finished and grooved plywood doors; mirrored wardrobe door in master bedroom	Five to six linear foot wardrobe; plain plywood sliding doors
Exterior features (9% of total cost)	Set on concrete and/or metal piers; axle and wheel assembly for each towable section	Set on concrete and/or metal piers; axle and wheel assembly for each towable section	Set on concrete and/or metal piers; axle and wheel assembly for each towable section	Set on concrete and/or metal piers; axle and wheel assembly for each towable section	Set on concrete and/or metal piers; axle and wheel assembly for each towable section

Manufactured Housing

A manufactured home is a structure in one or more sections that is transportable, with or without a permanent foundation. No recreational vehicle or method of transporting is included in these costs. They can be from 8 to 36 feet wide and up to 80 feet long. Manufactured homes assembled from two or three attached sections are referred to as double wide or triple wide.

Tip-out, expando, or tag-a-long units have one or more telescoping or attached rooms to the side. All sections are to be included in the total square footage computations.

Area modification factors should not be used when computing the cost of manufactured housing.

Estimating Procedure

1. Establish the structure quality class by applying the information on page 16.
2. Multiply the structure floor area (excluding the garage) by the appropriate square foot cost below.
3. Add, when appropriate, the cost of foundation, air conditioning, built-ins, porch, skirting, tie-downs, carport, screen walls and roof snow load capability. See the following page.

Square Foot Area

Quality Class	500	700	900	1100	1300	1500	1700	1900	2100	2300	2500
1, Best	95.51	94.32	93.16	91.95	90.78	89.59	88.44	87.23	86.07	84.90	83.71
1, & 2	89.92	88.72	87.57	86.43	85.18	84.00	82.78	81.66	80.46	79.31	78.10
2, Good	84.27	83.11	81.94	78.52	77.41	76.29	75.08	73.97	72.77	71.67	70.54
2 & 3	78.74	77.50	76.37	71.74	70.60	69.48	68.36	67.25	66.12	64.96	63.89
3, Average	73.40	72.26	70.98	66.67	63.69	62.56	61.51	60.42	59.32	58.24	57.13
3 & 4	68.68	67.48	66.35	62.21	59.32	58.24	57.13	56.03	54.94	53.85	52.74
4, Low Average	63.95	62.80	61.61	57.69	54.94	53.85	52.74	51.64	50.57	49.47	48.38
4 & 5	60.11	58.90	57.76	54.00	51.38	50.30	49.22	48.11	47.03	45.96	44.79
5 Lowest	56.56	55.43	54.24	49.22	48.11	47.03	45.96	44.79	43.72	42.64	41.56

Manufactured Housing, Class 1

Manufactured Housing, Class 3

Manufactured Housing, Class 4

Manufactured Housing, Class 5

Manufactured Housing

Additional Costs

Permanent Foundation

Single Story
Less than 1,000 square feet of floor area	$8,180 to $14,290
Over 1,000 square feet to 1,800 square feet of floor area	$14,290 to $26,060
Over 1,800 square feet to 2,500 square feet of floor area	$26,060 to $42,800

For two-story units, use the footprint of the first floor and select a figure higher in the range of costs. For difficult site conditions, such as a high water table, heavy clay soil, over 3' foundation depth or a sloping site, use a figure in the higher range of costs.

Air Conditioning

Central air for use by existing furnace and ducts	
2 ton, up to 1,100 S.F.	$3,530
2-1/2 to 3 ton, over 1,100 to 1,600 S.F.	$4,060
4 to 5 ton, over 1,600 to 2,500 S.F.	$4,460 to $5,240.
Cost per unit	
Thru-wall small unit 1/2 H.P., 6,000 Btu	$1,230
Thru-wall large unit 1 H.P., 12,000 Btu	$1,630
Evaporative cooler, roof mounted	$1,160 to $1,830
Wiring for air conditioning	$223 to $470

Built-Ins

Dishwasher (included in classes 1, 2 & 3)	$940 - $1,250
Garbage disposal (included in all base cost, deduct if missing)	$190 - $1,160
Built-in microwave oven	$525 - $730
Trash compactor	$855 - $1,080
Wet bar (walk-up--if not included in class)	$750 - $900
Wet bar (walk behind--if not included in class)	$2,465 - $2,690
Separate shower in master bath	$855 - $1,080
One-half bath: toilet, sink, and pullman	$1,695 - $1,800
Bathroom sink or laundry sink	$360
Fireplace (permanent--includes flue)	$3,300 - $4,485
Fireplace (free standing--includes flue)	$1,505 - $2,695
Built-in buffet-hutch (included in classes 1 and 2)	$1,140 - $1,435
Whirlpool tub in master bath	$1,380 - $1,685

Porches and Decks (no roofs included)

Wood deck at home floor level with handrail, skirting, steps and outdoor carpet, per square foot of porch or deck	$18.38 to $25.76

Skirting, cost per linear foot of skirt

Lightweight aluminum panels	$8.38
Lap aluminum siding	$14.95
Painted hardboard panels	$19.19
Flagstone-type aluminum panels	$14.95
Concrete composite panels	$25.05 - $31.31
Vinyl panels	$16.67
Brick or stone	$26.26

Storage Buildings, per S.F. of floor

Aluminum exterior	$20.01
Enameled steel exterior	$16.06
Hardboard panel exterior	$35.05

Tie Downs

Cork screw anchor and straps, per each	$105 - $155

Steps And Rails per flight to 36" high

Fiberglass steps	$265 - $415
Handrail	$60 - $90

Upgraded Components

Upgraded Carpets	$1,575 - $3,920
Upgraded Drapes	$1,620 - $3,365

Carport, Porch, or Deck Roof per S.F. covered

Aluminum supports and roof cover, free standing	$15.05 - $20.00
Aluminum supports and roof cover, attached to house	$9.70 - $14.05
Wood supports and enameled steel cover, free standing	$17.65 - $22.00

Screen Wall Enclosure per linear foot of 8' wall

Wood frame with screen walls and door	$69.00
Wood or aluminum frame with screen and glass walls, with door	$120.00

Roof Snowload Capability

Cost per square foot of roof	
30 pound design load	$.76 - $1.21
40 pound design load	$1.20 - $2.18
50 pound design load	$2.18 - $2.89
60 pound design load	$2.88 - $3.85
80 pound design load	$3.65 - $5.80
100 pound design load	$4.81 - $6.65
175 pound design load	$6.10 - $7.35

Multi-Family Residences

Quality Classification

	Class 1 Best Quality	Class 2 Good Quality	Class 3 High Average Quality	Class 4 Low Average Quality	Class 5 Minimum Quality
Foundation (9% of total cost)	Conventional crawl space built on a sloping site.	Conventional crawl space built on a sloping site.	Conventional crawl space, footing over 40" deep.	Concrete slab or crawl space with 30" footing.	Concrete slab.
Floor Structure (12% of total cost)	Engineered wood, steel or concrete exceeding code requirements, complex plan, changes in elevation.	Engineered wood or steel built to meet code requirements, changes in shape and elevation.	Standard wood frame with irregular shape and changes in elevation.	Standard wood frame or concrete slab, simple floor plan.	Simple slab on grade with no changes in elevation.
Walls and Exterior Finish (12% of total cost)	Complex wood or light steel frame, stone or masonry veneer, 10' average wall height.	Wood or light steel frame, masonry veneer at entrance, good wood or stucco siding.	Wood or light steel frame, decorative trim at entrance, plywood or stucco siding, simple framing plan.	Wood frame, some ornamental details at entrance, plywood or hardboard siding.	Wood frame, little or no ornamentation, inexpensive stucco or hardboard siding.
Roof & Cover (10% of total cost)	Complex roof plan, good insulation, tile or good shake cover.	Good insulation, good shake, tile or 5-ply built-up roof.	4-ply built-up roof, some portions heavy shake or tile.	4-ply built-up roof, some portions shake or composition shingles.	4-ply built-up roof or minimum grade composition single.
Windows and Doors (5% of total cost)	Many large, good quality vinyl or metal windows, architectural grade doors.	Large, good-quality vinyl or metal windows, commercial grade doors.	Good quality vinyl or metal windows, residential grade doors.	Standard residential-grade doors and windows.	Minimum grade doors and windows.
Interior Finish (8% of total cost)	Gypsum board with heavy texture or plaster, some paneled walls, cathedral ceiling at entry, built-in cases, several wall offsets and level changes.	Textured gypsum board, some paneled walls, decorative or stain grade trim at entrance or living room, several irregular walls and wall openings.	Textured 1/2" gypsum board, several irregular walls or wall openings, few ornamental details, standard grade trim and wall molding.	Textured 1/2" gypsum board, some wall-cover or hardboard paneling, most walls are rectangular, standard grade trim and wall molding.	1/2" gypsum board with smooth finish, no ornamental details, doors and windows are the only wall openings.
Floor Finish (5% of total cost)	Masonry or stone tile entry, good hardwood or deluxe carpet in most rooms, good sheet vinyl in other rooms.	Masonry or tile at entry, hardwood or good carpet in most rooms, sheet vinyl in other rooms.	Hardwood or tile at entry, standard carpet in most rooms, sheet vinyl in kitchen and bath.	Average quality carpet or hardwood in most rooms, sheet vinyl or resilient tile in kitchen.	Minimum carpet or resilient tile throughout.
Interior Features (5% of total cost)	Breakfast bar or nook, formal dining room, one walk-in closet, linen closet utility room or pantry.	Formal dining room ample closet space linen closet and utility closet, extra shelving.	Separate dining area, good closet space, linen closet and small utility closet.	Dining area is in the kitchen, small closet in each bedroom, linen closet.	Dining area is part of kitchen, minimum closet space, minimum shelving.
Bath Detail (4% of total cost)	Good tile shower, 8' simulated marble top.	Tile shower, 6' vanity cabinet and top.	Better vanity cabinet and good wall cabinet.	Good vanity cabinet, good medicine cabinet.	Vanity and one small medicine cabinet.
Kitchen (8% of total cost)	16 LF of better hardwood wall and base cabinets, synthetic stone top, 6 very good built-in appliances.	12 LF of good hardwood wall and base cabinets, tile or acrylic top, 5 good built-in appliances.	8 LF of standard hardwood wall and base cabinets, acrylic top, 4 standard grade built-in appliances.	6 LF of low-cost wall and base cabinets, laminate counter top, 4 standard grade appliances.	5 LF of low-cost. wall & base cabinets, laminate counter top, low cost appliances.
Electrical (10% of total cost)	Ample recessed lighting, task lighting in kitchen and bath, security & computer, networks, good chandelier.	Recessed lighting in most rooms, good task lighting in kitchen & bath, security & computer networks.	Recessed lighting in kitchen and living room, switched receptacles in bedrooms, wired for cable TV.	Low-cost recessed lighting in kitchen and living room, switched receptacles in other rooms, cable TV.	Fluorescent ceiling fixture in kitchen, switched receptacles in other rooms.
Plumbing (12% of total cost)	Four excellent fixtures per bathroom, copper supply and drain lines.	Three good fixtures per bathroom, copper supply and drain lines.	Three standard fixtures per bathroom, copper supply and plastic drain lines.	Three low cost fixtures per bathroom, plastic supply and drain lines.	Three minimum-grade fixtures per bathroom, plastic supply & drains.

Plumbing costs assume 1 bathroom per unit. See page 30 for the costs of additional bathrooms.

	Class 1	Class 2	Class 3	Class 4	Class 5
For Masonry Walls	Good textured block, tile or decorative brick.	Colored or detailed block tile or decorative brick.	Colored concrete block, tile or decorative brick.	Colored concrete block or brick.	Concrete block or common brick.

When masonry walls are used in lieu of wood or light steel frame walls, add 9% to the appropriate S.F. cost.

Note: Use the percent of total cost to help identify the correct quality classification. Exceptional class multi-family residences have architectural details and features uncommon in conventional apartment buildings. Many exceptional class multi-family structures are designed for sale or conversion to condominium ownership.

Multi-Family Residences

2 or 3 Units

Estimating Procedure

1. Establish the structure quality class by applying the information on page 19.
2. Multiply the average unit area by the appropriate square foot cost below. The average unit area is found by dividing the building area on all floors by the number of units in the building. The building area should include office and utility rooms, interior hallways and interior stairways.
3. Multiply the total from step 2 by the correct location factor listed on page 7 or 8.
4. Add, when appropriate, the cost of balconies, porches, garages, heating and cooling equipment, basements, fireplaces, carports, appliances and plumbing fixtures beyond that listed in the quality classification. See the cost of these items on pages 27 to 31.
5. Costs assume one bathroom per unit. Add the cost of additional bathrooms from page 30.

Multi-Family, Class 2

Multi-Family, Class 4

Average Unit Area in Square Feet

Quality Class	400	450	500	550	600	650	700	750	800	900	1,000
Exceptional	212.20	202.92	197.85	193.35	189.90	186.78	184.43	181.74	180.16	177.06	174.16
1, Best	186.44	178.21	173.79	169.84	166.74	164.11	162.04	159.66	158.29	155.46	153.03
1, & 2	163.50	156.30	152.38	148.89	146.29	143.92	142.06	140.10	138.79	136.27	134.14
2, Good	143.06	136.83	133.36	130.38	128.02	125.89	124.34	122.57	121.45	119.29	117.41
2 & 3	130.85	125.06	122.03	119.17	117.05	115.24	113.71	112.17	111.09	109.18	107.40
3, Hi Average	119.74	114.40	111.57	109.12	107.14	105.41	103.95	102.66	101.64	99.81	98.24
3 & 4	110.56	105.67	103.07	100.69	98.88	97.38	96.10	94.71	93.88	92.19	90.73
4, Lo Average	102.12	97.58	95.13	92.97	91.33	89.86	88.62	87.43	86.69	85.17	83.74
4 & 5	94.30	90.11	87.86	85.87	84.28	82.95	81.92	80.74	80.05	78.57	77.30
5 Minimum	87.03	83.26	81.15	79.31	77.93	76.63	75.58	74.64	73.92	72.50	71.40

Average Unit Area in Square Feet

Quality Class	1,100	1,200	1,300	1,400	1,500	1,600	1,700	1,800	1,900	2,000	2,200
Exceptional	172.18	170.32	168.80	167.54	166.47	165.48	164.64	163.89	163.19	162.65	162.14
1, Best	151.12	149.72	148.22	147.17	146.18	145.34	144.58	144.06	143.37	142.85	142.46
1, & 2	132.56	131.21	130.01	129.01	128.27	127.46	126.78	126.28	125.72	125.37	124.96
2, Good	115.97	114.83	113.80	112.94	112.25	111.54	110.99	110.48	110.02	109.61	109.34
2 & 3	106.18	104.93	104.18	103.30	102.67	102.02	101.51	101.15	100.64	100.33	100.00
3, Hi Average	97.08	96.10	95.24	94.45	93.89	93.32	92.84	92.56	92.03	91.76	91.47
3 & 4	89.67	88.65	87.90	87.22	86.72	86.16	85.81	85.34	84.99	84.77	84.48
4, Lo Average	82.80	81.92	81.16	80.55	80.07	79.58	79.16	78.80	78.48	78.24	77.99
4 & 5	76.45	75.67	75.03	74.35	73.94	73.48	73.09	72.83	72.46	72.25	72.02
5 Minimum	70.52	69.87	69.22	68.72	68.23	67.80	67.51	67.15	66.96	66.65	66.51

Note: Work outside metropolitan areas may cost 2 to 6% less. Add 2% to the costs for second floor areas and 4% for third floor areas. Add 9% when the exterior walls are masonry.

Multi-Family Residences

4 to 9 Units

Estimating Procedure

1. Establish the structure quality class by applying the information on page 19.
2. Multiply the average unit area by the appropriate square foot cost below. The average unit area is found by dividing the building area on all floors by the number of units in the building. The building area should include office and utility rooms, interior hallways and interior stairways.
3. Multiply the total from step 2 by the correct location factor listed on page 7 or 8.
4. Add, when appropriate, the cost of balconies, porches, garages, heating and cooling equipment, basements, fireplaces, carports, appliances and plumbing fixtures beyond that listed in the quality classification. See the cost of these items on pages 27 to 31.
5. Costs assume one bathroom per unit. Add the cost of additional bathrooms from page 30.

Multi-Family, Class 3 & 4

Multi-Family, Class 3

Average Unit Area in Square Feet

Quality Class	400	450	500	550	600	650	700	750	800	900	1,000
Exceptional	199.84	191.00	186.14	182.20	178.74	175.94	173.82	171.40	169.81	166.55	163.89
1, Best	175.64	167.82	163.52	160.06	157.11	154.58	152.67	150.58	149.20	146.40	144.06
1, & 2	153.93	147.16	143.36	140.40	137.69	135.53	133.92	132.00	130.85	128.38	126.28
2, Good	134.73	128.81	125.50	122.81	120.54	118.61	117.16	115.44	114.40	112.29	110.48
2 & 3	123.27	117.79	114.83	112.35	110.25	108.48	107.18	105.65	104.74	102.69	101.15
3, Hi Average	112.77	107.81	104.98	102.74	100.74	99.21	98.06	96.57	95.83	93.90	92.56
3 & 4	104.18	99.50	96.91	94.84	93.14	91.68	90.48	89.15	88.49	86.79	85.34
4, Lo Average	96.13	91.83	89.61	87.61	85.98	84.59	83.50	82.42	81.69	80.12	78.80
4 & 5	88.75	84.84	82.74	80.90	79.37	78.11	77.22	76.10	75.41	73.98	72.83
5 Minimum	81.97	78.32	76.30	74.72	73.31	72.14	71.33	70.28	69.57	68.27	67.15

Average Unit Area in Square Feet

Quality Class	1,100	1,200	1,300	1,400	1,500	1,600	1,700	1,800	1,900	2,000	2,200
Exceptional	162.27	160.51	159.07	157.79	156.81	155.74	154.98	154.35	153.58	153.04	152.67
1, Best	142.48	141.04	139.73	138.60	137.79	136.84	136.17	135.57	134.89	134.47	134.14
1, & 2	124.98	123.62	122.57	121.54	120.73	119.96	119.41	118.87	118.31	117.94	117.58
2, Good	109.38	108.22	107.26	106.33	105.67	105.01	104.53	104.01	103.54	103.17	102.90
2 & 3	100.07	98.99	98.06	97.24	96.74	96.13	95.60	95.18	94.66	94.34	94.14
3, Hi Average	91.55	90.48	89.69	89.07	88.49	87.86	87.42	87.03	86.61	86.40	86.09
3 & 4	84.54	83.50	82.82	82.13	81.64	81.15	80.74	80.41	80.05	79.67	79.53
4, Lo Average	78.01	77.22	76.50	75.90	75.41	74.92	74.64	74.26	73.92	73.61	73.41
4 & 5	72.04	71.33	70.66	70.03	69.57	69.19	68.82	68.56	68.19	67.95	67.77
5 Minimum	66.55	65.86	65.24	64.66	64.28	63.91	63.58	63.34	63.01	62.70	62.61

Note: Work outside metropolitan areas may cost 2 to 6% less. Add 2% to the costs for second floor areas and 4% for third floor areas. Add 9% when the exterior walls are masonry.

Multi-Family Residences

10 or More Units

Estimating Procedure

1. Establish the structure quality class by applying the information on page 19.
2. Multiply the average unit area by the appropriate square foot cost below. The average unit area is found by dividing the building area on all floors by the number of units in the building. The building area should include office and utility rooms, interior hallways and interior stairways.
3. Multiply the total from step 2 by the correct location factor listed on page 7 or 8.
4. Add, when appropriate, the cost of balconies, porches, garages, heating and cooling equipment, basements, fireplaces, carports, appliances and plumbing fixtures beyond that listed in the quality classification. See the cost of these items on pages 27 to 31.
5. Costs assume one bathroom per unit. Add the cost of additional bathrooms from page 30.

Multi-Family, Class 4

Multi-Family, Class 3 & 4

Average Unit in Square Feet

Quality Class	400	450	500	550	600	650	700	750	800	900	1,000
Exceptional	188.94	179.64	175.94	172.26	168.80	166.18	163.89	161.86	160.23	157.42	155.12
1, Best	165.89	157.83	154.58	151.28	148.22	146.01	144.06	142.20	140.70	138.36	136.25
1, & 2	145.45	138.41	135.53	132.69	130.01	128.08	126.28	124.63	123.44	121.21	119.51
2, Good	127.30	121.09	118.61	116.06	113.80	112.09	110.48	109.13	108.04	106.13	104.54
2 & 3	116.45	110.79	108.48	106.27	104.18	102.55	101.15	99.84	98.87	97.08	95.63
3, Hi Average	106.53	101.28	99.21	97.16	95.24	93.74	92.56	91.33	90.37	88.75	87.48
3 & 4	98.39	93.66	91.68	89.69	87.90	86.51	85.34	84.28	83.45	82.01	80.81
4, Lo Average	90.81	86.44	84.59	82.82	81.16	80.02	78.80	77.93	77.17	75.68	74.67
4 & 5	83.92	79.85	78.11	76.50	75.03	73.82	72.83	71.85	71.15	69.88	68.88
5 Minimum	77.45	73.70	72.14	70.66	69.22	68.17	67.15	66.40	65.68	64.54	63.60

Average Unit in Square Feet

Quality Class	1,100	1,200	1,300	1,400	1,500	1,600	1,700	1,800	1,900	2,000	2,200
Exceptional	153.18	151.66	150.19	149.05	147.87	147.08	146.48	145.77	145.13	144.48	144.18
1, Best	134.56	133.20	131.99	130.85	129.88	129.17	128.69	128.03	127.57	126.92	126.60
1, & 2	117.98	116.78	115.71	114.83	113.90	113.36	112.84	112.31	111.79	111.37	110.97
2, Good	103.27	102.24	101.28	100.42	99.59	99.16	98.69	98.25	97.76	97.38	97.16
2 & 3	94.55	93.55	92.66	91.92	91.05	90.68	90.34	89.86	89.49	89.10	88.88
3, Hi Average	86.44	85.59	84.77	84.05	83.38	82.95	82.65	82.22	81.88	81.54	81.22
3 & 4	79.85	78.99	78.31	77.62	76.93	76.63	76.21	75.96	75.58	75.25	75.10
4, Lo Average	73.70	72.96	72.25	71.67	71.13	70.76	70.40	70.05	69.86	69.49	69.36
4 & 5	68.07	67.46	66.77	66.21	65.66	65.27	65.02	64.77	64.45	64.21	64.00
5 Minimum	62.84	62.19	61.65	61.16	60.61	60.27	60.09	59.78	59.54	59.26	59.13

Note: Work outside metropolitan areas may cost 2 to 6% less. Add 2% to the costs for second floor areas and 4% for third floor areas. Add 9% when the exterior walls are masonry.

Motels

Quality Classification

	Class 1 Best Quality	Class 2 Good Quality	Class 3 Average Quality	Class 4 Low Quality
Foundation (4%) Foundation costs will vary greatly with substrate, type, and location.	Concrete slab	Concrete slab	Concrete slab	Concrete slab
Framing* (20% of total Cost)	Wood frame.	Wood frame.	Wood frame.	Wood frame.
Windows (2% of total Cost)	Large, good quality.	Average number and quality.	Average number and quality.	Small, few, low cost.
Roofing (8% of total Cost)	Heavy, shake, tile or slate.	Medium shake or good built-up with large rock, inexpensive tile.	Wood or good composition shingle, light shake, or good built-up with rock.	Inexpensive shingles or built-up with rock.
Overhang (2% of total Cost)	36" open or 24" closed.	30" open or small closed.	16" open.	12" to 16" open.
Exterior Walls (10% of total Cost)	Good wood or stucco, masonry veneer on front.	Good wood siding or stucco with some veneer.	Hardboard, wood shingle, plywood or stucco.	Low cost stucco, hardboard or plywood.
Flooring (5% of total Cost)	Good carpet, good sheet vinyl.	Good carpet, sheet vinyl or inlaid resilient.	Average carpet, average resilient tile in bath.	Minimum tile or low cost carpet.
Interior Finish (23% of total cost including finish carpentry, wiring, lighting, etc.)	Gypsum board with heavy texture or plaster with putty coat. Some good sheet wall cover or paneling.	Gypsum board, taped, textured and painted or plaster. Some wallpaper.	Gypsum board taped and textured or colored interior stucco.	Minimum gypsum board.
Baths (15% of total Cost)	Vinyl or foil wall cover, ceramic tile over tub with glass shower door, ample mirrors.	Ceramic tile over tub with glass shower door.	Plastic coated hardboard with low cost glass shower door.	Plastic coated hardboard with one small mirror.
Plumbing* (9% of total Cost)	Copper tube, good quality fixtures.	Galvanized pipe, good fixtures.	Average cost fixtures.	Plastic pipe, low cost fixtures.
Special Features (2% of total Cost)	8' sliding glass door, 8' to 10' tile pullman in bath.	8' sliding glass door, good tile or plastic top pullman in bath.	Small tile or plastic pullman in bath.	None.
*For Masonry Walls	8" textured face reinforced masonry.	8" colored or detailed reinforced masonry.	8" colored block or common brick, reinforced.	8" painted concrete block.

Note: When masonry walls are used in lieu of wood frame walls add 8% to the appropriate cost

Add the Following Amounts per Kitchen Unit **Kitchens	Good sink, 8' to 10' of good cabinets and drainboard - $3,670	Average sink and 6' to 8' average cabinet and drainboard - $3,400	Low cost sink, and 5' of cabinets and drainboard - $2,455	Minimum sink, cabinets and drainboard - $2,070

Add the cost of built-in kitchen fixtures from the table of costs for built-in appliances on page 29.

Note: Use the percent of total cost to help identify the correct quality classification.

Motels

9 Units or Less

Estimating Procedure

1. Establish the structure quality class by applying the information on page 23.
2. Multiply the average unit area by the appropriate cost below. The average unit area is found by dividing the total building area on all floors (including office and manager's area, utility rooms, interior hallways and stairway area) by the number of units in the building.
3. Multiply the total from step 2 by the correct location factor listed on page 7 or 8.
4. Add, when appropriate, the cost of heating and cooling equipment, porches, balconies, exterior stairs, garages, kitchens, built-in kitchen appliances and fireplaces. See pages 23 and 27 to 31.

Motel, Class 3 & 4

Average Unit Area in Square Feet

Quality Class	200	225	250	275	300	330	375	425	500	600	720
1, Best	154.33	148.81	144.46	140.78	137.78	134.79	131.18	128.00	124.46	121.05	118.26
1 & 2	141.77	136.67	132.68	129.34	126.59	123.79	120.42	117.56	114.29	111.23	108.62
2, Good	131.56	126.87	123.14	120.06	117.47	114.92	111.81	109.16	106.07	103.20	100.81
2 & 3	120.89	116.60	113.13	110.31	107.95	105.58	102.70	100.28	97.48	94.87	92.68
3, Average	112.18	108.17	105.02	102.36	100.15	97.94	95.33	93.01	90.44	87.99	85.98
3 & 4	102.96	99.28	96.38	93.94	91.95	89.90	87.47	85.42	82.99	80.78	78.87
4, Low	94.12	90.72	88.04	85.88	84.01	82.19	79.96	78.05	75.84	73.80	72.08

Note: Add 2% for work above the first floor. Work outside metropolitan areas may cost 2 to 6% less. Add 8% when the exterior walls are masonry. Deduct 2% for area built on a concrete slab.

Motels

10 to 24 Units

Estimating Procedure

1. Establish the structure quality class by applying the information on page 23.
2. Multiply the average unit area by the appropriate cost below. The average unit area is found by dividing the total building area on all floors (including office and manager's area, utility rooms, interior hallways and stairway area) by the number of units in the building.
3. Multiply the total from step 2 by the correct location factor listed on page 7 or 8.
4. Add, when appropriate, the cost of heating and cooling equipment, porches, balconies, exterior stairs, garages, kitchens, built-in kitchen appliances and fireplaces. See pages 23 and 27 to 31.

Motel, Class 3

Average Unit Area in Square Feet

Quality Class	200	225	250	275	300	330	375	425	500	600	720
1, Best	149.53	144.22	139.92	136.47	133.54	130.59	127.08	124.05	120.60	117.29	114.60
1 & 2	137.35	132.48	128.54	125.34	122.63	119.96	116.73	113.93	110.77	107.79	105.24
2, Good	127.58	123.05	119.35	116.37	113.90	111.40	108.39	105.77	102.82	100.07	97.78
2 & 3	117.16	112.98	109.57	106.86	104.59	102.22	99.54	97.13	94.42	91.86	89.74
3, Average	108.68	104.80	101.74	99.14	97.01	94.91	92.33	90.12	87.61	85.29	83.25
3 & 4	99.75	96.19	93.37	91.01	89.07	87.10	84.73	82.76	80.38	78.26	76.45
4, Low	91.18	87.89	85.33	83.21	81.41	79.66	77.45	75.62	73.53	71.55	69.89

Note: Add 2% for work above the first floor. Work outside metropolitan areas may cost 2 to 6% less. Add 8% when the exterior walls are masonry. Deduct 2% for area built on a concrete slab.

Motels

Over 24 Units

Estimating Procedure

1. Establish the structure quality class by applying the information on page 23.
2. Multiply the average unit area by the appropriate cost below. The average unit area is found by dividing the total building area on all floors (including office and manager's area, utility rooms, interior hallways and stairway area) by the number of units in the building.
3. Multiply the total from step 2 by the correct location factor listed on page 7 or 8.
4. Add, when appropriate, the cost of heating and cooling equipment, porches, balconies, exterior stairs, garages, kitchens, built-in kitchen appliances and fireplaces. See pages 23 and 27 to 31.

Motel, Class 2 & 3

Average Unit Area in Square Feet

Quality Class	200	225	250	275	300	330	375	425	500	600	720
1, Best	144.61	139.44	135.30	131.96	129.07	126.27	122.86	119.95	116.63	113.46	110.87
1 & 2	132.90	128.15	124.31	121.24	118.61	116.00	112.85	110.19	107.13	104.24	101.84
2, Good	123.35	119.01	115.45	112.58	110.17	107.74	104.89	102.30	99.51	96.79	94.58
2 & 3	113.32	109.24	106.02	103.39	101.12	98.92	96.27	93.90	91.35	88.91	86.86
3, Average	105.10	101.33	98.35	95.89	93.80	91.80	89.32	87.19	84.76	82.45	80.58
3 & 4	96.45	92.99	90.22	87.93	86.09	84.24	81.91	79.97	77.77	75.68	73.92
4, Low	88.19	85.01	82.47	80.40	78.68	76.99	74.88	73.10	71.09	69.20	67.56

Note: Add 2% for work above the first floor. Work outside metropolitan areas may cost 2 to 6% less. Add 8% when the exterior walls are masonry. Deduct 2% for area built on a concrete slab.

Additional Costs for Residential Structures

Covered Porches

Estimate covered porches by applying a fraction of the main building square foot cost.

Porch Description	Suggested Fraction
Ground level floor (usually concrete) without banister, with no ceiling and shed-type roof.	1/4 to 1/3
High (house floor level) floor (concrete or wood) with light banister, no ceiling and shed-type roof.	1/3 to 1/2
Same as above with a finished ceiling and roof like the residence (most typical).	1/2
Same as above but partially enclosed with screen or glass.	1/2 to 2/3
Enclosed lean-to (sleeping porch, etc.) with lighter foundation, wall structure, interior finish or roof than that of house to which it is attached.	1/2 to 3/4
Roofed, enclosed, recessed porch, under the same roof as the main building and with the same type and quality foundation (includes shape costs).	3/4
Roofed, enclosed, recessed porch with the same type roof and foundation as the main building (includes shape costs).	4/4
Good arbor or pergola with floor.	1/4 to 1/3

Uncovered Concrete Decks, cost per square foot, 4" thick concrete

	On Grade	1' High	2' High	3' High	4' High
Less than 100 square feet	$7.83	$10.95	$17.60	$24.71	$36.03
100 to 200 square feet	7.13	9.88	14.28	20.08	26.76
200 to 400 square feet	6.06	7.83	12.23	17.80	23.06
Over 400 square feet	5.87	7.13	10.75	14.28	18.58

Uncovered Wood Decks, cost per square foot, 2" thick deck with typical steps and railing

1' to 4' above ground.	$21.99 to $25.66
Over 4' to 6' above ground	25.48 to 32.92
Over 6' to 9' above ground	26.60 to 34.86
Over 9' to 12' above ground	27.62 to 36.48
Over 12' above ground	29.04 to 37.71

Porch Roofs, cost per square foot based on wood shingle cover

Type	Cost per Square Foot	Alternate Roof Covers	Cost Difference per S.F.		
Unceiled shed roof	$8.80 to $10.47	Corrugated aluminum	Deduct	$.79 to	$.99
Ceiled shed roof	14.83 to 16.81	Roll asphalt	Deduct	.79 to	.88
Unceiled gable roof	9.89 to 12.85	Fiberglass shingles	Deduct	.98 to	1.09
Ceiled gable roof	16.80 to 18.59	Wood shakes	Add	1.09 to	1.68
(See the figures at the right for other roof cover)		Clay or concrete tile	Add	6.33 to	7.72
		Slate	Add	6.92 to	9.54

Residential Basements, cost per square foot, including stairs

Size	Unfinished Basements	Finished Basements
Less than 400 square feet	$42 to $74	$62 to $96
400 - 1,000 square feet	32 to 45	53 to 65
Over 1,000 square feet	27 to 33	49 to 56

These basement costs assume normal soil conditions, 7' headroom, no plumbing, partitions or windows. Unfinished basements have reinforced concrete floors and concrete or concrete block walls, a floor drain, stairway with a landing and handrail, open ceilings and one switched fluorescent fixture. Finished residential basements have a tile ceiling, resilient flooring, wood panel walls and lighting similar to Class 5 residences. Residential basements are common in climates where footing depths must be 4' or more to prevent frost heaving. These figures assume the residence is in an area where minimum footing depth is 4 feet. Where climate doesn't influence footing depth, unfinished basement costs will be 20% to 50% higher.

Additional Costs for Residential Structures

Balconies, Standard Wood Frame, cost per square foot, including foundations

Supported by 4" x 4" posts, 2" wood floor, open on underside, open 2" x 4" railing.	$19.55 to $21.22
Supported by 4" x 4" posts, 2" wood floor, sealed on underside, solid stucco or wood siding on railing.	22.98 to 24.75
Supported by steel columns, lightweight concrete floor, sealed on underside, solid stucco or open grillwork railing	34.94 to 38.69

Heating and Cooling Equipment

Prices include wiring and minimum duct work.
Use the higher figures for smaller residences and in more extreme climates where greater heating and cooling density is required. Cost per square foot of heated or cooled area.

Type	Perimeter Outlets	Overhead Outlets
Central Ducted Air Systems, Single Family		
Forced air heating	$5.36 to $5.93	$4.19 to $4.79
Forced air heating and cooling	6.03 to 7.18	5.76 to 6.08
Gravity heat	3.86 to 5.20	—
Central Ducted Air Systems, Multi-Family		
Forced air heating	4.61 to 5.08	4.41 to 5.07
Forced air heating and cooling	6.38 to 7.03	5.62 to 6.01
Motel Units		
Forced air heating	5.52 to 5.84	5.31 to 5.76
Forced air heating and cooling	6.51 to 7.03	6.32 to 6.51
Circulating hot and cold water system	12.80 to 15.06	12.80 to 15.06

Floor and Wall Furnaces, cost each

Single floor unit	$1,240 to $1,415
Dual floor unit	2,205 to 2,370
Single wall unit	795 to 1,020
Dual wall unit	1,475 to 1,705
Thermostat control, add	115 to 138

Electric Baseboard Units, cost each

500 watts, 3'	$296 to $332
1,000 watts, 4'	411 to 456
1,500 watts, 6'	442 to 489
2,000 watts, 8'	536 to 614
2,500 watts, 10'	624 to 681
3,000 watts, 12'	750 to 815

Outside Stairways, cost per square foot of horizontal step area

Standard wood frame, wood steps with open risers, open on underside, open 2" x 4" railing, unpainted.	$17.58 to $19.34
Standard wood frame, solid wood risers, sealed on underside, solid stucco or wood siding on railing.	21.22 to 25.00
Precast concrete steps with open risers, steel frame, pipe rail with ornamental grillwork.	46.18 to 51.50

Window Type or Thru-the-Wall Refrigerated Room Coolers, cost each

1/3 ton	$756 to $888
1/2	885 to 1,065
3/4	916 to 1,416
1	1,060 to 1,225
1-1/2	1,276 to 1,550
2	1,545 to 1,890
Ton = 12,000 Btu	

Electric Wall Heaters, cost each

1,000 watts	$410 to $480
2,000	477 to 515
3,000	500 to 647
3,500	580 to 714
4,000	682 to 750
4,500	750 to 955
Add for circulating fan	79 to 115
Add for thermostat	52 to 115

Additional Costs for Residential Structures

Appliances. Add these costs only when the appliance is not included in the quality class. Includes installation.

Built-in single wall oven with broiler	$550 to $665	Range hood and fan	$165 to $390
Built-in double wall oven with microwave	995 to 1,870	Franklin or Buck stove	
Drop-in range with single oven, economy	440 to 665	Steel, cast iron front	1,320 to 1,990
Drop-in range with single oven, excellent	1,100 to 2,060	Steel, cast iron front, glass door	1,990 to 2,760
Range top, four elements		All cast iron, glass panel door	3,420 to 4,965
Residential grade, without grill	495 to 940	Under counter 5 CF refrigerator	610 to 885
Residential grade, with grill	720 to 1,385	Central vacuum, 3 to 5 outlets	1,880 to 3,755
Commercial grade	3,755 to 6,290	Dishwasher	300 to 1,110
Hot water circulator	610 to 660	Garbage disposal	200 to 467
Instant hot water dispenser	510 to 720	Trash compactor	377 to 633

Fireplaces, cost each, including reinforced foundation, flue, cap, gas line and valve.

	1 Story	**2 Story**
Freestanding wood burning heat circulating prefab metal fireplace with interior flue, base and cap	$1,965	$2,400
36" wide zero-clearance enclosed metal firebox, brick face, wood mantel	2,300	2,620
48" wide zero-clearance enclosed metal firebox, raised hearth, brick face and mantel	3,170	3,608
Masonry, 5' base, common brick or block on interior face, wood or brick mantle	5,025	5,680
Masonry, 6' base, used brick or natural stone on interior face, raised hearth	9,940	11,910
Masonry, 8' base, used brick or natural stone on interior face, raised hearth	12,000	17,470

Residential Garages and Carports

Attached and detached garages for single family dwellings usually fall in the same quality class as the main structure. Costs are per SF of floor based on wood or light steel construction. Add 8% if exterior walls are masonry. Attached garages assume a 20 foot wall in common with the main structure. Multiply the square foot cost below by the correct location factor on page 7 or 8 to find the square foot cost for any garage. Costs include interior finish and one light fixture per 300 SF of floor. Deduct 10% to 18% if interior walls are unfinished. Where dwelling and exterior garage walls are in vertical alignment with second floor walls, the garage cost per SF will be about 2/3 of the main dwelling cost per SF if finished and 1/2 of the main dwelling cost if unfinished. Carports with wood or steel posts, an asphalt floor, and built-up or metal roof will cost $15.50 to $17.90 per SF.

Square Foot Area for Attached Garages for Single Family Dwellings

Quality Class	220	260	280	320	360	400	440	480	540	600	720
1, Luxury	148.20	141.21	138.23	133.88	128.85	125.65	121.90	118.88	115.94	113.05	110.24
1, & 2	128.56	122.61	120.15	116.19	112.20	109.39	106.15	103.52	100.93	98.45	95.98
2, Semi-Luxury	96.63	92.29	90.54	87.59	84.58	82.48	80.03	78.05	76.12	74.20	72.36
2 & 3	78.18	73.23	72.10	71.14	68.70	67.00	64.99	63.40	61.82	60.28	58.79
3, Best Std.	64.98	62.14	61.02	59.08	57.23	55.81	54.16	52.79	51.49	50.20	48.96
3 & 4	55.03	52.80	51.89	50.33	48.51	47.29	45.88	44.74	43.63	42.55	41.50
4, Good Std.	48.71	46.48	45.65	44.40	42.93	41.86	40.61	39.60	38.62	37.66	36.73
4 & 5	45.97	43.49	42.50	41.11	39.63	38.65	37.49	36.57	35.65	34.78	33.90
5 Avg. Std.	43.05	40.41	39.46	37.96	36.33	35.42	34.37	33.51	32.69	31.87	31.08
5 & 6	38.20	36.07	35.26	33.89	32.64	31.82	30.87	30.11	29.36	28.63	27.91
6, Min. Std.	33.47	31.73	31.23	30.20	29.05	28.32	27.48	26.79	26.12	25.48	24.84

Square Foot Area for Detached Garages for Single Family Dwellings

Quality Class	220	260	280	320	360	400	440	480	540	600	720
1, Luxury	168.58	155.79	151.15	143.09	140.26	135.81	129.90	126.67	123.53	120.46	117.47
1, & 2	145.23	134.67	130.36	123.68	121.45	117.59	112.48	109.69	106.96	104.29	101.70
2, Semi-Luxury	108.25	100.65	97.67	92.71	91.10	88.21	84.35	82.28	80.24	78.24	76.29
2 & 3	87.52	81.29	78.82	74.86	73.64	71.29	68.19	66.51	64.85	63.24	61.67
3, Best Std.	72.46	67.28	65.31	62.11	61.10	59.16	56.58	55.18	53.79	52.47	51.17
3 & 4	64.18	59.74	57.94	55.16	54.34	52.59	50.32	49.07	47.85	46.64	45.50
4, Good Std.	56.61	52.72	51.13	48.62	47.90	46.37	44.36	43.25	42.18	41.13	40.11
4 & 5	52.30	48.67	47.26	44.52	44.34	42.93	41.05	40.03	39.04	38.06	37.12
5 Avg. Std.	49.42	45.24	43.63	41.13	40.24	38.97	37.27	36.34	35.43	34.55	33.70
5 & 6	41.58	38.40	37.08	35.16	34.58	33.48	32.01	31.22	30.44	29.69	28.94
6, Min. Std.	36.22	33.46	32.51	30.85	30.42	29.45	28.17	27.48	26.78	26.11	25.48

Additional Costs for Residential Structures

Costs for Multi-Family Residential Bathrooms beyond 1 per unit

	Class 1 Best Quality	Class 2 Good Quality	Class 3 High Average	Class 4 Low Average	Class 5 Minimum Quality
2 or 3 units					
2 fixture bath	$7,803	$6,280	$5,312	$4,425	$3,747
3 fixture bath	11,325	9,656	8,010	6,895	5,520
4 fixture bath	14,410	12,455	11,120	9,110	7,800
4 to 9 units					
2 fixture bath	7,200	5,970	4,990	4,170	3,438
3 fixture bath	10,190	8,850	7,618	6,332	5,096
4 fixture bath	14,100	11,940	9,870	8,205	6,795
10 or more units					
2 fixture bath	6,485	5,520	4,685	3,644	3,005
3 fixture bath	9,985	8,338	7,000	5,518	4,530
4 fixture bath	13,175	11,325	9,058	7,412	5,662

Half Story Areas

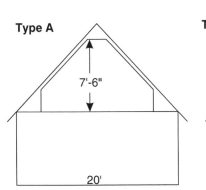

Type A — 7'-6" — 20'

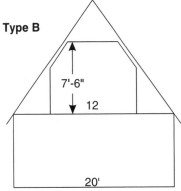

Type B — 7'-6" — 12 — 20'

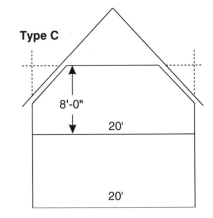

Type C — 8'-0" — 20' — 20'

Use a fraction of the basic square foot cost for figuring the reduced headroom floor area.
Type "C" includes typical dormers.

Type	Same Finish As Main Area	Lesser Quality Finish
A	1/3	1/4
B	1/2	1/3
C	2/3	1/2

Elevators, per shaft cost for car and machinery

Hydraulic based on two stops

Capacity	100 F.P.M.	200 F.P.M.
2,000 lbs.	$43,970	$72,760
2,500 lbs.	47,178	75,925
3,000 lbs.	49,020	81,310
3,500 lbs.	—	86,100
4,000 lbs.	—	88,900

Add for deluxe car, $8,325. Add for each additional stop over 2: $3,500, baked enamel doors $8,610, stainless steel doors $9,010.

Electric based on six stops

Capacity	200 F.P.M.	250 F.P.M.	300 F.P.M.
2,000 lbs.	$110,412	$116,880	$121,260
2,500 lbs.	116,880	123,350	130,835
3,000 lbs.	125,471	137,235	141,640
3,500 lbs.	137,235	145,825	153,362
4,000 lbs.	146,945	157,645	165,205

Add $8,540 for a deluxe car. Add $9,270 for each additional stop over 6.

Multi-Family and Motel Garages Cost Per Square Foot

Garages built at ground level under a multi-family or motel unit. The costs below include the following components:

1. A reinforced concrete floor in all areas.
2. Exterior walls, on one long side and two short sides, made up of a wood frame and good quality stucco, wood siding or masonry veneer.
3. A finished ceiling in all areas.
4. The difference between the cost of a standard wood frame floor structure at second floor level and one at ground level.
5. An inexpensive light fixture for each 600 square feet.

Where no exterior walls enclose the two short sides, use $^2/_3$ of the square foot cost.

Garages built as separate structures for multi-family or motel units. The costs below include the following components:

1. Foundations.
2. A reinforced concrete floor in all areas.
3. Exterior walls on one long side and two short sides, made up of a wood frame and good quality stucco, wood siding or masonry veneer.
4. Steel support columns supporting the roof.

5. A wood frame roof structure with composition tar and gravel, wood shingle or light shake cover. No interior ceiling finish.
6. An inexpensive light fixture for each 600 square feet.

Use the location modifiers on page 7 or 8 to adjust garage costs to any area.

Basement Garages

Costs listed below are per square foot of floor, including the horizontal area of stairs and the approach ramp. These costs assume a single-level garage is built on one level, approximately 5 feet below grade, directly below 2 to 4 story multi-family structure with perimeter walls in vertical alignment. These costs include:

1. Excavation to 5' below ground line.

2. Full wall enclosure.

3. Typical storage facilities.

4. Minimum lighting.

5. Concrete floors.

Use the location modifiers on page 7 or 8 to adjust garage costs to the site.

Ground Level Garages

Area	400	800	1,200	2,000	3,000	5,000	10,000	20,000
Cost	34.42	30.69	27.38	24.20	22.65	21.64	21.11	20.08

Separate Structure Garages

Area	400	800	1,200	2,000	3,000	5,000	10,000	20,000
Cost	39.50	35.20	32.22	30.58	29.23	28.00	26.86	26.35

Basement Garages

Type	5,000	7,500	10,000	15,000	20,000	30,000	40,000	60,000
Reinforced concrete exterior walls and columns. Flat concrete roof slab.	52.62	48.09	46.00	45.34	43.99	43.47	42.84	42.33
Concrete block exterior walls, reinforced concrete columns. Flat concrete roof slab.	52.20	48.88	45.66	44.50	43.45	42.95	42.33	41.30
Concrete block exterior walls, steel posts and beams, light concrete/metal roof fireproofed with spray plaster.	49.00	44.81	42.64	36.90	35.36	39.50	38.35	37.75
Concrete block exterior walls, wood posts and beams, light concrete/metal roof fireproofed with spray plaster.	43.65	41.50	38.90	36.20	35.15	34.62	34.11	33.48
Add for each security gate	3.28	2.38	2.01	1.42	1.26	1.02	.89	.78

Cabins and Recreational Dwellings

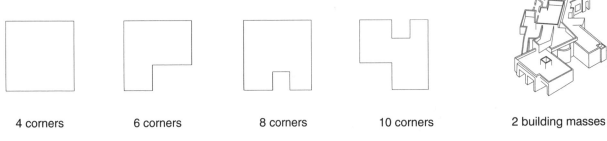

| 4 corners | 6 corners | 8 corners | 10 corners | 2 building masses |

Example of Dwelling Shapes

Cabins and recreational dwellings are designed for single family occupancy, usually on an intermittent basis. These structures are characterized by a more rustic interior and exterior finish and often have construction details which would not meet building requirements in metropolitan areas. Classify these structures into either "conventional type" or "A-frame" construction. Conventional dwellings have an exterior wall which is approximately 8 feet high on all sides. A-frame cabins have a sloping roof which reduces the horizontal area 8 feet above the first floor to between 50% and 75% of the first floor area.

Conventional recreational dwellings vary widely in quality and the quality of construction is the most significant factor influencing cost. Conventional recreational dwellings are listed in six quality classes. Class 1 is the most expensive commonly encountered and Class 6 is the minimum commonly encountered. Nearly all conventional recreational dwellings built from stock plans will fall into Class 3, 4, 5, or 6. For convenience, these classes are labeled *Best Standard, Good Standard, Average Standard* or *Minimum Standard*. Class 1 residences are labeled *Luxury*. Class 2 residences are labeled *Semi-Luxury*. Class 1 and 2 residences are designed by professional architects, usually to meet preferences of the first owner.

The shape of the outside perimeter also has a significant influence on cost: The more complex the shape, the more expensive the structure per square foot of floor. The shape classification of multiple story or split-level conventional recreational dwellings should be based on the outline formed by the outermost exterior walls, including the garage area, regardless of the story level. Most conventional recreational dwellings fall into Classes 3, 4, 5 or 6 and have 4, 6, 8 or 10 corners, as illustrated above. Small insets that do not require a change in the roof line can be ignored when evaluating the outside perimeter.

Class 1 and 2 *(Luxury and Semi-Luxury)* conventional recreational dwellings have more than ten corners and are best evaluated by counting the "building masses." A building mass is a group of contiguous rooms on one or more levels with access at varying angles from a common point or hallway. The illustration at the right above represents a conventional recreational dwelling with two building masses. Most Class 1 and Class 2 conventional recreational dwellings have from one to four building masses, ignoring any attached garage. For convenience, cost tables for Class 1 and 2 conventional recreational dwellings with one, two, three or four building masses have been appended to cost tables for Class 3, 4, 5 and 6 conventional recreational dwellings with 4, 6, 8 and 10 building corners.

Conventional recreational dwellings which have features of two or more quality classes can be placed between two of the six labeled classes. The tables have five half-classes (1 & 2, 2 & 3, etc.) which can be applied to conventional recreational dwellings with some characteristics of two or more quality classes. If a portion of a conventional recreational dwelling differs significantly in quality from other portions, evaluate the square footage of each portion separately.

Cabins and recreational dwellings are often built under difficult working conditions and in remote sites. Individual judgments may be necessary in evaluating the cost impact of the dwelling location. The costs assume construction by skilled professional craftsmen. Where non-professional labor or second quality materials are used, use the next lower quality classification that might otherwise apply. If the structure is assembled from prefabricated components, use costs for the next lower half class.

Conventional Recreational Dwellings

Quality Classification

	Class 1 Luxury	Class 2 Semi-Luxury	Class 3 Best Std.	Class 4 Good Std.	Class 5 Average Std	Class 6 Minimum Std.
Foundation (8% of total cost)	Reinforced concrete on a sloping site.	Reinforced concrete.	Reinforced concrete.	Reinforced concrete or concrete block.	Reinforced concrete or concrete block.	Wood piers, light concrete or block
Floor Structure (11% of total cost)	Engineered wood or steel, complex plan, elevation changes.	Engineered wood or steel trusses, good floor insulation.	Engineered wood or steel trusses, T&G sub-floor, good floor insulation.	Good wood frame with OSB sub-floor, some floor insulation.	Standard wood frame with OSB sub-floor, some floor insulation.	2" floor joists 16" on center with OSB sub-floor.
Wall Framing and Exterior Finish (14% of total cost)	Wood or steel, irregular walls, wood siding, stone, veneer, top-grade doors and windows.	Wood or steel, irregular walls, wood siding, stone veneer, better doors and windows.	Wood or steel, several wall offsets, plywood or lap siding, good grade doors and windows.	Wood or steel, shingle or plywood siding, some trim or veneer, average doors and windows.	Wood or steel, wood panel siding few or no offsets, commodity grade doors and windows.	Wood or steel, panel hardboard siding, minimum grade doors and windows.
Roof (13% of total cost)	Complex, heavy tile or metal cover, highly detailed.	Multi-pitch, shake, metal or good tile surface.	Dual-pitch, wood single or tile surface, gable over entrances.	Wood trusses, wood or good fiberglass shingle surface.	Simple wood frame, fiberglass shingle surface.	Wood frame, fiberglass shingle or roll roofing cover.
Floor Finish (5% of total cost)	Stone or masonry tile entry, inlaid hardwood or best carpet throughout.	Masonry entry, good hardwood or carpet in most rooms, good sheet vinyl elsewhere.	Hardwood or tile entry, carpet in most rooms sheet vinyl in kitchen and bathrooms.	Good sheet vinyl or average carpet in most areas, some hardwood or tile.	Sheet vinyl or tile on most areas, carpet in living room.	Composition tile or minimum grade sheet vinyl.
Interior Wall and Ceiling Finish (8% of total cost)	Top-grade paneling or wallboard with artistic finish, many offsets and wall openings, decorative details in most rooms.	Good wood paneling or textured wallboard with decorative details in most rooms, many wall openings, several racks and shelves.	Good hardwood veneer paneling or gypsum wallboard, some irregular walls, decorative details in living room, entry and kitchen.	1/2" gypsum wallboard with smooth finish, plywood paneling. at entry and living room, some decorative details.	1/2" gypsum wallboard with smooth finish, most walls are rectangular, doors and windows are the only openings.	Taped 1/2" gypsum wallboard, smooth or orange peel finish. Nearly all walls are regular, few decorative details.
Interior Features (5% of total cost)	Exposed beams or decorative details, 10' to 14' ceiling in great room, many sky widows, built-in shelving.	Great room has exposed beams, most rooms have windows on two sides, several framed openings.	Cathedral ceiling at entry or in master bedroom, floor level changes, several wall openings or pass-throughs.	Cathedral ceiling in master bedroom, sliding glass door, decorative wood molding and trim.	Rustic exposed ceiling beams, sliding closet doors, standard grade wood molding and trim.	Minimum grade molding and trim.
Bath Detail (4% of total cost)	At least 1 large tile shower, good tile counter in master bath.	Tile in 1 bathroom, glass block or good window in each bath, good vanity cabinet.	Tile or fiberglass shower, at least one built-in bathtub, good window in each bath.	Good plastic tub and shower in at least one bathroom, one small window in each bath.	Average plastic tub and shower in at least one bathroom, small vanity cabinet.	Minimum plastic tub and shower in one bathroom, minimum vanity.
Kitchen Detail (8% of total cost)	Over 20 LF of good custom wall & base cabinets, synthetic stone counter top, island work area.	15 to 18 LF of good custom base and wall cabinets, acrylic or tile counter top, desk with book shelf above.	12 to 15 LF of good stock wall and base cabinets, tile or acrylic counter top, desk and shelf or breakfast nook.	10 to 12 LF of stock standard grade wall and base cabinets, low-cost tile or laminated plastic counter top.	8 to 10 LF of stock standard grade wall and base cabinets, laminated plastic or resin coated hardboard top.	Less than 8 LF of low-cost wall and base cabinets, resin-coated hardboard counter top.
Plumbing (11% of total cost)	12 good fixtures, 2 water heaters, laundry room, copper piping.	10 good fixtures large water heater, laundry area, copper piping.	9 average grade fixtures, copper supply and plastic drain piping.	8 standard grade, fixtures, plastic supply and plastic drain lines.	7 low-cost fixtures, plastic supply and plastic drain lines.	6 or less minimum grade fixtures, plastic supply and drain lines.
Special Features (4% of total cost)	10 deluxe built-in appliances, good weather-protection throughout.	7 good built-in appliances, good wall and ceiling insulation.	6 good built-in appliances, good wall and ceiling insulation.	5 average built-in appliances, adequate wall and ceiling insulation.	4 standard grade kitchen appliances, adequate ceiling insulation.	3 minimum grade built-in kitchen appliances, limited insulation.
Electrical System (9% of total cost)	Ample area and track lighting in most rooms, task light in bathrooms.	Good area and track lighting, simple light fixture in each bathroom.	Good light fixtures in kitchen and baths, limited fixtures in other rooms.	Good light fixture in most rooms, switch-operated outlet in bedrooms.	Simple light fixture in most rooms, switch-operated plugs in bedrooms.	5 or less lighting fixtures, switch-operated plug outlet in most rooms.

Note: Use the percent of total cost to help identify the correct quality classification.

Conventional Recreational Dwellings

4 Corners (Classes 3, 4, 5, and 6) or
One Building Mass (Classes 1 and 2 Only)

Estimating Procedure

1. Establish the structure quality class by applying the information on page 33.
2. Multiply the structure floor area by the appropriate cost listed below.
3. Multiply the total from step 2 by the correct location factor listed on page 7 or 8.
4. Add, when appropriate, the cost of a deck or porch, paving, fireplace, garage or carport, heating, extra plumbing fixtures, supporting walls, half story areas, construction on hillside lots, and construction in remote areas. See page 42.

Conventional Recreational Dwelling, Class 5

Conventional Recreational Dwelling, Class 3

Square Foot Area

Quality Class	400	500	600	700	800	900	1,000	1,100	1,200	1,300	1,400
1, Luxury	—	—	—	—	378.28	361.85	348.15	337.21	327.87	319.78	312.46
1, & 2	—	—	—	350.53	332.47	318.09	305.99	296.55	288.11	281.23	274.74
2, Semi-Luxury	—	—	328.94	307.66	291.75	279.16	268.55	260.38	252.88	246.81	241.02
2 & 3	—	308.90	285.46	266.97	253.04	242.23	232.91	226.09	219.29	214.04	209.18
3, Best Std.	258.04	231.42	213.92	200.05	189.70	181.47	174.54	169.36	164.39	160.41	156.75
3 & 4	235.80	211.53	195.41	182.76	173.34	165.88	159.63	154.76	150.29	146.63	143.27
4, Good Std.	215.49	193.27	178.69	166.98	158.48	151.57	145.76	141.44	137.29	134.09	130.95
4 & 5	198.86	178.29	164.82	154.17	146.18	139.91	134.48	130.50	126.58	123.62	120.86
5 Avg. Std.	183.39	164.47	152.12	142.15	134.85	129.00	124.06	120.31	116.89	114.11	111.40
5 & 6	169.18	151.80	140.23	131.13	124.35	119.01	114.47	110.97	107.87	105.13	102.81
6, Min. Std.	156.01	139.99	129.45	120.94	114.70	109.86	105.60	102.47	99.37	97.08	94.87

Square Foot Area

Quality Class	1,500	1,600	1,700	1,800	2,000	2,200	2,400	2,600	2,800	3,000	3,200
1, Luxury	307.82	301.61	297.18	292.88	285.30	278.46	273.81	268.69	265.58	261.20	258.68
1, & 2	269.29	265.22	261.22	257.46	250.86	244.65	240.75	236.16	233.57	229.74	227.35
2, Semi-Luxury	237.30	232.86	229.27	226.01	220.23	214.61	211.37	207.30	204.95	201.64	199.51
2 & 3	205.73	202.05	198.91	196.05	190.99	186.22	183.30	179.87	177.85	174.91	173.10
3, Best Std.	154.27	151.33	149.03	146.94	143.17	139.58	137.48	134.71	133.26	131.10	129.65
3 & 4	140.88	138.33	136.22	134.28	130.73	127.52	125.53	123.22	121.77	119.75	118.58
4, Good Std.	128.76	126.46	124.42	122.74	119.52	116.46	114.74	112.60	111.38	109.46	108.33
4 & 5	118.77	116.58	114.97	113.15	110.18	107.48	105.89	103.82	102.75	100.97	—
5 Avg. Std.	109.60	107.62	105.93	104.45	101.68	99.24	97.74	95.80	94.75	—	—
5 & 6	101.11	99.28	97.76	96.42	93.88	91.51	90.13	88.32	—	—	—
6, Min. Std.	93.31	91.56	90.19	88.87	86.54	84.42	83.04	—	—	—	—

Note: Add 4% to the square foot cost for floors above the second floor level.

6 Corners (Classes 3, 4, 5, and 6) or Two Building Masses (Classes 1 and 2 Only)

Estimating Procedure

1. Establish the structure quality class by applying the information on page 33.
2. Multiply the structure floor area by the appropriate cost listed below.
3. Multiply the total from step 2 by the correct location factor listed on page 7 or 8.
4. Add, when appropriate, the cost of a deck or porch, paving, fireplace, garage or carport, heating, extra plumbing fixtures, supporting walls, half story areas, construction on hillside lots, and construction in remote areas. See page 42.

Conventional Recreational Dwelling, Class 4 & 5

Conventional Recreational Dwelling, Class 3

Square Foot Area

Quality Class	400	500	600	700	800	900	1,000	1,100	1,200	1,300	1,400
1, Luxury	—	—	—	—	386.60	369.95	355.93	345.64	336.04	328.11	320.98
1, & 2	—	—	—	357.78	339.97	325.33	312.93	303.93	295.34	288.33	282.00
2, Semi-Luxury	—	—	335.25	314.05	298.40	285.54	274.66	266.76	259.20	252.98	247.49
2 & 3	—	315.14	290.94	272.56	258.87	247.75	238.36	231.42	224.82	219.44	214.61
3, Best Std.	262.60	236.20	218.03	204.32	193.97	185.64	178.56	173.38	168.58	164.44	160.90
3 & 4	239.97	215.82	199.34	186.69	177.29	169.76	163.28	158.38	153.95	150.30	147.10
4, Good Std.	219.25	197.28	182.20	170.66	162.00	155.05	149.14	144.70	140.77	137.45	134.41
4 & 5	202.30	181.95	167.97	157.46	149.57	143.03	137.60	133.65	129.85	126.77	123.98
5 Avg. Std.	186.57	167.85	154.96	145.16	137.85	131.94	126.91	123.27	119.75	116.97	114.37
5 & 6	172.14	154.87	142.95	133.94	127.25	121.71	117.10	113.77	110.52	107.88	105.57
6, Min. Std.	158.87	142.83	131.88	123.56	117.40	112.36	108.07	104.89	101.93	99.49	97.33

Square Foot Area

Quality Class	1,500	1,600	1,700	1,800	2,000	2,200	2,400	2,600	2,800	3,000	3,200
1, Luxury	315.60	309.64	305.45	301.08	293.47	286.15	282.15	276.68	273.69	269.48	266.71
1, & 2	277.43	272.29	268.47	264.63	257.87	251.56	247.97	243.34	240.72	236.83	234.24
2, Semi-Luxury	243.42	239.11	235.62	232.32	226.40	220.83	217.55	213.62	211.37	207.94	205.54
2 & 3	211.09	207.59	204.47	201.50	196.30	191.57	188.70	185.32	183.30	180.34	178.21
3, Best Std.	158.27	155.54	153.29	151.11	147.11	143.53	141.40	138.80	137.48	135.16	133.54
3 & 4	144.61	142.07	140.05	138.04	134.48	131.13	129.27	126.92	125.53	123.56	122.06
4, Good Std.	132.18	129.91	128.07	126.21	122.92	119.85	118.13	116.00	114.74	112.99	111.56
4 & 5	121.99	119.75	118.13	116.42	113.40	110.56	108.95	107.06	105.89	104.21	—
5 Avg. Std.	112.46	110.52	108.95	107.44	104.52	102.06	100.53	98.72	97.74	—	—
5 & 6	103.81	101.93	100.53	99.09	96.49	94.09	92.72	91.11	—	—	—
6, Min. Std.	95.76	94.01	92.72	91.41	88.97	86.84	85.57	—	—	—	—

Note: Add 4% to the square foot cost for floors above the second floor level.

Conventional Recreational Dwellings

8 Corners (Classes 3, 4, 5, and 6) or
Three Building Masses (Classes 1 and 2 only)

Estimating Procedure

1. Establish the structure quality class by applying the information on page 33.
2. Multiply the structure floor area by the appropriate cost listed below.
3. Multiply the total from step 2 by the correct location factor listed on page 7 or 8.
4. Add, when appropriate, the cost of a deck or porch, paving, fireplace, garage or carport, heating, extra plumbing fixtures, supporting walls, half story areas, construction on hillside lots, and construction in remote areas.
   See page 42.

Conventional Recreational Dwelling, Class 3

Conventional Recreational Dwelling, Class 1 & 2

Square Foot Area

Quality Class	400	500	600	700	800	900	1,000	1,100	1,200	1,300	1,400
1, Luxury	—	—	—	—	396.79	378.02	364.24	353.91	343.88	336.42	328.61
1, & 2	—	—	—	365.28	348.72	332.47	320.17	311.17	302.30	295.79	288.92
2, Semi-Luxury	—	—	342.17	320.51	305.99	291.84	281.05	273.03	265.45	259.47	253.57
2 & 3	—	320.99	296.82	278.09	265.47	253.22	243.85	236.76	230.35	225.12	219.98
3, Best Std.	266.79	240.50	222.46	208.31	198.95	189.77	182.76	177.42	172.63	168.76	164.86
3 & 4	243.93	219.93	203.28	190.52	181.89	173.41	167.09	162.21	157.74	154.17	150.69
4, Good Std.	222.88	200.95	185.85	174.03	166.23	158.52	152.64	148.20	144.15	140.82	137.72
4 & 5	205.65	185.34	171.43	160.51	153.32	146.23	140.78	136.78	133.09	129.98	127.16
5 Avg. Std.	189.73	170.98	158.11	148.15	141.42	134.87	129.91	126.21	122.74	119.85	117.16
5 & 6	174.98	157.74	145.81	136.62	130.50	124.42	119.77	116.42	113.15	110.57	108.18
6, Min. Std.	161.39	145.50	134.53	126.05	120.31	114.74	110.56	107.44	104.45	102.06	99.83

Square Foot Area

Quality Class	1,500	1,600	1,700	1,800	2,000	2,200	2,400	2,600	2,800	3,000	3,200
1, Luxury	323.66	317.45	312.74	309.59	301.08	294.63	289.61	285.02	281.69	277.05	274.47
1, & 2	284.46	279.16	275.02	272.16	264.67	258.79	254.65	250.55	249.45	243.53	241.32
2, Semi-Luxury	249.74	245.10	241.50	238.75	232.40	227.03	223.50	219.76	217.20	213.77	211.82
2 & 3	216.56	212.56	209.47	207.12	201.60	196.85	193.94	190.68	188.40	185.44	183.79
3, Best Std.	162.28	159.24	156.97	155.21	151.15	147.53	145.36	142.92	141.24	139.04	137.69
3 & 4	148.39	145.59	143.37	141.86	138.22	134.87	132.81	130.66	129.04	127.15	125.91
4, Good Std.	135.60	133.09	131.12	129.65	126.29	123.27	121.39	119.40	117.98	116.01	115.07
4 & 5	125.00	122.74	120.91	119.77	116.45	113.77	112.01	110.12	108.83	107.10	—
5 Avg. Std.	115.35	113.17	111.56	110.33	107.45	104.89	103.40	101.58	100.39	—	—
5 & 6	106.36	104.47	103.01	101.68	99.12	96.70	95.32	93.69	—	—	—
6, Min. Std.	98.10	96.42	94.92	93.88	91.50	89.32	87.95	—	—	—	—

Note: Add 4% to the square foot cost for floors above the second floor level.

Conventional Recreational Dwellings

10 Corners (Classes 3, 4, 5, and 6) or Four Building Masses (Classes 1 and 2 only)

Estimating Procedure

1. Establish the structure quality class by applying the information on page 33.
2. Multiply the structure floor area by the appropriate cost listed below.
3. Multiply the total from step 2 by the correct location factor listed on page 7 or 8.
4. Add, when appropriate, the cost of a deck or porch, paving, fireplace, garage or carport, heating, extra plumbing fixtures, supporting walls, half story areas, construction on hillside lots, and construction in remote areas. See page 42.

Conventional Recreational Dwelling, Class 2 & 3

Conventional Recreational Dwelling, Class 1

Square Foot Area

Quality Class	400	500	600	700	800	900	1,000	1,100	1,200	1,300	1,400
1, Luxury	—	—	—	—	403.63	386.60	372.96	362.21	352.85	344.87	337.21
1, & 2	—	—	—	372.76	354.72	339.97	327.84	318.43	310.10	303.67	296.43
2, Semi-Luxury	—	—	348.72	327.19	311.24	298.40	287.70	279.47	272.08	265.86	260.17
2 & 3	—	326.67	302.63	283.88	269.98	258.87	249.50	242.40	235.92	230.54	225.71
3, Best Std.	271.52	244.87	226.76	212.74	202.37	193.97	186.95	181.72	176.85	172.74	169.06
3 & 4	248.15	223.88	207.29	194.46	184.89	177.29	170.98	165.97	161.63	158.07	154.51
4, Good Std.	226.68	204.52	189.42	177.75	168.99	162.00	156.30	151.80	147.74	144.36	141.28
4 & 5	209.22	188.74	174.76	163.92	155.90	149.57	144.06	139.99	136.24	133.18	130.31
5 Avg. Std.	193.06	174.03	161.21	151.20	143.88	137.85	132.91	129.22	125.70	122.80	120.21
5 & 6	178.06	160.51	148.68	139.48	132.70	127.25	122.70	119.10	115.98	113.39	110.85
6, Min. Std.	164.30	148.15	137.21	128.69	122.40	117.40	113.09	109.99	107.06	104.52	102.35

Square Foot Area

Quality Class	1,500	1,600	1,700	1,800	2,000	2,200	2,400	2,600	2,800	3,000	3,200
1, Luxury	332.54	326.46	321.30	316.96	309.86	302.27	298.27	292.73	289.67	283.46	281.91
1, & 2	292.40	286.98	282.50	278.71	272.42	265.63	262.24	257.49	254.81	249.27	248.06
2, Semi-Luxury	256.44	251.87	247.97	244.73	239.01	233.10	230.06	226.04	223.58	218.80	217.84
2 & 3	222.41	218.40	215.10	212.41	207.26	202.26	199.58	196.28	194.04	189.80	189.05
3, Best Std.	166.76	163.74	161.21	159.18	155.32	151.67	149.57	147.01	145.50	142.17	141.59
3 & 4	152.36	149.69	147.23	145.55	142.04	138.63	136.66	134.28	132.91	130.04	129.46
4, Good Std.	139.20	136.78	134.60	132.95	129.75	126.58	124.94	122.76	121.47	118.77	118.36
4 & 5	128.47	126.21	124.20	122.70	119.75	116.79	115.18	113.39	112.03	109.60	—
5 Avg. Std.	118.47	116.42	114.56	113.09	110.49	107.76	106.30	104.47	103.42	—	—
5 & 6	109.34	107.44	105.68	104.44	101.87	99.36	98.09	96.48	—	—	—
6, Min. Std.	100.86	99.09	97.43	96.31	93.94	91.59	90.45	—	—	—	—

Note: Add 4% to the square foot cost for floors above the second floor level.

"A-Frame" Cabins

Quality Classification

	Class 1 Best Quality	Class 2 Good Quality	Class 3 Average Quality	Class 4 Low Quality
Framing (10% of total cost)	Wood frame.	Wood frame.	Wood frame.	Wood frame.
Floor Framing (5% of total cost)	4" x 8" girders 48" o.c. with 2" T&G subfloor, or 2" x 6" to 2" x 8" joists 16" o.c. with 1" subfloor.	4" x 8" girders 48" o.c. with 1-1/4" plywood or 2" T&G subfloor, or 2" x 6" to 2" x 8" joists 16" o.c. with 1" subfloor.	4" x 6" girders 48" o.c. with 1-1/4" plywood or 2" T&G subfloor, or 2" x 6" joists 16" o.c. with 1" subfloor.	4" x 6" girders 48" o.c. with 1-1/4" plywood or 2" T&G subfloor, or 2" x 6" joists 16" o.c. with 1" subfloor.
Roof Framing (8% of total cost)	4" x 8" at 48" o.c. with 2" or 3" T&G sheathing.	4" x 8" at 48" o.c. with 2" or 3" T&G sheathing.	4" x 8" at 48" o.c. with 2" T&G sheathing.	4" x 8" at 48" o.c. with 1-1/4" plywood or 2" T&G sheathing.
Gable End Finish (5% of total cost)	Good plywood, lap board or board and batt.	Average to good plywood, or boards.	Average plywood, board or wood shingle.	Low cost plywood, shingle or composition siding.
Windows (2% of total cost)	Good quality large insulated wood or metal windows.	Average quality insulated wood or metal windows.	Average quality wood or metal windows.	Small glass area of low cost windows.
Roofing (10% of total cost)	Heavy wood shakes.	Medium wood or aluminum shakes.	Wood or composition shingles.	Low cost composition shingles.
Flooring (5% of total cost)	Good carpet or hardwood with sheet vinyl in kitchen and baths.	Average to good quality carpet with good tile or sheet vinyl in kitchen and baths.	Average quality carpet with resilient tile in kitchen and baths.	Composition tile.
Interior Finish (25% of total cost including finish carpentry, wiring, lighting, fireplace, etc.)	Good quality hardwood veneer paneling.	Good textured gypsum wallboard, good plywood or knotty pine paneling.	Textured gypsum wallboard or plywood paneling.	Low cost paneling or wallboard.
Bathrooms (5% of total cost)	Two 3-fixture baths and one 2-fixture bath, good fixtures.	Two 3-fixture baths, good fixtures.	Two 3-fixture baths, average fixtures.	One 3-fixture bath.
Kitchen (5% of total cost)	15' to 18' good quality hardwood veneer base cabinet with matching wall cabinets. 15' to 18' of good quality plastic or ceramic tile drain board.	12' to 16' of hardwood veneer base cabinet with matching wall cabinets. 12' to 16' of plastic or ceramic tile drainboard.	8' to 12' of average quality veneer or painted base cabinets with matching wall cabinets. 8' to 12' of plastic drainboard.	6' to 8' of minimum base cabinets with matching wall cabinets. 6' to 8' of minimum plastic drainboard.
Plumbing (15% of total cost)	Nine good quality fixtures and one larger or two 30 gallon water heaters. Copper supply piping.	Seven good quality fixtures and one water heater.	Seven average quality fixtures and one water heater.	Four low cost fixtures and one water heater. Plastic supply pipe.
Special Features (5% of total cost)	Built-in oven, range, dishwasher, disposer, range hood with good insulation, good lighting fixtures, insulated sliding glass door and ornate entry door.	Built-in range, oven and range hood, some insulation, 8' sliding glass door, average electric fixtures.	Drop-in range and hood, some insulation, low cost electric fixtures.	Minimum electric fixtures.

Note: Use the percent of total cost to help identify the correct quality classification.

"A-Frame" Cabins

4 Corners

Estimating Procedure

1. Establish the structure quality class by applying the information on page 38.
2. Multiply the structure floor area by the appropriate cost listed below.
3. Multiply the total from step 2 by the correct location factor listed on page 7 or 8.
4. Add, when appropriate, the cost of a deck or porch, paving, fireplace, garage or carport, heating, extra plumbing fixtures, supporting walls, half story areas, construction on hillside lots, and construction in remote areas. See page 42.

"A-Frame" Cabin, Class 3 & 4

Square Foot Area

Quality Class	400	500	600	700	800	900	1,000	1,100	1,200	1,300	1,400
1, Best	210.95	190.34	176.03	165.51	157.30	150.78	145.40	140.94	137.12	133.78	130.90
1 & 2	193.82	174.91	161.74	152.04	144.55	138.42	133.62	129.48	125.95	122.96	120.28
2, Good	177.85	160.47	148.47	139.51	132.69	127.12	122.63	118.79	115.62	112.82	110.38
2 & 3	167.88	151.49	140.13	131.72	125.22	120.02	115.71	112.20	109.12	106.51	104.19
3, Average	159.05	143.51	132.74	124.75	118.58	113.66	109.60	106.23	103.40	100.88	98.71
3 & 4	144.36	130.25	120.42	113.24	107.66	103.19	99.53	96.44	93.81	91.53	89.61
4, Low	129.48	116.86	108.09	101.64	96.61	92.57	89.29	86.55	84.15	82.14	80.36

Square Foot Area

Quality Class	1,500	1,600	1,700	1,800	2,000	2,200	2,400	2,600	2,800	3,000	3,200
1, Best	126.26	124.22	122.38	120.66	117.76	115.34	113.29	111.49	109.93	108.53	107.33
1 & 2	116.51	114.63	112.86	111.36	108.68	106.42	104.56	102.89	101.48	100.19	99.08
2, Good	107.52	105.73	104.14	102.71	100.27	98.20	96.45	94.93	93.56	92.39	91.40
2 & 3	102.04	100.35	98.88	97.54	95.15	93.25	91.52	90.12	88.84	87.76	86.73
3, Average	96.94	95.33	93.89	92.70	90.44	88.56	86.96	85.59	84.43	83.37	82.42
3 & 4	89.19	87.73	86.40	85.27	83.21	81.48	80.03	78.76	77.68	76.70	75.82
4, Low	79.78	78.21	77.42	76.33	75.36	73.80	72.47	71.30	70.32	69.45	68.67

"A-Frame" Cabins

6 Corners

Estimating Procedure

1. Establish the structure quality class by applying the information on page 38.
2. Multiply the structure floor area by the appropriate cost listed below.
3. Multiply the total from step 2 by the correct location factor listed on page 7 or 8.
4. Add, when appropriate, the cost of a deck or porch, paving, fireplace, garage or carport, heating, extra plumbing fixtures, supporting walls, half story areas, construction on hillside lots, and construction in remote areas. See page 42.

"A-Frame" Cabin, Class 2 & 3

Square Foot Area

Quality Class	400	500	600	700	800	900	1,000	1,100	1,200	1,300	1,400
1, Best	214.34	193.42	179.04	168.43	160.27	153.81	148.49	144.04	140.32	137.00	134.19
1 & 2	196.57	177.41	164.22	154.50	147.04	141.08	136.18	132.10	128.66	125.67	122.96
2, Good	180.58	162.96	150.87	141.89	135.00	129.54	125.10	121.34	118.19	115.44	113.08
2 & 3	170.53	153.84	142.41	133.96	127.52	122.38	118.12	114.57	111.54	109.02	106.75
3, Average	160.73	145.03	134.22	126.29	120.14	115.29	111.33	108.00	105.19	102.70	100.61
3 & 4	146.64	132.36	122.52	115.26	109.67	105.23	101.59	98.60	95.98	93.76	91.83
4, Low	131.28	118.47	109.64	103.19	98.20	94.21	90.95	88.24	85.90	83.90	82.17

Square Foot Area

Quality Class	1,500	1,600	1,700	1,800	2,000	2,200	2,400	2,600	2,800	3,000	3,200
1, Best	129.79	127.64	125.73	124.05	121.11	118.64	116.51	114.70	113.13	111.68	110.47
1 & 2	119.51	117.53	115.82	114.22	111.53	109.26	107.34	105.64	104.15	102.89	101.74
2, Good	110.27	108.44	106.85	105.42	102.92	100.83	99.03	97.49	96.14	94.96	93.87
2 & 3	104.64	102.92	101.40	100.01	97.68	95.67	93.94	92.52	91.26	90.08	89.12
3, Average	99.69	98.08	96.66	95.32	93.07	91.19	89.61	88.17	86.93	85.87	84.87
3 & 4	91.52	90.08	88.71	87.52	85.44	83.71	82.26	80.97	79.80	78.80	77.95
4, Low	81.46	80.26	79.18	77.28	75.70	74.40	73.17	72.21	71.28	70.49	69.41

"A-Frame" Cabins

8 Corners

Estimating Procedure

1. Establish the structure quality class by applying the information on page 38.
2. Multiply the structure floor area by the appropriate cost listed below.
3. Multiply the total from step 2 by the correct location factor listed on page 7 or 8.
4. Add, when appropriate, the cost of a deck or porch, paving, fireplace, garage or carport, heating, extra plumbing fixtures, supporting walls, half story areas, construction on hillside lots, and construction in remote areas. See page 42.

"A-Frame" Cabin, Class 2

Square Foot Area

Quality Class	400	500	600	700	800	900	1,000	1,100	1,200	1,300	1,400
1, Best	217.86	197.00	182.63	172.02	163.86	157.27	151.91	147.39	143.57	140.32	137.39
1 & 2	199.76	180.73	167.53	157.78	150.23	144.22	139.33	135.20	131.68	128.66	126.01
2, Good	183.15	165.64	153.61	144.61	137.78	132.25	127.70	123.94	120.74	117.98	115.50
2 & 3	172.86	156.35	144.96	136.52	130.01	124.78	120.54	116.98	113.94	111.33	109.03
3, Average	163.49	147.90	137.05	129.08	122.99	118.06	113.98	110.68	107.75	105.27	103.15
3 & 4	148.56	134.42	124.55	117.29	111.71	107.23	103.60	100.56	97.92	95.71	93.72
4, Low	133.18	120.43	111.63	105.14	100.16	96.12	92.87	90.12	87.78	85.76	84.01

Square Foot Area

Quality Class	1,500	1,600	1,700	1,800	2,000	2,200	2,400	2,600	2,800	3,000	3,200
1, Best	133.07	130.93	129.02	127.33	124.36	121.88	119.75	117.99	116.39	115.02	113.83
1 & 2	120.32	118.37	116.63	115.08	112.39	110.17	108.26	106.66	105.19	103.98	102.82
2, Good	113.06	111.18	109.57	108.15	105.62	103.50	101.74	100.19	98.85	97.68	96.64
2 & 3	107.05	105.27	103.77	102.39	100.00	97.99	96.37	94.88	93.56	92.50	91.48
3, Average	101.96	100.29	98.83	97.49	95.23	93.38	91.80	90.41	89.19	88.08	87.14
3 & 4	93.52	92.00	90.60	89.44	87.37	85.62	84.19	82.91	81.80	80.84	79.96
4, Low	83.37	82.14	81.07	79.16	77.58	76.22	75.07	74.08	73.17	72.46	71.33

Cabins and Recreational Dwellings

Additional Costs

Half-Story Costs

For conventional recreational dwellings, use the suggested fractions found on page 30 in the section "Additional Costs for Residential Structures." For "A-Frame" cabins, use one of the following costs: A simple platform with low cost floor cover, minimum partitions, and minimum lighting costs $65 to $95 per square foot. Average quality half story area with average quality carpet, average number of partitions finished with gypsum wallboard or plywood veneer and average lighting costs $95 to $105 per square foot. A good quality half story area with good carpet, decorative rustic partitions, ceiling beams and good lighting costs $125 to $145 per square foot.

Decks and Porches, per square foot

2" wood deck with steps and railing (300 S.F. base)	
1' to 4' above ground	$23.37 to $27.28
Over 4' to 6' above ground	27.07 to 35.00
Over 6' to 9' above ground	28.31 to 37.06
Over 9' to 12' above ground	29.34 to 38.81
Over 12' above ground	30.88 to 40.14

Fireplaces, 2-story, including foundation

Metal hood with concrete slab	$2,704 to $3,356
Prefabricated, zero clearance	3,890 to 5,834
Simple concrete block	4,750 to 7,893
Concrete block with stone facing	6,270 to 9,512
Simple natural stone	10,805 to 15,670

Extra Plumbing, cost each

Lavatory	$1,680 to $2,465
Water closet or bidet	2,050 to 2,516
Tub and shower	2,160 to 2,880
Stall shower	1,612 to 2,350
Laundry or utility sink	1,175 to 1,390

Heating, cost each

Wall furnace, 35,000 Btu	$1,330
Wall furnace, 65,000 Btu	1,630
Baseboard hot water, per SF*	5.20
Central heating, perimeter ducts, per S.F.*	7.28
*Cost is per SF of floor area heated.	

Garages, Carports and Basements

For garage, carport and basement costs for conventional recreational dwellings, see pages 27 and 29.

Flatwork, per square foot

Asphalt paving	$4.48 to $6.73
4" concrete	4.61 to 6.93
6" concrete	4.90 to 7.13

Reinforced concrete walls, per C.F.

Formed one side only	$18.50 to $21.42
Formed both sides	23.65 to 26.83

Supporting Wall Costs

Cabins and recreational dwellings built on sloping lots cost more than if they are built on level lots. The cost of supporting walls of a building that do not enclose any living area should be estimated by using the figures below. These costs include everything above a normal foundation (12" to 18" above ground) up to the bottom of the next floor structure where square foot costs can be applied. In addition to the cost of supporting walls, add the cost of any extra structural members and the higher cost of building on a slope. A good rule of thumb for this is to add $870 for each foot of vertical distance between the highest and the lowest points of intersection of foundation and ground level.

Wood posts, per foot of height

4" x 4"	$2.30 to $3.65
4" x 6"	3.65 to 6.25
6" x 6"	4.71 to 8.89
8" x 8"	10.64 to 16.54
10" x 10"	19.70 to 28.23
12" x 12"	29.62 to 41.20

Brick, per square foot of wall

8" common brick	$36.96 to $45.20
12" common brick	56.79 to 70.54
8" common brick, 1 side face brick	46.89 to 57.84
12" common brick, 1 side face brick	73.34 to 91.42

Reinforced concrete block, per square foot of wall

8" natural	$8.94 to $10.80
8" colored	12.31 to 14.45
8" detailed blocks, natural	10.18 to 13.35
8" detailed blocks, colored	13.86 to 15.68
8" sandblasted	10.80 to 12.65
8" splitface, natural	9.21 to 10.86
8" splitface, colored	14.44 to 16.30
8" slump block, natural	9.89 to 12.31
8" slump block, colored	13.72 to 15.88
12" natural	17.45 to 19.51

Life in Years and Depreciation for Residences

Quality Class	1	2	3	4	5	6
Single family residences	70	70	70	60	60	55
Manufactured housing	45	40	40	30	30	
Multi-family residences	60	60	55	55	50	
Motels	60	55	55	50		
Conventional recreational dwellings	70	60	60	55	55	50
A-frame cabins	60	55	55	50		

This table shows typical physical lives in years in the absence of unusual physical, functional or economic obsolescence. Raise half classes to the next higher whole class.

To Find the Present Value of an Existing Residence

Present value is the replacement cost less depreciation (inverse of the "% Good" column below). Multiply the appropriate figure in the "% good" column by the current replacement cost developed using this manual to find the present value. For newer residences, the chronological age ("Age" column) is usually the best indicator of percent good. The present value of older residences may be influenced more by physical, functional or economic obsolescence than by age. When physical, functional or economic conditions limit or extend the remaining useful life of a residence, estimate that life in years and use the "Rem. Life" column (rather than the "Age" column) to find the percent good.

Age	20 Years Rem. Life	20 Years % Good	25 Years Rem. Life	25 Years % Good	30 Years Rem. Life	30 Years % Good	40 Years Rem. Life	40 Years % Good	Age	45 Years Rem. Life	45 Years % Good	50 Years Rem. Life	50 Years % Good	55 Years Rem. Life	55 Years % Good	60 Years Rem. Life	60 Years % Good	70 Years Rem. Life	70 Years % Good
0	20	100	25	100	30	100	40	100	0	45	100	50	100	55	100	60	100	70	100
1	19	94	24	95	29	96	39	98	2	43	97	48	97	53	98	58	98	68	99
2	18	88	23	90	28	93	38	96	4	41	93	46	94	51	96	56	96	66	98
3	17	81	22	86	27	89	37	94	6	39	89	44	91	49	94	54	94	64	97
4	16	75	21	81	26	86	36	92	8	37	85	42	88	47	91	52	92	62	96
5	15	69	20	77	25	82	35	90	10	35	81	39	85	45	88	50	90	60	95
6	14	63	19	72	24	79	34	87	12	33	77	38	82	43	85	48	88	58	93
7	13	59	18	68	23	75	33	84	14	32	73	36	78	41	82	46	86	56	92
8	12	57	17	63	22	71	32	82	16	30	69	35	74	40	79	45	83	54	90
9	11	55	16	60	21	67	31	80	18	28	65	33	70	38	76	43	80	52	89
10	11	53	16	58	20	64	30	77	20	26	60	31	67	36	73	41	77	50	87
11	10	50	15	56	19	60	29	74	22	24	58	29	63	34	69	39	74	48	86
12	9	48	14	54	19	59	28	72	24	23	56	28	60	32	65	37	71	46	84
13	8	46	13	53	18	57	27	70	26	22	54	26	58	31	62	35	68	44	82
14	7	44	12	51	17	56	27	67	28	20	52	24	56	29	60	34	65	42	80
15	7	42	11	49	16	54	26	65	30	18	50	23	54	27	58	32	63	40	78
16	6	40	11	48	15	53	25	62	32	17	48	21	53	26	56	30	60	38	76
17	5	38	10	46	14	52	24	60	34	15	47	20	51	24	55	29	58	36	73
18	5	36	9	44	13	50	23	59	36	14	45	18	49	23	53	27	57	34	71
19	4	33	8	43	13	49	22	58	38	12	43	17	47	21	51	26	55	32	68
20	4	31	7	41	12	47	21	58	40	11	41	16	45	20	50	24	54	30	65
21	3	29	7	39	11	46	21	55	42	10	39	14	44	19	48	23	52	28	62
22	3	27	6	37	11	44	20	54	44	9	37	13	42	17	46	21	51	26	59
23	3	25	6	35	10	43	19	53	46	8	35	12	40	16	45	20	49	25	56
24	3	23	5	34	9	42	18	52	48	7	33	11	38	15	43	19	47	23	54
25	2	21	5	32	9	40	17	51	50	6	31	10	37	14	41	18	46	21	49
26	2	19	4	30	8	39	17	50	52	5	29	9	35	12	40	16	44	19	45
27	2	16	4	29	7	37	16	49	54	5	28	8	33	11	38	15	43	18	44
28	2	14	4	27	7	36	15	48	56	4	26	7	31	10	36	14	41	16	42
29	2	12	3	25	6	34	14	47	58	4	24	6	30	9	35	13	40	15	38
30	1	10	3	24	6	33	14	46	60	3	22	5	28	8	33	12	38	14	36
31	–	–	3	22	5	31	13	45	62	3	20	4	26	7	31	11	37	12	31
32	–	–	3	20	5	30	12	44	64	3	17	4	24	6	30	10	35	11	30
33	–	–	2	18	5	29	12	43	66	2	16	3	22	5	28	9	33	10	27
34	–	–	2	17	4	27	11	42	68	2	14	3	21	5	27	8	32	9	25
35	–	–	2	15	4	26	11	41	70	2	12	3	19	4	25	7	30	9	24
36	–	–	2	13	4	24	10	40	72	1	10	2	17	4	23	6	29	8	21
38	–	–	1	10	3	21	9	38	74	–	–	2	15	4	21	5	27	7	20
40	–	–	–	–	2	19	7	35	76	–	–	2	14	3	20	5	26	7	19
42	–	–	–	–	2	16	6	33	80	–	–	1	10	2	17	4	23	7	18
46	–	–	–	–	1	10	5	29	82	–	–	–	–	2	15	3	20	6	17
50	–	–	–	–	–	–	4	25	84	–	–	–	–	1	10	2	17	5	16
55	–	–	–	–	–	–	3	20	96	–	–	–	–	–	–	1	10	3	14
60	–	–	–	–	–	–	2	14	98	–	–	–	–	–	–	–	–	2	12
64	–	–	–	–	–	–	1	10	100	–	–	–	–	–	–	–	–	1	10

Quality Classification

	Class 1 Best Quality	Class 2 Good Quality	Class 3 Average Quality	Class 4 Low Quality
Foundation (7% of total cost)	Reinforced concrete, depth to 8'	Reinforced concrete, depth 6' to 8'.	Reinforced concrete, depth 4' to 6'.	Reinforced concrete, depth 4' or less.
Floor Structure (4% of total cost)	Concrete on steel beams and deck.	Lightweight concrete on steel beams.	6" thickened edge concrete slab on 6" rock base.	4" reinforced slab on rock base.
Exterior Walls (14% of total cost)	Decorative brick veneer with concrete block backup. Ornate brick or stone trim.	Decorative or colored concrete block. Some brick or stone veneer.	Colored concrete block with some brick or wood trim.	Painted tilt-up concrete wall panels. Few decorative details.
Roof Structure & Cover (29% of total cost)	Glu-lams or steel trusses on steel intermediate columns. Panelized roof system with elastomeric concrete tile or metal roof cover. Engineered for earthquake or high wind zones.	Glu-lams or steel beams on steel intermediate columns. Panelized roof system with 5-ply, built-up or concrete tile roof cover. Good insulation.	Wood or metal trusses on intermediate columns. Panelized roof system with built-up or good composition shingle roofing. Insulated.	Beams or trusses on steel supports. OSB. sheathing. Built-up or low cost membrane roofing. Foil insulation. Not designed for high wind or seismic zones.
Floor Finish (5% of total cost)	Hardwood with good sheet vinyl or carpet in offices. Ceramic tile in restrooms.	Hardwood or sheet vinyl in classrooms. Carpet in offices.	Standard grade sheet vinyl or good composition tile in most areas.	Minimum grade tile.
Windows & Doors (4% of total cost)	Large vinyl-clad or metal insulated low-E windows. Metal doors with glass panels. Institutional grade hardware. LEED certified.	Vinyl-clad insulated windows. Metal exterior doors with glass panels. Solid core interior doors. Commercial grade hardware.	Standard grade insulated windows. Metal exterior doors. Wood interior doors. Standard grade hardware.	Few standard grade metal windows. Low cost metal exterior doors. Low grade hardware.
Interior Wall Finish (13% of total cost)	Gypsum wallboard or lath and plaster finished with good paper or vinyl. Good metal or hardwood veneer wainscot and trim.	Textured gypsum wallboard covered with vinyl or good wallpaper. Good hardwood-veneer wainscot and wood trim in high traffic areas.	Textured and painted interior stucco or gypsum wallboard. Wood trim in high traffic areas.	Painted gypsum wallboard.
Ceiling Finish (2% of total cost)	Suspended good grade acoustical tile with gypsum wallboard backing.	Suspended acoustical tile with concealed grid system.	Suspended acoustical tile with exposed grid system.	Painted gypsum wallboard with acoustic texture.
Specialties (5% of total cost)	Central station alarm. Large chalkboards, cabinets, shelves and cases. Network connection.	Fire alarm and bell system. Network connection. Good chalkboards, map rail & shelving.	Fire alarm, bell and network connections. Some cabinets and shelves.	Minimum alarm system. Few cabinets and shelves.
Plumbing (7% of total cost)	6 good commercial fixtures per classroom. Copper supply & drain pipe. Metal toilet partitions.	5 standard fixtures per classroom. Copper supply & drain pipe. Metal toilet partitions.	4 standard fixtures per classroom. Plastic supply and drain pipe. Composition toilet partitions.	3 minimum fixtures per classroom. Plastic supply and drain pipe. Wood toilet partitions.
Lighting and Power (10% of total cost)	Recessed fluorescent lighting in modular plastic panels. Many task lights or indirect lighting fixtures.	Continuous recessed 4 tube fluorescent strips with egg crate diffusers, 8' O.C. Some task lighting or indirect light fixtures.	Continuous 4 tube fluorescent strips with egg crate diffusers, 8' O.C. Some ceiling downlights.	Continuous exposed 2 tube fluorescent strips, 8' O.C.

Note: Use the percent of total cost to help identify the correct quality classification.

Square foot costs include the following components: Foundations as required for normal soil conditions. Floor, wall and roof structures. Interior ceiling, wall and floor finishes (including carpet). Exterior wall finish and roof cover. Interior partitions. Basic lighting and electrical systems. Rough and finish plumbing. Design and engineering fees. Typical permit and hook-up fees. Contractor's mark-up.

Add the cost of: Canopies and canopy lighting. Public address, intercom and security systems. Docks and ramps. Elevators. Draperies. Fire extinguishers and fire sprinklers. Heating and cooling systems. Exterior signs. Walks, paving and curbing. Yard improvements. See the section "Additional Costs for Commercial, Industrial and Public Structures" beginning on page 236.

First Floor

Estimating Procedure

1. Use the tables in this section to estimate the cost of elementary schools (K-6) which are primarily classrooms and lack the extra office space, assembly, library, food service and recreational facilities common in secondary schools.
2. Establish the structure quality class by applying the information on page 44.
3. Calculate the area of the first floor. This should include all area within the building exterior walls and all inset areas outside the main walls but under the main building roof.
4. Find in the table below the square foot cost for the appropriate quality class and the nearest building area.
5. Use figures in the Wall Height Adjustment row to adjust that square foot cost for wall heights more or less than 10 feet.
6. Multiply the adjusted square foot cost by the area of the first floor.
7. Multiply that total by the location factor on page 7 or 8.
8. Add costs from the section Additional Costs for Commercial, Industrial and Public Buildings beginning on page 236.
9. Using figures on the next page, add the cost of any second or higher floors or a basement.

Elementary School, Class 2 & 3

First Floor - Square Foot Area

Quality Class	5,000	6,000	7,500	10,000	12,500	15,000	17,500	20,000	25,000	30,000	40,000
1, Best	301.00	287.67	277.09	268.52	261.23	254.98	249.62	240.70	233.41	227.51	218.20
1 & 2	269.92	258.01	248.55	240.78	234.22	228.61	223.86	215.77	209.35	204.11	195.63
2, Good	242.93	232.27	223.78	216.81	210.85	205.85	201.48	194.32	188.48	183.62	176.20
2 & 3	217.32	207.75	200.05	193.76	188.59	184.10	180.20	173.72	168.58	164.27	157.56
3, Average	194.86	186.28	179.49	173.90	169.09	165.16	161.63	155.82	151.18	147.33	141.31
3 & 4	170.07	162.58	156.61	151.76	147.61	144.16	141.10	136.00	131.88	128.61	123.34
4, Low	145.12	138.68	133.59	129.50	125.97	122.95	120.33	116.03	112.50	109.72	105.18
Wall Height Adjustment*	1.64	1.26	1.15	1.10	1.03	1.00	.92	.91	.88	.88	.88

*Wall Height Adjustment: Add or subtract the amount listed in this row to or from the square foot of floor cost for each foot of wall height more or less than 10 feet.

Upper Floors and Basements

Estimating Procedure

1. Establish the quality class for second and higher floors and the basement. The quality class will usually be the same as the first floor of the building. Square foot costs for unfinished basements will be nearly the same regardless of the structure quality class.
2. Calculate the area of any second or higher floor or a basement.
3. Find in the tables below the square foot cost for the appropriate quality class and the nearest area.
4. Use figures in the Wall Height Adjustment row to adjust the square foot cost for wall heights more or less than 10 feet.
5. Multiply the adjusted square foot cost by the area.
6. Multiply that total by the location factor on page 7 or 8.
7. Add costs from the section Additional Costs for Commercial, Industrial and Public Buildings beginning on page 236.
8. Add totals from this page to the cost for the first floor to find the total building cost.

Second and Higher Floors - Square Foot Area

Quality Class	5,000	6,000	7,500	10,000	12,500	15,000	17,500	20,000	25,000	30,000	40,000
1, Best	276.91	264.65	254.92	247.03	240.33	234.58	229.63	221.45	214.73	209.31	200.75
1 & 2	248.34	237.37	228.66	221.51	215.48	210.33	205.95	198.51	192.60	187.77	179.97
2, Good	223.48	213.68	205.88	199.45	193.98	189.38	185.38	178.77	173.39	168.93	162.11
2 & 3	199.93	191.13	184.04	178.27	173.51	169.37	165.78	159.81	155.09	151.13	144.96
3, Average	179.29	171.39	165.11	160.00	155.56	151.94	148.70	143.35	139.08	135.54	130.00
3 & 4	156.46	149.57	144.10	139.62	135.79	132.61	129.82	125.10	121.32	118.34	113.47
4, Low	133.49	127.58	122.91	119.14	115.89	113.11	110.70	106.73	103.50	100.93	96.77
Wall Height Adjustment*	1.52	1.16	1.06	1.01	.96	.92	.85	.83	.81	.81	.81

*Wall Height Adjustment: Add or subtract the amount listed in this row to or from the square foot of floor cost for each foot of wall height more or less than 10 feet.

Finished Basement - Square Foot Area

Quality Class	5,000	6,000	7,500	10,000	12,500	15,000	17,500	20,000	25,000	30,000	40,000
1, Best	169.21	161.71	155.76	150.93	146.84	143.34	140.32	135.31	131.20	127.89	122.66
2, Good	136.56	130.56	125.80	121.87	118.51	115.71	113.26	109.23	105.94	103.22	99.05
3, Average	109.54	104.71	100.88	97.76	95.05	92.84	90.85	87.59	84.98	82.81	79.44
4, Low	81.57	77.95	75.09	72.79	70.81	69.12	67.64	65.23	63.25	61.66	59.13

Unfinished Basements

Area	5,000	6,000	7,500	10,000	12,500	15,000	17,500	20,000	25,000	30,000	40,000
Cost	41.18	39.53	38.25	37.20	36.22	35.47	34.86	33.69	32.80	32.05	30.83

Wall Height Adjustment: Add or subtract the amount listed in this table to or from the square foot of floor cost for each foot of basement wall height more or less than 10 feet.

Area	5,000	6,000	7,500	10,000	12,500	15,000	17,500	20,000	25,000	30,000	40,000
Finished	.98	.89	.87	.85	.84	.81	.80	.75	.73	.73	.71
Unfinished	.89	.87	.84	.81	.80	.75	.75	.73	.71	.70	.67

Elementary Schools – Wood or Steel Frame

Quality Classification

	Class 1 Best Quality	Class 2 Good Quality	Class 3 Average Quality	Class 4 Low Quality
Foundation (7% of total cost)	Reinforced concrete, depth to 8'.	Reinforced concrete, depth 6' to 8'.	Reinforced concrete, depth 4' to 6'.	Reinforced concrete, depth 4' or less.
Floor Structure (4% of total cost)	Concrete on steel beams and deck.	Sheathing on wood or steel floor trusses.	6" thickened edge concrete slab on 6" rock base.	4" reinforced slab on rock base.
Exterior Walls (14% of total cost)	Braced wood or steel studs. Decorative brick or stone veneer with ornate details.	Wood or steel studs. Good wood or composition siding. Some masonry veneer.	Wood studs. Stucco with integral color. Some brick trim.	Wood studs. Painted stucco or inexpensive wood panel siding.
Roof Structure & Cover (29% of total cost)	Glu-lams or steel trusses on steel intermediate columns. Panelized roof system with elastomeric concrete tile or metal roof cover. Engineered for seismic or high wind zones.	Glu-lams or steel beams on steel intermediate columns. Panelized roof system with 5-ply, built-up or concrete tile roof cover. Good insulation.	Glu-lams on steel intermediate columns. Panelized roof system with built-up or good composition shingle roofing. Insulated. Adequate Insulation.	Beams or trusses on steel supports. OSB. sheathing. Built-up or composition shingle roofing. Foil insulation. Not designed for high wind or seismic zones.
Floor Finish (5% of total cost)	Hardwood with good sheet vinyl or carpet in offices. Ceramic tile in restrooms.	Hardwood or sheet vinyl in classrooms. Carpet in offices.	Standard grade sheet vinyl or good composition tile in most areas.	Minimum grade tile.
Windows & Doors (4% of total cost)	Large vinyl-clad or metal insulated low-E windows. Metal doors with glass panels. Institutional grade hardware. LEED certified.	Vinyl-clad insulated windows. Metal exterior doors with glass panels. Solid core interior doors. Commercial grade hardware.	Standard grade insulated windows. Metal exterior doors. Wood interior doors. Standard grade hardware.	Few standard grade metal windows. Low cost metal exterior doors. Low grade hardware.
Interior Wall Finish (13% of total cost)	Gypsum wallboard or lath and plaster finished with good paper or vinyl. Good metal or hardwood veneer wainscot and trim.	Textured gypsum wallboard covered with vinyl or good wallpaper. Good hardwood-veneer wainscot and wood trim in high traffic areas.	Textured and painted interior stucco or gypsum wallboard. Wood trim in high traffic areas.	Painted gypsum wallboard.
Ceiling Finish (2% of total cost)	Suspended good grade acoustical tile with gypsum wallboard backing.	Suspended acoustical tile with concealed grid system.	Suspended acoustical tile with exposed grid system.	Painted gypsum wallboard with acoustic texture.
Specialties (5% of total cost)	Central station alarm. Large chalkboards, cabinets, shelves and cases. Network connection.	Fire alarm and bell system. Network connection. Good chalkboards, map rail & shelving.	Fire alarm, bell and network connections. Some cabinets and shelves.	Minimum alarm system. Few cabinets and shelves.
Plumbing (7% of total cost)	6 good commercial fixtures per classroom. Copper supply & drain pipe. Metal toilet partitions.	5 standard fixtures per classroom. Copper supply & drain pipe. Metal toilet partitions.	4 standard fixtures per classroom. Plastic supply and drain pipe. Composition toilet partitions.	3 minimum fixtures per classroom. Plastic supply and drain pipe. Wood toilet partitions.
Lighting and Power (10% of total cost)	Recessed fluorescent lighting in modular plastic panels. Many task lights or indirect lighting fixtures.	Continuous recessed 4 tube fluorescent strips with egg crate diffusers, 8' O.C. Some task lighting or indirect light fixtures.	Continuous 4 tube fluorescent strips with egg crate diffusers, 8' O.C. Some ceiling downlights.	Continuous exposed 2 tube fluorescent strips, 8' O.C.

Note: Use the percent of total cost to help identify the correct quality classification.

Square foot costs include the following components: Foundations as required for normal soil conditions. Floor, wall and roof structures. Interior ceiling, wall and floor finishes (including carpet). Exterior wall finish and roof cover. Interior partitions. Basic lighting and electrical systems. Rough and finish plumbing. Design and engineering fees. Typical permit and hook-up fees. Contractor's mark-up.

Add the cost of: Canopies and canopy lighting. Public address, intercom and security systems. Docks and ramps. Elevators. Draperies. Fire extinguishers and fire sprinklers. Heating and cooling systems. Exterior signs. Walks, paving and curbing. Yard improvements. See the section "Additional Costs for Commercial, Industrial and Public Structures" beginning on page 236.

Elementary Schools – Wood or Steel Frame

First Floor

Estimating Procedure

1. Use the tables in this section to estimate the cost of elementary schools (K-6) which are primarily classrooms and lack the extra office space, assembly, library, food service and recreational facilities common in secondary schools.
2. Establish the structure quality class by applying the information on page 47.
3. Calculate the area of the first floor. This should include all area within the building exterior walls and all inset areas outside the main walls but under the main building roof.
4. Find in the table below the square foot cost for the appropriate quality class and the nearest building area.
5. Use figures in the Wall Height Adjustment row to adjust that square foot cost for wall heights more or less than 10 feet.
6. Multiply the adjusted square foot cost by the area of the first floor.
7. Multiply that total by the location factor on page 7 or 8.
8. Add costs from the section Additional Costs for Commercial, Industrial and Public Buildings beginning on page 236.
9. Using figures on the next page, add the cost of any second or higher floors or a basement.

Elementary School, Class 3

Square Foot Area

Quality Class	5,000	6,000	7,500	10,000	12,500	15,000	17,500	20,000	25,000	30,000	40,000
1, Best	267.34	255.51	246.12	238.49	232.01	226.48	221.71	213.79	207.30	202.06	193.79
1 & 2	239.75	229.15	220.76	213.86	208.03	203.06	198.83	191.65	185.94	181.27	173.76
2, Good	215.77	206.29	198.76	192.56	187.28	182.82	178.96	172.59	167.40	163.09	156.50
2 & 3	193.01	184.52	177.68	172.09	167.51	163.52	160.05	154.29	149.72	145.91	139.93
3, Average	173.08	165.45	159.40	154.46	150.18	146.69	143.55	138.38	134.27	130.84	125.50
3 & 4	128.88	123.18	118.66	115.02	111.88	109.20	106.86	103.04	99.93	97.45	93.42
4, Low	151.06	144.41	139.11	134.79	131.10	128.03	125.32	120.79	117.14	114.24	109.53
Wall Height Adjustment*	1.47	1.12	1.02	.97	.92	.88	.81	.80	.78	.78	.78

*Wall Height Adjustment: Add or subtract the amount listed in this table to or from the square foot of floor cost for each foot of wall height more or less than 10 feet.

Elementary Schools – Wood or Steel Frame

Upper Floor and Basement

Estimating Procedure

1. Establish the quality class for second floor and the basement. The quality class will usually be the same as the first floor of the building. Square foot costs for unfinished basements will be nearly the same regardless of the structure quality class.
2. Calculate the area of any second floor or basement.
3. Find in the tables below the square foot cost for the appropriate quality class and the nearest area.
4. Use figures in the Wall Height Adjustment row to adjust the square foot cost for wall heights more or less than 10 feet.
5. Multiply the adjusted square foot cost by the area.
6. Multiply that total by the location factor on page 7 or 8.
7. Add costs from the section Additional Costs for Commercial, Industrial and Public Buildings beginning on page 236.
8. Add totals from this page to the cost for the first floor to find the total building cost.

Second Floor - Square Foot Area

Quality Class	5,000	6,000	7,500	10,000	12,500	15,000	17,500	20,000	25,000	30,000	40,000
1, Best	226.83	216.80	208.82	202.36	196.86	192.17	188.12	181.39	175.91	171.46	164.43
1 & 2	203.42	194.44	187.32	181.46	176.52	172.30	168.71	162.60	157.76	153.82	147.44
2, Good	183.07	175.05	168.65	163.37	158.89	155.14	151.84	146.43	142.03	138.37	132.79
2 & 3	163.78	156.57	150.75	146.02	142.12	138.75	135.81	130.92	127.04	123.79	118.74
3, Average	146.86	140.39	135.25	131.05	127.43	124.46	121.80	117.44	113.93	111.02	106.49
3 & 4	128.17	122.53	118.03	114.37	111.24	108.65	106.32	102.48	99.39	96.93	92.94
4, Low	109.36	104.52	100.67	97.59	94.92	92.64	90.68	87.43	84.78	82.67	79.26
Wall height Adjustment*	1.24	.96	.86	.82	.77	.76	.71	.69	.68	.68	.68

*Wall Height Adjustment: Add or subtract the amount listed in this table to or from the square foot of floor cost for each foot of second and higher floor wall height more or less than 10 feet.

Finished Basements - Square Foot Area

Quality Class	5,000	6,000	7,500	10,000	12,500	15,000	17,500	20,000	25,000	30,000	40,000
1, Best	170.78	163.23	157.22	152.34	148.21	144.67	141.63	136.57	132.42	129.07	123.80
2, Good	137.84	131.78	126.96	123.00	119.62	116.78	114.32	110.25	106.92	104.19	99.98
3, Average	110.56	105.70	101.82	98.66	95.94	93.70	91.70	88.41	85.77	83.58	80.17
4, Low	82.33	78.68	75.80	73.47	71.47	69.76	68.27	65.83	63.84	62.23	59.68

Unfinished Basements

Area	5,000	6,000	7,500	10,000	12,500	15,000	17,500	20,000	25,000	30,000	40,000
Cost	41.55	39.90	38.60	37.53	36.56	35.80	35.18	34.01	33.11	32.34	31.12

Wall Height Adjustment: Add or subtract the amount listed in this table to or from the square foot of floor cost for each foot of basement wall height more or less than 10 feet.

Area	5,000	6,000	7,500	10,000	12,500	15,000	17,500	20,000	25,000	30,000	40,000
Finished	.99	.89	.87	.85	.84	.81	.80	.77	.75	.75	.73
Unfinished	.89	.87	.84	.81	.80	.77	.77	.75	.73	.72	.69

Temporary "bungalow" classrooms: One or two-story 24' x 40' prefabricated classrooms, including foundation and utility hookup will cost about $90,000 per classroom for units with standard grade lighting, doors, windows, exterior finish and electric space heating. Prefabricated 24' x 40' classrooms with better grade lighting, doors, windows, exterior finish and packaged A/C will cost about $130,000 each.

Secondary Schools – Masonry or Concrete

Quality Classification

	Class 1 Best Quality	Class 2 Good Quality	Class 3 Average Quality	Class 4 Low Quality
Foundation (7% of total cost)	Reinforced concrete, depth to 8'	Reinforced concrete, depth 6' to 8'.	Reinforced concrete, depth 4' to 6'.	Reinforced concrete, depth 4' or less.
Floor Structure (4% of total cost)	Concrete on steel beams and deck.	Lightweight concrete on steel beams.	6" thickened edge concrete slab on 6" rock base.	4" reinforced slab on rock base.
Exterior Walls (14% of total cost)	Decorative brick veneer with concrete block backup. Ornate brick or stone trim.	Decorative or colored concrete block. Some brick or stone veneer.	Colored concrete block with some brick or wood trim.	Painted tilt-up concrete wall panels. Few decorative details.
Roof Structure & Cover (29% of total cost)	Glu-lams or steel trusses on steel intermediate columns. Panelized roof system with elastomeric, concrete tile or metal roof cover. Engineered for earthquake or high wind zones.	Glu-lams or steel beams on steel intermediate columns. Panelized roof system with 5-ply, built-up or concrete tile roof cover. Good insulation.	Wood or metal trusses on intermediate columns. Panelized roof system with built-up or good composition shingle roofing. Insulated.	Beams or trusses on steel supports. OSB. sheathing. Built-up or low cost membrane roofing. Foil insulation. Not designed for high wind or seismic zones.
Floor Finish (5% of total cost)	Hardwood with good sheet vinyl or carpet in offices. Ceramic tile in restrooms.	Hardwood or sheet vinyl in classrooms. Carpet in offices.	Standard grade sheet vinyl or good composition tile in most areas.	Minimum grade tile.
Windows & Doors (4% of total cost)	Large vinyl-clad or metal insulated low-E windows. Metal doors with glass panels. Institutional grade hardware.	Vinyl-clad insulated windows. Metal exterior doors with glass panels. Solid core interior doors. Commercial grade hardware.	Standard grade insulated windows. Metal exterior doors. Wood interior doors. Standard grade hardware.	Few standard grade metal windows. Low cost metal exterior doors. Low grade hardware.
Interior Wall Finish (13% of total cost)	Gypsum wallboard or lath and plaster finished with good paper or vinyl. Good metal or hardwood veneer wainscot and trim.	Textured gypsum wallboard covered with vinyl or good wallpaper. Good hardwood-veneer wainscot and wood trim in high traffic areas.	Textured and painted interior stucco or gypsum wallboard. Wood trim in high traffic areas.	Painted gypsum wallboard.
Ceiling Finish (2% of total cost)	Suspended good grade acoustical tile with gypsum wallboard backing.	Suspended acoustical tile with concealed grid system.	Suspended acoustical tile with exposed grid system.	Painted gypsum wallboard with acoustic texture.
Specialties (5% of total cost)	Central station alarm. Large chalkboards, cabinets, shelves and cases. Network connection.	Fire alarm and bell system. Network connection. Good chalkboards, map rail & shelving.	Fire alarm, bell and network connections. Some cabinets and shelves.	Minimum alarm system. Few cabinets and shelves.
Plumbing (7% of total cost)	6 good commercial fixtures per classroom. Copper supply & drain pipe. Metal toilet partitions.	5 standard fixtures per classroom. Copper supply & drain pipe. Metal toilet partitions.	4 standard fixtures per classroom. Plastic supply and drain pipe. Composition toilet partitions.	3 minimum fixtures per classroom. Plastic supply and drain pipe. Wood toilet partitions.
Lighting and Power (10% of total cost)	Recessed fluorescent lighting in modular plastic panels. Many task lights or indirect lighting fixtures.	Continuous recessed 4 tube fluorescent strips with egg crate diffusers, 8' O.C. Some task lighting or indirect light fixtures.	Continuous 4 tube fluorescent strips with egg crate diffusers, 8' O.C. Some ceiling downlights.	Continuous exposed 2 tube fluorescent strips, 8' O.C.

Note: Use the percent of total cost to help identify the correct quality classification.

Square foot costs include the following components: Foundations as required for normal soil conditions. Floor, wall and roof structures. Interior ceiling, wall and floor finishes (including carpet). Exterior wall finish and roof cover. Interior partitions. Basic lighting and electrical systems. Rough and finish plumbing. Design and engineering fees. Typical permit and hook-up fees. Contractor's mark-up.

Add the cost of: Canopies and canopy lighting. Public address, intercom and security systems. Docks and ramps. Draperies. Fire extinguishers and fire sprinklers. Heating and cooling systems. Exterior signs. Walks, paving and curbing. Elevators. Kitchen equipment. Yard improvements. See the section "Additional Costs for Commercial, Industrial and Public Structures" beginning on page 236.

First Floor

Estimating Procedure

1. Use the tables in this section to estimate the cost of secondary schools and junior colleges which include classrooms, faculty and staff office space, assembly, library-media center, food service and recreational facilities.
2. Establish the structure quality class by applying the information on page 50.
3. Calculate the area of the first floor. This should include all area within the building exterior walls and all inset areas outside the main walls but under the main building roof.
4. Find in the table below the square foot cost for the appropriate quality class and the nearest building area.
5. Use figures in the Wall Height Adjustment row to adjust that square foot cost for wall heights more or less than 12 feet.
6. Multiply the adjusted square foot cost by the area of the first floor.
7. Multiply that total by the location factor on page 7 or 8.
8. Add costs from the section Additional Costs for Commercial, Industrial and Public Buildings beginning on page 236.
9. Using figures on the next page, add the cost of any second or higher floors or a basement.

Secondary School, Class 2

First Floor - Square Foot Area

Quality Class	20,000	25,000	30,000	35,000	40,000	45,000	50,000	60,000	70,000	80,000	100,000
1, Best	293.77	280.77	270.45	262.06	254.95	248.86	243.62	234.93	227.80	222.05	212.96
1 & 2	263.45	251.81	242.59	235.01	228.59	223.14	218.48	210.59	204.32	199.21	190.93
2, Good	237.09	226.69	218.41	211.60	205.80	200.90	196.65	189.65	183.94	179.21	171.97
2 & 3	212.10	202.77	195.25	189.11	184.06	179.67	175.87	169.54	164.52	160.33	153.77
3, Average	190.19	181.81	175.17	169.73	165.03	161.19	157.74	152.08	147.53	143.78	137.91
3 & 4	165.97	158.68	152.86	148.12	144.08	140.69	137.70	132.71	128.70	125.53	120.37
4, Low	141.62	135.35	130.39	126.40	122.94	119.99	117.43	113.24	109.80	107.08	102.65
Wall Height Adjustment*	1.41	1.08	.98	.93	.88	.85	.79	.77	.75	.75	.75

*Wall Height Adjustment: Add or subtract the amount listed in this row to or from the square foot of floor cost for each foot of wall height more or less than 12 feet.

Secondary Schools – Masonry or Concrete

Upper Floors and Basements

Estimating Procedure

1. Establish the quality class for second and higher floors and the basement. The quality class will usually be the same as the first floor of the building. Square foot costs for unfinished basements will be nearly the same regardless of the structure quality class.
2. Calculate the area of any second or higher floor or a basement.
3. Find in the tables below the square foot cost for the appropriate quality class and the nearest area.
4. Use figures in the Wall Height Adjustment row to adjust the square foot cost for wall heights more or less than 10 feet.
5. Multiply the adjusted square foot cost by the area.
6. Multiply that total by the location factor on page 7 or 8.
7. Add costs from the section Additional Costs for Commercial, Industrial and Public Buildings beginning on page 236.
8. Add totals from this page to the cost for the first floor to find the total building cost.

Second and Higher Floors - Square Foot Area

Quality Class	20,000	25,000	30,000	35,000	40,000	45,000	50,000	60,000	70,000	80,000	100,000
1, Best	264.40	252.69	243.40	235.87	229.46	223.98	219.26	211.44	205.02	199.84	191.66
1 & 2	237.10	226.62	218.34	211.49	205.73	200.82	196.64	189.53	183.89	179.29	171.84
2, Good	213.38	204.02	196.56	190.44	185.21	180.81	176.98	170.68	165.54	161.29	154.77
2 & 3	190.89	182.49	175.72	170.20	165.66	161.71	158.29	152.58	148.07	144.30	138.40
3, Average	171.17	163.62	157.64	152.76	148.52	145.06	141.97	136.87	132.78	129.41	124.12
3 & 4	149.39	142.81	137.57	133.31	129.65	126.61	123.94	119.45	115.84	112.99	108.33
4, Low	127.46	121.82	117.35	113.75	110.65	108.00	105.69	101.91	98.82	96.37	92.39
Wall Height Adjustment*	1.45	1.11	1.01	.96	.91	.88	.81	.79	.78	.78	.78

*Wall Height Adjustment: Add or subtract the amount listed in this row to or from the square foot of floor cost for each foot of wall height more or less than 10 feet.

Finished Basement - Square Foot Area

Quality Class	20,000	25,000	30,000	35,000	40,000	45,000	50,000	60,000	70,000	80,000	100,000
1, Best	161.57	154.43	148.74	144.14	140.23	136.88	134.00	129.21	125.29	122.12	117.13
2, Good	130.41	124.68	120.13	116.38	113.19	110.49	108.15	104.31	101.16	98.56	94.58
3, Average	104.60	99.99	96.34	93.35	90.76	88.65	86.76	83.64	81.14	79.08	75.85
4, Low	77.89	74.45	71.71	69.51	67.62	65.99	64.59	62.28	60.39	58.88	56.47

Unfinished Basements

Area	20,000	25,000	30,000	35,000	40,000	45,000	50,000	60,000	70,000	80,000	100,000
Cost	33.74	32.41	31.35	30.49	29.68	29.07	28.57	27.61	26.90	26.27	25.28

Wall Height Adjustment: Add or subtract the amount listed in this table to or from the square foot of floor cost for each foot of basement wall height more or less than 10 feet.

Area	20,000	25,000	30,000	35,000	40,000	45,000	50,000	60,000	70,000	80,000	100,000
Finished	.83	.75	.73	.71	.70	.68	.67	.64	.62	.62	.61
Unfinished	.68	.66	.64	.62	.61	.58	.58	.56	.55	.54	.52

Quality Classification

	Class 1 Best Quality	Class 2 Good Quality	Class 3 Average Quality	Class 4 Low Quality
Foundation (7% of total cost)	Reinforced concrete, depth to 8'	Reinforced concrete, depth 6' to 8'.	Reinforced concrete, depth 4' to 6'.	Reinforced concrete, depth 4' or less.
Floor Structure (4% of total cost)	Concrete on steel beams and deck.	Sheathing on wood or steel floor trusses.	6" thickened edge concrete slab on 6" rock base.	4" reinforced slab on rock base.
Exterior Walls (14% of total cost)	Braced wood or steel studs. Decorative brick or stone veneer with ornate details.	Wood or steel studs. Good wood or composition siding. Some masonry veneer.	Wood studs. Stucco with integral color. Some brick trim.	Wood studs. Painted stucco or inexpensive wood panel siding.
Roof Structure & Cover (29% of total cost)	Glu-lams or steel trusses on steel intermediate columns. Panelized roof system with elastomeric, concrete tile or metal roof cover. Engineered for seismic or high wind zones.	Glu-lams or steel beams on steel intermediate columns. Panelized roof system with 5-ply, built-up or concrete tile roof cover. Good insulation.	Glu-lams on steel intermediate columns. Panelized roof system with built-up or good composition shingle roofing. Insulated. Adequate Insulation.	Beams or trusses on steel supports. OSB. sheathing. Built-up or composition shingle roofing. Foil insulation. Not designed for high wind or seismic zones.
Floor Finish (5% of total cost)	Hardwood with good sheet vinyl or carpet in offices. Ceramic tile in restrooms.	Hardwood or sheet vinyl in classrooms. Carpet in offices.	Standard grade sheet vinyl or good composition tile in most areas.	Minimum grade tile.
Windows & Doors (4% of total cost)	Large vinyl-clad or metal insulated low-E windows. Metal doors with glass panels. Institutional grade hardware. LEED certified.	Vinyl-clad insulated windows. Metal exterior doors with glass panels. Solid core interior doors. Commercial grade hardware.	Standard grade insulated windows. Metal exterior doors. Wood interior doors. Standard grade hardware.	Few standard grade metal windows. Low cost metal exterior doors. Low grade hardware.
Interior Wall Finish (13% of total cost)	Gypsum wallboard or lath and plaster finished with good paper or vinyl. Good metal or hardwood veneer wainscot and trim.	Textured gypsum wallboard covered with vinyl or good wallpaper. Good hardwood-veneer wainscot and wood trim in high traffic areas.	Textured and painted interior stucco or gypsum wallboard. Wood trim in high traffic areas.	Painted gypsum wallboard.
Ceiling Finish (2% of total cost)	Suspended good grade acoustical tile with gypsum wallboard backing.	Suspended acoustical tile with concealed grid system.	Suspended acoustical tile with exposed grid system.	Painted gypsum wallboard with acoustic texture.
Specialties (5% of total cost)	Central station alarm. Large chalkboards, cabinets, shelves and cases. Network connection.	Fire alarm and bell system. Network connection. Good chalkboards, map rail & shelving.	Fire alarm, bell and network connections. Some cabinets and shelves.	Minimum alarm system. Few cabinets and shelves.
Plumbing (7% of total cost)	6 good commercial fixtures per classroom. Copper supply & drain pipe. Metal toilet partitions.	5 standard fixtures per classroom. Copper supply & drain pipe. Metal toilet partitions.	4 standard fixtures per classroom. Plastic supply and drain pipe. Composition toilet partitions.	3 minimum fixtures per classroom. Plastic supply and drain pipe. Wood toilet partitions.
Lighting and Power (10% of total cost)	Recessed fluorescent lighting in modular plastic panels. Many task lights or indirect lighting fixtures.	Continuous recessed 4 tube fluorescent strips with egg crate diffusers, 8' O.C. Some task lighting or indirect light fixtures.	Continuous 4 tube fluorescent strips with egg crate diffusers, 8' O.C. Some ceiling downlights.	Continuous exposed 2 tube fluorescent strips, 8' O.C.

Note: Use the percent of total cost to help identify the correct quality classification.

Square foot costs include the following components: Foundations as required for normal soil conditions. Floor, wall and roof structures. Interior ceiling, wall and floor finishes (including carpet). Exterior wall finish and roof cover. Interior partitions. Basic lighting and electrical systems. Rough and finish plumbing. Design and engineering fees. Typical permit and hook-up fees. Contractor's mark-up.

Add the cost of: Canopies and canopy lighting. Public address, intercom and security systems. Docks and ramps. Elevators. Draperies. Fire extinguishers and fire sprinklers. Heating and cooling systems. Exterior signs. Walks, paving and curbing. Kitchen equipment. Yard improvements. See the section "Additional Costs for Commercial, Industrial and Public Structures" beginning on page 236.

Secondary Schools – Wood or Steel Frame

First Floor

Estimating Procedure

1. Use the tables in this section to estimate the cost of secondary schools and junior colleges which include classrooms, faculty and staff office space, assembly, library-media center, food service and recreational facilities.
2. Establish the structure quality class by applying the information on page 53.
3. Calculate the area of the first floor. This should include all area within the building exterior walls and all inset areas outside the main walls but under the main building roof.
4. Find in the table below the square foot cost for the appropriate quality class and the nearest building area.
5. Use figures in the Wall Height Adjustment row to adjust that square foot cost for wall heights more or less than 12 feet.
6. Multiply the adjusted square foot cost by the area of the first floor.
7. Multiply that total by the location factor on page 7 or 8.
8. Add costs from the section Additional Costs for Commercial, Industrial and Public Buildings beginning on page 236.
9. Using figures on the next page, add the cost of any second or higher floors or a basement.

Secondary School, Class 3

Secondary School, Class 2

Square Foot Area

Quality Class	20,000	25,000	30,000	35,000	40,000	45,000	50,000	60,000	70,000	80,000	100,000
1, Best	260.92	249.36	240.20	232.75	226.44	221.03	216.37	208.66	202.32	197.22	189.14
1 & 2	233.98	223.65	215.46	208.72	203.03	198.18	194.05	187.03	181.46	176.92	169.58
2, Good	210.58	201.34	193.97	187.93	182.78	178.43	174.66	168.44	163.36	159.17	152.73
2 & 3	188.38	180.10	173.41	167.95	163.48	159.59	156.20	150.58	146.12	142.40	136.58
3, Average	168.92	161.47	155.57	150.74	146.57	143.16	140.11	135.06	131.04	127.70	122.49
3 & 4	147.42	140.93	135.77	131.56	127.95	124.96	122.30	117.88	114.32	111.49	106.90
4, Low	125.78	120.21	115.81	112.26	109.19	106.58	104.29	100.58	97.53	95.10	91.18
Wall Height Adjustment*	1.41	1.09	1.00	.95	.89	.86	.79	.78	.77	.77	.76

*Wall Height Adjustment: Add or subtract the amount listed in this table to or from the square foot of floor cost for each foot of wall height more or less than 12 feet.

Secondary Schools – Wood or Steel Frame

Upper Floor and Basement

Estimating Procedure

1. Establish the quality class for second floor and the basement. The quality class will usually be the same as the first floor of the building. Square foot costs for unfinished basements will be nearly the same regardless of the structure quality class.
2. Calculate the area of any second floor or basement.
3. Find in the tables below the square foot cost for the appropriate quality class and the nearest area.
4. Use figures in the Wall Height Adjustment row to adjust the square foot cost for wall heights more or less than 10 feet.
5. Multiply the adjusted square foot cost by the area.
6. Multiply that total by the location factor on page 7 or 8.
7. Add costs from the section Additional Costs for Commercial, Industrial and Public Buildings beginning on page 236.
8. Add totals from this page to the cost for the first floor to find the total building cost.

Second Floor - Square Foot Area

Quality Class	20,000	25,000	30,000	35,000	40,000	45,000	50,000	60,000	70,000	80,000	100,000
1, Best	216.39	206.81	199.21	193.04	187.79	183.31	179.45	173.05	167.80	163.56	156.86
1 & 2	194.05	185.48	178.70	173.10	168.40	164.36	160.93	155.13	150.50	146.73	140.65
2, Good	174.65	166.98	160.88	155.85	151.59	147.99	144.85	139.70	135.49	132.01	126.67
2 & 3	156.23	149.36	143.82	139.30	135.58	132.35	129.55	124.88	121.19	118.09	113.28
3, Average	140.09	133.92	129.02	125.03	121.56	118.73	116.20	112.02	108.69	105.91	101.59
3 & 4	122.26	116.90	112.59	109.11	106.12	103.64	101.44	97.76	94.81	92.48	88.66
4, Low	104.31	99.69	96.04	93.09	90.55	88.39	86.50	83.41	80.88	78.87	75.62
Wall height Adjustment*	1.19	.90	.82	.78	.75	.72	.67	.66	.63	.63	.63

*Wall Height Adjustment: Add or subtract the amount listed in this table to or from the square foot of floor cost for each foot of second and higher floor wall height more or less than 10 feet.

Finished Basements - Square Foot Area

Quality Class	20,000	25,000	30,000	35,000	40,000	45,000	50,000	60,000	70,000	80,000	100,000
1, Best	163.24	156.01	150.27	145.61	141.67	138.28	135.37	130.54	126.58	123.39	118.33
2, Good	131.74	125.96	121.36	117.57	114.35	111.62	109.27	105.37	102.20	99.59	95.56
3, Average	105.68	101.03	97.33	94.32	91.70	89.55	87.65	84.50	81.98	79.89	76.63
4, Low	78.70	75.20	72.45	70.23	68.31	66.67	65.25	62.92	61.01	59.50	57.03

Unfinished Basements

Area	20,000	25,000	30,000	35,000	40,000	45,000	50,000	60,000	70,000	80,000	100,000
Cost	34.06	32.71	31.65	30.77	29.96	29.34	28.84	27.87	27.14	26.51	25.51

Wall Height Adjustment: Add or subtract the amount listed in this table to or from the square foot of floor cost for each foot of basement wall height more or less than 10 feet.

Area	20,000	25,000	30,000	35,000	40,000	45,000	50,000	60,000	70,000	80,000	100,000
Finished	.77	.70	.68	.67	.66	.63	.62	.59	.57	.57	.56
Unfinished	.70	.68	.66	.63	.62	.59	.59	.57	.56	.55	.53

Temporary "bungalow" classrooms: One or two-story 24' x 40' prefabricated classrooms, including foundation and utility hookup will cost about $90,000 per classroom for units with standard grade lighting, doors, windows, exterior finish and electric space heating. Prefabricated 24' x 40' classrooms with better grade lighting, doors, windows, exterior finish and packaged A/C will cost about $130,000 each.

Quality Classification

	Class 1 Best Quality	Class 2 Good Quality	Class 3 Average Quality	Class 4 Low Quality
Foundation (7% of total cost)	Reinforced concrete, depth to 12'.	Reinforced concrete, depth 8' to 10'.	Reinforced concrete, depth 6' to 8'.	Reinforced concrete, depth 6' or less.
Floor Structure (5% of total cost)	Concrete on steel beams and deck.	Lightweight concrete on steel beams.	6" thickened edge concrete slab on 6" rock base.	4" reinforced slab on rock base.
Exterior Walls (12% of total cost)	Marble or polished granite, spandrel glass. Metal trim. Decorative atrium entrance.	Glass curtain wall. Textured-block, good brick or stone veneer. Atrium entrance.	Colored concrete block with some brick or wood trim. Decorative entrance.	Tilt-up concrete, brick or concrete block. Few decorative details.
Roof Structure & Cover (16% of total cost)	Glu-lams or steel trusses on steel intermediate columns. Panelized roof system with elastomeric concrete tile or metal roof cover. Engineered for earthquake or high wind zones.	Glu-lams or steel beams on steel intermediate columns. Panelized roof system with 5-ply, built-up or concrete tile roof cover. Good insulation.	Wood or metal trusses on intermediate columns. Panelized roof system with built-up or good composition shingle roofing. Insulated.	Beams or trusses on steel supports. OSB. sheathing. Built-up or low cost membrane roofing. Foil insulation. Not designed for high wind or seismic zones.
Floor Finish (8% of total cost)	Marble or good terrazzo in public rooms. Carpeted offices. Ceramic tile in restrooms.	Terrazzo or marble tile in public rooms. Carpet in offices. Vinyl in restrooms.	Good sheet vinyl in meeting rooms. Carpet in offices. Composition tile in restrooms.	Low cost sheet vinyl in public rooms. Floor Tile elsewhere.
Windows & Doors (6% of total cost)	Low-E glass in metal sash. Metal-frame laminated glass entrance doors. Metal interior doors. Institutional grade hardware. LEED certified.	Colored low-E glass. Decorative metal exterior doors. Solid core 8' high wood interior doors. Commercial grade hardware.	Insulated store front or glazed curtain wall. Metal exterior doors. Wood interior doors. Standard grade hardware.	Few standard grade metal windows. Low cost metal exterior doors. Low grade hardware.
Interior Wall Finish (14% of total cost)	Decorative plaster in public rooms. Plaster or vinyl covered wallboard in private offices. Decorative metal or hardwood veneer wainscot and trim.	Plaster or good paneling in public rooms. Vinyl-covered wallboard in hallways. Textured or vinyl-covered wallboard with good trim elsewhere.	Textured and painted interior stucco or gypsum wallboard. Wood trim in public meeting rooms.	Painted gypsum wallboard.
Ceiling Finish (6% of total cost)	Suspended decorative textured plaster in meeting rooms. Acoustic ceiling tile elsewhere.	Suspended acoustical tile in with concealed grid in meeting rooms. Acoustical tile elsewhere.	Suspended acoustical tile with exposed grid system.	Painted gypsum wallboard with acoustic texture.
Specialties (4% of total cost)	Security, alarm, PA and surveillance systems. Video and network connections.	Alarm and security systems. Network connections. Directory boards and built-in cabinetry.	Fire alarm, bell and network connections. Some cabinets and shelves.	Minimum alarm system. Few cabinets and shelves.
Plumbing (6% of total cost)	Institutional grade fixtures. Copper supply, vent & drain pipe. Metal or synthetic stone toilet partitions.	Good commercial grade fixtures. Copper supply & drain pipe. Metal toilet partitions.	Standard grade fixtures. PEX or PVC supply, vent and drain pipe. Composition toilet partitions.	Minimum fixtures. Plastic supply, vent & drain pipe. Plastic-faced toilet partitions.
Lighting and Power (16% of total cost)	Decorative indirect fixtures in public rooms. Many recessed task lights on separate controls. Recessed fluorescent fixtures in offices and hallways.	Indirect lighting fixtures in public rooms. Track lighting or recessed fluorescent fixtures with some task lighting in offices and hallways.	Continuous 4 tube fluorescent strips with decorative diffusers, 8' O.C. Some recessed ceiling fixtures.	Continuous exposed 2 tube fluorescent strip, fixtures 8' O.C.

Notes: Use the percent of total cost to help identify the correct quality classification. State and federal office buildings are usually Class 1 or Class 2 and rarely Class 3 or Class 4. Municipal office buildings are usually Class 3 or Class 4 and rarely Class 1 or Class 2. The figures in this section apply to government offices designed for public assembly (with committee hearing rooms or council chambers). For government offices serving walk-in clientele (motor vehicle department offices, post offices) use figures from either the section Urban Stores or the section Suburban Stores. For government offices used primarily by administrative staff (police stations, hall of records), use figures from the section General Office Buildings.

Square foot costs include the following components: Foundations as required for normal soil conditions. Floor, wall and roof structures. Interior ceiling, wall and floor finishes (including carpet). Exterior wall finish and roof cover. Interior partitions. Basic lighting and electrical systems. Rough and finish plumbing. Specialties as listed. Design and engineering fees. Typical utility hook-up. Contractor's mark-up.

Add the cost of: Canopies and canopy lighting. Public address, intercom and security systems beyond what appears in the quality classification above. Docks and ramps. Elevators. Draperies. Fire extinguishers and fire sprinklers. Heating and cooling systems. Exterior signs. Walks, paving and curbing. Yard improvements. See the section "Additional Costs for Commercial, Industrial and Public Structures" beginning on page 236.

Government Offices – Masonry or Concrete

First Floor

Estimating Procedure

1. Use the tables in this section to estimate the cost of buildings designed for occupancy by state, federal, or municipal agencies. Many government agencies occupy office space designed for use by commercial tenants rather than built for use by government officials. Use figures from the sections on Urban Stores, Suburban Stores or General Office Buildings when the structure was designed for commercial occupancy.
2. Establish the structure quality class by applying the information on page 56.
3. Calculate the area of the first floor. This should include all area within the building exterior walls and all inset areas outside the main walls but under the main building roof.
4. Find in the table below the square foot cost for the appropriate quality class and the nearest building area.
5. Use figures in the Wall Height Adjustment row to adjust that square foot cost for wall heights more or less than 12 feet.
6. Multiply the adjusted square foot cost by the area of the first floor.
7. Multiply that total by the location factor on page 7 or 8.
8. Add costs from the section Additional Costs for Commercial, Industrial and Public Buildings beginning on page 236.
9. Using figures on the next page, add the cost of any second or higher floors or a basement.

Government Office, Class1

First Floor - Square Foot Area

Quality Class	5,000	7,500	10,000	12,500	15,000	20,000	25,000	30,000	35,000	40,000	50,000
1, Best	300.14	279.10	266.49	257.88	251.46	242.52	236.35	231.77	228.26	225.41	220.95
1 & 2	278.29	258.68	247.12	239.03	233.08	224.74	219.07	214.85	211.52	208.90	204.94
2, Good	257.66	239.59	228.80	221.41	215.89	208.26	202.90	199.01	195.99	193.54	189.80
2 & 3	240.40	223.48	213.48	206.57	201.36	194.25	189.30	185.59	182.74	180.50	176.98
3, Average	225.95	210.18	200.64	194.11	189.30	182.65	177.83	174.45	171.81	169.66	166.32
3 & 4	204.97	190.50	181.92	176.09	171.71	165.62	161.39	158.24	155.80	153.91	150.93
4, Low	183.00	170.14	162.46	157.24	153.31	147.83	144.03	141.30	139.15	137.38	134.68
Wall Height Adjustment*	3.41	2.71	2.39	2.19	2.02	1.65	1.46	1.33	1.29	1.23	1.04

***Wall Height Adjustment:** Add or subtract the amount listed in this row to or from the square foot of floor cost for each foot of wall height more or less than 10 feet.

Government Offices – Masonry or Concrete

Upper Floors and Basements

Estimating Procedure

1. Establish the quality class for second and higher floors and the basement. The quality class will usually be the same as the first floor of the building. Square foot costs for unfinished basements will be nearly the same regardless of the structure quality class.
2. Calculate the area of any second or higher floor or a basement.
3. Find in the tables below the square foot cost for the appropriate quality class and the nearest area.
4. Use figures in the Wall Height Adjustment row to adjust the square foot cost for wall heights more or less than 10 feet.
5. Multiply the adjusted square foot cost by the area.
6. Multiply that total by the location factor on page 7 or 8.
7. Add costs from the section Additional Costs for Commercial, Industrial and Public Buildings beginning on page 236.
8. Add totals from this page to the cost for the first floor to find the total building cost.

Second and Higher Floors - Square Foot Area

Quality Class	5,000	7,500	10,000	12,500	15,000	20,000	25,000	30,000	35,000	40,000	50,000
1, Best	263.50	245.05	233.96	226.41	220.76	212.93	207.50	203.48	200.39	197.89	193.98
1 & 2	244.32	227.11	216.94	209.86	204.62	197.30	192.32	188.62	185.70	183.41	179.93
2, Good	226.22	210.34	200.87	194.38	189.54	182.85	178.13	174.72	172.06	169.91	166.63
2 & 3	211.05	196.22	187.43	181.37	176.78	170.54	166.20	162.93	160.44	158.48	155.39
3, Average	198.37	184.52	176.14	170.41	166.20	160.36	156.13	153.15	150.84	148.95	146.02
3 & 4	179.94	167.25	159.70	154.59	150.74	145.41	141.68	138.92	136.78	135.13	132.51
4, Low	160.66	149.38	142.62	138.05	134.59	129.79	126.45	124.04	122.16	120.61	118.25
Wall Height Adjustment*	3.00	2.39	2.10	1.93	1.77	1.45	1.28	1.16	1.12	1.09	.92

*Wall Height Adjustment: Add or subtract the amount listed in this row to or from the square foot of floor cost for each foot of wall height more or less than 10 feet.

Finished Basement - Square Foot Area

Quality Class	5,000	7,500	10,000	12,500	15,000	20,000	25,000	30,000	35,000	40,000	50,000
1, Best	163.47	152.01	145.14	140.44	136.95	132.08	128.71	126.23	124.31	122.76	120.33
2, Good	140.33	130.49	124.59	120.57	117.57	113.42	110.49	108.39	106.74	105.40	103.37
3, Average	123.05	114.46	109.27	105.71	103.09	99.47	96.85	95.00	93.56	92.40	90.58
4, Low	99.66	92.66	88.47	85.63	83.50	80.51	78.45	76.95	75.78	74.82	73.36

Unfinished Basements

Area	5,000	7,500	10,000	12,500	15,000	20,000	25,000	30,000	35,000	40,000	50,000
Cost	41.57	38.65	36.91	35.71	34.82	33.58	32.73	32.10	31.61	31.22	30.59

Wall Height Adjustment: Add or subtract the amount listed in this table to or from the square foot of floor cost for each foot of basement wall height more or less than 10 feet.

Area	5,000	7,500	10,000	12,500	15,000	20,000	25,000	30,000	35,000	40,000	50,000
Finished	.90	.71	.63	.58	.53	.44	.39	.35	.34	.33	.28
Unfinished	.81	.64	.56	.52	.48	.39	.35	.32	.31	.30	.24

Government Offices – Wood Frame

Quality Classification

	Class 1 Best Quality	Class 2 Good Quality	Class 3 Average Quality	Class 4 Low Quality
Foundation (7% of total cost)	Reinforced concrete, depth to 8'.	Reinforced concrete, depth 6' to 8'.	Reinforced concrete, depth 4' to 6'.	Reinforced concrete, depth 4' or less.
Floor Structure (5% of total cost)	Concrete on steel beams and deck.	Sheathing on wood or steel floor trusses.	6" thickened edge concrete slab on 6" rock base.	4" reinforced slab on rock base.
Exterior Walls (12% of total cost)	Braced wood or steel studs. Decorative brick or stone veneer with ornate details.	Wood or steel studs. Good wood or composition siding. Some masonry veneer.	Wood studs. Stucco with integral color. Some brick trim.	Wood studs. Painted stucco or inexpensive wood panel siding.
Roof Structure & Cover (16% of total cost)	Glu-lams or steel trusses on steel intermediate columns. Panelized roof system with elastomeric concrete tile or metal roof cover. Engineered for earthquake or high wind zones.	Glu-lams or steel beams on steel intermediate columns. Panelized roof system with 5-ply, built-up or concrete tile roof cover. Good insulation.	Wood or metal trusses on intermediate columns. Panelized roof system with built-up or good composition shingle roofing. Insulated.	Beams or trusses on steel supports. OSB sheathing. Built-up or low cost membrane roofing. Foil insulation. Not designed for high wind or seismic zones.
Floor Finish (8% of total cost)	Marble or good terrazzo in public rooms. Carpeted offices. Ceramic tile in restrooms.	Terrazzo or marble tile in public rooms. Carpet in offices. Vinyl in restrooms.	Good sheet vinyl in meeting rooms. Carpet in offices. Composition tile in restrooms.	Low cost sheet vinyl in public rooms. Floor Tile elsewhere.
Windows & Doors (6% of total cost)	Low-E glass in metal sash. Metal-frame laminated glass entrance doors. Metal interior doors. Institutional grade hardware. LEED certified.	Colored low-E glass. Decorative metal exterior doors. Solid core 8' high wood interior doors. Commercial grade hardware.	Insulated store front or glazed curtain wall. Metal exterior doors. Wood interior doors. Standard grade hardware.	Few standard grade metal windows. Low cost metal exterior doors. Low grade hardware.
Interior Wall Finish (14% of total cost)	Decorative plaster in public rooms. Plaster or vinyl covered wallboard in private offices. Decorative metal or hardwood veneer wainscot and trim.	Plaster or good paneling in public rooms. Vinyl-covered wallboard in hallways. Textured or vinyl-covered wallboard with good trim elsewhere.	Textured and painted interior stucco or gypsum wallboard. Wood trim in public meeting rooms.	Painted gypsum wallboard.
Ceiling Finish (6% of total cost)	Suspended decorative textured plaster in meeting rooms. Acoustic ceiling tile elsewhere.	Suspended acoustical tile in with concealed grid in meeting rooms. Acoustical tile elsewhere.	Suspended acoustical tile with exposed grid system.	Painted gypsum wallboard with acoustic texture.
Specialties (4% of total cost)	Security, alarm, PA and surveillance systems. Video and network connections.	Alarm and security systems. Network connections. Directory boards and built-in cabinetry.	Fire alarm, bell and network connections. Some cabinets and shelves.	Minimum alarm system. Few cabinets and shelves
Plumbing (6% of total cost)	Institutional grade fixtures. Copper supply, vent & drain pipe. Metal or synthetic stone toilet partitions.	Good commercial grade fixtures. Copper supply & drain pipe. Metal toilet partitions.	Standard grade fixtures. PEX or PVC supply, vent and drain pipe. Composition toilet partitions.	Minimum fixtures. Plastic supply, vent & drain pipe. Plastic-faced toilet partitions.
Lighting and Power (16% of total cost)	Decorative indirect fixtures in public rooms. Many recessed task lights on separate controls. Recessed fluorescent fixtures in offices and hallways.	Indirect lighting fixtures in public rooms. Track lighting or recessed fluorescent fixtures with some task lighting in offices and hallways.	Continuous 4 tube fluorescent strips with decorative diffusers, 8' O.C. Some recessed ceiling fixtures.	Continuous exposed 2 tube fluorescent strip, fixtures 8' O.C.

Notes: Use the percent of total cost to help identify the correct quality classification. State and federal office buildings are usually Class 1 or Class 2 and rarely Class 3 or Class 4. Municipal office buildings are usually Class 3 or Class 4 and rarely Class 1 or Class 2. The figures in this section apply to government offices designed for public assembly (with committee hearing rooms or council chambers). For government offices serving walk-in clientele (motor vehicle department offices, post offices) use figures from either the section Urban Stores or the section Suburban Stores. For government offices used primarily by administrative staff (police stations, hall of records), use figures from the section General Office Buildings.

Square foot costs include the following components: Foundations as required for normal soil conditions. Floor, wall and roof structures. Interior ceiling, wall and floor finishes (including carpet). Exterior wall finish and roof cover. Interior partitions. Basic lighting and electrical systems. Rough and finish plumbing. Specialties as listed. Design and engineering fees. Typical utility hook-up. Contractor's mark-up.

Add the cost of: Canopies and canopy lighting. Public address, intercom and security systems beyond what appears in the quality classification above. Docks and ramps. Elevators. Draperies. Fire extinguishers and fire sprinklers. Heating and cooling systems. Exterior signs. Walks, paving and curbing. Yard improvements. See the section "Additional Costs for Commercial, Industrial and Public Structures" beginning on page 236.

First Floor

Estimating Procedure

1. Use the tables in this section to estimate the cost of buildings designed for occupancy by state, federal, or municipal agencies. Many government agencies occupy office space designed for use by commercial tenants rather than built for use by government officials. Use figures from the sections on Urban Stores, Suburban Stores or General Office Buildings when the structure was designed for commercial occupancy.
2. Establish the structure quality class by applying the information on page 59.
3. Calculate the area of the first floor. This should include all area within the building exterior walls and all inset areas outside the main walls but under the main building roof.
4. Find in the table below the square foot cost for the appropriate quality class and the nearest building area.
5. Use figures in the Wall Height Adjustment row to adjust that square foot cost for wall heights more or less than 10 feet.
6. Multiply the adjusted square foot cost by the area of the first floor.
7. Multiply that total by the location factor on page 7 or 8.
8. Add costs from the section Additional Costs for Commercial, Industrial and Public Buildings beginning on page 236.
9. Using figures on the next page, add the cost of any second or higher floors or a basement.

Government Office, Class 3

Government Office, Class 3 & 4

Square Foot Area

Quality Class	5,000	7,500	10,000	12,500	15,000	20,000	25,000	30,000	35,000	40,000	50,000
1, Best	266.52	247.85	236.64	229.00	223.30	215.35	209.88	205.82	202.69	200.16	196.21
1 & 2	247.11	229.72	219.43	212.25	206.97	199.57	194.52	190.79	187.82	185.49	181.99
2, Good	228.81	212.76	203.16	196.61	191.71	184.94	180.17	176.73	174.03	171.86	168.54
2 & 3	213.47	198.47	189.57	183.44	178.81	172.50	168.10	164.81	162.28	160.28	157.16
3, Average	200.64	186.64	178.16	172.36	168.10	162.21	157.91	154.90	152.57	150.65	147.68
3 & 4	162.51	151.09	144.26	139.63	136.14	131.28	127.90	125.47	123.56	122.00	119.60
4, Low	182.01	169.16	161.54	156.37	152.47	147.07	143.31	140.51	138.35	136.68	134.04
Wall Height Adjustment*	3.03	2.40	2.12	1.94	1.79	1.46	1.29	1.18	1.14	1.10	.93

*Wall Height Adjustment: Add or subtract the amount listed in this table to or from the square foot of floor cost for each foot of wall height more or less than 10 feet.

Government Offices – Wood Frame

Upper Floor and Basement

Estimating Procedure

1. Establish the quality class for second floor and the basement. The quality class will usually be the same as the first floor of the building. Square foot costs for unfinished basements will be nearly the same regardless of the structure quality class.
2. Calculate the area of any second floor or basement.
3. Find in the tables below the square foot cost for the appropriate quality class and the nearest area.
4. Use figures in the Wall Height Adjustment row to adjust the square foot cost for wall heights more or less than 10 feet.
5. Multiply the adjusted square foot cost by the area.
6. Multiply that total by the location factor on page 7 or 8.
7. Add costs from the section Additional Costs for Commercial, Industrial and Public Buildings beginning on page 236.
8. Add totals from this page to the cost for the first floor to find the total building cost.

Second Floor - Square Foot Area

Quality Class	5,000	7,500	10,000	12,500	15,000	20,000	25,000	30,000	35,000	40,000	50,000
1, Best	234.09	217.69	207.84	201.14	196.12	189.17	184.34	180.77	178.04	175.81	172.33
1 & 2	217.05	201.77	192.73	186.43	181.79	175.28	170.86	167.58	164.98	162.93	159.84
2, Good	200.97	186.88	178.45	172.69	168.40	162.44	158.26	155.22	152.87	150.96	148.04
2 & 3	187.50	174.31	166.50	161.13	157.06	151.52	147.64	144.76	142.52	140.80	138.04
3, Average	176.23	163.92	156.49	151.39	147.64	142.46	138.70	136.05	134.00	132.33	129.72
3 & 4	159.86	148.57	141.90	137.34	133.92	129.18	125.87	123.42	121.52	120.05	117.72
4, Low	142.74	132.70	126.70	122.64	119.57	115.30	112.34	110.21	108.52	107.15	105.05
Wall height Adjustment*	2.66	2.12	1.86	1.72	1.58	1.28	1.13	1.03	1.00	.97	.81

Wall Height Adjustment: Add or subtract the amount listed in this table to or from the square foot of floor cost for each foot of second and higher floor wall height more or less than 10 feet.

Finished Basement - Square Foot Area

Quality Class	5,000	7,500	10,000	12,500	15,000	20,000	25,000	30,000	35,000	40,000	50,000
1, Best	164.98	153.42	146.48	141.75	138.22	133.31	129.92	127.40	125.47	123.90	121.45
2, Good	141.64	131.71	125.76	121.70	118.66	114.47	111.52	109.39	107.74	106.37	104.32
3, Average	124.20	115.52	110.29	106.70	104.05	100.40	97.75	95.89	94.44	93.27	91.43
4, Low	100.60	93.52	89.29	86.42	84.27	81.27	79.18	77.67	76.48	75.51	74.04

Unfinished Basements

Area	5,000	7,500	10,000	12,500	15,000	20,000	25,000	30,000	35,000	40,000	50,000
Cost	41.96	39.01	37.25	36.05	35.15	33.89	33.04	32.39	31.91	31.51	30.88

Wall Height Adjustment: Add or subtract the amount listed in this table to or from the square foot of floor cost for each foot of basement wall height more or less than 10 feet.

Area	5,000	7,500	10,000	12,500	15,000	20,000	25,000	30,000	35,000	40,000	50,000
Finished	.90	.73	.64	.59	.54	.44	.38	.34	.33	.32	.27
Unfinished	.81	.66	.57	.53	.48	.38	.34	.31	.30	.29	.25

Quality Classification

	Class 1 Best Quality	Class 2 Good Quality	Class 3 Average Quality	Class 4 Low Quality
Foundation (6% of total cost)	Reinforced concrete, depth to 12'.	Reinforced concrete, depth 8' to 10'.	Reinforced concrete, depth 6 to 8'.	Reinforced concrete, depth 6' or less.
Floor Structure (5% of total cost)	Concrete on steel beams and deck.	Lightweight concrete on steel beams.	6" thickened edge concrete slab on 6" rock base.	4" reinforced slab on rock base.
Exterior Walls (15% of total cost)	Marble or polished granite, spandrel glass. Metal trim. Decorative atrium entrance.	Glass curtain wall. Textured-block, good brick or stone veneer. Atrium entrance.	Colored concrete block with some brick or wood trim. Decorative entrance.	Tilt-up concrete, brick or concrete block. Few decorative details.
Roof Structure & Cover (18% of total cost)	Glu-lams or steel trusses on steel intermediate columns. Panelized roof system with elastomeric concrete tile or metal roof cover. Engineered for earthquake or high wind zones.	Glu-lams or steel beams on steel intermediate columns. Panelized roof system with 5-ply, built-up or concrete tile roof cover. Good insulation.	Wood or metal trusses on intermediate columns. Panelized roof system with built-up or good composition shingle roofing. Insulated.	Beams or trusses on steel supports. OSB. sheathing. Built-up or low cost membrane roofing. Foil insulation. Not designed for high wind or seismic zones.
Floor Finish (5% of total cost)	Marble or good terrazzo in public rooms. Carpeted offices. Ceramic tile in restrooms.	Terrazzo or marble tile in public rooms. Carpet in offices. Vinyl in restrooms.	Good sheet vinyl in meeting rooms. Carpet in offices. Composition tile in restrooms.	Low cost sheet vinyl in public rooms. Floor tile elsewhere.
Windows & Doors (6% of total cost)	Low-E glass in metal sash. Metal-frame laminated glass entrance doors. Metal interior doors. Institutional grade hardware. LEED certified.	Colored low-E glass. Decorative metal exterior doors. Solid core 8' high wood interior doors. Commercial grade hardware.	Insulated store front or glazed curtain wall. Metal exterior doors. Wood interior doors. Standard grade hardware.	Few standard grade metal windows. Low cost metal exterior doors. Low grade hardware.
Interior Wall Finish (13% of total cost)	Decorative plaster in public rooms. Plaster- or vinyl-covered wallboard in collection area. Decorative metal or hardwood veneer wainscot and trim.	Plaster or good paneling in public rooms. Vinyl-covered wallboard in hallways. Textured or vinyl-covered wallboard with good trim elsewhere.	Textured and painted interior stucco or gypsum wallboard. Wood trim in public meeting rooms.	Painted gypsum wallboard.
Ceiling Finish (2% of total cost)	Suspended decorative textured plaster in meeting rooms. Acoustic ceiling tile elsewhere.	Suspended acoustical tile in with concealed grid in meeting rooms. Acoustical tile elsewhere.	Suspended acoustical tile with exposed grid system.	Painted gypsum wallboard with acoustic texture.
Specialties (13% of total cost)	Wired or wireless security and surveillance systems, video and network connections, large circulation desk area.	Surveillance and security system. Network connections throughout. Dedicated information and circulation stations.	Data network and AV connections throughout. Some cabinets and shelves.	Minimum alarm system. Few cabinets and shelves.
Plumbing (7% of total cost)	Institutional grade fixtures. Copper supply, vent & drain pipe. Metal or synthetic stone toilet partitions.	Good commercial grade fixtures. Copper supply & drain pipe. Metal toilet partitions.	Standard grade fixtures. PEX or PVC supply, vent and drain pipe. Composition toilet partitions.	Minimum fixtures. Plastic supply, vent & drain pipe. Plastic-faced toilet partitions.
Lighting and Power (10% of total cost)	Decorative indirect fixtures in public rooms. Many recessed task lights on separate controls. Recessed fluorescent fixtures in offices and hallways.	Indirect lighting fixtures in public rooms. Track lighting or recessed fluorescent fixtures with some task lighting in offices and hallways.	Continuous 4 tube fluorescent strips with decorative diffusers, 8' O.C. Some recessed ceiling fixtures.	Continuous exposed 2 tube fluorescent strip, fixtures 8' O.C.

Notes: Use the percent of total cost to help identify the correct quality classification. Includes space for the library collection, seating, public access computer stations, staff work area, meeting rooms, circulation and information desks.

Square foot costs include the following components: Foundations as required for normal soil conditions. Floor, wall and roof structures. Interior ceiling, wall and floor finishes (including carpet). Exterior wall finish and roof cover. Interior partitions. Basic lighting and electrical systems. Rough and finish plumbing. Specialties as listed. Design and engineering fees. Typical utility hook-up. Contractor's mark-up.

Add the cost of: Book and media shelving and storage. Canopies and canopy lighting. Desks, tables and study carrels. Installed AV equipment, computer network and computers. Intercom and security systems beyond what appears in the quality classification above. Docks and ramps. Elevators. Draperies. Fire extinguishers and fire sprinklers. Heating and cooling systems. Exterior signs. Walks, paving and curbing. Yard improvements. See the section "Additional Costs for Commercial, Industrial and Public Structures" beginning on page 236.

Public Libraries – Masonry or Concrete

First Floor

Estimating Procedure

1. Use the tables in this section to estimate the cost of buildings designed for use as a public, academic or school library. Many community libraries occupy space designed for use by commercial tenants rather than built for use as a public library. Use figures from the sections on Urban Stores, Suburban Stores or General Office Buildings when the structure was designed for commercial occupancy.
2. Establish the structure quality class by applying the information on page 62.
3. Calculate the area of the first floor. This should include all area within the building exterior walls and all inset areas outside the main walls but under the main building roof.
4. Find in the table below the square foot cost for the appropriate quality class and the nearest building area.
5. Use figures in the Wall Height Adjustment row to adjust that square foot cost for wall heights more or less than 14 feet.
6. Multiply the adjusted square foot cost by the area of the first floor.
7. Multiply that total by the location factor on page 7.
8. Add costs from the section Additional Costs for Commercial, Industrial and Public Buildings beginning on page 236.
9. Using figures on the next page, add the cost of any second or higher floors or a basement.

Public Library, Class 2

Public Library, Class 1

First Floor - Square Foot Area

Quality Class	4,000	6,000	8,000	10,000	12,000	16,000	20,000	24,000	28,000	32,000	40,000
1, Best	305.01	291.50	280.79	272.08	264.70	258.39	252.94	243.92	236.50	230.53	221.11
1 & 2	273.52	261.45	251.87	243.99	237.35	231.66	226.84	218.63	212.13	206.82	198.24
2, Good	246.16	235.37	226.76	219.69	213.66	208.59	204.17	196.90	190.97	186.07	178.55
2 & 3	220.21	210.51	202.71	196.34	191.11	186.55	182.60	176.03	170.81	166.46	159.65
3, Average	197.47	188.76	181.86	176.22	171.35	167.36	163.78	157.89	153.19	149.29	143.19
3 & 4	172.34	164.75	158.70	153.78	149.57	146.08	142.98	137.79	133.62	130.34	124.97
4, Low	147.05	140.52	135.38	131.23	127.64	124.57	121.93	117.56	114.00	111.17	106.58
Wall Height Adjustment*	1.67	1.28	1.16	1.10	1.05	1.01	.93	.91	.89	.89	.89

Wall Height Adjustment: Add or subtract the amount listed in this row to or from the square foot of floor cost for each foot of wall height more or less than 14 feet.

Public Libraries – Masonry or Concrete

Upper Floors and Basements

Estimating Procedure

1. Establish the quality class for second and higher floors and the basement. The quality class will usually be the same as the first floor of the building. Square foot costs for unfinished basements will be nearly the same regardless of the structure quality class.
2. Calculate the area of any second or higher floor or a basement.
3. Find in the tables below the square foot cost for the appropriate quality class and the nearest area.
4. Use figures in the Wall Height Adjustment row to adjust the square foot cost for wall heights more or less than 10 feet.
5. Multiply the adjusted square foot cost by the area.
6. Multiply that total by the location factor on page 7.
7. Add costs from the section Additional Costs for Commercial, Industrial and Public Buildings beginning on page 236.
8. Add totals from this page to the cost for the first floor to find the total building cost.

Second and Higher Floors - Square Foot Area

Quality Class	4,000	6,000	8,000	10,000	12,000	16,000	20,000	24,000	28,000	32,000	40,000
1, Best	276.84	264.58	254.85	246.96	240.26	234.52	229.57	221.39	214.67	209.25	200.68
1 & 2	248.26	237.30	228.60	221.46	215.42	210.27	205.89	198.45	192.54	187.72	179.93
2, Good	223.43	213.63	205.82	199.40	193.93	189.32	185.31	178.71	173.34	168.88	162.05
2 & 3	199.87	191.08	183.99	178.20	173.46	169.33	165.73	159.77	155.05	151.09	144.90
3, Average	179.22	171.33	165.06	159.94	155.51	151.89	148.65	143.31	139.04	135.49	129.96
3 & 4	156.42	149.53	144.05	139.57	135.76	132.57	129.76	125.07	121.29	118.30	113.43
4, Low	133.46	127.54	122.87	119.11	115.86	113.08	110.67	106.71	103.47	100.90	96.74
Wall Height Adjustment*	1.50	1.16	1.06	1.00	.95	.91	.84	.83	.81	.81	.81

*Wall Height Adjustment: Add or subtract the amount listed in this row to or from the square foot of floor cost for each foot of wall height more or less than 10 feet.

Finished Basement - Square Foot Area

Quality Class	4,000	6,000	8,000	10,000	12,000	16,000	20,000	24,000	28,000	32,000	40,000
1, Best	166.04	158.68	152.85	148.12	144.10	140.65	137.69	132.77	128.74	125.49	120.37
2, Good	134.01	128.13	123.45	119.59	116.31	113.54	111.14	107.19	103.96	101.29	97.20
3, Average	107.49	102.76	99.00	95.93	93.27	91.10	89.16	85.95	83.40	81.27	77.94
4, Low	80.04	76.50	73.69	71.44	69.49	67.82	66.38	64.00	62.06	60.52	58.02

Unfinished Basements

Area	4,000	6,000	8,000	10,000	12,000	16,000	20,000	24,000	28,000	32,000	40,000
Cost	40.98	39.16	37.71	36.56	35.56	34.71	33.98	32.75	31.76	30.98	29.69

Wall Height Adjustment: Add or subtract the amount listed in this table to or from the square foot of floor cost for each foot of basement wall height more or less than 10 feet.

Area	4,000	6,000	8,000	10,000	12,000	16,000	20,000	24,000	28,000	32,000	40,000
Finished	.0.88	.67	.61	.58	.55	.53	.49	.48	.47	.47	.47
Unfinished	.79	.61	.55	.52	.51	.48	.44	.43	.42	.42	.42

Public Libraries – Wood or Steel Frame

Quality Classification

	Class 1 Best Quality	Class 2 Good Quality	Class 3 Average Quality	Class 4 Low Quality
Foundation (6% of total cost)	Reinforced concrete, depth to 8'.	Reinforced concrete, depth 6' to 8'.	Reinforced concrete, depth 4' to 6'.	Reinforced concrete, depth 4' or less.
Floor Structure (5% of total cost)	Concrete on steel beams and deck.	Sheathing on wood or steel floor trusses.	6" thickened edge concrete slab on 6" rock base.	4" reinforced slab on rock base.
Exterior Walls (15% of total cost)	Braced wood or steel studs. Decorative brick or stone veneer with ornate details.	Wood or steel studs. Good wood or composition siding. Some masonry veneer.	Wood studs. Stucco with integral color. Some brick trim.	Wood studs. Painted stucco or inexpensive wood panel siding.
Roof Structure & Cover (18% of total cost)	Glu-lams or steel trusses on steel intermediate columns. Panelized roof system with elastomeric concrete tile or metal roof cover. Engineered for earthquake or high wind zones.	Glu-lams or steel beams on steel intermediate columns. Panelized roof system with 5-ply, built-up or concrete tile roof cover. Good insulation.	Wood or metal trusses on intermediate columns. Panelized roof system with built-up or good composition shingle roofing. Insulated.	Beams or trusses on steel supports. OSB sheathing. Built-up or low cost membrane roofing. Foil insulation. Not designed for high wind or seismic zones.
Floor Finish (5% of total cost)	Marble or good terrazzo in public rooms. Carpeted offices. Ceramic tile in restrooms.	Terrazzo or marble tile in public rooms. Carpet in offices. Vinyl in restrooms.	Good sheet vinyl in meeting rooms. Carpet in offices. Composition tile in restrooms.	Low cost sheet vinyl in public rooms. Floor Tile elsewhere.
Windows & Doors (6% of total cost)	Low-E glass in metal sash. Metal-frame laminated glass entrance doors. Metal interior doors. Institutional grade hardware. LEED certified.	Colored low-E glass. Decorative metal exterior doors. Solid core 8' high wood interior doors. Commercial grade hardware.	Insulated store front or glazed curtain wall. Metal exterior doors. Wood interior doors. Standard grade hardware.	Few standard grade metal windows. Low cost metal exterior doors. Low grade hardware.
Interior Wall Finish (13% of total cost)	Decorative plaster in public rooms. Plaster- or vinyl-covered wallboard in private offices. Decorative metal or hardwood veneer wainscot and trim.	Plaster or good paneling in public rooms. Vinyl-covered wallboard in hallways. Textured or vinyl-covered wallboard with good trim elsewhere.	Textured and painted interior stucco or gypsum wallboard. Wood trim in public meeting rooms.	Painted gypsum wallboard.
Ceiling Finish (2% of total cost)	Suspended decorative textured plaster in meeting rooms. Acoustic ceiling tile elsewhere.	Suspended acoustical tile in with concealed grid in meeting rooms. Acoustical tile elsewhere.	Suspended acoustical tile with exposed grid system.	Painted gypsum wallboard with acoustic texture.
Specialties (13% of total cost)	Wired or wireless security and surveillance systems, video and network connections, large circulation desk area.	Surveillance and security system. Network connections throughout. Dedicated information and circulation stations.	Data network and AV connections throughout. Some cabinets and shelves.	Minimum alarm system. Few cabinets and shelves.
Plumbing (7% of total cost)	Institutional grade fixtures. Copper supply, vent & drain pipe. Metal or synthetic stone toilet partitions.	Good commercial grade fixtures. Copper supply & drain pipe. Metal toilet partitions.	Standard grade fixtures. PEX or PVC supply, vent and drain pipe. Composition toilet partitions.	Minimum fixtures. Plastic supply, vent & drain pipe. Plastic-faced toilet partitions.
Lighting and Power (10% of total cost)	Decorative indirect fixtures in public rooms. Many recessed task lights on separate controls. Recessed fluorescent fixtures in offices and hallways.	Indirect lighting fixtures in public rooms. Track lighting or recessed fluorescent fixtures with some task lighting in offices and hallways.	Continuous 4 tube fluorescent strips with decorative diffusers, 8' O.C. Some recessed ceiling fixtures.	Continuous exposed 2 tube fluorescent strip, fixtures 8' O.C.

Notes: Use the percent of total cost to help identify the correct quality classification. Includes space for the library collection, seating, public access computer stations, staff work area, meeting rooms, circulation and information desks.

Square foot costs include the following components: Foundations as required for normal soil conditions. Floor, wall and roof structures. Interior ceiling, wall and floor finishes (including carpet). Exterior wall finish and roof cover. Interior partitions. Basic lighting and electrical systems. Rough and finish plumbing. Specialties as listed. Design and engineering fees. Typical utility hook-up. Contractor's mark-up.

Add the cost of: Book and media shelving and storage. Canopies and canopy lighting. Desks, tables and study carrels. Installed AV equipment, computer network and computers. Public address, intercom and security systems beyond what appears in the quality classification above. Docks and ramps. Elevators. Draperies. Fire extinguishers and fire sprinklers. Heating and cooling systems. Exterior signs. Walks, paving and curbing. Yard improvements. See the section "Additional Costs for Commercial, Industrial and Public Structures" beginning on page 236.

Public Libraries – Wood or Steel Frame

First Floor

Estimating Procedure

1. Use the tables in this section to estimate the cost of buildings designed for use as public libraries. Many community libraries occupy space designed for use by commercial tenants rather than built for use as public libraries. Use figures from the sections on Urban Stores, Suburban Stores or General Office Buildings when the structure was designed for commercial occupancy.
2. Establish the structure quality class by applying the information on page 65.
3. Calculate the area of the first floor. This should include all area within the building exterior walls and all inset areas outside the main walls but under the main building roof.
4. Find in the table below the square foot cost for the appropriate quality class and the nearest building area.
5. Use figures in the Wall Height Adjustment row to adjust that square foot cost for wall heights more or less than 14 feet.
6. Multiply the adjusted square foot cost by the area of the first floor.
7. Multiply that total by the location factor on page 7.
8. Add costs from the section Additional Costs for Commercial, Industrial and Public Buildings beginning on page 236.
9. Using figures on the next page, add the cost of any second or higher floors or a basement.

Public Library, Class 4

Public Library, Class 1 & 2

Square Foot Area

Quality Class	4,000	6,000	8,000	10,000	12,000	16,000	20,000	24,000	28,000	32,000	40,000
1, Best	273.52	261.40	251.79	243.99	237.37	231.70	226.82	218.73	212.10	206.73	198.28
1 & 2	245.28	234.46	225.88	218.81	212.84	207.74	203.42	196.07	190.24	185.46	177.77
2, Good	220.75	211.07	203.35	197.01	191.60	187.05	183.09	176.58	171.26	166.86	160.12
2 & 3	197.48	188.79	181.78	176.07	171.38	167.29	163.75	157.85	153.18	149.27	143.17
3, Average	177.08	169.27	163.08	158.03	153.65	150.07	146.88	141.59	137.36	133.87	128.40
3 & 4	154.54	147.74	142.32	137.90	134.14	130.99	128.20	123.57	119.84	116.89	112.07
4, Low	131.86	126.03	121.40	117.68	114.46	111.72	109.34	105.42	102.23	99.69	95.58
Wall Height Adjustment*	1.50	1.15	1.04	.99	.94	.90	.83	.81	.79	.79	.79

***Wall Height Adjustment:** Add or subtract the amount listed in this table to or from the square foot of floor cost for each foot of wall height more or less than 14 feet.

Public Libraries – Wood or Steel Frame

Upper Floor and Basement

Estimating Procedure

1. Establish the quality class for the second floor and the basement. The quality class will usually be the same as the first floor of the building. Square foot costs for unfinished basements will be nearly the same regardless of the structure quality class.
2. Calculate the area of any second floor or basement.
3. Find in the tables below the square foot cost for the appropriate quality class and the nearest area.
4. Use figures in the Wall Height Adjustment row to adjust the square foot cost for wall heights more or less than 10 feet.
5. Multiply the adjusted square foot cost by the area.
6. Multiply that total by the location factor on page 7.
7. Add costs from the section Additional Costs for Commercial, Industrial and Public Buildings beginning on page 236.
8. Add totals from this page to the cost for the first floor to find the total building cost.

Second Floor - Square Foot Area

Quality Class	4,000	6,000	8,000	10,000	12,000	16,000	20,000	24,000	28,000	32,000	40,000
1, Best	240.16	229.52	221.08	214.23	208.42	203.44	199.15	192.05	186.22	181.52	174.09
1 & 2	215.35	205.86	198.32	192.11	186.87	182.41	178.61	172.15	167.02	162.83	156.08
2, Good	193.81	185.32	178.55	172.97	168.23	164.24	160.75	155.03	150.36	146.50	140.58
2 & 3	173.39	165.76	159.61	154.60	150.47	146.89	143.77	138.60	134.49	131.06	125.70
3, Average	155.47	148.62	143.19	138.76	134.90	131.76	128.96	124.32	120.61	117.54	112.74
3 & 4	135.69	129.71	124.96	121.08	117.77	115.00	112.57	108.49	105.22	102.63	98.39
4, Low	115.77	110.65	106.59	103.32	100.51	98.09	96.00	92.56	89.76	87.53	83.92
Wall height Adjustment*	1.31	1.01	.92	.86	.82	.79	.74	.72	.71	.71	.71

*Wall Height Adjustment: Add or subtract the amount listed in this table to or from the square foot of floor cost for each foot of second and higher floor wall height more or less than 10 feet.

Finished Basements - Square Foot Area

Quality Class	4,000	6,000	8,000	10,000	12,000	16,000	20,000	24,000	28,000	32,000	40,000
1, Best	168.73	161.26	155.33	150.52	146.44	142.95	139.92	134.93	130.83	127.54	122.31
2, Good	136.18	130.21	125.44	121.53	118.20	115.40	112.94	108.92	105.64	102.93	98.77
3, Average	109.24	104.43	100.61	97.49	94.79	92.57	90.60	87.35	84.74	82.59	79.22
4, Low	81.34	77.74	74.89	72.60	70.61	68.92	67.45	65.03	63.07	61.50	58.96

Unfinished Basements

Area	4,000	6,000	8,000	10,000	12,000	16,000	20,000	24,000	28,000	32,000	40,000
Cost	42.19	40.32	38.83	37.65	36.62	35.74	34.99	33.73	32.71	31.90	30.58

Wall Height Adjustment: Add or subtract the amount listed in this table to or from the square foot of floor cost for each foot of basement wall height more or less than 10 feet.

Area	4,000	6,000	8,000	10,000	12,000	16,000	20,000	24,000	28,000	32,000	40,000
Finished	.90	.69	.62	.59	.56	.54	.51	.50	.49	.49	.49
Unfinished	.81	.62	.56	.53	.52	.50	.46	.45	.44	.44	.44

Quality Classification

	Class 1 Best Quality	Class 2 Good Quality	Class 3 Average Quality	Class 4 Low Quality
Foundation (6% of total cost)	Reinforced concrete, depth to 12'.	Reinforced concrete, depth 8' to 10'.	Reinforced concrete, depth 6 to 8'.	Reinforced concrete, depth 6' or less.
Floor Structure (5% of total cost)	Concrete on steel beams and deck.	Lightweight concrete on steel beams.	6" thickened edge concrete slab on 6" rock base.	4" reinforced slab on rock base.
Exterior Walls (15% of total cost)	Decorative brick with store-front glazing. Metal trim. Decorative public entrance.	Insulated glass with textured-block, good brick or stone veneer. Public entrance.	Colored concrete block with some brick or wood trim. Plain entrance.	Tilt-up concrete, brick or concrete block. Few decorative details.
Roof Structure & Cover (18% of total cost)	Glu-lams or steel trusses on steel intermediate columns. Panelized roof system with elastomeric or metal roof cover. Patio or roof deck. Engineered for earthquake or high wind zones.	Glu-lams or steel beams on steel intermediate columns. Panelized roof system with 5-ply, built-up or elastomeric roof cover. Good insulation.	Wood or metal trusses on intermediate columns. Panelized roof system with built-up or good composition roofing. Adequate insulation.	Beams or trusses on steel supports. OSB sheathing. Built-up or low cost membrane roofing. Foil insulation. Not designed for high wind or seismic zones.
Floor Finish (5% of total cost)	Stone or good terrazzo in public rooms. Carpeted leisure-time rooms. Tile in restrooms.	Terrazzo or hardwood in public rooms. Carpet in offices. Vinyl in restrooms.	Good sheet vinyl in meeting rooms. Carpet in offices. Composition tile in restrooms.	Low cost sheet vinyl in public rooms. Floor tile elsewhere.
Windows & Doors (6% of total cost)	Low-E glass in metal sash. Metal-frame laminated glass entrance doors. Metal interior doors. Institutional grade hardware. LEED certified.	Colored low-E glass. Decorative metal exterior doors. Solid core 8' high wood interior doors. Commercial grade hardware.	Insulated store front or glazed curtain wall. Metal exterior doors. Wood interior doors. Standard grade hardware.	Few standard grade metal windows. Low cost metal exterior doors. Low grade hardware.
Interior Wall Finish (13% of total cost)	Decorative plaster in public rooms. Plaster- or vinyl-covered wallboard in leisure time areas. Decorative metal or hardwood veneer wainscot and trim.	Plaster or good paneling in public rooms. Vinyl-covered wallboard in hallways. Textured or vinyl-covered wallboard with good trim elsewhere.	Textured and painted interior stucco or gypsum wallboard. Wood trim in public meeting rooms.	Painted gypsum wallboard.
Ceiling Finish (2% of total cost)	Suspended decorative textured plaster in administrative rooms. Acoustic ceiling tile elsewhere.	Suspended acoustical tile with concealed grid in meeting rooms. Ceiling tile elsewhere.	Suspended acoustical tile with exposed grid. Wallboard in vehicle bays.	Painted gypsum wallboard with trowel texture.
Specialties (13% of total cost)	Wired security, PA and surveillance systems. Video and network connections. Good day room and dispatch areas.	Surveillance and security system. Network connections throughout. Recreation facilities and good vehicle maintenance area.	Data network and AV connections throughout. Some cabinets and shelves. Plain day room and storage.	Minimum alarm system. Few cabinets and shelves. Few built-ins.
Plumbing (7% of total cost)	Top grade commercial fixtures. Copper supply, vent & drain pipe. Metal or synthetic stone toilet partitions.	Good commercial grade fixtures. Copper supply & drain pipe. Metal toilet partitions.	Standard grade fixtures. PEX or PVC supply, vent and drain pipe. Composition toilet partitions.	Minimum fixtures. Plastic supply, vent & drain pipe. Plastic-faced toilet partitions.
Lighting and Power (10% of total cost)	Decorative indirect fixtures in public rooms. Many recessed task lights on separate controls. Recessed fluorescent fixtures in offices and hallways.	Indirect lighting fixtures in public rooms. Track lighting or recessed fluorescent fixtures with some task lighting in offices and hallways.	Continuous 4 tube fluorescent strips with decorative diffusers, 8' O.C. Some recessed ceiling fixtures.	Continuous exposed 2 tube fluorescent strip, fixtures 8' O.C.

Notes: Use the percent of total cost to help identify the correct quality classification. Includes vehicle and equipment bays, equipment storage and maintenance area, living accommodations, leisure time, administration and training facilities.

Square foot costs include the following components: Foundations as required for normal soil conditions. Floor, wall and roof structures. Interior ceiling, wall and floor finishes (including carpet). Exterior wall finish and roof cover. Interior partitions. Basic lighting and electrical systems. Rough and finish plumbing. Specialties as listed. Design and engineering fees. Typical utility hook-up. Contractor's mark-up.

Add the cost of: Canopies and canopy lighting. Installed PA and security systems beyond what appears in the quality classification above. Docks and ramps. Elevators. Draperies. Fire extinguishers and fire sprinklers. Heating and cooling systems. Exterior signs. Walks, paving and curbing. Yard improvements. See the section "Additional Costs for Commercial, Industrial and Public Structures" beginning on page 236.

Fire Stations – Masonry or Concrete

First Floor

Estimating Procedure

1. Use the tables in this section to estimate the cost of staffed fire stations including vehicle and equipment bays, equipment storage and maintenance areas, living accommodations, leisure time, administration and training facilities. Use the cost tables for Service Garages for volunteer fire stations with fire-fighting equipment bays but without living accommodations or administration facilities.
2. Establish the structure quality class by applying the information on page 68.
3. Calculate the area of the first floor. This should include all area within the building exterior walls and all inset areas outside the main walls but under the main building roof.
4. Find in the table below the square foot cost for the appropriate quality class and the nearest building area.
5. Use figures in the Wall Height Adjustment row to adjust that square foot cost for wall heights more or less than 14 feet in vehicle bays and 8 feet in other areas.
6. Multiply the adjusted square foot cost by the area of the first floor.
7. Multiply that total by the location factor on page 7.
8. Add costs from the section Additional Costs for Commercial, Industrial and Public Buildings beginning on page 236.
9. Using figures on the next page, add the cost of any second or higher floors or a basement.

Fire Station, Class 2

Fire Station, Class 3

First Floor - Square Foot Area

Quality Class	4,000	6,000	8,000	10,000	12,000	16,000	20,000	24,000	28,000	32,000	40,000
1, Best	224.90	214.94	207.04	200.63	195.18	190.52	186.51	179.85	174.40	169.99	163.03
1 & 2	201.68	192.78	185.72	179.91	175.00	170.82	167.27	161.22	156.42	152.50	146.18
2, Good	181.51	173.55	167.21	161.99	157.54	153.80	150.54	145.19	140.81	137.20	131.65
2 & 3	162.38	155.24	149.48	144.77	140.92	137.55	134.63	129.80	125.96	122.74	117.73
3, Average	145.60	139.19	134.10	129.94	126.34	123.40	120.77	116.42	112.95	110.08	105.58
3 & 4	127.07	121.48	117.03	113.40	110.29	107.71	105.42	101.61	98.53	96.10	92.15
4, Low	108.42	103.62	99.82	96.76	94.12	91.86	89.90	86.69	84.06	81.97	78.59
Wall Height Adjustment*	1.23	.94	.86	.81	.77	.74	.69	.67	.66	.66	.66

Wall Height Adjustment: Add or subtract the amount listed in this row to or from the square foot of floor cost for each foot of wall height more or less than 14 feet in equipment bays and 8 feet in other areas.

Fire Stations – Masonry or Concrete

Upper Floors and Basements

Estimating Procedure

1. Establish the quality class for second and higher floors and the basement. The quality class will usually be the same as the first floor of the building. Square foot costs for unfinished basements will be nearly the same regardless of the structure quality class.
2. Calculate the area of any second or higher floor or a basement.
3. Find in the tables below the square foot cost for the appropriate quality class and the nearest area.
4. Use figures in the Wall Height Adjustment row to adjust the square foot cost for wall heights more or less than 8 feet.
5. Multiply the adjusted square foot cost by the area.
6. Multiply that total by the location factor on page 7.
7. Add costs from the section Additional Costs for Commercial, Industrial and Public Buildings beginning on page 236.
8. Add totals from this page to the cost for the first floor to find the total building cost.

Second and Higher Floors - Square Foot Area

Quality Class	4,000	6,000	8,000	10,000	12,000	16,000	20,000	24,000	28,000	32,000	40,000
1, Best	197.50	188.75	181.82	176.18	171.41	167.32	163.78	157.93	153.15	149.29	143.17
1 & 2	177.11	169.30	163.09	157.98	153.68	150.01	146.88	141.57	137.36	133.93	128.37
2, Good	159.40	152.41	146.83	142.26	138.36	135.07	132.21	127.49	123.65	120.49	115.61
2 & 3	142.59	136.32	131.27	127.14	123.75	120.80	118.24	113.99	110.61	107.79	103.38
3, Average	127.86	122.23	117.76	114.11	110.95	108.36	106.05	102.24	99.19	96.67	92.71
3 & 4	111.58	106.68	102.77	99.58	96.86	94.58	92.58	89.23	86.53	84.40	80.92
4, Low	95.21	91.00	87.66	84.97	82.65	80.67	78.95	76.12	73.82	71.98	69.01
Wall Height Adjustment*	1.08	.83	.75	.72	.68	.65	.60	.59	.58	.58	.58

*Wall Height Adjustment: Add or subtract the amount listed in this row to or from the square foot of floor cost for each foot of wall height more or less than 8 feet.

Finished Basement - Square Foot Area

Quality Class	4,000	6,000	8,000	10,000	12,000	16,000	20,000	24,000	28,000	32,000	40,000
1, Best	122.52	117.10	112.79	109.30	106.33	103.80	101.61	97.98	95.01	92.61	88.82
2, Good	98.88	94.55	91.09	88.25	85.83	83.79	82.01	79.09	76.71	74.74	71.72
3, Average	79.33	75.82	73.05	70.79	68.82	67.23	65.79	63.43	61.53	59.97	57.51
4, Low	59.06	56.46	54.39	52.71	51.28	50.05	48.97	47.23	45.79	44.65	42.81

Unfinished Basements

Area	4,000	6,000	8,000	10,000	12,000	16,000	20,000	24,000	28,000	32,000	40,000
Cost	40.98	39.16	37.71	36.56	35.56	34.71	33.98	32.75	31.76	30.98	29.69

Wall Height Adjustment: Add or subtract the amount listed in this table to or from the square foot of floor cost for each foot of basement wall height more or less than 8 feet.

Area	4,000	6,000	8,000	10,000	12,000	16,000	20,000	24,000	28,000	32,000	40,000
Finished	0.88	.67	.61	.58	.55	.53	.49	.48	.47	.47	.47
Unfinished	.79	.61	.55	.52	.51	.48	.44	.43	.42	.42	.42

Fire Stations – Wood or Steel Frame

Quality Classification

	Class 1 Best Quality	Class 2 Good Quality	Class 3 Average Quality	Class 4 Low Quality
Foundation (6% of total cost)	Reinforced concrete, depth to 8'.	Reinforced concrete, depth 6' to 8'.	Reinforced concrete, depth 4' to 6'.	Reinforced concrete, depth 4' or less.
Floor Structure (5% of total cost)	Concrete on steel beams and deck.	Sheathing on wood or steel floor trusses.	6" thickened edge concrete slab on 6" rock base.	4" reinforced slab on rock base.
Exterior Walls (15% of total cost)	Braced wood or steel studs. Decorative brick or stone veneer with ornate details.	Wood or steel studs. Good wood or composition siding. Some masonry veneer.	Wood studs. Stucco with integral color. Some brick trim.	Wood studs. Painted stucco or inexpensive wood panel siding.
Roof Structure & Cover (18% of total cost)	Glu-lams or steel trusses on steel intermediate columns. Panelized roof system with elastomeric or metal roof cover. Patio or roof deck. Engineered for earthquake or high wind zones.	Glu-lams or steel beams on steel intermediate columns. Panelized roof system with 5-ply, built-up or elastomeric roof cover. Good insulation.	Wood or metal trusses on intermediate columns. Panelized roof system with built-up or good composition roofing. Adequate insulation.	Beams or trusses on steel supports. OSB sheathing. Built-up or low cost membrane roofing. Foil insulation. Not designed for high wind or seismic zones.
Floor Finish (5% of total cost)	Stone or good terrazzo in public rooms. Carpeted leisure-time rooms. Tile in restrooms.	Terrazzo or hardwood in public rooms. Carpet in offices. Vinyl in restrooms.	Good sheet vinyl in meeting rooms. Carpet in offices. Composition tile in restrooms.	Low cost sheet vinyl in public rooms. Floor tile elsewhere.
Windows & Doors (6% of total cost)	Low-E glass in metal sash. Metal-frame laminated glass entrance doors. Metal interior doors. Institutional grade hardware. LEED certified.	Colored low-E glass. Decorative metal exterior doors. Solid core 8' high wood interior doors. Commercial grade hardware.	Insulated store front or glazed curtain wall. Metal exterior doors. Wood interior doors. Standard grade hardware.	Few standard grade metal windows. Low cost metal exterior doors. Low grade hardware.
Interior Wall Finish (13% of total cost)	Decorative plaster in public rooms. Plaster- or vinyl-covered wallboard in leisure time areas. Decorative metal or hardwood veneer wainscot and trim.	Plaster or good paneling in public rooms. Vinyl-covered wallboard in hallways. Textured or vinyl-covered wallboard with good trim elsewhere.	Textured and painted interior stucco or gypsum wallboard. Wood trim in public meeting rooms.	Painted gypsum wallboard.
Ceiling Finish (2% of total cost)	Suspended decorative textured plaster in administrative rooms. Acoustic ceiling tile elsewhere.	Suspended acoustical tile with concealed grid in meeting rooms. Ceiling tile elsewhere.	Suspended acoustical tile with exposed grid. Wallboard in vehicle bays.	Painted gypsum wallboard with trowel texture.
Specialties (13% of total cost)	Wired security, PA and surveillance systems. Video and network connections. Good day room and dispatch areas.	Surveillance and security system. Network connections throughout. Recreation facilities and good vehicle maintenance area.	Data network and AV connections throughout. Some cabinets and shelves. Plain day room and storage.	Minimum alarm system. Few cabinets and shelves. Few built-ins.
Plumbing (7% of total cost)	Top grade commercial fixtures. Copper supply, vent & drain pipe. Metal or synthetic stone toilet partitions.	Good commercial grade fixtures. Copper supply & drain pipe. Metal toilet partitions.	Standard grade fixtures. PEX or PVC supply, vent and drain pipe. Composition toilet partitions.	Minimum fixtures. Plastic supply, vent & drain pipe. Plastic-faced toilet partitions.
Lighting and Power (10% of total cost)	Decorative indirect fixtures in public rooms. Many recessed task lights on separate controls. Recessed fluorescent fixtures in offices and hallways.	Indirect lighting fixtures in public rooms. Track lighting or recessed fluorescent fixtures with some task lighting in offices and hallways.	Continuous 4 tube fluorescent strips with decorative diffusers, 8' O.C. Some recessed ceiling fixtures.	Continuous exposed 2 tube fluorescent strip, fixtures 8' O.C.

Notes: Use the percent of total cost to help identify the correct quality classification. Includes vehicle and equipment bays, equipment storage and maintenance area, living accommodations, leisure time, administration and training facilities.

Square foot costs include the following components: Foundations as required for normal soil conditions. Floor, wall and roof structures. Interior ceiling, wall and floor finishes (including carpet). Exterior wall finish and roof cover. Interior partitions. Basic lighting and electrical systems. Rough and finish plumbing. Specialties as listed. Design and engineering fees. Typical utility hook-up. Contractor's mark-up.

Add the cost of: Canopies and canopy lighting. Installed PA and security systems beyond what appears in the quality classification above. Docks and ramps. Elevators. Draperies. Fire extinguishers and fire sprinklers. Heating and cooling systems. Exterior signs. Walks, paving and curbing. Yard improvements. See the section "Additional Costs for Commercial, Industrial and Public Structures" beginning on page 236.

First Floor

Estimating Procedure

1. Use the tables in this section to estimate the cost of staffed fire stations including vehicle and equipment bays, equipment storage and maintenance areas, living accommodations, leisure time, administration and training facilities. Use the cost tables for Service Garages for volunteer fire stations with fire-fighting equipment bays but without living accommodations or administration facilities.
2. Establish the structure quality class by applying the information on page 71.
3. Calculate the area of the first floor. This should include all area within the building exterior walls and all inset areas outside the main walls but under the main building roof.
4. Find in the table below the square foot cost for the appropriate quality class and the nearest building area.
5. Use figures in the Wall Height Adjustment row to adjust that square foot cost for wall heights more or less than 14 feet in equipment bays and 8 feet in other areas.
6. Multiply the adjusted square foot cost by the area of the first floor.
7. Multiply that total by the location factor on page 7.
8. Add costs from the section Additional Costs for Commercial, Industrial and Public Buildings beginning on page 236.
9. Using figures on the next page, add the cost of any second or higher floors or a basement.

Fire Station, Class 3

Fire Station, Class 2 & 3

Square Foot Area

Quality Class	4,000	6,000	8,000	10,000	12,000	16,000	20,000	24,000	28,000	32,000	40,000
1, Best	201.76	192.84	185.74	179.98	175.09	170.92	167.33	161.35	156.45	152.51	146.26
1 & 2	180.93	172.95	166.62	161.40	157.00	153.24	150.06	144.63	140.33	136.81	131.13
2, Good	162.83	155.69	150.01	145.33	141.34	137.98	135.05	130.24	126.33	123.07	118.10
2 & 3	145.67	139.27	134.10	129.88	126.41	123.41	120.79	116.45	113.00	110.12	105.61
3, Average	130.62	124.86	120.31	116.57	113.35	110.70	108.34	104.45	101.33	98.75	94.71
3 & 4	113.99	108.98	104.99	101.72	98.95	96.63	94.57	91.16	88.40	86.22	82.67
4, Low	97.26	92.97	89.54	86.81	84.43	82.41	80.65	77.76	75.41	73.54	70.50
Wall Height Adjustment*	1.10	.84	.77	.74	.70	.67	.61	.60	.59	.59	.59

Wall Height Adjustment: Add or subtract the amount listed in this table to or from the square foot of floor cost for each foot of wall height more or less than 14 feet in equipment bays and 8 feet in other areas.

Fire Stations – Wood or Steel Frame

Upper Floor and Basement

Estimating Procedure

1. Establish the quality class for second floor and the basement. The quality class will usually be the same as the first floor of the building. Square foot costs for unfinished basements will be nearly the same regardless of the structure quality class.
2. Calculate the area of any second floor or basement.
3. Find in the tables below the square foot cost for the appropriate quality class and the nearest area.
4. Use figures in the Wall Height Adjustment row to adjust the square foot cost for wall heights more or less than 8 feet.
5. Multiply the adjusted square foot cost by the area.
6. Multiply that total by the location factor on page 7.
7. Add costs from the section Additional Costs for Commercial, Industrial and Public Buildings beginning on page 236.
8. Add totals from this page to the cost for the first floor to find the total building cost.

Second Floor - Square Foot Area

Quality Class	4,000	6,000	8,000	10,000	12,000	16,000	20,000	24,000	28,000	32,000	40,000
1, Best	182.24	174.17	167.77	162.57	158.16	154.38	151.12	145.74	141.32	137.75	132.11
1 & 2	163.43	156.21	150.50	145.78	141.81	138.41	135.53	130.63	126.74	123.58	118.45
2, Good	147.08	140.63	135.48	131.26	127.66	124.62	121.99	117.64	114.10	111.18	106.68
2 & 3	131.58	125.79	121.12	117.31	114.18	111.46	109.11	105.18	102.07	99.46	95.40
3, Average	117.98	112.79	108.66	105.29	102.38	99.99	97.85	94.34	91.52	89.20	85.55
3 & 4	102.96	98.44	94.83	91.88	89.38	87.28	85.42	82.33	79.84	77.88	74.66
4, Low	87.86	83.96	80.88	78.41	76.26	74.43	72.85	70.24	68.11	66.42	63.68
Wall height Adjustment*	1.00	.77	.70	.67	.62	.60	.56	.54	.53	.53	.53

*Wall Height Adjustment: Add or subtract the amount listed in this table to or from the square foot of floor cost for each foot of second and higher floor wall height more or less than 8 feet.

Finished Basements - Square Foot Area

Quality Class	4,000	6,000	8,000	10,000	12,000	16,000	20,000	24,000	28,000	32,000	40,000
1, Best	124.89	119.36	114.96	111.40	108.38	105.80	103.57	99.87	96.84	94.40	90.53
2, Good	100.79	96.38	92.85	89.95	87.48	85.40	83.60	80.62	78.20	76.19	73.11
3, Average	80.85	77.28	74.46	72.16	70.15	68.53	67.06	64.65	62.72	61.13	58.62
4, Low	60.21	57.54	55.43	53.74	52.26	51.01	49.92	48.14	46.68	45.52	43.64

Unfinished Basements

Area	4,000	6,000	8,000	10,000	12,000	16,000	20,000	24,000	28,000	32,000	40,000
Cost	41.77	39.92	38.45	37.27	36.25	35.39	34.63	33.38	32.38	31.57	30.27

Wall Height Adjustment: Add or subtract the amount listed in this table to or from the square foot of floor cost for each foot of basement wall height more or less than 8 feet.

Area	4,000	6,000	8,000	10,000	12,000	16,000	20,000	24,000	28,000	32,000	40,000
Finished	.88	.69	.62	.59	.56	.54	.50	.49	.48	.48	.48
Unfinished	.80	.62	.56	.53	.51	.49	.45	.44	.43	.43	.43

Commercial Structures Section

Section Contents

Urban Stores

Urban store buildings are designed for retail sales and are usually found in strip or downtown commercial developments. Square foot costs in this section are representative of a building situation where construction activities are restricted to the immediate site. This restriction tends to make the cost slightly higher than suburban type stores where unlimited use of modern machinery and techniques is possible. Do not use these figures for department stores, discount houses or suburban stores. These building types are evaluated in later sections.

Costs are for shell-type buildings without permanent partitions and include all labor, material and equipment costs for the following:

1. Foundations as required for normal soil conditions.
2. Floor, rear wall, side wall and roof structures.
3. A front wall consisting of vertical support columns or pilasters and horizontal beams spanning the area between these members leaving an open space to receive a display front.
4. Interior floor, wall and ceiling finishes.
5. Exterior wall finish on the side and rear walls.
6. Roof cover.
7. Basic lighting and electrical systems.
8. Rough and finish plumbing.
9. Design and engineering fees.
10. Permits and fees.
11. Utility hook-up.
12. Contractor's contingency, overhead and profit.

The in-place costs of the following components should be added to the basic building cost to arrive at the total structure cost. See the section "Additional Costs for Commercial, Industrial and Public Structures" on page 236.

1. Heating and air conditioning systems.
2. Elevators and escalators.
3. Fire sprinklers and fire escapes.
4. All display front components.
5. Finish materials on the front wall.
6. Canopies, ramps and docks.
7. Interior partitions.
8. Exterior signs.
9. Mezzanines and basements.
10. Communication systems.

For valuation purposes, urban stores are divided into two building types: 1) masonry or concrete frame and, 2) wood or wood and steel frame. Masonry or concrete urban stores vary widely in cost. Consequently, 6 quality classifications are established. Wood or wood and steel frame urban stores are divided into 4 quality classes.

Quality Classification

	Class 1 Best Quality	Class 2 Good Quality	Class 3 High Average Quality	Class 4 Low Average Quality	Class 5 Low Quality	Class 6 Minimum Quality
Foundation (15% of total cost)	Reinforced concrete.	Reinforced concrete.	Reinforced concrete.	Reinforced concrete.	Reinforced concrete.	Reinforced concrete.
Floor Structure (15% of total cost)	6" reinforced concrete on 6" rock fill or 2" x 12" joists 16" o.c.	4" to 6" reinforced concrete on 6" rock fill or 2" x 10" joists 16" o.c.	4" reinforced concrete on 6" rock fill or 2" x 10" joists 16" o.c.	4" reinforced concrete on 6" rock fill or 2" x 8" joists 16" o.c.	4" reinforced concrete on 6" rock fill or 2" x 6" joists 16" o.c.	4" reinforced concrete on 4" rock fill or 2" x 6" joists 16" o.c.
Wall Structure (15% of total cost)	Reinforced 8" concrete or 12" common brick or block.	Reinforced 8" concrete or 12" common brick or block.	Reinforced 8" concrete or 12" common brick or block.	Reinforced 8" concrete or 12" common brick or block.	Reinforced 8" concrete block or reinforced 6" concrete.	Reinforced 8" concrete block or reinforced 6" concrete or 8" clay tile or 8" brick.
Roof Covering (10% of total cost)	5 ply composition roof on 1" sheathing with insulation.	5 ply composition roof on 1" sheathing with insulation.	5 ply composition roof on 1" sheathing with insulation.	5 ply composition roof on 1" sheathing with insulation.	4 ply composition roof on 1" sheathing.	4 ply composition roof on 1" sheathing.
Floor Finish (5% of total cost)	Combination solid vinyl tile and terrazzo or very good carpet.	Combination solid vinyl tile and terrazzo or very good carpet.	Solid vinyl tile with some terrazzo or good carpet.	Vinyl tile with small areas of terrazzo, carpet or solid vinyl tile.	Resilient tile.	Composition tile.
Interior Wall Finish (5% of total cost)	Plaster on gypsum or metal lath or 2 layers of 5/8" gypsum wallboard with expensive wallpaper or vinyl wall cover.	Plaster on gypsum or metal lath or 2 layers of 5/8" gypsum wallboard with average wallpaper or vinyl wall cover.	Plaster with putty coat finish on gypsum or metal lath, or 5/8" gypsum wallboard taped, textured and painted, some vinyl wall covering.	Plaster with putty coat finish or gypsum or metal lath, or 5/8" gypsum wallboard taped, textured and painted or with wallpaper.	Lath, 2 coats plaster with putty coat finish or 1/2" gypsum wallboard taped, textured and painted.	Interior plaster on masonry. Colored finish.
Ceiling Finish (5% of total cost)	Acoustical plaster or suspended anodized acoustical metal panels.	Acoustical plaster or suspended anodized acoustical metal panels.	Plaster with putty coat finish and some acoustical plaster or suspended acoustical tile with gypsum wallboard backing.	Plaster with putty coat finish or suspended acoustical tile.	Gypsum wallboard taped and textured or lath, 2 coats of plaster and putty coat finish.	Ceiling tile or gypsum wallboard and paint.
Exterior Wall Finish (5% of total cost)	Waterproofed and painted finish with face brick on exposed walls.	Waterproofed and painted finish with face brick on exposed walls.	Waterproofed and painted finish, face brick on exposed walls.	Painted finish, face brick on exposed wall.	Painted finish.	Unfinished.
Lighting (10% of total cost)	Encased modular units and custom designed chandeliers. Many spotlights.	Encased modular units and stock design chandeliers. Many spotlights.	Encased modular units and stock chandeliers. Many spotlights.	Quad open strip fixtures or triple encased louvered strip fixtures. Average number of spotlights.	Triple open strip fixtures or double encased louvered strip fixtures. Some spotlights.	Double open strip fluorescent fixtures.
Plumbing (Per each 5,000 S.F.) (12% of total cost)	6 good fixtures, metal or marble toilet partitions.	6 good fixtures, metal or marble toilet partitions.	6 standard fixtures, metal or marble toilet partitions.	6 standard fixtures, metal toilet partitions.	4 standard commercial fixtures, metal toilet partitions.	4 standard commercial fixtures, wood toilet partitions.
Bath Wall Finish (3% of total cost)	Ceramic tile or marble or custom mosaic tile.	Ceramic tile or marble or custom mosaic tile.	Ceramic tile or marble or plain mosaic tile.	Gypsum wallboard and paint, some ceramic tile or plastic finish wallboard.	Gypsum wallboard and paint.	Gypsum wallboard and paint.

Note: Use the percent of total cost to help identify the correct quality classification

Urban Stores – Masonry or Concrete

First Floor, Length Less than Twice Width

Estimating Procedure

1. Establish the structure quality class by applying the information on page 76.
2. Compute the building ground floor area. This should include everything within the exterior walls and all insets outside the walls but under the main roof.
3. Add to or subtract from the cost below the appropriate amount from the Wall Height Adjustment Table on page 81 if the first floor wall height is more or less than 16 feet for large stores or 12 feet for small stores.
4. Multiply the adjusted square foot cost by the building area.
5. Deduct, if appropriate, for common walls, using the figures on page 81.
6. Multiply the total cost by the location factor on page 7 or 8.
7. Add the cost of heating and cooling equipment, elevators, escalators, fire escapes, fire sprinklers, display fronts, canopies, ramps, docks, interior partitions, mezzanines, basements, and communication systems from pages 236 to 248.
8. Add the cost of second and higher floors from page 80.

Urban Store, Class 4 & 5

Smaller Stores - Square Foot Area

Quality Class	500	600	700	800	900	1,000	1,200	1,500	1,700	2,000	2,500
4, Low Avg.	141.21	134.18	128.66	124.35	120.65	117.56	112.58	107.05	104.22	100.80	96.52
4 & 5	132.72	126.12	120.96	116.81	113.36	110.49	105.79	100.59	97.93	94.73	90.68
5, Low	125.47	119.20	114.29	110.39	107.13	104.37	99.95	95.04	92.58	89.53	85.74
5 & 6	119.48	113.52	108.94	105.18	102.04	99.45	95.25	90.57	88.18	85.30	81.65
6, Minimum	114.04	108.35	103.93	100.40	97.42	94.92	90.90	86.47	84.19	81.42	77.97

Larger Stores - Square Foot Area

Quality Class	3,000	3,500	4,000	4,500	5,000	6,000	7,500	10,000	15,000	20,000
1, Best	140.46	132.60	129.55	127.07	124.99	121.72	118.17	114.15	109.52	106.82
1 & 2	128.00	124.43	121.57	119.25	117.30	114.21	110.86	107.12	102.80	100.23
2, Good	120.54	117.22	114.52	112.33	110.50	107.57	104.42	100.89	96.79	94.46
2 & 3	115.06	111.88	109.26	105.65	105.44	102.66	99.65	96.26	92.39	90.06
3, Hi. Avg.	108.30	104.87	101.87	100.35	98.55	95.87	93.78	90.96	86.87	84.64
3 & 4	102.21	99.29	96.93	94.98	93.41	90.75	87.88	84.71	80.94	78.68
4, Low Avg.	93.66	91.35	89.17	87.40	85.89	83.52	80.92	77.95	74.50	72.44
4 & 5	89.09	86.54	84.48	82.76	81.39	79.10	76.62	73.82	70.50	68.55
5, Low	84.82	82.35	80.41	78.85	77.49	75.29	72.93	70.29	67.12	65.33
5 & 6	80.40	78.06	76.20	74.68	73.42	72.94	68.90	66.64	63.67	61.90
Minimum	76.11	73.95	72.17	70.73	69.55	67.58	65.47	63.08	60.32	58.62

Urban Stores – Masonry or Concrete

First Floor, Length Between 2 and 4 Times Width

Estimating Procedure

1. Establish the structure quality class by applying the information on page 76.
2. Compute the building ground floor area. This should include everything within the exterior walls and all insets outside the walls but under the main roof.
3. Add to or subtract from the cost below the appropriate amount from the Wall Height Adjustment Table on page 81 if the first floor wall height is more or less than 16 feet for large stores or 12 feet for small stores.
4. Multiply the adjusted square foot cost by the building area.
5. Deduct, if appropriate, for common walls, using the figures on page 81.
6. Multiply the total cost by the location factor on page 7 or 8.
7. Add the cost of heating and cooling equipment, elevators, escalators, fire escapes, fire sprinklers, display fronts, canopies, ramps, docks, interior partitions, mezzanines, basements, and communication systems from pages 236 to 248.
8. Add the cost of second and higher floors from page 80.

Urban Store, Class 4
Smaller Stores - Square Foot Area

Quality Class	500	600	700	800	900	1,000	1,250	1,500	1,700	2,000	2,500
4, Low Avg.	154.86	148.50	142.00	136.80	132.49	128.91	121.81	116.64	113.38	109.43	104.51
4 & 5	147.82	139.85	133.77	128.81	124.80	121.34	114.73	109.84	106.80	102.99	98.41
5, Low	139.78	132.25	126.45	121.78	117.97	114.74	108.47	103.83	100.93	97.41	93.02
5 & 6	133.61	126.39	120.86	116.41	112.75	109.68	103.66	99.25	96.49	93.14	88.95
6, Minimum	128.05	121.22	115.87	111.63	108.07	105.12	99.38	95.17	92.49	89.29	85.27

Larger Stores - Square Foot Area

Quality Class	3,000	3,500	4,000	4,500	5,000	6,000	7,500	10,000	15,000	20,000
1, Best	146.14	141.83	138.40	135.57	133.18	129.35	125.10	120.37	114.75	111.41
1 & 2	137.52	133.53	130.33	127.63	125.43	121.76	117.82	113.33	108.03	104.83
2, Good	129.33	125.54	122.51	119.98	117.89	114.49	110.75	106.49	101.60	98.61
2 & 3	123.44	119.84	116.94	114.55	112.53	109.27	105.75	101.71	96.97	94.15
3, Hi. Avg.	116.84	115.16	112.37	110.06	108.13	105.02	101.60	97.72	93.14	90.48
3 & 4	110.43	106.93	104.11	101.82	99.85	96.74	93.39	89.49	84.99	82.34
4, Low Avg.	101.83	98.26	95.72	93.55	91.81	88.93	85.76	82.23	78.09	75.69
4 & 5	96.67	93.58	91.11	89.11	87.39	84.67	81.67	78.32	74.39	72.06
5, Low	91.86	88.92	86.57	84.69	83.08	80.47	77.61	74.45	70.69	68.49
5 & 6	87.00	84.20	82.02	80.19	78.61	76.18	73.51	70.48	66.94	64.83
Minimum	82.50	79.90	77.82	76.07	74.63	72.29	69.76	66.89	63.53	61.02

Urban Stores – Masonry or Concrete

First Floor, Length More Than 4 Times Width

Estimating Procedure

1. Establish the structure quality class by applying the information on page 76.
2. Compute the building ground floor area. This should include everything within the exterior walls and all insets outside the walls but under the main roof.
3. Add to or subtract from the cost below the appropriate amount from the Wall Height Adjustment Table on page 81 if the first floor wall height is more or less than 16 feet for large stores or 12 feet for small stores.
4. Multiply the adjusted square foot cost by the building area.
5. Deduct, if appropriate, for common walls, using the figures on page 81.
6. Multiply the total cost by the location factor on page 7 or 8.
7. Add the cost of heating and cooling equipment, elevators, escalators, fire escapes, fire sprinklers, display fronts, canopies, ramps, docks, interior partitions, mezzanines, basements, and communication systems from pages 236 to 248.
8. Add the cost of second and higher floors from page 80.

Urban Store, Class 3 & 4

Smaller Stores - Square Foot Area

Quality Class	500	600	700	800	900	1,000	1,200	1,500	1,700	2,000	2,500
4, Low Avg.	171.37	164.54	156.65	150.39	145.23	140.85	133.90	126.31	122.40	117.73	111.95
4 & 5	164.61	154.95	147.55	141.56	136.73	132.63	126.12	118.93	115.30	110.87	99.79
5, Low	155.63	146.52	139.48	133.90	129.30	125.47	119.24	112.45	109.01	104.87	99.71
5 & 6	149.30	140.50	133.80	128.43	124.00	120.32	114.37	107.88	104.54	100.53	95.65
6, Minimum	143.55	135.13	128.65	123.48	119.25	115.66	109.95	103.72	100.57	96.70	91.96

Larger Stores - Square Foot Area

Quality Class	3,000	3,500	4,000	4,500	5,000	6,000	7,500	10,000	15,000	20,000
1, Best	157.25	151.97	147.78	144.39	141.41	136.77	131.68	125.95	119.21	115.19
1 & 2	148.04	143.16	139.18	135.98	133.25	128.80	123.98	118.61	112.25	109.15
2, Good	139.23	134.62	130.86	127.84	125.28	121.18	116.58	111.53	105.50	102.02
2 & 3	128.01	123.76	120.33	117.51	115.16	111.36	107.20	102.53	97.02	93.79
3, Hi. Avg.	126.89	123.41	119.99	117.19	114.82	111.06	106.93	102.26	96.74	93.54
3 & 4	118.78	114.66	111.31	108.56	106.27	102.55	98.45	93.83	88.45	85.22
4, Low Avg.	109.73	105.86	102.83	100.27	98.13	94.74	90.91	86.70	81.67	78.70
4 & 5	104.26	100.61	97.66	95.25	93.21	89.96	86.34	82.38	77.57	74.79
5, Low	98.98	95.54	92.75	90.49	88.53	85.44	82.05	78.21	73.69	71.01
5 & 6	93.87	90.60	87.95	85.79	83.96	81.05	77.83	74.18	69.90	67.38
6, Minimum	89.09	85.97	83.28	81.42	78.79	75.64	72.80	69.49	66.34	63.93

Urban Stores – Masonry or Concrete

Second and Higher Floors

Estimating Procedure

1. Establish the structure quality class. The class for second and higher floors will usually be the same as the first floor.
2. Compute the square foot area of the second floor and each higher floor.
3. Add to or subtract from the square foot cost below the appropriate amount from the Wall Height Adjustment Table on page 81 if the wall height is more or less than 12 feet.
4. Multiply the adjusted square foot cost by the area of each floor.
5. Deduct, if appropriate, for common walls, using the figures on page 81.
6. Add 2% to the cost of each floor above the second floor. For example, the third floor cost would be 102% of the second floor cost and the fourth floor cost would be 104% of the second floor cost.
7. Multiply the total cost for each floor by the location factor on page 7 or 8.
8. Add the cost of heating and cooling equipment, escalators, fire escapes, fire sprinklers, and interior partitions from pages 236 to 248.

Length less than twice width - Square Foot Area

Quality Class	2,500	3,000	3,500	4,000	4,500	5,000	6,000	7,500	10,000	15,000	20,000
1, Best	126.13	122.54	119.74	117.51	115.67	114.13	111.63	108.86	105.71	101.99	99.81
1 & 2	117.68	114.34	111.74	109.68	107.92	106.49	104.17	101.57	98.66	95.14	93.14
2, Good	109.62	106.52	104.11	102.17	100.53	99.21	97.01	94.64	91.89	88.66	86.72
2 & 3	103.59	100.67	98.38	96.53	94.99	93.73	91.67	89.41	86.79	83.74	81.98
3, Hi. Avg.	98.69	95.88	93.71	91.95	90.54	89.29	87.34	85.17	82.70	79.82	78.06
3 & 4	91.07	88.25	86.02	84.27	82.79	81.56	79.54	77.35	74.88	71.91	70.17
4, Low Avg.	82.87	80.35	78.37	76.72	75.42	74.27	72.47	70.43	68.19	65.48	63.88
4 & 5	77.64	75.28	73.39	71.87	70.59	69.55	67.84	65.99	63.88	61.32	59.81
5, Low	72.49	70.26	68.49	67.08	65.88	64.93	63.36	61.59	59.57	57.25	55.80
5 & 6	68.44	66.30	64.68	63.29	62.22	61.27	59.77	58.14	56.25	54.01	52.69
6, Minimum	64.50	62.51	60.95	59.70	58.68	57.75	56.38	54.79	53.01	50.91	49.68

Length between 2 and 4 times width - Square Foot Area

Quality Class	2,500	3,000	3,500	4,000	4,500	5,000	6,000	7,500	10,000	15,000	20,000
1, Best	131.01	127.07	124.03	121.52	119.49	117.78	115.04	111.92	108.45	104.29	101.84
1 & 2	122.26	118.59	115.72	113.41	111.49	109.95	107.29	104.39	101.17	97.31	94.97
2, Good	113.79	110.39	107.73	105.61	103.83	102.31	99.90	97.22	94.21	90.63	88.46
2 & 3	107.70	104.46	101.94	99.94	98.29	96.81	94.50	92.01	89.12	85.70	83.67
3, Hi. Avg.	102.55	99.47	97.06	95.19	93.59	92.25	90.02	87.65	84.87	81.63	79.70
3 & 4	94.81	91.66	89.18	87.24	85.60	84.24	82.02	79.55	76.81	73.55	71.59
4, Low Avg.	86.29	83.43	81.25	79.37	77.94	76.70	74.66	72.47	69.91	66.91	65.19
4 & 5	80.95	78.24	76.17	74.49	73.09	71.92	70.00	67.93	65.59	62.73	61.13
5, Low	75.76	73.18	71.22	69.63	68.39	67.30	65.51	63.56	61.35	58.72	57.20
5 & 6	71.50	69.10	67.26	65.77	64.57	63.53	61.83	61.49	58.82	55.46	53.97
6, Minimum	67.37	65.17	63.39	62.02	60.84	59.86	58.28	56.55	54.60	52.30	50.87

Length over 4 times width - Square Foot Area

Quality Class	2,500	3,000	3,500	4,000	4,500	5,000	6,000	7,500	10,000	15,000	20,000
1, Best	136.26	132.71	129.74	127.29	125.16	123.33	120.28	116.71	112.49	107.24	103.97
1 & 2	127.07	123.78	121.07	118.75	116.77	115.05	112.18	108.88	104.93	100.04	96.98
2, Good	118.30	115.23	112.70	110.54	108.71	107.08	104.42	101.33	97.67	93.11	90.27
2 & 3	111.95	109.06	106.63	104.59	102.86	101.34	98.82	95.88	92.44	88.09	85.45
3, Hi. Avg.	106.54	103.81	101.55	99.56	97.91	96.48	94.10	91.33	87.98	83.89	81.37
3 & 4	99.12	96.17	93.76	91.70	90.03	88.53	86.03	83.22	79.90	75.79	73.26
4, Low Avg.	89.64	87.58	85.40	83.56	82.01	80.67	78.42	75.79	72.80	69.05	66.75
4 & 5	84.64	82.09	80.04	78.32	76.85	75.57	73.49	71.07	68.27	64.72	62.55
5, Low	79.32	76.93	74.99	73.38	71.97	70.85	68.85	66.57	63.93	60.61	58.59
5 & 6	74.86	72.62	70.83	69.29	67.96	66.85	65.03	62.87	60.37	57.28	55.31
6, Minimum	70.82	68.74	66.95	65.53	64.33	63.26	61.50	59.50	57.07	54.19	52.34

Urban Stores – Masonry or Concrete

Wall Height Adjustment

The square foot costs for urban stores are based on the wall heights listed on each page. The main or first floor height is the distance from the bottom of the floor slab or joists to the top of the roof slab or ceiling joists. Second and higher floors are measured from the top of the floor slab or floor joists to the top of the roof slab or ceiling joists. Add or subtract the amount listed to or from the square foot cost for each foot more or less than the standard wall height in the tables. For second and higher floors use only 75% of the wall height adjustment cost.

Area	500	600	700	800	900	1,000	1,250	1,500	1,750	2,000	2,500
Adjustment	4.05	3.71	3.41	3.24	3.06	2.88	2.65	2.33	2.18	2.07	1.85

Area	3,000	3,500	4,000	4,500	5,000	6,000	7,500	10,000	15,000	20,000
Adjustment	1.66	1.55	1.48	1.36	1.31	1.16	1.05	.93	.70	.64

Perimeter (Common) Wall Adjustment

A common wall exists when two buildings share one wall. Adjust for common walls by deducting the linear foot costs below from the total structure cost. In some structures one or more walls are not owned at all. In this case, deduct the "No Owner-ship" cost per linear foot of wall not owned.

Small Urban Stores (to 2,500 S.F.)
Common wall, deduct $128 per linear foot
No ownership, deduct $254 per linear foot

Large Urban Stores (over 2,500 S.F.)
Common wall, deduct $250 per linear foot
No ownership, deduct $500 per linear foot

Quality Classification

	Class 1 Best Quality	Class 2 Good Quality	Class 3 Average Quality	Class 4 Low Quality
Foundation (15% of total cost)	Reinforced concrete.	Reinforced concrete.	Reinforced concrete.	Reinforced concrete.
Floor Structure (15% of total cost)	4" reinforced concrete on 6" rock fill or 2" x 10" joists 16" o.c.	4" reinforced concrete on 6" rock fill or 2" x 8" joists 16" o.c.	4" reinforced concrete on 6" rock fill or 2" x 6" joists 16" o.c.	4" reinforced concrete on 4" rock fill or 2" x 6" joists 16" o.c.
Wall Structure (15% of total cost)	2" x 6" studs 16" o.c.	2" x 4" or 2" x 6" studs 16" o.c.	2" x 4" studs 16" o.c. up to 14' high, 2" x 6" studs 16" o.c. over 14' high.	2" x 4" studs 16" o.c. up to 14' high, 2" x 6" studs 16" o.c. over 14' high.
Roof Covering (10% of total cost)	5 ply composition roof on O.S.B. sheathing with insulation.	5 ply composition roof on O.S.B. sheathing with insulation.	4 ply composition roof on O.S.B. sheathing.	4 ply composition roof on O.S.B. sheathing.
Floor Finish (5% of total cost)	Sheet vinyl with some terrazzo or good carpet.	Resilient tile with small areas of terrazzo, carpet or solid vinyl tile.	Composition tile.	Minimum grade tile.
Interior Wall Finish (5% of total cost)	Plaster with putty coat finish on gypsum or metal lath, or 5/8" gypsum wallboard taped, textured and painted or some vinyl wall cover.	Plaster with putty coat finish on gypsum or metal lath, or 5/8" gypsum wallboard taped, textured and painted or with wallpaper.	Lath, 2 coats plaster with putty coat finish or 1/2" gypsum wallboard taped, textured and painted.	1/2" gypsum wallboard taped, textured and painted.
Ceiling Finish (5% of total cost)	Plaster with putty coat finish and some acoustical plaster or suspended acoustical tile with gypsum wallboard backing.	Plaster with putty coat finish or suspended acoustical tile with exposed grid.	Gypsum wallboard taped and textured or lath, 2 coats of plaster and putty coat finish.	Ceiling tile or gypsum wallboard and paint.
Exterior Wall Finish (5% of total cost)	Good wood siding.	Average wood siding.	Stucco or average wood siding.	Stucco or inexpensive wood siding.
Lighting (10% of total cost)	Encased modular units and stock chandeliers. Many spotlights.	Quad open strip fixtures or triple encased louvered strip fixtures. Average number of spotlights.	Triple open strip fixtures or double encased louvered strip fixtures. Some spotlights.	Double open strip fixtures.
Plumbing (12% of total cost) *(Per 5,000 S.F.)*	6 standard fixtures, metal or marble toilet partitions.	6 standard fixtures, metal toilet partitions.	4 standard commercial fixtures, metal toilet partitions.	4 standard commercial fixtures, wood toilet partitions.
Bath Wall Finish (3% of total cost)	Ceramic tile, marble or plain mosaic tile.	Gypsum wallboard and paint, some ceramic tile or plastic finish wallboard.	Gypsum wallboard and paint.	Gypsum wallboard and paint.

Note: Use the percent of total cost to help identify the correct quality classification

Urban Stores – Wood or Wood and Steel Frame

First Floor, Length Less Than Twice Width

Estimating Procedure

1. Establish the structure quality class by applying the information on page 82.
2. Compute the building ground floor area. This should include everything within the exterior walls and all insets outside the walls but under the main roof.
3. Add to or subtract from the cost below the appropriate amount from the Wall Height Adjustment Table on page 87 if the first floor wall height is more or less than 16 feet for large stores or 12 feet for small stores.
4. Multiply the adjusted square foot cost by the building area.
5. Deduct, if appropriate, for common walls, using the figures on page 87.
6. Multiply the total cost by the location factor on page 7 or 8.
7. Add the cost of heating and cooling equipment, elevators, escalators, fire escapes, fire sprinklers, display fronts, canopies, ramps, docks, interior partitions, mezzanines, basements, and communication systems from pages 236 to 248.
8. Add the cost of second and higher floors from page 86.

Urban Store, Class 3

Smaller Stores - Square Foot Area

Quality Class	500	600	700	800	900	1,000	1,250	1,500	1,750	2,000	2,500
2, Good	110.88	106.89	103.79	101.26	99.16	97.36	93.88	91.28	89.27	87.63	85.07
2 & 3	103.86	100.14	97.26	94.86	92.92	91.23	87.93	85.46	83.66	82.08	79.67
3, Average	97.55	94.02	91.29	89.04	87.26	85.66	82.56	80.32	78.46	77.05	74.85
3 & 4	89.50	86.28	83.78	81.76	80.05	78.60	75.78	73.68	72.01	70.72	68.69
4, Low	81.75	78.85	76.51	74.69	73.13	71.82	69.23	67.32	65.79	64.59	62.72

Larger Stores - Square Foot Area

Quality Class	3,000	3,500	4,000	4,500	5,000	6,000	7,500	10,000	15,000	20,000
1, Best	103.46	101.31	99.64	98.25	97.04	95.17	93.06	90.70	87.83	86.20
1 & 2	93.64	91.74	90.21	88.95	87.89	86.21	84.26	82.08	79.53	78.01
2, Good	84.78	83.04	81.63	80.52	79.50	77.99	76.24	74.32	72.00	70.61
2 & 3	79.39	77.76	76.45	75.41	74.50	73.07	71.46	69.60	67.41	66.14
3, Average	74.33	72.81	71.59	70.57	69.73	68.37	66.89	65.15	63.11	61.88
3 & 4	67.27	65.90	64.84	63.92	63.14	61.92	60.53	58.94	57.15	56.08
4, Low	61.61	60.38	59.36	58.56	57.83	56.69	55.47	54.00	52.34	51.32

Urban Stores – Wood or Wood and Steel Frame

First Floor, Length Between 2 and 4 Times Width

Estimating Procedure

1. Establish the structure quality class by applying the information on page 82.
2. Compute the building ground floor area. This should include everything within the exterior walls and all insets outside the walls but under the main roof.
3. Add to or subtract from the cost below the appropriate amount from the Wall Height Adjustment Table on page 87 if the first floor wall height is more or less than 16 feet for large stores or 12 feet for small stores.
4. Multiply the adjusted square foot cost by the building area.
5. Deduct, if appropriate, for common walls, using the figures on page 87.
6. Multiply the total cost by the location factor on page 7 or 8.
7. Add the cost of heating and cooling equipment, elevators, escalators, fire escapes, fire sprinklers, display fronts, canopies, ramps, docks, interior partitions, mezzanines, basements, and communication systems from pages 236 to 248.
8. Add the cost of second and higher floors from page 86.

Urban Store, Class 3

Smaller Stores - Square Foot Area

Quality Class	500	600	700	800	900	1,000	1,250	1,500	1,750	2,000	2,500
2, Good	119.90	115.11	111.40	108.41	105.96	103.84	99.78	96.77	94.45	92.58	89.69
2 & 3	111.70	107.22	103.78	101.02	98.71	96.76	92.94	90.15	87.95	86.24	83.60
3, Average	105.31	101.22	97.91	95.30	93.13	91.33	87.70	85.07	83.04	81.36	78.85
3 & 4	96.76	92.92	89.90	87.51	85.49	83.82	80.54	78.09	76.23	74.69	72.40
4, Low	88.18	84.62	81.91	79.72	77.92	76.36	73.40	71.17	69.47	68.06	65.99

Larger Stores - Square Foot Area

Quality Class	3,000	3,500	4,000	4,500	5,000	6,000	7,500	10,000	15,000	20,000
1, Best	107.62	105.91	103.92	101.63	100.53	98.51	96.21	93.38	90.08	88.10
1 & 2	98.95	96.71	94.88	93.38	92.14	90.11	87.87	85.30	82.26	80.41
2, Good	88.50	86.50	84.90	83.57	82.42	80.58	78.58	76.33	73.55	71.96
2 & 3	82.59	80.75	79.26	78.01	76.92	75.20	73.31	71.20	68.68	67.14
3, Average	77.69	75.95	74.54	73.40	72.36	70.76	68.96	66.98	64.59	63.15
3 & 4	71.31	69.67	68.41	67.34	66.42	64.93	63.28	61.47	59.31	58.00
4, Low	65.27	63.81	62.60	61.62	60.78	59.42	57.93	56.26	54.23	53.06

Urban Stores – Wood or Wood and Steel Frame

First Floor, Length More Than 4 Times Width

Estimating Procedure

1. Establish the structure quality class by applying the information on page 82.
2. Compute the building ground floor area. This should include everything within the exterior walls and all insets outside the walls but under the main roof.
3. Add to or subtract from the cost below the appropriate amount from the Wall Height Adjustment Table on page 87 if the first floor wall height is more or less than 16 feet for large stores or 12 feet for small stores.
4. Multiply the adjusted square foot cost by the building area.
5. Deduct, if appropriate, for common walls, using the figures on page 87.
6. Multiply the total cost by the location factor on page 7 or 8.
7. Add the cost of heating and cooling equipment, elevators, escalators, fire escapes, fire sprinklers, display fronts, canopies, ramps, docks, interior partitions, mezzanines, basements, and communication systems from pages 236 to 248.
8. Add the cost of second and higher floors from page 86.

Urban Store, Class 3

Smaller Stores - Square Foot Area

Quality Class	500	600	700	800	900	1,000	1,250	1,500	1,750	2,000	2,500
2, Good	132.15	125.65	120.75	116.92	113.80	111.18	106.19	102.68	99.95	97.79	94.57
2 & 3	123.46	117.38	112.83	109.23	106.27	103.80	99.25	95.90	93.34	91.40	88.35
3, Average	115.76	110.07	105.78	102.40	99.67	97.42	93.05	89.90	87.54	85.68	82.90
3 & 4	105.90	100.71	96.77	93.70	91.22	89.10	85.18	82.27	80.09	78.33	75.78
4, Low	96.80	92.04	88.49	85.66	83.36	81.43	77.85	75.23	73.18	71.68	69.31

Larger Stores - Square Foot Area

Quality Class	3,000	3,500	4,000	4,500	5,000	6,000	7,500	10,000	15,000	20,000
1, Best	116.96	113.90	111.45	109.43	107.71	105.00	101.98	98.61	94.63	92.32
1 & 2	106.85	104.06	101.84	99.98	98.39	95.94	93.18	90.10	86.46	84.35
2, Good	97.79	95.24	93.18	91.48	90.03	87.79	85.29	82.44	79.16	77.19
2 & 3	86.76	84.51	82.68	81.19	79.89	77.90	75.68	73.15	70.22	68.54
3, Average	82.62	80.49	78.74	77.28	76.10	74.19	72.07	69.67	66.90	65.25
3 & 4	74.45	72.49	70.94	69.63	68.60	66.84	64.93	62.74	60.24	58.78
4, Low	67.39	65.62	64.21	63.04	62.06	60.50	58.78	56.84	54.52	53.19

Urban Stores – Wood or Wood and Steel Frame

Second and Higher Floors

Estimating Procedure

1. Establish the structure quality class. The class for second and higher floors will usually be the same as the first floor.
2. Compute the square foot area of the second floor and each higher floor.
3. Add to or subtract from the square foot cost below the appropriate amount from the Wall Height Adjustment Table on page 87 if the wall height is more or less than 12 feet.
4. Multiply the adjusted square foot cost by the area of each floor.
5. Deduct, if appropriate, for common walls, using the figures on page 87.
6. Add 2% to the cost for each floor above the second floor. For example, the third floor cost would be 102% of the second floor cost and the fourth floor cost would be 104% of the second floor cost.
7. Multiply the total cost by the location factor on page 7 or 8.
8. Add the cost of heating and cooling equipment, escalators, fire escapes, fire sprinklers, and interior partitions from pages 236 to 248.

Length less than twice width - Square Foot Area

Quality Class	2,500	3,000	3,500	4,000	4,500	5,000	6,000	7,500	10,000	15,000	20,000
1, Best	89.92	88.10	86.57	85.39	84.42	83.61	82.24	80.79	79.10	77.12	75.92
1 & 2	81.69	79.93	78.60	77.54	76.67	75.92	74.67	73.32	71.83	70.01	68.93
2, Good	74.10	72.56	71.39	70.37	69.51	68.88	67.74	66.55	65.16	63.50	62.52
2 & 3	68.70	67.28	66.16	65.26	64.50	63.87	62.85	61.69	60.40	58.90	58.01
3, Average	64.05	62.72	61.70	60.87	60.16	59.57	58.61	57.52	56.35	54.90	54.07
3 & 4	60.35	59.06	58.08	57.28	56.67	56.12	55.23	54.19	53.11	51.73	50.89
4, Low	56.52	55.38	54.40	53.68	53.13	52.52	51.72	50.78	49.69	48.47	47.70

Length between 2 and 4 times width - Square Foot Area

Quality Class	2,500	3,000	3,500	4,000	4,500	5,000	6,000	7,500	10,000	15,000	20,000
1, Best	92.57	90.46	88.86	87.53	86.43	85.50	84.01	82.38	80.51	78.32	76.93
1 & 2	84.00	82.08	80.60	79.41	78.44	77.65	76.25	74.77	73.07	71.08	69.88
2, Good	76.21	74.45	73.11	72.07	71.17	70.41	69.17	67.82	66.27	64.49	63.35
2 & 3	70.76	69.16	67.94	66.94	66.09	65.42	64.24	63.02	61.57	59.86	58.84
3, Average	65.95	64.49	63.32	62.41	61.61	60.98	59.88	58.74	57.37	55.78	54.88
3 & 4	62.06	60.68	59.59	58.71	57.94	57.34	56.35	55.27	54.00	52.50	51.64
4, Low	58.18	56.87	55.82	55.00	54.34	53.77	52.79	51.79	50.64	49.21	48.25

Length over 4 times width - Square Foot Area

Quality Class	2,500	3,000	3,500	4,000	4,500	5,000	6,000	7,500	10,000	15,000	20,000
1, Best	96.53	94.03	92.14	90.60	89.36	88.23	86.48	84.56	82.39	79.80	78.30
1 & 2	87.67	85.39	83.70	82.27	81.10	80.12	78.55	76.79	74.82	72.49	71.09
2, Good	79.50	77.50	75.91	74.66	73.62	72.73	71.27	69.67	67.89	65.72	64.53
2 & 3	73.91	72.01	70.56	69.40	68.38	67.54	66.22	64.76	63.11	61.13	59.94
3, Average	68.82	67.08	65.72	64.64	63.73	62.94	61.71	60.32	58.77	56.91	55.81
3 & 4	64.85	63.17	61.88	60.88	60.01	59.32	58.10	56.86	55.38	53.64	52.57
4, Low	60.60	59.04	57.87	56.90	56.13	55.42	54.34	53.15	51.75	50.16	49.17

Urban Stores – Wood or Wood and Steel Frame

Wall Height Adjustment

The square foot costs for urban stores are based on the wall heights listed on each page. The main or first floor height is the distance from the bottom of the floor slab or joists to the top of the roof slab or ceiling joists. Second and higher floors are measured from the top of the floor slab or floor joists to the top of the roof slab or ceiling joists. Add or subtract the amount listed to or from the square foot cost for each foot more or less than the standard wall height in the tables. For second and higher floors use only 75% of the wall height adjustment cost.

Area	500	600	700	800	900	1,000	1,250	1,500	1,750	2,000	2,500
Adjustment	1.79	1.63	1.52	1.40	1.32	1.30	1.15	1.05	.97	.93	.82

Area		3,000	3,500	4,000	4,500	5,000	6,000	7,500	10,000	15,000	20,000
Adjustment		.71	.68	.67	.62	.59	.56	.54	.50	.47	.45

Perimeter (Common) Wall Adjustment

A common wall exists when two buildings share one wall. Adjust for common walls by deducting the linear foot costs below from the total structure cost. In some structures one or more walls are not owned at all. In this case, deduct the "No Ownership" cost per linear foot of wall not owned.

Small Urban Stores (2,500 S.F. or less)
Common wall, deduct $90 per linear foot
No ownership, deduct $179 per linear foot

Large Urban Stores (over 2,500 S.F.)
Common wall, deduct $132 per linear foot
No ownership, deduct $268 per linear foot

Suburban Stores

Suburban stores are usually built as part of shopping centers. They differ from urban stores in that they are built in open areas where modern construction techniques, equipment and more economical designs can be used. They are also subject to greater variations in size and shape than are urban stores. Do not use the figures in this section for department stores, discount houses or urban stores. These building types are evaluated in other sections.

Costs identified "building shell only" do not include permanent partitions, display fronts or finish materials on the front of the building. Costs for "multi-unit buildings" include partitions, display fronts and finish materials on the front of the building. All figures include the following costs:

1. Foundations as required for normal soil conditions.

2. Floor, rear wall, side wall and roof structures.

3. A front wall consisting of vertical support columns or pilasters and horizontal beams spanning the area between these members, leaving an open space to receive a display front.

4. Interior floor, wall and ceiling finishes.

5. Exterior wall finish on the side and rear walls.

6. Roof cover.

7. Basic lighting and electrical systems.

8. Rough and finish plumbing.

9. A usual or normal parapet wall.

10. Design and engineering fees.

11. Permits and fees.

12. Utility hook-ups.

13. Contractor's contingency, overhead and mark-up.

The in-place costs of these extra components should be added to the basic building cost to arrive at total structure cost. See the section "Additional Costs for Commercial, Industrial and Public Structures" on page 236.

1. Heating and air conditioning systems.

2. Fire sprinklers.

3. All display front components (shell-type buildings only).

4. Finish materials on the front wall of the building (shell-type building only).

5. Canopies.

6. Interior partitions (shell-type buildings only).

7. Exterior signs.

8. Mezzanines and basements.

9. Loading docks and ramps.

10. Miscellaneous yard improvements.

11. Communications systems.

For valuation purposes suburban stores are divided into two building types: masonry or concrete frame, or wood or wood and steel frame. Each building type is divided into four shape classes:

1. Buildings in which the depth is greater than the front.

2. Buildings in which the front is between one and two times the depth.

3. Buildings in which the front is between two and four times the depth.

4. Buildings in which the front is greater than four times the depth. Angular buildings should be classed by comparing the sum of the length of all wings to the width of the wings. All areas should be included, but no area should be included as part of two different wings. Note the example at the right.

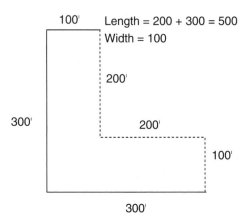

Suburban Stores – Masonry or Concrete

Quality Classification

	Class 1 Best Quality	Class 2 Good Quality	Class 3 Average Quality	Class 4 Low Quality
Foundation (15% of total cost)	Reinforced concrete.	Reinforced concrete.	Reinforced concrete.	Reinforced concrete.
Floor Structure (15% of total cost)	6" reinforced concrete on 6" rock base.	6" reinforced concrete on 6" rock base.	6" reinforced concrete on 6" rock base.	4" reinforced concrete on 6" rock base.
Wall Structure (15% of total cost)	8" reinforced decorative concrete block, 6" concrete tilt-up or 8" reinforced brick.	8" reinforced decorative concrete block, 6" concrete tilt-up or 8" reinforced brick.	8" reinforced concrete block, 6" concrete tilt-up or 8" reinforced common brick.	8" reinforced concrete block or 6" concrete tilt-up.
Roof (15% of total cost)	Glu-lam or steel beams on steel intermediate columns. Panelized roof system, 1/2" plywood sheathing, 5 ply built-up roof with insulation.	Glu-lam or steel beams on steel intermediate columns. Panelized roof system, 1/2" plywood sheathing, 5 ply built-up roof with insulation.	Glu-lam beams on steel intermediate columns. Panelized roof system, 1/2" plywood sheathing, 4 ply built-up roof.	Glu-lam beams on steel intermediate columns. Panelized roof system, 1/2" plywood sheathing, 4 ply built-up roof.
Floor Finish (5% of total cost)	Terrazzo, sheet vinyl or very good carpet.	Resilient tile with 50% solid vinyl tile, terrazzo, or good carpet.	Composition tile.	Minimum grade tile.
Interior Wall Finish (5% of total cost)	Inside of exterior walls furred out with gypsum wallboard or lath and plaster cover. Exterior walls and partitions finished with vinyl wall covers and hardwood veneers.	Interior stucco on inside of exterior walls, gypsum wallboard and texture or paper on partitions, some vinyl wall cover and plywood paneling.	Interior stucco on inside of exterior walls, gypsum wallboard and texture and paint on partitions.	Paint on inside of exterior walls, gypsum wallboard with texture and paint on partitions.
Ceiling Finish (5% of total cost)	Suspended good grade acoustical tile with gypsum wallboard backing.	Suspended acoustical tile with concealed grid system.	Suspended acoustical tile with exposed grid system.	Exposed beams with ceiling tile or paint.
Lighting (5% of total cost)	Recessed fluorescent lighting in modular plastic panels.	Continuous recessed 3 tube fluorescent strips with egg crate diffusers, 8' o.c.	Continuous 3 tube fluorescent strips with egg crate diffusers, 8' o.c.	Continuous exposed 2 tube fluorescent strips, 8' o.c.
Exterior (8% of total cost)	Face brick or stone veneer.	Exposed aggregate, some stone veneer.	Paint on exposed areas, some exposed aggregate.	Paint on exposed areas.
Plumbing (12% of total cost)	6 good fixtures per 5,000 S.F. of floor area, metal toilet partitions.	6 standard fixtures per 5,000 S.F. of floor area, metal toilet partitions.	4 standard fixtures per 5,000 S.F. of floor area, metal toilet partitions.	4 standard fixtures per 5,000 S.F. of floor area wood toilet partitions.

Note: Use the percent of total cost to help identify the correct quality classification.

The costs on pages 90 to 93, and 95 to 102 include display fronts. The quality of the display front will help establish the quality class of the building as a whole. Display fronts are classified as follows:

	Class 1 Best Quality	Class 2 Good Quality	Class 3 Average Quality	Class 4 Low Quality
Bulkhead (0 to 4' high)	Vitrolite, domestic marble or stainless steel.	Black flagstone, terrazzo or good ceramic tile.	Average ceramic tile, Roman brick or imitation flagstone.	Stucco, wood or common brick.
Window Frame	Bronze or stainless steel.	Heavy aluminum.	Aluminum.	Light aluminum with with stops.
Glass	1/4" float glass with mitered joints.	1/4" float glass, some mitered joints.	1/4" float glass.	Crystal or 1/4" float glass.
Sign Area (4' high)	Vitrolite, domestic marble or stainless steel.	Black flagstone, terrazzo, or good ceramic tile.	Average ceramic tile, Roman brick or imitation flagstone.	Stucco.
Pilasters	Vitrolite, domestic marble.	Black flagstone, terrazzo or good ceramic tile.	Average ceramic tile, Roman brick or imitation flagstone.	Stucco.

Suburban Stores – Masonry or Concrete

Building Shell Only

Estimating Procedure

1. Use these figures to estimate the cost of shell-type buildings without permanent partitions, display fronts or finish material on the front wall of the building.
2. Establish the structure quality class by applying the information on page 89.
3. Compute the building floor area. This should include everything within the exterior walls and all inset areas outside the main walls but under the main roof.
4. Add to or subtract from the cost below the appropriate amount from the Wall Height Adjustment Table (at the bottom of this page) if the wall height is more or less than 16 feet.
5. Multiply the adjusted square foot cost by the building area.
6. Deduct, if appropriate, for common walls, using the figures at the bottom of page 91.
7. Multiply the total cost by the location factor on page 7 or 8.
8. Add the cost of the appropriate additional components from page 236 to 248: heating and cooling equipment, fire sprinklers, display fronts, finish materials on the front wall, canopies, interior partitions, exterior signs, mezzanines and basements, loading docks and ramps, yard improvements, and communication systems.

Suburban Store, Class 2

Depth greater than length of front - Square Foot Area

Quality Class	500	1,000	2,000	2,500	3,000	4,000	5,000	7,500	10,000	12,500	15,000
1, Best	161.04	134.32	115.46	110.69	107.14	102.20	98.78	93.51	90.36	88.25	86.62
1 & 2	149.06	124.34	106.92	102.45	99.17	94.56	91.43	86.56	83.63	81.67	80.19
2, Good	139.55	116.40	100.05	95.89	92.86	88.56	85.63	81.04	78.30	76.47	75.07
2 & 3	132.14	110.24	94.78	90.84	87.95	83.85	81.08	76.76	74.17	72.40	71.09
3, Average	126.98	105.94	91.04	87.25	84.52	80.58	77.90	73.74	71.29	69.62	68.34
3 & 4	119.67	99.85	85.86	82.24	79.61	75.91	73.39	69.50	67.19	65.57	64.41
4, Low	114.00	95.05	81.71	78.32	75.83	72.29	69.87	66.20	63.94	62.46	61.31

Length of front between 1 and 2 times depth - Square Foot Area

Quality Class	500	1,000	2,000	3,000	5,000	7,500	10,000	15,000	20,000	25,000	35,000
1, Best	153.87	129.24	111.94	104.29	96.67	91.81	88.89	85.50	83.50	82.07	80.26
1 & 2	142.18	119.47	103.41	96.36	89.26	84.84	82.16	79.01	77.13	75.85	74.12
2, Good	133.12	111.83	96.87	90.24	83.57	79.41	76.89	73.98	72.23	70.97	69.43
2 & 3	125.98	105.85	91.65	85.41	79.11	75.09	72.78	69.95	68.30	67.22	65.69
3, Average	121.26	101.89	88.25	82.20	76.12	72.38	70.07	67.38	65.77	64.71	63.23
3 & 4	114.89	96.55	83.60	77.86	72.13	68.59	66.41	63.82	62.33	61.30	59.94
4, Low	108.39	91.07	78.84	73.41	68.03	64.67	62.63	60.21	58.78	57.77	56.51

Wall Height Adjustment: Costs above are based on a 16' wall height, measured from the bottom of the floor slab or floor joists to the top of the roof cover. Add or subtract the amount listed to or from the square foot cost for each foot more or less than 16 feet.

Area	500	1,000	2,000	2,500	3,000	4,000	5,000	7,500	10,000	12,500
Cost	1.75	1.62	1.51	1.33	1.18	1.05	.97	.77	.66	.58

Area	15,000	20,000	25,000	30,000	35,000	50,000	70,000	75,000	100,000	150,000
Cost	.55	.54	.50	.48	.46	.41	.36	.34	.25	.23

Suburban Stores – Masonry or Concrete

Building Shell Only

Estimating Procedure

1. Use these figures to estimate the cost of shell-type buildings without permanent partitions, display fronts or finish material on the front wall of the building.
2. Establish the structure quality class by applying the information on page 89.
3. Compute the building floor area. This should include everything within the exterior walls and all inset areas outside the main walls but under the main building roof.
4. Add to or subtract from the cost below the appropriate amount from the Wall Height Adjustment Table on page 90 if the wall height is more or less than 16 feet.
5. Multiply the adjusted square foot cost by the building area.
6. Deduct, if appropriate, for common walls, using the figures at the bottom of this page.
7. Multiply the total cost by the location factor on page 7 or 8.
8. Add the cost of the appropriate additional components from page 236 to 248: heating and cooling equipment, fire sprinklers, display fronts, finish materials on the front wall, canopies, interior partitions, exterior signs, mezzanines and basements, loading docks and ramps, yard improvements, and communication systems.

Suburban Store, Class 1

Length between 2 and 4 times depth - Square Foot Area

Quality Class	1,000	2,000	3,000	5,000	7,500	10,000	15,000	20,000	30,000	50,000	70,000
1, Best	134.05	115.63	107.49	99.33	94.14	91.12	87.50	85.08	82.72	80.15	78.74
1 & 2	123.46	106.45	98.95	91.44	86.70	83.89	80.53	78.55	76.14	73.81	72.50
2, Good	114.94	99.13	92.14	85.13	80.72	78.13	74.99	73.12	70.91	68.71	67.54
2 & 3	108.88	93.90	87.26	80.65	76.49	73.98	71.02	69.29	67.21	65.08	63.94
3, Average	104.56	90.24	83.92	77.48	73.50	71.05	68.23	66.60	64.53	62.50	61.46
3 & 4	99.33	85.69	79.63	73.58	69.78	67.53	64.78	63.18	61.30	59.37	58.32
4, Low	93.78	80.90	75.16	69.47	65.88	63.73	61.22	59.69	57.84	56.07	55.14

Length greater than 4 times depth - Square Foot Area

Quality Class	2,000	3,000	5,000	10,000	15,000	20,000	30,000	50,000	75,000	100,000	150,000
1, Best	121.98	112.77	103.57	94.28	90.18	87.73	84.86	81.95	80.14	79.03	77.79
1 & 2	111.10	102.71	94.30	85.81	82.09	79.93	77.28	74.61	72.95	71.99	70.82
2, Good	103.38	95.56	87.71	79.89	76.43	74.35	71.90	69.43	67.88	66.94	65.84
2 & 3	97.85	90.43	83.04	75.60	72.34	70.37	68.06	65.75	64.26	63.36	62.36
3, Average	93.99	86.93	79.79	72.65	69.47	67.59	65.38	63.16	61.76	60.92	59.92
3 & 4	88.84	82.18	75.46	68.68	65.67	63.91	61.79	59.71	58.35	57.58	56.66
4, Low	84.12	77.80	71.39	65.02	62.16	60.51	58.51	56.51	55.25	54.53	53.58

Perimeter Wall Adjustment: A common wall exists when two buildings share one wall. Adjust for common walls by deducting $235 per linear foot of common wall from the total structure cost. In some structures one or more walls are not owned at all. In this case, deduct $456 per linear foot of wall not owned.

Multi-Unit Buildings

Estimating Procedure

1. Use these square foot costs to estimate the cost of stores designed for multiple occupancy. These costs include all components of shell buildings plus the cost of display fronts, finish materials on the front of the building and normal interior partitions.
2. Establish the structure quality class by applying the information on page 89. Evaluate the quality of the display front to help establish the correct quality class of the building as a whole. See also pages 242 to 245.
3. Compute the building floor area. This should include everything within the building exterior walls and all inset areas outside the main walls but under the main building roof.
4. Add to or subtract from the cost below the appropriate amount from the Wall Height Adjustment Table (at the bottom of this page) if the wall height is more or less than 16 feet.
5. Multiply the adjusted square foot cost by the building area.
6. Deduct, if appropriate, for common walls, using the figures at the bottom of page 93.
7. Multiply the total cost by the location factor on page 7 or 8.
8. Add the cost of the appropriate additional components from page 236 to 248: heating and cooling equipment, fire sprinklers, canopies, exterior signs, mezzanines and basements, loading docks and ramps, yard improvements, and communications systems.

Depth greater than length of front - Square Foot Area

Quality Class	500	1,000	2,000	2,500	3,000	4,000	5,000	7,500	10,000	12,500	15,000
1, Best	229.31	187.19	157.47	149.88	144.26	136.47	131.13	122.78	117.79	114.44	111.92
1 & 2	205.39	167.71	141.08	134.29	129.25	122.26	117.43	110.01	105.56	102.53	100.28
2, Good	184.60	150.65	126.76	120.64	116.18	109.85	105.50	98.83	94.84	92.12	90.08
2 & 3	174.64	138.42	116.41	110.84	106.69	100.90	96.93	90.73	87.11	84.59	82.77
3, Average	156.84	128.02	107.72	102.53	98.74	93.34	89.65	84.00	80.59	78.30	76.58
3 & 4	145.44	118.74	99.86	95.07	91.50	86.56	83.12	77.86	74.71	72.57	70.97
4, Low	133.99	109.37	92.01	87.58	84.35	79.69	76.62	71.76	68.83	66.85	65.42

Length of front between 1 and 2 times depth - Square Foot Area

Quality Class	500	1,000	2,000	3,000	5,000	7,500	10,000	15,000	20,000	25,000	35,000
1, Best	252.28	204.26	170.07	154.81	139.50	129.81	124.00	117.17	113.08	110.24	106.60
1 & 2	224.21	181.51	151.11	137.59	123.95	115.36	110.22	104.09	100.47	97.96	94.75
2, Good	199.38	161.44	134.41	122.35	110.21	102.57	97.99	92.61	89.34	87.14	84.22
2 & 3	181.94	147.33	122.65	111.67	100.61	93.62	89.46	84.53	81.53	79.54	76.86
3, Average	173.16	140.20	116.74	106.25	95.77	89.14	85.15	80.42	77.64	75.68	73.15
3 & 4	163.85	132.68	110.45	100.58	90.63	84.30	80.59	76.10	73.42	71.62	69.25
4, Low	149.48	121.05	100.77	91.75	82.67	76.94	73.51	69.43	67.00	65.35	63.18

Wall Height Adjustment: Costs above are based on a 16' wall height, measured from the bottom of the floor slab or floor joists to the top of the roof cover. Add or subtract the amount listed to or from the square foot cost for each foot more or less than 16 feet.

Square Foot Area

Class	2,000	3,000	5,000	10,000	15,000	25,000	35,000	50,000	75,000	100,000	150,000
1, Best	6.51	5.29	4.11	2.87	2.40	1.84	1.58	1.38	1.17	1.11	1.03
2, Good	4.86	3.98	3.05	2.13	1.83	1.38	1.17	1.06	.90	.83	.74
3, Average	3.73	3.04	2.34	1.67	1.39	1.10	.95	.78	.67	.65	.61
4, Low	2.94	2.38	1.84	1.28	1.11	.84	.68	.63	.57	.49	.48

Suburban Stores – Masonry or Concrete

Multi-Unit Buildings

Estimating Procedure

1. Use these square foot costs to estimate the cost of stores designed for multiple occupancy. These costs include all components of shell buildings plus the cost of display fronts, finish materials on the front of the building and normal interior partitions.
2. Establish the structure quality class by applying the information on page 89. Evaluate the quality of the display front to help establish the correct quality class of the building as a whole. See also pages 236 to 248.
3. Compute the building floor area. This should include everything within the building exterior walls and all inset areas outside the main walls but under the main building roof.
4. Add to or subtract from the cost below the appropriate amount from the Wall Height Adjustment Table (at the bottom of page 92) if the wall height is more or less than 16 feet.
5. Multiply the adjusted square foot cost by the building area.
6. Deduct, if appropriate, for common walls, using the figures at the bottom of this page.
7. Multiply the total cost by the location factor on page 7 or 8.
8. Add the cost of the appropriate additional components from page 236 to 248: heating and cooling equipment, fire sprinklers, canopies, exterior signs, mezzanines and basements, loading docks and ramps, yard improvements, and communications systems.

Suburban Store, Class 3

Suburban Store, Class 4

Length of front between 2 and 4 times depth - Square Foot Area

Quality Class	1,000	2,000	3,000	5,000	7,500	10,000	15,000	20,000	30,000	50,000	70,000
1, Best	230.35	188.96	170.51	151.90	140.12	133.10	124.81	119.79	113.90	107.93	104.77
1 & 2	205.34	168.49	152.02	135.45	124.96	118.68	111.23	106.82	101.51	96.23	93.39
2, Good	181.92	149.22	134.64	119.95	110.65	105.11	98.53	94.60	89.92	85.21	82.71
2 & 3	165.06	135.43	122.22	108.90	100.45	95.42	89.45	85.87	81.59	77.37	75.07
3, Average	155.47	123.73	111.67	99.52	91.71	87.17	81.69	78.44	74.58	70.67	68.60
3 & 4	139.15	114.17	102.98	91.80	84.64	80.44	75.39	72.39	68.78	65.21	63.31
4, Low	127.36	104.46	94.28	84.02	77.50	73.61	68.94	66.24	62.95	59.69	57.92

Length of front greater than 4 times depth - Square Foot Area

Quality Class	2,000	3,000	5,000	10,000	15,000	20,000	30,000	50,000	75,000	100,000	150,000
1, Best	211.21	188.48	165.79	143.18	133.17	127.25	120.25	113.23	108.83	106.17	103.10
1 & 2	186.80	166.68	146.61	126.59	117.79	112.57	106.38	100.19	96.24	93.91	91.19
2, Good	165.19	147.39	129.68	111.97	104.21	99.57	94.04	88.59	85.10	83.08	80.63
2 & 3	149.64	133.54	117.49	101.44	94.38	90.20	85.20	80.21	77.12	75.27	73.05
3, Average	136.99	122.23	107.51	92.84	86.41	82.55	77.98	73.42	70.54	68.84	66.85
3 & 4	126.47	112.84	99.25	85.72	79.78	76.19	71.99	67.80	65.18	63.55	61.71
4, Low	115.41	102.97	90.59	78.21	72.78	69.54	65.67	61.86	59.47	58.00	56.34

Perimeter Wall Adjustment: A common wall exists when two buildings share one wall. Adjust for common walls by deducting $238 per linear foot of common wall from the total structure cost. In some structures one or more walls are not owned at all. In this case, deduct $479 per linear foot of wall not owned.

Suburban Stores – Wood or Wood and Steel Frame

Quality Classification

	Class 1 Best Quality	Class 2 Good Quality	Class 3 Average Quality	Class 4 Low Quality
Foundation (15% of total cost)	Reinforced concrete.	Reinforced concrete.	Reinforced concrete.	Reinforced concrete.
Floor Structure (15% of total cost)	6" reinforced concrete on 6" rock base.	6" reinforced concrete on 6" rock base.	6" reinforced concrete on 6" rock base.	4" reinforced concrete on 6" rock base.
Wall Structure (15% of total cost)	2" x 6" - 16" o.c.	2" x 6" - 16" o.c.	2" x 6" - 16" o.c.	2" x 4" - 16" o.c.
Roof (15% of total cost)	Glu-lams or steel beams on steel intermediate columns. Panelized roof system, 1/2" plywood sheathing, 5 ply built-up roof with insulation.	Glu-lams or steel beams on steel intermediate columns. Panelized roof system, 1/2" plywood sheathing, 5 ply built-up roof with insulation.	Glu-lams on steel intermediate columns. Panelized roof system, 1/2" plywood sheathing, 4 ply built-up roof.	Glu-lams on steel intermediate columns. Panelized roof system, 1/2" plywood sheathing, 4 ply built-up roof.
Floor Finish (5% of total cost)	Terrazzo, sheet vinyl, or very good carpet.	Resilient tile with 50% solid vinyl tile, terrazzo, or good carpet.	Composition tile.	Minimum grade tile.
Interior Wall Finish (5% of total cost)	Gypsum wallboard or lath and plaster on exterior walls and partitions, finished with vinyl wall covers and hardwood veneers.	Gypsum wallboard, texture and paper on exterior walls and partitions, some vinyl wall cover and plywood paneling.	Gypsum wallboard, texture and paint on interior walls and partitions.	Gypsum wallboard, texture and paint on interior walls and partitions.
Ceiling Finish (5% of total cost)	Suspended good grade acoustical tile with gypsum board backing.	Suspended acoustical tile with concealed grid system.	Suspended acoustical tile with exposed grid system.	Exposed beams with ceiling tile or painted.
Lighting (5% of total cost)	Recessed fluorescent lighting in modular plastic panels.	Continuous recessed 3 tube fluorescent strips with egg crate diffusers, 8' o.c.	Continuous 3 tube fluorescent strips with egg crate diffusers, 8' o.c.	Continuous exposed 2 tube fluorescent strips, 8' o.c.
Exterior (8% of total cost)	Face brick or stone veneer.	Wood siding, some stone veneer.	Stucco on exposed areas, some brick trim.	Stucco on exposed areas.
Plumbing (12% of total cost)	6 good fixtures per 5,000 S.F. of floor area, metal toilet partitions.	6 standard fixtures per 5,000 S.F. of floor area, metal toilet partitions.	4 standard fixtures per 5,000 S.F. of floor area, metal toilet partitions.	4 standard fixtures per 5,000 S.F. of floor area wood toilet partitions.

Note: Use the percent of total cost to help identify the correct quality classification

Strip and Island Suburban Stores

For estimating purposes, wood frame suburban stores should be divided into strip type units or island type units. Strip type buildings have a front wall made up of display fronts. The side and rear walls, except for delivery or walk-through doors, are made up of solid, continuous wood frame walls. If there are any display areas in the sides or rear of these buildings, the cost of the display front must be added to the building cost and the cost of the wall that it replaces must be deducted from the building costs.

Island type suburban store buildings have display fronts on the major portion of all four sides. Stores may be arranged so that one store fronts on two sides or they may be partitioned in such a way that there are two separate stores fronting on each side of the building.

Strip Type

Island Type

Suburban Stores – Wood or Wood and Steel Frame

Building Shell Only, Island Type

Estimating Procedure

1. Use these figures to estimate the cost of shell-type buildings without permanent partitions, display fronts or finish material on the front wall of the building.
2. Establish the structure quality class by applying the information on page 94.
3. Compute the building floor area. This should include everything within the exterior walls and all inset areas outside the main walls but under the main roof.
4. Add to or subtract from the square foot cost below the appropriate amount from the Wall Height Adjustment Table (at the bottom of this page) if the wall height is more or less than 16 feet.
5. Multiply the adjusted square foot cost by the building area.
6. Deduct, if appropriate, for common walls, using the figures at the bottom of this page.
7. Multiply the total cost by the location factor on page 7 or 8.
8. Add the cost of the appropriate additional components from page 236 to 248: heating and cooling equipment, fire sprinklers, display fronts, finish materials on the front wall, canopies, interior partitions, exterior signs, mezzanines and basements, loading docks and ramps, yard improvements, and communication systems.

Length less than 1-1/2 times depth - Square Foot Area

Quality Class	3,500	5,000	7,500	10,000	12,500	15,000	20,000	30,000	40,000	50,000	75,000
1, Best	96.75	95.15	93.58	92.68	92.04	91.54	90.93	90.11	89.64	89.36	88.86
1 & 2	87.66	86.20	84.77	83.96	83.34	82.94	82.37	81.62	81.22	80.92	80.51
2, Good	79.89	78.58	77.29	76.55	76.03	75.65	75.12	74.45	74.07	73.84	73.39
2 & 3	77.16	74.55	72.09	71.41	70.91	70.58	70.08	69.43	69.06	68.85	68.49
3, Average	70.49	69.35	68.19	67.53	67.07	66.70	66.24	65.71	65.37	65.11	64.73
3 & 4	64.70	63.65	62.58	61.95	61.53	61.27	60.79	60.28	59.94	59.75	59.39
4, Low	58.81	57.81	56.88	56.33	55.90	55.66	55.24	54.80	54.48	54.32	53.98

Length between 1-1/2 and 2 times depth - Square Foot Area

Quality Class	4,500	5,000	7,500	10,000	15,000	20,000	30,000	40,000	50,000	75,000	100,000
1, Best	96.28	95.75	93.90	92.91	91.71	91.06	90.22	89.80	89.50	89.02	88.77
1 & 2	87.18	86.68	85.04	84.04	83.03	82.40	81.72	81.30	81.03	80.59	80.39
2, Good	79.52	79.07	77.57	76.74	75.71	75.17	74.53	74.15	73.91	73.53	73.31
2 & 3	74.08	73.65	72.24	71.48	70.58	70.06	69.43	69.07	68.88	68.55	68.32
3, Average	70.06	69.63	68.31	67.60	66.67	66.21	65.67	65.35	65.10	64.75	64.59
3 & 4	64.29	63.89	62.71	62.00	61.24	60.78	60.30	59.94	59.76	59.48	59.26
4, Low	58.31	57.97	56.88	56.26	55.57	55.15	54.67	54.40	54.18	53.93	53.77

Wall Height Adjustment: Add or subtract the amount listed to or from the square foot costs above for each foot of wall height more or less than 16 feet.

Area	3,500	5,000	7,500	10,000	12,500	15,000	Over 20,000
Cost	.24	.22	.17	.15	.13	.12	.11

Perimeter Wall Adjustment: For common wall deduct $55.20 per linear foot of common wall. For no wall ownership, deduct $110.70 per linear foot of wall.

Suburban Stores – Wood or Wood and Steel Frame

Building Shell Only, Island Type

Estimating Procedure

1. Use these figures to estimate the cost of shell-type buildings without permanent partitions, display fronts or finish material on the front wall of the building.
2. Establish the structure quality class by applying the information on page 94.
3. Compute the building floor area. This should include everything within the exterior walls and all inset areas outside the main walls but under the main roof.
4. Add to or subtract from the square foot cost below the appropriate amount from the Wall Height Adjustment Table (at the bottom of this page) if the wall height is more or less than 16 feet.
5. Multiply the adjusted square foot cost by the building area.
6. Deduct, if appropriate, for common walls, using the figures at the bottom of this page.
7. Multiply the total cost by the location factor on page 7 or 8.
8. Add the cost of the appropriate additional components from page 236 to 248: heating and cooling equipment, fire sprinklers, display fronts, finish materials on the front wall, canopies, interior partitions, exterior signs, mezzanines and basements, loading docks and ramps, yard improvements, and communication systems.

Length between 2 and 3 times depth - Square Foot Area

Quality Class	10,000	15,000	20,000	30,000	40,000	50,000	75,000	100,000	150,000	200,000	250,000
1, Best	94.29	92.92	92.08	91.14	90.57	90.17	89.53	89.26	88.85	88.59	88.38
1 & 2	85.31	84.04	83.32	82.44	81.99	81.61	81.09	80.78	80.41	80.14	80.03
2, Good	77.48	76.33	75.61	74.86	74.37	74.06	73.59	73.26	72.95	72.76	72.61
2 & 3	72.18	71.12	70.49	69.75	69.35	68.99	68.59	68.26	68.00	67.77	67.67
3, Average	67.88	66.85	66.24	65.53	65.15	64.84	64.45	64.19	63.95	63.73	63.60
3 & 4	62.23	61.29	60.76	60.11	59.77	59.48	59.11	58.82	58.64	58.40	58.28
4, Low	56.42	55.64	55.15	54.55	54.19	53.97	53.64	53.40	53.16	53.00	52.89

Length greater than 3 times depth - Square Foot Area

Quality Class	7,500	10,000	15,000	20,000	30,000	40,000	50,000	75,000	100,000	150,000	200,000
1, Best	94.03	93.45	92.35	91.69	90.82	90.28	89.89	89.30	88.88	88.37	88.13
1 & 2	87.95	87.40	86.38	83.03	82.26	81.75	81.39	80.82	80.51	80.04	79.79
2, Good	77.19	76.74	75.78	75.26	74.55	74.10	73.79	73.26	73.00	72.60	72.32
2 & 3	71.99	71.51	70.64	70.13	69.50	69.06	68.81	68.28	68.02	67.65	67.40
3, Average	67.70	67.29	66.49	65.99	65.43	64.99	64.72	64.24	63.99	63.65	63.44
3 & 4	62.06	61.69	60.98	60.53	59.94	59.58	59.37	58.90	58.70	58.34	58.18
4, Low	56.39	56.05	55.38	54.96	54.44	54.12	53.92	53.55	53.30	52.99	52.83

Wall Height Adjustment: Add or subtract the amount listed to or from the square foot costs above for each foot of wall height more or less than 16 feet.

Area	3,500	5,000	7,500	10,000	12,500	15,000	Over 20,000
Cost	.25	.23	.18	.16	.14	.13	.12

Perimeter Wall Adjustment: For common wall, deduct $53.70 per linear foot of common wall. For no wall ownership, deduct $107.40 per linear foot of wall.

Suburban Stores – Wood or Wood and Steel Frame

Building Shell Only, Strip Type

Estimating Procedure

1. Use these figures to estimate the cost of shell-type buildings without permanent partitions, display fronts or finish material on the front wall of the building.
2. Establish the structure quality class by applying the information on page 94.
3. Compute the building floor area. This should include everything within the exterior walls and all inset areas outside the main walls but under the main roof.
4. Add to or subtract from the square foot cost below the appropriate amount from the Wall Height Adjustment Table (at the bottom of this page) if the wall height is more or less than 16 feet.
5. Multiply the adjusted square foot cost by the building area.
6. Deduct, if appropriate, for common walls, using the figures at the bottom of this page.
7. Multiply the total cost by the location factor on page 7 or 8.
8. Add the cost of the appropriate additional components from page 236 to 248: heating and cooling equipment, fire sprinklers, display fronts, finish materials on the front wall, canopies, interior partitions, exterior signs, mezzanines and basements, loading docks and ramps, yard improvements, and communication systems.

Length less than 1-1/2 times depth - Square Foot Area

Quality Class	500	1,000	2,000	2,500	3,000	4,000	5,000	7,500	10,000	12,500	15,000
1, Best	151.17	130.59	116.06	112.36	109.60	105.78	103.14	99.08	96.67	95.04	93.77
1 & 2	138.13	119.36	106.05	102.68	100.14	96.69	94.27	90.53	88.34	86.82	85.69
2, Good	126.77	109.54	97.35	94.26	91.89	88.71	86.51	83.10	81.06	79.65	78.60
2 & 3	120.27	103.92	92.35	89.42	87.19	84.17	82.10	78.82	76.90	75.57	74.59
3, Average	115.27	99.60	88.50	85.66	83.61	80.66	78.70	75.54	73.68	72.43	71.48
3 & 4	108.01	93.24	82.90	80.25	78.30	75.54	73.67	70.73	69.06	67.87	66.96
4, Low	100.69	86.93	77.27	74.82	73.05	70.43	68.71	65.99	64.36	63.24	62.44

Length between 1-1/2 and 2 times depth - Square Foot Area

Quality Class	500	1,000	2,000	3,000	5,000	6,000	7,500	10,000	15,000	20,000	35,000
1, Best	145.74	126.45	112.73	106.58	100.44	98.59	96.57	94.23	91.46	89.80	87.19
1 & 2	133.22	115.54	102.98	97.41	91.78	90.10	88.24	86.12	83.57	82.05	79.74
2, Good	122.34	106.10	94.57	89.44	84.27	82.71	81.03	79.08	76.77	75.37	73.15
2 & 3	115.87	100.54	89.55	84.70	79.82	78.35	76.74	74.89	72.70	71.42	69.35
3, Average	110.91	96.21	85.72	81.10	76.39	74.96	73.43	71.66	69.59	68.31	66.35
3 & 4	104.24	90.42	80.57	76.21	71.85	70.45	69.06	67.36	65.44	64.21	62.37
4, Low	97.53	84.60	75.42	71.35	67.15	65.94	64.58	63.02	61.17	60.07	58.34

Wall Height Adjustment: Add or subtract the amount listed to or from the square foot cost above for each foot of wall height more or less than 16 feet.

Area	500	1,000	2,000	2,500	3,000	4,000	5,000	7,500	10,000	12,500
Cost	1.73	1.22	.87	.80	.71	.66	.59	.54	.51	.48

Area	15,000	20,000	25,000	30,000	35,000	50,000	70,000	75,000	100,000	150,000
Cost	.38	.25	.23	.22	.20	.18	.17	.16	.15	.14

Perimeter Wall Adjustment: For a common wall, deduct $184 per linear foot of common wall. For no wall ownership, deduct $370 per linear foot of wall.

Suburban Stores – Wood or Wood and Steel Frame

Building Shell Only, Strip Type

Estimating Procedure

1. Use these figures to estimate the cost of shell-type buildings without permanent partitions, display fronts or finish material on the front wall of the building.
2. Establish the structure quality class by applying the information on page 94.
3. Compute the building floor area. This should include everything within the exterior walls and all inset areas outside the main walls but under the main roof.
4. Add to or subtract from the square foot cost below the appropriate amount from the Wall Height Adjustment Table (at the bottom of this page) if the wall height is more or less than 16 feet.
5. Multiply the adjusted square foot cost by the building area.
6. Deduct, if appropriate, for common walls, using the figures at the bottom of this page.
7. Multiply the total cost by the location factor on page 7 or 8.
8. Add the cost of the appropriate additional components from page 236 to 248: heating and cooling equipment, fire sprinklers, display fronts, finish materials on the front wall, canopies, interior partitions, exterior signs, mezzanines and basements, loading docks and ramps, yard improvements, and communication systems.

Length between 2 and 3 times depth - Square Foot Area

Quality Class	1,000	2,000	3,000	5,000	7,500	10,000	15,000	20,000	30,000	50,000	70,000
1, Best	128.36	114.45	108.24	102.04	98.18	95.86	93.05	91.42	89.46	87.53	86.46
1 & 2	117.31	104.56	98.89	93.28	89.75	87.61	85.06	83.54	81.76	79.96	79.03
2, Good	107.68	95.95	90.79	85.58	82.33	80.37	78.04	76.67	75.05	73.41	72.50
2 & 3	102.18	91.15	86.22	81.27	78.17	76.25	74.07	72.76	71.21	69.72	68.86
3, Average	101.55	90.07	82.71	78.02	74.96	73.23	71.10	69.89	68.35	66.90	66.06
3 & 4	92.22	82.20	77.75	73.28	70.50	68.81	66.85	65.67	64.25	62.89	62.09
4, Low	86.22	76.79	72.66	68.49	65.85	64.29	62.49	61.36	60.04	58.76	58.03

Length greater than 3 times depth - Square Foot Area

Quality Class	2,000	3,000	5,000	10,000	15,000	20,000	30,000	50,000	75,000	100,000	150,000
1, Best	118.24	111.35	104.53	97.67	94.62	92.83	90.70	88.57	87.18	86.39	85.43
1 & 2	107.35	101.15	94.91	88.67	85.90	84.31	82.37	80.42	79.16	78.46	77.57
2, Good	98.55	92.82	87.13	81.39	78.89	77.37	75.60	73.80	72.73	72.02	71.21
2 & 3	93.46	88.03	82.61	77.18	74.80	73.32	71.66	69.98	68.92	68.26	67.54
3, Average	89.62	84.39	79.26	74.02	71.75	70.36	68.72	67.10	66.06	65.50	64.75
3 & 4	84.52	79.61	74.72	69.86	67.65	66.37	64.85	63.27	62.36	61.79	61.09
4, Low	79.27	74.67	70.06	65.50	63.44	62.23	60.81	59.39	58.49	57.93	57.27

Wall Height Adjustment: Add or subtract the amount listed to or from the square foot cost above for each foot of wall height more or less than 16 feet.

Area	500	1,000	2,000	2,500	3,000	4,000	5,000	7,500	10,000	12,500
Cost	1.72	1.21	.87	.89	.71	.67	.60	.54	.50	.47

Area	15,000	20,000	25,000	30,000	35,000	50,000	70,000	75,000	100,000	150,000
Cost	.37	.24	.23	.22	.20	.18	.17	.16	.15	.14

Perimeter Wall Adjustment: For a common wall, deduct $182 per linear foot of common wall. For no wall ownership, deduct $367 per linear foot of wall.

Suburban Stores – Wood or Wood and Steel Frame

Multi-Unit, Island Type

Estimating Procedure

1. Use these figures to estimate the cost of stores designed for multiple occupancy. These costs include all components of shell buildings plus the cost of display fronts, finish materials on the front of the building and normal interior partitions.
2. Establish the structure quality class by applying the information on page 94. Evaluate the quality of the display front to help establish the correct quality class of the building as a whole. The building classes have display fronts as classified on page 89. See also pages 242 to 245.
3. Compute the building floor area. This should include everything within the exterior walls and all inset areas outside the main walls but under the main roof.
4. Add to or subtract from the square foot cost below the appropriate amount from the Wall Height Adjustment Table (at the bottom of this page) if the wall height is more or less than 16 feet.
5. Multiply the adjusted square foot cost by the building area.
6. Deduct, if appropriate, for common walls, using the figures at the bottom of this page.
7. Multiply the total cost by the location factor on page 7 or 8.
8. Add the cost of the appropriate additional components from page 236 to 248: heating and cooling equipment, fire sprinklers, canopies, exterior signs, mezzanines and basements, loading docks and ramps, yard improvements, and communication systems.

Length less than 1-1/2 times depth - Square Foot Area

Quality Class	3,500	5,000	7,500	10,000	12,500	15,000	20,000	30,000	40,000	50,000	75,000
1, Best	215.26	195.94	178.30	166.10	159.23	153.77	144.99	136.10	130.90	123.50	120.27
1 & 2	188.15	171.55	156.53	145.97	139.91	135.44	127.90	126.86	120.26	112.77	107.68
2, Good	162.45	149.00	136.28	128.69	123.44	119.58	114.18	107.70	103.80	101.18	97.06
2 & 3	142.08	130.34	119.25	112.59	108.00	104.61	99.89	94.24	90.85	88.57	84.93
3, Average	126.06	115.61	105.79	99.87	95.82	92.80	88.59	83.61	80.57	78.57	75.32
3 & 4	112.91	103.56	94.70	89.43	85.79	83.08	79.33	74.82	72.16	70.36	67.49
4, Low	99.86	91.58	83.76	79.10	75.91	73.49	70.18	66.21	63.84	62.20	59.69

Length between 1-1/2 and 2 times depth - Square Foot Area

Quality Class	4,500	5,000	7,500	10,000	15,000	20,000	30,000	40,000	50,000	75,000	100,000
1, Best	204.98	199.19	179.98	168.94	156.21	148.83	140.24	135.24	131.86	126.72	123.68
1 & 2	180.67	175.54	158.60	148.91	137.70	131.20	123.61	119.19	116.25	111.72	109.03
2, Good	158.22	153.72	138.88	130.34	120.54	114.83	108.23	104.41	101.80	97.80	95.56
2 & 3	139.89	135.91	122.79	115.25	106.59	101.55	95.75	92.32	90.00	86.44	84.40
3, Average	122.99	119.50	108.02	101.40	93.77	89.35	84.22	81.15	79.16	76.04	74.22
3 & 4	111.08	107.96	97.55	91.51	84.67	80.60	76.04	73.28	71.48	68.68	67.03
4, Low	99.04	96.22	86.92	81.62	75.46	71.91	67.78	65.35	63.73	61.24	59.73

Wall Height Adjustment: Add or subtract the amount listed to or from the square foot cost above for each foot of wall height more or less than 16 feet.

Square Foot Area

Quality Class	3,500	5,000	7,500	10,000	12,500	15,000	20,000	30,000	40,000	50,000	75,000	100,000	150,000
1	10.35	8.69	7.13	6.22	5.56	5.11	4.46	3.65	3.19	2.89	2.36	2.07	1.75
2	7.13	6.02	4.93	4.29	3.86	3.53	3.11	2.52	2.23	1.99	1.66	1.42	1.18
3	4.93	4.16	3.38	2.97	2.65	2.42	2.13	1.75	1.53	1.36	1.14	1.02	.80
4	3.63	3.05	2.49	2.15	1.97	1.78	1.56	1.30	1.09	.99	.83	.70	.61

Perimeter Wall Adjustment: For a common wall, deduct per linear foot: Class 1, $1022, Class 2, $674, Class 3, $479, Class 4, $314. For no wall ownership, deduct per linear foot: Class 1, $2,026, Class 2, $1,333, Class 3, $921, Class 4, $642.

Suburban Stores – Wood or Wood and Steel Frame

Multi-Unit, Island Type

Estimating Procedure

1. Use these figures to estimate the cost of stores designed for multiple occupancy. These costs include all components of shell buildings plus the cost of display fronts, finish materials on the front of the building and normal interior partitions.
2. Establish the structure quality class by applying the information on page 94. Evaluate the quality of the display front to help establish the correct quality class of the building as a whole. The building classes have display fronts as classified on page 89. See also pages 242 to 245.
3. Compute the building floor area. This should include everything within the exterior walls and all inset areas outside the main walls but under the main roof.
4. Add to or subtract from the square foot cost below the appropriate amount from the Wall Height Adjustment Table (at the bottom of this page) if the wall height is more or less than 16 feet.
5. Multiply the adjusted square foot cost by the building area.
6. Deduct, if appropriate, for common walls, using the figures at the bottom of this page.
7. Multiply the total cost by the location factor on page 7 or 8.
8. Add the cost of the appropriate additional components from page 236 to 248: heating and cooling equipment, fire sprinklers, canopies, exterior signs, mezzanines and basements, loading docks and ramps, yard improvements, and communication systems.

Length between 2 and 3 times depth - Square Foot Area

Quality Class	7,500	10,000	15,000	20,000	30,000	40,000	50,000	75,000	100,000	150,000	200,000
1, Best	181.29	170.79	158.27	150.79	141.84	136.50	132.78	127.09	123.69	119.60	117.22
1 & 2	160.24	150.94	139.83	133.23	125.31	120.60	117.34	112.29	109.29	105.74	103.56
2, Good	140.80	132.65	122.89	117.08	110.13	106.01	103.12	98.72	96.04	92.88	91.02
2 & 3	125.00	117.73	109.06	103.92	97.74	94.04	91.52	87.64	85.24	82.43	80.78
3, Average	110.62	104.22	96.57	91.97	86.52	83.26	81.06	77.55	75.48	73.04	71.51
3 & 4	99.46	93.70	86.82	82.69	77.79	74.85	72.88	69.72	67.87	65.59	64.29
4, Low	88.14	83.06	76.95	73.26	68.93	66.32	64.57	61.72	60.08	58.17	56.99

Length greater than 3 times depth - Square Foot Area

Quality Class	10,000	15,000	20,000	30,000	40,000	50,000	75,000	100,000	150,000	200,000	250,000
1, Best	179.87	165.35	156.79	146.62	140.60	136.51	130.10	126.32	121.82	119.14	117.31
1 & 2	159.01	146.21	138.60	129.63	124.29	120.68	115.03	111.70	107.70	105.29	103.69
2, Good	139.66	128.44	121.79	113.89	109.19	106.03	101.07	98.10	94.58	92.53	91.10
2 & 3	124.22	114.26	108.25	101.29	97.08	94.27	89.85	87.26	84.09	82.31	81.05
3, Average	109.99	101.12	95.86	89.66	86.01	83.44	79.52	77.19	74.48	72.84	71.75
3 & 4	98.89	90.99	86.25	80.66	77.36	75.07	71.55	69.49	67.02	65.52	64.53
4, Low	87.68	80.66	76.44	71.49	68.58	66.55	63.44	61.60	59.42	58.10	57.24

Wall Height Adjustment: Add or subtract the amount listed to or from the square foot cost above for each foot of wall height more or less than 16 feet.

Square Foot Area

Quality Class	7,500	10,000	12,500	15,000	20,000	30,000	40,000	50,000	75,000	100,000	150,000	200,000	250,000
1	6.74	5.85	5.27	4.78	4.16	3.39	2.97	2.70	2.20	1.91	1.60	1.40	1.24
2	4.72	4.07	3.68	3.32	2.94	2.40	2.11	1.86	1.57	1.33	1.12	.99	.87
3	3.27	2.85	2.56	2.32	2.04	1.65	1.47	1.30	1.07	.96	.77	.69	.61
4	2.37	2.12	1.85	1.75	1.50	1.23	1.06	.96	.79	.66	.60	.52	.49

Perimeter Wall Adjustment: For a common wall, deduct per linear foot: Class 1, $1,022, Class 2, $674, Class 3, $479, Class 4, $314. For no wall ownership, deduct per linear foot: Class 1, $2,027, Class 2, $1,333, Class 3, $921, Class 4, $642.

Suburban Stores – Wood or Wood and Steel Frame

Multi-Unit, Strip Type

Estimating Procedure

1. Use these figures to estimate the cost of stores designed for multiple occupancy. These costs include all components of shell buildings plus the cost of display fronts, finish materials on the front of the building and normal interior partitions.
2. Establish the structure quality class by applying the information on page 94. Evaluate the quality of the display front to help establish the correct quality class of the building as a whole. The building classes have display fronts as classified on page 89. See also pages 242 to 245.
3. Compute the building floor area. This should include everything within the exterior walls and all inset areas outside the main walls but under the main roof.
4. Add to or subtract from the square foot cost below the appropriate amount from the Wall Height Adjustment Table (at the bottom of this page) if the wall height is more or less than 16 feet.
5. Multiply the adjusted square foot cost by the building area.
6. Deduct, if appropriate, for common walls, using the figures at the bottom of this page.
7. Multiply the total cost by the location factor on page 7 or 8.
8. Add the cost of the appropriate additional components from page 236 to 248: heating and cooling equipment, fire sprinklers, canopies, exterior signs, mezzanines and basements, loading docks and ramps, yard improvements, and communication systems.

Length less than 1-1/2 times depth - Square Foot Area

Quality Class	500	1,000	2,000	2,500	3,000	4,000	5,000	7,500	10,000	12,500	15,000
1, Best	221.48	184.64	158.74	152.11	147.25	140.40	135.75	128.53	124.21	121.23	119.07
1 & 2	196.20	163.63	140.60	134.76	130.44	124.35	120.22	113.82	109.99	107.37	105.45
2, Good	172.99	144.24	123.93	118.76	115.01	109.62	106.04	100.37	97.00	94.64	92.96
2 & 3	157.48	131.28	112.86	108.13	104.71	99.80	96.52	91.35	88.26	86.22	84.62
3, Average	144.24	120.27	103.40	99.12	95.89	91.47	88.42	83.72	80.87	78.96	77.54
3 & 4	132.88	110.77	95.23	94.63	88.35	84.24	81.44	77.10	74.48	72.73	71.46
4, Low	120.76	100.69	86.51	82.92	80.26	76.51	74.00	70.06	67.70	66.12	64.89

Length between 1-1/2 and 2 times depth - Square Foot Area

Quality Class	500	1,000	2,000	3,000	5,000	7,500	10,000	15,000	20,000	25,000	35,000
1, Best	247.38	203.59	172.57	158.80	145.01	136.32	131.14	124.99	121.31	118.80	115.52
1 & 2	218.22	179.61	152.25	140.13	127.95	120.26	115.68	110.26	107.04	104.78	101.92
2, Good	191.68	157.74	133.67	123.06	112.38	105.60	101.65	96.87	94.00	92.08	89.51
2 & 3	174.00	143.17	121.36	111.70	102.01	95.87	92.22	87.89	85.29	83.57	81.26
3, Average	158.44	130.40	110.53	101.70	92.86	87.31	84.00	80.52	77.68	76.12	74.00
3 & 4	144.96	119.31	101.11	93.06	84.95	79.88	76.87	73.18	71.10	69.63	67.70
4, Low	131.71	108.35	91.80	84.52	77.17	72.53	69.78	66.51	64.57	63.22	61.47

Wall Height Adjustment: Add or subtract the amount listed to or from the square foot of floor cost for each foot of wall height more or less than 16 feet.

Square Foot Area

Quality Class	500	1,000	2,000	3,000	5,000	7,500	10,000	15,000	20,000	25,000	35,000
1, Best	15.06	10.49	7.39	6.02	4.71	3.82	3.32	2.77	2.38	2.14	1.96
2, Good	9.88	6.88	4.85	3.96	3.04	2.50	2.19	1.79	1.61	1.39	1.30
3, Average	7.23	5.04	3.55	2.92	2.30	1.84	1.63	1.31	1.15	1.06	.97
4, Low	5.27	3.63	2.55	2.11	1.64	1.32	1.15	.97	.79	.71	.69

Perimeter Wall Adjustment: For a common wall, deduct $183 per linear foot. For no wall ownership, deduct $366 per linear foot.

Multi-Unit, Strip Type

Estimating Procedure

1. Use these figures to estimate the cost of stores designed for multiple occupancy. These costs include all components of shell buildings plus the cost of display fronts, finish materials on the front of the building and normal interior partitions.

2. Establish the structure quality class by applying the information on page 94. Evaluate the quality of the display front to help establish the correct quality class of the building as a whole. The building classes have display fronts as classified on page 89. See also pages 242 to 245.

3. Compute the building floor area. This should include everything within the exterior walls and all inset areas outside the main walls but under the main roof.

4. Add to or subtract from the square foot cost below the appropriate amount from the Wall Height Adjustment Table (at the bottom of this page) if the wall height is more or less than 16 feet.

5. Multiply the adjusted square foot cost by the building area.

6. Deduct, if appropriate, for common walls, using the figures at the bottom of this page.

7. Multiply the total cost by the location factor on page 7 or 8.

8. Add the cost of the appropriate additional components from page 236 to 248: heating and cooling equipment, fire sprinklers, canopies, exterior signs, mezzanines and basements, loading docks and ramps, yard improvements, and communication systems.

Length between 2 and 3 times depth - Square Foot Area

Quality Class	1,000	2,000	3,000	5,000	7,500	10,000	15,000	20,000	30,000	50,000	70,000
1, Best	232.61	193.17	175.74	158.26	147.30	140.72	132.91	128.29	122.79	117.34	114.40
1 & 2	204.99	170.24	154.89	139.51	129.79	124.05	117.14	113.09	108.25	103.42	100.81
2, Good	179.47	149.02	135.61	122.10	113.62	108.56	102.60	99.01	94.75	90.51	88.25
2 & 3	162.50	134.92	122.76	110.58	102.90	98.34	92.91	89.64	85.82	81.99	79.93
3, Average	147.30	122.31	111.26	100.20	93.22	89.12	84.18	81.23	77.76	74.28	72.43
3 & 4	134.77	111.89	101.82	91.63	85.29	81.52	76.96	74.34	71.15	67.96	66.24
4, Low	121.99	101.28	92.19	83.03	77.19	73.83	69.73	67.28	64.48	61.53	60.00

Length greater than 3 times depth - Square Foot Area

Quality Class	2,000	3,000	5,000	10,000	15,000	20,000	30,000	50,000	75,000	100,000	150,000
1, Best	212.28	191.04	170.00	149.16	140.07	134.62	128.20	121.83	117.82	115.45	112.60
1 & 2	186.94	168.23	149.65	131.31	123.30	118.52	112.90	107.29	103.77	101.65	99.16
2, Good	163.45	147.11	130.92	114.88	107.84	103.68	98.75	93.85	90.73	88.91	86.74
2 & 3	142.71	128.41	114.31	100.26	94.19	90.51	86.22	81.90	79.26	77.65	75.70
3, Average	133.74	120.34	107.10	93.96	88.21	84.84	80.78	76.76	74.22	72.73	70.96
3 & 4	123.08	110.76	98.60	86.48	81.17	78.03	74.37	70.64	68.32	66.94	65.35
4, Low	112.08	100.87	89.78	78.79	73.96	71.10	67.72	64.34	62.23	61.02	59.50

Wall Height Adjustment: Add or subtract the amount listed to or from the square foot cost above for each foot of wall height more or less than 16 feet.

Square Foot Area

Quality Class	2,000	3,000	5,000	10,000	15,000	20,000	30,000	50,000	75,000	100,000	150,000
1, Best	7.17	5.84	4.56	3.28	2.74	2.36	1.93	1.62	1.31	1.18	1.04
2, Good	4.60	3.79	2.92	2.11	1.72	1.52	1.28	1.02	.84	.77	.63
3, Average	3.38	2.80	2.15	1.58	1.29	1.13	.95	.72	.63	.57	.49
4, Low	2.52	2.02	1.62	1.13	.96	.86	.68	.56	.48	.44	.35

Perimeter Wall Adjustment: For a common wall, deduct $183 per linear foot. For no wall ownership, deduct $366 per linear foot.

Supermarkets – Masonry or Concrete

Quality Classification

	Class 1 Best Quality	Class 2 Good Quality	Class 3 Average Quality	Class 4 Low Quality
Foundation (15% of total cost)	Reinforced concrete.	Reinforced concrete.	Reinforced concrete.	Reinforced concrete.
Floor Structure (12% of total cost)	4" reinforced concrete on 6" rock fill.	4" reinforced concrete on 6" rock fill.	4" reinforced concrete on 6" rock fill.	4" reinforced concrete on 6" rock fill.
Wall Structure (15% of total cost)	6" concrete tilt-up or ornamental block or brick.	6" concrete tilt-up, colored concrete block or brick.	6" concrete tilt-up or 8" concrete block.	6" concrete tilt-up or 8" concrete block.
Roof Structure (10% of total cost)	Glu-lams or steel "I" beams on steel intermediate columns, 2" x 12" purlins 16" o.c., 1/2" plywood sheathing.	Glu-lams or steel "I" beams on steel intermediate columns, 2" x 12" purlins 16" o.c., 1/2" plywood sheathing.	Glu-lams or steel "I" beams on steel intermediate columns, 2" x 12" purlins 16" o.c., 1/2" plywood sheathing.	Glu-lams or steel "I" beams on steel intermediate columns, 3" x 12" purlins 3' o.c., 1/2" plywood sheathing.
Floor Finish (5% of total cost)	Terrazzo in sales area. Sheet vinyl or carpet in cashiers' area.	Resilient tile in sales area. Terrazzo, solid vinyl tile or carpet in cashiers' area.	Composition tile in sales area.	Minimum grade tile in sales area.
Interior Wall Finish (5% of total cost)	Inside of exterior walls furred out with gypsum wallboard and paint or interior stucco, interior stucco or gypsum wallboard and vinyl wall cover on partitions.	Paint on inside of exterior walls, gypsum wallboard and paint or vinyl wall cover on partitions.	Paint on inside of exterior walls, wallboard and paint on partitions.	Paint on inside of exterior walls, wallboard and paint on partitions.
Ceiling Finish (5% of total cost)	Suspended acoustical tile, dropped ceiling over meat and produce departments.	Suspended acoustical tile or gypsum board and acoustical texture, dropped ceiling over meat and produce departments.	Ceiling tile on roof purlins, dropped ceiling over meat department.	Open.
Front (7% of total cost)	A large amount of float glass in good aluminum frames (18'-22' high for 3/4 of width), brick or stone veneer on remainder, 1 pair of good automatic doors per 7,000 S.F. of floor area, anodized aluminum sunshade over glass area, 8' canopy across front, 10'-12' raised walk across front.	A large amount of float glass in good aluminum frames (16'-18' high for 2/3 of width), brick or stone veneer on remainder, 1 pair of good automatic doors per 10,000 S.F. of floor area, 8' canopy across front, 10' raised walk across front.	A moderate amount of float glass in average quality aluminum frames (12'-16' high for 2/3 of width), exposed aggregate on remainder, 1 pair average automatic doors per 10,000 S.F. of floor area, 6' canopy across front, 8' raised walk across front.	Stucco or exposed aggregate with a small amount of float glass in an inexpensive aluminum frame (6'-10' high for 1/2 of width), 6' canopy across front, 6' ground level walk across front.
Exterior Finish (8% of total cost)	Large ornamental rock or brick veneer.	Large ornamental rock or brick veneer.	Paint, some exposed aggregate.	Paint.
Roof Cover (5% of total cost)	5 ply built-up roofing with large rock.	5 ply built-up roofing with tar and rock.	4 ply built-up roofing.	4 ply built-up roofing.
Plumbing (8% of total cost)	2 rest rooms with 3 fixtures, floor piping and drains to refrigerated cases, 2 double sinks with drain board.	2 rest rooms with 3 fixtures each, floor piping and drains to refrigerated cases, 2 double sinks with drain board.	2 rest rooms with 2 fixtures each, floor piping and drains to refrigerated cases, 2 double sinks.	1 rest room with 2 fixtures, floor piping and drains to refrigerated cases.
Electrical (5% of total cost)	Conduit wiring, recessed 4 tube fluorescent fixtures 8' o.c., 30-40 spotlights.	Conduit wiring, 4 tube fluorescent fixtures with diffusers 8' o.c., 30-40 spotlights.	Conduit wiring, 3 tube fluorescent fixtures, 8' o.c., 5 or 10 spotlights.	Conduit wiring, double tube fluorescent fixtures, 8' o.c.

Note: Use the percent of total cost to help identify the correct quality classification.

Square foot costs include the following components: Foundations as required for normal soil conditions. Floor, wall, and roof structures. Interior floor, wall and ceiling finishes. Exterior wall finish and roof cover. Display fronts. Interior partitions. Entry and delivery doors. A canopy and walk across the front of the building as described in the applicable building specifications. Basic lighting and electrical systems. Rough and finish plumbing. All plumbing, piping and wiring necessary to operate the usual refrigerated cases and vegetable cases. Design and engineering fees. Permits and hook-up fees. Contractor's mark-up.

Supermarkets – Masonry or Concrete

Estimating Procedure

1. Establish the structure quality class by using the information on page 103.
2. Compute the building floor area. This should include everything within the building exterior walls and all insets outside the main walls but under the main building roof.
3. Add to or subtract from the square foot cost below the appropriate amount from the Wall Height Adjustment Row (at the bottom of this page) if the wall height is more or less than 20 feet.
4. Multiply the adjusted square foot cost by the building area.
5. Deduct, if appropriate, for common walls, using the figures at the bottom of this page.
6. Multiply the total cost by the location factor listed on page 7 or 8.
7. Add the cost of heating and cooling equipment, fire sprinklers, exterior signs, yard improvements, loading docks, ramps and walk-in boxes if they are an integral part of the building. See pages 236 to 248.

Supermarket, Class 2

Square Foot Area

Quality Class	5,000	7,500	10,000	12,500	15,000	20,000	25,000	30,000	35,000	40,000	50,000
Exceptional	147.86	137.49	131.30	127.03	123.91	119.47	116.40	114.18	112.45	111.03	108.88
1, Best	140.91	131.04	125.11	121.07	118.06	113.86	110.97	108.81	107.16	105.83	103.73
1 & 2	130.64	121.45	116.02	112.22	109.43	105.50	102.85	100.87	99.31	98.07	96.22
2, Good	120.97	112.49	107.42	103.95	101.36	97.78	95.26	93.44	92.01	90.86	89.11
2 & 3	112.86	104.93	100.23	96.98	94.53	91.20	88.87	87.13	85.79	84.74	83.09
3, Average	106.08	98.68	94.20	91.13	88.87	85.75	83.50	81.90	80.66	79.65	78.08
3 & 4	96.23	89.44	85.41	82.67	80.61	77.75	75.77	74.30	73.14	72.27	70.86
4, Low	85.91	79.88	76.28	73.82	71.97	69.41	67.62	66.34	65.33	64.50	63.24
Wall Height Adjustment*	1.60	1.28	1.12	1.03	.95	.78	.68	.62	.60	.58	.49

*Wall Height Adjustment: Add or subtract the amount listed in this row to or from the square foot of floor cost for each foot of wall height more or less than 20 feet.

Perimeter Wall Adjustment: A common wall exists when two buildings share one wall. Adjust for common walls by deducting the linear foot costs below from the total structure cost. In some structures one or more walls are not owned at all. In this case, deduct the "No Ownership" cost per linear foot of wall not owned. For common wall, deduct $277 per linear foot. For no wall ownership, deduct $555 per linear foot.

Supermarkets – Wood and Steel Frame

Quality Classification

	Class 1 Best Quality	Class 2 Good Quality	Class 3 Average Quality	Class 4 Low Quality
Foundation (15% of total cost)	Reinforced concrete.	Reinforced concrete.	Reinforced concrete.	Reinforced concrete.
Floor Structure (12% of total cost)	4" reinforced concrete on 6" rock fill.	4" reinforced concrete on 6" rock fill.	4" reinforced concrete on 6" rock fill.	4" reinforced concrete on 6" rock fill.
Wall Structure (10% of total cost)	2" x 6" - 16" o.c.	2" x 6" - 16" o.c.	2" x 4" - 16" o.c.	2" x 4" - 16" o.c.
Roof Structure (10% of total cost)	Glu-lams or steel "I" beams on steel intermediate columns, 2" x 12" purlins 16" o.c., 1/2" plywood sheathing.	Glu-lams or steel "I" beams on steel intermediate columns, 2" x 12" purlins 16" o.c., 1/2" plywood sheathing.	Glu-lams or steel "I" beams on steel intermediate columns, 2" x 12" purlins 16" o.c., 1/2" plywood sheathing.	Glu-lams or steel "I" beams on steel intermediate columns, 3" x 12" purlins 3' o.c., 1/2" plywood sheathing.
Floor Finish (5% of total cost)	Terrazzo in sales area. Sheet vinyl or carpet in cashiers' area.	Resilient tile in sales area. Terrazzo, solid vinyl tile or carpet in cashiers' area.	Composition tile in sales area.	Minimum tile or inexpensive composition tile in sales area.
Interior Wall Finish (7% of total cost)	Gypsum wallboard and vinyl wall cover or interior stucco on inside of exterior walls and on partitions.	Gypsum wallboard, texture and paint or vinyl wall cover on inside of exterior walls, and on partitions.	Gypsum wallboard, texture and paint on inside of exterior walls, and on partitions.	Gypsum wallboard and paint on inside of exterior walls, and on partitions.
Ceiling Finish (5% of total cost)	Suspended acoustical tile, dropped ceiling over meat and produce departments.	Suspended acoustical tile or gypsum board and acoustical texture, dropped ceiling over meat and produce departments.	Ceiling tile on roof purlins, dropped ceiling over meat department.	Open.
Front (10% of total cost)	A large amount of float glass in good aluminum frames (18'-22' high for 3/4 of width), brick or stone veneer on remainder, 1 pair good automatic doors per 7,000 S.F. of floor area, anodized aluminum sunshade over glass area, 8' canopy across front, 10'-12' raised walk across front.	A large amount of float glass in good aluminum frames (16'-18' high for 2/3 of width), brick or stone veneer on remainder, 1 pair good automatic doors per 10,000 S.F. of floor area, 9' canopy across front, 10' raised walk across front.	Moderate amount of float glass in average quality aluminum frames (12'-16' high for 2/3 of width), wood siding on remainder, 1 pair average automatic doors per 10,000 S.F. of floor area, 6' canopy across front, 8' raised walk across front.	Stucco with small amount of float glass in an inexpensive aluminum frame (6'-10' high for 1/2 of width), 6' canopy across front, 6' ground level walk across front.
Exterior Finish (8% of total cost)	Large ornamental rock or brick veneer.	Good wood siding, some masonry veneer.	Stucco or wood siding.	Stucco.
Roof Cover (5% of total cost)	5 ply built-up roofing with large rock.	5 ply built-up roofing with tar and rock.	4 ply built-up roofing.	4 ply built-up roofing.
Plumbing (8% of total cost)	2 rest rooms with 3 fixtures each, floor piping and drains to refrigerated cases, 2 double sinks with drain board.	2 rest rooms with 3 fixtures each, floor piping and drains to refrigerated cases, 2 double sinks with drain board.	2 rest rooms with 2 fixtures each, floor piping and drains to refrigerated cases, 2 double sinks.	1 rest room with 2 fixtures, floor piping and drains to refrigerated cases.
Electrical (5% of total cost)	Conduit wiring, recessed 4 tube fluorescent fixtures, 8' o.c., 30 to 40 spotlights.	Conduit wiring, 4 tube fluorescent fixtures with diffusers, 8' o.c., 30 to 40 spotlights.	Conduit wiring, 3 tube fluorescent fixtures, 8' o.c., 5 or 10 spotlights.	Conduit wiring, double tube fluorescent fixtures, 8' o.c.

Note: Use the percent of total cost to help identify the correct quality classification.

Square foot costs include the following components: Foundations as required for normal soil conditions. Floor, wall, and roof structures. Interior floor, wall and ceiling finishes. Exterior wall finish and roof cover. Display fronts. Interior partitions. Entry and delivery doors. A canopy and walk across the front of the building as described in the applicable building specifications. Basic lighting and electrical systems. Rough and finish plumbing. All plumbing, piping and wiring necessary to operate the usual refrigerated cases and vegetable cases. Design and engineering fees. Permits and hook-up fees. Contractor's mark-up.

Supermarkets – Wood and Steel Frame

Estimating Procedure

1. Establish the structure quality class by using the information on page 105.
2. Compute the building floor area. This should include everything within the building exterior walls and all insets outside the main walls but under the main building roof.
3. Add to or subtract from the square foot cost below the appropriate amount from the Wall Height Adjustment Row (at the bottom of this page) if the wall height is more or less than 20 feet.
4. Multiply the adjusted square foot cost by the building area.
5. Deduct, if appropriate, for common walls, using the figures at the bottom of this page.
6. Multiply the total cost by the location factor listed on page 7 or 8.
7. Add the cost of heating and cooling equipment, fire sprinklers, exterior signs, yard improvements, loading docks, ramps and walk-in boxes if they are an integral part of the building. See pages 236 to 248.

Supermarket, Class 3

Square Foot Area

Quality Class	5,000	7,500	10,000	12,500	15,000	20,000	25,000	30,000	35,000	40,000	50,000
Exceptional	140.67	132.56	127.66	124.32	121.84	118.39	116.01	114.23	112.89	111.82	110.06
1, Best	134.20	126.45	121.78	118.63	116.27	112.92	110.69	109.01	107.68	106.64	105.02
1 & 2	123.29	116.21	111.88	108.99	106.80	103.76	101.70	100.15	98.94	97.94	96.48
2, Good	113.13	106.53	102.65	99.93	98.03	95.19	93.29	91.84	90.77	89.86	88.50
2 & 3	105.68	99.61	95.95	93.45	91.61	88.98	87.21	85.87	84.82	84.01	82.76
3, Average	99.53	93.80	90.32	87.92	86.20	83.76	82.04	80.80	79.86	79.03	77.85
3 & 4	91.16	85.90	82.75	80.57	78.96	76.71	75.17	74.04	73.15	72.46	71.33
4, Low	82.13	77.39	74.55	72.54	71.12	69.10	67.70	66.66	65.87	65.22	64.24
Wall Height Adjustment*	.89	.74	.66	.60	.55	.51	.49	.47	.44	.43	.38

***Wall Height Adjustment:** Add or subtract the amount listed in this row to or from the square foot of floor cost for each foot of wall height more or less than 20 feet.

Perimeter Wall Adjustment: A common wall exists when two buildings share one wall. Adjust for common walls by deducting the linear foot costs below from the total structure cost. In some structures one or more walls are not owned at all. In this case, deduct the "No Ownership" cost per linear foot of wall not owned. For common wall, deduct $200 per linear foot. For no wall ownership, deduct $399 per linear foot.

Small Food Stores – Masonry Construction

Quality Classification

	Class 1 Best Quality	Class 2 Good Quality	Class 3 Average Quality	Class 4 Low Quality
Foundation (15% of total cost)	Reinforced concrete.	Reinforced concrete.	Reinforced concrete.	Reinforced concrete.
Floor Structure (12% of total cost)	4" reinforced concrete on 6" rock fill.	4" reinforced concrete on 6" rock fill.	4" reinforced concrete on 6" rock fill.	4" reinforced concrete on 6" rock fill.
Wall Structure (10% of total cost)	6" concrete tilt-up or ornamental block or brick.	6" concrete tilt-up, colored concrete block or brick.	6" concrete tilt-up or 8" concrete block.	6" concrete tilt-up or 8" concrete block.
Roof Structure (10% of total cost)	Glu-lams or steel "I" beams on steel intermediate columns, 2" x 12" purlins 16" o.c., 1/2" plywood sheathing.	Glu-lams or steel "I" beams, 2" x 12" purlins 16" o.c., 1/2" plywood sheathing.	Glu-lams, 3" x 12" purlins 3' o.c., 1/2" plywood sheathing.	Glu-lams, 3" x 12" purlins 3' o.c., 1/2" plywood sheathing.
Floor Finish (5% of total cost)	Resilient tile in sales area.	Composition tile in sales area.	Minimum grade tile in sales area.	Concrete.
Interior Wall Finish (7% of total cost)	Paint on inside of exterior walls, gypsum wallboard, texture and paint or vinyl wall cover on partitions.	Paint on inside of exterior walls, gypsum wallboard, texture and paint on partitions.	Paint on inside of exterior walls, gypsum wallboard and paint on partitions.	Paint on inside of exterior walls, gypsum wallboard and paint on partitions.
Ceiling Finish (5% of total cost)	Suspended acoustical tile or gypsum board and acoustical texture.	Ceiling tile on roof purlins.	Open.	Open.
Front (10% of total cost)	A large amount of float glass in good aluminum frames (10'-12' high for 2/3 of width), brick or stone veneer on remainder, 1 pair good aluminum and glass doors per 3,000 S.F. of floor area, 8' canopy across front, 10' raised walk across front.	A moderate amount of float glass in average aluminum frames (8' to 10' high for 2/3 of width), exposed aggregate on remainder, 1 pair average aluminum and glass doors per 3,000 S.F. of floor area, 6' canopy across front, 8' raised walk across front.	Painted concrete block with a small amount of float glass in an inexpensive aluminum frame (6' to 8' high for 1/2 of width), 6' canopy across front, 6' ground level walk across front.	Painted concrete block with small amount of crystal glass in wood frames, wood and glass doors, small canopy over entrance, 6' ground level walk at entrances.
Exterior Finish (8% of total cost)	Colored block.	Paint.	Paint.	Paint.
Roof Cover (5% of total cost)	5 ply built-up roofing with tar and rock.	4 ply built-up roofing.	4 ply built-up roofing.	4 ply built-up roofing.
Plumbing (8% of total cost)	2 rest rooms with 3 fixtures each, floor piping and drains to refrigerated cases.	1 rest room with 3 fixtures, floor piping and drains to refrigerated cases.	1 rest room with 2 fixtures, floor piping and drains to refrigerated cases.	1 rest room with 2 fixtures, floor piping and drains to refrigerated cases.
Electrical (5% of total cost)	Conduit wiring, 4 tube fluorescent fixtures with diffusers, 8' o.c., 5 spotlights.	Conduit wiring, 3 tube fluorescent fixtures, 8' o.c.	Conduit wiring, double tube fluorescent fixtures, 8' o.c.	Conduit wiring, incandescent fixtures,10' o.c. or single tube fluorescent fixtures, 8' o.c.

Note: Use the percent of total cost to help identify the correct quality classification.

Square foot costs include the following components: Foundations as required for normal soil conditions. Floor, wall, and roof structures. Interior floor, wall and ceiling finishes. Exterior wall finish and roof cover. Display fronts. Interior partitions. Entry and delivery doors. A canopy and walk across the front of the building as described in the applicable building specifications. Basic lighting and electrical systems. Rough and finish plumbing. All plumbing, piping and wiring necessary to operate the usual refrigerated cases and vegetable cases. Design and engineering fees. Permits and hook-up fees. Contractor's mark-up.

Small Food Stores – Masonry Construction

Estimating Procedure

1. Establish the structure quality class by using the information on page 107.
2. Compute the building floor area. This should include everything within the building exterior walls and all insets outside the main walls but under the main building roof.
3. Add to or subtract from the square foot cost below the appropriate amount from the Wall Height Adjustment Row (at the bottom of this page) if the wall height is more or less than 12 feet.
4. Multiply the adjusted square foot cost by the building area.
5. Deduct, if appropriate, for common walls, using the figures at the bottom of this page.
6. Multiply the total cost by the location factor listed on page 7 or 8.
7. Add the cost of heating and cooling equipment, fire sprinklers, exterior signs, yard improvements, loading docks, ramps and walk-in boxes if they are an integral part of the building. See pages 236 to 248.

Small Food Store, Class 1 & 2

Small Food Store, Class 2

Square Foot Area

Quality Class	500	1,000	1,500	2,000	2,500	3,000	3,500	4,000	4,500	5,000	6,000
1, Best	217.93	165.12	144.38	132.74	125.14	119.72	115.67	112.37	109.73	107.51	104.02
1 & 2	200.73	152.44	133.45	122.81	115.85	110.86	107.10	104.17	101.69	99.68	96.47
2, Good	185.07	140.93	123.58	113.81	107.44	102.86	99.41	96.66	94.37	92.54	89.58
2 & 3	174.82	134.07	117.49	108.07	101.83	97.29	93.81	91.07	88.81	86.91	83.87
3, Average	165.15	126.36	110.74	101.90	96.05	91.86	88.66	86.17	84.05	82.29	79.50
3 & 4	136.77	115.23	103.42	95.80	90.31	86.14	82.72	80.04	77.71	75.74	72.44
4, Low	127.42	106.60	95.54	88.36	83.23	79.35	76.20	73.69	71.51	69.70	66.69
Wall Height Adjustment*	5.01	3.52	2.88	2.50	2.21	2.06	1.89	1.75	1.66	1.60	1.48

*Wall Height Adjustment: Add or subtract the amount listed in this row to or from the square foot of floor cost for each foot of wall height more or less than 12 feet.

Perimeter Wall Adjustment: For common wall, deduct $148 per linear foot. For no wall ownership, deduct $291 per linear foot.

Small Food Stores – Wood Frame Construction

Quality Classification

	Class 1 Best Quality	Class 2 Good Quality	Class 3 Average Quality	Class 4 Low Quality
Foundation (15% of total cost)	Reinforced concrete.	Reinforced concrete.	Reinforced concrete.	Reinforced concrete.
Floor Structure (12% of total cost)	4" reinforced concrete on 6" rock fill.	4" reinforced concrete on 6" rock fill.	4" reinforced concrete on 6" rock fill.	4" reinforced concrete on 6" rock fill.
Wall Structure (10% of total cost)	2" x 6" - 16" o.c.	2" x 6" - 16" o.c.	2" x 4" - 16" o.c.	2" x 4" - 16" o.c.
Roof Structure (10% of total cost)	Glu-lams or steel "I" beams on steel intermediate columns, 2" x 12" purlins 16" o.c., 1/2" plywood sheathing.	Glu-lams or steel "I" beams on steel intermediate columns, 2" x 12" purlins 16" o.c., 1/2" plywood sheathing.	Glu-lams, or steel "I" beams, 3" x 12" purlins 3' o.c., 1/2" plywood sheathing.	Glu-lams, 3" x 12" purlins 3' o.c. 1/2" plywood sheathing.
Floor Finish (5% of total cost)	Resilient tile in sales area.	Resilient tile in sales area.	Inexpensive composition tile in sales area.	Concrete.
Interior Wall Finish (7% of total cost)	Gypsum wallboard, texture and paint or vinyl wall cover on inside of exterior walls, and on partitions.	Gypsum wallboard, texture and paint on inside of exterior walls, and on partitions.	Gypsum wallboard and paint on inside of exterior walls, and on partitions.	Gypsum wallboard and paint on inside of exterior walls and on partitions.
Ceiling Finish (5% of total cost)	Suspended acoustical tile or gypsum board and acoustical texture.	Ceiling tile on roof purlins.	Open.	Open.
Front (10% of total cost)	A large amount of float glass in good aluminum frames (10'-12' high for 2/3 of width), brick or stone veneer on remainder, 1 pair good aluminum and glass doors per 3,000 S.F. of floor area, 8' canopy across front, 10' raised walk across front.	A moderate amount of float glass in average quality aluminum frames (8' to 10' high for 2/3 of width), ornamental concrete block on remainder, 1 pair average aluminum and glass doors per 3,000 S.F. of floor area, 6' canopy across front, 8' raised walk across front.	Painted stucco with a small amount of float glass in an inexpensive aluminum frame (6' to 8' high for 1/2 of width) 6' canopy across front. 6' ground level walk across front.	Stucco with small amount of crystal glass in wood frames, wood and glass doors, small canopy over entrance, 6' ground level walk at entrances.
Exterior Finish (8% of total cost)	Stucco and paint or wood siding.	Stucco and paint.	Stucco.	Stucco.
Roof Cover (5% of total cost)	5 ply built-up roofing with tar and rock.	4 ply built-up roofing.	4 ply built-up roofing.	4 ply built-up roofing.
Plumbing (8% of total cost)	2 rest rooms with 3 fixtures each, floor piping and drains to refrigerated cases.	1 rest room with 3 fixtures, floor piping and drains to refrigerated cases.	1 rest room with 2 fixtures, floor piping and drains to refrigerated cases.	1 rest room with 2 fixtures, floor piping and drains to refrigerated cases.
Electrical (5% of total cost)	Conduit wiring, 4 tube fluorescent fixtures with diffusers, 8' o.c., 5 spotlights.	Conduit wiring, 3 tube fluorescent fixtures, 8' o.c.	Conduit wiring, double tube fluorescent fixtures, 8' o.c.	Conduit wiring, incandescent fixtures, 10' o.c. or single tube fluorescent fixtures, 8' o.c.

Note: Use the percent of total cost to help identify the correct quality classification.

Square foot costs include the following components: Foundations as required for normal soil conditions. Floor, wall, and roof structures. Interior floor, wall and ceiling finishes. Exterior wall finish and roof cover. Display fronts. Interior partitions. Entry and delivery doors. A canopy and walk across the front of the building as described in the applicable building specifications. Basic lighting and electrical systems. Rough and finish plumbing. All plumbing, piping and wiring necessary to operate the usual refrigerated cases and vegetable cases. Design and engineering fees. Permits and hook-up fees. Contractor's mark-up.

Small Food Stores – Wood Frame Construction

Estimating Procedure

1. Establish the structure quality class by using the information on page 109.
2. Compute the building floor area. This should include everything within the building exterior walls and all insets outside the main walls but under the main building roof.
3. Add to or subtract from the square foot cost below the appropriate amount from the Wall Height Adjustment Row (at the bottom of this page) if the wall height is more or less than 12 feet.
4. Multiply the adjusted square foot cost by the building area.
5. Deduct, if appropriate, for common walls, using the figures at the bottom of this page.
6. Multiply the total cost by the location factor listed on page 7 or 8.
7. Add the cost of heating and cooling equipment, fire sprinklers, exterior signs, yard improvements, loading docks, ramps and walk-in boxes if they are an integral part of the building. See pages 236 to 248.

Small Food Store, Class 1

Small Food Store, Class 3

Square Foot Area

Quality Class	500	1,000	1,500	2,000	2,500	3,000	3,500	4,000	4,500	5,000	6,000
1, Best	199.93	152.35	134.38	124.54	118.15	113.70	110.35	107.74	105.58	103.84	101.04
1 & 2	184.81	141.15	124.60	115.54	109.78	105.64	102.58	100.18	98.18	96.57	94.03
2, Good	171.97	131.67	116.42	108.04	102.65	98.86	95.98	93.78	91.92	90.41	88.05
2 & 3	156.64	120.24	106.49	98.96	94.13	90.72	88.12	86.07	84.41	83.06	80.98
3, Average	143.20	110.32	97.85	91.07	86.67	83.58	81.24	79.45	78.02	76.73	74.80
3 & 4	129.78	100.20	88.93	82.85	78.87	76.13	74.02	72.37	71.05	69.92	68.24
4, Low	116.71	89.40	79.35	74.03	70.62	68.26	66.51	65.18	64.07	63.16	61.73
Wall Height Adjustment*	3.11	2.27	1.84	1.62	1.46	1.28	1.23	1.14	1.07	1.03	.96

*Wall Height Adjustment: Add or subtract the amount listed in this row to or from the square foot of floor cost for each foot of wall height more or less than 12 feet.

Perimeter Wall Adjustment: For common wall, deduct $101 per linear foot. For no wall ownership, deduct $200 per linear foot.

Discount Houses – Masonry or Concrete

Quality Classification

	Class 1 Best Quality	Class 2 Good Quality	Class 3 Average Quality	Class 4 Low Quality
Foundation (15% of total cost)	Reinforced concrete.	Reinforced concrete.	Reinforced concrete.	Reinforced concrete.
Floor Structure (12% of total cost)	4" reinforced concrete on 6" rock fill.	4" reinforced concrete on 6" rock fill.	4" reinforced concrete on 6" rock fill.	4" reinforced concrete on 6" rock fill.
Wall Structure (10% of total cost)	6" concrete tilt-up or ornamental block or brick.	6" concrete tilt-up, colored concrete block or brick.	6" concrete tilt-up or 8" concrete block.	6" concrete tilt-up or 8" concrete block.
Roof Structure (10% of total cost)	Glu-lams or steel "I" beams on steel intermediate columns, plywood sheathing.	Glu-lams or steel "I" beams on steel intermediate columns, plywood sheathing.	Glu-lams, or steel "I" beams on steel intermediate columns, plywood sheathing.	Glu-lams, or steel "I" beams on steel intermediate columns, plywood sheathing.
Floor Finish (5% of total cost)	Terrazzo, sheet vinyl or good carpet in sales area.	Resilient tile in sales area with some terrazzo, solid vinyl tile, or carpet.	Composition tile in sales area.	Inexpensive composition tile in sales area.
Interior Wall Finish (7% of total cost)	Inside of exterior walls furred out with gypsum wallboard and paint or interior stucco or gypsum wallboard and vinyl wall cover on partitions.	Paint on inside of exterior walls, gypsum wallboard and paint or vinyl wall cover on partitions.	Paint on inside of exterior walls, gypsum wallboard and paint on partitions.	Paint on inside of exterior walls, gypsum wallboard and paint on partitions.
Ceiling Finish (5% of total cost)	Suspended acoustical tile, dropped ceilings in some areas.	Suspended acoustical tile or gypsum board and acoustical texture, dropped ceilings in some areas.	Ceiling tile on roof purlins, dropped ceiling over some areas.	Open.
Front (10% of total cost)	A large amount of float glass in good aluminum frames (18'-22' high for 3/4 of width), brick or stone veneer on remainder, 1 pair good automatic doors per 7,000 S.F. of floor area, anodized aluminum sunshade over glass area, 8' canopy across front, 10'-12' raised walk across front.	A large amount of float glass in good aluminum frames (16'-18' high for 2/3 of width), brick or stone veneer on remainder, 1 pair good automatic doors per 10,000 S.F. of floor area, 8' canopy across front, 10' raised walk across front.	A moderate amount of float glass in average quality aluminum frames (12'-16' high extending 20' on each side of entrances), exposed aggregate on remainder, 1 pair average automatic doors per 20,000 S.F. of floor area, 6' canopy over glass area.	Stucco or exposed aggregate with a small amount of float glass in inexpensive aluminum frames (6'-10' high for 1/2 of width), 6' canopy at entrances, 6' ground level walk across front.
Exterior Finish (8% of total cost)	Large ornamental rock or brick veneer on exposed walls.	Exposed aggregate on exposed walls.	Paint, some exposed aggregate.	Paint.
Roof Cover (5% of total cost)	5 ply built-up roofing with large rock.	5 ply built-up roofing with tar and rock.	4 ply built-up roofing.	4 ply built-up roofing.
Plumbing (8% of total cost)	2 rest rooms with 8 fixtures each, floor piping and drains to refrigerated cases.	2 rest rooms with 6 fixtures each, floor piping and drains to refrigerated cases.	2 rest rooms with 4 fixtures each, floor piping and drains to refrigerated cases.	2 rest rooms with 2 fixtures each, floor piping and drains to refrigerated cases.
Electrical (5% of total cost)	Conduit wiring, recessed 4 tube fluorescent fixtures 8' o.c., 60-80 spotlights.	Conduit wiring, 4 tube fluorescent fixtures with diffusers 8' o.c., 60-80 spotlights.	Conduit wiring, 3 tube fluorescent fixtures 8' o.c., 20 to 40 spotlights.	Conduit wiring, double tube fluorescent fixtures, 8' o.c.

Note: Use the percent of total cost to help identify the correct quality classification.

Square foot costs include the following components: Foundations as required for normal soil conditions. Floor, wall, and roof structures. Interior floor, wall and ceiling finishes. Exterior wall finish and roof cover. Display fronts. Interior partitions. Entry and delivery doors. A canopy and walk across the front of the building as described in the applicable building specifications. Basic lighting and electrical systems. Rough and finish plumbing. Design and engineering fees. Permits and hook-up fees. Contractor's mark-up.

Discount Houses – Masonry or Concrete

Estimating Procedure

1. Establish the structure quality class by using the information on page 111.
2. Compute the building floor area. This should include everything within the building exterior walls and all insets outside the main walls but under the main building roof.
3. Add to or subtract from the square foot cost below the appropriate amount from the Wall Height Adjustment Row (at the bottom of this page) if the wall height is more or less than 20 feet.
4. Multiply the adjusted square foot cost by the building area.
5. Deduct, if appropriate, for common walls, using the figures at the bottom of this page.
6. Multiply the total cost by the location factor listed on page 7 or 8.
7. Add the cost of heating and cooling equipment, fire sprinklers, exterior signs, yard improvements, loading docks, ramps and walk-in boxes if they are an integral part of the building. See pages 236 to 248.

Discount House, Class 3

Discount House, Class 4

Square Foot Area

Quality Class	15,000	20,000	25,000	30,000	35,000	40,000	50,000	75,000	100,000	150,000	200,000
1, Best	90.75	87.64	85.54	83.97	82.72	81.71	80.20	77.80	76.40	74.64	73.57
1 & 2	85.28	82.42	80.42	78.94	77.75	76.85	75.41	73.10	71.76	70.20	69.22
2, Good	81.51	78.73	76.82	75.42	74.32	73.40	72.05	69.89	68.60	67.02	66.17
2 & 3	75.79	73.18	71.46	70.14	69.12	68.27	66.99	64.98	63.77	62.37	61.48
3, Average	71.33	68.94	67.27	66.00	65.05	64.26	63.07	61.18	60.06	58.71	57.86
3 & 4	65.22	62.98	61.48	60.33	59.44	58.72	57.59	55.89	54.87	53.65	52.88
4, Low	58.93	56.92	55.56	54.51	53.73	53.09	52.11	50.52	49.56	48.49	47.78
Wall Height Adjustment*	.93	.84	.67	.61	.58	.56	.52	.43	.41	.38	.37

*Wall Height Adjustment: Add or subtract the amount listed in this row to or from the square foot of floor cost for each foot of wall height more or less than 20 feet.

Perimeter Wall Adjustment: A common wall exists when two buildings share one wall. Adjust for common walls by deducting the linear foot costs below from the total structure cost. In some structures one or more walls are not owned at all. In this case, deduct the "No Ownership" cost per linear foot of wall not owned. For common wall, deduct $231 per linear foot. For no wall ownership, deduct $459 per linear foot.

Discount Houses – Wood or Wood and Steel Frame

Quality Classification

	Class 1 Best Quality	Class 2 Good Quality	Class 3 Average Quality	Class 4 Low Quality
Foundation (15% of total cost)	Reinforced concrete.	Reinforced concrete.	Reinforced concrete.	Reinforced concrete.
Floor Structure (12% of total cost)	4" reinforced concrete on 6" rock fill.	4" reinforced concrete on 6" rock fill.	4" reinforced concrete on 6" rock fill.	4" reinforced concrete on 6" rock fill.
Wall Structure (10% of total cost)	2" x 6" - 16" o.c.	2" x 6" - 16" o.c.	2" x 6" - 16" o.c.	2" x 4" - 16" o.c.
Roof Structure (10% of total cost)	Glu-lams or steel "I" beams on steel intermediate columns, plywood sheathing.	Glu-lams or steel "I" beams on steel intermediate columns, plywood sheathing.	Glu-lams, or steel "I" beams on steel intermediate columns, plywood sheathing.	Glu-lams, or steel "I" beams on steel intermediate columns, plywood sheathing.
Floor Finish (5% of total cost)	Terrazzo, sheet vinyl or good carpet in sales area.	Resilient tile in sales area with some terrazzo, solid vinyl tile or carpet.	Resilient tile in sales area.	Inexpensive composition tile in sales area.
Interior Wall Finish (5% of total cost)	Gypsum wallboard and vinyl wall cover or interior stucco on inside of walls and on partitions.	Gypsum wallboard, texture and paint or vinyl wall cover on inside of exterior walls and on partitions.	Gypsum wallboard, texture and paint on inside of exterior walls and on partitions.	Gypsum wallboard and paint on inside of exterior walls and on partitions.
Ceiling Finish (5% of total cost)	Suspended acoustical tile, dropped ceilings over some areas.	Suspended acoustical tile or gypsum board and acoustical texture, dropped ceilings in some areas.	Ceiling tile on roof purlins, dropped ceiling over some areas.	Open.
Front (10% of total cost)	A large amount of float glass in good aluminum frames (18'-22' high for 3/4 of width), brick or stone veneer on remainder, 1 pair good automatic doors 1 per 7,000 S.F. of floor area, anodized aluminum sunshade over glass area, 8' canopy across front, 10'-12' raised walk across front.	A large amount of float glass in good aluminum frames (16'-18' high for 2/3 of width), brick or stone veneer on remainder, 1 pair good automatic doors per 10,000 S.F. of floor area, 8' canopy across front, 10' raised walk across front.	A moderate amount of float glass in average quality aluminum frames (12'-16' high extending 20' on each side of entrances), exposed aggregate on remainder, 1 pair average automatic doors per 20,000 S.F. of floor area, 6' canopy over glass areas.	Stucco or exposed aggregate with a small amount of float glass in inexpensive aluminum frames (6'-10' high for 1/2 of width), 6' canopy at entrances, 6' ground level walk across front.
Exterior Finish (7% of total cost)	Good wood siding or masonry veneer.	Wood siding, some masonry veneer.	Stucco, some masonry trim.	Stucco.
Roof Cover (5% of total cost)	5 ply built-up roofing with large rock.	5 ply built-up roofing with tar and rock.	4 ply built-up roofing.	4 ply built-up roofing.
Plumbing (10% of total cost)	2 rest rooms with 8 fixtures each, floor piping and drains to refrigerated cases.	2 rest rooms with 6 fixtures each, floor piping and drains to refrigerated cases.	2 rest rooms with 4 fixtures each, floor piping and drains to refrigerated cases.	2 rest rooms with 2 fixtures each, floor piping and drains to refrigerated cases.
Electrical (6% of total cost)	Conduit wiring, recessed 4 tube fluorescent fixtures 8' o.c., 60-80 spotlights.	Conduit wiring, 4 tube fluorescent fixtures with diffusers 8' o.c., 60-80 spotlights.	Conduit wiring, 3 tube fluorescent fixtures 8' o.c., 20 to 40 spotlights.	Conduit wiring, double tube fluorescent fixtures, 8' o.c.

Note: Use the percent of total cost to help identify the correct quality classification.

Square foot costs include the following components: Foundations as required for normal soil conditions. Floor, wall, and roof structures. Interior floor, wall and ceiling finishes. Exterior wall finish and roof cover. Display fronts. Interior partitions. Entry and delivery doors. A canopy and walk across the front of the building as described in the applicable building specifications. Basic lighting and electrical systems. Rough and finish plumbing. Design and engineering fees. Permits and hook-up fees. Contractor's mark-up.

Discount Houses – Wood or Wood and Steel Frame

Estimating Procedure

1. Establish the structure quality class by using the information on page 113.
2. Compute the building floor area. This should include everything within the building exterior walls and all insets outside the main walls but under the main building roof.
3. Add to or subtract from the square foot cost below the appropriate amount from the Wall Height Adjustment Row at the bottom of this page) if the wall height is more or less than 20 feet.
4. Multiply the adjusted square foot cost by the building area.
5. Deduct, if appropriate, for common walls, using the figures at the bottom of this page.
6. Multiply the total cost by the location factor listed on page 7 or 8.
7. Add the cost of heating and cooling equipment, fire sprinklers, exterior signs, yard improvements, loading docks, ramps and walk-in boxes if they are an integral part of the building. See pages 236 to 248.

Discount House, Class 2

Discount House, Class 2 & 3

Square Foot Area

Quality Class	15,000	20,000	25,000	30,000	35,000	40,000	50,000	75,000	100,000	150,000	200,000
1, Best	91.76	89.47	87.92	86.81	85.89	85.17	84.07	82.34	81.32	80.09	79.33
1 & 2	86.49	84.34	82.89	81.81	80.98	80.26	79.24	77.60	76.67	75.50	74.81
2, Good	82.53	80.45	79.08	78.03	77.24	76.62	75.62	74.06	73.13	72.03	71.36
2 & 3	76.77	74.87	73.59	72.61	71.91	71.27	70.32	68.92	68.03	67.02	66.42
3, Average	72.16	70.43	69.24	68.28	67.57	67.03	66.15	64.78	63.97	63.03	62.45
3 & 4	65.98	64.34	63.23	62.43	61.72	61.26	60.44	59.21	58.48	57.60	57.09
4, Low	59.37	57.91	56.92	56.20	55.58	55.18	54.44	53.32	52.61	51.82	51.33
Wall Height Adjustment*	.54	.52	.47	.46	.43	.42	.41	.33	.31	.22	.21

*Wall Height Adjustment: Add or subtract the amount listed in this row to or from the square foot of floor cost for each foot of wall height more or less than 20 feet.

Perimeter Wall Adjustment: A common wall exists when two buildings share one wall. Adjust for common walls by deducting the linear foot costs below from the total structure cost. In some structures one or more walls are not owned at all. In this case, deduct the "No Ownership" cost per linear foot of wall not owned. For common wall, deduct $174 per linear foot. For no wall ownership, deduct $344 per linear foot.

Banks and Savings Offices – Masonry or Concrete

Quality Classification

	Class 1 Best Quality	Class 2 Good Quality	Class 3 High Average Quality	Class 4 Low Average Quality	Class 5 Low Quality
Foundation (11% of total cost)	Reinforced concrete.	Reinforced concrete.	Reinforced concrete.	Reinforced concrete.	Reinforced concrete.
Floor Structure (10% of total cost)	Reinforced concrete.	Reinforced concrete.	Reinforced concrete.	Reinforced concrete.	Reinforced concrete.
Wall Structure (10% of total cost)	12" reinforced brick, 8" reinforced concrete or concrete columns with noncombustible filler walls.	12" reinforced brick, 8" reinforced concrete or concrete columns with noncombustible filler walls.	6" concrete tilt-up, 12" reinforced brick, 8" reinforced con. or concrete columns with noncombustible filler walls.	8" decorative concrete block, 6" concrete tilt-up, 8" reinforced brick or concrete columns with noncombustible filler walls.	8" concrete block, 6" reinforced concrete, 6" concrete tilt-up or 8" reinforced brick.
Roof & Cover (7% of total cost)	5 ply built-up roof, some portions copper or slate.	5 ply built-up roof, some portions heavy shake or mission tile.	4 ply built-up roof, some portions heavy shake or mission tile.	4 ply built-up roof, some portions shake or composition shingles.	4 ply built-up roof.
Exterior Wall Finish (9% of total cost)	Expensive veneers.	Ornamental brick or stone veneer.	Brick, or ornamental block veneer.	Ornamental rock imbedded in tilt-up panels or stucco with masonry trim.	Exposed aggregate or stucco.
Interior Wall Finish (7% of total cost)	Ornamental plaster painted with murals or designs. Ornamental moldings, marble and similar expensive finishes.	Ornamental plaster furred out from walls. Ornamental moldings, some hardwood panels or marble finishes.	Hard plaster furred out from walls. Ornamental cove at ceiling. Vinyl wall covering. Some hardwood veneer.	Plaster on lath with putty coat finish. Gypsum wallboard, texture and paint. Some vinyl wall cover.	Plaster on lath with putty coat finish or gypsum wallboard, texture and paint.
Glass (5% of total cost)	Tinted float glass in customized frames, (50% of exterior wall area.)	Tinted float glass in bronze frames, (50% of exterior wall area).	Tinted float glass in heavy anodized aluminum frames or custom wood frames, (50% of exterior wall area).	Moderate amount of float glass in heavy frames, (25% of exterior wall area).	Small to moderate amount of float glass in average aluminum frames, (5 to 10% of exterior wall area).
Overhang (4% of total cost)	4' closed overhang with copper gutters.	4' closed overhang with copper gutters.	4' closed overhang with painted gutters.	3' closed overhang with painted gutters.	None.
Floor Finish Public Area: (7% of total cost)	Terrazzo and marble.	Detailed terrazzo.	Detailed terrazzo.	Plain terrazzo.	Sheet vinyl or vinyl tile.
Officers, Area: (3% of total cost)	Excellent carpet.	Very good carpet.	Very good carpet.	Good carpet.	Average quality carpet.
Work area: (2% of total cost)	Good sheet vinyl or carpet.	Average sheet vinyl, tile or carpet.	Resilient tile.	Resilient tile.	Composition tile.
Ceiling Finish (8% of total cost)	Ornamental plaster with exposed ornamental beams.	Ornamental plaster.	Suspended acoustical tile with gypsum wallboard backing or acoustical plaster.	Suspended acoustical tile with exposed grid system.	Acoustical tile on wood furring.
Lighting (5% of total cost)	Recessed panelized fluorescent lighting ,custom light fixtures or chandeliers, and many spotlights.	Recessed panelized fluorescent lighting. Many spotlights.	Recessed panelized fluorescent lighting. Many spotlights.	Recessed panelized fluorescent lighting. Some spotlights.	Nonrecessed panelized lighting.
Plumbing (12% of total cost)	2 or more rest rooms with special fixtures, good ceramic tile, marble or terrazzo wainscot walls. Hard plaster with putty coat and enamel paint. Marble toilet screens.	2 or more rest rooms with many good fixtures, good ceramic tile, marble or terrazzo wainscot walls. Hard plaster with putty coat and enamel paint. Marble toilet screens.	2 rest rooms with 4 or more fixtures, ceramic tile or terrazzo floors. Ceramic tile or terrazzo wainscot. Hard plaster walls with putty coat and enamel paint. Marble or metal toilet screens.	2 rest rooms with 4 or more fixtures each. Ceramic tile or terrazzo floor. Ceramic tile or terrazzo wainscot plaster walls with putty coat. Enamel paint. Good metal toilet partitions.	2 rest rooms with 4 fixtures each. Ceramic tile or vinyl asbestos tile floors. Plaster walls with enamel paint. Metal toilet screens.

Note: Use the percent of total cost to help identify the correct quality classification.

Square foot costs include the following components: Foundations as required for normal soil conditions. Floor, wall, and roof structures. Interior floor, wall and ceiling finishes. Exterior wall finish and roof cover. All glass and glazing. Interior partitions. Roof overhang as described above. Basic electrical systems and lighting fixtures. Rough and finish plumbing. Typical bank vault. Alarm systems. Night depository. Typical record vault and fire doors. Fire exits. Design and engineering fees. Permits and hook-up fees. Contractor's mark-up.

Length Less Than Twice Width

Estimating Procedure

1. Establish the structure quality class by using the information on page 115.
2. Compute the building floor area. This should include everything within the building exterior walls and all insets outside the main walls but under the main building roof.
3. Add to or subtract from the square foot cost below the appropriate amount from the Wall Height Adjustment Table on page 119 if the wall height is more or less than 16 feet for the first floor or 12 feet for higher floors.
4. Multiply the adjusted square foot cost by the building area.
5. Deduct, if appropriate, for common walls, using the figures on page 119.
6. Multiply the total cost by the location factor listed on page 7 or 8.
7. Add the cost of heating and cooling equipment, fire sprinklers, exterior signs, elevators, and yard improvements from pages 236 to 248. Add the cost of mezzanines, bank fixtures, external windows, safe deposit boxes and vault doors from page 125.

Savings Office, Class 3

First Story - Square Foot Area

Quality Class	2,500	3,000	3,500	4,000	4,500	5,000	6,000	7,500	10,000	15,000	20,000
1, Best	349.39	338.65	329.26	320.97	313.65	307.16	296.07	282.87	266.79	246.14	233.01
1 & 2	328.86	318.73	309.90	302.05	295.20	289.10	278.65	266.24	251.09	231.62	219.30
2, Very Good	312.56	302.97	294.54	287.15	280.62	274.78	264.85	253.09	238.67	220.22	208.48
2 & 3	292.55	283.51	275.69	268.75	262.64	257.22	247.92	236.86	223.38	206.12	195.10
3, Good	277.65	269.13	261.69	255.15	249.28	244.16	235.35	224.96	212.03	195.59	185.17
3 & 4	261.83	253.82	246.77	240.59	235.09	230.26	221.87	212.05	199.96	184.49	174.64
4, Average	249.29	241.64	234.90	229.00	223.82	219.17	211.28	201.83	190.33	175.65	166.25
4 & 5	230.21	223.15	216.94	211.48	206.65	202.34	195.04	186.35	175.78	162.19	153.51
5, Low	209.75	203.30	197.65	192.69	188.34	184.40	177.77	169.83	160.24	147.78	139.91

Second and Higher Stories - Square Foot Area

Quality Class	500	750	1,000	1,500	2,000	3,000	4,000	5,000	7,500	10,000	20,000
1, Best	284.84	255.18	237.63	217.04	204.79	190.34	181.80	176.02	166.96	161.62	151.52
1 & 2	269.35	241.25	224.68	205.16	193.62	179.95	171.89	166.42	157.86	152.77	143.26
2, Very Good	258.61	231.63	215.71	196.99	185.94	172.84	165.10	159.81	151.61	146.74	137.60
2 & 3	243.60	218.21	203.22	185.60	175.15	162.78	155.47	150.52	142.82	138.24	129.58
3, Good	233.19	208.90	194.52	177.63	167.66	155.83	148.83	144.10	136.71	132.30	124.04
3 & 4	219.94	197.02	183.48	167.56	158.08	146.97	140.38	135.89	128.92	124.81	116.96
4, Average	209.69	187.84	174.94	159.76	150.75	140.15	133.85	129.56	122.88	119.00	111.52
4 & 5	197.83	177.27	165.05	150.75	142.28	132.20	126.28	122.21	115.93	112.26	105.23
5, Low	184.75	165.50	154.16	140.75	132.85	123.45	117.90	114.15	108.29	104.81	98.26

Banks and Savings Offices – Masonry or Concrete

Length Between 2 and 4 Times Width

Estimating Procedure

1. Establish the structure quality class by using the information on page 115.
2. Compute the building floor area. This should include everything within the building exterior walls and all insets outside the main walls but under the main building roof.
3. Add to or subtract from the square foot cost below the appropriate amount from the Wall Height Adjustment Table on page 119 if the wall height is more or less than 16 feet for the first floor or 12 feet for higher floors.
4. Multiply the adjusted square foot cost by the building area.
5. Deduct, if appropriate, for common walls, using the figures on page 119.
6. Multiply the total cost by the location factor listed on page 7 or 8.
7. Add the cost of heating and cooling equipment, fire sprinklers, exterior signs, elevators, and yard improvements from pages 236 to 248. Add the cost of mezzanines, bank fixtures, external windows, safe deposit boxes and vault doors from page 125.

Savings Office, Class 4

First Story - Square Foot Area At 16 Foot Wall Height

Quality Class	2,500	3,000	3,500	4,000	4,500	5,000	6,000	7,500	10,000	15,000	20,000
1, Best	372.29	353.08	338.65	327.45	318.33	310.84	299.07	286.55	272.89	257.53	248.80
1 & 2	351.58	333.14	319.35	308.57	299.89	292.60	281.37	269.42	256.30	241.54	233.14
2, Very Good	335.64	317.70	304.28	293.76	285.28	278.28	267.34	255.67	243.00	228.71	220.58
2 & 3	315.22	297.76	284.76	274.68	266.58	259.91	249.52	238.52	226.72	213.55	206.21
3, Good	299.99	283.54	271.27	261.69	253.96	247.52	237.54	226.81	215.20	202.16	194.77
3 & 4	282.38	266.83	255.28	246.25	238.98	232.97	223.55	213.56	202.78	190.65	183.75
4, Average	268.35	253.52	242.48	233.90	226.95	221.27	212.43	203.00	192.82	181.52	175.15
4 & 5	247.04	233.38	223.22	215.35	209.07	203.84	195.76	187.19	177.98	167.81	162.13
5, Low	224.19	211.84	202.71	195.65	189.94	185.29	178.03	170.42	162.23	153.22	148.19

Second and Higher Stories - Square Foot Area

Quality Class	500	750	1,000	1,500	2,000	3,000	4,000	5,000	7,500	10,000	20,000
1, Best	304.74	272.32	252.93	229.76	215.97	199.53	189.69	182.98	172.54	166.26	154.43
1 & 2	288.67	257.97	239.58	217.69	204.59	188.97	179.65	173.32	163.43	157.49	146.29
2, Very Good	277.08	247.58	229.92	208.93	196.37	181.40	172.48	166.31	156.85	151.18	140.42
2 & 3	260.54	232.84	216.23	196.46	184.64	170.58	162.19	156.42	147.49	142.16	132.02
3, Good	247.61	221.30	205.54	186.74	175.52	162.14	154.17	148.69	140.20	135.13	125.51
3 & 4	234.33	209.38	194.46	176.72	166.09	153.41	145.85	140.72	132.63	127.84	118.74
4, Average	223.38	199.65	185.44	168.47	158.32	146.26	139.08	134.15	126.47	121.92	113.23
4 & 5	210.42	188.05	174.63	158.64	149.11	137.75	130.98	126.33	119.18	114.78	106.64
5, Low	196.37	175.43	162.97	148.08	139.15	128.54	122.21	117.89	111.19	107.12	99.51

Length More Than 4 Times Width

Estimating Procedure

1. Establish the structure quality class by using the information on page 115.
2. Compute the building floor area. This should include everything within the building exterior walls and all insets outside the main walls but under the main building roof.
3. Add to or subtract from the square foot cost below the appropriate amount from the Wall Height Adjustment Table on page 119 if the wall height is more or less than 16 feet for the first floor or 12 feet for higher floors.
4. Multiply the adjusted square foot cost by the building area.
5. Deduct, if appropriate, for common walls, using the figures on page 119.
6. Multiply the total cost by the location factor listed on page 7 or 8.
7. Add the cost of heating and cooling equipment, fire sprinklers, exterior signs, elevators, and yard improvements from pages 236 to 248. Add the cost of mezzanines, bank fixtures, external windows, safe deposit boxes and vault doors from page 125.

Bank, Class 5

First Story - Square Foot Area

Quality Class	2,500	3,000	3,500	4,000	4,500	5,000	6,000	7,500	10,000	15,000	20,000
1, Best	397.68	374.53	357.39	344.09	333.40	324.54	310.90	296.46	280.90	263.67	253.96
1 & 2	374.49	352.68	336.55	324.05	313.97	305.67	292.76	279.18	264.54	248.31	239.17
2, Very Good	355.91	335.23	319.87	307.92	298.40	290.50	278.24	265.32	251.43	235.99	227.32
2 & 3	333.81	314.37	299.99	288.82	279.83	272.45	260.96	248.84	235.77	221.30	213.19
3, Good	317.10	298.67	284.96	274.38	265.87	258.82	247.92	236.39	223.99	210.19	202.51
3 & 4	298.15	280.78	267.93	257.96	249.92	243.33	233.10	222.27	210.56	197.67	190.37
4, Average	282.72	266.32	254.12	244.62	237.03	230.79	221.05	210.75	199.69	187.44	180.55
4 & 5	260.16	245.02	233.83	225.11	218.10	212.36	203.39	193.92	183.75	172.48	166.16
5, Low	235.71	222.03	211.85	204.00	197.64	192.42	184.31	175.75	166.54	156.31	150.58

Second and Higher Stories - Square Foot Area

Quality Class	500	750	1,000	1,500	2,000	3,000	4,000	5,000	7,500	10,000	20,000
1, Best	337.24	298.46	275.43	248.12	231.83	212.57	201.11	193.29	181.12	173.89	160.21
1 & 2	319.26	282.51	260.73	234.87	219.44	201.24	190.35	182.97	171.46	164.60	151.64
2, Very Good	305.47	270.33	249.48	224.73	210.02	192.57	182.16	175.11	164.07	157.49	145.12
2 & 3	286.86	253.85	234.24	211.02	197.20	180.81	171.05	164.42	154.07	147.88	136.24
3, Good	273.44	242.01	223.27	201.12	187.95	172.37	163.05	156.70	146.81	140.95	129.82
3 & 4	257.08	227.48	209.93	189.15	176.74	162.04	153.33	147.33	138.08	132.54	122.14
4, Average	243.85	215.81	199.15	179.42	167.60	153.72	145.44	139.77	131.00	125.76	115.83
4 & 5	229.76	203.32	187.57	168.99	157.90	144.80	136.96	131.64	123.38	118.45	109.10
5, Low	214.28	189.63	174.97	157.63	147.30	135.08	127.72	122.81	115.06	110.49	101.82

Banks and Savings Offices – Masonry or Concrete

Wall Adjustments

Wall Height Adjustment

Add or subtract the amount listed in this table to the square foot of floor cost for each foot of wall height more or less than 16 feet, if adjusting for a first floor, and 12 feet if adjusting for upper floors.

Square Foot Area

Quality Class	500	750	1,000	1,500	2,000	2,500	3,000	3,500
1, Best	13.79	11.30	9.85	8.03	9.98	6.27	5.70	5.29
2, Very Good	12.43	10.19	8.88	7.30	6.29	5.65	5.15	4.78
3, Good	11.15	9.13	7.95	6.50	5.64	5.06	4.62	4.25
4, Average	9.32	7.64	6.63	5.45	4.72	4.21	3.88	3.57
5, Low	7.37	6.07	5.25	4.29	3.75	3.38	3.03	2.82

Quality Class	4,000	4,500	5,000	6,000	7,500	10,000	15,000	20,000
1, Best	4.97	4.66	4.44	4.06	3.61	3.12	2.51	2.15
2, Very Good	4.44	4.20	3.99	3.62	3.24	2.82	2.27	1.95
3, Good	4.05	3.75	3.58	3.28	2.91	2.50	2.06	1.75
4, Average	3.37	3.11	2.99	2.71	2.43	2.10	1.70	1.48
5, Low	2.65	2.47	2.33	2.14	1.89	1.63	1.31	1.14

Perimeter (Common) Wall Adjustment

First Story

Class	For a Common Wall, Deduct Per L.F.	For No Wall Ownership, Deduct Per L.F.	For Lack of Exterior Finish, Deduct Per L.F.
1	$795	$1,592	$541
2	666	1,320	436
3	548	1,096	300
4	331	674	204
5	270	551	57

Second and Higher Stories

Class	For a Common Wall, Deduct Per L.F.	For No Wall Ownership, Deduct Per L.F.	For Lack of Exterior Finish, Deduct per L.F.
1	$477	$1,302	$265
2	400	773	200
3	317	636	129
4	270	539	89
5	200	381	61

Note: First floor costs include the cost of overhang as described on page 115. Second floor costs do not include any allowance for overhang.

Quality Classification

	Class 1 Best Quality	Class 2 Good Quality	Class 3 High Average Quality	Class 4 Low Average Quality	Class 5 Low Quality
Foundation (10% of total cost)	Reinforced concrete.	Reinforced concrete.	Reinforced concrete.	Reinforced concrete.	Reinforced concrete.
Floor Structure (10% of total cost)	Reinforced concrete.	Reinforced concrete.	Reinforced concrete.	Reinforced concrete.	Reinforced concrete.
Wall Structure (10% of total cost)	2" x 6" - 16" o.c. brick or concrete columns with combustible filler walls.	2" x 6" - 16" o.c. brick or concrete columns with combustible filler walls.	2" x 6" - 16" o.c.	2" x 6" - 16" o.c.	2" x 6" - 16" o.c.
Roof & Cover (10% of total cost)	Copper or slate.	Mission tile or heavy shakes.	5 ply built-up roof. Some portions heavy shake or mission tile.	4 ply built-up roof. Some portions shingle or composition shingles.	4 ply built-up roof.
Exterior Wall Finish (7% of total cost)	Expensive veneers.	Expensive ornamental veneer filler walls.	Wood siding combined with brick or stone veneers.	Good wood siding.	Good stucco or wood siding.
Interior Wall Finish (7% of total cost)	Ornamental plaster painted with murals or designs, ornamental moldings, marble and similar expensive finishes.	Ornamental plaster ornamental moldings, some hardwood panels or marble finishes.	Hard plaster, ornamental cove at ceiling, vinyl wall covering, some hardwood veneer.	Plaster on lath with putty coat finish. Gypsum wallboard, texture and paint. Some vinyl wall cover.	Plaster on lath with putty coat finish. Gypsum wallboard, texture and paint.
Glass (5% of total cost)	Tinted float glass in customized frames (50% of exterior wall area).	Tinted float glass in bronze frames (50% of exterior wall area).	Tinted float glass in heavy anodized aluminum frames or custom wood frames (50% of exterior wall area).	Moderate amount of float glass in heavy frames (25% of exterior wall area).	Small to moderate amount of float glass in average aluminum frames (5 to 10% of exterior wall area).
Overhang (4% of total cost)	4' closed overhang with copper gutters.	4' closed overhang with copper gutters.	4' closed overhang with painted gutters.	3' closed overhang with painted gutters.	None.
Floor Finish Public Area: (7% of total cost)	Terrazzo and marble.	Detailed terrazzo.	Detailed terrazzo.	Plain terrazzo.	Sheet vinyl or resilient tile.
Officers Area: (3% of total cost)	Excellent carpet.	Very good carpet.	Very good carpet.	Good carpet.	Average quality carpet.
Work Area: (2% of total cost)	Good sheet vinyl or carpet.	Average sheet vinyl or carpet.	Resilient tile.	Composition tile.	Composition tile.
Ceiling Finish (8% of total cost)	Ornamental plaster with exposed ornamental beams.	Ornamental plaster.	Suspended acoustical tile with gypsum wallboard backing or plain acoustical plaster.	Suspended acoustical tile with exposed grid system.	Acoustical tile on wood strips.
Lighting (5% of total cost)	Recessed panelized fluorescent light fixtures, custom light fixtures or chandeliers. Many spotlights.	Recessed panelized fluorescent lighting. Custom chandeliers. Many spotlights.	Recessed panelized fluorescent lighting. Many spotlights.	Recessed panelized fluorescent lighting. Some spotlights.	Nonrecessed panelized lighting.
Plumbing (12% of total cost)	2 or more rest rooms with special fixtures. Good ceramic tile, marble or terrazzo wainscot walls. Hard plaster with putty coat and enamel paint. Marble toilet screens. toilet screens.	2 or more rest rooms with many good fixtures. Good ceramic tile, marble or terrazzo wainscot walls. Hard plaster with putty coat and enamel paint. Marble screens.	2 rest rooms with 4 or more fixtures. Ceramic tile or terrazzo wainscot, hard plaster walls with putty coat and enamel paint. Marble or metal toilet screens.	2 rest rooms with 4 or more fixtures each. Ceramic tile or terrazzo floor. Ceramic tile or terrazzo wainscot plaster walls with putty coat. Enamel paint. Good metal toilet partitions.	2 rest rooms with 4 fixtures each. Metal toilet screens. Ceramic tile or vinyl asbestos tile floors. Plaster walls with enamel paint.

Note: Use the percent of total cost to help identify the correct quality classification.

Square foot costs include the following components: Foundations as required for normal soil conditions. Floor, wall, and roof structures. Interior floor, wall and ceiling finishes. Exterior wall finish and roof cover. All glass and glazing. Interior partitions. Roof overhang as described above. Basic electrical systems and lighting fixtures. Rough and finish plumbing. Typical bank vault. Alarm systems. Night depository. Typical record vault and fire doors. Fire exits. Design and engineering fees, permits and hook-up fees, contractor's mark-up.

Banks and Savings Offices – Wood Frame

Length Less Than Twice Width

Estimating Procedure

1. Establish the structure quality class by using the information on page 120.
2. Compute the building floor area. This should include everything within the building exterior walls and all insets outside the main walls but under the main building roof.
3. Add to or subtract from the square foot cost below the appropriate amount from the Wall Height Adjustment Table on page 124 if the wall height is more or less than 16 feet for the first floor or 12 feet for higher floors.
4. Multiply the adjusted square foot cost by the building area.
5. Deduct, if appropriate, for common walls, using the figures on page 124.
6. Multiply the total cost by the location factor listed on page 7 or 8.
7. Add the cost of heating and cooling equipment, fire sprinklers, exterior signs, elevators, and yard improvements from pages 236 to 248. Add the cost of mezzanines, bank fixtures, external windows, safe deposit boxes and vault doors from page 125.

Savings Office, Class 5

First Story - Square Foot Area

Quality Class	2,500	3,000	3,500	4,000	4,500	5,000	6,000	7,500	10,000	15,000	20,000
1, Best	359.18	339.65	325.49	314.74	306.21	299.36	288.83	278.08	266.93	255.20	248.91
1 & 2	338.93	320.52	307.15	297.02	289.03	282.50	272.60	262.43	251.92	240.79	234.89
2, Very Good	319.96	302.50	289.92	280.30	272.74	266.59	257.25	247.69	237.73	227.24	221.71
2 & 3	286.55	270.99	259.68	251.14	244.30	238.85	230.48	221.89	212.95	203.61	198.62
3, Good	282.69	267.38	256.24	247.77	241.07	235.64	227.38	218.92	210.11	200.88	195.93
3 & 4	263.42	249.11	238.71	230.82	224.56	219.52	211.84	203.99	195.75	187.16	182.57
4, Average	247.77	234.30	224.54	217.17	211.28	206.60	199.32	191.87	184.15	176.01	171.76
4 & 5	226.92	214.64	205.70	198.87	193.51	189.14	182.52	175.72	168.64	161.22	157.29
5, Low	205.23	194.08	186.00	179.85	175.01	171.06	165.07	158.90	152.55	145.80	142.23

Second and Higher Stories - Square Foot Area

Quality Class	500	750	1,000	1,500	2,000	3,000	4,000	5,000	7,500	10,000	20,000
1, Best	247.74	224.79	211.11	194.91	185.19	173.74	166.89	162.26	154.95	150.61	142.42
1 & 2	230.99	210.37	198.12	183.67	175.05	164.84	158.76	154.64	148.21	144.45	137.17
2, Very Good	218.35	199.57	188.41	175.17	167.35	157.99	152.46	148.67	142.80	139.29	132.68
2 & 3	201.74	185.09	175.18	163.54	156.60	148.37	143.47	140.14	134.93	131.87	126.01
3, Good	187.64	173.09	164.44	154.19	148.06	140.78	136.50	133.61	128.99	126.26	121.10
3 & 4	172.92	159.96	152.32	143.31	137.94	131.56	127.77	125.23	121.26	118.88	114.38
4, Average	160.02	148.94	142.27	134.44	129.78	124.22	120.87	118.64	115.16	113.06	109.10
4 & 5	148.09	138.41	132.68	125.78	121.73	116.95	114.07	112.15	109.09	107.29	103.94
5, Low	138.75	128.82	123.22	116.95	113.36	109.31	106.96	105.38	102.99	101.59	99.06

Length Between 2 and 4 Times Width

Estimating Procedure

1. Establish the structure quality class by using the information on page 120.
2. Compute the building floor area. This should include everything within the building exterior walls and all insets outside the main walls but under the main building roof.
3. Add to or subtract from the square foot cost below the appropriate amount from the Wall Height Adjustment Table on page 124 if the wall height is more or less than 16 feet for the first floor or 12 feet for higher floors.
4. Multiply the adjusted square foot cost by the building area.
5. Deduct, if appropriate, for common walls, using the figures on page 124.
6. Multiply the total cost by the location factor listed on page 7 or 8.
7. Add the cost of heating and cooling equipment, fire sprinklers, exterior signs, elevators, and yard improvements from pages 236 to 248. Add the cost of mezzanines, bank fixtures, external windows, safe deposit boxes and vault doors from page 125.

Bank, Class 4

First Story - Square Foot Area

Quality Class	2,500	3,000	3,500	4,000	4,500	5,000	6,000	7,500	10,000	15,000	20,000
1, Best	368.41	349.40	335.32	324.41	315.70	308.50	297.38	285.56	272.96	259.11	251.37
1 & 2	347.76	329.88	316.56	306.26	297.97	291.24	280.71	269.61	257.71	244.64	237.21
2, Very Good	329.89	312.85	300.27	290.45	282.65	276.24	266.28	255.73	244.46	231.98	225.02
2 & 3	307.76	291.83	280.11	271.01	263.73	257.68	248.41	238.60	228.05	216.44	210.00
3, Good	290.24	275.27	264.19	255.58	248.70	243.04	234.25	225.01	215.09	204.13	198.02
3 & 4	269.28	255.33	245.03	237.11	230.70	225.47	217.32	208.70	199.53	189.36	183.70
4, Average	252.86	239.78	230.15	222.59	216.64	211.72	204.05	196.01	187.32	177.85	172.50
4 & 5	230.87	218.97	210.14	203.32	197.80	193.34	186.35	178.98	171.01	162.35	157.52
5, Low	208.55	197.77	189.77	183.60	178.67	174.62	168.32	161.63	154.49	146.64	142.23

Second and Higher Stories - Square Foot Area

Quality Class	500	750	1,000	1,500	2,000	3,000	4,000	5,000	7,500	10,000	20,000
1, Best	250.24	229.12	216.58	201.71	192.80	182.28	176.06	171.77	165.16	161.19	153.68
1 & 2	237.01	217.00	205.10	191.02	182.62	172.68	166.74	162.70	156.44	152.64	145.59
2, Very Good	225.59	206.65	195.24	181.85	173.86	164.35	158.71	154.87	148.91	145.32	138.55
2 & 3	210.84	193.11	182.45	169.96	162.54	153.62	148.37	144.76	139.20	135.81	129.52
3, Good	198.89	182.14	172.16	160.32	153.32	144.92	139.91	136.52	131.29	128.15	122.16
3 & 4	184.94	169.32	160.04	149.12	142.58	134.79	130.11	126.97	122.05	119.11	113.57
4, Average	173.77	159.14	150.42	140.13	133.89	126.65	122.27	119.30	114.70	111.96	106.72
4 & 5	162.90	149.18	140.97	131.31	125.55	118.73	114.63	111.85	107.49	104.93	100.07
5, Low	151.81	139.01	131.39	122.38	117.00	110.64	106.82	104.21	100.22	97.79	93.26

Banks and Savings Offices – Wood Frame

Length More Than 4 Times Width

Estimating Procedure

1. Establish the structure quality class by using the information on page 120.
2. Compute the building floor area. This should include everything within the building exterior walls and all insets outside the main walls but under the main building roof.
3. Add to or subtract from the square foot cost below the appropriate amount from the Wall Height Adjustment Table on page 124 if the wall height is more or less than 16 feet for the first floor or 12 feet for higher floors.
4. Multiply the adjusted square foot cost by the building area.
5. Deduct, if appropriate, for common walls, using the figures on page 124.
6. Multiply the total cost by the location factor listed on page 7 or 8.
7. Add the cost of heating and cooling equipment, fire sprinklers, exterior signs, elevators, and yard improvements from pages 236 to 248. Add the cost of mezzanines, bank fixtures, external windows, safe deposit boxes and vault doors from page 125.

Bank, Class 4 & 5

First Story - Square Foot Area

Quality Class	2,500	3,000	3,500	4,000	4,500	5,000	6,000	7,500	10,000	15,000	20,000
1, Best	387.04	365.81	350.10	337.94	328.31	320.33	308.02	295.08	281.33	266.21	257.80
1 & 2	365.46	345.36	330.49	319.04	309.92	302.41	290.78	278.60	265.62	251.31	243.40
2, Very Good	346.39	327.40	313.30	302.41	293.76	286.69	275.63	264.08	251.74	238.20	230.68
2 & 3	323.88	306.03	292.95	282.76	274.65	268.04	257.69	246.92	235.41	222.74	215.75
3, Good	305.20	288.41	276.05	266.47	258.85	252.57	242.89	232.67	221.81	209.87	203.27
3 & 4	282.91	267.36	255.91	247.02	239.93	234.12	225.12	215.68	205.61	194.53	188.36
4, Average	264.22	249.70	239.00	230.68	224.08	218.64	210.26	201.43	192.03	181.71	175.98
4 & 5	240.33	227.15	217.38	209.85	203.85	198.88	191.24	183.24	174.67	165.32	160.04
5, Low	216.04	204.15	195.40	188.64	183.21	178.78	171.90	164.68	156.97	148.54	143.87

Second and Higher Stories - Square Foot Area

Quality Class	500	750	1,000	1,500	2,000	3,000	4,000	5,000	7,500	10,000	20,000
1, Best	287.49	257.11	239.01	217.56	204.83	189.74	180.76	174.63	165.11	159.43	148.68
1 & 2	268.11	240.57	224.23	204.84	193.34	179.68	171.54	165.99	157.36	152.26	142.59
2, Very Good	250.70	225.90	211.19	193.75	183.40	171.11	163.79	158.79	151.09	146.50	137.78
2 & 3	230.27	208.43	195.41	180.03	170.84	160.02	153.56	149.18	142.32	138.23	130.57
3, Good	212.68	193.50	182.10	168.63	160.54	151.03	145.36	141.44	135.45	131.88	125.09
3 & 4	194.84	177.96	167.88	156.00	149.00	140.58	135.60	132.17	126.92	123.78	117.82
4, Average	179.33	164.55	155.75	145.40	139.20	131.91	127.57	124.59	120.04	117.29	112.18
4 & 5	164.72	151.91	144.34	135.30	129.99	123.70	119.95	117.32	113.39	111.01	106.55
5, Low	150.04	139.22	132.79	125.17	120.65	115.36	112.20	110.03	106.69	104.68	100.93

Wall Adjustments

Wall Height Adjustment

Add or subtract the amount listed in this table to or from the square foot of floor cost for each foot of wall height more or less than 16 feet, if adjusting for first floor, and 12 feet if adjusting for upper floors.

Square Foot Area

Quality Class	500	750	1,000	1,500	2,000	2,500	3,000	3,500
1, Best	12.04	9.91	8.59	7.07	6.09	5.47	4.99	4.67
2, Very Good	10.86	8.93	7.76	6.34	5.52	4.97	4.51	4.23
3, Good	9.65	7.94	6.88	5.61	4.87	4.34	4.06	3.69
4, Average	6.55	5.40	4.71	3.87	3.35	3.01	2.78	2.50
5, Low	4.33	3.52	3.11	2.52	2.25	1.96	1.79	1.66

Square Foot Area

Quality Class	4,000	4,500	5,000	6,000	7,500	10,000	15,000	20,000
1, Best	4.54	4.20	3.92	3.49	3.12	2.66	2.28	2.00
2, Very Good	4.09	3.76	3.52	3.14	2.78	2.40	1.97	1.79
3, Good	3.58	3.33	3.10	2.81	2.43	2.12	1.79	1.59
4, Average	2.44	2.32	2.17	1.93	1.68	1.47	1.27	1.12
5, Low	1.66	1.56	1.48	1.30	1.12	.96	.81	.71

Perimeter (Common) Wall Adjustment

First Story

Class	For a Common Wall, Deduct Per L.F.	For No Wall Ownership, Deduct Per L.F.	For Lack of Exterior Finish, Deduct Per L.F.
1	$570	$1,121	$553
2	493	955	477
3	394	806	328
4	290	575	232
5	133	272	81

Second and Higher Stories

Class	For a Common Wall, Deduct Per L.F.	For No Wall Ownership, Deduct Per L.F.	For Lack of Exterior Finish, Deduct Per L.F.
1	$347	$711	$315
2	296	575	233
3	246	477	153
4	153	304	106
5	106	216	55

Note: First floor costs include the cost of overhang as described on page 120. Second floor costs do not include any allowance for overhang.

Banks and Savings Offices Additional Costs

Mezzanines Without Partitions

Quality Class	1, Best	2, Good	3, High Avg.	4, Low Avg.	5, Low
S.F. Cost	$91.06	$88.42	$76.43	$70.66	$63.84

With Partitions

Quality Class	1, Best	2, Good	3, High Avg.	4, Low Avg.	5, Low
S.F. Cost	$119.96	$109.58	$97.60	$91.06	$79.68

Mezzanine costs include: Floor system, floor finish, typical stairway, lighting and structural support costs.

Fixtures, cost per square foot of floor

Shell-type counters, plastic finish, no counter screens or drawers.	$24.44 to $27.66
Counters with drawers, good hardwood, plain counter screens.	28.70 to 39.31
Counters with drawers, good hardwood, plastic countertops, average counter screens.	39.31 to 57.82
Counters with drawers, terrazzo or marble finish, marble counter tops, fancy counter screens.	57.82 to 96.93

Costs include counters, screens, and partitions. The square-foot cost should be applied only to the first floor area. Office areas used for purposes other than conducting bank business related to the immediate site should be excluded.

External Access Facilities, cost each unit

Drive-up teller, flush window	$12,900 to $17.600
Drive-up teller, projected window	15,470 to 23,260
Walk-up teller, flush window	8,100 to 9,500
Automatic teller, cash dispensing, with phone	63,850 to 76,520
Night deposit vault whole chest	14,480 to 15,570

Safe Deposit Boxes, cost per box

Box Sizes	Modular Unit		Custom Built	
3" x 5"	$109 to	$129	$172 to	$184
5" x 5"	136 to	141	176 to	226
3" x 10"	119 to	152	202 to	237
5" x 10"	156 to	182	250 to	299
10" x 10"	220 to	252	332 to	426

Bank fixtures and safe deposit boxes are part of the structure cost only if they are fixed to the building.

Vault Doors Record Storage

Description	3' x 7', 2 hour	3' x 7', 4 hour	4' x 7', 2 hour	4' x 7', 4 hour
In Place Cost	$4,595	$5,150	$6,970	$7,440

Prices include frames, time locks, and architrave.

Department Stores – Reinforced Concrete

Quality Classification

	Class 1 Best Quality	Class 2 Good Quality	Class 3 Average Quality	Class 4 Low Quality
Foundation (17% of total cost)	Reinforced concrete.	Reinforced concrete.	Reinforced concrete.	Reinforced concrete.
Ground Floor Structure (10% of total cost)	6" reinforced concrete on 6" rock base.	6" reinforced concrete on 6" rock base.	6" reinforced concrete on 6" rock base.	4" reinforced concrete on 6" rock base.
Wall Structure (10% of total cost)	Reinforced concrete.	Reinforced concrete.	Reinforced concrete.	Reinforced concrete.
Upper Floor Structure (12% of total cost)	Reinforced concrete.	Reinforced concrete.	Reinforced concrete.	Reinforced concrete.
Roof & Cover (10% of total cost)	Reinforced concrete with 5 ply built-up roofing and insulation.	Reinforced concrete with 5 ply built-up roofing and insulation.	Reinforced concrete with 4 ply built-up roofing.	Reinforced concrete with 4 ply built-up roofing.
Floor Finish (5% of total cost)	Terrazzo and very good carpet.	Resilient tile with 50% vinyl tile, terrazzo or good carpet.	Composition tile.	Minimum grade tile.
Interior Wall Finish (5% of total cost)	Gypsum wallboard or lath and plaster finished with good paper or vinyl wall cover on hardwood veneer paneling.	Gypsum wallboard and texture or paper. Some vinyl wall cover or hardwood veneer paneling.	Interior stucco or gypsum wallboard, texture and paint.	Gypsum wallboard, texture and paint.
Ceiling Finish (5% of total cost)	Suspended good grade acoustical tile with gypsum wallboard backing.	Suspended acoustical tile with concealed grid system.	Suspended acoustical tile with exposed grid system.	Painted.
Lighting (6% of total cost)	Recessed fluorescent lighting in modular plastic panels. Many spotlights.	Continuous recessed 3 tube fluorescent strips with egg crate diffusers 8' o.c. Average number of spotlights.	Continuous 3 tube fluorescent strips with egg crate diffusers, 8' o.c. Some spotlights.	Continuous exposed 2 tube fluorescent strips, 8' o.c.
Display Fronts (6% of total cost)	Best quality front as described on page 77. 15 to 25% of the first floor exterior wall is made up of display fronts.	Good quality front as described on page 77. 15 to 25% of the first floor exterior wall is made up of display fronts.	Average quality front as described on page 77. 10 to 20% of the first floor exterior wall is made up of display fronts.	Low quality flat type as described on page 77. 10 to 20% of the first floor exterior wall is made up of display fronts.
Exterior Wall Finish (8% of total cost)	Ornamental block or brick, some marble veneer.	Decorative block, some stone veneer.	Paint.	Paint.
Plumbing (6% of total cost)	6 good fixtures per 20,000 square feet of floor area. Metal toilet partitions.	6 standard fixtures per 20,000 square feet of floor area. Metal toilet partitions.	4 standard fixtures per 20,000 square feet of floor area. Metal toilet partitions.	4 standard fixtures per 20,000 square feet of floor area. Wood toilet partitions.

Note: Use the percent of total cost to help identify the correct quality classification.

Square foot costs include the following components: Foundations as required for normal soil conditions. Floor, wall and roof structures. Interior ceiling, wall and floor finishes (including carpet). Exterior wall finish and roof cover. Display fronts. Interior partitions (including perimeter wall partitions). Entry and delivery doors. Basic lighting and electrical systems. Rough and finish plumbing. Design and engineering fees. Permits and hook-up fees. Contractor's mark-up.

The in-place cost of these extra components should be added to the basic building cost to arrive at the total structure cost. See the section "Additional Costs for Commercial Structures" on page 236 to 248. Heating and air conditioning systems. Elevators and escalators. Fire sprinklers. Exterior signs. Canopies and walks. Paving and curbing. Loading docks or ramps. Miscellaneous yard improvements. Mezzanines.

Department Stores – Reinforced Concrete

First Floor

Estimating Procedure

1. Use these square foot costs to estimate the cost of retail stores designed to sell a wider variety of goods. These buildings differ from discount houses in that they have more interior partitions and more elaborate interior and exterior finishes.
2. Establish the structure quality class by using the information on page 126.
3. Compute the building floor area. This should include everything within the building exterior walls and all inset areas outside the main walls but under the main building roof.
4. Add to or subtract from the square foot cost below the appropriate amount from the Wall Height Adjustment Table shown below if the wall height is more or less than 20 feet.
5. Multiply the adjusted square foot cost by the building area.
6. Deduct, if appropriate, for common walls, using the figures at the bottom of this page.
7. Multiply the total cost by the location factor listed on page 7 or 8.
8. Add the cost of appropriate additional components from page 236 to 248: heating and air conditioning systems, elevators and escalators, fire sprinklers, exterior signs, canopies and walks, paving and curbing, loading docks and ramps, miscellaneous yard improvements, and mezzanines.
9. Add the cost of second and higher floors and basements from page 128.

Department Store, Class 1

First Floor - Square Foot Area

Quality Class	20,000	25,000	30,000	35,000	40,000	45,000	50,000	60,000	70,000	80,000	100,000
1, Best	213.96	205.59	198.77	193.15	188.37	184.21	180.63	174.63	169.78	165.76	159.42
1 & 2	199.03	191.63	185.63	180.60	176.37	172.77	169.59	164.25	159.96	156.41	150.82
2, Good	187.44	180.88	175.53	171.13	167.41	164.19	161.37	156.70	152.91	149.82	144.90
2 & 3	173.37	167.72	163.18	159.41	156.22	153.46	151.13	147.13	143.91	141.27	137.05
3, Average	162.18	157.40	153.47	150.32	147.69	145.37	143.41	140.18	137.48	135.28	131.89
3 & 4	146.66	142.82	139.75	137.19	135.11	133.30	131.72	129.11	127.02	125.32	122.55
4, Low	133.04	130.25	128.01	126.22	124.59	123.26	122.02	120.07	118.46	117.11	115.02

Perimeter (Common) Wall Adjustment - First Floor

Class	For a Common Wall, Deduct Per L.F.	For No Wall Ownership, Deduct Per L.F.	For Lack of Exterior Finish, Deduct Per L.F.
1	$738	$1,480	$486
2	565	1,110	287
3	414	803	129
4	278	558	78

Wall Height Adjustment: Add or subtract the amount listed to or from the square foot of floor cost for each foot of first and upper story wall height more or less than 20 feet.

Square Foot Area

Quality Class	20,000	25,000	30,000	35,000	40,000	45,000	50,000	60,000	70,000	80,000	100,000
1, Best	2.21	1.85	1.66	1.53	1.42	1.32	1.28	1.16	1.13	1.10	1.08
2, Good	1.55	1.29	1.14	1.07	.98	.95	.92	.84	.81	.72	.70
3, Average	1.28	1.08	.98	.92	.78	.72	.69	.64	.63	.62	.61
4, Low	1.04	.93	.78	.66	.63	.62	.60	.58	.56	.54	.49

Department Stores – Reinforced Concrete

Estimating Procedure

1. Establish the basement and upper floor quality class. The quality class will usually be the same as the first floor of the building. Square foot costs for unfinished basements will be nearly the same regardless of the structure quality class.
2. Compute the floor area.
3. Add to or subtract from the square foot cost below the appropriate amount from the Wall Height Adjustment Table on page 127 for second and higher floors and from the bottom of this page for basements for each foot of wall height more or less than 20 feet for second and higher floors and 16 feet for basements.
4. Multiply the adjusted square foot cost from one of the three tables below by the floor area.
5. Deduct, if appropriate, for common or unfinished upper floor walls, using the costs in the table below titled "Second and Higher Floor Perimeter Wall Adjustments."
6. Multiply the total cost by the location factor listed on page 7 or 8.
7. Add the cost of appropriate additional components from page 236 to 248: heating and air conditioning systems, elevators and escalators, fire sprinklers, and mezzanines.
8. Add the total from this page to the total from page 127 to find the building cost.

Second and Higher Stories - Square Foot Area

Quality Class	20,000	25,000	30,000	35,000	40,000	45,000	50,000	60,000	70,000	80,000	100,000
1, Best	191.80	183.93	177.47	172.14	167.57	163.64	160.21	154.46	149.80	145.89	139.78
1 & 2	178.90	171.78	166.09	161.27	157.26	153.76	150.66	145.55	141.39	138.00	132.58
2, Good	168.84	162.49	157.38	153.14	149.51	146.42	143.72	139.23	135.59	132.57	127.83
2 & 3	156.65	151.24	146.84	143.19	140.18	137.49	135.23	131.36	128.27	125.66	121.68
3, Average	147.17	142.49	138.77	135.68	133.11	130.83	128.89	125.67	123.06	120.89	117.51
3 & 4	134.34	130.50	127.48	124.97	122.86	121.10	119.59	116.96	114.97	113.23	110.55
4, Low	120.65	117.68	115.33	113.49	111.92	110.64	109.49	107.61	106.09	104.88	102.97

Second and Higher Floor Perimeter (Common) Wall Adjustment

Class	For a Common Wall, Deduct Per L.F.	For No Wall Ownership, Deduct Per L.F.	For Lack of Exterior Finish, Deduct Per L.F.
1	$568	$1,125	$388
2	420	828	232
3	302	604	110
4	265	509	79

Finished Basements - Square Foot Area

Quality Class	20,000	25,000	30,000	35,000	40,000	45,000	50,000	60,000	70,000	80,000	100,000
1, Best	163.45	158.28	153.95	150.31	147.19	144.49	142.08	138.12	134.85	132.11	127.80
1 & 2	153.07	148.44	144.61	141.37	138.65	136.26	134.19	130.70	127.87	125.52	121.75
2, Good	147.75	143.43	139.91	136.90	134.36	132.20	130.28	127.03	124.44	122.29	118.79
2 & 3	137.88	134.19	131.15	128.64	126.53	124.65	123.04	120.36	118.22	116.37	113.51
3, Average	132.48	129.62	127.16	124.98	122.91	121.47	120.03	117.59	115.55	113.86	111.16
3 & 4	122.42	119.73	117.55	115.78	114.33	113.06	111.96	110.13	108.69	107.43	105.50
4, Low	111.29	109.13	107.49	106.14	105.08	104.24	103.43	102.16	101.18	100.31	99.12

Unfinished Basements

Area	20,000	25,000	30,000	35,000	40,000	45,000	50,000	60,000	70,000	80,000	100,000
Cost	76.00	74.63	73.48	72.69	71.93	71.51	70.94	70.17	69.59	69.20	68.40

Basement Wall Height Adjustment: Add or subtract the amount listed to or from the square foot of floor cost for each foot of basement wall height more or less than 16 feet.

Area	20,000	25,000	30,000	35,000	40,000	45,000	50,000	60,000	70,000	80,000	100,000
Finished	1.05	.95	.81	.69	.66	.64	.63	.62	.61	.60	.60
Unfinished	.96	.81	.66	.64	.62	.60	.59	.58	.56	.56	.54

Department Stores – Masonry or Concrete

Quality Classification

	Class 1 Best Quality	Class 2 Good Quality	Class 3 Average Quality	Class 4 Low Quality
Foundation (20% of total cost)	Reinforced concrete.	Reinforced concrete.	Reinforced concrete.	Reinforced concrete.
Floor Structure (15% of total cost)	6" reinforced concrete on 6" rock base.	6" reinforced concrete on 6" rock base.	6" reinforced concrete on 6" rock base.	4" reinforced concrete on 6" rock base.
Wall Structure (12% of total cost)	8" reinforced decorative concrete block, 6" concrete tilt-up or 8" reinforced brick.	8" reinforced decorative concrete block, 6" concrete tilt-up or 8" reinforced brick.	8" reinforced concrete. block, 6" concrete tilt-up or 8" reinforced common brick.	8" reinforced concrete block or 6" concrete tilt-up.
Roof & Cover (12% of total cost)	Glu-lams or steel beams on steel intermediate columns. Panelized roof system, 1/2" plywood sheathing, 5 ply built-up roof with insulation.	Glu-lams or steel beams on intermediate columns. Panelized roof system, 1/2" plywood sheathing, 5 ply built-up roof with insulation.	Glu-lams on steel intermediate columns. Panelized roof system, 1/2" plywood sheathing, 4 ply built-up roof.	Glu-lams on steel intermediate columns. Panelized roof system, 1/2" plywood sheath-ing, 4 ply built-up roof.
Floor Finish (5% of total cost)	Terrazzo and very good carpet.	Resilient tile with 50% sheet vinyl, terrazzo or good carpet.	Composition tile.	Minimum grade tile.
Interior Wall Finish (5% of total cost)	Gypsum wallboard or lath and plaster, finished with good paper or vinyl wall covers, or hardwood veneer paneling.	Gypsum wallboard and texture or paper, some vinyl wall cover or hardwood veneer paneling.	Interior stucco or gypsum wallboard, texture and paint.	Gypsum wallboard, texture and paint.
Ceiling Finish (5% of total cost)	Suspended good grade acoustical tile with gypsum wallboard backing.	Suspended acoustical tile with concealed grid system.	Suspended acoustical tile with exposed grid system.	Painted.
Lighting (6% of total cost)	Recessed fluorescent lighting in modular plastic panels. Many spotlights.	Continuous recessed 3 tube fluorescent strips with egg crate diffusers, 8' o.c. Average number of spotlights.	Continuous 3 tube fluorescent strips with egg crate diffusers, 8' o.c. Some spotlights.	Continuous exposed 2 tube fluorescent strips, 8' o.c.
Display Fronts (6% of total cost)	Best quality front as described on page 77. 15 to 25% of the first floor exterior wall is made up of display fronts.	Good quality front as described on page 77. 15 to 25% of the first floor exterior wall is made up of display fronts.	Average quality front as described on page 77. 10 to 20% of the first floor exterior wall is made up of display fronts.	Low quality flat type as described on page 77. 10 to 20% of the first floor exterior wall is made up of display fronts.
Exterior Wall Finish (8% of total cost)	Ornamental block or large rock imbedded in tilt-up panels, some stone veneer.	Exposed aggregate or decorative block. Some stone veneer.	Paint, some exposed aggregate.	Paint.
Plumbing (6% of total cost)	6 good fixtures per 20,000 square feet of floor area. Metal toilet partitions.	6 standard fixtures per 20,000 square feet of floor area. Metal toilet partitions.	4 standard fixtures per 20,000 square feet of floor area. Metal toilet partitions.	4 standard fixtures per 20,000 square feet of floor area. Wood toilet partitions.

Note: Use the percent of total cost to help identify the correct quality classification.

Square foot costs include the following components: Foundations as required for normal soil conditions. Floor, wall and roof structures. Interior ceiling, wall and floor finishes (including carpet). Exterior wall finish and roof cover. Display fronts. Interior partitions (including perimeter wall partitions). Entry and delivery doors. Basic lighting and electrical systems. Rough and finish plumbing. Design and engineering fees. Permits and hook-up fees. Contractor's mark-up.

The in-place cost of these extra components should be added to the basic building cost to arrive at the total structure cost. See the section "Additional Costs for Commercial Structures" on page 236 to 248. Heating and air conditioning systems. Elevators and escalators. Fire sprinklers. Exterior signs. Canopies and walks. Paving and curbing. Loading docks or ramps. Miscellaneous yard improvements. Mezzanines.

Department Stores – Masonry or Concrete

First Floor

Estimating Procedure

1. Use these square foot costs to estimate the cost of retail stores designed to sell a wider variety of goods. These buildings differ from discount houses in that they have more interior partitions and more elaborate interior and exterior finishes.
2. Establish the structure quality class by using the information on page 129.
3. Compute the building floor area. This should include everything within the building exterior walls and all inset areas outside the main walls but under the main building roof.
4. Add to or subtract from the square foot cost below the appropriate amount from the Wall Height Adjustment Row (near the bottom of this page) if the wall height is more or less than 16 feet.
5. Multiply the adjusted square foot cost by the building area.
6. Deduct, if appropriate, for common or unfinished walls, using the figures at the bottom of this page.
7. Multiply the total cost by the location factor listed on page 7 or 8.
8. Add the cost of appropriate additional components from page 236 to 248: heating and air conditioning systems, elevators and escalators, fire sprinklers, exterior signs, canopies and walks, paving and curbing, loading docks and ramps, miscellaneous yard improvements, and mezzanines.
9. Add the cost of second and higher floors and basements from page 131.

Department Store, Class 1 & 2

Department Store, Class 2 & 3

First Floor - Square Foot Area

Quality Class	20,000	25,000	30,000	35,000	40,000	45,000	50,000	60,000	70,000	80,000	100,000
1, Best	162.14	154.95	149.27	144.63	140.71	137.35	134.47	129.65	125.72	122.54	117.52
1 & 2	145.40	138.99	133.90	129.69	126.16	123.16	120.57	116.23	112.76	109.95	105.38
2, Good	130.86	125.11	120.53	116.78	113.57	110.88	108.52	104.67	101.52	98.91	94.91
2 & 3	117.07	111.91	107.76	104.37	101.59	99.16	97.06	93.58	90.80	88.50	84.86
3, Average	104.97	100.34	96.68	93.68	91.08	88.95	87.07	83.93	81.44	79.37	76.11
3 & 4	91.61	87.58	84.37	81.74	79.51	77.64	76.00	73.26	71.03	69.29	66.43
4, Low	78.16	74.71	71.96	69.76	67.85	66.23	64.81	62.50	60.60	59.10	56.65
Wall Height Adjustment*	.89	.68	.62	.59	.56	.54	.51	.49	.48	.47	.46

*Wall Height Adjustment: Add or subtract the amount listed in this row to or from the square foot of floor cost for each foot of wall height more or less than 16 feet.

Perimeter Wall Adjustment: For common wall, deduct $241 per linear foot. For no wall ownership, deduct $485 per linear foot.

Department Stores – Masonry or Concrete

Upper Floors and Basements

Estimating Procedure

1. Establish the basement and upper floor quality class. The quality class will usually be the same as the first floor of the building. Square foot costs for unfinished basements will be nearly the same regardless of the structure quality class.
2. Compute the floor area.
3. Add to or subtract from the square foot cost below the appropriate amount from the Wall Height Adjustment Row for each foot of wall height more or less than 12 feet for second and higher floors and 12 feet for basements.
4. Multiply the adjusted square foot cost by the floor area.
5. Deduct, if appropriate, for common or unfinished upper floor walls, using the Perimeter Wall Adjustment costs listed below.
6. Multiply the total cost by the location factor listed on page 7 or 8.
7. Add the cost of the appropriate additional components from page 236 to 248: heating and air conditioning systems, elevators and escalators, fire sprinklers, and mezzanines.
8. Add the total from this page to the total from page 130 to find the building cost.

Second and Higher Floors - Square Foot Area

Quality Class	20,000	25,000	30,000	35,000	40,000	45,000	50,000	60,000	70,000	80,000	100,000
1, Best	141.94	136.72	131.93	127.65	123.87	120.48	117.49	112.31	108.05	104.42	98.57
1 & 2	125.20	120.62	116.38	112.64	109.26	106.33	103.67	99.13	95.32	92.12	86.91
2, Good	110.66	106.54	102.85	99.52	96.56	93.91	91.61	87.56	84.24	81.42	76.83
2 & 3	98.23	94.61	91.33	88.35	85.74	83.41	81.31	77.79	74.79	72.27	68.24
3, Average	86.61	83.41	80.47	77.86	75.58	73.49	71.63	68.50	65.91	63.72	60.14
3 & 4	71.34	68.72	66.28	64.11	62.26	60.56	59.05	56.44	54.33	52.49	49.54
4, Low	57.60	55.71	54.22	52.92	51.87	50.90	50.17	48.78	47.72	46.80	45.38
Wall Height Adjustment*	.62	.57	.49	.47	.46	.44	.43	.42	.42	.41	.41

*Wall Height Adjustment: Add or subtract the amount listed in this row to or from the square foot of floor cost for each foot of wall height more or less than 12 feet.

Perimeter Wall Adjustment: For common wall, deduct $130 per linear foot. For no wall ownership, deduct $258 per linear foot.

Finished Basement - Square Foot Area

Quality Class	20,000	25,000	30,000	35,000	40,000	45,000	50,000	60,000	70,000	80,000	100,000
1, Best	126.13	121.06	116.96	113.57	110.74	108.35	106.19	102.68	99.83	97.44	93.76
2, Good	101.06	97.00	93.71	91.00	88.77	86.78	85.10	82.26	80.00	78.10	75.10
3, Average	82.05	78.71	76.08	73.95	72.06	70.44	69.08	66.80	64.93	63.42	60.99
4, Low	58.75	56.41	54.50	52.91	51.57	50.48	49.45	47.82	46.53	45.42	43.67

Unfinished Basements

Area	20,000	25,000	30,000	35,000	40,000	45,000	50,000	60,000	70,000	80,000	100,000
Cost	34.73	33.07	31.91	31.04	30.29	29.69	29.18	28.44	27.78	27.35	26.54

Wall Height Adjustment: Add or subtract the amount listed in this table to or from the square foot of floor cost for each foot of basement wall height more or less than 12 feet.

Area	20,000	25,000	30,000	35,000	40,000	45,000	50,000	60,000	70,000	80,000	100,000
Finished	.69	.65	.64	.62	.61	.61	.60	.59	.59	.58	.56
Unfinished	.66	.63	.62	.61	.60	.59	.59	.58	.56	.56	.54

Department Stores – Wood Frame

Quality Classification

	Class 1 Best Quality	Class 2 Good Quality	Class 3 Average Quality	Class 4 Low Quality
Foundation (20% of total cost)	Reinforced concrete.	Reinforced concrete.	Reinforced concrete.	Reinforced concrete.
Floor Structure (10% of total cost)	6" reinforced concrete on 6" rock base.	6" reinforced concrete on 6" rock base.	6" reinforced concrete on 6" rock base.	4" reinforced concrete on 6" rock base.
Wall Structure (9% of total cost)	2" x 6", 16" o.c.	2" x 6", 16" o.c.	2" x 6", 16" o.c.	2" x 4", 16" o.c.
Roof & Cover (12% of total cost)	Glu-lams or steel beams on steel intermediate columns. Panelized roof system, 1/2" plywood sheathing, 5 ply built-up roof with insulation.	Glu-lams or steel beams on steel intermediate columns. Panelized roof system, 1/2" plywood sheathing, 5 ply built-up roof with insulation.	Glu-lams on steel intermediate columns. Panelized roof system, 1/2" plywood sheathing, 4 ply built-up roof.	Glu-lams on steel intermediate columns. Panelized roof system, 1/2" plywood sheathing, 4 ply built-up roof.
Floor Finish (6% of total cost)	Terrazzo and very good carpet.	Resilient tile with 50% sheet vinyl, terrazzo or good carpet.	Composition tile.	Minimum grade tile.
Interior Wall Finish (5% of total cost)	Gypsum wallboard or lath and plaster finished with good paper or vinyl wall covers, or hardwood veneer paneling.	Gypsum wallboard, texture or paper, some vinyl wall cover or hardwood veneer paneling.	Interior stucco or gypsum wallboard. Texture and paint.	Gypsum wallboard. Texture and paint.
Ceiling Finish (5% of total cost)	Suspended good grade acoustical tile with gypsum wallboard backing.	Suspended acoustical tile with concealed grid system.	Suspended acoustical tile with exposed grid system.	Painted.
Lighting (8% of total cost)	Recessed fluorescent lighting in modular plastic panels. Many spotlights.	Continuous recessed 3 tube fluorescent strips with egg crate diffusers, 8' o.c. Average number of spotlights.	Continuous 3 tube fluorescent strips with egg crate diffusers, 8' o.c. Some spotlights.	Continuous exposed 2 tube fluorescent strips, 8' o.c.
Display Fronts (8% of total cost)	Best quality fronts as described on page 77. 15 to 25% of the first floor exterior wall is made up of display fronts.	Good quality front as described on page 77. 15 to 25% of the first floor exterior wall is made up of display fronts.	Average quality front as described on page 77. 10 to 20% of the first floor exterior wall is made up of display fronts.	Low quality flat type as described on page 77. 10 to 20% of the first floor exterior wall is made up of display fronts.
Exterior Wall Finish (10% of total cost)	Good wood siding. Extensive stone veneer.	Wood siding. Some brick or stone veneer.	Stucco. Some brick trim.	Stucco.
Plumbing (7% of total cost)	6 good fixtures per 20,000 square feet of floor area. Metal toilet partitions.	6 standard fixtures per 20,000 square feet of floor area. Metal toilet partitions.	4 standard fixtures per 20,000 square feet of floor area. Metal toilet partitions.	4 standard fixtures per 20,000 square feet of floor area. Wood toilet partitions.

Note: Use the percent of total cost to help identify the correct quality classification.

Square foot costs include the following components: Foundations as required for normal soil conditions. Floor, wall and roof structures. Interior ceiling, wall and floor finishes (including carpet). Exterior wall finish and roof cover. Display fronts. Interior partitions (including perimeter wall partitions). Entry and delivery doors. Basic lighting and electrical systems. Rough and finish plumbing. Design and engineering fees. Permits and hook-up fees. Contractor's mark-up.

The in-place cost of these extra components should be added to the basic building cost to arrive at the total structure cost. See the section "Additional Costs for Commercial Structures" on page 236 to 248. Heating and air conditioning systems. Elevators and escalators. Fire sprinklers. Exterior signs. Canopies and walks. Paving and curbing. Loading docks or ramps. Miscellaneous yard improvements. Mezzanines.

Department Stores – Wood Frame

First Floor

Estimating Procedure

1. Use these square foot costs to estimate the cost of retail stores designed to sell a wider variety of goods. These buildings differ from discount houses in that they have more interior partitions and more elaborate interior and exterior finishes.
2. Establish the structure quality class by applying the information on page 132.
3. Compute the floor area. This should include everything within the building exterior walls and all inset areas outside the main walls but under the main building roof.
4. Add to or subtract from the square foot cost below the appropriate amount from the Wall Height Adjustment Row (near the bottom of this page) if the wall height is more or less than 16 feet.
5. Multiply the adjusted square foot cost by the building area.
6. Deduct, if appropriate, for common walls or no wall ownership, using the figures at the bottom of this page.
7. Multiply the total cost by the location factor on page 7 or 8.
8. Add the cost of appropriate additional components from page 236 to 248: heating and air conditioning systems, elevators and escalators, fire sprinklers, exterior signs, canopies and walks, paving and curbing, loading docks and ramps, miscellaneous yard improvements, and mezzanines.
9. Add the cost of second and higher floors and basements from page 134.

Department Store, Class 2

Square Foot Area

Quality Class	20,000	25,000	30,000	35,000	40,000	45,000	50,000	60,000	70,000	80,000	100,000
1, Best	164.01	157.33	151.95	147.50	143.76	140.48	137.66	132.94	129.08	125.93	120.91
1 & 2	147.33	141.37	136.52	132.54	129.18	126.26	123.72	119.46	116.00	113.21	108.67
2, Good	131.89	126.53	122.21	118.63	115.63	112.99	110.73	106.93	103.82	101.28	97.29
2 & 3	117.73	112.99	109.09	105.91	103.19	100.86	98.80	95.43	92.71	90.41	86.85
3, Average	105.75	101.46	97.95	95.09	92.71	90.55	88.72	85.65	83.22	81.22	78.00
3 & 4	91.83	88.10	85.08	82.60	80.48	78.67	77.05	74.41	72.32	70.53	67.70
4, Low	77.85	74.71	72.19	70.02	68.22	66.72	65.35	63.12	61.30	59.80	57.43
Wall Height Adjustment*	.45	.44	.43	.38	.37	.37	.35	.34	.33	.30	.21

*Wall Height Adjustment: Add or subtract the amount listed in this table to or from the square foot of floor cost for each foot of wall height more or less than 16 feet.

Perimeter Wall Adjustment: For common wall, deduct $53 per linear foot. For no wall ownership, deduct $102 per linear foot.

Department Stores – Wood Frame

Upper Floors and Basements

Estimating Procedure

1. Establish the basement and upper floor quality class. The quality class will usually be the same as the first floor of the building. Square foot costs for unfinished basements will be nearly the same regardless of the structure quality class.
2. Compute the floor area.
3. Add to or subtract from the square foot cost below the appropriate amount from the Wall Height Adjustment Row for each foot of wall height more or less than 12 feet.
4. Multiply the adjusted square foot cost by the floor area.
5. Deduct, if appropriate, for common upper floor walls and walls not owned, using the Perimeter Wall Adjustment costs.
6. Multiply the total cost by the location factor on page 7 or 8.
7. Add the cost of appropriate additional components from page 236 to 248: heating and air conditioning systems, elevators and escalators, fire sprinklers, and mezzanines.
8. Add the total from this page to the total from page 133 to find the building cost.

Second and Higher Floors - Square Foot Area

Quality Class	20,000	25,000	30,000	35,000	40,000	45,000	50,000	60,000	70,000	80,000	100,000
1, Best	135.94	131.15	127.08	123.58	120.63	118.01	115.67	111.79	108.62	105.96	101.75
1 & 2	120.40	116.12	112.55	109.44	106.79	104.53	102.48	99.06	96.19	93.85	90.17
2, Good	106.85	103.12	99.88	97.19	94.84	92.78	90.94	87.90	85.43	83.31	79.98
2 & 3	94.95	91.60	88.72	86.34	84.25	82.41	80.81	78.12	75.85	74.02	71.08
3, Average	84.33	81.32	78.81	76.64	74.84	73.17	71.75	69.36	67.37	65.73	63.13
3 & 4	71.52	68.96	66.79	64.98	63.40	62.07	60.83	58.82	57.17	55.74	53.54
4, Low	58.49	56.37	54.64	53.21	51.90	50.76	49.84	48.15	46.75	45.60	43.78
Wall Height Adjustment*	.43	.37	.34	.30	.27	.23	.21	.17	.16	.14	.11

***Wall Height Adjustment:** Add or subtract the amount listed in this table to or from the square foot of floor cost for each foot of wall height more or less than 12 feet.

Perimeter Wall Adjustment: For common wall, deduct $132 per linear foot. For no wall ownership, deduct $266 per linear foot.

Finished Basements - Square Foot Area

Quality Class	20,000	25,000	30,000	35,000	40,000	45,000	50,000	60,000	70,000	80,000	100,000
1, Best	132.93	128.68	124.63	120.91	117.63	114.69	112.02	107.38	103.54	100.26	94.91
2, Good	106.58	103.19	99.89	96.96	94.33	91.92	89.82	86.10	82.99	80.34	76.12
3, Average	87.14	84.39	81.73	79.33	77.18	75.20	73.44	70.44	67.90	65.72	62.24
4, Low	60.30	58.35	56.51	54.88	53.36	52.02	50.78	48.72	46.97	45.46	43.08

Unfinished Basements

Area	20,000	25,000	30,000	35,000	40,000	45,000	50,000	60,000	70,000	80,000	100,000
Cost	34.06	32.71	31.65	30.77	29.96	29.34	28.84	27.87	27.14	26.51	25.51

Wall Height Adjustment: Add or subtract the amount listed in this table to or from the square foot of floor cost for each foot of basement wall height more or less than 12 feet.

Area	20,000	25,000	30,000	35,000	40,000	45,000	50,000	60,000	70,000	80,000	100,000
Finished	.77	.70	.68	.67	.66	.63	.62	.59	.57	.57	.56
Unfinished	.70	.68	.66	.63	.62	.59	.59	.57	.56	.55	.53

General Office Buildings – Masonry or Concrete

Quality Classification

	Class 1 Best Quality	Class 2 Good Quality	Class 3 Average Quality	Class 4 Low Quality
Foundation (12% of total cost)	Reinforced concrete.	Reinforced concrete.	Reinforced concrete.	Reinforced concrete.
First Floor Structure (8% of total cost)	Reinforced concrete slab on grade or standard wood frame.	Reinforced concrete slab on grade or standard wood frame.	Reinforced concrete slab on grade or 4" x 6" girders with plywood sheathing.	Reinforced concrete slab on grade.
Upper Floor Structures (9% of total cost)	Standard wood frame, plywood and 1-1/2" light weight concrete sub floor.	Standard wood frame, plywood and 1-1/2" lightweight concrete sub floor.	Standard wood frame, 5/8" plywood sub floor.	Standard wood frame, 5/8" plywood sub floor.
Walls (10% of total cost)	8" decorative concrete block or 6" concrete tilt-up.	8" decorative concrete block or 6" concrete tilt-up.	8" reinforced concrete block or 8" reinforced brick or 8"" clay tile.	8" reinforced concrete block or 8" clay tile.
Roof Structure (6% of total cost)	Standard wood frame, flat or low pitch.	Standard wood frame, flat or low pitch.	Standard wood frame, flat or low pitch.	Standard wood frame, flat or low pitch.
Exterior Wall Finish (8% of total cost)	Decorative block or large rock imbedded in tilt-up panels with 10 - 20% brick or stone veneer.	Decorative block or exposed aggregate and 10 - 20% brick or stone veneer.	Stucco or colored concrete block.	Painted concrete block or tile.
Windows (5% of total cost)	Average number in good aluminum frame. Fixed float glass in good frame on front side.	Average number in good aluminum frame. Some fixed float glass in front.	Average number of average aluminum sliding type.	Average number of low cost aluminum sliding type.
Roof Cover (5% of total cost)	5 ply built-up roofing on flat roofs. Heavy shake or tile on sloping roofs.	5 ply built-up roofing on flat roofs. Average shake or composition, tar and large rock on sloping roofs.	4 ply built-up roofing on flat roofs. Wood shingle or composition, tar and pea gravel on sloping roofs.	3 ply built-up roofing on flat roofs. Composition shingle on sloping roofs.
Overhang (3% of total cost)	3' closed overhang, fully guttered.	2' closed overhang, fully guttered.	None on flat roofs. 18" open on sloping roofs. Fully guttered.	None on flat roofs. 12" to 16" open on sloping roofs. Gutters over entrances.
Floor Finishes:				
Offices (3% of total cost)	Very good carpet.	Good carpet.	Average grade carpet.	Minimum grade tile.
Corridors (2% of total cost)	Solid vinyl tile or carpet.	Resilient tile.	Composition tile.	Minimum grade tile.
Bathrooms (1% of total cost)	Sheet vinyl or ceramic tile.	Sheet vinyl or ceramic tile.	Vinyl asbestos tile.	Minimum grade tile.
Interior Wall Finishes:				
Offices (6% of total cost)	Good hardwood veneer.	Hardwood veneer paneling or vinyl wall cover.	Gypsum wallboard, texture and paint.	Gypsum wallboard, texture and paint.
Corridors (4% of total cost)	Good hardwood veneer.	Gypsum wallboard and vinyl wall cover	Gypsum wallboard, texture and paint	Gypsum wallboard, texture and paint.
Bathrooms (2% of total cost)	Gypsum wallboard and enamel with ceramic tile wainscot.	Gypsum wallboard and enamel or vinyl wall covering	Gypsum wallboard and enamel.	Gypsum wallboard and texture and paint.
Ceiling Finish (4% of total cost)	Suspended "T" bar and acoustical tile.	Gypsum wallboard and acoustical tile.	Gypsum wallboard and acoustical texture.	Gypsum walboard and paint.
Plumbing (6% of total cost)	Copper tubing and top quality fixtures.	Copper tubing and good fixtures.	Copper tubing and standard fixtures.	Copper tubing and economy fixtures.
Lighting (6% of total cost)	Conduit wiring, good fixtures.	Conduit wiring, good fixtures.	Romex or conduit wiring, average fixtures.	Romex wiring, economy fixtures.

Note: Use the percent of total cost to help identify the correct quality classification.

Square foot costs include the following components: Foundations as required for normal soil conditions. Floor, wall and roof structures. Interior ceiling, wall and floor finishes. Exterior wall finish and roof cover. Interior partitions. Cabinets, doors and windows. Basic electrical systems and lighting fixtures. Rough plumbing and fixtures. Permits and fees. Contractor's mark-up.

General Office Buildings – Masonry or Concrete

Exterior Suite Entrances, Length Less Than Twice Width

Estimating Procedure

1. Use these figures to estimate general office buildings in which access to each suite is through an exterior entrance. Medical and dental offices have smaller rooms and more plumbing fixtures than general offices and should be estimated with figures from the Medical and Dental Buildings Section. See page 151.

2. Establish the building quality class by applying the information on page 135.

3. Compute the first floor area. This should include everything within the exterior walls and all insets outside the main walls but under the main roof.

4. If the first floor wall height is more or less than 10 feet, add to or subtract from the first floor square foot cost below the appropriate amount from the Wall Height Adjustment Table on page 142.

5. Multiply the adjusted square foot cost by the first floor area.

6. Deduct, if appropriate, for common walls or no wall finish, Use the figures on page 142.

7. If there are second or higher floors, compute the square foot area on each floor. Locate the appropriate square foot cost from the table at the bottom of this page. Adjust this figure for a wall height more or less than 9 feet, using the figures on page 142. Multiply the adjusted cost by the square foot area on each floor. Use the figures on page 142 to deduct for common walls or no wall finish. Add the result to the cost from step 6 above.

8. Multiply the total cost by the location factor on page 7 or 8.

9. Add the cost of heating and air conditioning systems, elevators, fire sprinklers, exterior signs, paving and curbing, miscellaneous yard improvements. See pages 236 to 248.

First Story - Square Foot Area

Quality Class	1,000	1,500	2,000	2,500	3,000	4,000	5,000	7,500	10,000	15,000	20,000
Exceptional	224.20	205.77	195.13	188.10	182.97	175.87	171.14	163.85	159.62	154.65	151.75
1, Best	206.86	189.83	180.07	173.49	168.78	162.23	157.87	151.19	147.27	142.65	140.01
1 & 2	187.75	172.32	163.48	157.52	153.26	147.34	143.33	137.29	133.74	129.56	127.13
2, Good	173.68	159.40	151.18	145.65	141.74	136.24	132.54	126.94	123.64	119.81	117.55
2 & 3	158.50	145.48	137.96	133.00	129.35	124.37	120.99	115.86	112.86	109.34	107.28
3, Average	146.59	134.52	127.55	122.95	119.64	115.00	111.88	107.12	104.35	101.13	99.22
3 & 4	132.60	121.69	115.42	111.25	108.18	104.02	101.19	96.92	94.39	91.46	89.76
4, Low	117.40	107.73	102.21	98.50	95.83	92.09	89.63	85.83	83.61	80.97	79.49

Second and Higher Stories - Square Foot Area

Quality Class	1,000	1,500	2,000	2,500	3,000	4,000	5,000	7,500	10,000	15,000	20,000
Exceptional	203.20	187.64	178.55	172.44	167.94	161.73	157.54	151.05	147.21	142.72	140.08
1, Best	191.00	176.37	167.84	162.07	157.87	151.98	148.08	141.96	138.36	134.15	131.60
1 & 2	174.49	161.12	153.34	148.08	144.22	138.86	135.23	129.69	126.39	122.51	120.28
2, Good	162.50	150.10	142.82	137.91	134.33	129.32	125.99	120.77	117.73	114.13	111.96
2 & 3	147.88	136.63	129.96	125.51	122.22	117.71	114.64	109.95	107.12	103.87	101.92
3, Average	135.59	125.23	117.83	115.05	112.08	107.92	105.06	100.77	98.19	95.24	93.45
3 & 4	121.39	112.11	106.69	102.99	100.31	96.58	94.15	90.23	87.95	85.29	83.66
4, Low	108.15	99.88	95.03	91.75	89.39	86.02	83.80	80.36	78.32	75.92	74.50

General Office Buildings – Masonry or Concrete

Exterior Suite Entrances, Length Between 2 and 4 Times Width

Estimating Procedure

1. Use these figures to estimate general office buildings in which access to each suite is through an exterior entrance. Medical and dental offices have smaller rooms and more plumbing fixtures than general offices and should be estimated with figures from the Medical and Dental Buildings Section. See page 151.
2. Establish the building quality class by applying the information on page 135.
3. Compute the first floor area. This should include everything within the exterior walls and all insets outside the main walls but under the main roof.
4. If the first floor wall height is more or less than 10 feet, add to or subtract from the first floor square foot cost below the appropriate amount from the Wall Height Adjustment Table on page 142.
5. Multiply the adjusted square foot cost by the first floor area.
6. Deduct, if appropriate, for common walls or no wall finish. Use the figures on page 142.
7. If there are second or higher floors, compute the square foot area on each floor. Locate the appropriate square foot cost from the table at the bottom of this page. Adjust this figure for a wall height more or less than 9 feet, using the figures on page 142. Multiply the adjusted cost by the square foot area on each floor. Use the figures on page 142 to deduct for common walls or no wall finish. Add the result to the cost from step 6 above.
8. Multiply the total cost by the location factor on page 7 or 8.
9. Add the cost of heating and air conditioning systems, elevators, fire sprinklers, exterior signs, paving and curbing, miscellaneous yard improvements. See pages 236 to 248.

First Story - Square Foot Area

Quality Class	1,000	1,500	2,000	2,500	3,000	4,000	5,000	7,500	10,000	15,000	20,000
Exceptional	243.53	219.89	206.50	197.74	191.38	182.76	177.05	168.37	163.36	157.57	154.19
1, Best	224.66	202.86	190.57	182.43	176.59	168.63	163.35	155.37	150.72	145.37	142.30
1 & 2	204.25	184.41	173.24	165.80	160.50	153.32	148.48	141.26	137.04	132.19	129.32
2, Good	188.79	170.47	160.12	153.31	148.40	141.68	137.25	130.54	126.64	122.18	119.59
2 & 3	172.54	155.76	146.29	140.08	135.59	129.48	125.44	119.29	115.75	111.63	109.23
3, Average	159.38	144.04	135.26	129.49	125.40	119.73	115.92	110.26	107.01	103.19	101.00
3 & 4	144.69	130.67	122.76	117.49	113.74	108.58	105.21	100.09	97.10	93.64	91.66
4, Low	128.54	116.08	108.99	104.34	101.00	96.47	93.45	88.87	86.26	83.18	81.41

Second and Higher Stories - Square Foot Area

Quality Class	1,000	1,500	2,000	2,500	3,000	4,000	5,000	7,500	10,000	15,000	20,000
Exceptional	224.94	203.59	191.59	183.68	177.97	170.22	165.10	157.30	152.79	147.64	144.59
1, Best	207.28	187.67	176.56	169.28	164.06	156.87	152.12	144.96	140.85	136.07	133.26
1 & 2	189.96	171.95	161.77	155.12	150.29	143.73	139.37	132.86	129.03	124.64	122.15
2, Good	176.63	159.84	150.49	144.22	139.76	133.66	129.62	123.49	119.96	115.90	113.51
2 & 3	160.63	145.38	136.80	131.15	127.07	121.49	117.84	112.30	109.10	105.40	103.27
3, Average	146.72	132.83	124.97	119.83	116.12	111.04	107.70	102.63	99.68	96.32	94.33
3 & 4	133.30	120.72	113.55	108.83	105.46	100.87	97.80	93.21	90.56	87.45	85.68
4, Low	117.98	106.79	98.70	96.36	93.33	89.29	86.57	82.49	80.18	77.43	75.80

General Office Buildings – Masonry or Concrete

Exterior Suite Entrances, Length More Than 4 Times Width

Estimating Procedure

1. Use these figures to estimate general office buildings in which access to each suite is through an exterior entrance. Medical and dental offices have smaller rooms and more plumbing fixtures than general offices and should be estimated with figures from the Medical and Dental Buildings Section. See page 151.
2. Establish the building quality class by applying the information on page 135.
3. Compute the first floor area. This should include everything within the exterior walls and all insets outside the main walls but under the main roof.
4. If the first floor wall height is more or less than 10 feet, add to or subtract from the first floor square foot cost below the appropriate amount from the Wall Height Adjustment Table on page 142.
5. Multiply the adjusted square foot cost by the first floor area.
6. Deduct, if appropriate, for common walls or no wall finish. Use the figures on page 142.
7. If there are second or higher floors, compute the square foot area on each floor. Locate the appropriate square foot cost from the table at the bottom of this page. Adjust this figure for a wall height more or less than 9 feet, using the figures on page 142. Multiply the adjusted cost by the square foot area on each floor. Use the figures on page 142 to deduct for common walls or no wall finish. Add the result to the cost from step 6 above.
8. Multiply the total cost by the location factor on page 7 or 8.
9. Add the cost of heating and air conditioning systems, elevators, fire sprinklers, exterior signs, paving and curbing, miscellaneous yard improvements. See pages 236 to 248.

First Story - Square Foot Area

Quality Class	1,000	1,500	2,000	2,500	3,000	4,000	5,000	7,500	10,000	15,000	20,000
Exceptional	266.08	237.39	221.22	210.63	202.98	192.64	185.76	175.40	169.47	162.55	158.57
1, Best	244.81	218.37	203.53	193.73	186.74	177.24	170.90	161.36	155.88	149.53	145.89
1 & 2	223.16	199.05	185.48	176.60	170.22	161.53	155.76	147.07	142.10	136.30	132.96
2, Good	205.68	183.46	170.98	162.78	156.89	148.86	143.59	135.59	130.98	125.62	122.54
2 & 3	188.26	167.95	156.49	148.98	143.61	136.26	131.39	124.07	119.88	115.04	112.21
3, Average	174.95	156.10	145.47	138.44	133.49	126.67	122.17	115.37	111.44	106.87	104.26
3 & 4	158.32	141.25	131.60	125.31	120.78	114.62	110.55	104.35	100.83	96.73	94.33
4, Low	140.87	125.63	117.12	111.48	107.49	101.97	98.36	92.89	89.71	86.02	83.91

Second and Higher Stories - Square Foot Area

Quality Class	1,000	1,500	2,000	2,500	3,000	4,000	5,000	7,500	10,000	15,000	20,000
Exceptional	244.34	218.21	203.55	193.91	187.07	177.63	171.43	162.13	156.70	150.51	146.88
1, Best	225.38	201.27	187.77	178.85	172.51	163.85	158.09	149.49	144.57	138.81	135.48
1 & 2	206.55	184.43	172.07	163.90	158.11	150.16	144.91	137.04	132.48	127.24	124.13
2, Good	192.75	172.17	160.57	152.98	147.56	140.19	135.23	127.90	123.63	118.71	112.49
2 & 3	176.05	157.24	146.65	139.75	134.77	127.99	123.50	116.79	112.92	108.44	105.83
3, Average	162.52	145.20	135.41	129.03	124.41	118.17	114.04	107.86	104.25	100.10	97.72
3 & 4	147.42	131.67	122.82	117.05	112.86	107.18	103.42	97.79	94.57	90.81	88.59
4, Low	131.54	117.44	109.52	104.35	100.67	95.59	92.29	87.25	84.37	81.00	79.04

General Office Buildings – Masonry or Concrete

Interior Suite Entrances, Length Less Than Twice Width

Estimating Procedure

1. Use these figures to estimate general office buildings in which access to each suite is through an interior corridor. Medical and dental offices have smaller rooms and more plumbing fixtures than general offices and should be estimated with figures from the Medical and Dental Buildings Section. See page 151.
2. Establish the building quality class by applying the information on page 135.
3. Compute the first floor area. This should include everything within the exterior walls and all insets outside the main walls but under the main roof.
4. If the first floor wall height is more or less than 10 feet, add to or subtract from the first floor square foot cost below the appropriate amount from the Wall Height Adjustment Table on page 142.
5. Multiply the adjusted square foot cost by the first floor area.
6. Deduct, if appropriate, for common walls or no wall finish. Use the figures on page 142.
7. If there are second or higher floors, compute the square foot area on each floor. Locate the appropriate square foot cost from the table at the bottom of this page. Adjust this figure for a wall height more or less than 9 feet, using the figures on page 142. Multiply the adjusted cost by the square foot area on each floor. Use the figures on page 142 to deduct for common walls or no wall finish. Add the result to the cost from step 6 above.
8. Multiply the total cost by the location factor on page 7 or 8.
9. Add the cost of heating and air conditioning systems, elevators, fire sprinklers, exterior signs, paving and curbing, miscellaneous yard improvements. See pages 236 to 248.

First Story - Square Foot Area

Quality Class	2,000	2,500	3,000	4,000	5,000	7,500	10,000	15,000	20,000	30,000	40,000
Exceptional	189.28	182.35	177.31	170.35	165.69	158.58	154.43	149.55	146.71	143.40	141.40
1, Best	174.55	168.15	163.49	157.10	152.75	146.19	142.41	137.93	135.30	132.22	130.42
1 & 2	160.07	154.20	149.94	144.08	140.09	134.13	130.61	126.48	124.06	121.27	119.63
2, Good	149.53	144.08	140.09	134.60	130.90	125.29	122.00	118.20	115.91	113.32	111.73
2 & 3	136.68	131.66	127.99	122.96	119.63	114.45	111.48	108.02	105.94	103.54	102.13
3, Average	126.33	121.71	118.32	113.68	110.55	105.84	103.03	99.84	97.92	95.71	94.34
3 & 4	114.09	109.94	106.88	102.70	99.85	95.56	93.09	90.17	88.46	86.42	85.24
4, Low	100.83	97.13	94.48	90.73	88.30	84.47	82.26	79.66	78.16	76.42	75.32

Second and Higher Stories - Square Foot Area

Quality Class	2,000	2,500	3,000	4,000	5,000	7,500	10,000	15,000	20,000	30,000	40,000
Exceptional	176.78	170.53	165.94	159.65	155.45	148.99	145.21	140.77	138.18	135.08	133.26
1, Best	163.07	157.31	153.14	147.30	143.42	137.40	133.95	129.88	127.44	124.59	122.91
1 & 2	150.02	144.73	140.88	135.57	131.95	126.46	123.26	119.47	117.26	114.62	113.10
2, Good	140.34	134.50	131.79	126.80	123.42	118.32	115.26	111.75	109.69	107.24	105.80
2 & 3	127.90	123.38	120.05	115.51	112.46	107.80	105.02	101.84	99.95	97.73	96.83
3, Average	117.48	113.34	110.34	106.12	103.32	99.03	96.50	93.56	91.81	89.77	88.55
3 & 4	105.79	102.02	99.31	95.53	92.99	89.15	86.85	84.24	82.67	80.80	79.72
4, Low	93.20	89.91	87.50	84.21	81.99	78.55	76.57	74.22	72.88	71.22	70.28

Interior Suite Entrances, Length Between 2 and 4 Times Width

Estimating Procedure

1. Use these figures to estimate general office buildings in which access to each suite is through an interior corridor. Medical and dental offices have smaller rooms and more plumbing fixtures than general offices and should be estimated with figures from the Medical and Dental Buildings Section. See page 151.
2. Establish the building quality class by applying the information on page 135.
3. Compute the first floor area. This should include everything within the exterior walls and all insets outside the main walls but under the main roof.
4. If the first floor wall height is more or less than 10 feet, add to or subtract from the first floor square foot cost below the appropriate amount from the Wall Height Adjustment Table on page 142.
5. Multiply the adjusted square foot cost by the first floor area.
6. Deduct, if appropriate, for common walls or no wall finish. Use the figures on page 142.
7. If there are second or higher floors, compute the square foot area on each floor. Locate the appropriate square foot cost from the table at the bottom of this page. Adjust this figure for a wall height more or less than 9 feet, using the figures on page 142. Multiply the adjusted cost by the square foot area on each floor. Use the figures on page 142 to deduct for common walls or no wall finish. Add the result to the cost from step 6 above.
8. Multiply the total cost by the location factor on page 7 or 8.
9. Add the cost of heating and air conditioning systems, elevators, fire sprinklers, exterior signs, paving and curbing, miscellaneous yard improvements. See pages 236 to 248.

General Offices, Class 1 & 2

First Story - Square Foot Area

Quality Class	2,000	2,500	3,000	4,000	5,000	7,500	10,000	15,000	20,000	30,000	40,000
Exceptional	200.64	192.06	185.89	177.42	171.77	163.20	158.28	152.51	149.13	145.18	142.86
1, Best	185.06	177.16	171.46	163.66	158.46	150.58	146.00	140.70	137.52	133.93	131.79
1 & 2	169.51	162.46	157.25	150.09	145.32	138.05	133.89	128.97	126.14	122.80	120.80
2, Good	148.74	142.51	138.11	132.01	127.96	121.81	118.22	114.05	111.62	108.79	107.08
2 & 3	144.95	138.78	134.32	128.19	124.09	117.93	114.36	110.15	107.75	104.90	103.23
3, Average	134.11	128.37	124.25	118.57	114.81	109.10	105.79	101.90	99.68	97.02	95.48
3 & 4	121.31	116.14	112.39	107.26	103.90	98.72	95.71	92.25	90.17	87.79	86.36
4, Low	107.35	102.79	99.42	94.93	91.93	87.32	84.70	81.58	79.77	77.68	76.44

Second and Higher Stories - Square Foot Area

Quality Class	2,000	2,500	3,000	4,000	5,000	7,500	10,000	15,000	20,000	30,000	40,000
Exceptional	186.64	178.96	173.31	165.71	160.58	152.86	148.36	143.15	140.08	136.48	134.36
1, Best	172.05	164.87	159.77	152.70	148.03	140.90	136.76	131.96	129.13	125.83	123.91
1 & 2	158.44	151.88	147.14	140.64	136.32	129.75	125.97	121.49	118.93	115.86	114.13
2, Good	148.74	142.51	138.11	132.01	127.96	121.81	118.22	114.05	111.62	108.79	107.08
2 & 3	135.37	129.75	125.72	120.21	116.49	110.86	107.61	103.81	101.62	99.03	97.50
3, Average	124.45	119.38	115.70	110.57	107.19	102.03	99.04	95.54	93.54	91.13	89.76
3 & 4	112.51	107.86	104.48	99.87	96.78	92.13	89.42	86.27	84.46	82.26	81.00
4, Low	99.42	95.30	92.36	88.30	85.57	81.43	79.02	76.24	74.62	72.75	71.61

General Office Buildings – Masonry or Concrete

Interior Suite Entrances, Length More Than 4 Times Width

Estimating Procedure

1. Use these figures to estimate general office buildings in which access to each suite is through an interior corridor. Medical and dental offices have smaller rooms and more plumbing fixtures than general offices and should be estimated with figures from the Medical and Dental Buildings Section. See page 151.
2. Establish the building quality class by applying the information on page 135.
3. Compute the first floor area. This should include everything within the exterior walls and all insets outside the main walls but under the main roof.
4. If the first floor wall height is more or less than 10 feet, add to or subtract from the first floor square foot cost below the appropriate amount from the Wall Height Adjustment Table on page 142.
5. Multiply the adjusted square foot cost by the first floor area.
6. Deduct, if appropriate, for common walls or no wall finish. Use the figures on page 142.
7. If there are second or higher floors, compute the square foot area on each floor. Locate the appropriate square foot cost from the table at the bottom of this page. Adjust this figure for a wall height more or less than 9 feet, using the figures on page 142. Multiply the adjusted cost by the square foot area on each floor. Use the figures on page 142 to deduct for common walls or no wall finish. Add the result to the cost from step 6 above.
8. Multiply the total cost by the location factor on page 7 or 8.
9. Add the cost of heating and air conditioning systems, elevators, fire sprinklers, exterior signs, paving and curbing, miscellaneous yard improvements. See pages 236 to 248.

First Story - Square Foot Area

Quality Class	2,000	2,500	3,000	4,000	5,000	7,500	10,000	15,000	20,000	30,000	40,000
Exceptional	214.92	204.26	196.65	186.30	179.44	169.14	163.22	156.42	152.47	147.87	145.21
1, Best	198.31	188.46	181.43	171.83	165.56	156.05	150.59	144.28	140.67	136.45	133.96
1 & 2	181.80	172.78	166.31	157.56	151.75	143.07	138.04	132.30	128.95	125.05	122.81
2, Good	169.79	161.37	155.33	147.18	141.76	133.61	128.93	123.53	120.43	116.83	114.73
2 & 3	155.21	147.48	141.96	134.47	129.55	122.10	117.83	112.92	110.06	106.78	104.83
3, Average	143.91	136.76	131.67	124.70	120.14	113.26	109.26	104.75	102.05	99.03	97.22
3 & 4	130.41	123.94	119.30	113.03	108.88	102.66	99.05	94.92	92.51	89.72	88.06
4, Low	115.79	110.08	105.96	100.34	96.71	91.11	87.95	84.27	82.17	79.66	78.26

Second and Higher Stories - Square Foot Area

Quality Class	2,000	2,500	3,000	4,000	5,000	7,500	10,000	15,000	20,000	30,000	40,000
Exceptional	197.33	187.67	180.89	171.82	166.00	157.55	152.79	147.49	144.48	141.09	139.15
1, Best	180.55	171.68	165.45	157.26	151.90	144.18	139.83	134.95	132.20	129.11	127.33
1 & 2	167.28	159.13	153.37	145.69	140.78	133.58	129.59	125.05	122.48	119.65	117.95
2, Good	157.51	149.79	144.38	137.16	132.52	125.76	121.99	117.75	115.33	112.64	111.05
2 & 3	143.35	136.32	131.38	124.85	120.64	114.44	111.04	107.17	104.96	102.53	101.13
3, Average	132.60	126.13	121.51	115.48	111.58	105.86	102.71	99.12	97.11	94.82	93.53
3 & 4	130.61	124.15	119.72	113.72	109.85	104.27	101.15	97.60	95.64	93.35	92.07
4, Low	106.43	101.21	97.59	92.72	89.55	84.99	82.45	79.57	77.96	76.11	75.06

General Office Buildings – Masonry or Concrete

Wall Height Adjustments

The square foot costs for general offices are based on the wall heights of 10 feet for first floors and 9 feet for higher floors. The main or first floor height is the distance from the bottom of the floor slab or joists to the top of the roof slab or ceiling joists. Second and higher floors are measured from the top of the floor slab or floor joists to the top of the roof slab or ceiling joists. Add or subtract the amount listed in this table to or from the square foot of floor cost for each foot of wall height more or less than 10 feet, if adjusting for a first floor, and 9 feet, if adjusting for upper floors.

Square Foot Area

Quality Class	1,000	1,500	2,000	3,000	4,000	5,000	7,500	10,000	15,000	20,000	40,000
1, Best	6.00	4.71	3.99	3.15	2.69	2.39	1.91	1.64	1.35	1.13	.84
2, Good	5.21	4.07	3.43	2.72	2.36	2.07	1.68	1.43	1.14	1.01	.69
3, Average	4.59	3.59	3.03	2.43	2.07	1.83	1.43	1.24	1.04	.89	.62
4, Low	4.07	3.14	2.71	2.15	1.84	1.62	1.29	1.13	.93	.72	.58

Perimeter (Common) Wall Adjustment

A common wall exists when two buildings share one wall. Adjust for common walls by deducting the linear foot cost below from the total structure cost. In some structures one or more walls are not owned at all. In this case, deduct the "No Ownership" cost per linear foot of wall not owned. Where a perimeter wall remains unfinished, deduct the "lack of exterior finish" cost.

First Story

Class	For a Common Wall, Deduct Per L.F.	For No Wall Ownership, Deduct Per L.F.	For Lack of Exterior Finish, Deduct Per L.F.
1	$306	$615	$237
2	255	509	152
3	193	373	97
4	147	295	57

Second and Higher Stories

Class	For a Common Wall, Deduct Per L.F.	For No Wall Ownership, Deduct Per L.F.	For Lack of Exterior Finish, Deduct Per L.F.
1	$295	$587	$240
2	255	494	152
3	193	373	97
4	183	361	58

General Office, Class 3

General Office Buildings – Wood Frame

Quality Classification

	Class 1 Best Quality	Class 2 Good Quality	Class 3 Average Quality	Class 4 Low Quality
Foundation (12% of total cost)	Reinforced concrete.	Reinforced concrete.	Reinforced concrete.	Reinforced concrete.
First Floor Structure (8% of total cost)	Reinforced concrete slab on grade or standard wood frame.	Reinforced concrete slab on grade or standard wood frame.	Reinforced concrete slab on grade or 4" x 6" girders with 2" T&G subfloor.	Reinforced concrete slab on grade.
Upper Floor Structure (10% of total cost)	Standard wood frame. Plywood and 1-1/2" light-weight concrete subfloor.	Standard wood frame. Plywood and 1-1/2" light-weight concrete subfloor.	Standard wood frame. 5/8" plywood subfloor.	Standard wood frame. 5/8" plywood subfloor.
Walls (9% of total cost)	Standard wood frame.	Standard wood frame.	Standard wood frame.	Standard wood frame.
Roof Structure (6% of total cost)	Standard wood frame, flat or low pitch.	Standard wood frame, flat or low pitch.	Standard wood frame, flat or low pitch.	Standard wood frame, flat or low pitch.
Exterior Wall Finish (8% of total cost)	Good wood siding with 10 to 20% brick or stone veneer.	Average wood siding or stucco and 10 to 20% brick or stone veneer.	Stucco with some wood trim or cheap wood siding.	Stucco.
Windows (5% of total cost)	Average number in good aluminum frame. Fixed float glass in good frame on front side.	Average number in good aluminum frame. Some fixed float glass in front.	Average number of average aluminum sliding type.	Average number of low cost aluminum sliding type.
Roof Cover (5% of total cost)	5 ply built-up roofing on flat roofs. Heavy shake or tile on sloping roofs.	5 ply built-up roofing on flat roofs. Average shake or composition, tar and large rock on sloping roofs.	4 ply built-up roofing on flat roofs. Wood shingle or composition, tar and pea gravel on sloping roofs.	3 ply built-up roofing on flat roofs. Composition shingle on sloping roofs.
Overhang (3% of total cost)	3' closed overhang, fully guttered.	2' closed overhang, fully guttered.	None on flat roofs. 18" on sloping roofs, fully guttered.	None on flat roofs. 12" to 16" open on sloping roofs, gutters over entrances.
Floor Finishes:				
Offices (3% of total cost)	Very good carpet.	Good carpet.	Average grade carpet.	Minimum grade tile.
Corridors (2% of total cost)	Solid vinyl tile or carpet.	Resilient tile.	Composition tile.	Minimum grade tile.
Bathrooms (1% of total cost)	Sheet vinyl or ceramic tile.	Sheet vinyl or ceramic tile.	Composition tile.	Minimum grade tile.
Interior Wall Finish:				
Offices (6% of total cost)	Good hardwood veneer paneling.	Hardwood veneer paneling or vinyl wall cover.	Gypsum wallboard, texture and paint.	Gypsum wallboard, texture and paint.
Corridors (4% of total cost)	Good hardwood veneer paneling.	Gypsum wallboard and vinyl wall cover.	Gypsum wallboard, texture and paint.	Gypsum wallboard, texture and paint.
Bathrooms (2% of total cost)	Gypsum wallboard and enamel with ceramic tile wainscot.	Gypsum wallboard and enamel or vinyl wall covering.	Gypsum wallboard and enamel.	Gypsum wallboard, texture and paint.
Ceiling Finish (4% of total cost)	Suspended "T" bar and acoustical tile.	Gypsum wallboard and acoustical tile.	Gypsum wallboard and acoustical texture.	Gypsum wallboard and paint.
Plumbing (6% of total cost)	Copper tubing, top quality fixtures.	Copper tubing, good fixtures.	Copper tubing, standard fixtures.	Copper tubing, economy fixtures.
Lighting (6% of total cost)	Conduit wiring, good fixtures.	Conduit wiring, good fixtures.	Romex or conduit wiring, average fixtures.	Romex wiring economy fixtures.

Note: Use the percent of total cost to help identify the correct quality classification.

Square foot costs include the following components: Foundations as required for normal soil conditions. Floor, wall and roof structures. Interior floor, wall and ceiling finishes. Exterior wall finish and roof cover. Interior partitions. Cabinets, doors and windows. Basic electrical systems and lighting fixtures. Rough plumbing and fixtures. Permits and fees. Contractor's mark-up.

Exterior Suite Entrances, Length Less Than Twice Width

Estimating Procedure

1. Use these figures to estimate general office buildings in which access to each suite is through an exterior entrance. Medical and dental offices have smaller rooms and more plumbing fixtures than general offices and should be estimated with figures from the Medical and Dental Buildings Section. See page 151.
2. Establish the building quality class by applying the information on page 143.
3. Compute the first floor area. This should include everything within the exterior walls and all insets outside the main walls but under the main roof.
4. If the first floor wall height is more or less than 10 feet, add to or subtract from the first floor square foot cost below the appropriate amount from the Wall Height Adjustment Table on page 150.
5. Multiply the adjusted square foot cost by the first floor area.
6. Deduct, if appropriate, for common walls or no wall finish. Use the figures on page 150.
7. If there are second or higher floors, compute the square foot area on each floor. Locate the appropriate square foot cost from the table at the bottom of this page. Adjust this figure for a wall height more or less than 9 feet, using the figures on page 150. Multiply the adjusted cost by the square foot area on each floor. Use the figures on page 150 to deduct for common walls or no wall finish. Add the result to the cost from step 6 above.
8. Multiply the total cost by the location factor on page 7 or 8.
9. Add the cost of heating and air conditioning systems, elevators, fire sprinklers, exterior signs, paving and curbing, miscellaneous yard improvements. See pages 236 to 248.

General Offices, Class 1 & 2

First Story - Square Foot Area

Quality Class	1,000	1,500	2,000	2,500	3,000	4,000	5,000	7,500	10,000	15,000	20,000
Exceptional	194.76	184.17	178.11	174.03	171.10	167.04	164.35	160.24	157.86	155.01	153.38
1, Best	179.72	169.92	164.33	160.60	157.87	154.15	151.64	147.88	145.61	143.03	141.45
1 & 2	162.78	153.86	148.80	145.45	142.95	139.61	137.34	133.89	131.88	129.55	128.17
2, Good	148.29	140.25	135.62	132.48	130.34	127.19	125.14	122.04	120.16	118.06	116.79
2 & 3	135.32	127.99	123.77	120.92	118.88	116.08	114.17	111.36	109.69	107.73	106.57
3, Average	123.82	117.08	113.20	110.64	108.77	106.16	104.46	101.84	100.31	98.53	97.49
3 & 4	110.67	104.64	101.14	98.86	97.18	94.91	93.38	91.01	89.68	88.04	87.10
4, Low	96.82	91.60	88.57	86.51	85.09	83.06	81.72	79.70	78.49	77.13	76.25

Second and Higher Stories - Square Foot Area

Quality Class	1,000	1,500	2,000	2,500	3,000	4,000	5,000	7,500	10,000	15,000	20,000
Exceptional	170.16	163.36	159.45	156.85	154.99	152.42	150.64	148.04	146.53	144.72	143.68
1, Best	156.77	150.47	146.85	144.55	142.80	140.40	138.80	136.36	134.95	133.28	132.36
1 & 2	143.09	137.39	134.11	131.91	130.35	128.17	126.71	124.52	123.20	121.71	120.81
2, Good	130.71	125.51	122.52	120.53	119.05	117.04	115.71	113.79	112.55	111.12	110.36
2 & 3	117.92	113.20	110.51	108.68	107.39	105.63	104.44	102.60	101.52	100.27	99.57
3, Average	106.00	101.75	99.36	97.71	96.56	94.96	93.87	92.22	91.30	90.17	89.51
3 & 4	93.79	90.00	87.89	86.46	85.42	84.03	83.05	81.61	80.75	79.79	79.20
4, Low	81.62	78.37	76.51	75.23	74.33	73.10	72.25	70.98	70.25	69.41	68.93

General Office Buildings – Wood Frame

Exterior Suite Entrances, Length Between 2 and 4 Times Width

Estimating Procedure

1. Use these figures to estimate general office buildings in which access to each suite is through an exterior entrance. Medical and dental offices have smaller rooms and more plumbing fixtures than general offices and should be estimated with figures from the Medical and Dental Buildings Section. See page 151.
2. Establish the building quality class by applying the information on page 153.
3. Compute the first floor area. This should include everything within the exterior walls and all insets outside the main walls but under the main roof.
4. If the first floor wall height is more or less than 10 feet, add to or subtract from the first floor square foot cost below the appropriate amount from the Wall Height Adjustment Table on page 150.
5. Multiply the adjusted square foot cost by the first floor area.
6. Deduct, if appropriate, for common walls or no wall finish. Use the figures on page 150.
7. If there are second or higher floors, compute the square foot area on each floor. Locate the appropriate square foot cost from the table at the bottom of this page. Adjust this figure for a wall height more or less than 9 feet, using the figures on page 150. Multiply the adjusted cost by the square foot area on each floor. Use the figures on page 150 to deduct for common walls or no wall finish. Add the result to the cost from step 6 above.
8. Multiply the total cost by the location factor on page 7 or 8.
9. Add the cost of heating and air conditioning systems, elevators, fire sprinklers, exterior signs, paving and curbing, miscellaneous yard improvements. See pages 236 to 248.

General Offices, Class 3

First Story - Square Foot Area

Quality Class	1,000	1,500	2,000	2,500	3,000	4,000	5,000	7,500	10,000	15,000	20,000
Exceptional	205.76	192.31	184.66	179.68	176.02	171.10	167.85	162.92	160.04	156.76	154.82
1, Best	189.78	177.38	170.32	165.73	162.38	157.82	154.85	150.24	147.61	144.61	142.82
1 & 2	171.77	160.49	154.16	149.97	146.98	142.85	140.14	136.00	133.62	130.82	129.22
2, Good	156.57	146.32	140.48	136.66	133.94	130.19	127.70	123.95	121.75	119.30	117.80
2 & 3	143.03	133.65	128.38	124.86	122.40	118.98	116.68	113.29	111.30	109.01	107.64
3, Average	130.85	122.27	117.43	114.23	111.97	108.85	106.72	103.57	101.77	99.67	98.46
3 & 4	117.17	109.44	105.13	102.26	100.21	97.44	95.59	92.75	91.15	89.24	88.16
4, Low	102.71	95.93	92.11	89.71	87.88	85.40	83.77	81.30	79.90	78.22	77.26

Second and Higher Stories - Square Foot Area

Quality Class	1,000	1,500	2,000	2,500	3,000	4,000	5,000	7,500	10,000	15,000	20,000
Exceptional	177.15	168.20	163.24	159.97	157.73	154.55	152.53	149.47	147.74	145.68	144.53
1, Best	163.42	155.14	150.59	147.58	145.45	142.59	140.67	137.91	136.28	134.45	133.36
1 & 2	148.56	141.21	137.01	134.31	132.38	129.79	128.07	125.52	124.02	122.36	121.34
2, Good	135.57	128.68	124.86	122.41	120.66	118.30	116.68	114.37	113.04	111.49	110.60
2 & 3	123.03	116.79	113.35	111.07	109.49	107.34	105.91	103.77	102.59	101.17	100.35
3, Average	110.81	105.19	102.10	100.07	98.61	96.65	95.38	93.48	92.39	91.19	90.43
3 & 4	97.75	92.86	90.10	88.34	87.05	85.35	84.21	82.51	81.56	80.40	79.80
4, Low	85.59	81.28	78.85	77.29	76.18	74.70	73.70	72.22	71.39	70.40	69.88

Exterior Suite Entrances, Length More Than 4 Times Width

Estimating Procedure

1. Use these figures to estimate general office buildings in which access to each suite is through an exterior entrance. Medical and dental offices have smaller rooms and more plumbing fixtures than general offices and should be estimated with figures from the Medical and Dental Buildings Section. See page 151.

2. Establish the building quality class by applying the information on page 153.

3. Compute the first floor area. This should include everything within the exterior walls and all insets outside the main walls but under the main roof.

4. If the first floor wall height is more or less than 10 feet, add to or subtract from the first floor square foot cost below the appropriate amount from the Wall Height Adjustment Table on page 150.

5. Multiply the adjusted square foot cost by the first floor area.

6. Deduct, if appropriate, for common walls or no wall finish. Use the figures on page 150.

7. If there are second or higher floors, compute the square foot area on each floor. Locate the appropriate square foot cost from the table at the bottom of this page. Adjust this figure for a wall height more or less than 9 feet, using the figures on page 150. Multiply the adjusted cost by the square foot area on each floor. Use the figures on page 150 to deduct for common walls or no wall finish. Add the result to the cost from step 6 above.

8. Multiply the total cost by the location factor on page 7 or 8.

9. Add the cost of heating and air conditioning systems, elevators, fire sprinklers, exterior signs, paving and curbing, miscellaneous yard improvements. See pages 236 to 248.

General Offices, Class 2

First Story - Square Foot Area

Quality Class	1,000	1,500	2,000	2,500	3,000	4,000	5,000	7,500	10,000	15,000	20,000
Exceptional	218.91	202.19	192.80	186.65	182.22	176.29	172.27	166.37	162.92	159.00	156.71
1, Best	201.93	186.51	177.84	172.15	168.10	162.59	158.92	153.46	150.24	146.65	144.56
1 & 2	182.90	168.96	161.08	155.94	152.30	147.24	143.97	138.98	136.15	132.84	130.85
2, Good	166.51	153.77	146.59	141.93	138.58	133.99	131.07	126.50	123.92	120.90	119.13
2 & 3	152.26	140.60	134.11	129.81	126.73	122.56	119.82	115.67	113.33	110.58	109.00
3, Average	139.63	128.96	122.96	119.05	116.27	112.41	109.86	106.07	103.95	101.38	99.92
3 & 4	124.98	115.44	110.06	106.57	104.06	100.67	98.36	94.99	93.01	90.81	89.44
4, Low	109.72	101.31	96.64	93.53	91.31	88.35	86.32	83.38	81.63	79.70	78.51

Second and Higher Stories - Square Foot Area

Quality Class	1,000	1,500	2,000	2,500	3,000	4,000	5,000	7,500	10,000	15,000	20,000
Exceptional	184.83	174.20	168.23	164.33	161.52	157.75	155.18	151.35	149.23	146.69	145.19
1, Best	170.49	160.73	155.24	151.61	149.02	145.50	143.18	139.67	137.64	135.32	133.96
1 & 2	155.33	146.41	141.37	138.10	135.75	132.53	130.45	127.20	125.38	123.25	122.05
2, Good	142.24	134.00	129.46	126.45	124.30	121.36	119.41	116.49	114.82	112.85	111.73
2 & 3	128.65	121.24	117.10	114.37	112.41	109.77	107.98	105.35	103.81	102.09	101.07
3, Average	116.08	109.44	105.75	103.24	101.48	99.08	97.53	95.12	93.75	92.18	91.27
3 & 4	103.49	97.57	94.22	92.04	90.43	88.35	86.92	84.77	83.56	82.15	81.29
4, Low	90.01	84.85	81.97	80.04	78.72	76.81	75.61	73.76	72.64	71.43	70.75

General Office Buildings – Wood Frame

Interior Suite Entrances, Length Less Than Twice Width

Estimating Procedure

1. Use these figures to estimate general office buildings in which access to each suite is through an interior corridor. Medical and dental offices have smaller rooms and more plumbing fixtures than general offices and should be estimated with figures from the Medical and Dental Buildings Section. See page 151.
2. Establish the building quality class by applying the information on page 153.
3. Compute the first floor area. This should include everything within the exterior walls and all insets outside the main walls but under the main roof.
4. If the first floor wall height is more or less than 10 feet, add to or subtract from the first floor square foot cost below the appropriate amount from the Wall Height Adjustment Table on page 150.
5. Multiply the adjusted square foot cost by the first floor area.
6. Deduct, if appropriate, for common walls or no wall finish. Use the figures on page 150.
7. If there are second or higher floors, compute the square foot area on each floor. Locate the appropriate square foot cost from the table at the bottom of this page. Adjust this figure for a wall height more or less than 9 feet, using the figures on page 150. Multiply the adjusted cost by the square foot area on each floor. Use the figures on page 150 to deduct for common walls or no wall finish. Add the result to the cost from step 6 above.
8. Multiply the total cost by the location factor on page 7 or 8.
9. Add the cost of heating and air conditioning systems, elevators, fire sprinklers, exterior signs, paving and curbing, miscellaneous yard improvements. See page 236 to 248.

General Offices, Class 3 & 4

First Story - Square Foot Area

Quality Class	2,000	2,500	3,000	4,000	5,000	7,500	10,000	15,000	20,000	30,000	40,000
Exceptional	171.86	167.92	165.10	161.17	158.49	154.48	152.12	149.30	147.69	145.71	144.57
1, Best	158.33	154.73	152.12	148.50	146.05	142.27	140.15	137.57	136.06	134.30	133.22
1 & 2	152.02	141.68	139.25	135.92	133.71	130.33	128.27	125.95	124.56	122.96	121.96
2, Good	133.81	130.75	128.58	125.52	123.41	120.26	118.45	116.29	115.02	113.50	112.61
2 & 3	122.15	119.36	117.37	114.57	112.65	109.81	108.11	106.13	104.97	103.59	102.76
3, Average	111.73	109.20	107.35	104.78	103.05	100.42	98.90	97.08	95.98	94.76	94.05
3 & 4	100.15	97.88	96.20	93.89	92.35	90.01	88.60	87.04	86.08	84.91	84.26
4, Low	87.63	85.62	84.21	82.16	80.84	78.76	77.55	76.16	75.31	74.31	73.76

Second and Higher Stories - Square Foot Area

Quality Class	2,000	2,500	3,000	4,000	5,000	7,500	10,000	15,000	20,000	30,000	40,000
Exceptional	153.35	150.87	149.02	146.52	144.81	142.22	140.72	138.89	137.92	136.65	135.96
1, Best	141.43	139.20	137.46	135.14	133.61	131.22	129.81	128.18	127.19	126.07	125.43
1 & 2	130.27	128.15	126.55	124.46	123.04	120.81	119.54	118.01	117.15	116.07	115.48
2, Good	119.94	117.97	116.51	114.55	113.24	111.14	110.02	108.65	107.85	106.88	106.32
2 & 3	111.61	109.86	105.25	103.53	102.29	100.47	99.43	98.18	97.45	96.58	96.09
3, Average	97.79	96.17	95.05	93.41	92.32	90.69	89.73	88.58	87.90	87.13	86.69
3 & 4	87.00	85.57	84.54	83.11	82.16	80.67	79.82	78.78	78.22	77.52	77.16
4, Low	75.54	74.30	73.37	72.19	71.32	70.04	69.30	68.42	67.94	67.31	66.99

General Office Buildings – Wood Frame

Interior Suite Entrances, Length Between 2 and 4 Times Width

Estimating Procedure

1. Use these figures to estimate general office buildings in which access to each suite is through an interior corridor. Medical and dental offices have smaller rooms and more plumbing fixtures than general offices and should be estimated with figures from the Medical and Dental Buildings Section. See page 151.

2. Establish the building quality class by applying the information on page 153.

3. Compute the first floor area. This should include everything within the exterior walls and all insets outside the main walls but under the main roof.

4. If the first floor wall height is more or less than 10 feet, add to or subtract from the first floor square foot cost below the appropriate amount from the Wall Height Adjustment Table on page 150.

5. Multiply the adjusted square foot cost by the first floor area.

6. Deduct, if appropriate, for common walls or no wall finish. Use the figures on page 150.

7. If there are second or higher floors, compute the square foot area on each floor. Locate the appropriate square foot cost from the table at the bottom of this page. Adjust this figure for a wall height more or less than 9 feet, using the figures on page 150. Multiply the adjusted cost by the square foot area on each floor. Use the figures on page 150 to deduct for common walls or no wall finish. Add the result to the cost from step 6 above.

8. Multiply the total cost by the location factor on page 7 or 8.

9. Add the cost of heating and air conditioning systems, elevators, fire sprinklers, exterior signs, paving and curbing, miscellaneous yard improvements. See page 236 to 248.

First Story - Square Foot Area

Quality Class	2,000	2,500	3,000	4,000	5,000	7,500	10,000	15,000	20,000	30,000	40,000
Exceptional	177.90	173.31	169.96	165.32	162.18	157.29	154.41	151.04	149.02	146.67	145.25
1, Best	165.25	161.01	157.88	153.55	150.63	146.12	143.44	140.32	138.43	136.23	134.93
1 & 2	150.05	146.19	143.41	139.41	136.80	132.68	130.25	127.39	125.66	123.70	122.53
2, Good	138.42	134.91	132.31	128.65	126.18	122.41	120.16	117.53	115.95	114.12	113.04
2 & 3	126.50	123.24	120.89	117.56	115.30	111.85	109.81	107.39	105.96	104.25	103.29
3, Average	115.85	112.85	110.69	107.66	105.58	102.38	100.52	98.34	97.03	95.46	94.58
3 & 4	103.92	101.16	99.26	96.51	94.66	91.83	90.17	88.19	87.04	85.63	84.79
4, Low	90.93	88.59	86.88	84.49	82.91	80.38	78.88	77.21	76.18	74.95	74.22

Second and Higher Stories - Square Foot Area

Quality Class	2,000	2,500	3,000	4,000	5,000	7,500	10,000	15,000	20,000	30,000	40,000
Exceptional	157.29	154.15	151.90	148.81	146.79	143.74	141.96	139.89	138.74	137.31	136.49
1, Best	145.16	142.22	140.16	137.32	135.45	132.61	130.96	129.08	127.95	126.69	125.92
1 & 2	133.38	130.72	128.87	126.27	124.53	121.88	120.40	118.66	117.63	116.47	115.78
2, Good	123.07	120.60	118.85	116.44	114.86	112.43	111.05	109.49	108.49	107.44	106.78
2 & 3	111.24	109.02	107.40	105.24	103.81	101.64	100.35	98.92	98.08	97.09	96.55
3, Average	100.52	98.53	97.08	95.13	93.83	91.86	90.72	89.43	88.66	87.76	87.27
3 & 4	89.54	87.79	86.50	84.72	83.58	81.84	80.85	79.67	79.00	78.16	77.76
4, Low	77.48	76.00	74.87	73.35	72.37	70.83	70.00	68.95	68.36	67.67	67.28

General Office Buildings – Wood Frame

Interior Suite Entrances, Length More Than 4 Times Width

Estimating Procedure

1. Use these figures to estimate general office buildings in which access to each suite is through an interior corridor. Medical and dental offices have smaller rooms and more plumbing fixtures than general offices and should be estimated with figures from the Medical and Dental Buildings Section. See page 151.
2. Establish the building quality class by applying the information on page 153.
3. Compute the first floor area. This should include everything within the exterior walls and all insets outside the main walls but under the main roof.
4. If the first floor wall height is more or less than 10 feet, add to or subtract from the first floor square foot cost below the appropriate amount from the Wall Height Adjustment Table on page 150.
5. Multiply the adjusted square foot cost by the first floor area.
6. Deduct, if appropriate, for common walls or no wall finish. Use the figures on page 150.
7. If there are second or higher floors, compute the square foot area on each floor. Locate the appropriate square foot cost from the table at the bottom of this page. Adjust this figure for a wall height more or less than 9 feet, using the figures on page 150. Multiply the adjusted cost by the square foot area on each floor. Use the figures on page 150 to deduct for common walls or no wall finish. Add the result to the cost from step 6 above.
8. Multiply the total cost by the location factor on page 7 or 8.
9. Add the cost of heating and air conditioning systems, elevators, fire sprinklers, exterior signs, paving and curbing, miscellaneous yard improvements. See page 236 to 248.

General Offices, Class 2

First Story - Square Foot Area

Quality Class	2,000	2,500	3,000	4,000	5,000	7,500	10,000	15,000	20,000	30,000	40,000
Exceptional	186.47	180.43	176.06	170.19	166.28	160.44	157.09	153.20	150.98	148.30	146.78
1, Best	172.00	166.40	162.40	156.97	153.43	147.89	144.86	141.30	139.25	136.80	135.39
1 & 2	157.23	152.16	148.50	143.54	140.24	135.29	132.44	129.36	127.24	125.10	123.79
2, Good	145.00	140.30	136.91	132.34	129.30	124.72	122.14	119.09	117.37	115.32	114.12
2 & 3	132.60	128.25	125.17	121.06	118.23	114.05	111.65	109.00	107.35	105.48	104.43
3, Average	121.57	117.64	114.83	110.99	108.42	104.63	102.39	99.88	98.40	96.67	95.75
3 & 4	108.98	105.42	102.82	99.44	97.17	93.79	91.80	89.50	88.20	86.66	85.77
4, Low	95.66	92.56	90.32	87.30	85.32	82.28	80.58	78.58	77.39	76.08	75.31

Second and Higher Stories - Square Foot Area

Quality Class	2,000	2,500	3,000	4,000	5,000	7,500	10,000	15,000	20,000	30,000	40,000
Exceptional	161.88	158.07	155.34	151.61	149.13	145.44	143.28	140.82	139.38	137.69	136.75
1, Best	149.71	146.19	143.66	140.20	137.92	134.49	132.49	130.20	128.90	127.36	126.43
1 & 2	137.91	134.65	132.32	129.08	127.00	123.85	122.05	119.94	118.72	117.30	116.47
2, Good	127.07	124.02	121.87	118.92	117.00	114.11	112.39	110.48	109.36	108.05	107.24
2 & 3	114.97	112.25	110.29	107.66	105.91	103.29	101.76	100.01	98.96	97.77	97.12
3, Average	104.06	101.63	99.81	97.47	95.85	93.45	92.06	90.48	89.61	88.50	87.86
3 & 4	92.82	90.55	89.04	86.90	85.45	83.37	82.13	80.68	79.90	78.93	78.38
4, Low	80.75	78.84	77.46	75.62	74.36	72.51	71.47	70.22	69.53	68.67	68.18

General Office Buildings – Wood Frame

Wall Height Adjustment

The square foot costs for general offices are based on the wall heights of 10 feet for first floors and 9 feet for higher floors. Add to or subtract from the amount listed in this table the square foot of floor cost for each foot of wall height more or less than 10 feet, if adjusting for a first floor, and 9 feet, if adjusting for upper floors.

Square Foot Area

Quality Class	1,000	1,500	2,000	3,000	4,000	5,000	7,500	10,000	15,000	20,000	40,000
1, Best	2.20	1.86	1.63	1.37	1.16	1.06	.83	.69	.56	.48	.21
2, Good	1.93	1.61	1.42	1.20	1.06	.86	.71	.66	.49	.43	.16
3, Average	1.67	1.42	1.28	1.04	.86	.80	.66	.56	.45	.37	.16
4, Low	1.55	1.28	1.14	.94	.79	.70	.59	.50	.38	.33	.14

Perimeter (Common) Wall Adjustment

A common wall exists when two buildings share one wall. Adjust for common walls by deducting the linear foot cost below from the total structure cost. In some structures one or more walls are not owned at all. In this case, deduct the "No Ownership" cost per linear foot of wall not owned. Where a perimeter wall remains unfinished, deduct the "Lack of Exterior Finish" cost.

First Story

Class	For a Common Wall, Deduct Per L.F.	For No Wall Ownership, Deduct Per L.F.	For Lack of Exterior Finish, Deduct Per L.F.
1	$366	$738	$324
2	316	614	283
3	292	565	227
4	217	417	166

Second and Higher Stories

Class	For a Common Wall, Deduct Per L.F.	For No Wall Ownership, Deduct Per L.F.	For Lack of Exterior Finish, Deduct Per L.F.
1	$249	$475	$324
2	208	393	283
3	198	375	227
4	184	358	166

Medical-Dental Buildings – Masonry or Concrete

	Class 1 Best Quality	Class 2 Good Quality	Class 3 Average Quality	Class 4 Low Quality
First Floor Structure (10% of total cost)	Reinforced concrete slab on grade or standard wood frame.	Reinforced concrete slab on grade or standard wood frame.	Reinforced concrete slab on grade.	Reinforced concrete slab on grade.
Upper Floor Structure (8% of total cost)	Standard wood frame, plywood and 1-1/2" lightweight concrete subfloor.	Standard wood frame, plywood and 1-1/2" lightweight concrete subfloor.	Standard wood frame. 5/8" plywood subfloor.	Standard wood frame 5/8" plywood subfloor.
Walls (9% of total cost)	8" decorative concrete block or 6" concrete tilt-up.	8" decorative concrete block or 6" concrete tilt-up.	8" reinforced concrete block or 8" reinforced brick.	8" reinforced concrete block or clay tile.
Roof Structure (6% of total cost)	Standard wood frame, flat or low pitch.	Standard wood frame, flat or low pitch.	Standard wood frame, flat or low pitch.	Standard wood frame, flat or low pitch.
Exterior Wall Finish (8% of total cost)	Decorative block or large rock imbedded in tilt-up panels with 10 to 20% brick or stone veneer.	Decorative block or exposed aggregate and 10 to 20% brick or stone veneer.	Stucco or colored concrete block.	Painted.
Windows (5% of total cost)	Average number in good aluminum frame. Fixed float glass in good frame on front.	Average number in good aluminum frame. Some fixed float glass in front.	Average number of average aluminum sliding type.	Average number of low cost aluminum sliding type.
Roof Cover (5% of total cost)	5 ply built-up roofing on flat roofs. Heavy shake or tile on on sloping roofs.	5 ply built-up roofing on flat roofs. Average shake or composition, tar and large rock on sloping roofs.	4 ply built-up roofing on flat roofs. Wood shingle or composition, tar and pea gravel on sloping roofs.	3 ply built-up roofing on flat roofs. Composition shingle on sloping roofs.
Overhang (3% of total cost)	3' closed overhang, fully guttered.	2' closed overhang, fully guttered.	None on flat roofs. 18" open on sloping roofs, fully guttered.	None on flat roofs. 12" to 16" open on sloping roofs, gutters over entrances.
Business Offices (3% of total cost)	Good hardwood veneer paneling. Solid vinyl or carpet.	Hardwood paneling or vinyl wall cover. Resilient tile or carpet.	Gypsum wallboard, texture and paint. composition tile.	Gypsum wallboard, texture and paint. Minimum grade tile.
Corridors (6% of total cost)	Good hardwood veneer paneling. Solid vinyl or carpet.	Gypsum wallboard and vinyl wall cover. Resilient tile.	Gypsum wallboard, texture and paint. Composition tile.	Gypsum wallboard, texture and paint. Minimum grade tile.
Waiting Rooms (7% of total cost)	Good hardwood veneer paneling. Carpet.	Hardwood paneling. Carpet.	Gypsum wallboard, some paneling. Resilient tile or carpet.	Gypsum wallboard, texture and paint. Minimum grade tile.
Private Offices (2% of total cost)	Good hardwood veneer paneling. Carpet.	Textured wall cover and hardwood paneling. Carpet.	Gypsum wallboard and paper, wood paneling. Resilient tile or carpet.	Gypsum wallboard, texture and paint. Minimum grade tile.
Treatment Rooms (5% of total cost)	Gypsum wallboard and vinyl wall covering. Sheet vinyl or carpet.	Gypsum wallboard and enamel. Sheet vinyl.	Gypsum wallboard and enamel. Resilient tile.	Gypsum wallboard, texture and paint. Minimum grade tile.
Bathrooms (3% of total cost)	Gypsum wallboard and enamel with ceramic tile wainscot. Sheet vinyl or ceramic tile.	Gypsum wallboard and enamel or vinyl wall covering. Sheet vinyl or ceramic tile.	Gypsum wallboard and enamel. Resilient tile.	Gypsum wallboard, texture and paint. Minimum grade tile.
Ceiling Finish (4% of total cost)	Suspended "T" bar and acoustical tile.	Gypsum wallboard and acoustical tile.	Gypsum wallboard and acoustical tile.	Gypsum wallboard and paint.
Utilities				
Plumbing (6% of total cost)	Copper tubing, good economy fixtures.	Copper tubing, good fixtures.	Copper tubing, average fixtures.	Copper tubing, fixtures.
Lighting (6% of total cost)	Conduit wiring, good fixtures.	Conduit wiring, good fixtures.	Romex or conduit wiring, average fixtures.	Romex wiring, economy fixtures.
Cabinets (4% of total cost)	Formica faced with formica tops.	Good grade of hardwood with formica tops.	Average amount of painted wood or low grade hardwood with formica top.	Minimum amount of painted wood with formica top.

Note: Use the percent of total cost to help identify the correct quality classification.

Square foot costs include the following components: Foundations as required for normal soil conditions. Floor, wall and roof structures. Interior floor, wall and ceiling finishes. Exterior wall finish and roof cover. Interior partitions. Cabinets, doors and windows. Basic electrical systems and lighting fixtures. Rough plumbing and fixtures. Permits and fees. Contractor's mark-up. In addition to the above components, costs for buildings with more than 10,000 feet include the cost of lead shielding for typical x-ray rooms.

Exterior Suite Entrances, Length Less Than Twice Width

Estimating Procedure

1. Use these figures to estimate medical, dental, psychiatric, optometry and similar professional buildings in which access to each office suite is through an exterior entrance. Buildings in this section have more plumbing fixtures per square foot of floor and smaller room sizes than general office buildings. Note also that buildings with more than 10,000 square feet are assumed to have lead shielded x-ray rooms.
2. Establish the building quality class by applying the information on page 151.
3. Compute the first floor area. This should include everything within the exterior walls and all insets outside the main walls but under the main roof.
4. If the first floor wall height is more or less than 10 feet, add to or subtract from the first floor square foot cost below the appropriate amount from the Wall Height Adjustment Table on page 158.
5. Multiply the adjusted square foot cost by the first floor area.
6. Deduct, if appropriate, for common walls or no wall finish. Use the figures on page 158.
7. If there are second or higher floors, compute the square foot area on each floor. Locate the appropriate square foot cost from the table at the bottom of this page. Adjust this figure for a wall height more or less than 9 feet, using the figures on page 158. Multiply the adjusted cost by the square foot area on each floor. Use the figures on page 158 to deduct for common walls or no wall finish. Add the result to the cost from step 6 above.
8. Multiply the total cost by the location factor listed on page 7 or 8.
9. Add the cost of heating and air conditioning systems, elevators, fire sprinklers, exterior signs, paving and curbing, miscellaneous yard improvements. See page 236 to 248.

Medical-Dental Building, Class 2

First Story - Square Foot Area

Quality Class	1,000	1,500	2,000	2,500	3,000	4,000	5,000	7,500	10,000	15,000	20,000
Exceptional	252.38	237.48	228.82	223.05	218.75	212.91	208.93	202.90	199.30	195.09	192.64
1, Best	233.60	219.79	211.79	206.40	202.48	197.07	193.40	187.79	184.46	180.58	178.31
1 & 2	221.48	208.36	200.81	195.72	191.98	186.83	183.38	178.06	174.92	171.22	169.03
2, Good	211.51	199.05	191.79	186.95	183.38	178.47	175.15	170.05	167.06	163.56	161.46
2 & 3	195.54	183.96	177.28	172.77	169.48	164.92	161.89	157.18	154.41	151.16	149.24
3, Average	183.35	172.70	166.37	162.18	159.06	153.25	151.90	147.50	144.90	141.85	140.06
3 & 4	172.85	162.65	156.72	152.71	149.86	145.83	143.10	138.95	136.50	133.62	131.93
4, Low	160.97	151.52	145.99	142.30	139.54	135.83	133.31	129.44	127.16	124.45	122.85

Second and Higher Stories - Square Foot Area

Quality Class	1,000	1,500	2,000	2,500	3,000	4,000	5,000	7,500	10,000	15,000	20,000
Exceptional	225.96	210.84	202.67	197.44	193.78	188.90	185.73	181.19	178.58	175.70	174.03
1, Best	220.61	205.89	197.92	192.81	189.25	184.51	181.42	176.89	174.37	171.58	169.93
1 & 2	209.61	195.58	188.05	183.18	179.80	175.27	172.32	168.07	165.67	162.98	161.47
2, Good	202.28	188.78	181.47	176.80	173.51	169.13	166.33	162.20	159.84	157.30	155.82
2 & 3	186.77	174.33	167.56	163.20	160.20	156.22	153.56	149.75	147.64	145.28	143.86
3, Average	175.35	163.64	157.30	153.23	150.46	146.62	144.20	140.59	138.59	136.33	135.08
3 & 4	165.12	154.07	148.11	144.27	141.60	138.08	135.71	132.39	130.23	128.37	127.16
4, Low	153.89	143.62	138.05	134.51	132.02	128.66	126.53	123.41	121.60	119.70	118.57

Medical-Dental Buildings – Masonry or Concrete

Exterior Suite Entrances, Length Between 2 and 4 Times Width

Estimating Procedure

1. Use these figures to estimate medical, dental, psychiatric, optometry and similar professional buildings in which access to each office suite is through an exterior entrance. Buildings in this section have more plumbing fixtures per square foot of floor and smaller room sizes than general office buildings. Note also that buildings with more than 10,000 square feet are assumed to have lead shielded x-ray rooms.
2. Establish the building quality class by applying the information on page 151.
3. Compute the first floor area. This should include everything within the exterior walls and all insets outside the main walls but under the main roof.
4. If the first floor wall height is more or less than 10 feet, add to or subtract from the first floor square foot cost below the appropriate amount from the Wall Height Adjustment Table on page 158.
5. Multiply the adjusted square foot cost by the first floor area.
6. Deduct, if appropriate, for common walls or no wall finish. Use the figures on page 158.
7. If there are second or higher floors, compute the square foot area on each floor. Locate the appropriate square foot cost from the table at the bottom of this page. Adjust this figure for a wall height more or less than 9 feet, using the figures on page 158. Multiply the adjusted cost by the square foot area on each floor. Use the figures on page 158 to deduct for common walls or no wall finish. Add the result to the cost from step 6 above.
8. Multiply the total cost by the location factor listed on page 7 or 8.
9. Add the cost of heating and air conditioning systems, elevators, fire sprinklers, exterior signs, paving and curbing, miscellaneous yard improvements. See page 236 to 248.

Medical-Dental Building, Class 3 & 4

First Story - Square Foot Area

Quality Class	1,000	1,500	2,000	2,500	3,000	4,000	5,000	7,500	10,000	15,000	20,000
Exceptional	272.03	251.89	240.57	233.06	227.69	220.33	215.49	208.15	203.85	198.93	196.04
1, Best	252.23	233.57	223.00	216.07	211.12	204.28	199.76	192.95	189.04	184.46	181.80
1 & 2	237.19	219.69	209.79	203.25	198.58	192.19	187.90	181.52	177.80	173.49	171.01
2, Good	226.34	209.64	200.14	193.93	189.47	183.35	179.36	173.22	169.67	165.58	163.18
2 & 3	209.20	193.73	184.98	179.23	175.11	169.44	165.71	160.06	156.81	152.98	150.78
3, Average	196.42	181.88	173.68	168.29	164.42	159.12	155.60	150.26	147.19	143.61	141.56
3 & 4	184.93	171.22	163.49	158.40	154.75	149.79	146.44	141.48	138.57	135.24	133.29
4, Low	172.22	159.47	152.28	147.57	144.14	139.50	136.36	131.72	129.09	125.93	124.09

Second and Higher Stories - Square Foot Area

Quality Class	1,000	1,500	2,000	2,500	3,000	4,000	5,000	7,500	10,000	15,000	20,000
Exceptional	250.72	233.10	223.18	216.60	211.87	205.45	201.21	194.77	190.99	186.68	184.16
1, Best	232.46	216.31	206.90	200.77	196.42	190.41	186.53	180.51	177.04	173.02	170.71
1 & 2	220.78	205.23	196.46	190.72	186.58	180.88	177.11	171.44	168.17	164.38	162.09
2, Good	212.98	197.94	189.54	183.96	179.98	174.49	170.87	165.40	162.20	158.57	156.40
2 & 3	196.60	182.80	174.99	169.84	166.16	161.13	157.74	152.69	149.77	146.40	144.40
3, Average	184.55	171.58	164.25	159.42	155.91	151.22	148.11	143.31	140.57	137.40	135.57
3 & 4	173.84	161.65	154.74	150.23	146.96	142.45	139.50	135.03	132.47	129.42	127.66
4, Low	162.16	150.77	144.30	140.09	137.04	132.88	130.11	125.93	123.48	120.74	119.14

Exterior Suite Entrances, Length More Than 4 Times Width

Estimating Procedure

1. Use these figures to estimate medical, dental, psychiatric, optometry and similar professional buildings in which access to each office suite is through an exterior entrance. Buildings in this section have more plumbing fixtures per square foot of floor and smaller room sizes than general office buildings. Note also that buildings with more than 10,000 square feet are assumed to have lead shielded x-ray rooms.
2. Establish the building quality class by applying the information on page 151.
3. Compute the first floor area. This should include everything within the exterior walls and all insets outside the main walls but under the main roof.
4. If the first floor wall height is more or less than 10 feet, add to or subtract from the first floor square foot cost below the appropriate amount from the Wall Height Adjustment Table on page 158.
5. Multiply the adjusted square foot cost by the first floor area.
6. Deduct, if appropriate, for common walls or no wall finish. Use the figures on page 158.
7. If there are second or higher floors, compute the square foot area on each floor. Locate the appropriate square foot cost from the table at the bottom of this page. Adjust this figure for a wall height more or less than 9 feet, using the figures on page 158. Multiply the adjusted cost by the square foot area on each floor. Use the figures on page 158 to deduct for common walls or no wall finish. Add the result to the cost from step 6 above.
8. Multiply the total cost by the location factor listed on page 7 or 8.
9. Add the cost of heating and air conditioning systems, elevators, fire sprinklers, exterior signs, paving and curbing, miscellaneous yard improvements. See page 236 to 248.

Medical-Dental Building, Class 2 & 3

First Story - Square Foot Area

Quality Class	1,000	1,500	2,000	2,500	3,000	4,000	5,000	7,500	10,000	15,000	20,000
Exceptional	293.20	267.80	253.63	244.35	237.71	228.74	222.84	213.98	208.86	203.02	199.63
1, Best	271.82	248.31	235.11	226.51	220.41	212.06	206.58	198.35	193.65	188.21	185.06
1 & 2	255.25	233.08	220.72	212.66	206.94	199.06	193.89	186.18	181.75	176.72	173.73
2, Good	244.23	223.06	211.26	203.53	198.02	190.55	185.63	178.19	173.93	169.09	166.30
2 & 3	224.75	205.28	194.40	187.28	182.21	175.30	170.81	164.00	160.09	155.62	152.98
3, Average	210.79	192.51	182.28	175.65	170.87	164.43	160.17	153.77	150.15	145.92	143.48
3 & 4	198.40	181.14	171.60	165.29	160.86	154.75	150.77	145.32	141.27	137.34	135.05
4, Low	184.71	168.69	159.76	153.90	149.74	144.10	140.33	134.77	131.54	127.87	125.70

Second and Higher Stories - Square Foot Area

Quality Class	1,000	1,500	2,000	2,500	3,000	4,000	5,000	7,500	10,000	15,000	20,000
Exceptional	268.17	246.53	234.31	226.32	220.52	212.66	207.38	199.53	194.92	189.63	186.58
1, Best	247.58	227.61	216.36	208.91	203.59	196.33	191.47	184.20	179.98	175.11	172.27
1 & 2	236.00	216.97	206.23	199.16	194.06	187.13	182.53	175.55	171.57	166.90	164.16
2, Good	227.56	209.24	198.86	192.00	187.16	180.47	176.03	169.32	165.44	160.94	158.35
2 & 3	210.15	193.23	183.63	177.32	172.79	166.59	162.49	156.34	152.71	148.60	146.17
3, Average	197.19	181.31	172.30	166.45	162.19	156.40	152.52	146.71	143.34	139.46	137.19
3 & 4	186.05	170.98	162.54	156.95	152.95	147.49	143.88	138.38	135.23	131.52	129.38
4, Low	173.24	159.26	151.37	146.18	142.45	137.34	133.95	128.90	125.93	122.53	120.48

Interior Suite Entrances, Length Less Than Twice Width

Estimating Procedure

1. Use these figures to estimate medical, dental, psychiatric, optometry and similar professional buildings in which access to each office suite is through an interior corridor. Buildings in this section have more plumbing fixtures per square foot of floor and smaller room sizes than general office buildings. Note also that buildings with more than 10,000 square feet are assumed to have lead shielded x-ray rooms.
2. Establish the building quality class by applying the information on page 151.
3. Compute the first floor area. This should include everything within the exterior walls and all insets outside the main walls but under the main roof.
4. If the first floor wall height is more or less than 10 feet, add to or subtract from the first floor square foot cost below the appropriate amount from the Wall Height Adjustment Table on page 158.
5. Multiply the adjusted square foot cost by the first floor area.
6. Deduct, if appropriate, for common walls or no wall finish. Use the figures on page 158.
7. If there are second or higher floors, compute the square foot area on each floor. Locate the appropriate square foot cost from the table at the bottom of this page. Adjust this figure for a wall height more or less than 9 feet, using the figures on page 158. Multiply the adjusted cost by the square foot area on each floor. Use the figures on page 158 to deduct for common walls or no wall finish. Add the result to the cost from step 6 above.
8. Multiply the total cost by the location factor listed on page 7 or 8.
9. Add the cost of heating and air conditioning systems, elevators, fire sprinklers, exterior signs, paving and curbing, miscellaneous yard improvements. See page 236 to 248.

Medical-Dental Building, Class 3 & 4

First Story - Square Foot Area

Quality Class	2,000	2,500	3,000	4,000	5,000	7,500	10,000	15,000	20,000	30,000	40,000
Exceptional	213.33	207.57	203.53	198.55	193.72	187.82	184.37	180.31	177.95	175.20	173.54
1, Best	203.29	197.81	193.78	188.34	184.62	179.01	175.73	171.83	169.63	166.95	165.40
1 & 2	191.79	186.60	182.78	177.62	174.19	168.82	165.75	162.07	159.99	157.49	156.05
2, Good	183.55	178.57	174.97	170.04	166.68	161.58	158.62	155.17	153.14	150.71	149.31
2 & 3	170.11	165.53	162.18	157.57	154.49	149.77	147.06	143.80	141.93	139.69	138.39
3, Average	158.72	154.43	151.30	147.04	144.14	139.76	137.15	134.17	132.43	130.37	129.11
3 & 4	150.23	146.15	143.20	139.15	136.36	132.24	129.81	126.98	125.32	123.36	122.20
4, Low	140.82	136.97	134.21	130.41	127.87	123.95	121.69	119.06	117.46	115.66	114.55

Second and Higher Stories - Square Foot Area

Quality Class	2,000	2,500	3,000	4,000	5,000	7,500	10,000	15,000	20,000	30,000	40,000
Exceptional	201.69	196.53	192.79	187.66	184.20	178.94	175.86	172.29	170.21	167.70	166.27
1, Best	192.35	187.43	183.89	178.98	175.70	170.68	167.73	164.39	162.34	159.96	158.62
1 & 2	182.54	177.91	174.49	169.86	166.76	161.96	159.22	156.00	154.07	151.81	150.51
2, Good	175.87	171.41	168.15	163.64	160.60	156.08	153.39	150.26	148.42	146.29	144.98
2 & 3	162.60	158.44	155.42	151.33	148.49	144.28	141.83	138.92	137.24	135.24	134.07
3, Average	152.63	148.76	145.93	141.99	139.40	135.44	133.14	130.44	128.84	126.94	125.85
3 & 4	143.58	139.86	137.26	133.59	131.18	127.48	125.20	122.76	121.22	119.42	118.42
4, Low	135.22	131.72	129.24	125.78	123.46	119.94	117.93	115.52	114.13	112.45	111.48

Medical-Dental Buildings – Masonry or Concrete

Interior Suite Entrances, Length Between 2 and 4 Times Width

Estimating Procedure

1. Use these figures to estimate medical, dental, psychiatric, optometry and similar professional buildings in which access to each office suite is through an interior corridor. Buildings in this section have more plumbing fixtures per square foot of floor and smaller room sizes than general office buildings. Note also that buildings with more than 10,000 square feet are assumed to have lead shielded x-ray rooms.
2. Establish the building quality class by applying the information on page 151.
3. Compute the first floor area. This should include everything within the exterior walls and all insets outside the main walls but under the main roof.
4. If the first floor wall height is more or less than 10 feet, add to or subtract from the first floor square foot cost below the appropriate amount from the Wall Height Adjustment Table on page 158.
5. Multiply the adjusted square foot cost by the first floor area.
6. Deduct, if appropriate, for common walls or no wall finish. Use the figures on page 158.
7. If there are second or higher floors, compute the square foot area on each floor. Locate the appropriate square foot cost from the table at the bottom of this page. Adjust this figure for a wall height more or less than 9 feet, using the figures on page 158. Multiply the adjusted cost by the square foot area on each floor. Use the figures on page 158 to deduct for common walls or no wall finish. Add the result to the cost from step 6 above.
8. Multiply the total cost by the location factor listed on page 7 or 8.
9. Add the cost of heating and air conditioning systems, elevators, fire sprinklers, exterior signs, paving and curbing, miscellaneous yard improvements. See page 236 to 248.

Medical-Dental Building, Class 3

First Story - Square Foot Area

Quality Class	2,000	2,500	3,000	4,000	5,000	7,500	10,000	15,000	20,000	30,000	40,000
Exceptional	223.32	216.21	211.06	204.02	199.34	192.23	188.11	183.29	180.48	177.23	175.26
1, Best	212.85	206.10	201.21	194.47	190.00	183.21	179.31	174.69	172.00	168.86	167.02
1 & 2	200.60	194.25	189.62	183.26	179.04	172.68	168.94	164.68	162.09	159.21	157.46
2, Good	191.79	185.72	181.34	175.26	171.23	165.15	161.58	157.46	155.07	152.24	150.56
2 & 3	177.64	172.00	167.88	162.35	158.61	152.90	149.59	145.82	143.59	140.95	139.45
3, Average	165.62	160.34	156.53	151.30	147.82	142.56	139.48	135.92	133.83	131.43	129.95
3 & 4	156.88	151.88	148.33	143.34	140.03	135.07	132.14	128.70	126.81	124.46	123.19
4, Low	146.84	142.17	138.80	134.16	131.07	126.43	123.74	120.48	118.68	116.50	115.23

Second and Higher Stories - Square Foot Area

Quality Class	2,000	2,500	3,000	4,000	5,000	7,500	10,000	15,000	20,000	30,000	40,000
Exceptional	210.49	204.13	199.59	193.30	189.12	182.78	179.11	174.83	172.32	169.47	167.68
1, Best	200.62	194.55	190.20	184.24	180.19	174.27	170.69	166.62	164.22	161.49	159.82
1 & 2	190.32	184.59	180.45	174.78	171.01	165.23	161.92	158.09	155.81	153.20	151.63
2, Good	183.42	177.91	173.86	168.38	164.78	159.32	156.10	152.39	150.17	147.63	146.14
2 & 3	169.33	164.22	160.55	155.50	152.12	147.08	144.09	140.64	138.66	136.26	134.95
3, Average	158.85	154.11	150.56	145.86	142.71	137.93	135.13	131.93	130.05	127.86	126.53
3 & 4	150.42	145.86	142.58	138.13	135.13	130.61	127.99	124.93	123.12	121.01	119.81
4, Low	140.94	136.70	133.65	129.46	126.65	122.41	119.91	117.11	115.42	113.48	112.30

Medical-Dental Buildings – Masonry or Concrete

Interior Suite Entrances, Length More Than 4 Times Width

Estimating Procedure

1. Establish the building quality class by applying the information on page 151.
3. Compute the first floor area. This should include everything within the exterior walls and all insets outside the main walls but under the main roof.
4. If the first floor wall height is more or less than 10 feet, add to or subtract from the first floor square foot cost below the appropriate amount from the Wall Height Adjustment Table on page 158.
5. Multiply the adjusted square foot cost by the first floor area.
6. Deduct, if appropriate, for common walls or no wall finish. Use the figures on page 158.
7. If there are second or higher floors, compute the square foot area on each floor. Locate the appropriate square foot cost from the table at the bottom of this page. Adjust this figure for a wall height more or less than 9 feet, using the figures on page 158. Multiply the adjusted cost by the square foot area on each floor. Use the figures on page 158 to deduct for common walls or no wall finish. Add the result to the cost from step 6 above.
8. Multiply the total cost by the location factor listed on page 7 or 8.
9. Add the cost of heating and air conditioning systems, elevators, fire sprinklers, exterior signs, paving and curbing, miscellaneous yard improvements. See page 236 to 248.

Medical-Dental Building, Class 2 & 3

First Story - Square Foot Area

Quality Class	2,000	2,500	3,000	4,000	5,000	7,500	10,000	15,000	20,000	30,000	40,000
Exceptional	236.13	227.20	220.81	212.14	206.42	197.83	192.86	187.16	183.81	180.02	177.79
1, Best	225.04	216.53	210.48	202.18	196.71	188.52	183.80	178.38	175.20	171.58	169.38
1 & 2	211.93	203.94	198.19	190.37	185.26	177.55	173.14	168.00	165.04	161.57	159.54
2, Good	202.48	194.87	189.41	181.93	177.02	169.63	165.40	160.48	157.66	154.35	152.43
2 & 3	187.33	180.23	175.20	168.30	163.77	156.92	153.02	148.47	145.85	142.84	141.03
3, Average	176.10	169.49	164.72	158.24	153.94	147.55	143.85	139.60	137.13	134.22	132.58
3 & 4	166.62	160.34	155.81	149.74	145.66	139.56	136.11	132.09	129.74	127.01	125.48
4, Low	156.07	150.16	145.97	140.23	136.43	130.74	127.44	123.74	121.49	118.99	117.46

Second and Higher Stories - Square Foot Area

Quality Class	2,000	2,500	3,000	4,000	5,000	7,500	10,000	15,000	20,000	30,000	40,000
Exceptional	221.41	213.48	207.77	200.05	194.96	187.33	182.94	177.92	174.97	171.60	169.63
1, Best	211.15	203.56	198.13	190.77	185.95	178.60	174.45	169.65	166.81	163.59	161.68
1 & 2	200.22	193.02	187.88	180.92	176.32	169.38	165.44	160.86	158.23	155.15	153.34
2, Good	192.86	185.96	180.98	174.30	169.84	163.19	159.37	154.95	152.42	149.44	147.71
2 & 3	177.90	171.54	166.92	160.74	156.65	150.54	147.01	142.97	140.59	137.81	136.25
3, Average	167.09	161.10	156.83	151.00	147.16	141.39	138.11	134.22	132.04	129.49	127.96
3 & 4	158.20	152.50	148.42	142.94	139.25	133.85	130.67	127.07	124.99	122.54	121.14
4, Low	148.23	142.96	139.08	133.93	130.50	125.47	122.47	119.14	117.13	114.83	113.50

Medical-Dental Buildings – Masonry or Concrete

Wall Height Adjustment

The square foot costs for medical-dental buildings are based on the wall heights of 10 feet for first floors and 9 feet for higher floors. The main or first floor height is the distance from the bottom of the floor slab or joists to the top of the roof slab or ceiling joists. Second and higher floors are measured from the top of the floor slab or floor joists to the top of the roof slab or ceiling joists. Add or subtract the amount listed in this table to or from the square foot of floor cost for each foot of wall height more or less than 10 feet, if adjusting for a first floor, and 9 feet, if adjusting for upper floors.

Square Foot Area

Quality Class	1,000	1,500	2,000	3,000	4,000	5,000	7,500	10,000	15,000	20,000	40,000
1, Best	6.39	4.98	4.20	3.29	2.78	2.49	1.96	1.69	1.38	1.13	.83
2, Good	5.50	4.31	3.61	2.88	2.43	2.18	1.72	1.46	1.16	1.03	.68
3, Average	4.82	3.76	3.13	2.51	2.14	1.89	1.53	1.28	1.05	.92	.62
4, Low	4.22	3.37	2.81	2.19	1.88	1.64	1.31	1.14	.93	.72	.56

Perimeter (Common) Wall Adjustment

A common wall exists when two buildings share one wall. Adjust for common walls by deducting the linear foot costs below from the total structure cost. In some structures, one or more walls are not owned at all. In this case, deduct the "No Ownership" cost per linear foot of wall not owned. If a wall has no exterior finish, deduct the "Lack of Exterior Finish" cost.

First Story

Class	For a Common Wall, Deduct Per L.F.	For No Wall Ownership, Deduct Per L.F.	For Lack of Exterior Finish, Deduct Per L.F.
1	$365	$739	$280
2	287	501	184
3	207	414	100
4	155	317	63

Second and Higher Stories

Class	For a Common Wall, Deduct Per L.F.	For No Wall Ownership, Deduct Per L.F.	For Lack of Exterior Finish, Deduct Per L.F.
1	$342	$667	$280
2	280	541	186
3	207	414	100
4	184	365	63

Medical-Dental Buildings – Wood Frame

	Class 1 Best Quality	Class 2 Good Quality	Class 3 Average Quality	Class 4 Low Quality
Foundation (9% of total cost)	Reinforced concrete.	Reinforced concrete.	Reinforced concrete.	Reinforced concrete.
First Floor Structure (4% of total cost)	Reinforced concrete slab on grade or standard wood frame.	Reinforced concrete slab on grade or standard wood frame.	Reinforced concrete slab on grade or 4" x 6" girders with 2" T&G subfloor.	Reinforced concrete slab on grade.
Upper Floor Structure (6% of total cost)	Standard wood frame, plywood and 1-1/2" light-weight concrete subfloor.	Standard wood frame, plywood and 1-1/2" light-weight concrete subfloor.	Standard wood frame, 5/8" plywood subfloor.	Standard wood frame, 5/8" plywood subfloor.
Walls (9% of total cost)	Standard wood frame.	Standard wood frame.	Standard wood frame.	Standard wood frame.
Roof Structure (6% of total cost)	Standard wood frame, flat or low pitch.	Standard wood frame, flat or low pitch.	Standard wood frame, flat or low pitch.	Standard wood frame, flat or low pitch.
Exterior Finishes:				
Walls (8% of total cost)	Good wood siding with 10 to 20% brick or stone veneer.	Average wood siding or stucco and 10 to 20% brick or stone veneer.	Stucco with some wood trim or cheap wood siding.	Stucco.
Windows (5% of total cost)	Average number in good aluminum frame. Fixed float glass in good frame on front.	Average number in good aluminum frame. Some fixed float glass in front.	Average amount of average aluminum sliding type.	Average number of low cost aluminum sliding type.
Roof Cover (5% of total cost)	5 ply built-up roofing on flat roofs. Heavy shake or tile on sloping roofs.	5 ply built-up roofing on flat roofs. Avg. shake or composition, tar and large rock on sloping roofs.	4 ply built-up roofing on flat roofs. Wood shingle or composition, tar and pea gravel on sloping roofs.	3 ply built-up roofing on flat roofs. Composition shingle on sloping roofs.
Overhang (3% of total cost)	3' sealed overhang, fully guttered.	2' sealed overhang, fully guttered.	None on flat roofs. 18" unsealed on sloping roofs, fully guttered.	None on flat roofs. 12" to 16" unsealed on sloping roofs, gutters over entrances.
Floor Finishes:				
Business Offices (3% of total cost)	Solid vinyl tile or carpet.	Resilient tile or carpet.	Composition tile.	Minimum grade tile.
Corridors (2% of total cost)	Solid vinyl tile or carpet.	Resilient tile or carpet.	Composition tile.	Minimum grade tile.
Waiting Rooms (1% of total cost)	Carpet.	Carpet.	Composition tile or carpet.	Minimum grade tile.
Private Offices (2% of total cost)	Carpet.	Carpet.	Composition tile or carpet.	Minimum grade tile.
Treatment Rooms (2% of total cost)	Sheet vinyl or carpet.	Sheet vinyl.	Composition tile.	Minimum grade tile.
Bathrooms (1% of total cost)	Sheet vinyl or ceramic tile.	Sheet vinyl or ceramic tile.	Composition tile.	Minimum grade tile.
Interior Wall Finishes:				
Business Offices (3% of total cost)	Good hardwood veneer paneling.	Hardwood paneling or vinyl wall cover.	Gypsum wallboard, texture and paint.	Gypsum wallboard, texture and paint.
Corridors (2% of total cost)	Good hardwood veneer paneling.	Gypsum wallboard and vinyl wall cover.	Gypsum wallboard, texture and paint.	Gypsum wallboard, texture and paint.
Waiting Rooms (1% of total cost)	Good hardwood veneer paneling.	Hardwood paneling.	Gypsum wallboard and paper, some wood paneling.	Gypsum wallboard, texture and paint.
Treatment Rooms (3% of total cost)	Gypsum wallboard and vinyl wall covering.	Gypsum wallboard and enamel.	Gypsum wallboard and enamel.	Gypsum wallboard, texture and paint.
Bathrooms (2% of total cost)	Gypsum wallboard and enamel with ceramic tile wainscot.	Gypsum wallboard and enamel or vinyl wall covering.	Gypsum wallboard and enamel.	Gypsum wallboard, texture and paint.
Ceiling Finish (4% of total cost)	Suspended "T" bar and acoustical tile.	Gypsum wallboard and acoustical tile.	Gypsum wallboard and acoustical tile.	Gypsum wallboard and paint.
Plumbing (6% of total cost)	Copper tubing, good fixtures.	Copper tubing, good fixtures.	Copper tubing, average fixtures.	Copper tubing, economy fixtures.
Lighting (6% of total cost)	Conduit wiring, good fixtures.	Conduit wiring, good fixtures.	Romex or conduit wiring, average fixtures.	Romex wiring, economy fixtures.
Cabinets (7% of total cost)	Formica faced with formica tops.	Good grade of hardwood with formica tops.	Average amount of painted wood or low grade hardwood with formica top.	Minimum amount of painted wood with formica top.

Note: Use the percent of total cost to help identify the correct quality classification.

Square foot costs include the following components: Foundations as required for normal soil conditions. Floor, wall and roof structures. Interior floor, wall and ceiling finishes. Exterior wall finish and roof cover. Interior partitions. Cabinets, doors and windows. Basic electrical systems and lighting fixtures. Rough plumbing and fixtures. Permits and fees. Contractor's mark-up. In addition to the above components, costs for buildings with more than 10,000 feet include the cost of lead shielding for typical x-ray rooms.

Medical-Dental Buildings – Wood Frame

Exterior Suite Entrances, Length Less Than Twice Width

Estimating Procedure

1. Use these figures to estimate medical, dental, psychiatric, optometry and similar professional buildings in which access to each office suite is through an exterior entrance. Buildings in this section have more plumbing fixtures per square foot of floor and smaller room sizes than general office buildings. Note also that buildings with more than 10,000 square feet are assumed to have lead shielded x-ray rooms.
2. Establish the building quality class by applying the information on page 159.
3. Compute the first floor area. This should include everything within the exterior walls and all insets outside the main walls but under the main roof.
4. If the first floor wall height is more or less than 10 feet, add to or subtract from the first floor square foot cost below the appropriate amount from the Wall Height Adjustment Table on page 166.
5. Multiply the adjusted square foot cost by the first floor area.
6. Deduct, if appropriate, for common walls or no wall finish. Use the figures on page 166.
7. If there are second or higher floors, compute the square foot area on each floor. Locate the appropriate square foot cost from the table at the bottom of this page. Adjust this figure for a wall height more or less than 9 feet, using the figures on page 166. Multiply the adjusted cost by the square foot area on each floor. Use the figures on page 166 to deduct for common walls or no wall finish. Add the result to the cost from step 6 above.
8. Multiply the total cost by the location factor listed on page 7 or 8.
9. Add the cost of heating and air conditioning systems, elevators, fire sprinklers, exterior signs, paving and curbing, miscellaneous yard improvements. See page 236 to 248.

Medical-Dental Building, Class 2 & 3

First Story - Square Foot Area

Quality Class	1,000	1,500	2,000	2,500	3,000	4,000	5,000	7,500	10,000	15,000	20,000
Exceptional	233.92	224.84	219.63	216.14	213.67	210.23	207.95	204.50	202.50	200.08	198.73
1, Best	214.74	206.36	201.66	198.45	196.20	193.03	190.96	187.78	185.88	183.73	182.44
1 & 2	202.47	194.58	190.13	187.13	184.98	182.00	180.00	177.01	175.19	173.17	171.98
2, Good	191.52	184.06	179.82	177.00	174.98	172.14	170.28	167.43	165.81	163.84	162.71
2 & 3	177.85	170.93	166.96	164.35	162.46	159.82	158.15	155.44	153.96	152.10	151.07
3, Average	166.47	159.99	156.29	153.82	152.07	149.62	148.01	145.53	144.09	142.41	141.41
3 & 4	155.59	149.56	146.07	143.78	142.14	139.81	138.36	136.04	134.68	133.12	132.15
4, Low	145.27	139.65	136.45	134.28	132.76	130.64	129.20	127.08	125.80	124.31	123.44

Second and Higher Stories - Square Foot Area

Quality Class	1,000	1,500	2,000	2,500	3,000	4,000	5,000	7,500	10,000	15,000	20,000
Exceptional	208.55	203.25	200.17	198.07	196.55	194.41	192.95	190.70	189.37	187.81	186.90
1 Best	191.70	186.82	184.01	182.10	180.71	178.77	177.42	175.31	174.13	172.67	171.83
1 & 2	179.29	174.80	172.14	170.35	169.01	167.18	165.91	164.05	162.86	161.48	160.74
2, Good	174.64	170.27	167.72	165.92	164.66	162.88	161.68	159.78	158.58	157.34	156.57
2 & 3	161.41	157.30	154.95	153.34	152.10	150.46	149.34	147.61	146.56	145.39	144.67
3, Average	150.23	147.00	144.22	142.69	141.61	140.09	139.01	137.39	136.45	135.35	134.68
3 & 4	140.41	136.85	134.80	133.38	132.35	130.90	129.93	128.47	127.56	126.46	125.89
4, Low	131.36	128.02	126.12	124.76	123.81	122.50	121.51	120.14	119.34	118.33	117.71

Medical-Dental Buildings – Wood Frame

Exterior Suite Entrances, Length Between 2 and 4 Times Width

Estimating Procedure

1. Use these figures to estimate medical, dental, psychiatric, optometry and similar professional buildings in which access to each office suite is through an exterior entrance. Buildings in this section have more plumbing fixtures per square foot of floor and smaller room sizes than general office buildings. Note also that buildings with more than 10,000 square feet are assumed to have lead shielded x-ray rooms.
2. Establish the building quality class by applying the information on page 159.
3. Compute the first floor area. This should include everything within the exterior walls and all insets outside the main walls but under the main roof.
4. If the first floor wall height is more or less than 10 feet, add to or subtract from the first floor square foot cost below the appropriate amount from the Wall Height Adjustment Table on page 166.
5. Multiply the adjusted square foot cost by the first floor area.
6. Deduct, if appropriate, for common walls or no wall finish. Use the figures on page 166.
7. If there are second or higher floors, compute the square foot area on each floor. Locate the appropriate square foot cost from the table at the bottom of this page. Adjust this figure for a wall height more or less than 9 feet, using the figures on page 166. Multiply the adjusted cost by the square foot area on each floor. Use the figures on page 166 to deduct for common walls or no wall finish. Add the result to the cost from step 6 above.
8. Multiply the total cost by the location factor listed on page 7 or 8.
9. Add the cost of heating and air conditioning systems, elevators, fire sprinklers, exterior signs, paving and curbing, miscellaneous yard improvements. See page 236 to 248.

Medical-Dental Building, Class 1 & 2

First Story - Square Foot Area

Quality Class	1,000	1,500	2,000	2,500	3,000	4,000	5,000	7,500	10,000	15,000	20,000
Exceptional	238.93	227.66	221.30	217.13	214.19	210.04	207.33	203.21	200.86	198.07	196.46
1, Best	219.33	209.00	203.17	199.35	196.57	192.81	190.35	186.57	184.40	181.85	180.40
1 & 2	206.48	196.79	191.30	187.67	185.11	181.55	179.19	175.68	173.58	171.27	170.74
2, Good	195.01	186.08	180.80	177.42	175.02	171.63	169.45	166.05	164.12	161.86	160.60
2 & 3	181.20	172.70	167.82	164.69	162.40	159.28	157.24	154.15	152.32	150.24	149.04
3, Average	169.52	161.60	157.09	154.14	151.96	149.04	147.12	144.22	142.52	140.52	139.44
3 & 4	158.35	150.94	146.71	143.97	141.98	139.25	137.44	134.71	133.15	131.36	130.27
4, Low	147.90	140.93	136.98	134.42	132.53	130.04	128.36	125.77	124.31	122.61	121.60

Second and Higher Stories - Square Foot Area

Quality Class	1,000	1,500	2,000	2,500	3,000	4,000	5,000	7,500	10,000	15,000	20,000
Exceptional	211.07	204.34	200.48	197.93	196.05	193.50	191.77	189.14	187.64	185.84	184.82
1, Best	193.77	187.57	184.05	181.70	180.00	177.62	176.06	173.63	172.26	170.61	169.68
1 & 2	184.12	178.28	174.92	172.65	171.04	168.83	167.34	165.00	163.71	162.18	161.22
2, Good	176.73	171.10	167.87	165.74	164.16	161.97	160.61	158.41	157.12	155.58	154.74
2 & 3	163.42	158.24	155.29	153.25	151.79	149.81	148.52	146.44	145.27	143.87	143.07
3, Average	151.39	146.61	143.83	142.02	140.68	138.84	137.64	135.72	134.60	133.36	132.58
3 & 4	142.32	137.85	135.18	133.43	132.17	130.49	129.30	127.56	126.55	125.35	124.62
4, Low	132.08	127.90	125.54	123.86	122.73	121.11	120.04	118.42	117.47	116.33	115.66

Medical-Dental Buildings – Wood Frame

Exterior Suite Entrances, Length More Than 4 Times Width

Estimating Procedure

1. Use these figures to estimate medical, dental, psychiatric, optometry and similar professional buildings in which access to each office suite is through an exterior entrance. Buildings in this section have more plumbing fixtures per square foot of floor and smaller room sizes than general office buildings. Note also that buildings with more than 10,000 square feet are assumed to have lead shielded x-ray rooms.
2. Establish the building quality class by applying the information on page 159.
3. Compute the first floor area. This should include everything within the exterior walls and all insets outside the main walls but under the main roof.
4. If the first floor wall height is more or less than 10 feet, add to or subtract from the first floor square foot cost below the appropriate amount from the Wall Height Adjustment Table on page 166.
5. Multiply the adjusted square foot cost by the first floor area.
6. Deduct, if appropriate, for common walls or no wall finish. Use the figures on page 166.
7. If there are second or higher floors, compute the square foot area on each floor. Locate the appropriate square foot cost from the table at the bottom of this page. Adjust this figure for a wall height more or less than 9 feet, using the figures on page 166. Multiply the adjusted cost by the square foot area on each floor. Use the figures on page 166 to deduct for common walls or no wall finish. Add the result to the cost from step 6 above.
8. Multiply the total cost by the location factor listed on page 7 or 8.
9. Add the cost of heating and air conditioning systems, elevators, fire sprinklers, exterior signs, paving and curbing, miscellaneous yard improvements. See page 236 to 248.

Medical-Dental Building, Class 1

First Story - Square Foot Area

Quality Class	1,000	1,500	2,000	2,500	3,000	4,000	5,000	7,500	10,000	15,000	20,000
Exceptional	249.81	235.93	228.20	223.10	219.46	214.49	211.27	206.28	203.46	200.18	198.30
1, Best	229.82	217.09	209.99	205.31	201.93	197.37	194.40	189.84	187.22	184.17	182.43
1 & 2	216.13	204.15	197.43	193.03	189.85	185.61	182.76	178.53	176.02	173.19	171.57
2, Good	204.04	192.77	186.41	182.28	179.28	175.25	172.62	168.54	166.18	163.55	161.96
2 & 3	189.35	178.82	172.97	169.10	166.39	162.59	160.14	156.35	154.17	151.72	150.29
3, Average	177.06	167.33	161.73	158.16	155.57	152.06	149.70	146.22	144.22	141.89	140.52
3 & 4	165.29	156.16	151.04	147.67	145.22	141.95	139.78	136.53	134.62	132.48	131.27
4, Low	154.28	145.74	140.95	137.82	135.54	132.46	130.48	127.40	125.63	123.69	122.50

Second and Higher Stories - Square Foot Area

Quality Class	1,000	1,500	2,000	2,500	3,000	4,000	5,000	7,500	10,000	15,000	20,000
Exceptional	218.16	209.55	204.68	201.53	199.30	196.16	194.10	191.05	189.25	187.20	185.98
1, Best	200.39	192.47	188.05	185.12	183.04	180.21	178.31	175.46	173.85	171.93	170.85
1 & 2	190.20	182.66	178.43	175.72	173.74	170.98	169.20	166.52	164.93	163.19	162.20
2, Good	181.94	174.71	170.72	168.01	166.14	163.57	161.84	159.28	157.79	156.11	155.07
2 & 3	168.15	161.48	157.76	155.33	153.55	151.16	149.60	147.20	145.78	144.27	143.33
3, Average	156.30	150.17	146.70	144.42	142.77	140.58	139.09	136.85	135.60	134.16	133.27
3 & 4	146.24	140.43	137.27	135.11	133.60	131.51	130.11	128.04	126.87	125.54	124.69
4, Low	136.54	131.21	128.10	126.17	124.74	122.78	121.49	119.60	118.45	117.17	116.44

Medical-Dental Buildings – Wood Frame

Interior Suite Entrances, Length Less Than Twice Width

Estimating Procedure

1. Use these figures to estimate medical, dental, psychiatric, optometry and similar professional buildings in which access to each office suite is through an interior corridor. Buildings in this section have more plumbing fixtures per square foot or floor and smaller room sizes than general office buildings. Note also that buildings with more than 10,000 square feet are assumed to have lead shielded x-ray rooms.
2. Establish the building quality class by applying the information on page 159.
3. Compute the first floor area. This should include everything within the exterior walls and all insets outside the main walls but under the main roof.
4. If the first floor wall height is more or less than 10 feet, add or subtract from the first floor square foot cost below the appropriate amount from the Wall Height Adjustment Table on page 166.
5. Multiply the adjusted square foot cost by the first floor area.
6. Deduct, if appropriate, for common walls or no wall finish. Use the figures on page 166.
7. If there are second or higher floors, compute the square foot area on each floor. Locate the appropriate square foot cost from the table at the bottom of this page. Adjust this figure for a wall height more or less than 9 feet, using the figures on page 166. Multiply the adjusted cost by the square foot area on each floor. Use the figures on page 166 to deduct for common walls or no wall finish. Add the result to the cost from step 6 above.
8. Multiply the total cost by the location factor listed on page 7 or 8.
9. Add the cost of heating and air conditioning systems, elevators, fire sprinklers, exterior signs, paving and curbing, miscellaneous yard improvements. See page 236 to 248.

Medical-Dental Building, Class 3

First Story - Square Foot Area

Quality Class	2,000	2,500	3,000	4,000	5,000	7,500	10,000	15,000	20,000	30,000	40,000
Exceptional	198.10	194.90	192.52	189.29	187.16	183.86	181.94	179.68	178.32	176.75	175.91
1, Best	187.57	184.52	182.25	179.22	177.13	174.03	172.22	170.11	168.85	167.37	166.51
1 & 2	177.15	174.28	172.15	169.29	167.36	164.38	162.72	160.66	159.45	158.05	157.29
2, Good	168.05	165.36	163.35	160.61	158.74	155.94	154.30	152.45	151.29	150.02	149.21
2 & 3	156.11	153.55	151.70	149.18	147.44	144.85	143.31	141.45	140.52	139.29	138.62
3, Average	146.41	144.03	142.25	139.85	138.28	135.83	134.43	132.78	131.79	130.70	129.99
3 & 4	137.70	135.42	133.81	131.53	130.07	127.75	126.40	124.86	123.93	122.86	122.22
4, Low	129.50	127.39	125.85	123.73	122.30	120.16	118.91	117.47	116.51	115.58	114.97

Second and Higher Stories - Square Foot Area

Quality Class	2,000	2,500	3,000	4,000	5,000	7,500	10,000	15,000	20,000	30,000	40,000
Exceptional	181.65	179.68	178.25	176.23	174.91	172.82	171.60	170.19	169.35	168.42	167.82
1, Best	172.24	170.35	169.01	167.08	165.84	163.88	162.73	161.41	160.62	159.68	159.11
1 & 2	163.54	161.74	160.40	158.64	157.41	155.56	154.50	153.24	152.46	151.61	150.55
2, Good	156.18	154.43	153.20	151.50	150.33	148.55	147.58	146.32	145.61	144.77	144.25
2 & 3	144.28	142.69	141.58	139.97	138.87	137.29	136.32	135.20	134.53	133.78	133.31
3, Average	134.23	132.78	131.66	130.19	129.20	127.70	126.79	125.77	125.14	124.43	124.02
3 & 4	126.17	124.78	123.81	122.56	121.48	120.07	119.19	118.24	117.63	116.97	116.58
4, Low	118.49	117.20	116.28	114.97	114.11	112.76	111.99	111.06	110.49	109.87	109.49

Interior Suite Entrances, Length Between 2 and 4 Times Width

Estimating Procedure

1. Use these figures to estimate medical, dental, psychiatric, optometry and similar professional buildings in which access to each office suite is through an interior corridor. Buildings in this section have more plumbing fixtures per square foot of floor and smaller room sizes than general office buildings. Note also that buildings with more than 10,000 square feet are assumed to have lead shielded x-ray rooms.
2. Establish the building quality class by applying the information on page 159.
3. Compute the first floor area. This should include everything within the exterior walls and all insets outside the main walls but under the main roof.
4. If the first floor wall height is more or less than 10 feet, add to or subtract from the first floor square foot cost below the appropriate amount from the Wall Height Adjustment Table on page 166.
5. Multiply the adjusted square foot cost by the first floor area.
6. Deduct, if appropriate, for common walls or no wall finish. Use the figures on page 166.
7. If there are second or higher floors, compute the square foot area on each floor. Locate the appropriate square foot cost from the table at the bottom of this page. Adjust this figure for a wall height more or less than 9 feet, using the figures on page 166. Multiply the adjusted cost by the square foot area on each floor. Use the figures on page 166 to deduct for common walls or no wall finish. Add the result to the cost from step 6 above.
8. Multiply the total cost by the location factor listed on page 7 or 8.
9. Add the cost of heating and air conditioning systems, elevators, fire sprinklers, exterior signs, paving and curbing, miscellaneous yard improvements. See page 236 to 248.

Medical-Dental Building, Class 1 & 2

First Story - Square Foot Area

Quality Class	2,000	2,500	3,000	4,000	5,000	7,500	10,000	15,000	20,000	30,000	40,000
Exceptional	203.06	199.12	196.31	192.42	189.84	185.90	183.66	180.94	179.46	177.61	176.58
1, Best	192.94	189.18	186.50	182.83	180.35	176.61	174.43	171.92	170.49	168.73	167.72
1 & 2	181.96	178.40	175.90	172.38	170.06	166.58	164.53	162.18	160.78	159.17	158.16
2, Good	172.45	169.11	166.70	163.40	161.20	157.87	155.93	153.68	152.40	150.86	149.97
2 & 3	160.24	157.12	154.90	151.81	149.75	146.67	144.88	142.77	141.58	140.14	139.33
3, Average	150.11	147.19	145.09	142.22	140.36	137.39	135.72	133.76	132.66	131.30	130.50
3 & 4	141.68	138.92	136.91	134.22	132.44	129.69	128.07	126.25	125.12	123.90	123.16
4, Low	132.74	130.12	128.32	125.68	124.05	121.48	119.98	118.29	117.25	116.08	115.36

Second and Higher Stories - Square Foot Area

Quality Class	2,000	2,500	3,000	4,000	5,000	7,500	10,000	15,000	20,000	30,000	40,000
Exceptional	185.59	182.86	180.91	178.31	176.60	174.05	172.65	170.98	170.06	168.98	168.32
1, Best	176.84	174.26	172.43	169.94	168.29	165.89	164.53	162.92	162.05	160.96	160.39
1 & 2	167.04	164.58	162.83	160.47	158.95	156.71	155.41	153.94	153.05	152.10	151.53
2, Good	159.45	157.12	155.45	153.21	151.73	149.57	148.30	146.93	146.12	145.19	144.67
2 & 3	147.89	145.71	144.20	142.10	140.73	138.75	137.55	136.24	135.49	134.62	134.14
3, Average	137.11	135.04	133.65	131.70	130.48	128.59	127.52	126.30	125.61	124.78	124.34
3 & 4	129.50	127.58	126.22	124.43	123.22	121.46	120.43	119.34	118.63	117.89	117.42
4, Low	121.07	119.30	118.02	116.33	115.22	113.52	112.62	111.53	110.98	110.26	109.82

Medical-Dental Buildings – Wood Frame

Interior Suite Entrances, Length More Than 4 Times Width

Estimating Procedure

1. Use these figures to estimate medical, dental, psychiatric, optometry and similar professional buildings in which access to each office suite is through an interior corridor. Buildings in this section have more plumbing fixtures per square foot of floor and smaller room sizes than general office buildings. Note also that buildings with more than 10,000 square feet are assumed to have lead shielded x-ray rooms.
2. Establish the building quality class by applying the information on page 159.
3. Compute the first floor area. This should include everything within the exterior walls and all insets outside the main walls but under the main roof.
4. If the first floor wall height is more or less than 10 feet, add to or subtract from the first floor square foot cost below the appropriate amount from the Wall Height Adjustment Table on page 166.
5. Multiply the adjusted square foot cost by the first floor area.
6. Deduct, if appropriate, for common walls or no wall finish. Use the figures on page 166.
7. If there are second or higher floors, compute the square foot area on each floor. Locate the appropriate square foot cost from the table at the bottom of this page. Adjust this figure for a wall height more or less than 9 feet, using the figures on page 166. Multiply the adjusted cost by the square foot area on each floor. Use the figures on page 166 to deduct for common walls or no wall finish. Add the result to the cost from step 6 above.
8. Multiply the total cost by the location factor listed on page 7 or 8.
9. Add the cost of heating and air conditioning systems, elevators, fire sprinklers, exterior signs, paving and curbing, miscellaneous yard improvements. See page 236 to 248.

Medical-Dental Building, Class 2

First Story - Square Foot Area

Quality Class	2,000	2,500	3,000	4,000	5,000	7,500	10,000	15,000	20,000	30,000	40,000
Exceptional	210.96	206.24	202.85	198.03	194.76	189.70	186.72	183.23	181.05	178.58	177.12
1, Best	200.02	195.60	192.36	187.79	184.69	179.87	177.06	173.66	171.67	169.31	167.92
1 & 2	188.50	184.33	181.26	176.97	174.02	169.53	166.82	163.71	161.79	159.61	158.29
2, Good	178.46	174.54	171.61	167.55	164.78	160.52	157.97	155.00	153.20	151.10	149.84
2 & 3	166.57	162.86	160.20	156.33	153.81	149.81	147.41	144.67	142.98	140.97	139.87
3, Average	155.26	151.82	149.29	145.75	143.36	139.65	137.40	134.87	133.23	131.42	130.36
3 & 4	150.52	147.21	144.74	141.34	138.98	135.39	133.26	130.72	129.21	127.48	126.39
4, Low	137.02	133.99	131.79	128.66	126.56	123.25	121.34	119.05	117.63	116.02	115.06

Second and Higher Stories - Square Foot Area

Quality Class	2,000	2,500	3,000	4,000	5,000	7,500	10,000	15,000	20,000	30,000	40,000
Exceptional	189.40	186.35	184.15	181.14	179.15	176.10	174.45	172.45	171.34	169.94	169.18
1, Best	179.60	176.71	174.62	171.77	169.88	167.04	165.38	163.54	162.40	161.17	160.37
1 & 2	170.47	167.67	165.70	162.96	161.19	158.49	156.94	155.16	154.13	152.87	152.17
2, Good	162.68	160.04	158.16	155.56	153.84	151.29	149.79	148.09	147.07	145.98	145.27
2 & 3	151.09	148.62	146.85	144.47	142.89	140.49	139.09	137.52	136.59	135.57	134.93
3, Average	139.85	137.64	135.98	133.74	132.30	130.07	128.84	127.36	126.48	125.52	124.89
3 & 4	132.07	129.92	128.40	126.28	124.90	122.81	121.60	120.24	119.26	118.49	117.96
4, Low	123.40	121.43	120.04	118.02	116.74	114.83	113.70	112.37	111.58	110.76	110.25

Medical-Dental Buildings – Wood Frame

Wall Height Adjustment

The square foot costs for medical and dental buildings are based on the wall heights of 10 feet for first floors and 9 feet for higher floors. The first floor height is the distance from the bottom of the floor slab or joists to the top of the roof slab or ceiling joists. Second and higher floors are measured from the top of the floor slab or floor joists to the top of the roof slab or ceiling joists. Add or subtract the amount listed in this table to or from the square foot of floor cost for each foot of wall height more or less than 10 feet, if adjusting for first floor, and 9 feet, if adjusting for upper floors.

Square Foot Area

Quality Class	1,000	1,500	2,000	3,000	4,000	5,000	7,500	10,000	15,000	20,000	40,000
1, Best	2.20	1.76	1.49	1.18	1.04	.89	.70	.63	.53	.48	.33
2, Good	1.94	1.48	1.29	1.05	.86	.79	.63	.56	.47	.43	.30
3, Average	1.71	1.30	1.12	.92	.78	.68	.57	.49	.44	.35	.17
4, Low	1.51	1.16	1.01	.79	.68	.63	.49	.45	.35	.30	.17

Perimeter (Common) Wall Adjustment

A common wall exists when two buildings share one wall. Adjust for common walls by deducting the linear foot costs below from the total structure cost. In some structures, one or more walls are not owned at all. In this case, deduct the "No Ownership" cost per linear foot of wall not owned. If a wall has no exterior finish, deduct the "Lack of Exterior Finish" cost.

First Story

Class	For a Common Wall, Deduct Per L.F.	For No Wall Ownership, Deduct Per L.F.	For Lack of Exterior Finish, Deduct Per L.F.
1	$282	$545	$239
2	227	437	189
3	183	352	130
4	140	290	101

Second and Higher Stories

Class	For a Common Wall, Deduct Per L.F.	For No Wall Ownership, Deduct Per L.F.	For Lack of Exterior Finish, Deduct Per L.F.
1	$189	$364	$239
2	141	282	189
3	130	275	130
4	127	257	101

Convalescent Hospitals – Masonry or Concrete

Quality Classification

	Class 1 Best Quality	Class 2 Good Quality	Class 3 Average Quality	Class 4 Low Quality
Foundation (18% of total cost)	Reinforced concrete.	Reinforced concrete.	Reinforced concrete.	Reinforced concrete.
Floor Structure (10% of total cost)	Reinforced concrete.	Reinforced concrete.	Reinforced concrete.	Reinforced concrete.
Roof & Cover (7% of total cost)	Standard wood frame and composition roofing with large colored rock or tile. 4' to 6' sealed overhang.	Standard wood frame and composition roofing with large colored rock or asbestos shingles. 3' to 4' sealed overhang.	Standard wood frame and composition roofing small colored rock. 4' exposed or 3' sealed overhang.	Standard wood frame and composition roofing pea gravel or composition shingles. 2' exposed overhang.
Exterior Finishes				
Walls (12% of total cost)	8" colored concrete block.	8" colored concrete block.	8" colored concrete block.	8" colored concrete block.
Front (5% of total cost)	Brick or stone veneer and float glass in aluminum frame.	Stone or brick veneer. Small amount of float glass in aluminum frame.	Rustic siding or some brick or stone veneer.	Stucco and small amount siding.
Windows (5% of total cost)	Good aluminum sliding glass doors or anodized aluminum casement windows.	Good aluminum sliding glass doors with aluminum jalousie window for vent.	Average aluminum sliding type. 6' sliding glass door in bedrooms.	Low cost aluminum sliding type.
Doors (5% of total cost)	Anodized aluminum entry doors.	Aluminum and glass entry doors.	Good hardwood slab door with side lights or aluminum and glass entry door.	Wood slab door.
Interior Finishes				
Floors (5% of total cost)	Resilient tile. Good carpet in entry and day room. Quarry tile or epoxy type floor in kitchen.	Resilient tile. Good carpet in day room. May have coved sheet vinyl in kitchen.	Composition tile. Day room may have average grade carpet.	Low cost tile. Composition tile in kitchen. Concrete in storage areas.
Walls (10% of total cost)	Gypsum wallboard and enamel. Large amount of plastic wall cover. Some wood paneling or glass walls in entry and day rooms. 4' ceramic tile wainscot in kitchen. Gypsum wallboard and paint in storage areas.	Gypsum wallboard and enamel. Gypsum wallboard and some plastic wall cover or wood paneling in entry, bedrooms, dining room, day room, and kitchen. Gypsum wallboard and paint in storage areas.	Gypsum wallboard and enamel. Some plastic wall cover or wood paneling in entry and day room. Gypsum wallboard and paint in storage areas.	Gypsum wallboard and texture. Gypsum wallboard and enamel in kitchen. Unfinished gypsum wallboard in storage areas.
Ceilings (8% of total cost)	Acoustical tile. Washable acoustical tile in kitchen. Gypsum wallboard and paint in storage areas.	Gypsum wallboard and enamel. Acoustical tile in corridor. Open beam ceilings with wood decking in entry and day room. Gypsum wallboard and paint in storage areas.	Gypsum wallboard & enamel or acoustical texture. Open beams with wood decking. Gypsum wallboard and paint in storage areas.	Gypsum wallboard and texture. Gypsum wallboard and acoustical texture in entry. Gypsum wallboard and enamel in kitchen. Unfinished gypsum in storage areas.
Bath Finish Detail				
Main Bath & Showers (10% of total cost)	Ceramic tile floors. Ceramic tile walls. Gypsum wallboard and enamel ceilings.	Ceramic tile floors. 6' ceramic tile wainscot. Gypsum wallboard and enamel walls and ceilings.	Ceramic tile floors. 4' ceramic tile wainscot. Gypsum wallboard and enamel walls and ceilings.	Resilient tile floors. Gypsum wallboard and enamel walls and ceilings.
Toilet Rooms (5% of total cost)	Sheet vinyl or ceramic tile floors. 4' ceramic tile wainscot. Gypsum wallboard and enamel walls and ceilings.	Sheet vinyl floors. 4' plastic or ceramic tile wainscot.	Resilient tile or linoleum floors. 4' plastic or marlite wainscot.	Composition tile floors. Gypsum wallboard and enamel walls and ceilings.

Note: Use the percent of total cost to help identify the correct quality classification.

Square foot costs include the following components: Foundations as required for normal soil conditions. Floor, wall and roof structures. Interior floor, wall and ceiling finishes. Exterior wall finish and roofing. Interior partitions. Cabinets, doors and windows. Basic electrical systems and all plumbing. Permits and fees. Contractor's mark-up. Cost of nurses' built-in station desks and cabinets. Nurses' call system. Emergency lighting system. Cubicle curtain tracks. Kitchen range hood.

The in-place cost of these extra components should be added to the basic building cost to arrive at the total structure cost. See the section "Additional Costs for Commercial Buildings" on page 236 to 248. Heating and air conditioning systems. Elevators. Fire sprinklers. Dumbwaiters. Fireplaces. *Square foot costs do not include the following items:* Drapes. Cubicle curtains. Incinerators. Laundry or kitchen equipment, other than the range hood.

Estimating Procedure

1. Use these figures to estimate institutions such as nursing or rest homes which have facilities limited to bed care for people unable to care for themselves.

2. Establish the building quality class by applying the information on page 167.

3. Compute the floor area. This should include everything within the exterior walls and all insets outside the main walls but under the main roof. Areas such as storage rooms which have a substantially inferior finish or any area with a slightly interior finish and which does not perform a function related to the hospital operation should be estimated at 1/2 to 3/4 of the square foot costs listed.

4. Estimate second stories and basements at 100% of the first floor cost if they are of the same general quality. A storage area of the same or slightly inferior quality located in the basement, second floor or separate building should be estimated at 100% of the building square foot cost.

5. Multiply the appropriate square foot cost below by the floor area.

6. Multiply the total cost by the location factor on page 7 or 8.

7. Add the cost of heating and air conditioning systems, fire sprinklers, drapes, incinerators, elevators, dumbwaiters, and fireplaces. See the section beginning on page 236.

Convalescent Hospital, Class 2

Convalescent Hospital, Class 2

Square Foot Area

Quality Class	5,000	6,000	7,000	8,000	9,000	10,000	12,500	15,000	17,500	20,000	25,000	30,000
Exceptional	193.54	187.46	183.08	179.81	177.31	175.27	171.67	169.28	167.57	166.29	164.57	163.24
1, Best	182.70	176.91	172.84	169.72	167.35	165.44	162.05	159.78	158.20	156.95	155.33	154.21
1 & 2	172.23	166.77	162.90	159.94	157.76	155.96	152.75	150.62	149.13	147.97	146.40	145.37
2, Good	162.48	157.33	153.67	150.93	148.82	147.14	144.13	142.13	140.72	139.61	138.14	137.15
2 & 3	150.01	145.29	141.91	139.38	137.45	135.83	133.07	131.25	129.88	128.92	127.52	126.64
3, Average	141.49	137.05	133.90	131.49	129.68	128.19	125.51	123.81	122.54	121.60	120.33	119.48
3 & 4	129.65	125.54	122.67	120.43	118.77	117.44	115.05	113.40	112.26	111.41	110.21	109.47
4, Low	118.65	114.89	112.23	110.24	108.69	107.45	105.23	103.75	102.77	101.91	100.89	100.14

Convalescent Hospitals – Wood Frame

Quality Classification

	Class 1 Best Quality	Class 2 Good Quality	Class 3 Average Quality	Class 4 Low Quality
Foundation (18% of total cost)	Reinforced concrete.	Reinforced concrete.	Reinforced concrete.	Reinforced concrete.
Floor Structure (10% of total cost)	Reinforced concrete.	Reinforced concrete.	Reinforced concrete.	Reinforced concrete.
Roof & Cover (7% of total cost)	Standard wood frame and composition roofing with large colored rock or tile. 4' to 6' sealed overhang.	Standard wood frame and composition roofing with large colored rock or asbestos shingles. 3' to 4' sealed overhang.	Standard wood frame and composition roofing small colored rock. 4' exposed or 3' sealed overhang.	Standard wood frame and composition with pea gravel or composition shingles. 2' exposed overhang.
Exterior Finishes				
Walls (12% of total cost)	Wood siding or stucco with extensive trim.	Stucco or wood siding.	Stucco or good plywood siding.	Stucco.
Front (5% of total cost)	Brick or stone veneer and float glass in aluminum frame.	Stone or brick veneer. Small amount of float glass in aluminum frame.	Rustic siding or some brick or stone veneer.	Stucco and small amount siding.
Windows (5% of total cost)	Good aluminum sliding glass doors or anodized aluminum casement windows.	Good aluminum sliding glass doors with aluminum jalousie window for vent.	Average aluminum sliding type. 6 sliding glass door in bedrooms.	Low cost aluminum sliding type.
Doors (5% of total cost)	Anodized aluminum entry doors.	Aluminum and glass entry doors.	Good hardwood slab door with side lights or aluminum and glass entry door.	Wood slab door.
Interior Finishes				
Floors (5% of total cost)	Resilient tile. Good carpet in entry and day room. Quarry tile or epoxy type floor in kitchen.	Resilient tile. Good carpet in day room. May have coved sheet vinyl in kitchen.	Composition tile. Day room may have average grade carpet.	Low cost tile. Composition tile in kitchen. Concrete in storage areas.
Walls (10% of total cost)	Gypsum wallboard and enamel. Large amount of plastic wall cover. Some wood paneling or glass walls in entry and day rooms. 4' ceramic tile wainscot in kitchen. Gypsum wallboard and paint in storage areas.	Gypsum wallboard and enamel. Gypsum wallboard and some plastic wall cover or wood paneling in entry, bedrooms, dining room, day room, and kitchen. Gypsum wallboard and paint in storage areas.	Gypsum wallboard and enamel. Some plastic wall cover or wood paneling in entry and day room. Gypsum wallboard and paint in storage areas.	Gypsum wallboard and texture. Gypsum wallboard and enamel in kitchen. Unfinished gypsum wallboard in storage areas.
Ceilings (8% of total cost)	Acoustical tile. Washable acoustical tile in kitchen. Gypsum wallboard and paint in storage areas.	Gypsum wallboard and enamel. Acoustical tile in corridor. Open beam ceilings with wood decking in entry and day room. Gypsum wallboard and paint in storage areas.	Gypsum wallboard & enamel or acoustical texture. Open beams with wood decking. Gypsum wallboard and paint in storage areas.	Gypsum wallboard and texture. Gypsum wallboard and acoustical texture in entry. Gypsum wallboard and enamel in kitchen. Unfinished gypsum in storage areas.
Bath Finish Detail				
Main Bath & Showers (10% of total cost)	Ceramic tile floors. Ceramic tile walls. Gypsum wallboard and enamel ceilings.	Ceramic tile floors. 6' ceramic tile wainscot. Gypsum wallboard and enamel walls and ceilings.	Ceramic tile floors. 4' ceramic tile wainscot. Gypsum wallboard and enamel walls and ceilings.	Resilient tile floors. Gypsum wallboard and enamel walls and ceilings.
Toilet Rooms (5% of total cost)	Vinyl or ceramic tile floors. 4' ceramic tile wainscot. Gypsum wallboard and enamel walls and ceilings.	Vinyl floors. 4' plastic or ceramic tile wainscot.	Resilient tile or linoleum floors. 4' plastic wainscot.	Composition tile floors. Gypsum wallboard and enamel walls and ceilings.

Note: Use the percent of total cost to help identify the correct quality classification.

Square foot costs include the following components: Foundations as required for normal soil conditions. Floor, wall and roof structures. Interior floor, wall and ceiling finishes. Exterior wall finish and roofing. Interior partitions. Cabinets, doors and windows. Basic electrical systems and all plumbing. Permits and fees. Contractor's mark-up. Cost of nurses' built-in station desks and cabinets. Nurses' call system. Emergency lighting system. Cubicle curtain tracks. Kitchen range hood.

The in-place cost of these extra components should be added to the basic building cost to arrive at the total structure cost. See the section "Additional Costs for Commercial Buildings" on page 236 to 248. Heating and air conditioning systems. Elevators. Fire sprinklers. Dumbwaiters. Fireplaces. *Square foot costs do not include the following items:* Drapes. Cubicle curtains. Incinerators. Laundry or kitchen equipment, other than the range hood.

Convalescent Hospitals – Wood Frame

Estimating Procedure

1. Use these figures to estimate institutions such as nursing or rest homes which have facilities limited to bed care for people unable to care for themselves.

2. Establish the building quality class by applying the information on page 169.

3. Compute the floor area. This should include everything within the exterior walls and all insets outside the main walls but under the main roof. Areas such as storage rooms which have a substantially inferior finish or any area with a slightly interior finish and which does not perform a function related to the hospital operation should be estimated at 1/2 to 3/4 of the square foot costs listed.

4. Estimate second stories and basements at 100% of the first floor cost if they are of the same general quality. A storage area of the same or slightly inferior quality located in a basement, second floor or separate building should be estimated at 100% of the building square foot cost.

5. Multiply the appropriate square foot cost below by the floor area.

6. Multiply the total cost by the location factor on page 7 or 8.

7. Add the cost of heating and air conditioning systems, fire sprinklers, drapes, therapy facilities, cubicle curtains, incinerators, elevators, dumbwaiters, fireplaces, laundry equipment and kitchen equipment other than a range hood. See the section beginning on page 236.

Convalescent Hospital, Class 4

Convalescent Hospital, Class 3

Square Foot Area

Quality Class	5,000	6,000	7,000	8,000	9,000	10,000	12,500	15,000	17,500	20,000	25,000	30,000
Exceptional	178.79	173.16	169.10	165.98	163.55	161.63	158.06	155.69	153.90	152.57	150.66	149.39
1, Best	169.10	163.77	159.93	157.01	154.73	152.87	149.51	147.24	145.61	144.31	142.52	141.32
1 & 2	158.93	153.94	150.27	147.59	145.40	143.70	140.52	138.34	136.84	135.67	133.96	132.68
2, Good	150.33	145.60	142.16	139.60	137.51	135.92	132.93	130.89	129.41	128.27	126.71	125.60
2 & 3	140.41	135.97	132.80	130.35	128.42	126.94	124.10	122.27	120.89	119.82	118.33	117.31
3, Average	130.96	126.90	123.92	121.61	119.88	118.46	115.86	114.06	112.76	111.84	110.43	109.49
3 & 4	117.85	114.17	111.46	109.43	107.86	106.56	104.22	102.63	101.48	100.61	99.31	98.48
4, Low	110.38	106.92	104.32	102.45	100.99	99.80	97.61	96.12	94.98	94.21	93.01	92.22

Funeral Homes

Quality Classification

	Class 1 Best Quality	Class 2 Good Quality	Class 3 High Average Quality	Class 4 Low Average Quality	Class 5 Low Quality
Foundation (15% of total cost)	Reinforced concrete.	Reinforced concrete.	Reinforced concrete.	Reinforced concrete.	Reinforced concrete.
Floor Structure (7% of total cost)	Standard wood frame or reinforced concrete.	Standard wood frame or reinforced concrete.	Standard wood frame or reinforced concrete.	Standard wood frame or reinforced concrete.	Standard wood frame or reinforced concrete.
Wall Structure (12% of total cost)	Standard wood frame.	Standard wood frame.	Standard wood frame.	Standard wood frame.	Standard wood frame.
Roof & Cover (8% of total cost)	Standard wood frame with slate and 3' sealed overhang.	Standard wood frame with bar tile and 3' sealed overhang.	Standard wood frame with heavy shake and 3' sealed overhang.	Standard wood frame with composition roofing and large colored rock, asbestos shingles or medium shake, 3' exposed overhang.	Standard wood frame with compositon roofing and small colored rock or good composition shingles, 2' exposed overhang.
Exterior Finishes					
Walls (5% of total cost)	Brick or stone veneer.	Good wood siding, brick or stone veneer.	Wood siding or stucco with extensive wood trim.	Stucco or wood siding.	Stucco.
Front (5% of total cost)	Brick or stone veneer. Some tinted float glass in bronze frames.	Brick or stone veneer. Some tinted float glass in anodized aluminum frames.	Brick or stone veneer. Some tinted float glass in anodized aluminum frames.	Stone or brick veneer. Some tinted crystal or float glass in wood frame.	Wood siding or stucco with stone brick veneer. Some colored veneer windows with wood frame (bottle glass type).
Windows (5% of total cost)	Good anodized aluminum windows. Extensive stained glass in chapel.	Good aluminum sliding type. Stained glass in chapel.	Good aluminum sliding type. Leaded glass in chapel.	Good aluminum sliding type. Mock leaded glass in chapel.	Average aluminum sliding type. Colored plastic in chapel.
Doors (5% of total cost)	Elaborate hardwood entry doors.	Custom-built hardwood entry doors.	Custom hardwood or anodized aluminum and glass.	Good hardwood or anodized aluminum and glass doors.	Good hardwood slab or aluminum and glass entry doors.
Interior Finishes					
Floors (6% of total cost)	Excellent carpet. Good tile in kitchen.	Excellent carpet. Good carpet in living quarters. Good tile in kitchen.	Good carpet. Good tile in kitchen.	Good carpet. Average carpet in living quarters. Tile in kitchen.	Average carpet. Composition tile in hallways and living quarters.
Walls (12% of total cost)	Hardwood paneling, extensive brick or stone work in lobby and chapel. Gypsum wallboard and texture in living quarters.	Good hardwood veneer with brick or stone work in lobby and chapel. Gypsum wallboard and texture in living quarters.	Gypsum wallboard and embossed wallpaper or fabric textured wallcover. Hardwood in chapel. Gypsum wallboard and texture in living quarters.	Gypsum wallboard and wallpaper. Hardwood veneer in chapel.	Gypsum wallboard and texture. Some hardwood veneer in chapel.
Ceilings (8% of total cost)	Acoustical plaster. Exposed ornamental beams with ornamental hardwood decking or ornamental acoustical plaster in chapel.	Acoustical plaster. Exposed ornamental beams with ornamental wood decking or acoustical plaster in chapel.	Gypsum wallboard and heavy acoustical texture. Exposed architectural glu-lams w/ deck in chapel. Gypsum wallboard and texture in living quarters.	Gypsum wallboard and acoustical texture. Exposed wood beam with wood deck in chapel.	Gypsum wallboard and acoustical texture. Exposed beam with wood deck in chapel.
Special Lighting					
Fixtures (3% of total cost)	Two expensive chandeliers in lobby (4' to 6' diameter). Recessed and spotlighting in chapel.	Two expensive chandeliers in lobby (4' to 6' diameter). Recessed and spotlighting in chapel.	Two good chandeliers in lobby (4' diameter). Recessed and spotlighting in chapel.	Two average chandeliers in lobby (3' diameter).	One average chandelier in lobby.
Bath Detail (9% of total cost)	Ceramic tile floors and walls. Gypsum wallboard and enamel ceilings. Excellent fixtures.	Ceramic tile floors. 4' ceramic tile wainscot. Gypsum wallboard and enamel ceilings. Excellent fixtures.	Ceramic tile floors. Gypsum wallboard and enamel walls and ceilings. Good fixtures.	Good tile floors. Gypsum wallboard and enamel walls and ceilings. Average fixtures.	Tile floors. Gypsum wallboard and enamel walls and ceilings. Average fixtures.

Note: Use the percent of total cost to help identify the correct quality classification.

Square foot costs include the following components: Foundations as required for normal soil conditions. Floor, wall and roof structures. Interior floor, wall and ceiling finishes. Exterior wall finish and roof cover. Interior partitions. Cabinets, doors and windows. Basic electrical system and plumbing system. Special lighting fixtures. Bath detail. Permits and fees. Contractor's mark-up.

Estimating Procedure

1. Use these figures to estimate mortuaries and buildings designed for care of the dead and funeral services.
2. Establish the building quality class by applying the information on page 171.
3. Compute the first floor area under the main roof and inside the exterior walls. Include lobby, chapel and living sections, but exclude garages, whether internal, external or attached.
4. Add to the first floor area between 1/3 and 1/4 of the actual garage area. Use the higher value for better quality garages.
5. Add to the first floor area all finished basement and second floor area if it is similar in quality to the first floor area. Inferior quality second floor area should be reclassified as to quality and calculated separately. Unfinished funeral home basements should be estimated from the figures on page 237.
6. Finished space within the area formed by the roof but with an exterior wall height less than 7 feet (half story area) should be included at 1/3 to 1/2 of the actual floor area. Exclude half story area when selecting a square foot cost from the table.
7. Multiply the sum from steps 3 to 6 above by the appropriate square foot cost below.
8. Add 8% if the exterior walls are brick or block and 12% if the exterior walls are concrete. Add 2% if the building has more than 16 corners or if the length is more than twice with width.
9. Multiply the building cost by the location factor listed on page 7 or 8.
10. Add the cost of heating and cooling systems, elevators, fireplaces, pews, drapes, signs and yard improvement. See the section beginning on page 236.

Funeral Home, Class 5

Square Foot Area

Quality	2,000	2,500	3,000	4,000	5,000	7,500	10,000	12,500	15,000	20,000	25,000	30,000
Exceptional	—	—	—	—	165.09	159.34	156.74	154.86	153.65	152.06	150.91	150.08
1, Best	—	—	—	—	157.82	152.07	149.04	147.07	145.74	143.97	142.81	142.03
1 & 2	—	—	—	—	146.95	141.64	138.80	136.97	135.72	134.00	132.96	132.19
2, Good	—	—	—	—	139.29	134.25	131.55	129.82	128.68	127.08	126.07	125.34
2 & 3	—	—	145.59	136.36	131.40	126.19	124.63	122.96	122.16	121.40	120.29	119.26
3, Average	—	—	137.58	128.90	124.20	117.30	116.79	115.87	115.45	115.22	115.36	115.59
3 & 4	141.71	134.14	129.00	122.62	118.76	113.52	110.86	109.21	108.14	106.75	105.93	105.30
4, Low	133.96	126.79	122.00	115.92	112.29	107.34	104.85	103.28	102.24	100.95	100.16	99.59

Ecclesiastic Buildings

Quality Classification

	Class 1 Best Quality	Class 2 Good Quality	Class 3 High Average Quality	Class 4 Low Average Quality	Class 5 Low Quality
Foundation (12% of total cost)	Reinforced concrete.	Reinforced concrete.	Reinforced concrete.	Reinforced concrete.	Block masonry or reinforced concrete.
Floor Structure (6% of total cost)	Engineered wood frame or reinforced concrete.	Engineered wood frame or reinforced concrete.	Engineered wood frame or reinforced concrete.	Standard wood frame or reinforced concrete.	Standard wood frame or reinforced concrete.
Wall Structure (13% of total cost)	Engineered wood frame. First floor wall is 16' high.	Engineered wood frame. First floor wall is 14' high.	Engineered wood frame. First floor wall is 12' high.	Standard wood frame. First floor wall is 10' high.	Standard wood frame. First floor wall is 8' high.
Roof & Cover (8% of total cost)	Steep pitch glu-lam or steel frame with slate, concrete tile or standing seam sheet metal surface, Closed decorative soffit over windows and doors. Includes an attached clarion tower or steeple.	Steep pitch glu-lam wood frame over sanctuary. High pitch over other rooms. Concrete tile or heavy shake surface. Closed soffit over windows and doors. With a tower or steeple.	High pitch wood frame over sanctuary. Heavy shake or architectural composition tile surface, Closed soffit over entrances. Includes a roof steeple.	Standard wood frame with wood or composition shingle surface. Open soffit over entrances.	Standard wood frame with inexpensive composition single surface.
Exterior Finish (5% of total cost)	Brick or stone veneer.	Good wood siding, brick or stone veneer.	Wood siding or stucco with extensive wood trim.	Stucco or wood siding.	Stucco.
Front (5% of total cost)	Brick or stone veneer surrounding tinted or faceted glass set in metal frame. Highly decorative or starkly original architectural design elements.	Brick or stone veneer. Some tinted or faceted glass set in metal frame. Decorative design elements at the main entrance.	Brick or stone veneer. Some tinted float glass set in a metal frame.	Some masonry veneer or applied wood trim accents. Tinted glass set in a wood frame. Wall-mounted or roof-mounted signage.	Wood siding or stucco with applied wood trim. Wall-mounted signage.
Doors and Windows (8% of total cost)	Elaborate hardwood entry doors at all exits. Large insulated float glass windows.	Custom-built hardwood doors at sanctuary exits. Insulated float glass windows	Custom hardwood or insulated metal doors with glass insets. Commercial grade windows.	Good hardwood or insulated metal doors. Good quality windows.	Average hardwood or metal entry doors. Residential quality windows.
Floors (7% of total cost)	Terrazzo or excellent carpet. Good sheet vinyl in food service rooms.	Excellent carpet in the sanctuary. Good carpet in meeting rooms. Sheet vinyl or tile in other rooms.	Good carpet in the sanctuary. Good sheet vinyl or tile in meeting and food service rooms.	Good carpet in the sanctuary. Average sheet vinyl, tile or coated concrete in meeting and food service rooms.	Average carpet in the sanctuary. Composition tile or coated concrete in other rooms.
Walls (13% of total cost)	Decorative paneling with extensive brick or stone veneer in the narthex and sanctuary. Embossed or textured gypsum wallboard in hallways and meeting rooms.	Good paneling with brick or stone accents in the narthex and sanctuary. Textured or vinyl-covered gypsum wallboard in other rooms.	Textured or embossed gypsum wallboard or good paneling in the sanctuary. Textured gypsum wallboard in other rooms.	Textured or embossed gypsum wallboard or inexpensive paneling in the sanctuary Gypsum wallboard in other rooms.	Gypsum wallboard throughout.
Ceilings (7% of total cost)	Decorative exposed beams with ornamental accents, Ornamental acoustic plaster in the sanctuary.	Exposed beams with acoustical plaster or tile in the sanctuary. Acoustical tile in other rooms.	Exposed beams or trusses in the sanctuary, Ceiling finished with acoustic tile. Textured gypsum wallboard in other rooms.	Textured gypsum wallboard or acoustic tile in the sanctuary. Gypsum wallboard in other rooms.	Gypsum wallboard.
Lighting Fixtures (4% of total cost)	Highly decorative chandeliers in the narthex. Recessed and indirect lighting with spotlights in the sanctuary. Decorative fluorescent ceiling fixtures in other rooms.	Decorative chandeliers in the narthex. Recessed lighting and spotlights in the sanctuary. Good quality fluorescent fixtures in other rooms.	Decorative chandeliers or suspended fluorescent fixtures in the narthex. Recessed lighting in the sanctuary. Standard fluorescent fixtures in other rooms.	Decorative fluorescent fixtures throughout.	Standard fluorescent fixtures.
Chancel (5% of total cost)	Terrazzo, marble or good hardwood on a platform raised three steps above the nave. Two highly decorative altars or lecterns. Ample choir seating. Hardwood or marble railings	Excellent carpet on a raised platform. Decorative altar or lectern. Limited choir seating. Hardwood railings.	Good carpet on a raised platform. Decorative altar or lectern. Limited choir seating. Hardwood railings.	Good carpeted on a raised platform. Simple altar or lectern. Limited or no choir seating. Simple railings.	Wood or simulated wood pulpit on a raised platform..
Bath Detail (7% of total cost)	Simulated marble or terrazzo floors and walls. Gypsum wallboard and enamel ceilings. Excellent fixtures.	Terrazzo or ceramic tile floors. Ceramic tile wainscot. Gypsum wallboard and enamel ceilings. Excellent fixtures.	Ceramic tile floors. Plastic-coated wainscot. Gypsum wallboard and enamel walls and ceilings. Good fixtures.	Low cost ceramic tile or good vinyl floors. Gypsum wallboard and enamel walls and ceilings. Average fixtures.	Resilient tile floors. Gypsum wallboard and enamel walls and ceilings. Minimum fixtures.

Square foot costs include the following components: Foundations as required for normal soil conditions. Floor, wall and roof structures. Interior floor, wall and ceiling finishes. Exterior wall finish and roof cover. Interior partitions. Cabinets, doors and windows. Electrical, sound and plumbing systems. Special lighting fixtures. Building permits. Contractor's markup.

Ecclesiastic Buildings

Estimating Procedure

1. Use these figures to estimate religious buildings designed for worship or devotional purposes.
2. Establish the building quality class by applying the information on page 173.
3. Compute the first floor area under the main roof and inside the exterior walls. Include narthex (lobby), chancel and nave (sanctuary), meeting rooms, food preparation rooms and bathrooms but exclude garages, whether internal, external or attached.
4. Add to the first floor area between 1/4 and 1/3 of the actual garage area. Add to the first floor area 1/3 to 2/3 of any horizontal balcony area. Use higher values for better interior finish in the garage or balcony.
5. Add to the first floor area all finished basement (undercroft) and second floor area if similar in quality to the first floor area. Inferior quality second floor area should be reclassified as to quality and calculated separately. Unfinished ecclesiastic building basements should be estimated with the figures on page 237.
6. Finished space within the area formed by the roof but with an exterior wall height less than 7 feet (half story area) should be included at 1/3 to 1/2 of the actual floor area.
7. Multiply the sum from steps 3 to 6 above by the appropriate square foot cost below.
8. Add 4% if the building has more than 10 corners. Add 2% if the length is more than twice with the width. Add 8% if the exterior walls are masonry. Add 12% if the exterior walls are concrete.
9. Multiply the building cost by the location factor listed on page 7 or 8.
10. Add the cost of heating and cooling systems, elevators, fireplaces, pews, drapes, signs and yard improvement. See the section beginning on page 236.

Ecclesiastic Building, Class 1 & 2

Ecclesiastic Building, Class 5

Square Foot Area

Quality	2,000	2,500	3,000	4,000	5,000	7,500	10,000	12,500	15,000	20,000	25,000	30,000
Exceptional	265.61	255.74	245.82	233.54	226.48	216.70	211.23	208.14	206.35	203.27	202.03	200.70
1, Best	242.91	229.92	221.03	210.01	203.61	194.79	189.96	187.15	185.50	182.79	181.64	180.45
1 & 2	220.86	209.06	200.99	190.98	185.13	177.08	172.72	170.16	168.65	166.23	165.13	164.09
2, Good	200.52	189.80	182.49	173.40	168.07	160.73	156.82	154.50	153.09	150.96	149.93	148.99
2 & 3	181.75	172.02	165.42	157.21	152.33	145.66	142.17	140.06	138.75	136.84	135.88	135.05
3, Average	164.44	155.66	149.70	142.27	137.83	131.78	128.66	126.73	125.52	123.84	122.95	122.20
3 & 4	148.52	140.59	135.21	128.51	124.48	119.00	116.20	114.46	113.35	111.87	111.04	110.38
4, Low	133.84	126.68	121.88	115.85	112.18	107.22	104.75	103.18	102.15	100.85	100.07	99.49

Self Service Restaurants

Quality Classification

	Class 1 Best Quality	Class 2 Good Quality	Class 3 Average Quality	Class 4 Low Quality
Foundation (15% of total cost)	Reinforced concrete.	Reinforced concrete.	Reinforced concrete.	Reinforced concrete.
Floor Structure (7% of total cost)	Reinforced concrete or standard wood frame.	Reinforced concrete or standard wood frame.	Reinforced concrete or standard wood frame.	Reinforced concrete or standard wood frame.
Wall Structure (12% of total cost)	Standard wood frame.	Standard wood frame.	Standard wood frame.	Standard wood frame.
Roof & Cover (9% of total cost)	Complex angular structure, with concrete tile, mission tile, or heavy shake.	Standard wood frame structure, low or medium pitch, with composition tar and gravel or medium shake.	Standard wood frame structure, low pitch shed or gable type with composition tar and gravel.	Standard wood frame structure, low pitch shed or gable type with composition or composition shingle.
Floor Finish (7% of total cost)	Terrazzo in dining areas. Quarry tile in kitchen.	Vinyl tile in dining area. Terrazzo or quarry tile in kitchen.	Resilient tile in dining area. Grease proof tile in kitchen.	Composition tile in dining area. Grease proof tile in kitchen.
Walls, *Exterior Finish* (12% of total cost)	Very good wood siding; ornamental brick or natural stone veneer. Minimum 60% of front and side walls have float glass in heavy metal frames or rabbeted timbers.	Good wood siding or plywood; ornamental brick or concrete block; good stucco with color finish and with 2' to 4' brick, or natural stone veneer bulkheads. 50% to 75% of front and side walls have float glass set in good wood or metal frames.	Stucco or average wood siding with 2' to 4' brick or stone veneer bulkheads. Float glass front from waist high to roof line running along service front. Glassed area from 40% to 70% of front and side walls.	Stucco, low cost wood siding or plywood. 4' to 6' fixed glass waist high with sliding aluminum window opening running along service front. Glassed area from 30% to 40% of front and side walls.
Interior Finish (11% of total cost)	Plaster with putty coat finish; plastic coated paneling.	Plaster with putty coat finish; plastic coated paneling.	Plaster putty coat finish; textured gypsum wallboard with portions of wall finished with natural wood or plastic coated veneers.	Painted plaster or gypsum wallboard.
Ceilings (10% of total cost)	Complex angular structure with acoustical plaster.	Multi-level structure with good plaster or acoustical tile.	Flat or low slope with textured gypsum wallboard or acoustical tile.	Flat or low slope with textured gypsum wallboard or acoustical tile.
Plumbing (9% of total cost)	Good fixtures with metal or marble toilet partitions. Full wall height ceramic tile wainscot. Numerous floor drains.	Commercial fixtures with metal toilet partitions. Ceramic tile wainscot. Numerous floor drains in kitchen and dishwasher area.	4 to 6 standard commercial fixtures with metal toilet partitions. Floor drains in kitchen and dishwashing area.	4 to 6 standard commercial fixtures with wood toilet partitions. Minimum floor drainage in kitchen area.
Lighting (8% of total cost)	Triple encased fluorescent fixtures or decorative and ornate incandescent fixtures.	Triple encased fluorescent fixtures or decorative incandescent fixtures.	Triple open or double encased louvered fluorescent fixtures with some decorative incandescent fixtures.	Double open strip fluorescent fixtures or low cost incandescent fixtures.

Note: Use the percent of total cost to help identify the correct quality classification.

Square foot costs include the following components: Foundations as required for normal soil conditions. Floor, wall and roof structures. Interior floor, wall and ceiling finishes. Exterior wall finish and roof cover. All glass and glazing. Interior partitions. Basic electrical systems and lighting fixtures. Rough and finish plumbing. Permits and fees. Contractor's mark-up.

The in-place cost of these extra components should be added to the basic building cost to arrive at the total structure cost. See the section beginning on page 236. Heating and air conditioning systems. Booths and counters. Kitchen equipment. Fire sprinklers. Exterior signs. Paving and curbing. Yard improvements. Canopies and overhang.

Self Service Restaurants – Masonry

Estimating Procedure

1. Use these figures to estimate the cost of self-service or drive-in restaurants. These restaurants specialize in rapid service, may or may not have an interior eating area, have a large amount of glass on the front and side walls and usually are well lighted.
2. Establish the structure quality class by applying the information on page 175.
3. Compute the building floor area. This should include everything within the exterior walls and all insets outside the main walls but under the main roof.
4. Multiply the floor area by the appropriate cost below.
5. Multiply the total cost by the factor listed on page 7 or 8.
6. Add the cost of heating and air conditioning systems, fire sprinklers, exterior signs, paving and curbing, yard improvements and canopies. See the section beginning on page 236.

Self Service Restaurant, Class 2

Self Service Restaurant, Class 3

Square Foot Area

Quality Class	400	500	600	700	800	900	1,000	1,100	1,200	1,300	1,400
1, Best	420.87	388.49	364.44	345.51	330.21	317.41	306.58	297.20	289.03	281.81	275.30
1 & 2	364.08	336.17	315.26	298.90	285.63	274.63	265.27	257.11	250.05	243.77	238.19
2, Good	322.75	297.99	279.48	264.99	253.20	243.41	235.10	227.97	221.60	216.09	211.14
2 & 3	279.17	257.74	241.73	229.23	219.05	210.57	203.37	197.14	191.75	186.86	182.62
3, Average	246.25	227.35	213.25	202.17	193.20	185.70	179.42	173.89	169.12	164.86	161.06
3 & 4	212.99	196.63	184.42	174.89	167.12	160.64	155.17	150.44	146.26	142.59	139.33
4, Low	185.14	170.90	160.29	151.98	145.25	139.61	134.85	130.74	127.13	123.92	121.10

Square Foot Area

Quality Class	1,500	1,600	1,700	1,800	2,000	2,200	2,400	2,600	2,800	3,000	3,400
1, Best	270.16	266.79	263.58	260.57	254.03	249.98	245.43	241.25	237.47	234.00	227.72
1 & 2	233.83	230.88	228.12	225.50	219.82	216.35	212.38	208.80	205.51	202.49	197.10
2, Good	207.14	204.56	202.11	199.78	194.77	191.71	188.19	185.02	182.12	179.42	174.63
2 & 3	179.19	176.94	174.83	172.84	168.50	165.80	162.77	160.04	157.51	155.23	151.07
3, Average	158.01	156.07	154.20	152.43	148.63	146.25	143.55	141.13	138.92	136.87	133.25
3 & 4	136.73	135.01	133.37	131.85	128.54	126.49	124.26	122.14	120.22	118.42	115.24
4, Low	118.81	117.39	115.90	114.61	111.74	109.94	107.99	106.14	104.45	102.91	100.15

Self Service Restaurants – Wood Frame

Estimating Procedure

1. Use these figures to estimate the cost of self-service or drive-in restaurants. These restaurants specialize in rapid service, may or may not have an interior eating area, have a large amount of glass on the front and side walls and usually are well lighted.

2. Establish the structure quality class by applying the information on page 175.

3. Compute the building floor area. This should include everything within the exterior walls and all insets outside the main walls but under the main roof.

4. Multiply the floor area by the appropriate cost below.

5. Multiply the total cost by the factor listed on page 7 or 8.

6. Add the cost of heating and air conditioning systems, booths and counters, kitchen equipment, fire sprinklers, exterior signs, paving and curbing, yard improvements and canopies. See the section beginning on page 236.

Self Service Restaurant, Class 1 & 2

Self Service Restaurant, Class 1 & 2

Square Foot Area

Quality Class	400	500	600	700	800	900	1,000	1,100	1,200	1,300	1,400
1, Best	444.82	410.68	385.14	365.18	348.97	335.50	324.04	314.14	305.47	297.87	290.98
1 & 2	384.80	355.24	333.18	315.85	301.87	290.24	280.28	271.79	264.24	257.64	251.72
2, Good	339.30	313.24	293.79	278.52	266.20	255.95	247.17	239.65	233.00	227.21	222.01
2 & 3	293.36	270.80	253.99	240.79	230.13	221.23	213.67	207.15	201.46	196.44	191.94
3, Average	257.20	237.40	222.68	211.16	201.76	193.96	187.31	181.68	176.61	172.15	168.25
3 & 4	222.73	205.60	192.86	182.86	174.68	167.96	162.25	157.30	152.98	149.15	145.68
4, Low	193.47	178.58	167.50	158.82	151.78	145.92	140.97	136.65	132.88	129.55	126.56

Square Foot Area

Quality Class	1,500	1,600	1,700	1,800	2,000	2,200	2,400	2,600	2,800	3,000	3,400
1, Best	286.78	282.38	278.47	274.85	268.50	263.15	258.50	254.43	250.80	247.61	242.04
1 & 2	247.79	244.02	240.61	237.49	232.07	227.41	223.39	219.88	216.75	213.96	209.16
2, Good	218.77	215.34	212.36	209.64	204.78	200.73	197.16	194.07	191.31	188.83	184.65
2 & 3	189.16	186.26	183.66	181.27	177.15	173.59	170.51	167.79	165.43	163.28	159.65
3, Average	165.92	163.42	161.14	159.09	155.44	152.32	149.62	147.25	145.14	143.28	140.15
3 & 4	143.57	141.37	139.43	137.58	134.42	131.78	129.43	127.42	125.54	123.99	121.22
4, Low	124.73	122.80	121.13	119.55	116.79	114.46	112.43	110.68	109.11	107.72	105.28

Coffee Shop Restaurants

Quality Classification

	Class 1 Best Quality	Class 2 Good Quality	Class 3 Average Quality	Class 4 Low Quality
Foundation (15% of total cost)	Reinforced concrete.	Reinforced concrete.	Reinforced concrete.	Reinforced concrete.
Floor Structure (7% of total cost)	Reinforced concrete or standard wood frame.	Reinforced concrete or standard wood frame.	Reinforced concrete or standard wood frame.	Reinforced concrete or standard wood frame.
Wall Structure (12% of total cost)	Standard wood frame or concrete block.	Standard wood frame or concrete block.	Standard wood frame or concrete block.	Standard wood frame or concrete block.
Roof & Cover (9% of total cost)	Complex angular structure with concrete tile, mission tile, or heavy shake.	Standard wood frame structure, low or medium pitch, with composition tar and gravel roofing or medium shake.	Standard wood frame, low pitch shed or gable type with composition tar and gravel roofing	Standard wood frame, low pitch shed or gable type with composition tar and gravel or roofing.
Floor Finish (7% of total cost)	Terrazzo or good carpeting in dining area. Quarry tile in kitchen. Terrazzo or natural flagstone in entry vestibule.	Good tile or average carpeting in dining area. Terrazzo or quarry tile in kitchen. Terrazzo entry vestibule.	Good tile in dining area. Grease proof tile in kitchen area. Terrazzo in entry vestibule.	Composition tile in dining area. Grease proof tile in kitchen area.
Exterior Wall Finish (12% of total cost)	Very good wood siding; ornamental brick or natural stone veneer. Minimum 60% of front and side walls in float glass in heavy metal frames or rabbeted timbers. Entry vestibule with decorative screens of ornamental concrete block or natural stone panels.	Good wood siding; ornamental brick or concrete blocks. Good stucco with color finish and with 2' to 4' brick, or natural stone veneer bulkheads. 50% to 75% of front and side walls have float glass set in good wood or metal frames. Double entry doors, recessed entries with decorative screen of concrete block.	Stucco or average wood siding with 2' to 4' brick or stone veneer bulkheads. 50% to 60% of front and side walls in float glass set in average quality wood or aluminum frames. Double entry doors of metal or wood.	Stucco, low cost wood siding or plywood. 40% to 60% of front and side walls in crystal or float glass set in low-cost wood or metal frames. Double entry doors.
Interior Finish (11% of total cost)	Select and matched wood paneling, decorative wallpaper or synthetic fabrics.	Plaster with putty coat finish. Wood or plastic coated veneer paneling. Decorative wallpapers or fabrics.	Plaster putty coat finish textured gypsum wallboard with portions of wall finished with natural wood or plastic coated veneers.	Painted plaster or gypsum wallboard.
Ceilings (10% of total cost)	Complex angular structure with acoustical plaster.	Multi-level structure with good plaster or acoustical tile.	Flat or low slope with textured gypsum wallboard or acoustical tile.	Flat or low slope with textured gypsum wallboard or acoustical tile.
Plumbing (9% of total cost)	Good fixtures with metal or marble toilet partitions. Full wall height ceramic tile wainscot. Numerous floor drains.	Commercial fixtures with metal toilet partitions; ceramic tile wainscot. Numerous floor drains in kitchen and dishwasher area.	4 to 6 standard commercial fixtures with metal toilet partitions. Floor drains in kitchen and dishwashing area.	4 to 6 standard commercial fixtures with wood toilet partitions. Minimum floor drainage in kitchen.
Lighting (8% of total cost)	Triple encased fluorescent fixtures or decorative and ornate incandescent fixtures.	Triple encased fluorescent fixtures or decorative incandescent fixtures.	Triple open or double encased louvered fluorescent fixtures with some decorative incandescent fixtures.	Double open strip fluorescent fixtures or low cost incandescent fixtures.

Note: Use the percent of total cost to help identify the correct quality classification.

Square foot costs include the following components: Foundations as required for normal soil conditions. Floor, wall and roof structures. Interior floor, wall and ceiling finishes. Exterior wall finish and roof cover. All glass and glazing. Interior partitions. Basic electrical systems and lighting fixtures. Rough and finish plumbing. Permits and fees. Contractor's mark-up.

The in-place cost of these extra components should be added to the basic building cost to arrive at the total structure cost. See the section beginning on page 236: Heating and air conditioning systems. Booths and counters. Kitchen equipment. Fire sprinklers. Exterior signs. Paving and curbing. Yard improvements. Canopies and overhang.

Coffee Shop Restaurants – Masonry

Estimating Procedure

1. Use these figures to estimate the cost of restaurants with counters, or with counter, booth and table seating. A lounge or bar may be part of the building. Higher quality coffee shops usually have cut-up or complex sloping ceiling and roof structures. Coffee shops have extensive exterior glass and good lighting.
2. Establish the structure quality class by applying the information on page 178.
3. Compute the building floor area. This should include everything within the exterior walls and all insets outside the main walls but under the main roof.
4. Multiply the floor area by the appropriate cost below.
5. Multiply the total cost by the factor listed on page 7 or 8.
6. Add the cost of heating and air conditioning systems, booths and counters, kitchen equipment, fire sprinklers, exterior signs, paving and curbing, yard improvements and canopies. See the section beginning on page 236.

Coffee Shop Restaurant, Class 1

Coffee Shop Restaurant, Class 3

Square Foot Area

Quality Class	1,000	1,200	1,400	1,600	1,800	2,000	2,200	2,400	2,600	2,800	3,000
1, Best	291.39	269.73	254.13	242.23	232.93	225.33	219.13	213.84	209.35	205.50	202.06
1 & 2	252.50	233.78	220.23	209.93	201.81	195.29	189.84	185.28	181.45	178.06	175.13
2, Good	222.33	205.91	193.92	184.86	177.77	171.97	167.22	163.19	159.77	156.83	154.21
2 & 3	193.56	179.20	168.84	160.95	154.72	149.70	145.54	142.03	139.09	136.51	134.25
3, Average	170.50	157.87	148.73	141.77	136.27	131.85	128.21	125.11	122.48	120.24	118.25
3 & 4	147.49	136.60	128.65	122.64	117.93	114.09	110.96	108.28	105.97	104.04	102.29
4, Low	128.16	118.68	111.83	106.53	102.46	99.12	96.37	94.06	92.09	90.38	88.89

Square Foot Area

Quality Class	3,200	3,400	3,600	3,800	4,000	4,400	4,800	5,200	5,600	6,000	8,000
1, Best	196.77	194.55	192.63	190.78	189.11	186.12	183.52	181.22	179.16	177.36	170.38
1 & 2	170.21	168.33	166.61	165.05	163.58	161.01	158.75	156.73	154.98	153.40	147.41
2, Good	150.28	148.63	147.10	145.71	144.45	142.17	140.18	138.40	136.83	135.48	130.16
2 & 3	130.66	129.20	127.90	126.67	125.54	123.56	121.85	120.34	119.00	117.76	113.18
3, Average	115.24	113.98	112.78	111.74	110.75	108.98	107.48	106.14	104.93	103.88	99.81
3 & 4	99.68	98.57	97.59	96.70	95.84	94.31	92.99	91.82	90.76	89.85	86.34
4, Low	86.64	85.66	84.80	84.02	83.27	81.98	80.80	79.77	78.88	78.09	75.05

Coffee Shop Restaurants – Wood Frame

Estimating Procedure

1. Use these figures to estimate the cost of restaurants with counters, or with counter, booth and table seating. A lounge or bar may be part of the building. Higher quality coffee shops usually have cut-up or complex sloping ceiling and roof structures. Coffee shops have extensive exterior glass and good lighting.
2. Establish the structure quality class by applying the information on page 178.
3. Compute the building floor area. This should include everything within the exterior walls and all insets outside the main walls but under the main roof.
4. Multiply the floor area by the appropriate cost below.
5. Multiply the total cost by the factor listed on page 7 or 8.
6. Add the cost of heating and air conditioning systems, booths and counters, kitchen equipment, fire sprinklers, exterior signs, paving and curbing, yard improvements and canopies. See the section beginning on page 236.

Coffee Shop Restaurant, Class 3

Coffee Shop Restaurant, Class 2

Square Foot Area

Quality Class	1,000	1,200	1,400	1,600	1,800	2,000	2,200	2,400	2,600	2,800	3,000
1, Best	312.49	289.09	272.28	259.48	249.46	241.39	234.70	229.11	224.31	220.18	216.54
1 & 2	270.51	250.29	235.67	224.68	216.00	209.02	203.21	198.39	194.20	190.64	187.57
2, Good	238.59	220.77	207.85	198.05	190.44	184.27	179.16	174.91	171.27	168.10	165.37
2 & 3	206.23	190.87	179.71	171.28	164.68	159.31	154.91	151.22	148.03	145.36	142.93
3, Average	180.98	167.47	157.75	150.31	144.48	139.79	135.94	132.68	129.91	127.54	125.46
3 & 4	156.52	144.83	136.36	129.97	124.96	120.87	117.59	114.75	112.39	110.26	108.45
4, Low	135.95	125.80	118.45	112.95	108.53	105.03	102.12	99.65	97.60	95.82	94.21

Square Foot Area

Quality Class	3,200	3,400	3,600	3,800	4,000	4,400	4,800	5,200	5,600	6,000	8,000
1, Best	211.15	208.80	206.74	204.78	202.98	199.79	196.99	194.53	192.36	190.37	182.88
1 & 2	182.63	180.65	178.82	177.13	175.65	172.84	170.41	168.29	166.40	164.69	158.24
2, Good	161.01	159.27	157.73	156.20	154.82	152.40	150.27	148.41	146.73	145.23	139.50
2 & 3	139.29	137.79	136.36	135.08	133.86	131.81	129.98	128.27	126.86	125.58	120.66
3, Average	122.17	120.82	119.65	118.51	117.47	115.63	114.02	112.57	111.34	110.17	105.87
3 & 4	105.67	104.55	103.46	102.54	101.64	100.00	98.61	97.34	96.29	95.31	91.51
4, Low	91.75	90.75	89.85	88.97	88.25	86.87	85.63	84.56	83.60	82.76	79.52

Conventional Restaurants

Quality Classification

	Class 1 Best Quality	Class 2 Good Quality	Class 3 Average Quality	Class 4 Low Quality
Foundation (15% of total cost)	Reinforced concrete.	Reinforced concrete.	Reinforced concrete.	Reinforced concrete.
Floor Structure (7% of total cost)	Reinforced concrete or standard wood frame.	Reinforced concrete or standard wood frame.	Reinforced concrete or standard wood frame.	Reinforced concrete or standard wood frame.
Wall Structure (12% of total cost)	Standard wood frame or concrete block.	Standard wood frame or concrete block.	Standard wood frame or concrete block.	Standard wood frame or concrete block.
Roof & Cover (9% of total cost)	Complex angular structure, with concrete tile, mission tile, or heavy shake.	Standard wood frame structure, low or medium pitch, with composition tar and gravel roofing or medium shake.	Standard wood frame, low pitch shed or gable type. composition tar and gravel roofing	Standard wood frame, low pitch shed or gable type, with composition tar and gravel roofing.
Floor Finish (7% of total cost)	Terrazzo or good carpeting in dining area. Quarry tile in kitchen. Terrazzo or natural flagstone in entry vestibule.	Vinyl tile or average carpeting in dining area. Terrazzo or quarry tile in kitchen. Terrazzo in entry vestibule.	Good tile in dining area. Grease proof tile in kitchen area. Terrazzo in entry vestibule.	Composition tile in dining area. Grease proof tile in kitchen area.
Exterior Wall Finish (12% of total cost)	Very good wood siding, ornamental brick or natural stone veneer. 10% of front and side walls in float glass in heavy metal frames or rabbeted timbers. Entry vestibule with decorative screens of ornamental concrete block or natural stone panels.	Good wood siding or plywood; ornamental brick or concrete block. Good stucco with color finish and with 2' to 4' brick, or natural stone veneer bulkheads. 10% to 20% of front and side walls in float glass set in good wood or metal frames. Double entry doors, recessed entries with decorative screen of concrete block.	Stucco or average wood siding with 2' to 4' brick or stone veneer bulkheads. 10% to 20% of front and side walls in float glass set in wood or aluminum extrusions. Double entry doors of metal or wood.	Stucco, low cost wood siding or plywood. 10% to 20% of front & side walls in crystal float glass set in low-cost wood or metal frames. Double entry doors.
Interior Finish (11% of total cost)	Select and matched wood paneling, decorative wallpaper or synthetic fabrics.	Plaster with putty coat finish; wood or plastic coated veneer paneling; decorative wallpapers or fabrics.	Plaster putty coat finish; textured gypsum wallboard with portions of wall finished with natural wood or plastic coated veneer.	Painted plaster or gypsum wallboard.
Ceilings (10% of total cost)	Multi-level structure with acoustical plaster.	Multi-level structure with good plaster or acoustical tile.	Flat or low slope with textured gypsum wallboard or acoustical tile.	Flat or low slope with textured gypsum wallboard or acoustical tile
Plumbing (9% of total cost)	Good fixtures with metal or marble toilet partitions. Full wall height ceramic tile wainscot. Numerous floor drains.	Commercial fixtures with metal toilet partitions. Ceramic tile wainscot. Numerous floor drains in kitchen and dishwasher area.	4 to 6 standard commercial fixtures with metal toilet partitions. Floor drains in kitchen and dishwashing area.	4 to 6 standard commercial fixtures with wood toilet partitions. Minimum floor drainage in kitchen area.
Lighting (8% of total cost)	Decorative and ornate incandescent fixtures.	Decorative incandescent fixtures.	Double encased louvered fluorescent fixtures with decorative incandescent fixtures.	Double open strip fluorescent fixtures or low cost incandescent fixtures.

Note: Use the percent of total cost to help identify the correct quality classification.

Square foot costs include the following components: Foundations as required for normal soil conditions. Floor, wall and roof structures. Interior floor, wall and ceiling finishes. Exterior wall finish and roof cover. All glass and glazing. Interior partitions. Basic electrical systems and lighting fixtures. Rough and finish plumbing. Permits and fees. Contractor's mark-up.

The in-place cost of these extra components should be added to the basic building cost to arrive at the total structure cost. See the section beginning on page 236: Heating and air conditioning systems. Booths and counters. Kitchen equipment. Fire sprinklers. Exterior signs. Paving and curbing. Yard improvements. Canopies and overhang.

Estimating Procedure

1. Use these figures to estimate the cost of restaurants with limited use of glass as exterior walls and subdued lighting. Roof and ceiling structures are simple and conventional. Seating may be any combination of counter, stools, booths or tables. A lounge or bar is often a part of a building of this type.
2. Establish the structure quality class by applying the information on page 181.
3. Compute the building floor area. This should include everything within the exterior walls and all insets outside the main walls but under the main roof.
4. Multiply the floor area by the appropriate cost below.
5. Multiply the total cost by the factor listed on page 7 or 8.
6. Add the cost of heating and air conditioning systems, booths and counters, kitchen equipment, fire sprinklers, exterior signs, paving and curbing, yard improvements and canopies. See the section beginning on page 236.

Conventional Restaurant, Class 2

Masonry - Square Foot Area

Quality Class	1,000	1,500	2,000	2,500	3,000	3,500	4,000	5,000	6,000	8,000	10,000
1, Best	302.08	270.13	252.34	240.66	232.36	226.03	221.03	213.60	208.26	200.91	196.05
1 & 2	261.28	233.68	218.25	208.18	200.93	195.50	191.20	184.71	180.12	173.77	169.59
2, Good	230.43	206.11	192.50	183.62	177.23	172.44	168.64	162.99	158.86	153.30	149.57
2 & 3	199.26	178.21	166.49	158.76	153.30	149.13	145.86	140.95	137.38	132.60	129.34
3, Average	174.88	156.41	146.06	139.35	134.52	130.82	127.96	123.65	120.59	116.30	113.49
3 & 4	151.21	135.20	126.29	120.52	116.30	113.14	110.66	106.92	104.22	100.58	98.14
4, Low	131.41	117.53	109.76	104.68	101.05	98.29	96.15	92.86	90.58	87.37	85.30

Wood Frame - Square Foot Area

Quality Class	1,000	1,500	2,000	2,500	3,000	3,500	4,000	5,000	6,000	8,000	10,000
1, Best	310.44	277.62	259.32	247.34	238.75	232.28	227.16	219.50	214.03	206.48	201.51
1 & 2	268.61	240.13	224.27	213.97	206.59	200.90	196.50	189.88	185.14	178.62	174.24
2, Good	236.79	211.78	197.80	188.71	182.11	177.16	173.25	167.46	163.25	157.49	153.69
2 & 3	204.85	183.16	171.04	163.18	157.54	153.32	149.87	144.83	141.24	136.27	132.93
3, Average	179.78	160.72	150.11	143.20	138.25	134.51	131.54	127.07	123.92	119.55	116.68
3 & 4	155.43	139.00	129.84	123.81	119.55	116.30	113.78	109.94	107.19	103.39	100.87
4, Low	135.01	120.73	112.80	107.60	103.90	101.04	98.79	95.51	93.13	89.80	87.66

"A-Frame" Restaurants

Quality Classification

	Class 1 Best Quality	Class 2 Good Quality	Class 3 Average Quality	Class 4 Low Quality
Foundation (19% of total cost)	Reinforced concrete.	Reinforced concrete.	Reinforced concrete.	Reinforced concrete.
Floor Structure (8% of total cost)	Reinforced concrete or standard wood frame.	Reinforced concrete or standard wood frame.	Reinforced concrete or standard wood frame.	Reinforced concrete or standard wood frame.
Roof & Cover (12% of total cost)	Wood frame or post and beam, high pitch with concrete tile or heavy wood shake.	Wood frame or post and beam, high pitch with aluminum shake or medium wood shake.	Standard wood frame or post and beam, high pitch with wood or composition shingles.	Standard wood frame or post and beam, high pitch with composition shingles.
Floor Finish (10% of total cost)	Terrazzo or good carpeting in dining area. Quarry tile in kitchen. Terrazzo or natural flagstone in entry vestibule.	Vinyl tile or average carpeting in dining area Terrazzo or quarry tile in kitchen, terrazzo in entry vestibule.	Good tile in dining area. Grease proof tile in kitchen area. Terrazzo in entry vestibule.	Composition tile in dining area. Grease proof tile in kitchen area.
Interior Finish (12% of total cost)	Select and matched wood paneling, decorative wallpapers or synthetic fabrics.	Plaster with putty coat finish, wood or plastic coated veneer paneling, decorative wallpapers or fabrics.	Plaster, putty coat finish; textured gypsum wallboard with portions of wall finished with natural wood or plastic coated veneer.	Painted plaster or gypsum wallboard.
End Walls (10% of total cost)	Very good wood siding; ornamental brick or natural stone veneer. 60% on front in float glass in heavy metal extrusions or rabbeted timbers. Entry vestibule with decorative screens of ornamental concrete block or natural stone panels.	Good wood siding; ornamental brick or concrete blocks. Good stucco with color finish and with 2' to 4' brick or natural stone veneer bulkheads. 50% of front in float glass set in good wood or metal frames. Double entry doors, recessed entries with decorative screen of concrete block.	Stucco or average wood siding with 2' to 4' brick or stone veneer bulkheads. 50% to 60% of front in float glass set in average quality wood or aluminum frames. Double entry doors of metal or wood.	Stucco, low cost wood siding or plywood. 40% to 60% of front in crystal glass set in low cost wood or metal frames.
Ceilings (9% of total cost)	Decorative wood.	Natural wood, good plaster or acoustical tile.	Painted wood, textured gypsum wallboard or tile.	Painted wood, textured gypsum wallboard or acoustical tile.
Plumbing (10% of total cost)	Good fixtures with metal or marble toilet partitions. Full wall height ceramic tile wainscot. Numerous floor drains.	Commercial fixtures with metal toilet partitions. Ceramic tile wainscot. Numerous floor drains in kitchen and dishwashing area.	4 to 6 standard commercial fixtures with metal toilet partitions. Floor drains in kitchen and dishwashing area.	4 to 6 standard commercial fixtures with wood toilet partitions. Minimum floor drainage in kitchen area.
Lighting (10% of total cost)	Triple encased fluorescent fixtures or decorative and ornate incandescent fixtures.	Triple encased fluorescent or decorative incandescent fixtures.	Triple open, double encased louvered fluorescent fixtures or average incandescent fixtures.	Double open strip fluorescent fixtures or low cost incandescent fixtures.

Note: Use the percent of total cost to help identify the correct quality classification.

Square foot costs include the following components: Foundations as required for normal soil conditions. Floor, wall and roof structures. Interior floor, wall and ceiling finishes. Exterior wall finish and roof cover. All glass and glazing. Interior partitions. Basic electrical systems and lighting fixtures. Rough and finish plumbing. Permits and fees. Contractor's mark-up.

The in-place cost of these extra components should be added to the basic building cost to arrive at the total structure cost. See the section beginning on page 236: Heating and air conditioning systems. Booths and counters. Kitchen equipment. Fire sprinklers. Exterior signs. Paving and curbing. Yard improvements. Canopies and overhang.

"A-Frame" Restaurants – Wood Frame

Estimating Procedure

1. Use these figures to estimate the cost of restaurants with a sloping roof that forms two or more exterior walls. Either conventional or self service may be used and a lounge or bar may be part of the building.
2. Establish the structure quality class by applying the information on page 183.
3. Compute the building floor area. This should include everything within the exterior walls and all insets outside the main walls but under the main roof.
4. Multiply the floor area by the appropriate cost below.
5. Multiply the total cost by the factor listed on page 7 or 8.
6. Add the cost of heating and air conditioning systems, booths and counters, kitchen equipment, fire sprinklers, exterior signs, paving and curbing, yard improvements and canopies. See the section beginning on page 236.

"A-Frame" Restaurant, Class 1

Square Foot Area

Quality Class	400	500	600	800	1,000	1,200	1,400	1,600	1,800	2,000	2,400
1, Best	398.52	354.30	324.46	286.54	263.38	247.66	236.25	227.55	220.66	215.11	206.75
1 & 2	344.65	306.48	280.68	247.88	227.81	214.19	204.30	196.80	190.85	186.10	178.79
2, Good	303.98	270.30	247.53	218.61	200.92	188.95	180.21	173.58	168.37	164.12	157.73
2 & 3	262.97	233.82	214.18	189.13	173.84	163.40	155.91	150.18	145.62	141.98	136.41
3, Average	230.83	205.23	188.00	166.02	152.55	143.45	136.84	131.83	127.84	124.62	119.75
3 & 4	199.43	177.37	162.38	143.42	131.87	123.93	118.24	113.88	110.47	107.68	103.46
4, Low	173.37	154.14	141.17	124.68	114.59	107.73	102.76	98.99	95.98	93.56	89.94

Square Foot Area

Quality Class	2,800	3,200	3,600	4,000	4,500	5,000	6,000	7,000	8,000	9,000	10,000
1, Best	200.62	196.07	192.40	189.35	186.24	182.72	179.51	176.47	174.08	172.10	170.51
1 & 2	173.54	169.57	166.40	163.77	161.03	158.80	155.28	152.63	150.57	148.88	147.49
2, Good	153.09	149.58	146.79	144.46	142.06	140.09	136.98	134.62	132.80	131.30	130.07
2 & 3	132.31	129.50	127.09	125.10	123.03	121.28	118.59	116.54	114.98	113.66	112.61
3, Average	116.25	113.55	111.46	109.69	107.87	106.40	104.01	102.19	100.81	99.69	98.76
3 & 4	100.40	98.13	96.25	94.72	93.16	91.86	89.87	88.35	87.10	86.15	85.33
4, Low	87.38	85.39	83.77	82.45	81.09	79.96	78.20	76.87	75.78	74.96	74.20

Theaters – Masonry or Concrete

Quality Classification

	Class 1 Best w/ Balcony	Class 2 Very Good w/ Balcony	Class 3 Good Quality	Class 4 Average Quality	Class 5 Low Quality
Foundation (12% of total cost)	Reinforced concrete.	Reinforced concrete.	Reinforced concrete.	Reinforced concrete.	Reinforced concrete.
Floor Structure (7% of total cost)	6" reinforced concrete on 6" rock fill or 2" x 12" joists, 16" o.c.	4" to 6" reinforced concrete on 6" rock fill or 2" x 10" joists, 16" o.c.	4" reinforced concrete on 6" rock fill or 2" x 10" joists, 16" o.c.	4" reinforced concrete on 6" rock fill or 2" x 8" joists, 16" o.c.	4" reinforced concrete on 6" rock fill or 2" x 6" joists, 16" o.c.
Wall Structure (15% of total cost)	8" reinforced concrete or 12" common brick.	8" reinforced concrete or 12" common brick.	8" reinforced concrete or 12" common brick.	8" reinforced concrete or 12" common brick.	8" reinforced concrete block or 6" reinforced concrete.
Roof Framing (7% of total cost)	2" x 10" joists 16" o.c. Trusses on heavy pilasters 20' o.c. 2" x 12" rafters or purlins 16" o.c.	2" x 10" joists 16" o.c. Trusses on heavy pilasters 20' o.c. 2" x 12" rafters or purlins 16" o.c.	2" x 10" joists 16" o.c. Trusses on heavy pilasters 20' o.c. 2" x 12" rafters or purlins 16" o.c.	2" x 10" joists 16" o.c. Trusses on heavy pilasters 20' o.c. 2" x 10" rafters or purlins 16" o.c.	2" x 10" joists 16" o.c. Trusses on pilasters 20' o.c. 2" x 10" rafters or purlins 16" o.c.
Roof Covering (5% of total cost)	5 ply composition roof on 1" sheathing with insulation.	5 ply composition roof on 1" sheathing with insulation.	5 ply composition roof on 1" sheathing with insulation.	5 ply composition roof on 1" sheathing with insulation.	4 ply composition roof on 1" sheathing.
Front (3% of total cost)	Highly ornamental stucco or plaster finishes, custom select stone veneers or highly ornamental terra cotta.	Ornamental stucco, custom select brick, natural stone veneers or marble.	Highly ornamental stucco or custom brick or natural stone or terra cotta veneers.	Ornamental stucco or select brick veneers or partial terra cotta veneers.	Plain or colored stucco or common brick or carrara glass veneers.
Floors, Entry (3% of total cost)	Custom terrazzo with intricate and ornamental designs, custom select natural stone, marble or very good carpet.	Custom terrazzo with highly ornamental designs, natural stone veneers, marble or very good carpet.	Custom designed terrazzo with ornamental designs with portions natural stone veneers, marble or good carpet.	Colored terrazzo with designs, or average carpet.	Colored concrete with some plain colored terrazzo.
Floors, Interior (5% of total cost)	Concrete with carpet throughout.	Concrete with carpet throughout.	Concrete with carpet throughout.	Concrete with carpet throughout.	Concrete with carpet runners at aisles.
Restrooms (8% of total cost)	Per code requirement capacity. Custom select ornamental ceramic tile, terrazzo or natural stone on floors and walls.	Per code requirement capacity. Custom ceramic tile or terrazzo on floor and walls.	Per code requirement capacity. Ceramic tile on floors and walls or terrazzo floors and walls.	Per code requirement capacity. Ceramic tile on walls and floors or terrazzo on floors.	Per code requirement capacity. Ceramic or vinyl tile on floors.
Walls, Interior (11% of total cost)	Painted or custom select canvas backed or custom molded cloth tapestry wallpapers or ornamental plaster finished with detailed sirocco type moldings and trim, walls with selected matched wood veneers.	Painted or custom canvas backed, custom molded cloth tapestry wallpapers or ornamental plaster finished with custom moldings and trimmings. Portions of wall select matched wood veneers.	Painted or finished with custom canvas backed wallpapers or molded tapestry finished wallpapers or select wood veneer matched full height at lobby.	Painted or finished with durable canvas or select quality wood veneers on gypsum board or plaster.	Painted and papered with durable canvas materials with portion wood veneers on gypsum board or plaster.
Ceiling (6% of total cost)	Suspended acoustical with highly ornate moldings and trim with acoustical baffles.	Suspended acoustical with highly ornate moldings and trim with acoustical baffles.	Suspended acoustical with ornate plaster cove moldings and trim with acoustical baffles.	Suspended acoustical with plaster moldings and sound baffles.	Suspended acoustical tile.
Lighting (10% of total cost)	Incandescent or recessed lights throughout. Interior with ornate chandelier type fixtures throughout. All dimmer controlled.	Incandescent or recessed lights throughout. Interior with ornate chandelier type fixtures throughout. All dimmer controlled.	Incandescent fixtures with chandelier and recessed lights at theater area, dimmer controlled.	Incandescent fixtures in lobby with fluorescent or chandelier type fixtures in theater area, recessed lighting, dimmer controlled.	Incandescent fixtures with recessed fixtures, dimmer controlled.
Seating (8% of total cost)	Main floor and balcony seating.	Main floor and balcony seating.	May or may not have balcony.	May or may not have balcony.	May or may not have balcony.

Note: Use the percent of total cost to help identify the correct quality classification.

Square foot costs include the following components: Foundations as required for normal soil conditions. Floor, wall, and roof structures. Interior floor, wall and ceiling finishes. Exterior wall finish and roof cover. Display fronts. Interior partitions. All doors. Ticket booth. Basic lighting and electrical systems. Rough and finish plumbing. A mezzanine floor projection booth. A frame-work for mounting a picture screen. A balcony in auditorium type theaters. Permits and fees. Contractor's mark-up.

Theaters with Balcony – Masonry or Concrete

Estimating Procedure

1. Establish the structure quality class by applying the information on page 185.
2. Compute the building floor area. This should include everything within the main walls and all insets outside the main walls but under the main roof.
3. Add to or subtract from the square foot cost below the appropriate amount from the Wall Height Adjustment Table on page 190 if the wall height is more or less than 28 feet.
4. Multiply the adjusted square foot cost by the building floor area.
5. Deduct, if appropriate, for common walls, using the figures on page 190.
6. Multiply the total cost by the location factor listed on page 7 or 8.
7. Add the cost of heating and air conditioning systems, fire extinguishers, exterior signs, paving and curbing. See the section beginning on page 236.

Length less than twice width - Square Foot Area

Quality Class	5,000	6,000	7,000	8,000	9,000	10,000	12,000	15,000	20,000	24,000	30,000
1 Best	223.18	215.01	208.78	203.85	199.92	196.57	191.34	185.65	179.40	175.90	172.19
1 & 2	214.80	206.90	200.91	196.24	192.38	189.18	184.16	178.64	172.62	169.32	165.71
2, Very Good	212.92	205.07	199.15	194.50	190.70	187.51	182.53	177.08	171.13	167.82	164.25
2 & 3	204.27	196.78	191.15	186.64	182.99	179.93	175.15	169.93	164.21	161.04	157.60
3, Good	199.52	192.21	186.61	182.26	178.66	175.74	171.02	165.94	160.34	157.27	153.94
3 & 4	190.11	183.14	177.87	173.71	170.28	167.45	162.98	158.11	152.77	149.86	146.65
4, Average	184.75	177.95	172.79	168.78	165.47	162.72	158.36	153.66	148.48	145.62	142.51
4 & 5	174.69	168.26	163.40	159.55	156.46	153.84	149.74	145.32	140.42	137.72	134.77
5, Low	165.76	159.64	155.12	151.42	148.46	146.00	142.09	137.82	133.25	130.67	127.90

Length between 2 and 4 times width - Square Foot Area

Quality Class	5,000	6,000	7,000	8,000	9,000	10,000	12,000	15,000	20,000	24,000	30,000
1, Best	237.63	228.86	222.25	217.07	212.83	209.27	203.66	197.65	190.93	187.30	183.29
1 & 2	228.67	220.32	213.94	208.89	204.82	201.43	196.01	190.20	183.79	180.24	176.42
2, Very Good	226.76	218.42	212.10	207.15	203.07	199.67	194.35	188.58	182.24	178.76	174.94
2 & 3	217.50	209.48	203.45	198.68	194.78	191.56	186.41	180.89	174.78	171.42	167.79
3, Good	212.44	204.61	198.70	194.06	190.22	187.09	182.08	176.71	170.71	167.43	163.86
3 & 4	200.79	193.42	187.83	183.44	179.86	176.84	172.15	167.01	161.37	158.31	154.93
4, Average	196.83	189.61	184.12	179.80	176.29	173.32	168.73	163.69	158.21	155.17	151.85
4 & 5	186.07	179.19	174.04	169.92	166.61	163.84	159.48	154.74	149.51	146.64	143.53
5, Low	176.49	170.04	165.15	161.25	158.08	155.44	151.31	146.81	141.83	139.14	136.19

Length more than 4 times width - Square Foot Area

Quality Class	5,000	6,000	7,000	8,000	9,000	10,000	12,000	15,000	20,000	24,000	30,000
1, Best	253.07	243.77	236.77	231.28	226.73	222.96	217.00	210.48	203.37	199.38	195.09
1 & 2	243.48	234.64	227.89	222.56	218.21	214.59	208.79	202.61	195.71	191.91	187.77
2, Very Good	241.38	232.59	225.89	220.63	216.29	212.68	207.03	200.81	194.04	190.22	186.12
2 & 3	231.80	222.20	216.88	211.82	207.71	204.20	198.76	192.81	186.28	182.61	178.68
3, Good	226.13	217.88	211.57	206.64	202.64	199.22	193.88	188.11	181.70	178.15	174.38
3 & 4	215.55	207.67	201.72	196.99	193.13	189.92	184.83	179.32	173.22	169.84	166.19
4, Average	210.24	202.55	196.75	192.16	188.38	185.23	180.29	174.93	168.93	165.67	162.13
4 & 5	198.01	190.78	185.26	180.97	177.44	174.49	169.78	164.74	159.16	156.07	152.65
5, Low	187.73	181.04	175.84	171.70	168.33	165.58	161.13	156.34	151.00	148.11	144.89

Theaters without Balcony – Masonry or Concrete

Length Less Than Twice Width

Estimating Procedure

1. Establish the structure quality class by applying the information on page 185.
2. Compute the building floor area. This should include everything within the main walls and all insets outside the main walls but under the main roof.
3. Add to or subtract from the square foot cost below the appropriate amount from the Wall Height Adjustment Table on page 190 if the wall height is more or less than 20 feet.
4. Multiply the adjusted square foot cost by the building floor area.
5. Deduct, if appropriate, for common walls, using the figures on page 190.
6. Multiply the total cost by the location factor listed on page 7 or 8.
7. Add the cost of heating and air conditioning systems, fire extinguishers, exterior signs, paving and curbing. See the section beginning on page 236.

Theater Without Balcony, Class 4

Square Foot Area

Quality Class	3,000	3,500	4,000	5,000	6,000	7,000	8,000	10,000	12,000	15,000	20,000
3, Good	129.62	125.51	122.33	117.61	114.34	111.88	109.95	107.12	105.12	102.97	100.70
3 & 4	124.42	120.44	117.42	112.92	109.75	107.40	105.50	102.85	100.89	98.83	96.57
4, Average	122.42	118.53	115.50	111.06	107.99	105.66	103.86	101.18	99.29	97.22	95.03
4 & 5	118.21	114.44	111.52	107.24	104.24	101.97	100.24	97.67	95.85	93.88	91.78
5, Low	114.34	110.72	107.91	103.74	100.87	98.70	97.01	94.50	92.74	90.82	88.81

Theaters without Balcony – Masonry or Concrete

Length Between 2 and 4 Times Width

Estimating Procedure

1. Establish the structure quality class by applying the information on page 185.
2. Compute the building floor area. This should include everything within the main walls and all insets outside the main walls but under the main roof.
3. Add to or subtract from the square foot cost below the appropriate amount from the Wall Height Adjustment Table on page 190 if the wall height is more or less than 20 feet.
4. Multiply the adjusted square foot cost by the building floor area.
5. Deduct, if appropriate, for common walls, using the figures on page 190.
6. Multiply the total cost by the location factor listed on page 7 or 8.
7. Add the cost of heating and air conditioning systems, fire extinguishers, exterior signs, paving and curbing. See the section beginning on page 236.

Theater Without Balcony, Class 3

Square Foot Area

Quality Class	3,000	3,500	4,000	5,000	6,000	7,000	8,000	10,000	12,000	15,000	20,000
3, Good	139.77	133.85	129.56	123.76	120.11	117.61	115.83	113.54	112.21	111.00	110.00
3 & 4	134.21	128.52	124.38	118.78	115.30	112.96	111.27	109.07	107.71	106.53	105.59
4, Average	132.20	126.59	122.50	117.06	113.57	111.23	109.56	107.42	106.13	104.97	104.04
4 & 5	127.60	122.20	118.28	112.99	109.68	107.39	105.80	103.67	102.39	101.33	100.40
5, Low	123.61	118.35	114.52	109.42	106.18	104.02	102.41	100.45	99.22	98.13	97.21

Theaters without Balcony – Masonry or Concrete

Length More Than 4 Times Width

Estimating Procedure

1. Establish the structure quality class by applying the information on page 185.
2. Compute the building floor area. This should include everything within the main walls and all insets outside the main walls but under the main roof.
3. Add to or subtract from the square foot cost below the appropriate amount from the Wall Height Adjustment Table on page 190 if the wall height is more or less than 20 feet.
4. Multiply the adjusted square foot cost by the building floor area.
5. Deduct, if appropriate, for common walls, using the figures on page 190.
6. Multiply the total cost by the location factor listed on page 7 or 8.
7. Add the cost of heating and air conditioning systems, fire extinguishers, exterior signs, paving and curbing. See the section beginning on page 236.

Theater Without Balcony, Class 3 & 4

Square Foot Area

Quality Class	3,000	3,500	4,000	5,000	6,000	7,000	8,000	10,000	12,000	15,000	20,000
3, Good	146.07	141.31	137.61	132.25	128.47	125.76	123.56	120.39	118.20	115.83	113.33
3 & 4	139.56	135.01	131.49	126.38	122.81	120.21	118.12	115.08	112.97	110.69	108.26
4, Average	137.96	133.49	129.95	124.92	121.39	118.74	116.74	113.72	111.62	109.43	107.05
4 & 5	133.17	128.81	125.48	120.55	117.19	114.60	112.72	109.78	107.76	105.64	103.32
5, Low	128.89	124.64	121.41	116.71	113.36	110.92	109.03	106.28	104.27	102.23	99.95

Theaters – Masonry or Concrete

Wall Height Adjustment

Add or subtract the appropriate amount listed in this table to or from the square foot of floor cost for each foot of wall height more or less than 28 feet, if adjusting for a theater with balcony, or 20 feet, if adjusting for a theater without a balcony.

Square Foot Area

Quality Class	3,000	3,500	4,000	5,000	6,000	7,000	8,000	10,000	12,000	15,000	20,000
1, Best	3.84	3.72	3.62	3.50	3.41	3.34	3.27	3.16	3.13	3.08	3.02
2, Very Good	3.62	3.55	3.48	3.34	3.20	3.13	3.11	3.03	2.99	2.89	2.83
3, Good	3.50	3.40	3.29	3.14	3.06	3.01	2.97	2.88	2.86	2.78	2.69
4, Average	3.28	3.12	3.08	2.98	2.89	2.86	2.73	2.69	2.66	2.58	2.53
5, Low	3.06	2.97	2.88	2.77	2.71	2.65	2.56	2.50	2.47	2.43	2.36

Perimeter (Common) Wall Adjustment

A common wall exists when two buildings share one wall. Adjust for common walls by deducting the linear foot costs below from the total structure cost. In some structures one or more walls are not owned at all. In this case, deduct the "No Ownership" cost per linear foot of wall not owned. For Common Wall, deduct $293 per linear foot. For no Wall Ownership, deduct $584 per linear foot.

Theaters – Wood Frame

Quality Classification

	Class 1 Best Quality	Class 2 Good Quality	Class 3 Average Quality	Class 4 Low Quality
Foundation (12% of total cost)	Reinforced concrete.	Reinforced concrete.	Reinforced concrete.	Reinforced concrete.
Floor Structure (7% of total cost)	4" reinforced concrete on 6" rock fill or 2" x 10" joists, 16" o.c.	4" reinforced concrete on 6" rock fill or 2" x 8" joists, 16" o.c.	4" reinforced concrete on 6" rock fill or 2" x 6" joists, 16" o.c.	4" reinforced concrete on 4" rock fill or 2" x 6" joists, 16" o.c.
Wall Structure (15% of total cost)	2" x 6", 16" o.c.	2" x 4" or 2" x 6", 16" o.c.	2" x 4", 16" o.c. up to 14' high, 2" x 6", 16" o.c. over 14' high.	2" x 4", 16" o.c. up to 14' high, 2" x 6", 16" o.c. over 14' high.
Roof Framing (7% of total cost)	2" x 10" joists, 16" o.c. Trusses on heavy pilasters, 20' o.c. 2" x 12" rafters or purlins, 16" o.c.	2" x 10" joists, 16" o.c. Trusses on heavy pilasters, 20' o.c. 2" x 10" rafters or purlins.	2" x 10" joists, 16" o.c. Steel trusses on pilasters, 20' o.c. 2" x 10" rafters or purlins, 16" o.c.	2" x 10" joists, 16" o.c. Wood trusses, 2" x 8" purlins, 16" o.c.
Roof Covering (5% of total cost)	5 ply composition roof on 1" x 6" sheathing with insulation.	5 ply composition roof on 1" x 6" sheathing with insulation.	4 ply composition roof on 1" x 6" sheathing.	4 ply composition roof on 1" x 6" sheathing.
Front (3% of total cost)	Highly ornamental stucco or custom brick or natural stone or terra cotta veneers.	Ornamental stucco or select brick veneers or partial terra cotta veneers.	Plain or colored stucco or common brick or ornamental wood.	Plain stucco.
Floors, Entry & Lobby (3% of total cost)	Custom designed terrazzo with ornamental designs with portions natural stone veneers, marble or good carpet.	Colored terrazzo with designs or average carpet.	Colored concrete and portions terrazzo, plain colored.	Plain or colored concrete.
Floors, Interior (5% of total cost)	Concrete with carpet throughout.	Concrete with carpet throughout.	Concrete with carpet runners at aisles.	Plain or colored concrete.
Restrooms (8% of total cost)	As per code requirement capacity. Ceramic tile on floors and walls or terrazzo floors and walls.	As per code requirement capacity. Ceramic tile on walls and floors or terrazzo on floors.	As per code requirement capacity. Ceramic or vinyl tile on floors.	As per code requirement capacity. Plain concrete floors and walls, painted.
Walls, Interior (11% of total cost)	Painted and finished with custom backed wallpapers or molded tapestry finished wallpapers or select wood veneer, matched full height at lobby.	Painted and finished with durable canvas or wood veneers, select quality on gypsum wallboard or plaster.	Painted and papered with durable canvas materials with portion wood veneers on gypsum wallboard or plaster.	Painted with or without stencil type painted molded designs on gypsum wallboard taped and textured.
Ceilings (6% of total cost)	Suspended acoustical, ornate cove moldings and trim with acoustical baffles.	Suspended acoustical with plaster moldings and sound baffles.	Suspended acoustical tile.	Gypsum wallboard taped, textured and painted.
Lighting (10% of total cost)	Incandescent fixtures with chandelier fixtures, recessed at theater area, dimmer controlled.	Incandescent fixtures in lobby with fluorescent or chandelier type fixtures in theater area, recessed lighting, dimmer controlled.	Incandescent recessed fixtures, dimmer controlled.	Plain incandescent fixtures, with dimmers.
Seating (8% of total cost)	Main floor and balcony seating.	Main floor and balcony seating.	May or may not have balcony.	May or may not have balcony.

Note: Use the percent of total cost to help identify the correct quality classification.

Square foot costs include the following components: Foundations as required for normal soil conditions. Floor, wall, and roof structures. Interior floor, wall and ceiling finishes. Exterior wall finish and roof cover. Display fronts. Interior partitions. All doors. Ticket booth. Basic lighting and electrical systems. Rough and finish plumbing. A mezzanine floor projection booth. A frame-work for mounting a picture screen. A balcony in auditorium type theaters. Permits and fees. Contractor's mark-up.

Theaters – Wood Frame

Length Less Than Twice Width

Estimating Procedure

1. Establish the structure quality class by applying the information on page 191.
2. Compute the building floor area. This should include everything within the main walls and all insets outside the main walls but under the main roof.
3. Add to or subtract from the square foot cost below the appropriate amount from the Wall Height Adjustment Table on page 195 if the wall height is more or less than 20 feet.
4. Multiply the adjusted square foot cost by the building floor area.
5. Deduct, if appropriate, for common walls, using the figures on page 195.
6. Multiply the total cost by the location factor listed on page 7 or 8.
7. Add the cost of heating and air conditioning systems, fire extinguishers, exterior signs, paving and curbing. See the section beginning on page 236.

Theater, Class 4 Front, Class 3 Rear

Square Foot Area

Quality Class	3,000	3,500	4,000	5,000	6,000	7,000	8,000	10,000	12,000	15,000	20,000
1, Best	114.98	111.34	108.49	104.31	101.48	99.26	97.58	95.05	93.31	91.40	89.32
1 & 2	111.40	107.85	105.08	101.09	98.26	96.13	94.46	92.05	90.34	88.50	86.48
2, Good	109.90	106.41	103.70	99.75	96.93	94.87	93.25	90.86	89.11	87.34	85.37
2 & 3	106.40	103.01	100.35	96.61	93.83	91.84	90.28	87.91	86.25	84.52	82.60
3, Average	104.22	100.95	98.35	94.62	91.93	89.98	88.44	86.17	84.54	82.84	80.97
3 & 4	101.10	97.92	95.39	91.81	89.20	87.30	85.77	83.60	82.00	80.33	78.52
4, Low	98.20	95.09	92.68	89.07	86.61	84.76	83.30	81.14	79.63	78.03	76.28

Theaters – Wood Frame

Length Between 2 and 4 Times Width

Estimating Procedure

1. Establish the structure quality class by applying the information on page 191.
2. Compute the building floor area. This should include everything within the main walls and all insets outside the main walls but under the main roof.
3. Add to or subtract from the square foot cost below the appropriate amount from the Wall Height Adjustment Table on page 195 if the wall height is more or less than 20 feet.
4. Multiply the adjusted square foot cost by the building floor area.
5. Deduct, if appropriate, for common walls, using the figures on page 195.
6. Multiply the total cost by the location factor listed on page 7 or 8.
7. Add the cost of heating and air conditioning systems, fire extinguishers, exterior signs, paving and curbing. See the section beginning on page 236.

Theater, Class 3

Square Foot Area

Quality Class	3,000	3,500	4,000	5,000	6,000	7,000	8,000	10,000	12,000	15,000	20,000
1, Best	122.54	118.68	115.63	111.18	108.11	105.76	103.95	101.25	99.35	97.33	95.11
1 & 2	118.61	114.86	111.96	107.68	104.64	102.39	100.61	97.99	96.16	94.21	92.06
2, Good	117.00	113.29	110.36	106.18	103.20	100.96	99.22	96.65	94.84	92.90	90.81
2 & 3	113.21	109.60	106.79	102.71	99.82	97.71	96.02	93.53	91.75	89.86	87.83
3, Average	111.06	107.53	104.80	100.79	97.95	95.85	94.22	91.81	90.04	88.19	86.21
3 & 4	107.69	104.24	100.66	97.57	94.97	92.94	91.31	88.95	87.34	85.46	83.60
4, Low	104.37	101.09	98.51	94.71	92.05	90.08	88.54	86.23	84.58	82.89	81.01

Theaters – Wood Frame

Length More Than 4 Times Width

Estimating Procedure

1. Establish the structure quality class by applying the information on page 191.
2. Compute the building floor area. This should include everything within the main walls and all insets outside the main walls but under the main roof.
3. Add to or subtract from the square foot cost below the appropriate amount from the Wall Height Adjustment Table on page 195 if the wall height is more or less than 20 feet.
4. Multiply the adjusted square foot cost by the building floor area.
5. Deduct, if appropriate, for common walls, using the figures on page 195.
6. Multiply the total cost by the location factor listed on page 7 or 8.
7. Add the cost of heating and air conditioning systems, fire extinguishers, exterior signs, paving and curbing. See the section beginning on page 236.

Theater, Class 3

Square Foot Area

Quality Class	3,000	3,500	4,000	5,000	6,000	7,000	8,000	10,000	12,000	15,000	20,000
1, Best	130.34	126.16	122.98	118.29	114.96	112.47	110.51	107.73	105.67	103.54	101.14
1 & 2	126.19	122.23	119.09	114.51	111.35	108.98	107.08	104.31	102.38	100.28	97.99
2, Good	124.56	120.59	117.52	113.04	109.86	107.52	105.67	102.94	100.98	98.99	96.75
2 & 3	120.57	116.74	113.81	109.41	106.36	104.09	102.27	99.63	97.82	95.82	93.64
3, Average	118.33	114.51	111.63	107.36	104.40	102.12	100.34	97.82	95.96	93.98	91.87
3 & 4	114.66	111.01	108.18	104.05	101.14	98.99	97.26	94.71	92.98	91.04	89.02
4, Low	111.99	108.42	105.67	101.67	98.83	96.66	95.01	92.61	90.86	88.97	86.95

Theaters – Wood Frame

Wall Height Adjustment

Add or subtract the amount listed in this table to or from the square foot of floor cost for each foot of wall height more or less than 20 feet.

Square Foot Area

Quality Class	3,000	3,500	4,000	5,000	6,000	7,000	8,000	10,000	12,000	15,000	20,000
1, Best	3.05	2.98	2.92	2.79	2.75	2.67	2.62	2.58	2.49	2.43	2.37
2, Good	2.95	2.87	2.82	2.65	2.58	2.53	2.49	2.43	2.40	2.34	2.31
3, Average	2.81	2.72	2.66	2.53	2.49	2.43	2.40	2.34	2.32	2.28	2.18
4, Low	2.59	2.49	2.43	2.36	2.33	2.31	2.28	2.17	2.12	2.10	1.99

Perimeter (Common) Wall Adjustment

A common wall exists when two buildings share one wall. Adjust for common walls by deducting the linear foot costs below from the total structure cost. In some structures one or more walls are not owned at all. In this case, deduct the "No Ownership" cost per linear foot of wall not owned.

For common wall, deduct $155 per linear foot. For no wall ownership, deduct $309 per linear foot.

Mobile Home Parks

Quality Classification

	Class 1 Best Quality	Class 2 Good Quality	Class 3 Average Quality	Class 4 Low Quality
Engineering, Plans, Permits, Surveying (10% of total cost)	Good planning, necessary permits, good engineering; designed by architect.	Good planning, necessary permits, good engineering; designed by architect.	Average planning, necessary permits, engineered and designed.	Fair planning, necessary permits, minimum surveying.
Grading (10% of total cost)	Fully graded.	Fully graded.	Fully graded.	Minimum site leveling; grades not engineered; road grading.
Street Paving (10% of total cost)	2" thick asphalt surface on good base, concrete curbs, 30' width.	2" thick asphalt surface on good base, concrete curbs, 25' width.	20' roads, 2" asphalt on rock base; concrete or wood edging.	Narrow streets, 2" asphalt on ground; no curbs or edging.
Patios & Walks (5% of total cost)	Patios, 300 to 500 S.F. of good concrete. Walks to utility rooms, pools and recreation areas.	Patios, 200 to 300 S.F. of good concrete. Walks to utility rooms, pools and recreation areas.	Patios, approximately 150 S.F. average concrete or average grade asphalt. Walks to utility buildings.	Some patios, concrete or asphalt paving. No walks.
Trailer Pad & Parking (3% of total cost)	Concrete or good asphalt pad and driveway.	Asphalt under trailer and extended to one side for driveway.	Gravel under trailer and small asphalt driveway.	Gravel under trailer.
Sewer (10% of total cost)	8" lines, 10" mains. Meets all code requirements. Storm drain system.	8" lines, 10" mains. Meets all code requirements.	4" to 6" and 8" lines. Meets code requirements in most areas.	3" to 6" lines, inadequate. Below good code requirements.
Water (10% of total cost)	Engineered system for equalized pressure throughout park. Sprinkler system in common areas.	Adequate line size, designed and properly sized for equalized pressure.	Adequate line size; has required valves at each space.	Small lines; has required valves at each space.
Gas (10% of total cost)	Supplied to each space, sized to code requirements.	Supplied to each space, sized to code requirements.	None except in utility buildings and recreation buildings	None except in utility buildings.

Quality Classification continued

	Class 1 Best Quality	Class 2 Good Quality	Class 3 Average Quality	Class 4 Low Quality
Electric (10% of total cost)	Underground service, designed for larger modern trailers with adequate size to enlarge to take care of future needs. Approximately 100 amp or more. Speaker system, underground television system to each space.	Underground service, designed for larger modern trailers with facilities to enlarge capacity to 100 amp. Approximately 70 amp service or more. Speaker system, underground television system to each space.	Underground services, not designed for more capacity. Approximately 30 amp service or more. Speaker system.	Overhead system wired for 15 amp service at each space.
Outdoor Lighting (4% of total cost)	Lamp post each five spaces, ornate type.	Lamp post each five spaces, inexpensive type.	Overhead street lights at each corner.	Few overhead street lights.
Telephone (8% of total cost)	Underground to each space.	Underground to each space.	None.	None.
Sign (1% of total cost)	Large expensive sign.	Good sign.	Average sign.	Inexpensive sign.
Garbage (1% of total cost)	Built-in ground.	Built-in ground.	None.	None.
Mail Boxes (1% of total cost)	Good mail box and post each space.	Inexpensive mail box and post each space.	None.	None.
Fences and Gates (3% of total cost)	Good wood or cyclone. Ornamental fence or wall in front.	Good wood or cyclone. Block wall in front.	Inexpensive wood or wire.	None or inexpensive wire.
Pools (4% of total cost)	Good quality.	Good quality, adequate size for park.	Small with few extras.	None or inexpensive.
Utility Building (See page 185)	Wood frame and good stucco. Board batt redwood siding or concrete block exterior. Best composition shingle or tar and rock roofing. Good interior plaster or gypsum wallboard. Well finished concrete floors with vinyl tile. Good lighting. Good heating. Showers ceramic tile or fiberglass walls with ceramic tile floor. Glass shower doors. Good quality plumbing fixtures. Good workmanship throughout.	Wood frame and good stucco or concrete block exterior. Thick butt composition shingles or tar and gravel roof. Good exterior or plaster or gypsum wallboard. Well finished concrete floors. Good lighting. Good heating. Showers ceramic tile walls with ceramic tile base. Good quality plumbing fixtures. Good workmanship throughout.	Wood frame, average stucco exterior. Composition shingle or roll roofing. Gypsum wallboard taped and textured or plaster interior. Average concrete floors. Average lighting. Fair heating. Metal stall with showers or showers with enameled cement plaster walls and tile floor with tile base. Average plumbing fixtures. Average workmanship throughout.	Wood frame, fair stucco or fair siding exterior. Plastic interior. Composition roll roofing. Fair concrete finish. Fair lighting. Inexpensive heating. Showers enameled cement plaster walls and tile floors. Fair plumbing fixtures and fair workmanship throughout.
Recreation Building (See page 185)	Wood frame and stucco. Board and batt redwood siding or concrete block exterior. Best composition shingles or tar and rock roofing. Good interior plaster or gypsum wallboard taped, textured and painted. Well finished concrete floors with vinyl tile. Good heating. Good lighting. Rest room for each sex containing at least one each of the following fixtures: Shower, water closet & lavatory. Showers ceramic tile floors and walls or fiberglass walls and tilefloor with glass shower doors. Good quality plumbing fixtures. Kitchen sink, range, refrigerator, cabinets and drainboard of formica or equal material. Large glass area in community room.	Wood frame and good stucco or concrete block exterior. Thick butt composition shingles or tar and gravel roof. Good exterior or plaster or gypsum wallboard. Well finished concrete floors. Good heating. Good lighting. Ceramic tile stall showers with ceramic tile base. Good quality plumbing fixtures. Kitchen with tile drain board and some hardwood cabinets. Small office area. Large glass windows in community room.	Wood frame, average stucco or siding exterior. Composition shingle or roll roofing. Gypsum wallboard taped and textured or plaster interior. Average concrete floors. Average lighting. Average heating. Showers with enameled cement plaster walls and ceramic tile base. Water closets and lavatories. One rest room for each sex with at least 1 each shower, water closet and lavatory. Average grade of plumbing fixtures. Ceiling of gypsum wallboard. Average workmanship throughout.	None.

Note: Use the percent of total cost to help identify the correct quality classification.

Mobile Home Parks

Estimating Procedure

1. Establish the park quality class by applying the information on pages 195 and 196.
2. Compute the square foot area per home space. This should include the mobile home space, streets, recreation and other community use areas but exclude excess land not improved or not in use as a part of the park operation. Divide this total area by the number of home spaces. The result is the average area per home space.
3. Multiply the appropriate cost below by the number of home spaces.
4. Determine the quality class and area of recreation and utility buildings. Compute the total cost of these buildings and add this amount to or subtract it from the total from step 3 to adjust for more or fewer buildings than included in the quality specification.
5. Multiply the total building costs by the location factor listed on page 7 or 8.
6. Add the cost of septic tank systems, wells, and covered areas built at the individual spaces.

Space costs with community facilities include the cost of the following components: Grading associated with a level site under normal soil conditions. Street paving and curbs. Patios and walks. Pads and parking paving. Sewer, electrical, gas and water systems including normal hook-up costs. Outdoor lighting. Signs. Mail boxes. Fences and gates. Contractor's mark-up.

Space costs with community facilities and buildings include the cost of all the above components plus these components in amounts proportionate to the size of the park: Recreation, administrative and utility buildings adequate for the size of the park. Recreation facilities such as pools, shuffle board courts, playground equipment, fire pits, etc. Telephones. Restrooms.

The cost of the following components are not included in the basic building cost: Septic tank systems. Wells. Structures or covered areas on individual spaces. The cost of grading beyond that associated with a level site.

Parks Without Community Facilities or Buildings - Square Foot Area

Quality Class	1,500	2,000	2,500	3,000	3,500	4,000	4,500	5,000	5,500	6,000	6,500
1, Best	—	—	—	—	—	13,003	13,244	13,756	14,411	14,567	14,567
1 & 2	—	—	—	11,772	12,370	12,626	12,862	13,169	13,403	13,403	13,403
2, Good	—	—	8,906	9,683	9,444	10,563	10,777	10,777	10,777	10,777	—
2 & 3	5,428	5,971	6,534	6,953	7,332	7,654	7,654	7,654	7,654	—	—

Parks With Community Facilities and Buildings - Square Foot Area

Quality Class	1,500	2,000	2,500	3,000	3,500	4,000	4,500	5,000	5,500	6,000	6,500
1, Best	—	—	—	—	—	19,029	19,944	20,548	21,129	21,715	22,063
2, Good	—	—	—	17,983	18,419	18,843	19,204	19,535	20,275	20,275	20,275
3, Average	—	—	14,494	14,494	15,207	15,452	15,630	15,630	15,630	15,630	—
4, Low	9,848	9,984	10,268	10,715	11,092	11,318	11,295	11,295	11,295	—	—

Square Foot Costs for Building Alone

	Recreational Buildings	Utility Buildings
1, Best	$66.86 to $96.74	$64.25 to $77.40
2, Good	$59.20 to $74.71	$47.65 to $64.69
3, Average	$47.94 to $68.87	$45.04 to $48.53
4, Low	—	$41.16 to $47.08

Quality Classification

	Wood Frame	Masonry or Concrete	Painted Steel, Good	Painted Steel, Average	Painted Steel, Low
Foundation & Floor (25% of total cost)	Reinforced concrete.	Reinforced concrete.	Reinforced concrete.	Reinforced concrete.	Reinforced concrete.
Walls (15% of total cost)	Wood frame 2 x 4, 16" o.c.	8" concrete block.	Steel frame.	Steel frame.	Steel frame.
Roof Structure (6% of total cost)	Light wood frame, flat or shed type.	Light wood frame, flat or shed type.	Steel frame, flat or shed type.	Steel frame, flat or shed type.	Steel frame, flat or shed type.
Exterior Finish (10% of total cost)	Painted wood siding or stucco.	Painted concrete block.	Painted steel.	Painted steel.	Painted steel.
Roof Cover (5% of total cost)	Composition.	Composition.	Steel deck.	Steel deck.	Steel deck.
Glass Area (5% of total cost)	Small area, painted wood frames.	Small area, painted steel frames.	Large area, painted steel frames.	Average area, painted steel frames.	Small area, painted steel frames.
Lube Room Doors (5% of total cost)	Folding steel gate.	Folding steel gate.	Painted steel sectional roll up.	Painted steel sectional roll up.	Folding steel gate.
Floor Finish (5% of total cost)	Concrete.	Concrete.	Concrete, colored concrete in office.	Concrete.	Concrete.
Interior Wall Finish (5% of total cost)	Exposed studs, painted.	Concrete block, painted.	Exposed structure painted. Painted steel panels in office.	Exposed structure painted. Painted steel panels in office.	Exposed structure painted. Painted steel panels in office.
Ceiling Finish (3% of total cost)	Exposed structure painted.	Exposed structure painted.	Exposed structure painted. Painted steel panels in office.	Exposed structure painted. Painted steel panels in office.	Exposed structure painted.
Rest Room Finish (5% of total cost)	Wallboard and paint walls and ceilings.	Concrete block and paint walls, wallboard and paint ceilings.	Ceramic tile floors, 4' ceramic tile wainscot, painted steel ceilings.	Ceramic tile floors, 4' ceramic tile wainscot, painted steel ceilings.	Concrete floors, painted steel walls, painted steel ceilings.
Rest Room Fixtures (8% of total cost)	4 low cost fixtures.	4 low cost fixtures.	5 average cost fixtures.	5 average cost fixtures.	4 low cost fixtures.
Exterior Appointments (3% of total cost)	None.	None.	2' overhang on 3 sides, 3' raised walk on 3 sides, fluorescent soffit lights on 3 sides.	1' overhang on 2 sides, 3' raised walk on 2 sides.	None.

Note: Use the percent of total cost to help identify the correct quality classification.

Square foot costs include the cost of the following components: Foundations as required for normal soil conditions. Floor, wall and roof structure. Interior floor, wall and ceiling finishes as described above. Interior partitions. Exterior finish and roof cover. A built-in work bench, tire rack and shelving. Electrical services and fixtures contained within the building. Air and water lines within the building. That portion of rough plumbing serving the building and plumbing fixtures within the building. Roof overhangs and raised walks as described above. Lube room doors. Permits and fees. Contractor's mark-up.

The in-place cost of these extra components should be added to the basic building cost to arrive at the total structure cost. See the section "Additional Costs for Service Stations" beginning on Page 204. Canopies. Pumps, dispensers and turbines. Air and water services outside the building. Island lighters. Gasoline storage tanks. Hoists. Compressors. Yard lights. Signs. Paving. Curbs and fences. Miscellaneous equipment and accessories. Island office and storage buildings. Site improvements. Heating and cooling systems

Land improvement costs: Most service stations sites require an expenditure of $10,000 or more for items such as leveling, excavation, curbs, driveways, relocation of power poles, replacement of sidewalks with reinforced walks and street paving.

Service Stations – Wood, Masonry or Painted Steel

Estimating Procedure

1. Establish the structure quality class by applying the information on page 198.
2. Compute the building floor area.
3. Multiply the square foot cost by the building floor area.
4. Multiply the total cost by the location factor listed on page 7 or 8.
5. Add the cost of appropriate equipment and fixtures from the section "Additional Costs for Service Stations" beginning on page 204.

Wood Frame

Masonry

Painted Steel, Good

Painted Steel, Average

Painted Steel, Low

Square Foot Area

Quality Class	500	600	700	800	900	1,000	1,100	1,200	1,300	1,400	1,800
Wood Frame	114.76	105.41	98.59	93.63	89.71	86.58	84.01	81.92	80.08	78.51	74.04
Masonry or Concrete	127.35	116.67	109.21	103.65	99.29	95.88	93.06	90.69	88.69	86.95	81.99
Painted Steel, Good	213.67	196.10	183.62	174.25	166.97	161.20	156.35	152.42	149.05	146.22	137.86
Painted Steel, Avg.	191.43	176.99	166.51	157.25	150.65	144.57	139.51	133.93	130.55	127.29	124.41
Painted Steel, Low	167.66	153.93	144.12	136.80	131.06	126.49	122.75	119.66	117.01	114.09	108.24

Quality Classification

	Good Quality	Average Quality	Low Quality
Foundation & Floor (20% of total cost)	Reinforced concrete.	Reinforced concrete.	Reinforced concrete.
Walls (15% of total cost)	Steel frame.	Steel frame.	Steel frame.
Roof Structure (8% of total cost)	Steel frame, flat or shed type.	Steel frame, flat or shed type.	Steel frame, flat or shed type.
Exterior Finish (10% of total cost)	Porcelain and steel.	Porcelain and steel.	Porcelain and steel.
Roof Cover (6% of total cost)	Steel deck.	Steel deck.	Steel deck.
Glass Area (7% of total cost)	Large area, aluminum frames.	Large area, aluminum frames.	Average area, painted steel frames.
Lube Room Doors (3% of total cost)	Aluminum and glass sectional roll up.	Aluminum and glass sectional roll up.	Painted steel and glass sectional roll up.
Floor Finish (5% of total cost)	Concrete floors, ceramic tile in office.	Concrete floors, colored concrete in office.	Concrete floors, colored concrete in office.
Interior Wall Finish (5% of total cost)	Porcelain steel panels. Painted steel panels in office.	Exposed structure painted. Painted steel panels in office.	Exposed structure painted.
Ceiling Finish (3% of total cost)	Exposed structure painted. Porcelain steel panels in office.	Exposed structure painted. Painted steel panels in office.	Exposed structure painted. Painted steel panels in office.
Rest Room Finish (5% of total cost)	Ceramic tile floors, 8' ceramic tile or porcelain panel. Painted steel ceiling.	Ceramic tile floors, 5' ceramic tile wainscot. Painted steel ceiling.	Ceramic tile floors, 5' ceramic tile wainscot. Painted steel ceiling.
Rest Room Fixtures (10% of total cost)	5 good fixtures.	5 good fixtures.	5 good fixtures.
Exterior Appointments (3% of total cost)	3' to 4' overhang on 3 sides, 6' x 8' sign pylon, 3' raised walk on 3 sides, fluorescent soffit lights on 3 sides.	3' to 4' overhang on 3 sides, 6' x 8' sign pylon, 3' raised walk on 3 sides, fluorescent soffit lights on 3 sides.	3' raised walk on 3 sides, fluorescent soffit lights on 3 sides.

Note: Use the percent of total cost to help identify the correct quality classification.

Square foot costs include the cost of the following components: Foundations as required for normal soil conditions. Floor, wall and roof structure. Interior floor, wall and ceiling finishes as described above. Interior partitions. Exterior finish and roof cover. A built-in work bench, tire rack and shelving. Electrical services and fixtures contained within the building. Air and water lines within the building. That portion of rough plumbing serving the building and plumbing fixtures within the building. Roof overhangs and raised walks as described above. Lube room doors. Permits and fees. Contractor's mark-up.

The in-place cost of these extra components should be added to the basic building cost to arrive at the total structure cost. See the section "Additional Costs for Service Stations" beginning on page 204. Canopies. Pumps, dispensers and turbines. Air and water services outside the building. Island lighters. Gasoline storage tanks. Hoists. Compressors. Yard lights. Signs. Paving. Curbs and fences. Miscellaneous equipment and accessories. Island office and storage buildings. Site improvements. Heating and cooling systems

Land improvement costs: Most service station sites require an expenditure of $10,000 or more for items such as leveling, excavation, curbs, driveways, relocation of power poles, replacement of sidewalks with reinforced walks and street paving.

Estimating Procedure

1. Establish the structure quality class by applying the information on page 200.
2. Compute the building floor area.
3. Multiply the square foot cost by the building floor area.
4. Multiply the total cost by the location factor listed on page 7 or 8.
5. Add the cost of appropriate equipment and fixtures from the section "Additional Costs for Service Stations" beginning on page 204.

Good Quality

Average Quality

Low Quality

Square Foot Area

Quality Class	1,000	1,100	1,200	1,300	1,400	1,500	1,600	1,700	1,800	2,000	2,400
Good	200.39	193.45	187.95	183.46	179.84	176.95	174.41	172.35	170.62	167.93	164.47
Average	191.74	185.07	179.76	175.52	172.09	169.21	166.86	164.88	163.22	160.61	157.36
Low	174.18	168.10	163.26	159.45	156.34	153.71	151.56	149.83	148.27	145.92	142.98

Service Stations – Ranch or Rustic Type

Quality Classification

	Best Quality	Good Quality	Average Quality	Low Quality
Foundation & Floor (20% of total cost)	Reinforced concrete.	Reinforced concrete.	Reinforced concrete.	Reinforced concrete.
Walls (12% of total cost)	Steel frame.	Steel frame.	Steel frame, wood frame or masonry.	Steel frame, wood frame or masonry.
Roof Structure (8% of total cost)	Steel frame, hip or gable type.	Steel frame, hip or gable type.	Steel or wood frame, hip or gable type.	Steel or wood frame, hip or gable type.
Exterior Finish (10% of total cost)	Natural stone veneer.	Used brick veneer.	Painted steel and masonry veneer.	Painted steel or wood siding.
Roof Cover (6% of total cost)	Shingle tile or mission tile.	Heavy wood shakes or shingle tile.	Wood shakes or tar and rock.	Composition shingle or tar and gravel.
Glass Area (7% of total cost)	Large area float glass in heavy aluminum frame.	Large area float glass in heavy aluminum frame.	Large area, painted steel frame.	Average area, painted steel frame.
Lube Room Doors (5% of total cost)	Painted steel or aluminum and glass sectional roll up.	Painted steel or aluminum and glass sectional roll up.	Painted steel sectional roll up.	Painted steel sectional roll up.
Floor Finish (5% of total cost)	Concrete floors, ceramic tile in office.	Concrete floors, ceramic tile in office.	Concrete floors.	Concrete floors.
Interior Wall Finish (5% of total cost)	Painted steel panels or gypsum wallboard and paint.	Painted steel panels or gypsum wallboard and paint.	Painted steel panels or gypsum wallboard and paint.	Painted steel panels or gypsum wallboard and paint.
Ceiling Finish (3% of total cost)	Painted steel panels.	Painted steel panels.	Painted steel panels, gypsum wallboard, or "V" rustic and paint.	Painted steel panels, gypsum wallboard or "V" rustic and paint.
Restroom Finish (5% of total cost)	Ceramic tile floors, ceramic tile walls, painted steel ceiling.	Ceramic tile floors, ceramic tile walls, painted steel ceiling.	Ceramic tile floors, 5' ceramic tile wainscot, painted steel ceiling.	Ceramic tile floors, 5' ceramic tile wainscot, painted steel ceiling.
Restroom Fixtures (10% of total cost)	5 good fixtures.	5 good fixtures.	5 good fixtures.	5 good fixtures.
Exterior Appointments (4% of total cost)	3' to 6' overhang on all sides, 3' raised walk on 3 sides, fluorescent soffit lights on all sides.	3' to 6' overhang on all sides, 3' raised walk on 3 sides, fluorescent soffit lights on all sides.	3' to 6' overhang on 3 sides, 6' x 8' sign pylon, 3' raised walk on 3 sides, fluorescent soffit lights on 3 sides.	2' to 3' overhang on 3 sides, 3' raised walk on 3 sides, fluorescent soffit lights on 3 sides.

Note: Use the percent of total cost to help identify the correct quality classification.

Square foot costs include the cost of the following components: Foundations as required for normal soil conditions. Floor, wall and roof structure. Interior floor, wall and ceiling finishes as described above. Interior partitions. Exterior finish and roof cover. A built-in work bench, tire rack and shelving. Electrical services and fixtures contained within the building. Air and water lines within the building. That portion of rough plumbing serving the building and plumbing fixtures within the building. Roof overhangs and raised walks as described above. Lube room doors. Permits and fees. Contractor's mark-up.

The in-place cost of these extra components should be added to the basic building cost to arrive at the total structure cost. See the section "Additional Costs for Service Stations" beginning on page 204. Canopies. Pumps, dispensers and turbines. Air and water services outside the building. Island lighters. Gasoline storage tanks. Hoists. Compressors. Yard lights. Signs. Paving. Curbs and fences. Miscellaneous equipment and accessories. Island office and storage buildings. Site improvements. Heating and cooling systems

Land improvement costs: Most service stations sites require an expenditure of $10,000 or more for items such as leveling, excavation, curbs, driveways, relocation of power poles, replacement of sidewalks with reinforced walks and street paving.

Service Stations – Ranch or Rustic Type

Estimating Procedure

1. Establish the structure quality class by applying the information on page 202.
2. Compute the building floor area.
3. Multiply the square foot cost by the building floor area.
4. Multiply the total cost by the location factor listed on page 7 or 8.
5. Add the cost of appropriate equipment and fixtures from the section "Additional Costs for Service Stations" beginning on page 204.

Best Quality

Good Quality

Average Quality

Low Quality

Square Foot Area

Quality Class	1,000	1,100	1,200	1,300	1,400	1,500	1,600	1,700	1,800	2,000	2,400
Best	222.54	214.65	208.42	203.45	199.46	196.09	193.39	191.08	189.18	186.21	182.58
Good	213.51	205.93	199.95	195.19	191.31	188.14	185.49	183.37	181.44	178.70	175.17
Average	204.92	197.60	191.92	187.31	183.56	180.51	178.04	175.90	174.18	171.42	168.10
Low	193.50	186.68	181.28	176.96	173.41	170.58	168.13	166.20	164.49	161.91	158.77

Additional Costs for Service Stations

A portion of the typical plumbing or electrical cost has been added to each item of equipment requiring these services. It will not be necessary except in rare instances to add extra cost for these items.

Canopies, cost per square foot

Type	Less than 500 S.F.	500 to 1,000 S.F.	Over 1,000 S.F.
Painted steel	$34.30 to $38.60	$31.31 to $38.60	$27.00 to $30.02
Porcelain and steel	39.48 to 41.05	34.30 to 38.31	31.14 to 34.02
Ranch style or gable roof type	44.65 to 48.67	35.17 to 41.64	31.72 to 35.74

Deluxe steel with illuminated plastic signs on sides or in gables.
Also includes illuminated plastic island lighters.

Round type, good steel	67.58 to 79.26		

Costs include cost of foundation, steel support column or columns, complete canopy, painting or porcelaining, light fixtures, and electrical service. Ranch or gable roof types include the cost of a rock or shake roof cover. Concrete pads under canopies or masonry trim on support columns are not included in these costs.

Island Office and Storage buildings, cost per square foot

Type	Area						
	Under 30	31 - 40	41 - 50	51 - 60	61 - 80	81 - 100	101 - 120
Steel and glass or concrete block	440.16	421.15	375.65	334.37	297.31	279.26	225.41
Wood frame with stucco and glass	365.25	342.51	283.12	265.29	202.86	189.04	179.14

These buildings are usually found at self-service stations. Add $1,660 per unit for any plumbing fixtures in these buildings. Steel island offices cost about $1,760

Pumps, Dispensers and Turbines, cost each

Type	Installed Cost	Type	Installed Cost
Single pump	$6,008	Blendomatic pump	$9,868
Twin pump	8,154	Blendomatic dispenser	8,096
Single dispenser	4,578	Turbine pump, 1/3 HP	1,704
Twin dispenser	7,654	Turbine pump, 3/4 HP	2,361

Installed cost includes the cost of the pump or dispenser, installation cost, electrical hookup cost, a portion of the piping cost and a portion of the island block cost. Concrete islands 4" to 6" thick cost from $11.59 to $14.04 per square foot.

All of the above pump and dispenser costs are for the computing type. Add for electronic remote control totalizer, per hose, $1,860. Add for vapor control system, per hose/dispenser, $1,940.

Dispenser cost does not include the cost of the pump. Turbine pump costs must be added. 1/3 HP turbines will serve a single product up to four dispensers. 3/4 HP turbines will serve a single product up to eight dispensers.

Additional Costs for Service Stations

Air and Water Services

Type	Air Only		Air and Water	
	Equipment Cost	Installed Cost	Equipment Cost	Installed Cost
Underground disappearing hose type	$ 505	$ 745.38	$ 540.35	$1,127.16
Post type with auto inflator	$ 795	$1,173.62	$ 1,004.95	$1,595.80
Post type with auto inflator and disappearing hoses	$1,330	$1,810	$2,030	$2,480

Costs include cost of installation and a portion of the cost of air and water lines.

Island Lighters

Width	Length	4 Tubes	6 Tubes
42"	9'-5"	$2,140 ea.	$2,580 ea.
42"	11'-5"	2,660 ea.	3,380 ea.
42"	15'-6"	3,470 ea.	3,812 ea.
42"	19'-6"	4,220 ea.	4,550 ea.
36"	30'-0"	—	5,330 ea.

Cost includes foundation, davit poles or steel support columns and electrical service.

Cash Boxes complete, with pedestal $342 each

Gasoline Storage Tanks (Fiberglass)

Capacity in Gallons	Tank Cost	Installed Cost	Capacity in Gallons	Tank Cost	Installed Cost
110	$779	$1,368	5,300	$7,912	$10,279
150	960	1,640	6,300	8,298	10,606
280	1,154	1,877	7,400	10,265	11,465
550	1,528	2,391	8,400	10,588	11,564
1,000	2,882	4,944	10,500	10,631	13,772
2,000	5,390	6,583	12,600	13,501	17,151
4,000	7,204	10,843	—	—	—

Installed cost includes cost of tank, excavation (4' bury and soil disposal), placing backfill, fill box (concrete slab over tank), tank piping and vent piping.

Miscellaneous Lube Room Equipment

Air hose reel	$1,149	Pneumatic tube changer	$12,359
Water hose reel	1,185	Automatic lube equipment	9,179
Grease pit for trucks	$455 to $521 per L.F.	5 hose reel assembly	11,475

Yard Lights

High pressure sodium luminaires. Costs include electrical connection and mounting on a building soffit. For pole mounted yard lights, add pole mounting costs from page 195. Cost per light fixture.

70 Watt	100 Watt	200 Watt	300 Watt	400 Watt
$475	$496	$514	$558	$662

Additional Costs for Service Stations

Vehicle Hoist

Type	Equipment Cost	Installed Cost
One post 8,000 lb. semi hydraulic hoist	$4,925	$10,705
One post 8,000 lb. fully hydraulic hoist	5,256	11,113
Two post 11,000 lb. semi hydraulic hoist	7,457	17,187
Two post 11,000 fully hydraulic hoist	7,521	17,264
Two post 11,000 lb. pneumatic hoist	9,590	15,757
Two post 24,000 lb. pneumatic hoist	13,569	23,211

Air Compressors

Horsepower	Equipment Cost	Installed Cost	Horsepower	Equipment Cost	Installed Cost
1/2	$2,476	$2,795	2	$2,670	$2,992
3/4	2,508	2,851	3	2,815	3,619
1	2,545	2,905	5	2,992	3,685
1-1/2	2,634	2,966	7-1/2	5,115	5,422

Costs include compressor and tank only.

Paving, cost per S.F.

Asphalt, 2" with 4" base	$2.86 to $3.71
Concrete 4", with base	3.48 to 4.88
Concrete 6", with base	4.40 to 5.68
Oil macadam	2.73
Pea gravel	1.39

Site Improvement

Vertical curb and gutter	$7.37 to $23.69 LF
Concrete apron	9.14 to 20.31 SF
6" reinforced concrete sidewalks	5.64 to 7.37 SF
Standard 4" sidewalk	4.58 to 5.07 SF

The above costs are normally included in land value.

Fencing and Curbing, cost per L.F.

Heavy 2 rail fence, 2" x 6"	$1.01 to $11.82
Rails on 4" x 4" posts 6' to 8' o.c.	10.20 to 12.75
Chain link 3' to 4' high	10.15 to 15.03
Solid board 3' to 4' high	10.30 to 12.34
Log barrier	8.98 to 16.32
Metal guard rail on wood posts	37.97 to 69.71
6" x 6" doweled wood bumper strip	9.74 to 12.80
6" x 6" concrete bumper strip	8.34 to 11.87
Cable railing on wood posts	10.54 to 12.73
6" x 12" concrete curb and gutter	19.01 to 21.88
6" concrete block walls, per S.F.	7.74 to 11.07

plus $9.80/LF for foundation

Service Station Signs, cost per square foot of sign area measured on one side

Painted sheet metal with floodlights	$66.59 to $88.36
Porcelain enamel with floodlights	72.65 to 97.72
Plastic with interior lights	82.92 to 126.20
Simple rectangular neon with painted sheet metal faces and a moderate amount of plain letters	87.59 to 155.69
Round or irregular neon with porcelain enamel faces and more elaborate lettering	126.34 to 192.04

All of the above sign costs are for single faced signs. Add 50% to these costs for double faced signs. Sign costs include costs of installation and normal electrical hookup. They do not include the post cost. See page 195. These costs are intended for use on **service station signs only** and are based on volume production. Costs of custom-built signs will be higher.

Rotators, cost per sign for rotating mount

Small signs	Less than 50 S.F.	$2,680 to $2,880
Medium signs	50 to 100 S.F.	2,830 to 5,740
Large signs	100 to 200 S.F.	5,660 to 10,410
Extra large signs	Over 200 S.F.	$59.49 per S.F. of sign area

Post Mounting Costs

Post Height	Pole Diameter at Base					
	4"	6"	8"	10"	12"	14"
15	$1,304	$1,550	$2,284	$3,079	$4,791	$4,791
20	1,546	1,844	2,640	3,193	5,700	6,409
25	1,673	2,085	2,735	3,799	6,351	7,003
30	1,930	2,481	2,837	4,157	6,705	7,755
35	—	2,708	3,193	4,524	7,599	8,278
40	—	2,864	3,900	4,892	7,883	9,285
45	—	—	4,566	5,572	8,604	9,610
50	—	—	4,892	6,351	9,158	10,533
55	—	—	—	6,705	9,610	11,470
60	—	—	—	7,089	10,307	11,993
65	—	—	—	—	11,045	12,744

Horizontal Mount   **Vertical Mount**   **Cantilevered Mount**

If signs are mounted on separate posts, post mounting costs must be added. Post mounting costs include the installed cost of a galvanized steel post and foundation. On horizontally mounted signs, post height is the distance from the ground to the bottom of the sign. On vertically mounted signs, post height is the distance to the top of the post.

For cantilevered posts, use one and one-half to two times the conventional post cost.

All of the above post costs are for single posts. Use 90% of the single post costs for each additional post.

If signs are mounted on buildings or canopies and if, because of the extra weight of the sign, extra heavy support posts or foundations are required, 125% of the post mounting cost should be used.

For example, the cost of a 4' x 25' plastic sign mounted on a 15' by 6" post shared by an adjacent canopy might be estimated as follows:

Sign Cost (100 x $100)	$10,000
Post Cost ($1,550 x 1/2)	775
Total Cost	**$10,755**

If this sign were mounted on an 8" post 20' above the canopy with extra supports not needed, thecost might be estimated as follows:

Sign Cost (100 x $100)	$10,000
Post Cost ($2,640 x 1)	2,640
Total Cost	**$12,640**

Quality Classification

	Class 1 Best Quality	Class 2 Good Quality	Class 3 Average Quality	Class 4 Low Quality
Foundation (25% of total cost)	Reinforced concrete or masonry.	Reinforced concrete or masonry.	Reinforced concrete or masonry.	Unreinforced concrete or masonry.
Floor Structure (15% of total cost)	6" rock fill, 4" concrete with reinforcing mesh.	6" rock fill, 4" concrete with reinforcing mesh.	4" rock fill, 4" concrete with reinforcing mesh.	Unreinforced 4" concrete.
Walls (15% of total cost)	8" reinforced concrete block, 12" common brick.	8" reinforced concrete block, 6" reinforced concrete.	8" reinforced concrete block, 6" reinforced concrete or 8" common brick.	8" unreinforced concrete block or 8" clay tile.
Roof Structure (12% of total cost)	Glu-lams or steel trusses on heavy pilasters 20' o.c. 2" x 10" purlins 16" o.c.	Glu-lams or steel trusses on pilasters 20' o.c., 2" x 10" purlins 16" o.c.	Glu-lams or wood trusses with 2" x 8" purlins 16" o.c.	Glu-lams or light wood trusses, 2" x 8" rafters 24" o.c.
Roof Cover (8% of total cost)	5 ply built-up roof on wood sheathing, with small rock.	4 ply built-up roof on wood sheathing, with small rock.	4 ply built-up roof on wood sheathing.	4 ply built-up roof on wood sheathing.
Restrooms (10% of total cost)	Two rest rooms with three average fixtures each.	Two rest rooms with two average fixtures each.	One rest room with two low cost fixtures.	One rest room with two low cost fixtures.
Lighting (10% of total cost)	One incandescent fixture per 300 square feet of floor area.	One incandescent fixture per 300 square feet of floor area.	One incandescent fixture per 300 square feet of floor area.	One incandescent fixture per 300 square feet of floor area.
Windows (5% of total cost)	3% to 5% of wall area.	3% to 5% of wall area.	3% to 5% of wall area.	3% to 5% of wall area.

Note: Use the percent of total cost to help identify the correct quality classification.

Square foot costs include the cost of the following components: Foundations as required for normal soil conditions. Floor, wall and roof structures. Exterior wall finish and roof cover. Entry doors. Basic lighting and electrical systems. Rough and finish plumbing. Permits and fees. Contractor's mark-up.

The in-place cost of these extra components should be added to the basic building cost to arrive at the total structure cost. See page 236 to 248. Heating and air conditioning systems. Fire sprinklers. Interior finish costs. Interior partitions. Drive-through doors. Canopies and walks. Exterior signs. Paving and curbing. Miscellaneous yard improvements. Hoists, gas pump and compressor costs are listed in the section "Additional Costs for Service Stations" beginning on page 204.

Service Garage – Masonry or Concrete

Length Less Than Twice Width

Estimating Procedure

1. Use these figures to estimate buildings designed primarily for motor vehicle repair. Sales area should be figured separately. Use the costs for urban stores beginning on page 75.
2. Establish the building quality class by applying the information on page 208.
3. Compute the floor area.
4. If the wall height is more or less than 18 feet, add to or subtract from the square foot costs below the appropriate amount from the Wall Height Adjustment Table on page 212.
5. Multiply the adjusted square foot cost by the floor area.
6. Deduct for common walls or no wall ownership. Use the figures on page 212.
7. Multiply the total cost by the location factor on page 7 or 8.
8. Add the cost of heating and air conditioning systems, fire sprinklers, interior finish and partitions, drive-thru doors, canopies and walks, exterior signs, paving, curbing, and yard improvements. See page 236 to 248. Add the cost of hoists, pumps and compressors beginning on page 204.

Service Garage (rear portion), Class 2

Square Foot Area

Quality Class	2,000	2,500	3,000	4,000	5,000	6,000	7,500	10,000	15,000	20,000	30,000
1, Best	61.14	55.53	51.54	46.23	42.69	40.22	37.51	34.57	31.26	29.31	27.14
1 & 2	58.69	53.33	49.45	44.36	40.98	38.56	36.02	33.23	30.01	28.17	26.03
2, Good	57.49	52.21	48.46	43.44	40.13	37.77	35.28	32.54	29.35	27.57	25.50
2 & 3	54.68	49.69	46.12	41.35	38.22	35.98	33.59	30.96	27.96	26.29	24.27
3, Average	53.12	48.24	44.77	40.12	37.07	34.91	32.59	30.03	27.13	25.49	23.56
3 & 4	50.25	45.61	42.33	37.95	35.08	33.04	30.84	28.41	25.64	24.06	22.27
4, Low	47.59	43.26	40.14	36.02	33.27	31.30	29.21	26.96	24.35	22.83	21.14

Service Garage – Masonry or Concrete

Length Between 2 and 4 Times Width

Estimating Procedure

1. Use these figures to estimate buildings designed primarily for motor vehicle repair. Sales area should be figured separately. Use the costs for urban stores beginning on page 75.
2. Establish the building quality class by applying the information on page 208.
3. Compute the floor area.
4. If the wall height is more or less than 18 feet, add to or subtract from the square foot costs below the appropriate amount from the Wall Height Adjustment Table on page 212.
5. Multiply the adjusted square foot cost by the floor area.
6. Deduct for common walls or no wall ownership. Use the figures on page 212.
7. Multiply the total cost by the location factor on page 7 or 8.
8. Add the cost of heating and air conditioning systems, fire sprinklers, interior finish and partitions, drive-thru doors, canopies and walks, exterior signs, paving, curbing, and yard improvements. See page 236 to 248. Add the cost of hoists, pumps and compressors beginning on page 204.

Service Garage, Class 3

Square Foot Area

Quality Class	2,000	2,500	3,000	4,000	5,000	6,000	7,500	10,000	15,000	20,000	30,000
1, Best	65.15	59.12	54.91	49.24	45.47	42.82	39.97	36.84	33.29	31.23	28.89
1 & 2	62.38	56.65	52.56	47.09	43.53	41.00	38.28	35.30	31.86	29.90	27.62
2, Good	61.06	55.46	51.51	46.14	42.61	40.15	37.46	34.52	31.19	29.27	27.06
2 & 3	58.09	52.76	48.97	43.88	40.58	38.18	35.59	32.79	29.63	27.83	25.71
3, Average	54.42	50.95	47.31	42.40	39.20	36.95	34.46	31.74	28.65	26.91	24.88
3 & 4	53.28	48.35	44.87	40.22	37.18	35.02	32.68	30.11	27.19	24.93	23.61
4, Low	50.46	45.85	42.51	38.15	35.30	33.19	30.97	28.55	25.79	24.17	22.35

Service Garage – Masonry or Concrete

Length More Than 4 Times Width

Estimating Procedure

1. Use these figures to estimate buildings designed primarily for motor vehicle repair. Sales area should be figured separately. Use the costs for urban stores beginning on page 75.
2. Establish the building quality class by applying the information on page 208.
3. Compute the floor area.
4. If the wall height is more or less than 18 feet, add to or subtract from the square foot costs below the appropriate amount from the Wall Height Adjustment Table on page 212.
5. Multiply the adjusted square foot cost by the floor area.
6. Deduct for common walls or no wall ownership. Use the figures on page 212.
7. Multiply the total cost by the location factor on page 7 or 8.
8. Add the cost of heating and air conditioning systems, fire sprinklers, interior finish and partitions, drive-thru doors, canopies and walks, exterior signs, paving curbing, and yard improvements. See page 236 to 248. Add the cost of hoists, pumps and compressors beginning on page 204.

Service Garage, Class 3 & 4

Square Foot Area

Quality Class	2,000	2,500	3,000	4,000	5,000	6,000	7,500	10,000	15,000	20,000	30,000
1, Best	69.40	62.95	58.48	52.41	48.40	45.59	42.52	39.22	35.42	33.29	30.75
1 & 2	66.79	60.61	56.24	50.41	46.60	43.87	40.94	37.69	34.07	32.00	29.60
2, Good	65.10	59.07	54.80	49.09	45.41	42.69	39.91	36.77	33.22	31.19	28.85
2 & 3	62.01	56.27	52.25	46.77	43.27	40.74	38.00	35.02	31.68	29.73	27.52
3, Average	60.11	54.54	50.62	45.38	41.86	39.46	36.85	33.96	30.66	28.83	26.64
3 & 4	56.77	51.50	47.79	42.82	39.55	37.26	34.78	32.09	28.97	27.19	25.16
4, Low	56.64	48.76	45.25	40.57	37.46	35.31	32.93	30.32	27.41	25.71	23.81

Service Garage – Masonry or Concrete

Wall Height Adjustment

Add or subtract the amount listed in this table to or from the square foot of floor cost for each foot of wall height more or less than 18 feet.

Area	2,000	2,500	3,000	4,000	5,000	6,000	7,500	10,000	15,000	20,000	30,000
Cost	.65	.61	.58	.48	.45	.43	.41	.21	.17	.14	.07

Perimeter (Common) Wall Adjustment

A common wall exists when two buildings share one wall. Adjust for common walls by deducting the linear foot costs below from the total structure cost. In some structures, one or more walls are not owned at all. In this case, deduct the "No Ownership" cost per linear foot of wall not owned.

For common wall, deduct $183 per linear foot.

For no wall ownership, deduct $366 per linear foot.

Service Garage – Wood Frame

Quality Classification

	Class 1 Best Quality	Class 2 Good Quality	Class 3 Average Quality	Class 4 Low Quality
Foundation (25% of total cost)	Concrete, heavily reinforced.	Reinforced concrete.	Masonry or reinforced concrete.	Masonry or concrete.
Floor Structure (12% of total cost)	4" reinforced concrete on 6" rock fill.	4" reinforced concrete on 6" rock fill.	4" concrete on 6" rock fill.	4" concrete on 4" rock fill.
Walls (12% of total cost)	2" x 4" studs 16" o.c. in walls 14' high; 2" x 6" studs 16" o.c. in walls over 14' high; 3" sill, double plate, adequate blocking and bracing.	2" x 4" studs 16" o.c. in walls 14' high; 2" x 6" studs 16" o.c. in walls over 14' high; 2" sill, double plate, adequate blocking and bracing.	2" x 4" studs 16" o.c. in walls to 14' high; 2" x 6" studs 16" o.c. in walls over 14' high; 2" sill, double plate, minimum blocking and bracing.	2" x 4" studs 24" o.c.; 2" x 4" sill, double 2" x 4" plate, minimum diagonal bracing.
Exterior (9% of total cost)	Good corrugated iron or board and batt.	Good corrugated iron or board and batt.	Average corrugated iron or board and batt.	Light corrugated iron or board and batt.
Roof Structures (12% of total cost)	Glu-lams, trusses or tapered steel girders on steel intermediate columns; 2" x 10" rafters 16" o.c.	Glu-lams, average wood trusses, tapered steel girders on steel intermediate columns; 2" x 8" purlins or rafters 16" o.c.	Glu-lams or light wood trusses, on wood posts 18' o.c.; 2" x 8" rafters on purlins 24" o.c.	Light trussed rafters, clear span in small buildings, post and beam support in large buildings.
Roof Cover (5% of total cost)	Good quality 4 ply composition roofing on wood sheathing.	Average quality 4 ply composition roofing on wood sheathing.	Average quality 3 ply composition roofing on wood sheathing, or good corrugated aluminum.	Light weight 3 ply composition roofing on wood sheathing, or heavy corrugated iron.
Rest Rooms (10% of total cost)	Two restrooms with three average fixtures each.	Two restrooms with three average fixtures each.	One restroom with two low cost fixtures.	One restroom with two low cost fixtures.
Lighting (10% of total cost)	One incandescent fixture per 300 square feet of floor area.	One incandescent fixture per 300 square feet of floor area.	One incandescent fixture per 300 square feet of floor area.	One incandescent fixture per 300 square feet of floor area.
Windows (5% of total cost)	3% to 5% of wall area.	3% to 5% of wall area.	3% to 5% of wall area.	3% to 5% of wall area.

Note: Use the percent of total cost to help identify the correct quality classification.

Square foot costs include the cost of the following components: Foundations as required for normal soil conditions. Floor, wall and roof structure. Exterior wall finish and roof cover. Entry doors. Basic lighting and electrical systems. Rough and finish plumbing. Permits and fees. Contractor's mark-up.

The in-place cost of these extra components should be added to the basic building cost to arrive at the total structure cost. See page 236 to 248. Heating and air conditioning systems. Fire sprinklers. Interior finish costs. Interior partitions. Drive-through doors. Canopies and walks. Exterior signs. Paving and curbing. Miscellaneous yard improvements. Hoists, gas pump and compressor costs are listed in the section "Additional Costs for Service Stations" beginning on page 204.

Service Garage – Wood Frame

Length Less Than Twice Width

Estimating Procedure

1. Use these figures to estimate buildings designed primarily for motor vehicle repair. Sales area should be figured separately. Use the costs for urban stores beginning on page 75.
2. Establish the building quality class by applying the information on page 213.
3. Compute the floor area.
4. If the wall height is more or less than 16 feet, add to or subtract from the square foot costs below the appropriate amount from the Wall Height Adjustment Table on page 217.
5. Multiply the adjusted square foot cost by the floor area.
6. Deduct for common walls or no wall ownership. Use the figures on page 217.
7. Multiply the total cost by the location factor on page 7 or 8.
8. Add the cost of heating and air conditioning systems, fire sprinklers, interior finish and partitions, drive-thru doors, canopies and walks, exterior signs, paving, curbing, and yard improvements. See page 236 to 248. Add the cost of hoists, pumps and compressors beginning on page 204.

Service Garage, Class 3

Square Foot Area

Quality Class	2,000	2,500	3,000	4,000	5,000	6,000	7,500	10,000	15,000	20,000	30,000
1, Best	42.53	38.60	35.84	32.13	29.68	27.92	26.09	24.06	21.79	20.46	18.88
1 & 2	40.35	36.62	34.00	30.46	28.13	26.51	24.78	22.81	20.63	19.38	17.90
2, Good	38.96	35.36	32.82	29.42	27.20	25.60	23.90	22.04	19.90	18.72	17.34
2 & 3	36.66	33.23	30.85	27.66	25.58	24.04	22.47	20.69	18.76	17.59	16.27
3, Average	34.82	31.60	29.37	26.29	24.28	22.87	21.34	19.70	17.78	16.71	15.51
3 & 4	32.68	29.67	27.58	24.71	22.85	21.44	20.06	18.47	16.70	15.70	14.56
4, Low	30.74	27.89	25.94	23.20	21.44	20.22	18.88	17.37	15.67	14.77	13.68

Service Garage – Wood Frame

Length Between 2 and 4 Times Width

Estimating Procedure

1. Use these figures to estimate buildings designed primarily for motor vehicle repair. Sales area should be figured separately. Use the costs for urban stores beginning on page 75.
2. Establish the building quality class by applying the information on page 213.
3. Compute the floor area.
4. If the wall height is more or less than 16 feet, add to or subtract from the square foot costs below the appropriate amount from the Wall Height Adjustment Table on page 217.
5. Multiply the adjusted square foot cost by the floor area.
6. Deduct for common walls or no wall ownership. Use the figures on page 217.
7. Multiply the total cost by the location factor on page 7 or 8.
8. Add the cost of heating and air conditioning systems, fire sprinklers, interior finish and partitions, drive-thru doors, canopies and walks, exterior signs, paving, curbing, and yard improvements. See page 236 to 248. Add the cost of hoists, pumps and compressors beginning on page 204.

Service Garage (rear portion) Class 2 & 3

Square Foot Area

Quality Class	2,000	2,500	3,000	4,000	5,000	6,000	7,500	10,000	15,000	20,000	30,000
1, Best	45.23	41.07	38.13	34.18	31.60	29.76	27.78	25.60	23.12	21.70	20.11
1 & 2	42.96	39.02	36.18	32.46	30.00	28.26	26.40	24.29	21.99	20.63	19.07
2, Good	41.43	37.66	34.98	31.29	28.92	27.27	25.46	23.43	21.21	19.90	18.41
2 & 3	38.99	35.40	32.88	29.47	27.26	25.68	23.94	22.09	19.96	18.77	17.37
3, Average	37.21	33.84	31.37	28.13	26.02	24.50	22.86	21.08	19.03	17.89	16.55
3 & 4	34.70	31.49	29.27	26.25	24.25	22.85	21.30	19.62	17.72	16.66	15.40
4, Low	32.21	29.26	27.14	24.30	22.48	21.21	19.73	18.20	16.48	15.43	14.33

Service Garage – Wood Frame

Length More Than 4 Times Width

Estimating Procedure

1. Use these figures to estimate buildings designed primarily for motor vehicle repair. Sales area should be figured separately. Use the costs for urban stores beginning on page 75.
2. Establish the building quality class by applying the information on page 213.
3. Compute the floor area.
4. If the wall height is more or less than 16 feet, add to or subtract from the square foot costs below the appropriate amount from the Wall Height Adjustment Table on page 217.
5. Multiply the adjusted square foot cost by the floor area.
6. Deduct for common walls or no wall ownership. Use the figures on page 217.
7. Multiply the total cost by the location factor on page 7 or 8.
8. Add the cost of heating and air conditioning systems, fire sprinklers, interior finish and partitions, drive-thru doors, canopies and walks, exterior signs, paving, curbing, and yard improvements. See page 236 to 248. Add the cost of hoists, pumps and compressors beginning on page 204.

Service Garage, Class 3

Square Foot Area

Quality Class	2,000	2,500	3,000	4,000	5,000	6,000	7,500	10,000	15,000	20,000	30,000
1, Best	48.27	43.84	40.66	36.45	33.71	31.74	29.60	27.29	24.67	23.12	21.38
1 & 2	45.83	41.62	38.63	34.64	32.02	30.13	28.12	25.94	23.43	22.03	20.33
2, Good	44.31	40.19	37.33	33.44	30.92	29.13	27.20	25.06	22.63	21.25	19.62
2 & 3	41.67	37.86	35.17	31.53	29.14	27.41	25.59	23.61	21.32	20.03	18.47
3, Average	39.63	36.06	33.42	30.00	27.74	26.10	24.30	22.45	20.30	19.03	17.60
3 & 4	37.00	33.59	31.20	27.92	25.88	24.30	22.70	20.89	18.94	17.76	16.43
4, Low	34.54	31.36	29.11	26.11	24.12	22.68	21.16	19.57	17.66	16.57	15.31

Service Garage – Wood Frame

Wall Height Adjustment

Add or subtract the amount listed in this table to or from the square foot cost for each foot of wall height more or less than 16 feet.

Area	2,000	2,500	3,000	4,000	5,000	6,000	7,500	10,000	15,000	20,000	30,000
Cost	.56	.48	.44	.35	.30	.21	.17	.14	.11	.09	.07

Perimeter (Common) Wall Adjustment

A common wall exists when two buildings share one wall. Adjust for common walls by deducting the linear foot costs below from the total structure cost. In some structures one or more walls are not owned at all. In this case, deduct the "No Ownership" cost per linear foot of wall not owned.

For common wall, deduct $67 per linear foot.

For no wall ownership, deduct $135 per linear foot.

Auto Service Centers – Masonry or Concrete

Quality Classification

	Class 1 Best Quality	Class 2 Good Quality	Class 3 Average Quality	Class 4 Low Quality
Foundation (20% of total cost)	Reinforced concrete.	Reinforced concrete.	Reinforced concrete.	Reinforced concrete.
Floor Structure (10% of total cost)	4" reinforced concrete on 6" rock fill.	4" reinforced concrete on 6" rock fill.	4" reinforced concrete on 6" rock fill.	4" reinforced concrete on 6" rock fill.
Walls (15% of total cost)	8" reinforced decorative colored concrete block.	8" reinforced detailed concrete block.	8" reinforced concrete block.	8" reinforced concrete block.
Roof Structures (5% of total cost)	Steel open web joists, steel deck.	Glu-lams, 3" x 12" purlins 3' o.c., or wood open web joists (truss joists) 4' o.c.	Glu-lams, 3" x 12" purlins 3' o.c., or wood open web joists (truss joists) 4' o.c., 1/2" plywood sheathing.	Glu-lams, 3" x 12" purlins 3' o.c., or wood open web joists (truss joists) 4' o.c., 1/2" plywood sheathing.
Floor Finish (5% of total cost)	Concrete in work area, resilient tile in sales area.	Concrete in work area, resilient tile in sales area.	Concrete in work area, minimum grade tile in sales area.	Concrete.
Interior Wall Finish (5% of total cost)	Painted concrete block in work area; gypsum wallboard, texture and paint in sales area.	Painted concrete block in work area and sales area.	Unfinished in work area, painted concrete block in sales area	Unfinished.
Ceiling Finish (3% of total cost)	Open in work area, acoustical tile suspended in exposed grid in sales area.	Open in work area, acoustical tile suspended in exposed grid in sales area.	Open in work area. Celotex tile in sales area.	Open.
Exterior Finish (5% of total cost)	Decorative colored concrete block.	Colored or painted detailed block.	Painted concrete block.	Unpainted concrete block.
Display Front *(Covers about 25% of the exterior wall)* (7% of total cost)	1/4" float glass in good aluminum frame. Good aluminum and glass doors.	1/4" float glass in average aluminum frame. Aluminum and glass doors.	1/4" float glass in light aluminum frame. Wood and glass door.	Crystal glass in wood frame, wood door.
Roof and Cover (7% of total cost)	5 ply built-up roofing with insulation.	4 ply built-up roofing.	4 ply built-up roofing.	4 ply built-up roofing.
Plumbing (10% of total cost)	Two rest rooms with three good fixtures. Metal toilet partitions.	Two rest rooms with two average fixtures. Wood toilet partitions.	One rest room with two fixtures.	One rest room with two fixtures.
Electrical & Wiring (8% of total cost)	Conduit wiring with triple tube fluorescent strips, 8' o.c.	Conduit wiring with triple tube fluorescent strips, 8' o.c.	Conduit wiring, double tube fluorescent strips, 8' o.c.	Conduit wiring, incandescent fixtures, 10' o.c. or single tube fluorescent strips, 8' o.c.

Note: Use the percentage of total cost to help identify the correct quality classification.

Square foot costs include the cost of the following components: Foundations as required for normal soil conditions. Floor, wall and roof structures. Interior floor, wall and ceiling finishes (in sales area). Exterior wall finish and roof cover. Display windows. Interior partitions. Entry doors. Basic lighting and electrical systems. Rough and finish plumbing. Permits and fees. Contractor's mark-up.

Wall Height Adjustment: Add or subtract the amount listed in this table to or from the square foot of floor cost for each foot of wall height more or less than 16 feet.

Area	1,500	2,000	2,500	3,000	3,500	4,000	5,000	6,000	7,500	10,000	15,000
Cost	2.00	1.73	1.49	1.34	1.25	1.18	1.08	1.02	.82	.75	.67

Perimeter Wall Adjustment: For common wall, deduct $143 per linear foot. For no wall ownership, deduct $286 per linear foot.

Auto Service Centers – Masonry or Concrete

Length Less Than Twice Width

Estimating Procedure

1. Use these figures to estimate buildings designed for selling and installing automobile accessories. The square foot costs below allow for a sales area occupying 25% of the building space. The sales area has finished floors, walls and ceiling as described in the quality classification. The remaining 75% of the building is service area and has no interior finish.
2. Establish the building quality class by applying the information on page 218.
3. Compute the floor area. This should include everything within the exterior walls.
4. If the wall height is more or less than 16 feet, add to or subtract from the square foot costs below the appropriate amount from the Wall Height Adjustment Table on page 218.
5. Deduct for common walls or no wall ownership. See page 218.
6. Multiply the total cost by the location factor on page 7 or 8.
7. Add the cost of heating and air conditioning systems, fire sprinklers, canopies, walks, exterior signs, paving, curbing, loading docks, ramps, and yard improvements. See page 236 to 248. Add the cost of service station equipment beginning on 204.

Auto Service Center, Class 2

Square Foot Area

Quality Class	1,500	2,000	2,500	3,000	3,500	4,000	5,000	6,000	7,500	10,000	15,000
Exceptional	119.67	109.49	102.81	98.00	94.30	91.46	87.08	83.90	80.49	76.70	72.29
1, Best	114.52	104.78	98.36	93.76	90.27	87.49	83.30	80.30	77.01	73.38	69.17
1 & 2	109.49	100.14	94.03	89.63	86.29	83.62	79.62	76.72	73.61	70.12	66.12
2, Good	106.25	97.18	91.24	87.00	83.74	81.15	77.28	74.49	71.46	68.08	64.12
2 & 3	101.30	92.66	87.01	82.93	79.85	77.37	73.70	70.99	68.12	64.91	61.20
3, Average	98.40	90.02	84.50	80.55	77.52	75.15	71.57	68.94	66.19	63.04	59.44
3 & 4	93.59	85.65	80.41	76.65	73.78	71.52	68.12	65.64	62.93	59.99	56.54
4, Low	89.69	82.07	77.04	73.48	70.70	68.53	65.29	62.91	60.36	57.49	54.17

Length Between 2 and 4 Times Width

Estimating Procedure

1. Use these figures to estimate buildings designed for selling and installing automobile accessories. The square foot costs below allow for a sales area occupying 25% of the building space. The sales area has finished floors, walls and ceiling as described in the quality classification. The remaining 75% of the building is service area and has no interior finish.
2. Establish the building quality class by applying the information on page 218.
3. Compute the floor area. This should include everything within the exterior walls.
4. If the wall height is more or less than 16 feet, add to or subtract from the square foot costs below the appropriate amount from the Wall Height Adjustment Table on page 218.
5. Deduct for common walls or no wall ownership. See page 218.
6. Multiply the total cost by the location factor on page 7 or 8.
7. Add the cost of heating and air conditioning systems, fire sprinklers, canopies, walks, exterior signs, paving, curbing, loading docks, ramps, and yard improvements. See page 236 to 248. Add the cost of service station equipment beginning on 204.

Auto Service Center, Class 2

Square Foot Area

Quality Class	1,500	2,000	2,500	3,000	3,500	4,000	5,000	6,000	7,500	10,000	15,000
Exceptional	127.19	115.77	108.28	102.93	98.82	95.58	90.75	87.29	83.50	79.31	74.46
1, Best	121.73	110.78	103.66	98.48	94.60	91.50	86.86	83.52	79.89	75.85	71.31
1 & 2	116.23	105.77	98.90	94.03	90.29	87.34	82.93	79.73	76.29	72.46	68.01
2, Good	112.64	102.49	95.86	91.11	87.51	84.66	80.38	77.32	73.96	70.25	65.95
2 & 3	107.58	97.88	91.58	87.05	83.58	80.91	76.78	73.82	70.64	67.08	62.99
3, Average	104.17	94.80	88.65	84.27	80.93	78.26	74.31	71.48	68.36	64.96	60.98
3 & 4	99.46	90.56	84.71	80.47	77.32	74.77	70.98	68.27	65.31	62.03	58.23
4, Low	94.86	86.34	80.75	76.78	73.74	71.32	67.72	65.07	62.30	59.12	55.53

Auto Service Centers – Masonry or Concrete

Length More Than 4 Times Width

Estimating Procedure

1. Use these figures to estimate buildings designed for selling and installing automobile accessories. The square foot costs below allow for a sales area occupying 25% of the building space. The sales area has finished floors, walls and ceiling as described in the quality classification. The remaining 75% of the building is service area and has no interior finish.
2. Establish the building quality class by applying the information on page 218.
3. Compute the floor area. This should include everything within the exterior walls.
4. If the wall height is more or less than 16 feet, add to or subtract from the square foot costs below the appropriate amount from the Wall Height Adjustment Table on page 218.
5. Deduct for common walls or no wall ownership. See page 218.
6. Multiply the total cost by the location factor on page 7 or 8.
7. Add the cost of heating and air conditioning systems, fire sprinklers, canopies, walks, exterior signs, paving, curbing, loading docks, ramps, and yard improvements. See page 236 to 248. Add the cost of service station equipment beginning on 204.

Auto Service Center, Class 3

Square Foot Area

Quality Class	1,500	2,000	2,500	3,000	3,500	4,000	5,000	6,000	7,500	10,000	15,000
Exceptional	137.16	124.70	116.41	110.43	105.82	102.16	96.56	92.53	88.06	83.12	77.30
1, Best	131.18	119.29	111.36	105.63	101.20	97.67	92.38	88.49	84.23	79.51	73.94
1 & 2	125.14	113.83	106.33	100.78	96.57	93.20	88.14	84.46	80.38	75.84	70.52
2, Good	121.46	110.50	103.16	97.82	93.75	90.49	85.53	81.97	78.03	73.61	68.47
2 & 3	115.85	105.36	98.38	93.25	89.41	86.28	81.56	78.10	74.41	70.23	65.31
3, Average	112.48	102.25	95.50	90.56	86.75	83.75	79.21	75.87	72.23	68.13	63.37
3 & 4	107.29	97.59	91.11	86.45	82.76	79.88	75.56	72.37	68.90	65.00	60.49
4, Low	102.31	93.03	86.85	82.41	78.95	76.19	72.04	68.98	65.71	62.00	57.67

Industrial Structures Section

Section Contents

Warehouse, Class 3

Light Industrial, Class 2

Quality Classification

	Class 1 Best Quality	Class 2 Good Quality	Class 3 Average Quality	Class 4 Low Quality
Foundations (22% of total cost)	Continuous reinforced concrete.	Continuous reinforced concrete.	Continuous reinforced concrete.	Reinforced concrete pads under pilasters.
Floor Structure (15% of total cost)	6" rock base, 6" concrete with reinforcing mesh or bars.	6" rock base, 6" concrete with reinforcing mesh or bars.	6" rock base, 5" concrete with reinforcing mesh or bars.	6" rock base, 4" concrete with reinforcing mesh.
Wall Structure (25% of total cost)	8" reinforced concrete block or brick with pilasters 20' o.c., painted sides and rear exterior, front wall brick veneer.	8" reinforced concrete block or brick with pilasters 20' o.c., painted sides and rear exterior, stucco and some brick veneer on front.	8" reinforced concrete block or brick, unpainted.	8" reinforced concrete block or brick, unpainted.
Roof Structure (12% of total cost)	Glu-lams, wood or steel trusses on steel intermediate columns, span exceeds 70'.	Glu-lams, wood or steel trusses on steel intermediate columns, span exceeds 70'.	Glu-lams or steel beams on steel intermediate columns, short span.	Glu-lams on steel intermediate columns, short span.
Roof Cover (7% of total cost)	Panelized roof system, 1/2" plywood sheathing, 5 ply built-up roof.	Panelized roof system, 1/2" plywood sheathing, 4 ply built-up roof.	Panelized roof system, 1/2" plywood sheathing, 4 ply built-up roof.	Panelized roof system, 1/2" plywood sheathing, 4 ply built-up roof.
Skylights (1% of total cost)	48 S.F. of skylight per 2500 S.F. of floor area (1-6' x 8' skylight 40' to 50' o.c.).	32 S.F. of skylight per 2500 S.F. of floor area (1-4' x 8' skylight 40' to 50' o.c.).	24 S.F. of skylight per 2500 S.F. of floor area (1-4' x 6' skylight 40' to 50' o.c.).	10 S.F. of skylight per 2500 S.F. of floor area (1-2' x 4' skylight 40' to 50' o.c.).
Ventilators (2% of total cost)	1 large rotary vent per 2500 S.F. of floor area.	1 medium rotary vent per 2500 S.F. of floor area.	1 medium rotary vent per 2500 S.F. of floor area.	1 small rotary vent per 2500 S.F. of floor area.
Rest Rooms, Finish (3% of total cost)	Good vinyl asbestos tile floors enameled gypsum wallboard partitions.	Vinyl asbestos tile floors, enameled gypsum wallboard partitions.	Concrete floors, painted gypsum wallboard partitions.	Concrete floors, unfinished wallboard partitions.
Fixtures (5% of total cost)	2 rest rooms, 3 good fixtures in each.	2 rest rooms, 3 average fixtures in each.	2 rest rooms, 2 average fixtures in each.	1 rest room, 2 low cost fixtures in each.
Lighting (8% of total cost)	4' single tube fluorescent fixtures 10' x 12' spacing.	Low cost single tube fluorescent fixtures 12' x 20' spacing.	Low cost 4' single tube fluorescent fixtures 20' x 20' spacing.	Low cost incandescent fixtures 20' x 30' spacing.

Note: Use the percent of total cost to help identify the correct quality classification.

Square foot costs include the following components: Foundations as required for normal soil conditions. Floor, wall and roof structures. Exterior wall finish and roof cover. Basic lighting and electrical systems. Rough and finish plumbing. A usual or normal parapet wall. Walk-through doors. Contractors' mark-up.

Warehouses

Estimating Procedure

1. Establish the structure quality class by applying the information on page 223.
2. Compute the building floor area.
3. Add to or subtract from the square foot cost below the appropriate amount from the Wall Height Adjustment Table (at the bottom of page 226) if the wall height is more or less than 20 feet.
4. Multiply the adjusted square foot cost by the building floor area.
5. Deduct, if appropriate, for common walls, using the figures at the bottom of page 226.
6. Multiply the total cost by the location factor on page 7 or 8.
7. Add the cost of heating and air conditioning equipment, fire sprinklers, interior offices, drive-through or delivery doors, canopies, interior partitions, docks and ramps, paving and curbing, and miscellaneous yard improvements. See the section beginning on page 236.

Length less than twice width - Square Foot Area

Quality Class	3,000	4,000	5,000	7,500	10,000	15,000	20,000	30,000	50,000	100,000	200,000
1, Best	105.88	96.89	90.87	81.65	76.26	69.93	66.24	61.84	57.56	53.25	50.25
1 & 2	98.57	90.22	84.62	76.05	71.01	65.17	61.70	57.64	53.57	49.58	46.80
2, Good	93.15	85.21	79.94	71.83	67.08	61.52	58.25	54.42	50.59	46.81	44.19
2 & 3	87.11	79.65	74.74	67.21	62.72	57.57	54.50	50.88	47.35	43.76	41.31
3, Average	81.97	75.00	70.30	63.23	59.04	54.17	51.30	47.88	44.52	41.25	38.89
3 & 4	76.67	70.20	65.77	59.17	55.23	50.68	47.95	44.82	41.65	38.54	36.33
4, Low	71.44	65.36	61.32	55.09	51.47	47.20	44.70	41.72	38.85	35.91	33.92

Length between 2 and 4 times width - Square Foot Area

Quality Class	3,000	4,000	5,000	7,500	10,000	15,000	20,000	30,000	50,000	100,000	200,000
1, Best	112.94	102.82	96.09	85.83	79.89	72.88	68.78	63.96	59.27	54.59	51.33
1 & 2	105.46	96.05	89.74	80.15	74.52	68.04	64.22	59.74	55.35	50.95	47.90
2, Good	99.56	90.67	84.70	75.69	70.39	64.26	60.61	56.43	52.28	48.12	45.20
2 & 3	93.15	84.83	79.26	70.74	65.81	60.12	56.71	52.79	48.84	45.00	42.30
3, Average	87.64	79.81	74.52	66.62	61.93	56.53	53.39	49.66	45.99	42.37	39.77
3 & 4	82.00	74.65	69.77	62.34	57.99	52.90	49.93	46.45	43.03	39.61	37.26
4, Low	76.19	69.37	64.84	57.91	53.87	49.23	46.42	43.17	39.95	36.78	34.61

Length more than 4 times width - Square Foot Area

Quality Class	3,000	4,000	5,000	7,500	10,000	15,000	20,000	30,000	50,000	100,000	200,000
1, Best	122.35	111.18	103.66	92.09	85.27	77.28	72.52	67.02	61.50	56.00	52.11
1 & 2	117.37	103.84	96.77	85.98	79.58	72.17	67.74	62.61	57.44	52.32	48.64
2, Good	111.01	98.08	91.43	81.21	75.23	68.20	63.97	59.12	54.27	49.42	46.00
2 & 3	101.02	91.77	85.53	75.99	70.38	63.78	59.87	55.30	50.79	46.23	43.02
3, Average	95.04	86.38	80.51	71.51	66.21	60.01	56.39	52.03	47.79	43.46	40.47
3 & 4	88.81	80.68	75.23	66.80	61.90	56.09	52.63	48.61	44.62	40.61	37.85
4, Low	82.69	75.14	70.06	62.25	57.61	52.25	49.04	45.30	41.56	37.85	35.24

Light Industrial Buildings

Estimating Procedure

1. Establish the structure quality class by applying the information on page 223.
2. Compute the building floor area.
3. Add to or subtract from the square foot cost below the appropriate amount from the Wall Height Adjustment Table (at the bottom of page 226) if the wall height is more or less than 20 feet.
4. Multiply the adjusted square foot cost by the building floor area.
5. Deduct, if appropriate, for common walls, using the figures at the bottom of page 226.
6. Multiply the total cost by the location factor on page 7 or 8.
7. Add the cost of heating and air conditioning equipment, fire sprinklers, interior offices, drive-through or delivery doors, canopies, interior partitions, docks and ramps, paving and curbing, and miscellaneous yard improvements. See the section beginning on page 236.

Length less than twice width - Square Foot Area

Quality Class	3,000	4,000	5,000	7,500	10,000	15,000	20,000	30,000	50,000	100,000	200,000
1, Best	104.87	96.83	91.42	83.10	78.22	72.51	69.15	65.19	61.26	57.38	54.60
1 & 2	97.85	90.32	85.24	77.53	72.97	67.66	64.52	60.82	57.14	53.49	50.90
2, Good	91.52	84.52	79.77	72.52	68.31	63.32	60.38	56.90	53.49	50.06	47.66
2 & 3	86.50	79.89	75.39	68.59	64.57	59.81	57.03	53.80	50.54	47.31	45.03
3, Average	80.55	74.42	70.24	63.83	60.15	55.70	53.13	50.11	47.08	44.10	41.96
3 & 4	75.48	69.69	65.80	59.80	56.32	52.23	49.78	46.93	44.14	41.28	39.32
4, Low	70.26	64.86	61.22	55.68	52.42	48.59	46.34	43.70	41.04	38.42	36.59

Length between 2 and 4 times width - Square Foot Area

Quality Class	3,000	4,000	5,000	7,500	10,000	15,000	20,000	30,000	50,000	100,000	200,000
1, Best	111.53	102.40	96.32	87.07	81.60	75.28	71.53	67.18	62.88	58.61	55.59
1 & 2	104.30	95.80	90.08	81.41	76.35	70.40	66.90	62.84	58.83	54.80	51.97
2, Good	97.91	89.91	84.56	76.43	71.67	66.10	62.83	58.97	55.24	51.47	48.82
2 & 3	91.49	84.02	79.00	71.38	66.92	61.74	58.69	55.09	51.51	48.05	45.61
3, Average	85.74	78.72	74.06	66.92	62.73	57.90	55.03	51.70	48.36	45.04	42.72
3 & 4	80.33	73.80	69.37	62.68	58.76	54.21	51.50	48.39	45.34	42.20	40.05
4, Low	74.71	68.63	64.52	58.33	54.66	50.44	47.93	45.04	42.14	39.28	37.26

Length more than 4 times width - Square Foot Area

Quality Class	3,000	4,000	5,000	7,500	10,000	15,000	20,000	30,000	50,000	100,000	200,000
1, Best	120.15	109.87	103.01	92.52	86.38	79.11	74.85	69.84	64.88	59.94	56.45
1 & 2	112.49	102.96	96.48	86.63	80.89	74.13	70.12	65.42	60.79	56.15	52.87
2, Good	105.37	96.38	90.37	81.18	75.75	69.38	65.66	61.26	56.90	52.55	49.50
2 & 3	98.70	90.31	84.64	76.03	70.92	65.03	61.49	57.40	53.34	49.25	46.41
3, Average	92.58	84.74	79.42	71.32	66.58	60.98	57.68	53.85	50.01	46.18	43.53
3 & 4	86.47	79.10	74.15	66.62	62.14	56.95	53.88	50.31	46.69	43.13	40.61
4, Low	80.50	73.65	69.08	62.02	57.84	52.99	50.20	46.84	43.47	40.19	37.83

Factory Buildings

Estimating Procedure

1. Establish the structure quality class by applying the information on page 223.
2. Compute the building floor area.
3. Add to or subtract from the square foot cost below the appropriate amount from the Wall Height Adjustment Table (at the bottom of this page) if the wall height is more or less than 20 feet.
4. Multiply the adjusted square foot cost by the building floor area.
5. Deduct, if appropriate, for common walls, using the figures at the bottom of this page.
6. Multiply the total cost by the location factor on page 7 or 8.
7. Add the cost of heating and air conditioning equipment, fire sprinklers, interior offices, drive-through or delivery doors, canopies, interior partitions, docks and ramps, paving and curbing, and miscellaneous yard improvements. See the section beginning on page 236.

Length less than twice width - Square Foot Area

Quality Class	3,000	4,000	5,000	7,500	10,000	15,000	20,000	30,000	50,000	100,000	200,000
1, Best	103.84	96.46	91.49	83.91	79.50	74.31	71.25	67.62	64.08	60.53	58.05
1 & 2	97.49	90.58	85.89	78.79	74.64	69.76	66.85	63.50	60.17	56.84	54.54
2, Good	91.86	85.35	80.93	74.27	70.28	65.71	63.02	59.85	56.68	53.56	51.37
2 & 3	86.03	79.93	75.85	69.54	65.83	61.55	58.99	56.03	53.10	50.18	48.16
3, Average	80.90	75.10	71.25	65.33	61.89	57.82	55.49	52.63	49.89	47.15	45.26
3 & 4	75.53	70.18	66.60	61.03	57.78	54.02	51.80	49.24	46.59	44.05	42.22
4, Low	70.22	65.21	61.83	56.71	53.67	50.25	48.17	45.70	43.32	40.94	39.27

Length between 2 and 4 times width - Square Foot Area

Quality Class	3,000	4,000	5,000	7,500	10,000	15,000	20,000	30,000	50,000	100,000	200,000
1, Best	109.68	101.43	95.88	87.52	82.56	76.81	73.40	69.47	65.59	61.67	58.90
1 & 2	102.88	95.13	90.01	82.05	77.48	72.04	68.89	65.18	61.52	57.82	55.29
2, Good	97.18	89.84	84.94	77.52	73.14	68.04	65.07	61.54	58.05	54.62	52.23
2 & 3	90.96	84.11	79.54	72.54	68.46	63.72	60.90	57.61	54.36	51.15	48.86
3, Average	85.45	79.01	74.69	68.15	64.30	59.79	57.20	54.11	51.05	48.02	45.92
3 & 4	79.86	73.84	69.81	63.72	60.12	55.93	53.47	50.55	47.70	44.88	42.88
4, Low	74.14	68.60	64.82	59.12	55.79	51.92	49.65	46.98	44.34	41.63	39.84

Length more than 4 times width - Square Foot Area

Quality Class	3,000	4,000	5,000	7,500	10,000	15,000	20,000	30,000	50,000	100,000	200,000
1, Best	117.42	108.23	102.02	92.52	86.92	80.38	76.50	71.92	67.39	62.83	59.69
1 & 2	110.34	101.74	95.85	86.93	81.66	75.53	71.85	67.58	63.32	59.06	56.08
2, Good	104.04	95.91	90.38	81.99	77.03	71.19	67.75	63.72	59.71	55.69	52.85
2 & 3	97.49	89.85	84.68	76.79	72.17	66.70	63.50	59.71	55.95	52.23	49.54
3, Average	91.56	84.48	79.61	72.23	67.85	62.72	59.66	56.09	52.55	49.01	46.51
3 & 4	85.56	78.85	74.34	67.37	63.30	58.53	55.70	52.40	49.09	45.81	43.48
4, Low	79.41	73.19	68.95	62.58	58.76	54.34	51.74	48.61	45.53	42.51	40.35

Wall Height Adjustment: Industrial building costs are based on a 20' wall height, measured from the bottom of the floor slab to the top of the roof cover. Add or subtract the amount listed to the square foot cost for each foot more or less than 20 feet.

Area	3,000	4,000	5,000	7,500	10,000	15,000	20,000	30,000	50,000	100,000	200,000
Cost	.81	.70	.64	.58	.49	.44	.40	.32	.14	.06	.03

Perimeter Wall Adjustment: A common wall exists when two buildings share one wall. Adjust for common walls by deducting $105 per linear foot from the total structure cost. In some structures one or more walls are not owned at all. In this case, deduct $210 per liner foot of wall not owned.

Internal Offices

Internal offices are office areas built into the interior area of an industrial building. Add the square foot costs in this section to the basic building cost. The costs include floor finish, partition framing, wall finish, trim and doors, counter, ceiling structure, ceiling finish, and the difference between the cost of lighting and windows in an industrial building and the cost of lighting and windows in an office building.

Plumbing costs are not included in these internal office costs. if a building has fixtures in excess of those listed in the quality classification for the main building, add $1,380 to $1,700 for each extra fixture. For two-story internal offices, apply a square foot cost based on the total area of both floor levels.

	Best	Good	Average	Low Cost
Floor Finish (15% of total cost)	Carpet, some vinyl tile or terrazzo.	Resilient tile, some carpet.	Composition tile.	Colored concrete.
Wall Finish (25% of total cost)	Hardwood veneer, some textured cloth wall cover.	Gypsum board, texture and paint, some hardwood veneer.	Gypsum board, texture and paint.	Plywood and paint.
Ceiling Finish (15% of total cost)	Illuminated plastic ceilings.	Suspended "T" bar and acoustical tile.	Gypsum board, texture and paint.	Exposed or plywood and paint.
Doors - Interior (10% of total cost)	Good grade hardwood.	Good grade hardwood.	Low cost hardwood.	Standard paint grade.
Doors - Exterior (5% of total cost)	Pair aluminum entry doors with extensive sidelights.	Aluminum entry door with sidelights.	Wood store door.	Standard paint grade.
Windows (5% of total cost)	Average amount in good aluminum frame, fixed float glass in good frame in front.	Average amount in good aluminum frame, some fixed float glass.	Average amount of average cost aluminum sliding type.	Average amount of low cost aluminum sliding type.
Counters (15% of total cost)	Good grade hardwood counter, good shelving below.	Good grade plastic counter, average amount of shelving below.	Low cost plastic counter, average amount of shelving.	Paint grade counter, small amount of shelving.
Lighting (10% of total cost)	Illuminated ceilings.	Recessed fluorescent fixtures.	Average amount of fluorescent fixtures.	One incandescent per each 150 S.F.
S.F. Costs	$57.72 to $81.19	$45.49 to $58.85	$36.82 to $47.94	$17.95 to $26.42

Note: Use the percent of total cost to help identify the correct quality classification.

The range of costs is primarily due to the density of partitions in the office area. Use the lower costs for offices with larger rooms and fewer partitions.

	Best	Good	Average	Low Cost
Wall Height Adjustment*	$.78 to $1.08	$.70 to $1.01	$.65 to $.95	$.61 to $.92

***Wall Height Adjustment:** Add or subtract the amount listed in this column to or from the square foot cost for each foot when the office wall height is more or less than 8 feet.

External Offices

External offices outside the main building walls have one side that is common to the main building. Square foot costs for external office areas should be estimated with the figures for general office buildings with interior suite entrances. See pages 139 to 142 or 147 to 150.

In selecting a square foot cost for the external office area as well as the main building area, the area of each portion should be used separately for area classification. The area and the perimeter formed by these individual areas is used for shape classification of the main area and for calculating the area and perimeter relationship of the office area. A "no wall ownership" deduction based on the office wall cost should be made for the length of the common side. Wall height adjustments should be made for each area individually.

Steel Buildings

Engineered steel buildings are constructed to serve as warehouses, factories, airplane hangars, garages, and stores, among other uses. They are generally either high-profile (4 in 12 rise roof) or low-profile (1 in 12 rise roof).

The square foot costs for the basic building include: Foundations as required for normal soil conditions. A 4 inch concrete floor with reinforcing mesh and a 2 inch sand fill. A steel building made up of steel frames or bents set 20 or 24 feet on centers, steel roof purlins 4-1/2 to 5-1/2 feet on centers, steel wall girts 3-1/2 to 4-1/2 feet on centers, post and beam type end wall frames, 26-gauge galvanized steel on ends, sides, and roof, window area equal to 2% of the floor area. Basic wiring and minimum lighting fixtures. One small or medium gravity vent per 2,500 square feet of floor area.

Steel Buildings

Estimating Procedure

1. Compute the building area.

2. Add to or subtract from the square foot cost below $.33 for each foot of wall height at the eave more or less than 14 feet. Subtract $.53 from the square foot cost below for low profile buildings.

3. Multiply the adjusted square foot cost by the building area.

4. Multiply the total by the appropriate live load adjustment. The basic building costs are for a 12 pound live load usually built where snow load is not a design factor. A 20 pound live load building is usually found in light snow areas, and a 30 pound live load building is usually found in heavy snow areas.

5. Add or subtract alternate costs from pages 230 to 232. Alternate costs reflect the difference between unit costs of components that are included in the basic building square foot costs and the unit costs of alternate components. Total alternate cost is found by multiplying the alternate cost by the area or number of alternate components.

6. Add the appropriate costs from pages 233 to 234, "Alternate Costs for Steel Buildings." These costs reflect the in-place cost of components that are not included in the basic square foot cost but are often found as part of steel buildings. The cost of items that alter or replace a portion of the building reflect the net added cost of the component in-place. The cost of the item that is replaced has been deducted from the total cost of the additive components. No further deduction is necessary.

7. Add the cost of heating and air conditioning systems, fire sprinklers, plumbing, additional electrical work, alternate interior partitions and offices, dock height additive costs, loading docks or ramps, paving and curbing, and miscellaneous yard improvements. See the section beginning on page 236.

High Profile Rigid Steel Buildings
Square Foot Cost

	Length			
Width	60'	80'	120'	Over 140'
20'	$34.39	$32.34	$32.34	$30.31
30'	32.25	30.65	28.29	26.13
40'	29.91	27.64	25.58	24.73
50' to 70'	26.05	23.42	21.83	21.65
80' to 140'	—	22.11	21.09	19.97

Deduct $.53 per square foot for low profile buildings.

Live Load Adjustment Factors (multiply base cost by factor shown)

	High Profile				Low Profile			
Building Width	20 lb. Live Load		30 lb. Live Load		20 lb. Live Load		30 lb. Live Load	
	20' Bays	24' Bays	20' Bays	24' Bays	20' Bays	24' Bays	20' Bays	24' Bays
20'	1.00	1.01	1.05	1.07	1.00	1.00	1.03	1.04
24'	1.01	1.02	1.06	1.08	1.00	1.00	1.07	1.09
28'	1.01	1.02	1.06	1.08	—	—	—	—
30'	1.01	1.02	1.06	1.08	1.01	1.02	1.09	1.10
32'	1.01	1.02	1.07	1.09	1.01	1.02	1.10	1.11
36'	1.01	1.02	1.08	1.10	1.01	1.02	1.10	1.11
40'	1.02	1.03	1.08	1.11	1.01	1.02	1.10	1.11
50'	1.04	1.06	1.10	1.15	1.02	1.03	1.10	1.12
60'	1.05	1.07	1.12	1.18	1.03	1.04	1.15	1.18
70'	1.07	1.09	1.14	1.20	1.03	1.04	1.15	1.19
80'	1.08	1.10	1.15	1.21	1.04	1.05	1.16	1.20
90'	1.09	1.10	1.16	1.22	1.04	1.05	1.17	1.21
100'	1.09	1.10	1.17	1.23	1.04	1.05	1.17	1.22
110'	1.10	1.11	1.18	1.24	1.05	1.06	1.18	1.24
120'	1.11	1.12	1.19	1.25	1.06	1.07	1.19	1.27
130'	—	—	—	—	1.07	1.08	1.20	1.30
140'	1.13	1.14	1.20	1.27	1.08	1.09	1.22	1.33
150'	—	—	—	—	1.09	1.10	1.24	1.35

Alternate Costs for Steel Buildings

Floors, cost difference per square foot

4" concrete with reinforced mesh and 2" sand fill	0
5" concrete with reinforced mesh and 2" sand fill	+.50
6" concrete with reinforced mesh and 2" sand fill	+.98
6" concrete with 1/2" rebars, 12" x 12" o.c. and 2" sand fill	+1.94
3" plant mix asphalt on 4" untreated rock base	-.68
2" plant mix asphalt on 4" untreated rock base	-.87
Gravel (compacted)	-1.45
Dirt (compacted)	-2.00

Roof Covering,
cost difference per square foot

26 gauge galvanized steel	0
24 gauge galvanized steel	+.26
22 gauge galvanized steel	+.92
26 gauge colored steel	+.70
24 gauge colored steel	+1.09
.024 aluminum	+.59
.032 aluminum	+1.19
.032 colored aluminum	+1.77
No roof cover (just purlins)	-1.99

Wall Covering,
cost difference per square foot

26 gauge colored steel	+.65
24 gauge colored steel	+1.01
26 gauge galvanized steel	0
24 gauge galvanized steel	+.30
22 gauge galvanized steel	+.85
26 gauge aluminum and steel	+.53
24 gauge aluminum and steel	+.90
.024 aluminum	+.62
.032 aluminum	+1.18
.032 colored aluminum	+1.86
26 gauge galvanized steel insulated panel	+.83
26 gauge colored steel insulated panel	+1.59
26 gauge aluminum steel insulated panel	+1.28
26 gauge galvanized steel mono panel	+1.61
26 gauge colored steel mono panel	+2.49
No wall cover (just girts)	-2.35

These costs are to be added to or subtracted from the building square foot costs on page 217.

Open Endwall (includes ridged frame in lieu of post and beam), low profile building

Cost Deduction Per Each Endwall
Eave Heights

Width	10'	12'	14'	16'	18'	20'	24'
20'	$774	$932	$1,124	1,293	—	—	—
24'	1,124	1,176	1,489	1,546	—	—	—
30'	1,340	1,565	1,826	2,193	—	—	—
32'	1,434	1,677	1,995	2,314	2,476	2,788	4,224
36'	1,545	1,771	—	—	—	—	—
40'	1,667	1,958	2,360	2,689	2,933	3,457	4,264
50'	1,826	2,193	2,669	3,083	3,589	4,121	4,975
60'	2,170	2,397	2,893	3,429	4,273	4,985	6,278
70'	—	2,659	2,971	3,896	4,711	5,473	6,952
80'	—	2,792	3,429	4,283	5,156	5,846	8,094
90'	—	—	3,762	4,181	5,454	6,004	8,576
100'	—	—	3,051	4,081	5,126	6,032	8,827
110'	—	—	2,857	3,843	4,820	5,957	8,926
120'	—	—	2,558	3,336	4,209	5,957	8,926
130'	—	—	2,165	3,234	4,432	5,790	8,926
140'	—	—	1,592	2,689	4,301	5,426	8,658
150'	—	—	1,293	2,417	3,673	4,935	8,453

These costs are to be subtracted from the basic building cost.

Open Sidewalls, per linear foot of wall

Eave Height	10'	12'	14'	16'	18'	20'	24'
	$4.22	$5.05	$5.94	$6.76	$7.58	$8.30	$10.12

These costs are to be subtracted from the basic building cost.

Alternate Costs for Steel Buildings

Open Endwall (includes ridged frame in lieu of post and beam), high profile building

Cost Deduction Per Each Endwall - Eave Heights

Width	10'	12'	14'	16'	18'	20'	24'
20'	917	973	1,398	—	—	—	—
24'	1,059	1,486	1,723	—	—	—	—
28'	1,565	1,761	2,023	—	—	—	—
30'	1,695	1,874	2,230	—	—	—	—
32'	1,790	1,977	2,342	2,651	3,111	3,486	4,990
36'	2,033	2,203	2,652	—	—	—	—
40'	2,427	2,595	2,998	3,498	3,992	4,378	5,019
50'	3,074	3,386	3,926	4,358	4,721	5,039	6,569
60'	4,005	4,358	5,019	5,426	6,089	6,877	8,290
70'	4,685	5,772	5,911	6,952	7,628	8,390	10,248
80'	5,529	6,541	6,867	7,628	8,390	9,257	11,188
90'	—	7,992	9,052	9,591	9,614	11,411	13,883
100'	—	8,271	9,709	10,510	11,523	12,690	15,232
110'	—	—	12,554	13,983	15,268	16,262	19,123

Ridged Frame Endwall in lieu of post and beam, low profile building

Cost Deduction Per Each Endwall - Eave Heights

Width	10'	12'	14'	16'	18'	20'	24'
20'	874	932	1,005	—	—	—	—
24'	922	990	1,021	—	—	—	—
28'	1,005	1,097	1,097	—	—	—	—
30'	1,059	1,115	1,071	—	—	—	—
32'	1,115	1,199	1,236	1,396	1,565	1,658	1,921
36'	1,321	1,386	1,442	—	—	—	—
40'	1,452	1,565	1,658	1,761	1,939	1,977	2,445
50'	1,977	2,101	2,249	2,370	2,402	2,633	3,064
60'	2,473	2,652	2,783	3,008	3,149	3,176	3,655
70'	3,429	3,524	4,047	3,889	4,119	4,015	4,432
80'	3,889	3,990	4,432	4,432	4,769	5,103	5,454
90'	—	4,995	5,547	5,866	5,866	5,208	7,425
100'	—	6,171	6,700	6,435	7,455	7,759	8,499
110'	—	—	7,768	8,499	8,509	8,929	9,877

Ridged Frame Endwall in lieu of post and beam, high profile building

Cost Deduction Per Each Endwall - Eave Heights

Width	10'	12'	14'	16'	18'	20'	24'
20'	1,018	1,059	1,115	1,115	—	—	—
24'	1,087	1,097	1,115	1,199	—	—	—
30'	1,115	1,143	1,443	—	—	—	—
32'	1,380	1,396	1,481	1,509	1,593	1,612	1,790
36'	1,509	1,565	—	—	—	—	—
40'	1,555	1,658	1,743	1,827	1,921	1,967	2,249
50'	2,156	2,286	2,324	2,435	2,514	2,679	3,101
60'	2,726	2,839	2,998	2,445	3,149	3,270	3,634
70'	—	3,664	3,982	4,097	4,007	4,319	4,767
80'	—	4,432	4,835	4,995	5,163	5,332	5,547
90'	—	4,432	5,315	4,995	5,163	6,770	7,035
100'	—	—	7,460	7,618	7,768	7,899	8,336
110'	—	—	9,163	9,163	9,377	9,506	10,277
120'	—	—	10,718	10,950	11,383	11,625	11,998
130'	—	—	11,988	12,647	12,926	12,423	14,309
140'	—	—	14,616	14,896	15,554	15,601	16,281

Alternate Costs for Steel Buildings

Canopies (sidewall location), cost per linear foot

Type and Size	5'	6'	8'	10'	12'	15'
High profile 20' bays	$42.84	$48.80	$61.08	$70.87	$77.85	$88.19
High profile 24' bays	41.72	46.93	58.76	67.23	73.56	84.18
Low profile 20' bays	33.62	38.65	49.63	58.85	69.19	79.71
Low profile 24' bays	32.31	36.87	47.49	56.34	65.09	75.71
Cost Per Each Canopy						
Basic end cost	$320	$390	$540	$719	$970	$1,240

The above costs are for 26 gauge galvanized metal canopy.

Canopies (endwall location), add the following to sidewall location costs above.

Eave Height	10'	12'	14'	16'	18'	20'	24'
Cost	$372	$427	$484	$542	$605	$635	$862

Sliding Sidewall Doors, cost per opening, including framed opening.

Single Doors	10'	12'	14'	16'	18'	20'	24'
8' x 9'	$1,518	$1,518	$1,488	$1,684	$1,694	$1,831	$1,831
10' x 9'	1,586	1,694	1,655	1,831	1,890	1,909	1,939
10' x 11'	—	1,655	1,665	1,890	1,939	1,939	1,968
10' x 13'	—	—	1,606	1,909	1,968	1,968	1,998
12' x 9'	2,164	2,243	2,164	2,536	2,458	2,497	2,448
12' x 11'	—	—	2,213	2,478	2,536	2,565	2,565
12' x 13'	—	—	2,164	2,536	2,565	2,585	2,614
12' x 15'	—	—	—	2,527	2,614	2,732	2,800
14' x 9'	2,497	2,429	2,369	2,674	2,732	2,761	2,772
14' x 11'	—	2,644	2,213	2,644	2,761	2,702	2,898
14' x 13'	—	—	2,360	2,800	2,977	2,732	2,947
14' x 15'	—	—	—	2,674	2,957	3,045	3,065
16' x 9'	2,674	2,898	2,869	3,045	3,094	3,094	3,065
16' x 11'	—	2,761	2,898	3,094	3,133	3,163	3,163
16' x 13'	—	—	2,723	3,182	—	—	—

The above costs are for 26 gauge colored sliding. Doors in eave heights listed at the top of each column. If door is in an endwall, use the lowest cost of size desired and add $330.

Hollow Metal Walk-Thru Doors, cost per opening including framed opening.

Door Size	1-3/8" Thick Flush Galvanized	Colored	1-3/8" Thick Half Glass Galvanized	Colored	1-3/4" Thick Flush Galvanized	Colored	1-3/4" Thick Half Glass Galvanized	Colored
2'0" x 6'8" single	$680	$737	$837	$893	—	—	—	—
2'6" x 6'8" single	695	737	837	893	—	—	—	—
3'0" x 6'8" single	680	794	867	994	$998	$1,107	$1,136	$1,205
3'0" x 7'0" single	680	794	867	994	998	1,107	1,136	1,263
3'4" x 7'0" single	—	—	—	—	1,019	1,165	1,194	1,303
4'0" x 7'0" single	—	—	—	—	1,136	1,303	1,352	1,478
6'0" x 6'8" pair	1,145	1,352	1,401	1,576	1,576	1,792	1,939	2,076
6'0" x 7'0" pair	1,224	1,450	1,459	1,674	1,684	1,880	1,929	2,164
8'0" x 7'0" pair	—	—	—	—	1,802	1,998	2,164	2,438

Half glass doors include glazing.

Additives: When walk-thru door is used as a pilot in a sliding door, **add** $100 to the costs above.

Heavy duty lockset	Add $153 each	Panic hardware, pair	Add $1,459 pair
Door closer	Add $211 each	Weatherstripping, bronze	
Panic hardware, single	Add $732 each	and neoprene	Add $18.00/LF

Alternate Costs for Steel Buildings

These costs are to be added to the basic building cost.

Framed Openings, cost per opening

Location	Eave Height 10'	12'	14'	16'	18'	20'	24'
Sidewalls	$477	$492	$520	$543	$712	$798	$1,205
Endwalls	685	723	737	774	824	941	1,072

These costs are for the standard widths of 8', 10', 12', 14', 16', 18', and 20'. If the width is other than standard, add $108. per opening. If there is only one opening per building, add $158.

Gutters and Downspouts,
cost per linear foot

Eave gutter (4")	
24 gauge galvanized steel	$11.76
24 gauge colored steel	12.26
.032 aluminum	10.88
Valley gutter (6")	
12 gauge galvanized steel	23.42
24 gauge galvanized steel	20.10
Downspouts	
4" x 4" x 26 gauge galvanized steel	8.19
4" x 4" x 26 gauge colored steel	8.70
6" x 6" x 24 gauge galvanized steel	9.08
6" x 6" x 24 gauge colored steel	10.48

Door Hoods, cost each

Width of Door	Galvanized	Colored
12'	$237	$267
16'	304	336
20'	349	383

Louvers, cost each, including screens

Size	Fixed Galvanized	Color	Adjustable Galvanized	Color
3' x 2'	$405	$422	$528	$550
3' x 3'	422	551	567	622
5' x 5'	511	693	790	872

Insulation, cost per square foot of surface area

Size and Type	Roof Thickness 1"	1-1/2"	2"	Wall Thickness 1"	1-1/2"	2"
.6 pound density						
White vinyl faced	$1.33	$1.39	$1.46	$1.39	$1.39	$1.68
Colored vinyl faced	1.53	1.62	1.73	1.68	1.73	1.96
Aluminum faced	1.68	1.73	1.96	1.82	1.96	2.10
.75 pound density						
White vinyl faced	1.39	1.46	1.62	1.46	1.62	1.73
Colored vinyl faced	1.68	1.68	1.82	1.73	1.82	2.10
Aluminum faced	1.82	1.82	2.10	1.96	2.10	2.22

Overhangs (sidewall location), cost per linear foot of overhang, 26 gauge galvanized

Size and Type	20' Bays 3'	4'	5'	24' Bays 3'	4'	5'
No soffit	27.85	33.76	38.91	25.61	30.56	34.16
Soffit	60.05	70.63	78.30	58.21	66.56	79.07
Color, soffit	67.14	70.63	80.53	60.44	70.63	78.30
Color, no soffit	29.79	36.38	42.30	27.85	33.37	39.19
Color, galvanized soffit	62.87	75.58	82.67	60.44	70.63	80.53
Color, color soffit	64.62	74.90	84.61	92.85	70.63	82.75

Overhangs (endwall location), cost per linear foot of overhang, 26 gauge galvanized

Size and Type	3'	4'	5'	6'
No soffit	17.85	29.59	29.01	33.96
Galvanized soffit	43.27	53.56	63.35	71.11
Color, soffit	54.04	52.59	65.87	73.54
Color, no soffit	19.60	25.23	31.92	38.22
Color, galvanized soffit	44.43	57.63	65.87	75.58
Color, color soffit	46.96	57.63	67.82	73.54

Alternate Costs for Steel Buildings

These costs are to be added to the basic building cost

Skylights, Polycarbonate, with curb

	2' x 2'	4' x 4'	4' x 8'
Single dome	$155	$412	$517
Double dome	182	468	602
Triple dome	227	539	875
Double, ventilating	445	763	991

Partitions, Interior, 26 gauge steel, cost per square foot of partition with two sides finished

Painted drywall finish	$3.90
Painted plywood, fire retardant	5.70

Ventilators, round type, includes screen (gravity type), cost each

Diameter	Stationary Galvanized	Stationary Colored	Stationary Aluminum	Rotary Galvanized	Rotary Colored	Rotary Aluminum
12"	$230	$249	$411	$366	$411	$517
16"	321	335	480	458	502	641
20"	386	410	550	559	589	730
24"	417	441	611	624	662	834

Ventilators, ridge type, includes screen and damper

Throat Size	4"	9"	12"	14"
Cost per linear foot, galvanized	$60	$89	$113	$130
Cost per linear foot, colored	62	98	122	140

Ventilator-Dampers, cost each

Diameter	12"	16"	20"	24"
Damper only	$85	$115	$120	$139
Dampers with cords and pulleys	169	212	261	301

Continuous Ridge Ventilator, includes screen and damper, cost per 10 foot unit

Size & Type	First 10' Galvanized	First 10' Color	Each Additional 10' Galvanized	Each Additional 10' Color
9" throat	$852	$975	$804	$902
10" throat	975	1,070	865	975
12" throat	628	1,400	1,155	1,226

Steel Sliding Windows, includes glass and screens, cost per window

3' x 2'6"	$436
6' x 2'6"	539
6' x 3'8"	623

Smoke and Heat Vents, automatic control, cost per 10 foot unit

Size & Type	First 10' Galvanized	First 10' Color	Each Additional 10' Galvanized	Each Additional 10' Color
9" ridge mounted	$3,233	$3,417	$2,672	$2,744
9" slope mounted	3,335	3,580	2,744	2,876

Add for operators:

One or two 10 foot sections	Add $107.00
Two to seven 10 foot sections	Add $224.00

Aluminum Industrial Windows, includes glass and screens, cost per window

Size and Type	Project Out	Fixed
3' x 2'6"	$412	$301
2' x 2'8"	441	330
6' x 2'6"	610	404
6' x 3'8"	740	513

Aluminum Sliding Windows, includes glass and screens, cost per window

Width	Height 2'	Height 2'6"	Height 3'	Height 3'6"	Height 4'
2'	$307	$335	$343	$362	$383
3'	335	356	362	383	397
4'	—	374	397	397	439
5'	—	397	412	505	523
6'	—	439	505	544	585

If window is fixed, deduct $5.55 per window. For mullions add $11.00 each.

Commercial, Industrial, and Public Structures

Typical Physical Lives in Years by Quality Class

Building Type	Masonry or Concrete						Wood or Wood and Steel Frame				
	1	2	3	4	5	6	1	2	3	4	5
Public Buildings	70	70	70	60	60	60	70	60	60	60	–
Urban Stores	70	70	70	60	60	60	70	60	60	60	–
Suburban Stores	70	60	60	60	60	–	60	50	50	45	–
Supermarkets	70	60	60	60	–	–	60	50	50	45	–
Small Food Stores	60	60	60	60	–	–	50	50	45	45	–
Discount Houses	70	60	60	60	–	–	60	50	50	45	–
Banks and Savings Offices	70	70	70	60	60	–	60	60	60	50	50
Department Stores	70	60	60	60	–	–	60	50	50	45	–
General Office Buildings	60	60	60	60	–	–	60	50	50	45	–
Medical-Dental Buildings	60	60	60	50	–	–	60	50	50	45	–
Convalescent Hospitals	60	60	60	50	–	–	55	50	50	45	–
Funeral Homes	70	70	70	60	60	–	60	60	60	50	50
Restaurants	70	60	60	60	–	–	60	50	50	45	–
Theaters	50	50	50	50	–	–	50	45	45	40	–
Service Garages	60	60	50	50	–	–	45	45	40	40	–
Auto Service Centers	50	50	45	45	–	–	–	–	–	–	–
Warehouses	55	55	50	50	–	–	–	–	–	–	–
Light Industrial Buildings	55	55	50	50	–	–	–	–	–	–	–
Factory Buildings	40	40	35	35	–	–	–	–	–	–	–

Service Stations located on main highways or in high land value areas can be expected to become obsolete in 20 years. Other service stations can be expected to become obsolete in 25 years. Reinforced Concrete Department Stores have a typical physical life of 80 years for class one structures and 70 years for lower quality class structures. Steel Buildings have a typical physical life of 50 years

Normal Percent Good Table

Average Life in Years

Age	20 Years Life	Good	25 Years Life	Good	30 Years Life	Good	35 Years Life	Good
0	20	100	25	100	30	100	35	100
1	19	95	24	97	29	98	34	99
2	18	90	23	93	28	96	33	97
3	17	85	22	90	27	93	32	95
4	16	79	21	86	26	90	31	93
5	15	73	20	82	25	88	30	91
6	14	67	19	78	24	85	29	89
7	13	61	18	74	23	82	28	87
8	12	56	17	70	22	79	27	85
9	11	51	16	65	21	75	26	83
10	10	49	15	60	20	72	25	80
11	9	48	14	56	19	68	24	78
12	9	46	13	52	18	65	23	75
13	8	44	12	50	17	61	22	72
14	7	43	11	48	16	58	21	69
15	6	43	10	47	15	54	20	66
16	6	41	9	46	14	50	19	63
17	5	39	8	45	13	49	18	60
18	5	38	8	44	12	48	17	57
19	5	37	7	43	12	47	16	54
20	4	35	7	42	11	47	15	51
21	4	34	6	41	11	46	14	50
22	4	33	6	40	10	45	13	49
23	3	32	5	39	10	44	13	48
24	3	30	5	38	9	43	12	47
25	3	29	5	37	9	43	12	47
26	3	28	4	36	8	42	11	46
27	2	27	4	35	8	41	11	45
28	2	25	4	34	7	40	10	44
29	2	24	4	33	7	39	10	43
30	2	22	3	32	6	38	9	43
31	2	21	3	31	6	37	9	42
32	1	20	3	30	5	36	8	42
33	–	–	3	29	5	35	8	41
34	–	–	3	28	5	35	7	40
35	–	–	2	27	5	34	7	39
36	–	–	2	26	4	33	6	38
38	–	–	2	24	4	32	6	37
40	–	–	2	22	3	30	5	36
42	–	–	1	20	3	28	5	34
45	–	–	–	–	2	26	4	32
48	–	–	–	–	2	23	3	30
52	–	–	–	–	1	20	3	27
56	–	–	–	–	–	–	2	24
62	–	–	–	–	–	–	1	20

Age	40 Years Life	Good	45 Years Life	Good	50 Years Life	Good	55 Years Life	Good
0	40	100	45	100	50	100	55	100
2	38	98	43	99	48	99	53	99
4	36	96	41	97	46	98	51	98
6	34	93	39	95	44	97	49	97
8	32	90	37	93	42	95	47	96
10	30	86	35	90	40	93	45	95
12	28	82	33	87	38	91	43	94
14	26	78	31	84	36	88	41	92
16	24	73	29	81	34	85	39	90
18	22	68	27	77	32	82	37	88
20	20	63	25	73	30	80	35	86
22	18	58	23	69	28	77	33	83
24	17	53	21	65	26	73	31	80
26	15	50	20	60	24	69	29	77
28	14	48	18	55	23	65	27	74
30	13	47	17	50	21	61	26	71
32	11	45	15	49	20	57	24	67
34	10	44	14	48	18	53	22	63
36	9	43	13	47	17	50	21	59
38	8	42	12	46	16	48	19	55
40	8	40	11	44	14	47	18	52
42	7	39	10	43	13	46	17	50
44	6	38	9	42	12	45	16	49
46	6	36	8	41	11	44	15	48
49	5	35	7	40	10	43	14	47
50	5	34	7	38	10	42	13	45
52	4	32	6	37	9	41	12	44
54	4	31	6	36	8	40	11	43
56	3	30	5	35	8	39	10	42
58	3	29	5	34	7	38	9	41
60	3	27	4	32	7	37	9	40
62	2	26	4	31	6	36	8	39
64	2	25	4	30	6	35	8	38
66	2	24	3	29	5	34	7	37
68	2	22	3	28	5	33	7	36
70	2	21	3	27	4	32	6	36
72	1	20	3	25	4	31	6	35
74	–	–	2	24	4	30	5	34
76	–	–	2	23	3	28	5	32
82	–	–	1	20	3	26	4	30
84	–	–	–	–	2	24	4	29
88	–	–	–	–	2	22	3	27
92	–	–	–	–	1	20	2	25
96	–	–	–	–	–	–	2	23
102	–	–	–	–	–	–	1	20

Age	60 Years Life	Good	70 Years Life	Good
0	60	100	70	100
2	58	99	68	99
4	56	99	66	99
6	54	98	64	99
8	52	97	62	98
10	50	96	60	98
12	48	95	58	97
14	46	94	56	96
16	44	93	54	96
18	42	92	52	95
20	40	89	50	94
22	38	87	48	93
24	36	85	46	92
26	34	83	45	91
28	32	81	42	89
30	30	78	40	87
32	29	75	39	85
34	27	72	37	83
36	25	69	35	81
38	24	66	33	79
40	22	63	31	76
42	21	60	30	73
44	20	56	29	70
46	18	52	27	67
48	17	49	26	64
50	16	48	25	61
52	15	47	23	58
54	14	46	22	56
56	13	46	21	54
58	12	45	20	52
60	11	44	19	50
64	10	42	17	48
68	9	40	15	46
72	8	38	13	44
76	7	36	12	43
80	6	35	11	41
86	5	32	9	39
92	4	29	8	36
100	3	25	6	33
108	2	22	4	29
112	1	20	3	27
122	–	–	2	24
130	–	–	1	20

Additional Costs for
Commercial, Industrial, and Public Structures

Section Contents

Additional Structure Costs

Basements

Cost includes concrete floor and walls, open ceiling, minimum lighting, no plumbing, and no wall finish. Cost per square foot of floor at 12' wall height.

Area	500	1,000	1,500	2,000	3,000	4,000	5,000	7,500	10,000	15,000	20,000
Cost	54.12	48.37	42.21	38.17	37.16	32.41	31.30	30.20	26.56	25.34	23.83

Add or subtract the amount listed in the table below to or from the square foot of floor cost for each foot of wall height more or less than 12 feet.

Wall Height Adjustment
Square Foot Area

Area	500	1,000	1,500	2,000	3,000	4,000	5,000	7,500	10,000	15,000	20,000
Cost	3.61	2.66	2.35	1.91	1.56	1.44	1.35	1.04	.85	.66	.62

Canopies, per S.F. of canopy area

Light frame, flat roof underside, plywood and paint or cheap stucco supported by wood or light steel posts, 4" to 6" wood fascia.	$19.49 to $21.01
Average frame, underside of good stucco, flat roof, cantilevered from building or supported by steel posts, 6" to 12" metal fascia.	$21.81 to $29.48
Same as above but with sloping shake or tile roof.	$22.92 to $31.71
Corrugated metal on steel frame.	$19.69 to $29.48

Canopy Lights, per S.F. based on one row of lights for 5' canopy

Recessed spots (1 each 6 linear feet)	$3.18
Single tube fluorescent	5.83
Double tube fluorescent	8.18

Public Address Systems, speakers attached to building. No conduit included.

Base cost, master control	$904 to $1,757
Per indoor speaker	188
Per outdoor speaker	376

Sound Systems, cost per unit

Voice only, per unit	$101 to $171
Music (add to above), small units	101 to 131
Music (add to above), large units	131 to 394
Larger installations cost the least per unit.	

Docks for unloading trucks. Cost per S.F. of dock at 4' height

L x W	10'	20'	30'	50'	100'	200'
5'	33.53	29.80	27.17	24.54	22.73	21.11
10'	29.80	25.86	22.62	20.30	18.79	18.18
15'	26.16	21.92	19.39	16.77	15.55	14.44
20'	23.43	18.79	16.26	15.05	14.04	13.23

Cost includes compacted fill, three concrete walls, concrete floor, and rock base.

Intercommunication Systems

Master control, base cost	$1,896	to	$5,708
Cost per station	145	to	217
Nurses call system, per station	217	to	397

Security Systems

Control panel	$155	to	$309
Each door or window secured	31	to	69
Heat detectors, each	10	to	51
Smoke detectors, each	20	to	101
Motion detectors, each	20	to	41

Loading Ramps, cost per S.F. of ramp

Size	
Under 300 S.F.	$9.65
Over 300 S.F.	9.25

Dock Levelers and Lifts, cost each

Dock leveler, manual	$7,575
Dock leveler, mechanical	3,687
Powered platform dock leveler	
6' x 6' recessed	3,287
6' x 8' recessed	3,717
Electro-hydraulic, pit recessed scissor lift	
5,000 lb. capacity, 6' x 8'	9,849
10,000 lb. capacity, 8' x 10'	17,412
20,000 lb. capacity, 8' x 12'	28,745

Additional Structure Costs

Doors, with hardware

Exterior, commercial, cost per door

Glass in wood (3' x 7')	$943 to	$1,474
1/4" plate in aluminum (3' x 7')	1,525 to	2,473
Automatic, tempered glass (3' x 7')	7,253 to	11,023
Residential type (3' x 7')	359 to	660

Interior, commercial and industrial, cost per S.F.

Hollow core wood	$15.25 to	$15.97
Solid wood	15.35 to	19.88
Hollow core metal	33.48 to	39.63

Fire, cost per S.F.

Hollow metal, 1-3/4"	$52.82 to	$69.99
Metal clad, rolling	43.23 to	70.80
Metal clad, swinging	61.81 to	88.38

Elevators, Freight, Electric, car and equipment, per shaft, car speed in feet per minute, 2 stop

Capacity	50 to 75	100 to 150	200
2,500 lbs	$63,276	—	—
3,000	66,780	$76,500	$88,455
3,500	80,240	80,189	90,040
4,000	74,935	83,430	96,450
5,000	80,140	91,470	103,232
6,000	88,330	100,110	111,300
8,000	100,050	111,440	126,495
10,000	114,902	126,445	144,990

For manual doors, **add** $5,560 for each stop. For power operated doors, **add** $8,430 for each additional stop. **Add** $8,430 per car for self-leveling cars. **Add** for double center opening doors, per stop $355. **Add** for deluxe cab (raised panel, interior, drop ceiling) $4,220.

Elevators, Freight,

Hydraulic, 100 F.P.M.

Shaft, car, machinery	
2,500 lb. capacity	$55,500
6,000 lb. capacity	93,400
Cost per stop	
Manual doors	9,490
Automatic doors	20,673

Roll-Up Metal Warehouse Door with chain operator, cost each

10' x 10'	$2,000
12' x 12'	2,656
14' x 14'	3,030
Fusible link (add to above)	563
Motor controlled (add to above)	285

Draperies, cost per square yard of opening

	54" high	68" high	96" high
Minimum	$22.90	$23.00	$25.80
Good quality	51.60	52.80	61.80
Better quality	62.90	68.80	84.50

Escalators, cost per flight up or down

Total Rise	32" W	40" W	48" W
10' to 13'	$133,000	$136,000	$148,000
14'	137,000	143,000	155,000
15'	142,000	149,000	161,000
16'	146,000	159,000	161,000
17'	152,000	161,000	164,000
18'	155,000	166,000	164,000
19'	160,000	167,000	165,000
20'	166,000	172,000	170,000
21'	171,000	174,000	174,000

Add for glass side enclosure: $15,219 - $17,923.

Dumbwaiters, includes door, traction type

	1st Two Stops		Add'l. Stops
Hand operated, 25 fpm (no doors)			
25 lb.	$2,355 to	$4,284	$1,790
75 lb.	3,162 to	5,310	1,790
Electrical, with machinery above, floor loading			
100 lb., 50 fpm	$8,796 to	$14,190	$3,370
300 lb., 50 fpm	9,160 to	14,140	3,370
500 lb., 50 fpm	9,635 to	15,310	3,370
500 lb., 100 fpm	14,140 to	22,800	(5 stop)

Elevators, Passenger, Electric, car and machinery cost, per shaft*

Capacity	200 F.P.M., 10 Stops	350 F.P.M., 5 Stops	500 F.P.M., 5 Stops
2,000 lbs.	$100,680	$107,460	$230,200
2,500 lbs.	123,600	114,620	237,600
3,000 lbs.	124,820	121,990	240,100
3,500 lbs.	125,330	128,360	241,400
4,000 lbs.	126,130	136,210	244,400
4,000 lbs (Hospital)	127,790	139,810	251,990

*Add for each additional stop: 200 or 350 F.P.M. units, $7,180; 500 F.P.M. units, $11,816. Deduct for multi-shaft applications, $3,393 to $7,180 per additional shaft. Add for rear-opening door: $10,200 to base cost, plus $7,360 per door.

Additional Structure Costs

Fill, compacted under raised floor, includes perimeter retaining wall but not slab, per C.F.

Up to 10,000 S.F.	$1.06 to $1.70
Over 10,000 to 50,000 S.F	.90 to 1.32

Fire Extinguishers, cost each

Fire hose and cabinet	$371 to $733
Extinguisher cabinets	98 to 216
Extinguishers, chemical	78 to 192
Extinguishers, carbon dioxide	221 to 436

Fire Escapes

Type	Unit	Cost
Second story	Each	$4,222 to $5,767
Additional floors	Per story	2,485 to 3,727

Fire Sprinklers, cost per S.F.
of area served

	Wet Pipe System	
Area	**Normal**	**Special***
to 2,000	$4.53	$5.60
2,001 to 4,000	3.15	4.53
4,001 to 10,000	2.79	3.85
Over 10,000	2.45	3.53

	Dry Pipe System	
Area	**Normal**	**Special***
to 2,000	$4.90	$5.94
2,001 to 4,000	3.15	4.27
4,001 to 10,000	3.02	4.20
Over 10,000	2.79	3.84

Costs include normal installation, service lines, permit and valves.

*Special hazard systems are custom engineered to meet code or insurance requirements and are usually so identified by a metal plate attached to the riser.

Overhead Suspended Heaters, per unit

25 MBTU	$1,071 to	$1,293
50	1,246 to	1,384
75	1,384 to	1,525
100	1,576 to	1,798
150	1,929 to	2,071
200	2,232 to	2,333
250	2,485 to	2,495

Fireplace

	1 Story	2 Story
Freestanding wood burning heat circulating prefab fireplace, with interior flue, base and cap.	$1,646	—
Zero-clearance, insulated prefab metal fireplace, brick face.	2,353	$3,101
5' base, common brick, on interior face.	3,131	3,515
6' base, common brick, used brick, face brick or natural stone on interior face with average wood mantle.	4,878	5,232
8' base, common brick, used brick or natural stone on interior face, raised hearth.	6,818	7,656

Electric Heating Units

Baseboard, per linear foot	$15.45 to	$30.90
Add for thermostat		41.20
Cable in ceiling, per S.F.	2.33 to	2.98
Wall heaters, per K.W.	51.50 to	103.00

Heating and Cooling Systems

Cost per S.F. of Floor Area**

Type and Use	Heating Only		Heating & Cooling	
Elementary schools	$6.89 to	$10.69	$12.54 to	$19.45
Secondary schools	7.36 to	11.40	13.38 to	20.75
Government offices	11.92 to	18.49	21.69 to	33.63
Libraries	8.14 to	14.84	14.84 to	22.96
Fire stations	7.21 to	13.07	11.33 to	17.61
Urban stores	4.54 to	7.01	8.25 to	12.78
Suburban stores	3.64 to	5.62	6.59 to	10.23
Small food stores	3.86 to	5.98	7.01 to	10.88
Supermarkets	4.50 to	6.97	8.21 to	12.70
Discount houses	3.33 to	5.18	6.06 to	9.42
Bank and savings	6.07 to	9.40	11.00 to	17.05
Department stores	4.26 to	6.60	7.76 to	12.02
Reinforced concrete	5.36 to	8.32	9.77 to	15.13
General offices				
Forced air	5.31 to	8.24	9.65 to	14.98
Hot & chilled water	—		11.17 to	17.34
Medical-Dental				
Forced air	5.78 to	8.96	10.50 to	16.29
Hot & chilled water	—		11.85 to	18.39
Convalescent hospitals				
Forced air	5.36 to	8.32	9.77 to	15.12
Hot & chilled water	—		11.50 to	17.86
Funeral homes	7.73 to	11.95	14.02 to	21.72
Ecclesiastic buildings	5.97 to	9.25	10.84 to	16.70
Restaurants	7.96 to	12.35	14.57 to	22.49
Theaters	5.32 to	8.27	9.70 to	15.03
Industrial buildings	2.30 to	5.72	—	
Interior offices	2.61 to	3.67	4.74 to	7.35

**Use the higher figures where more heating and cooling density is required.

Additional Structure Costs

Kitchen Equipment, cost per linear foot of stainless steel fixture

Work tables	$837 to $1,017
Serving fixtures	347 to 1,939

Mezzanines, cost per S.F. of floor

Unfinished (min. lighting and plumbing)	2.60 to 31.10
Store mezzanines	43.10 to 54.70
Office mezzanines (without partitions)	46.60 to 60.50
Office mezzanines (with partitions)	60.50 to 95.00

Costs include floor system, floor finish, stairways, lighting, and partitions where applicable.

Seating, cost per seat space

Theater, economy	$168
Theater, lodge	308
Pews, bench type	81
Pews, seat type	113

Partitions, cost per S.F. of surface

Gypsum on wood frame, (finished both sides) 2" x 4" wood studs, 24" on center with 1/2" gypsum board, taped, textures and painted. **$5.82**

Plaster on wood frame (finished both sides) 2" x 4" wood studs, 24" on center with 2 coats plaster over gypsum lath, painted with primer and 1 coat enamel. **$10.80**

Pneumatic Tube Systems

Twin tube, two station system

2-1/4" round, 500 to 1,500 feet	$19,988 to $36,360
3" round, 500 to 1,500 feet	20,604 to 39,663
4" round, 500 to 1,500 feet	21,432 to 45,743
4" x 7" oval, 500 to 1,500 feet	34,098 to 56,762

Automatic System, twin tube, cost per station

4" round, 500 to 1,500 feet	$25,452 to $33,795
4" x 7" oval, 500 to 1,500 feet	34,098 to 36,885

Skylights, Plastic Rectangular Domes, cost per unit

	Single Plastic Panel		Double Plastic Panel	
Size	Skylight Only	With 4" or 9" Insulated Curb	Skylight Only	With 4" or 9" Insulated Curb
16" x 16"	$176	$300	$215	$317
16" x 24"	201	339	242	331
16" x 48"	228	391	317	469
24" x 24"	228	364	339	358
24" x 32"	242	391	371	469
24" x 48"	282	443	391	532
28" x 92"	482	715	762	883
32" x 32"	242	391	339	469
32" x 48"	326	455	434	540
32" x 72"	416	644	709	817
39" x 39"	339	455	455	534
39" x 77"	507	715	883	949
40" x 61"	469	644	709	962
48" x 48"	364	532	532	657
48" x 64"	507	793	793	949
48" x 72"	587	912	912	1,072
48" x 92"	768	982	1,175	1,494
48" x 122"	1,082	1,298	1,484	1,731
58" x 58"	587	807	949	1,092
60" x 72"	735	982	1,143	1,308
60" x 92"	936	1,195	1,422	1,216
64" x 64"	748	949	1,030	1,638
77" x 77"	1,072	1,349	1,731	1,896
94" x 94"	1,906	2,225	3,122	3,461

Triple dome skylights cost about 30% more than double dome skylights.

Additional Structure Costs

Plastic Circular Dome Skylights, cost each

| | Single Plastic Panel | | Double Plastic Panel | | Additives | |
Size	4" Curb	9" Curb	4" Curb	9" Curb	Ceiling Dome	Wall Liner
30"	$703	$716	$831	$871	$337	$337
36"	716	750	871	937	429	361
48"	951	1,040	1,216	1,278	575	429
60"	1,205	1,256	1,617	1,638	840	443
72"	1,803	1,783	2,401	2,504	1,072	534
84"	2,473	2,637	3,461	3,647	1,535	631
96"	3,637	3,802	5,068	5,419	1,680	750

The above costs are for single skylights. For three or more, deduct 20%.

Plastic Pyramid Skylights, cost each

| | | Installed Cost | |
Size	Height	2 or Less	3 or More
39" x 39"	34"	$1,143	$951
48" x 48"	42"	1,617	1,349
58" x 58"	49"	1,793	1,957

Plastic Continuous Vaulted Skylights, cost per L.F.

Width	Single Panel	Double Panel
16"	$119	$175
20"	127	182
24"	148	208
30"	182	250
36"	195	262
42"	208	273
48"	250	303
54"	262	328
60"	273	349
72	303	374
84"	361	489

Ventilators, Roof, Power Type, cost each

Throat Dia.	2 or Less	3 or More	Add for Insulated Curb
6"	$528	$513	$94
8"	852	771	132
10"	1,028	952	161
12"	1,143	1,112	166
18"	1,247	1,175	179
24"	1,415	1,309	218
30"	2,435	2,216	232
36"	2,601	2,257	238
48"	5,732	5,098	293

Above costs are for a single-speed motor installation. Dampers and bird screens are included. Add: Explosive-proof units, add $390 each. Two-speed motors, add $679 to $1,004 each. Plastic coating, depending on size of unit, add $139 to $211 each.

Plastic Ridge Type Skylights,
cost per linear foot

Width*	Single Panel	Double Panel
18"	$269	$401
24"	298	484
30"	372	552
36"	470	640
42"	484	772
48"	509	993

*Width is from ridge to curb following slope of roof.

Wire Glass Skylights,
Exterior Aluminum Frame, cost each

24" x 48"	$429
24" x 72"	517
24" x 96"	690
48" x 48"	697
48" x 72"	857
48" x 96"	1,037

Ventilators, Roof, Gravity Type,
cost each

Throat Dia.	2 or Less	3 or More	Add for Insulated Curb
8"	$230	$217	$112
12"	252	230	125
18"	387	378	177
24"	459	438	190

Heat and Smoke Vents, cost each

Size	Plastic Dome Lid	Aluminum Covered Lid
32" x 32"	$1,090	$1,236
32" x 48"	1,298	1,329
50" x 50"	1,474	1,525
50" x 62"	1,675	1,916
50" x 74"	1,535	1,999
50" x 92"	2,019	2,225
50" x 98"	2,359	2,380
62" x 104"	2,998	3,070
74" x 104"	3,358	3,689

Additional Structure Costs

Walk-In Boxes, cost per S.F. of floor area

Temperature Range	50	100	200	300	400	500	600
Over 45°	$156	$106	$82	$70	$67	$61	$60
25.50° to 45°	174	124	97	83	74	70	67
0° to 25°	207	154	112	97	83	77	73
-25.50° to 0°	226	184	147	123	106	99	91

Cost Includes:
Painted wood exterior facing, insulation as required for temperature, interior plaster, one 4 x 7 door per 300 S.F. of floor area. Costs are based upon 8' exterior wall height. Costs do not include machinery and wiring. Figure refrigeration machinery at $1,800.00 per ton capacity.

Material Handling Systems

Belt type conveyors, 24" wide.	
Horizontal sections, per linear foot	$222
Elevating, descending sections, per flight	369
Mail conveyors, automatic, electronic.	
Horizontal, per linear foot	1,761
Vertical, per 12' floor	22,767
Mail chutes, cost per floor, 5" x 14", aluminum	1,110
Linen chutes, 18 gauge steel, 30" diameter, per 10' floor	1,823
Disinfecting and sanitizing unit, each	750

Display Fronts

Display front costs may be estimated by calculating the in-place cost of each component or by estimating a cost per linear foot of bulkhead and multiplying by the bulkhead length. This section contains data for both methods. For most fronts, the cost per linear foot method is best suited for rapid preliminary estimates.

Bulkhead length is the distance from the inside of the pilaster and following along the bulkhead or glass to the inside of the opposite pilaster. This measurement includes the distance across entryways.

The cost per linear foot of bulkhead is estimated using the storefront specifications and costs in this section. This manual suggests linear foot costs for four quality types: low cost, average, good, and very good. Costs are related for each quality type in terms of flat or recessed type fronts.

Recessed type fronts include all components described in the specifications. Flat front costs do not include the following components: vestibule floor, vestibule and display area ceiling framing, back trim, display platform, lighting. The cost of automatic door openers is not included in front costs.

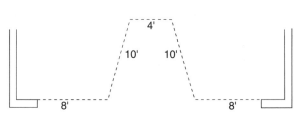

Bulkhead or storefront length 8'+10'+4'+10'+8' = 40'

Display Fronts

Display Front, Best

Display Front, Best

Display Front, Good

Display Front, Good

Display Front, Average

Display Front, Average

Display Front, Low Cost

Display Front, Low Cost

Display Fronts

All front costs are based upon a height of 10 feet from the floor level to the top of the display window. Variations from this standard should be adjusted by using the display window height adjustment costs shown with the front foot costs. These amounts are added or deducted for each foot of variation from the standard.

Bulkhead height variations will not require adjustment. Cost differentials, due to variations in bulkhead height, will be compensated for by equal variations in display window height if overall heights are equal.

Sign areas are based upon 4 foot heights. Cost adjustments are given for flat type and for recessed type fronts. A cost range is given for recessed type fronts because deeply recessed fronts will have lower linear foot costs for sign area components than will moderately recessed fronts because this cost is spread over a longer distance when recesses are deep.

Display island costs are estimated by applying 60 to 80 percent of the applicable linear foot cost to the island bulkhead length. Window height adjustments should be made, but sign height adjustments will not be necessary.

Components	Best	Good	Average	Low Cost
Bulkhead *(0 to 4' high)* (10% of total cost)	Vitrolite domestic marble or stainless steel.	Black Carrera flagstone, terrazzo or good ceramic tile.	Average ceramic tile, Roman brick or imitation flagstone.	Stucco, wood or common brick.
Window Area (30% of total cost)	Bronze or stainless steel. 1/4" float glass with mitered joints.	Heavy aluminum. 1/4" float glass, some mitered joints.	Aluminum. 1/4" float glass.	Light aluminum with wood stops. Crystal or 1/4" float glass.
Sign Area *(4' high)* (10% of total cost)	Vitrolite, domestic marble or stainless steel.	Black Carrera flagstone, terrazzo or good ceramic tile.	Average ceramic tile, Roman brick or imitation flagstone.	Stucco.
Pilasters (5% of total cost)	Vitrolite, domestic marble.	Black Carrera flagstone, terrazzo or good ceramic tile.	Average ceramic tile, Roman brick or imitation flagstone.	Stucco.
Vestibule Floor* (5% of total cost)	Decorative terrazzo.	Decorative terrazzo.	Plain terrazzo.	Concrete.
Vestibule and Display Area Ceilings* (10% of total cost)	Stucco or gypsum wallboard and texture.	Stucco or gypsum wallboard and texture.	Stucco or gypsum wallboard and texture.	Gypsum wallboard and texture.
Back Trim* (5% of total cost)	Hardwood veneer on average frame.	Gypsum wallboard and texture or light frame.	None.	None.
Display Platform Cover* (10% of total cost)	Excellent carpet.	Good carpet.	Average carpet.	Plywood with tile.
Lighting* (10% of total cost)	1 recessed spot per linear foot of bulkhead.	1 recessed spot per linear foot of bulkhead.	1 exposed spot per 2 linear feet of bulkhead.	1 exposed spot per 4 linear feet of bulkhead.
Doors (5% of total cost)	3/4" glass double doors.	Good aluminum and glass double door or single 3/4" glass door.	Average aluminum and glass double door.	Wood and glass.

Note: Use the percent of total cost to help identify the correct quality classification.

	Best	Good	Average	Low Cost
Costs, Flat Fronts	$1,142/linear foot.	$766/linear foot.	$492/linear foot.	$430/linear foot.
Costs, Recessed Fronts	$1,213/linear foot.	$1,033/linear foot.	$586/linear foot.	$476/linear foot.
Display Window *Adjustment per Foot of Height*	$52.30/linear foot.	$48.60/linear foot.	$46.20/linear foot.	$45.20/linear foot.
Flat Front, Sign Area *Adjustment per Foot of Height*	$51.90/linear foot.	$32.70/linear foot.	$12.99/linear foot.	$4.32/linear foot.
Recessed Front, Sign Area *Adjustment per Foot of Height*	$18.30 to $24.35/ linear foot.	$11.20 to $14.28/ linear foot.	$4.88 to 6.98/ linear foot.	$2.59 to $2.87/ linear foot.

*Not included in flat front costs.

Display Fronts

Lighting, cost per fixture

Open incandescent	$58.67 to $84.80
Recessed incandescent	84.60 to 170.66
Fluorescent exposed, 4' single	183.70 to 271.70
Fluorescent recessed, 4' single	195.70 to 348.10

Bulkhead Walls, cost per S.F. of wall

Up to 5' high, nominal 6" thick	
Concrete	$16.48 to $24.44
Concrete block	11.51 to 17.10
Wood frame	7.10 to 12.56

Ceiling, cost per S.F. of floor

Dropped ceiling framing	$2.39 to $3.35
Acoustical tile on wood strips	3.71 to 4.61
Acoustical plaster including lath	3.43 to 5.02
Gypsum board, texture and paint	2.67 to 3.94
Plaster and paint including lath	3.82 to 5.25

Entrances, cost per entrance

Aluminum and 1/4" float glass	
Single door, 3' x 7'	$1,785 to $2,950
Double door, 6' x 7'	3,160 to 4,360
Stainless steel and 1/4" float glass	
Single door, 3' x 7'	3,520 to 5,530
Double door, 6' x 7'	4,850 to 7,916
3/4" tempered glass	
Single door, 3' x 7'	3,690 to 5,290
Double door, 6' x 7'	6,180 to 7,800

Includes door, glass, lock handles, hinges, sill and frame.

Exterior Wall Finish, cost per S.F. of wall

Aluminum sheet baked enamel finish	$4.85 to $7.85
Brick veneer	
Common brick	$9.56 to $12.48
Roman	12.39 to 18.21
Norman	12.39 to 18.21
Glazed	15.09 to 22.68
Carrera glass	
Black	23.92 to 36.93
Red	25.70 to 39.01
Flagstone veneer	
Imitation	16.33 to 20.91
Natural	25.18 to 40.05
Marble	
Plain colors	36.97 to 48.82
With color variations	67.36 to 79.40
Stucco	3.74 to 4.88
Terrazzo	24.56 to 33.71
Tile, ceramic	15.50 to 22.68

Display Platforms,
cost per S.F. of platform area

Framing up to 5' high	$7.43 to $11.53
Hardwood cover	4.48 to 7.31
Plywood cover	2.99 to 4.12

Glass and Window Frames,
per S.F. of glass

Glass only installed	
1/4" float	$8.69 to $12.06
1/4" float, tempered	11.43 to 15.35
1/4" float, colored	8.93 to 15.35
Store front, 1/4" glass in aluminum frame	
Anodized, 8' high	28.80 to 39.40
Anodized, 6' high	34.70 to 46.10
Anodized, 3' high	42.85 to 54.14
Satin bronze, 6' high	40.30 to 52.82
Satin bronze, 3' high	49.20 to 61.60

Satellite Receiver Systems

Satellite receiver systems are common in mountain and rural areas, where TV reception is limited. They are also often installed in residential or commercial areas, for homes, motels or hotels, restaurants and businesses. Installed cost for an all-automatic, motorized system, including wiring to one interior outlet.

Exterior disk plus electronics	$190 to $500

Signs

Lighted Display Signs, Cost per S.F. of sign area

Painted sheet metal with floodlights	$91.10 to $117.30
Porcelain enamel with floodlights	97.10 to 132.60
Plastic with interior lights	110.30 to 172.00
Simple rectangular neon with painted sheet metal faces and a moderate amount of plain letters	116.60 to 210.00
Round or irregular neon with porcelain enamel faces and more elaborate lettering	172.00 to 252.00
Channel letters - individual neon illuminated metal letters with translucent plastic faces, (per upright inch, per letter)	14.60 to 21.90

All of the above sign costs are for double-faced signs. Use 2/3 of those costs for single-faced signs. Sign costs include costs of installation and normal electrical hookup. They do not include the cost of a post. If signs are mounted on separate posts, post mounting costs must be added. These costs are for custom-built signs (one-at-a-time orders). Mass-produced signs will have lower costs.

Post Mounting Costs for Signs

Horizontally Mounted   Vertically Mounted   Cantilever

Post Mounting Costs

Pole Diameter at Base

Post Height	4"	6"	8"	10"	12"	14"
15	$1,330	$1,580	$2,330	$3,140	$4,890	$4,890
20	1,580	1,880	2,690	3,250	5,810	6,535
25	1,700	2,120	2,790	3,880	6,470	7,140
30	1,970	2,535	2,900	4,230	6,830	7,900
35	—	2,760	3,250	4,620	7,750	8,430
40	—	2,920	3,980	4,990	8,040	9,460
45	—	—	4,660	5,677	8,770	9,800
50	—	—	5,000	6,470	9,330	10,720
55	—	—	—	6,830	9,800	11,750
60	—	—	—	7,220	10,500	12,260
65	—	—	—	—	11,260	12,980

If signs are mounted on separate posts, post mounting costs must be added. Post mounting costs include the installed cost of the post and foundation. On horizontally mounted signs, post height is the distance from the ground to the bottom of the sign. On vertically mounted signs, post height is the distance to the top of the post. For cantilevered posts, use one and one-half to two times the conventional post cost.

All of the above post costs are for single posts. Use 90% of the single post costs for each additional post.

Signs

If signs are mounted on buildings or canopies and if, because of the extra weight of the sign, extra heavy support posts or foundations are required, 125% of the post mounting cost should be used.

Sample calculations:

For example, the cost of a 4' x 25' plastic sign mounted on a 15' by 6" post shared by an adjacent canopy might be estimated as follows:

Sign cost 100 S.F. at $100.00	$10,000
Post cost $1,700 x 1/2	850
Total cost	**$10,850**

If this sign were mounted on a 8" post 20' high above the canopy with extra supports not needed, the cost might be estimated as follows:

Sign cost	$10,000
Post cost $2,532 x 1	2,690
Total cost	**$12,690**

Rotators, cost per sign for rotating mount

Small signs	Less than 50 S.F.	$2,707 to $2,919
Medium signs	50 to 100 S.F.	2,858 to 5,797
Large signs	100 to 200 S.F.	5,717 to 10,504
Extra large signs	Over 200 S.F.	$59.50 per S.F. of sign area

Yard Improvements

Bumpers, pre-cast concrete or good quality painted wood.

Typical 4-foot lengths $11.50 to $17.00 per linear foot.

Asphaltic Concrete Paving, cost per square foot

	Under 1,000	1,000 to 2,000	2,000 to 5,000	5,000 to 12,000	12,000 or more
2", no base	$3.80	$1.87	$1.61	$1.41	$1.28
3", no base	4.19	2.39	1.97	1.79	1.69
4", no base	4.60	2.92	2.50	2.39	1.97
2", 4" base	6.47	3.66	3.01	2.79	2.50
3", 6" base	7.08	4.27	3.66	3.40	3.09

Concrete Paving,
small quantities, per S.F.

4" concrete (without wire mesh) no base	$3.25
4" concrete (without wire mesh) 4" base	3.71
5" concrete (with wire mesh) no base	4.13
6" concrete (with wire mesh) no base	4.50
Add for color	.47

Gates, coin or card operated

Single gate, 10' arm	$4,060 to $6,770
Lane spikes, 6' wide	1,630 to 2,040

Striping

Parking spaces		
Single line between spaces	$ 7.84	per space
Double line between spaces	12.30	per space
Pavement line marking, 4"	.44	per LF

Curbs, per linear foot

Asphalt 6" high berm	$7.00 to $8.50
Concrete 6" wide x 12" high	10.70 to 13.70
Concrete 6" wide x 18" high	13.30 to 16.60
Wood bumper rail 6" x 6"	12.50 to 14.30

Lighting

Fluorescent arm-type fixtures

	One arm unit, pole height			Two arm unit, pole height			Add for 3-fixture unit
	12 ft.	**16 ft.**	**30 ft.**	**12 ft.**	**16 ft.**	**30 ft.**	
2 tube, 60"	$1,710	$1,860	—	$2,174	$2,195	—	$867
4 tube, 48"	1,740	2,059	—	2,251	2,620	—	1,013
4 tube, 72"	1,980	2,195	$2,524	2,451	2,640	$3,027	1,167
6 tube, 72"	2,195	2,378	2,711	2,701	2,859	3,475	1,368
4 tube, 96"	2,280	2,461	2,849	2,809	3,027	3,477	1,360
6 tube, 96"	2,364	2,609	3,049	2,862	3,340	3,830	1,462

Mercury vapor

	1-fixture unit, pole height			2-fixture unit, pole height			4-fixture unit, pole height		
	12 ft.	**16 ft.**	**30 ft.**	**12 ft.**	**16 ft.**	**30 ft.**	**12 ft.**	**16 ft.**	**30 ft.**
400 watt	$3,430	$3,565	$4,808	$4,819	$5,168	$6,383	$8,665	$9,545	$10,840
1,000 watt	—	4,474	5,004	—	6,044	7,610	—	—	12,531

Incandescent scoop reflector

	1-fixture unit, pole height			2-fixture unit, pole height			Add for 3-fixture unit
	12 ft.	**16 ft.**	**30 ft.**	**12 ft.**	**16 ft.**	**30 ft.**	
500 watt	$1,026	$1,207	$1,545	$1,356	$1,441	$1,870	$362
1,000 watt	1,280	1,439	1,860	1,722	1,795	2,212	446

Mall and garden lighting

	1-fixture unit, pole height		
	3 ft.*	**5 - 7 ft.**	**10 ft.**
Incandescent 60-200 watt	$881	$1,292	$1,356
Mercury vapor 100-250 watt	1,012	1,661	3,490

*Area lights usually found in service stations.

Chain Link Fences, 9 gauge 2" mesh with top rail line posts 10' on center, per linear foot.

Height	Under 150 LF	150 to 1,000 LF	1,000 to 2,000 LF	Over 2,000 LF	3 strands barbed wire	Add for line posts 8' or less o.c.	Deduct For: No top rail	Deduct For: #11 gauge wire
4'	$16.81	$14.01	$13.28	$12.62	$1.42	$1.92	$2.91	$1.64
5'	17.62	14.63	13.96	13.38	1.42	2.12	2.91	1.71
6'	18.53	15.28	14.63	13.97	1.42	2.32	2.91	1.76
8'	20.12	16.83	16.05	15.20	1.42	2.51	2.91	1.92
10'	23.33	19.31	18.36	17.31	1.42	2.68	2.91	2.23
12'	26.83	22.42	21.22	20.06	1.42	2.91	2.91	2.59

Add for gates, per square foot of frame area $6.12 to $7.83   Add for gate hardware   per walkway gate $31.40 to $39.51
per driveway gate $61.08 to $74.42

Drainage, per linear foot, runs to 50'

6" non-reinforced concrete pipe	$7.39 to $8.59
8" non-reinforced concrete pipe	9.98 to 11.92
10" non-reinforced concrete pipe	11.01 to 20.71
12" non-reinforced concrete pipe	13.84 to 25.76

The cost varies with the depth of the pipe in the ground.

Drainage Items

Size and Type	Cost	
Catch basin 4' x 4' x 4' deep	$2,585	ea.
For each additional foot in depth, add	138	ea.
Drop inlets	609 to 1,050	ea.
Manholes 4' diameter x 6' deep	1,884	ea.
For each additional foot in depth, add	174	per ft.

Wood Fences, per linear foot

4' high Redwood board	$17.50
6' high Redwood board	22.40
4' basketweave	23.10
6' basketweave	24.00
4' board and batt	12.50
6' board and batt	16.20
3' split rail	6.59
4' split rail	7.88
3' two rail Redwood picket	10.20
5' three rail Redwood picket	12.40
Typical 3' wide gate, 4' to 6' high	118.00

Agricultural Structures Section

Section Contents

General Purpose Barns

Quality Classification

General Purpose Barn, Class 1

General Purpose Barn, Class 3

Component	Class 1 Good Quality	Class 2 Average Quality	Class 3 Low Quality
Foundation (20% of total cost)	Continuous concrete.	Concrete or masonry piers.	Redwood or cedar mudsills.
Floor (5% of total cost)	Concrete.	Dirt, leveled & compacted.	Dirt, leveled & compacted.
Wall Structure (25% of total cost)	Good wood frame, 10' eave height.	Average wood frame, 10' eave height.	Light wood frame, 10' eave height.
Exterior Wall Cover (25% of total cost)	Good wood siding, painted.	Standard gauge corrugated iron, aluminum or average wood siding.	Light aluminum or low cost boards.
Roof Construction (9% of total cost)	Medium to high pitch, good wood trusses.	Medium to high pitch, average wood trusses.	Medium to high pitch, 2" x 4" rafters 24" to 36" o.c. or light wood trusses.
Roof Cover (5% of total cost)	Wood shingles.	Standard gauge corrugated iron or aluminum.	Light aluminum.
Electrical (8% of total cost)	Four outlets per 1,000 S.F.	Two outlets per 1,000 S.F.	None.
Plumbing (3% of total cost)	Two cold water outlets.	One cold water outlet.	None.

Note: Use the percent of total cost to help identify the correct quality classification.

Square Foot Area

Quality Class	1,000	2,000	3,000	4,000	5,000	6,000	7,000	8,000	9,000	10,000	11,000
1, Good	35.25	32.47	30.07	28.87	27.68	26.47	25.61	25.03	24.54	24.05	23.64
2, Average	26.16	23.60	21.87	21.01	20.18	19.46	18.90	18.54	18.22	17.94	17.64
3, Low	17.06	14.73	13.67	13.09	12.70	12.45	12.20	12.05	11.87	11.78	11.65

Hay Storage Barns

Quality Classification

Hay Storage Barn, Class 2
Length between one and two times width

Component	Class 1 Good Quality	Class 2 Average Quality	Class 3 Low Quality
Foundation (25% of total cost)	Continuous concrete.	Concrete or masonry piers.	Redwood or cedar mudsills.
Floor (5% of total cost)	Concrete.	Dirt, leveled & compacted.	Dirt, leveled & compacted.
Wall Structure (25% of total cost)	Good wood frame, 20' eave height.	Average wood frame, 20' eave height.	Light wood frame, 20' eave height.
Exterior Wall Cover (30% of total cost)	Good wood siding, painted.	Standard gauge corrugated iron or aluminum.	Light aluminum or low cost boards.
Roof Construction (10% of total cost)	Low to medium pitch, good wood trusses.	Low to medium pitch, average wood trusses.	Low to medium pitch, 2" x 4" rafters 24" to 36" o.c. or light wood trusses.
Roof Cover (5% of total cost)	Wood shingles.	Standard gauge corrugated iron or aluminum.	Light aluminum.
Electrical	None.	None.	None.
Plumbing	None.	None.	None.

Note: Use the percent of total cost to help identify the correct quality classification.

Square Foot Area

Quality Class	1,000	2,000	3,000	4,000	5,000	6,000	7,000	8,000	9,000	10,000	11,000
1, Good	27.37	24.64	22.81	21.38	20.50	19.75	19.24	18.76	18.37	18.01	17.62
2, Average	16.81	15.05	13.94	13.18	12.69	12.24	11.81	11.43	11.18	10.95	10.81
3, Low	14.62	13.12	12.24	11.60	11.06	10.64	10.30	10.06	9.88	9.58	9.37

Feed Barns

Quality Classification

Feed Barn, Class 2

Component	Class 1 Good Quality	Class 2 Average Quality	Class 3 Low Quality
Foundation (20% of total cost)	Continuous concrete.	Concrete or masonry piers.	Redwood or cedar mudsills.
Floor (5% of total cost)	Concrete in center section.	Concrete in center section.	Dirt.
Wall Structure (25% of total cost)	Good wood frame, 8' eave height at drip line.	Average wood frame, 8' eave height at drip line.	Light wood frame, 8' eave eight at drip line.
Exterior Wall Cover (25% of total cost)	Open sides, good siding painted on ends.	Open sides, standard gauge corrugated iron, aluminum or average wood siding on ends.	Open sides and ends.
Roof Construction (9% of total cost)	Medium to low pitch, good wood trusses.	Medium to low pitch, average wood trusses.	Medium to low pitch, 2" x 4" rafters 24" to 36" o.c. or light wood trusses.
Roof Cover (5% of total cost)	Wood shingles.	Standard gauge corrugated iron or aluminum.	Light gauge corrugated iron or aluminum.
Electrical (7% of total cost)	Four outlets per 1,000 S.F.	Two outlets per 1,000 S.F.	None.
Plumbing (4% of total cost)	Two cold water outlets.	One cold water outlet.	None.

Note: Use the percent of total cost to help identify the correct quality classification.

Square Foot Area

Quality Class	1,000	2,000	3,000	4,000	5,000	6,000	7,000	8,000	9,000	10,000	11,000
1, Good	17.18	16.24	15.81	15.56	15.37	15.24	15.12	15.06	15.00	14.96	14.94
2, Average	14.81	14.06	13.62	13.32	13.12	13.00	12.94	12.88	12.81	12.78	12.75
3, Low	9.37	8.94	8.64	8.37	8.24	8.18	8.13	8.09	8.06	8.03	8.00

Shop Buildings

Quality Classification

Shop, Class 2
Length between one and two times width

Component	Class 1 Good Quality	Class 2 Average Quality	Class 3 Low Quality
Foundation (20% of total cost)	Continuous concrete.	Light concrete.	Light concrete.
Floor (5% of total cost)	Concrete.	Concrete.	Concrete.
Wall Structure (20% of total cost)	Good wood frame, 15' eave height.	Average wood frame, 15' eave height.	Light wood frame, 15' eave height.
Exterior Wall Cover (25% of total cost)	Good wood siding, painted.	Standard gauge corrugated iron, aluminum or average wood siding.	Light aluminum or low cost boards.
Roof Construction (5% of total cost)	Low to medium pitch, good wood trusses.	Low to medium pitch, average wood trusses.	Low to medium pitch, 2" x 4" rafters 24" to 36" o.c. or light wood trusses.
Roof Cover (5% of total cost)	Wood shingles.	Standard gauge corrugated iron or aluminum.	Light gauge corrugated iron or aluminum.
Electrical (5% of total cost)	Four outlets per 1,000 S.F.	Two outlets per 1,000 S.F.	Two outlets per 1,000 S.F.
Plumbing (7% of total cost)	Two cold water outlets.	One cold water outlet.	None.
Doors (5% of total cost)	One drive-thru door per 1,000 S.F. plus one walk-thru door.	One average sliding or swinging door per 2,000 S.F.	One light sliding or swinging door per 2,000 S.F.
Windows (3% of total cost)	Five percent of floor area.	None or few low cost.	None.

Note: Use the percent of total cost to help identify the correct quality classification.

Square Foot Area

Quality Class	1,000	1,500	2,000	2,500	3,000	4,000	5,000	6,000	8,000	10,000
1, Good	28.96	28.96	27.42	26.24	25.09	24.33	23.55	22.79	22.01	21.17
2, Average	25.09	23.17	21.62	20.85	20.08	19.17	18.40	18.03	17.63	17.24
3, Low	20.07	18.39	17.24	16.34	15.58	15.23	14.80	14.04	14.03	13.65

Machinery and Equipment Sheds

Quality Classification

Equipment Shed, Class 3
Usually elongated, width between 15 and 30 feet, any length

Component	Class 1 Good Quality	Class 2 Average Quality	Class 3 Low Quality
Foundation (22% of total cost)	Continuous concrete.	Concrete or masonry piers.	Redwood or cedar mudsills.
Floor (5% of total cost)	Concrete.	Concrete.	Dirt, leveled & compacted
Wall Structure (25% of total cost)	Good wood frame, 10' eave height.	Average wood frame, 10' eave height.	Light wood frame, 10' eave height.
Exterior Wall Cover (30% of total cost)	Good wood siding, painted.	Standard gauge corrugated iron, aluminum or average wood siding.	Light aluminum or low cost boards.
Roof Construction (10% of total cost)	Low to medium pitch, gable or shed type, good wood framing.	Low to medium pitch, gable or shed type, average wood framing.	Low to medium pitch, shed type, light wood framing.
Roof Cover (5% of total cost)	Wood shingles.	Standard gauge corrugated iron or aluminum.	Light aluminum.
Electrical (3% of total cost)	Four outlets per 1,000 S.F.	Two outlets per 1,000 S.F.	None.

Note: Use the percent of total cost to help identify the correct quality classification.

All Sides Closed - Square Foot Area

Quality Class	500	1,000	1,500	2,000	2,500	3,000	3,500	4,000	4,500	5,000	6,000
1, Good	23.83	21.50	20.00	19.62	19.17	19.18	18.96	18.73	18.57	18.44	18.20
2, Average	18.38	16.05	15.27	14.95	14.60	14.60	14.24	14.13	14.06	13.98	13.85
3, Low	12.54	11.24	10.47	10.10	10.27	10.25	9.79	9.70	9.58	9.47	9.35

One Side Open - Square Foot Area

Quality Class	500	1,000	1,500	2,000	2,500	3,000	3,500	4,000	4,500	5,000	6,000
1 Good	19.47	18.34	17.69	16.95	16.48	16.27	16.14	15.96	15.90	15.81	15.75
2, Average	16.83	14.43	13.33	12.94	12.56	12.45	12.24	12.17	12.10	11.98	11.88
3, Low	11.00	9.24	8.69	8.38	8.24	8.14	8.06	7.98	7.91	7.84	7.78

Small Sheds

Quality Classification

Usually elongated, width between 6 and 12 feet, any length

Component	Class 1 Good Quality	Class 2 Average Quality	Class 3 Low Quality
Foundation (25% of total cost)	Continuous concrete.	Concrete or masonry piers.	Redwood or cedar mudsills.
Floor (5% of total cost)	Concrete.	Boards.	Dirt, leveled & compacted.
Wall Structure (25% of total cost)	Good wood frame, 8' eave height.	Average wood frame, 8' eave height.	Light wood frame, 8' eave height.
Exterior Wall Cover (30% of total cost)	Good wood siding, painted.	Standard gauge corrugated iron, aluminum or average wood siding.	Light aluminum or low cost boards.
Roof Construction (10% of total cost)	Low to medium pitch, gable or shed type, good wood framing.	Low to medium pitch, gable or shed type, average wood framing.	Low to medium pitch, shed type, light wood framing.
Roof Cover (5% of total cost)	Wood shingles.	Standard gauge corrugated iron or aluminum.	Light aluminum.
Electrical	None.	None.	None.

Note: Use the percent of total cost to help identify the correct quality classification.

All Sides Closed - Square Foot Area

Quality Class	50	60	80	100	120	150	200	250	300	400	500
1, Good	30.62	27.49	26.24	24.59	22.88	21.15	19.89	19.12	18.20	17.81	17.37
2, Average	24.96	22.43	20.32	18.71	17.79	16.95	16.18	15.32	14.40	14.00	13.58
3, Low	17.79	16.09	14.39	12.29	11.81	11.04	10.62	10.19	10.84	9.34	8.88

One Side Open - Square Foot Area

Quality Class	50	60	80	100	120	150	200	250	300	400	500
1, Good	23.43	21.04	20.32	19.06	17.79	16.95	16.24	15.17	14.42	13.59	13.18
2, Average	18.73	17.37	16.09	15.17	14.42	13.58	12.68	11.81	11.37	11.05	10.90
3, Low	12.65	11.81	11.05	10.19	9.28	8.88	8.24	7.75	7.38	6.90	6.75

Pole Barns

These prices are for pole barns with a low pitch corrugated iron or aluminum covered roof supported by light wood trusses and poles 15' to 20' o.c. The gable end is enclosed and the roof overhangs about 2' on two sides. Wall height is 18 feet. Where sides are enclosed, the wall consists of a light wood frame covered with corrugated metal.

All Sides Open - Side Length

End Width	34	51	68	85	102	119	136	153	170	187
20	9.03	8.69	8.52	8.46	8.39	8.30	8.28	8.28	8.27	8.26
25	8.48	8.15	8.00	7.92	7.89	7.81	7.78	7.77	7.76	7.75
30	8.10	7.77	7.67	7.56	7.53	7.48	7.47	7.44	7.44	7.44
35	7.78	7.53	7.41	7.30	7.26	7.20	7.19	7.18	7.16	7.16
40	7.69	7.41	7.26	7.16	7.14	7.11	7.09	7.02	7.02	7.00
45	7.54	7.26	7.14	7.02	6.98	6.95	6.93	6.91	6.89	6.89
50	7.37	7.10	6.93	6.88	6.81	6.80	6.77	6.76	6.76	6.74
60	7.34	7.04	6.89	6.81	6.78	6.76	6.74	6.73	6.70	6.70
70	7.26	6.95	6.85	6.78	6.74	6.70	6.69	6.67	6.66	6.66
80	7.20	6.93	6.80	6.74	6.69	6.67	6.62	6.62	6.59	6.56

Ends and One Side Closed, One Side Open - Side Length

End Width	34	51	68	85	102	119	136	153	170	187
20	16.29	14.35	13.38	12.85	12.54	12.30	12.11	11.93	11.83	11.77
25	14.90	13.14	12.30	11.77	11.42	11.21	11.10	10.95	10.83	10.73
30	13.99	12.32	11.50	11.08	10.71	10.53	10.40	10.27	10.16	10.09
35	13.26	11.72	10.95	10.49	10.20	10.00	9.88	9.80	9.66	9.59
40	12.78	11.30	10.55	10.11	9.88	9.63	9.50	9.41	9.30	9.25
45	12.45	10.99	10.22	9.86	9.52	9.39	9.23	9.15	9.04	8.99
50	12.11	10.62	9.95	9.52	9.26	9.09	8.99	8.86	8.77	8.73
60	11.77	10.33	9.68	9.26	9.04	8.86	8.73	8.61	8.55	8.49
70	11.50	10.11	9.43	9.07	8.86	8.68	8.51	8.45	8.38	8.28
80	11.24	9.82	9.23	8.89	8.60	8.46	8.32	8.26	8.17	8.10

All Sides Closed - Side Length

End Width	34	51	68	85	102	119	136	153	170	187
20	19.52	17.55	16.56	15.96	15.58	15.29	15.11	14.95	14.84	14.72
25	17.45	15.68	14.77	14.27	13.89	13.66	13.47	13.30	13.22	13.14
30	15.97	14.36	13.58	13.07	12.77	12.55	12.40	12.29	12.16	12.09
35	15.04	13.52	12.73	12.31	11.97	11.75	11.60	11.52	11.40	11.33
40	14.27	12.86	12.12	11.69	11.40	11.21	11.08	10.95	10.83	10.74
45	13.70	12.31	11.59	11.20	10.95	10.71	10.58	10.48	10.41	10.30
50	13.15	11.83	11.17	10.73	10.48	10.31	10.19	10.07	9.98	9.92
60	12.57	11.28	10.62	10.28	10.02	9.86	9.73	9.61	9.52	9.46
70	12.19	10.95	10.32	9.98	9.70	9.52	9.41	9.29	9.23	9.18
80	11.75	10.53	9.98	9.61	9.32	9.20	9.09	8.99	8.93	8.87

Side sheds tying into one side of a pole barn are priced as follows. The shed consists of one row of poles 14' to 16' high, spaced 15' to 20' o.c. A light wood truss covered with a low pitch sheet metal roof spans the distance between the poles and the barn side. If the sides are open, the cost will be between $7.86 and $10.50 per square foot of area covered. If all sides are enclosed with sheet metal and a light wood frame, the square foot cost will be $12.58 to $16.49.

Low Cost Dairy Barns

1" x 4" or 1" x 6" spaced sheathing

2" x 4" rafters 16" o.c.

Concrete block 6" x 8" x 16" exterior walls

2" x 6" rafter 30" o.c.

Concrete foundation and partial wall

Breezeway

Milk house

Hay storage (dirt floor)

4" x 6" 10'0" o.c.

Concrete footing & 4" thick slab

Wood manger

Wood stanchions

Cow stand (6" concrete)

	Milk House	**Dairy Barn**
Foundation (20% of total cost)	Concrete.	Light concrete.
Floors (15% of total cost)	Concrete slab.	Concrete cow stands.
Walls (30% of total cost)	6" or 8" concrete block 36" high 2" x 4" @16" o.c. framing above.	Box frame, 4" x 6", 10' o.c.
Roof (15% of total cost)	Average wood frame, corrugated iron or aluminum cover.	Average wood frame, wood shingles, corrugated iron or aluminum cover.
Windows (5% of total cost)	Metal sash or metal louvers, on 5% of wall area.	Barn sash.
Interior (10% of total cost)	Smooth finish plaster.	Unfinished, wood stanchions.
Electrical (3% of total cost)	Minimum grade, fair fixtures.	None.
Plumbing (2% of total cost)	One wash basin.	None.
Square Foot Cost	$42.91 to $52.98 (including breezeway).	$19.79 to $23.73 (exclusive of milking equipment).

Component parts of this dairy:
A Milking barn
B Feed room
C Milk, wash and equipment room

Cow stand

Cow alley

Wash room

A

B

2" x 6" studs 16" o.c.

Double 2" x 4" plate

Exterior plaster

Ramp concrete

36" high concrete or 6" concrete block

Feed alley

4" concrete slab

C

Milk room

Equipment or machine room

	Feed Room	Milk, Wash and Equipment Room	Milking Barn
Foundation (20% of total cost)	Reinforced concrete.	Reinforced concrete.	Reinforced concrete.
Floors (15% of total cost)	Concrete slab.	Concrete slab.	Concrete, well formed gutters and mangers.
Walls (30% of total cost)	2" x 4" or 2" x 6" @16" o.c. framing.	6" or 8" concrete block 36" high with 2" x 6" @16" o.c. framing above.	6" or 8" concrete block or reinforced concrete 36" high with 2" x 6" @ 16" o.c. framing above.
Roofs (15% of total cost)	Average wood frame, corrugated iron or aluminum cover.	Average wood frame, corrugated iron or aluminum cover.	Average wood frame, iron or aluminum cover.
Windows (5% of total cost)	None.	Metal sash or metal louvers on 10% of wall area.	Metal sash or metal louvers.
Interior (5% of total cost)	Unfinished.	Smooth finish plaster, cove base.	Smooth plaster 36" high, metal stanchions.
Electrical (4% of total cost)	Conduit, average fixtures.	Conduit, average fixtures.	Conduit, average fixtures.
Plumbing (6% of total cost)	None.	One wash basin with floor drains.	Floor drains and hose bibs.
Square Foot Costs	$19.19 to $31.58.	$46.43 to $56.18 (including breezeway).	$34.31 to $39.30 (exclusive of milking equipment).

Walk-Through Dairy Barns

A Milking barn
Milking barn
Wash room
Cow alley
Ramp
36" high concrete or 6" concrete block
Exit alley
Cow stand
4" concrete slab
Equipment or machine room
Milk room
B

Component parts of this dairy:
A Milking barn
B Milk, wash and equipment room

	Milking Barn	Milk, Wash, and Equipment Room
Foundation (20% of total cost)	Reinforced concrete.	Reinforced concrete.
Floors (15% of total cost)	Concrete, well-formed gutters and mangers.	Concrete slab
Walls (30% of total cost)	6" or 8" concrete block or reinforced concrete 36" high with 2" x 6" @16" o.c. framing above or all concrete block.	6" or 8" concrete block 36" high with 2" x 6" @16" o.c. framing above, or all concrete block.
Roofs (15% of total cost)	Average wood frame, corrugated iron or aluminum cover.	Average wood frame, corrugated iron or aluminum cover.
Windows (5% of total cost)	Metal sash or metal louvers.	Metal sash or metal louvers on 10% of wall area.
Interior (5% of total cost)	Smooth plaster 36" high, metal stanchions.	Smooth finish plaster, cove base.
Electrical (4% of total cost)	Conduit, average fixtures.	Conduit, average fixtures.
Plumbing (6% of total cost)	Floor drains and hose bibs.	One wash basin, floor drains.
Square Foot Costs	$37.88 to $41.18 (exclusive of milking equipment).	$39.40 to $42.36 (including breezeway).

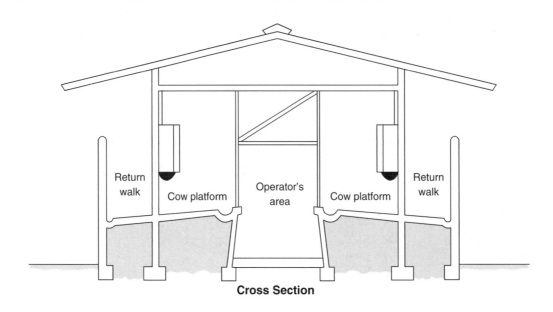

Cross Section

Milking Barn

Foundation (15% of total cost)	6" Reinforced concrete.
Floors (15% of total cost)	Concrete, well-formed gutters and mangers.
Walls (30% of total cost)	6" or 8" concrete block or reinforced concrete 60" high with 2" x 6" @16" o.c. framing above or all concrete block.
Roof (15% of total cost)	Average wood frame, corrugated iron or steel beams. steel roofing, skylights.
Windows (5% of total cost)	Metal sash or metal louvers.
Interior (5% of total cost)	Smooth plaster on entire block walls or tile and plaster.
Electrical (4% of total cost)	Conduit, average fixtures. Not major supply for milking equipment.
Plumbing (6% of total cost)	Floor drains and hose bibs.
Stanchions (5% of total cost)	Metal stanchions.
Cost per SF $46.40	Excluding stalls, gates, feeding system and milking equipment.
Feed Systems & Stalls	Per double ten barn, $53,450

Milk, Wash, and Equipment Room

	Average Quality	Good Quality
Foundation (20% of total cost)	Reinforced concrete.	Reinforced concrete.
Floors (15% of total cost)	Concrete slab.	Reinforced concrete slab.
Walls (25% of total cost)	8" concrete block with 2" x 6", 16" o.c. framing above or all concrete block.	8" concrete block with 2" x 6" @16" o.c. framing above or all concrete block.
Exterior (10% of total cost)	Stucco or concrete block.	Stucco and masonry veneer.
Roof (10% of total cost)	Wood frame, corrugated iron or aluminum.	Wood frame, or steel beams, steel roofing or tile, skylights, and gutters.
Windows (5% of total cost)	Metal sash on 10% of wall area.	Tile floors and walls in many areas.
Interior (5% of total cost)	Smooth finish plaster, cove base.	Smooth finish plaster, cove base.
Electrical (4% of total cost)	Conduit, average fixtures.	Conduit, better lighting and ample outlets.
Plumbing (6% of total cost)	One wash basin, one water closet, one lavatory, floor drains.	One wash basin, one water closet, ¾ bath, vinyl floors, floor drains.
Square Foot Costs	$59.61 to $66.67	$66.67 to $74.61

Note: Use the percent of total cost to help identify the correct quality classification.

Miscellaneous Dairy Costs

Holding Corral and Wash Area Costs

Components	Cost
Floor or Ramp	Sloping concrete with abrasive finish, $4.35 to $4.84 per square foot.
Wall	5' to 6' high plastered interior, $43.66 to $61.21 per linear foot.
Metal rail fence	Welded pipe, posts 10' o.c. in concrete, top rail and 3 cables, $13.36 to $15.82 per linear foot.
Cable fence	Pipe posts 10' o.c. set in concrete, $10.92 + $.76 per linear foot per cable.
Gates	54" high, pipe with necessary bracing, $184 to $220 ea.
Sprinklers	Hooded rainbird, $184 to $232 each, including plumbing and pump.
Roof	Pipe column supports, average wood frame, corrugated iron or aluminum cover, open sides, $6.25 to $8.70 per square foot.
Typical wash area (without sprinkler)	Sloped concrete floors, 5' concrete block exterior walls, welded pipe interior fences and gates, usual floor drains $29.38/S.F. with roof, $20.50/S.F. without roof.

Milk Line, 3" stainless steel

40-cow conventional barn	$26,560 total $664 per cow
Double ten herringbone barn	$16,050 total $803 per cow
Dual milk pump, add	$2,726
Incline filter, add	$2,995
Incline cold plate, add	$6,690 to $9,749

Refrigeration Compressors

7-1/2 HP	$7,878
10 HP	10,373
15 HP	13,069

Corral Costs

Components	Cost
4" concrete flatwork	$4.20 to 6.32 per square foot.
6" concrete flatwork	$4.43 to 6.64 per square foot.
8" curb	$10.50 per linear foot.
Cable fence	$9.45 per linear foot.
Water tank, concrete typical	$630.24 each.
Steel stanchions	$63.80 each. $28.32 to $30.40 per linear foot.
Steel lockable stanchions	$60.70 to $65.41 each. $32.30 to $35.54 per linear foot.
Light standards	$2,960 each.
Sump pumps, each 3 HP	$3,322
4 HP	$4,262
10 HP	$7,140
Hay shelters	$6.58 to $7.90 per square foot.
Loafing sheds	$6.12 to $7.76 per square foot.
Typical 80-cow corral	$36,774 to $42,026 total. $459 to $525 per cow.

Refrigerated Holding Tanks

1,530 gallon	$37,720
2,040 gallon	42,610
2,550 gallon	45,730
3,060 gallon	49,540
3,570 gallon	55,750
4,080 gallon	58,140
5,100 gallon	61,720

Vacuum Pumps (air pumps)

Units	Cost
8	$5,250
12	8,830
20	14,500

Poultry Houses

Conventional Lay Cage Type

 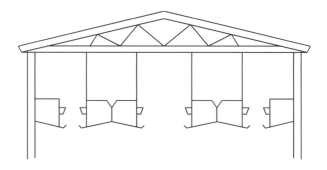

Basic Building

Component	Good Quality	Average Quality	Low Quality
Floors (20% of total cost)	2" concrete.	Dirt with 4' concrete walkways.	Dirt, leveled and compacted.
Foundations (15% of total cost)	Thickened slab.	Concrete piers.	Wood piers.
Frame (20% of total cost)	Light steel or average wood frame.	Average wood frame.	Light wood frame.
Roof Cover (5% of total cost)	Aluminum or corrugated iron.	Light aluminum or composition.	Light aluminum or composition.
Exterior (8% of total cost)	Plywood.	Vinyl curtains.	Wood lath.
Lighting (20% of total cost)	Good system, automatic controls.	Average system, automatic controls.	Minimum system, manual controls.
Plumbing (10% of total cost)	Good system.	Average system.	Fair system.
Insulation (2% of total cost)	Roof only.	None.	None.
Basic Building Cost Per S.F.	$13.99 to $16.92	$9.35 to $12.50	$8.04 to $9.39

Note: Use the percent of total cost to help identify the correct quality classification.

Equipment

Component	Best Quality	Good Quality	Average Quality	Low Quality
Cages (35% of total cost)	12" x 20" double deck.	12" x 20" single deck.	12" x 20" single deck.	12" x 12" single deck.
Water System (20% of total cost)	Automatic cup system.	Automatic cup system.	Simple "V" trough.	Simple "V" trough.
Feed System (30% of total cost)	Automatic system.	V trough.	V trough.	V trough.
Egg Gathering	Manual.	Manual.	Manual.	Manual.
Cooling (15% of total cost)	Pad and fan system.	Pad and fan system.	Simple fogging system.	Simple fogging system.
Cost Per S.F.	$23.50 to $24.74	$14.35 to $17.02	$10.29 to $13.31	$8.75 to $12.17

Note: Use the percent of total cost to help identify the correct quality classification.

Modern Controlled Environment Type

Basic Building

Foundation (20% of total cost)	Concrete.
Floor (15% of total cost)	3-1/2 concrete slab.
Wall Frame (20% of total cost)	2" x 4" @ 24" o.c.
Roof & Cover (10% of total cost)	Wood trusses with 2" x 4" purlins @24" o.c., corrugated iron or aluminum cover
Exterior (18% of total cost)	Two rib aluminum or corrugated iron.
Interior (7% of total cost)	4" fiberglass roll with aluminum foil facing or 3/4" insulation.
Lighting (5% of total cost)	Fluorescent or good automatic incandescent system.
Plumbing (5% of total cost)	Good basic system.
Basic Building Cost Per S.F.	$28.31 to $31.38

	Equipment	
Component	**Single Deck**	**Stair Step**
Cages (45% of total cost)	12" x 20" single deck.	12" x 20" double deck.
Watering System (30% of total cost)	Automatic cup system.	Automatic cup system.
Feeding System	Manual.	Manual.
Egg Gathering System	Manual.	Manual.
Cooling (25% of total cost)	Evaporative coolers.	Evaporative coolers.
Heating	None.	None.
Building & Equipment Square Foot Cost	$36.82 to $41.27	$39.88 to $44.79

Single-deck cage system

Double-deck cage system

Poultry Houses

High Rise Type

Basic Building

Foundation (25% of total cost)	Concrete piers.
Floors (5% of total cost)	Dirt, leveled and compacted.
Wall Frame (20% of total cost)	2" x 4" @24" o.c.
Roof & Cover (15% of total cost)	Wood trusses with 2" x 4" purlins @24" o.c., corrugated iron or aluminum cover.
Exterior (18% of total cost)	Two rib aluminum or corrugated iron.
Interior (7% of total cost)	3/4" insulation.
Lighting (5% of total cost)	Fluorescent or good automatic incandescent system.
Plumbing (5% of total cost)	Good basic system.
Basic Building Cost Per S.F.	$53.24 to $59.09

Component	Equipment Flat Deck	Stair Step
Cages (33% of total cost)	12" x 20".	12" x 20".
Watering System (20% of total cost)	Automatic cup system.	Automatic cup system.
Feeding (25% of total cost)	Automatic system.	Automatic system.
Egg Gathering (15% of total cost)	Automatic system.	Automatic system.
Cooling (7% of total cost)	Negative pressure system.	Negative pressure system.
Heating	None.	None.
Building & Equipment Square Foot Cost	$68.39 to $76.60	$72.75 to $82.15

Flat-deck cage system

Poultry Houses

Deep Pit Type

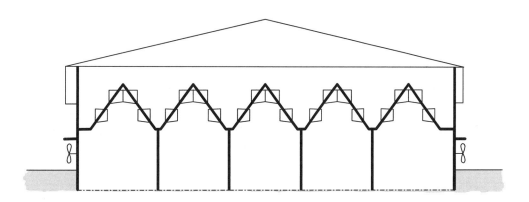

Basic Building

Foundation (25% of total cost)	Concrete piers.
Floors (15% of total cost)	Concrete with waterproof membrane.
Wall Frame (15% of total cost)	2" x 4" @24" o.c.
Roof & Cover (15% of total cost)	Wood trusses with 2" x 4" purlins @24" o.c., corrugated iron aluminum cover.
Exterior (15% of total cost)	Two rib aluminum or corrugated iron.
Interior (5% of total cost)	3/4" insulation.
Lighting (5% of total cost)	Fluorescent or good incandescent.
Plumbing (5% of total cost)	Good basic system.
Basic Building Cost Per S.F.	$31.47 to $34.98

Equipment

Component	Flat Deck	Stair Step
Cages (33% of total cost)	12" x 20".	12" x 20".
Watering (20% of total cost)	Automatic cup system.	Automatic cup system.
Feeding (25% of total cost)	Automatic system.	Automatic system.
Egg Gathering (15% of total cost)	Automatic system.	Automatic system.
Cooling (7% of total cost)	Negative pressure system.	Negative pressure system.
Heating	None.	None.
Building & Equipment Square Foot Cost	$40.17 to $43.55	$41.96 to $45.35

Poultry Houses

Equipment Costs

Add these costs to the basic building cost

Component	Serving One Row of Cages	Serving Two Rows of Cages
Automatic feeders	$2.22 per bird	$1.27 per bird
Automatic egg gathering	1.71 per bird	.95 per bird
Automatic water cup system	1.66 per bird	.80 per bird
	5.30 per cup	3.40 per cup
"V" water trough	.43 per bird	.31 per bird
16" feed trough	.51 per bird	.33 per bird

Foggers

1/2" galvanized pipe	$2.40/linear foot
3/4" galvanized pipe	2.52/linear foot
1" galvanized pipe	2.61/linear foot

Roof sprinklers

$2.71 per linear foot

Evaporative coolers

$786 each. $1.99 per S.F. of building

Fans

36"	$403 each
48"	525 each
50"	585 each

Negative pressure air conditioning system

$1.61 to $2.07 per S.F. of building.

Cooling pads in walls

$.95 per S.F. of surface.

Heating systems

$2,244 per unit.

Cages, 12" x 20" or 18"

$8.26 each. $2.14 per bird.

Greenhouses

Greenhouse, Class 3

Greenhouse, Class 1

Quality Classification

Component	Class 1 High Quality	Class 2 Average Quality	Class 3 Low Quality
Wall and roof	Heavy steel frame, 8' wall, glass or multi-wall polycarbonate cover.	Galvanized steel frame, 8' wall, double polycarbonate or fiberglass cover.	Light pipe, 4' wall, single light polyethylene cover, fiberglass ends.
Floor	Finished concrete walks, concrete foundation.	Gravel, some plain concrete walks.	Dirt, some gravel.
Interior	Good lighting, running water, roof vents, and exhaust fans.	Average lighting, water, and roof vents.	Light wood frame, 10' eave height.

Note: Use the percent of total cost to help identify the correct quality classification.

Square Foot Area

Quality Class	5,000	7,500	10,000	15,000	20,000	25,000	30,000	35,000	40,000	45,000	50,000
High	25.87	24.96	24.12	22.60	21.20	20.43	19.86	19.29	18.73	18.39	18.30
Average	19.44	18.85	18.22	16.57	15.47	14.98	14.62	14.19	14.05	13.76	13.56
Low	4.45	4.21	3.99	3.90	3.85	3.79	3.72	3.46	3.23	3.09	2.97

Migrant Worker Housing

Quality Classification

	Class 1 Best Quality	Class 2 Prefabricated	Class 3 Good Quality	Class 4 Average Quality	Class 5 Low Quality
Slab Foundation (15% of total cost)	Spread footing around perimeter and thickened slab at partitions.	Spread footing around perimeter.	Thickened around perimeter.	Thickened around perimeter.	Thickened around perimeter.
Floor (10% of total cost)	4" concrete slab reinforced.	4" concrete slab reinforced.	4" concrete slab.	4" concrete slab.	4" concrete slab.
Walls (20% of total cost)	Masonry exterior walls, wood frame interior partitions and ceiling.	Metal building, prefabricated.	2" x 4" studs @16" o.c., 2" x 4" stud partitions.	Box construction 4" x 4" at 48" o.c.	Box construction 2" x 4" at 48" o.c.
Exterior Cover (15% of total cost)	Natural blocks.	Prefabricated metal building.	Average grade redwood board and batt or horizontal siding or stucco finish.	Fair grade redwood or fir board and batt or horizontal board.	Poor grade of redwood or fir, vertical or horizontal.
Interior Finish (15% of total cost)	Gypsum wallboard.	None.	Gypsum wallboard.	Plywood partitions.	None.
Roof Framing (10% of total cost)	Rafters, collar beams and ceiling joists.	Prefabricated metal building.	Rafters, collar beams and ceiling joists.	Very simple truss.	Rafters and tie at plate line.
Roofing (5% of total cost)	Composition shingles.	Metal.	Aluminum or wood.	Composition or sheet metal.	Composition or used sheet metal.
Doors (3% of total cost)	1 metal door and metal frame each room.	Metal doors.	1 average door each room.	3 or 4 average doors.	2 or 3 cheap doors.
Windows (2% of total cost)	1 steel sash or aluminum window in each room.	Approximately 20% of floor area.	1 steel or aluminum window in each room.	1 window each room.	Few and small.
Electrical (5% of total cost)	1 good light and plug in each room.	1 light, 1 plug for each 300 S.F.	1 light, 1 plug in each room.	1 pull chain light and plug for each 400 S.F.	1 pull chain light for each 500 S.F.

Note: Use the percent of total cost to help identify the correct quality classification.

Migrant Worker Housing, Class 1

Migrant Worker Housing, Class 4

Square Foot Area

Quality Class	400	600	800	1,000	1,200	1,500	2,000	2,500	3,000
1, Best	56.87	52.52	50.16	48.71	47.62	46.54	45.37	44.63	44.06
2, Prefabricated	52.11	48.14	46.00	44.62	43.67	42.63	41.59	40.88	40.36
3, Good	48.64	44.91	42.90	41.66	40.76	39.82	38.83	38.16	37.75
4, Average	40.95	37.83	36.12	35.10	34.34	33.56	32.71	32.10	31.74
5, Low	33.73	31.12	29.77	28.86	28.20	27.61	26.94	26.45	26.14

Costs do not include any plumbing. Add $765 to $915 per fixture.

Miscellaneous Agricultural Structures

Livestock Scales

Type	Size	Capacity	In-Place
Full-capacity beam	16' x 8'	5 ton	$12,470
Printing beam	16' x 8'	5 ton	15,600
Full-capacity beam	22' x 8'	10 ton	16,500
Printing beam	22' x 8'	10 ton	19,950

Additional Costs for Livestock Scales

Types and Size	Cost
Each foot arm is removed from scale	$150/L.F.
Angle iron stock rack for 16' x 8' scale	4,080 ea.
Angle iron stock rack (wood) for 16' x 8'	606 ea.
Angle iron stock rack for 22' x 8' scale	7,110 ea.

Scale pit has 4" concrete walls and slab poured in place. May be poured in or on top of the ground. If on top, compacted ramps and steps to the scale beam are included.

Motor Truck Scales

Five inch reinforced concrete platform. All-steel structure and scale mechanism. Reinforced concrete pit. Motor truck scales are of two general types, the beam type (either manual or type registering) and the full-automated dial type. The construction of both, insofar as the weight-carrying mechanism is concerned is very similar. The method of recording and weight capacity make the cost vary.

Capacity	Platform Size	Total Cost
20 tons	24' x 10'	$25,600
30 tons	34' x 10'	32,370
40 tons	40' x 10'	35,600
50 tons	45' x 10'	40,550
50 tons	50' x 10'	42,300
50 tons	60' x 10'	48,400
50 tons	70' x 10'	52,600

Above costs are for full-capacity beam scales.
Add $860 for the registering type beam.

Septic Tanks

2 bedroom home with 1,200 gallon tank	$2,210
3 bedroom home with 1,500 gallon tank	2,330
4 bedroom home with 2,000 gallon tank	2,475

Bulk Feed Tanks

Size and Type	Cost
5 Ton	$2,270
9 Ton	3,210
10.5 Ton	3,415
13 Ton	3,760
15 Ton	4,425
20 Ton	5,635
25 Ton	6,160
31 Ton	7,100
34 Ton	7,435
40 Ton	8,585
45 Ton	9,850
60 Ton	11,030

Tanks are equipped with a scissor-type opening chute

Domestic Water Systems.
Submersible pump, installed at 105' depth. Add the costs below for well (with casing) and pressure tank (if installed.)

	Typical Installation		
	1/2 HP	3/4 HP	1 HP
Total cost	$2,405	$2,675	$3,140
Pressure tank size	82 gal.	82 gal.	120 gal.
Cost per ft. above or below 105' depth	$2.97	$3.33	$3.72
	1-1/2 HP	2 HP	3 HP
Total cost	$3,585	$4,555	$5,495
Pressure tank size	220 gal.	220 gal.	315 gal.
Cost per ft. above or below 105' depth	$3.88	$5.59	$7.54

6" wells average $37.47 per foot of depth
8" wells average $45.25 per foot or depth.

Pressure Tank Sizes and Installed Costs

42 gal. 16" dia. x 48" depth	$298 to $ 414
82 gal. 20" dia. x 60" depth	418 to 489
120 gal. 24" dia. x 60" depth	490 to 737
220 gal. 30" dia. x 72" depth	1,210 to 1,365
315 gal. 36" dia. x 72" depth	1,696 to 1,910
525 gal. 36" dia. x 120" depth	2,200 to 2,495

Typical Physical Lives in years for agricultural structures

Building Type	Good	Average	Low
Barns	40	30	20
Dairy barns	25	25	—
Dairy barns, low cost	—	20	20
Storage sheds	40	30	20
Poultry houses, modern	30	25	—
Poultry houses, conventional	—	25	20

To determine the useful life remaining, use the percent good table for residential structures on page 43.

Military Construction Costs

The Office of the Under Secretary of Defense prepared the following square foot guidelines to reflect the cost of military construction for fiscal 2010. The costs are based on construction of permanent facilities built on military bases worldwide. Use the "Construction Cost Indices" at the end of this section to adapt the square foot costs to any other area. The "Size Cost Adjustment Chart" should be used to determine the approximate cost of a structure larger or smaller than the typical size shown.

Included in these costs are all items of equipment which are permanently built-in or attached to the structure, including items with fixed utility connections.

The costs include items such as the following:

Furniture, cabinets and shelving, built-in.

Venetian blinds and shades.

Window screens and screen doors.

Elevators and escalators.

Drinking water coolers.

Telephone, fire alarm and intercom systems.

Theater seats.

Pneumatic tube systems.

Heating, ventilating and air conditioning installations.

Electrical generators and auxiliary gear.

Waste disposers such as incinerators.

Food preparation & serving equipment, built-in.

Raised flooring.

Hoods and vents.

Chapel pews and pulpit.

Refrigerators, built-in.

Laboratory furniture, built-in.

Cranes and hoists, built-in.

Dishwashers.

The costs listed are the estimated contract award costs, excluding contingencies, supervision, and administration. They include construction to the five-foot line only, but do not include the cost of outside utilities or other site improvements.

Figures listed do not include the cost of piles or other special foundations which are considered as an additional supporting item. The cost of air conditioning is included to the extent authorized by the Construction Criteria Manual.

The costs of equipment such as furniture and furnishings which are loose, portable, or can be detached from the structure without tools are excluded from the unit costs. The cost of permanently attached equipment related directly to the operating function for which the structure is being provided, such as technical, scientific, production and processing equipment, is normally excluded from these costs. The following items are excluded from the costs on the following page.

Furniture, loose.

Furnishings, including rugs, loose.

Filing cabinets and portable safes.

Office machines, portable.

Wall clocks, plug-in

Food preparation and serving equipment, including appliances, portable.

Training aids and equipment, including simulators.

Shop equipment.

Bowling lanes, including automatic pin spotting equipment, score table and players' seating.

Automatic data processing equipment.

Communications equipment.

Photographic equipment, portable.

Any operational equipment for which installation, mounting and connections are provided in building design and which are detachable without damage to the building or equipment.

Estimating Procedure

Determine the area relationship of the proposed building by dividing the gross area by the typical size as shown in the Square Foot Cost Table. Locate the quotient on the Area Relationship scale and trace vertically to the Factor Line, then trace horizontally to the Cost Relationship scale. This value is then multiplied by the unit cost in the Square Foot Cost Table and factored by the Construction Cost Index to determine the adjusted unit cost for the building.

Military Construction Costs

Facilities	Typical size Gross S.F.	Unit cost per S.F. FY 2011
Administrative office		
Multi-purpose	25,000	194.00
Data processing	21,000	283.00
Aircraft operations		
without tower	25,000	333.00
tower only	4,500	924.00
Applied instruction building		
General instruction	25,000	225.00
High Tech (Auto-Aid)	25,000	256.00
Barracks, dormitory		
(No Kitchenette equip)	99,500	203.00
Bowling alley, 8 lanes,	7,800	243.00
Chapel center	15,000	314.00
Commissary		
(sales store/equipment)	85,000	204.00
Family housing, U.S.	None	116.00
Family housing, outside U.S.	None	151.00
Family support		
Child development center	15,000	253.00
Education center	10,000	249.00
Youth center	15,000	241.00
Family service center	5,000	231.00
Fire and rescue station (airfield)	8,000	305.00
Fire Station, community	8,000	255.00
Hangars		
Maintenance/Gen. purpose	23,000	235.00
High bay Maintenance	35,000	248.00
Library	12,000	244.00
Main Exchange		
with mall service shops	80,000	165.00
Medical facility		
Station hospital	N/A	364.00
Regional medical center	N/A	394.00
Medical clinic	50,000	275.00
Dental clinic	20,000	346.00
Ambulatory clinic	30,000	320.00

Facilities	Typical size Gross S.F.	Unit cost per S.F. FY 2011
Dining facility		
(with kitchen equipment)	21,500	324.00
Operations building		
General purpose	25,000	204.00
Squadron	36,000	238.00
Physical fitness		
training center	30,000	231.00
Recreation center	20,000	241.00
Reserve Center	20,000	199.00
Satellite Communications center	6,000	728.00
Service club	22,500	331.00
School for dependents		
Elementary	None	209.00
Jr. high/middle	None	211.00
High school	None	222.00
Shops		
Vehicle maint. (wheeled)	30,000	206.00
Vehicle maint. (tracked)	25,000	226.00
Aircraft avionics	23,000	204.00
Installation maintenance	31,000	144.00
Parachute and dinghy	8,000	241.00
Aircraft machine shop	20,000	249.00
Storage facility		
Cold storage warehouse		
w/processing	11,000	180.00
Cold storage warehouse	6,000	241.00
General purpose warehouse		
low bay	40,000	105.00
General purpose warehouse		
high bay	100,000	121.00
General purpose magazine		
w/o crane	10,000	293.00
High Explosive magazine	5,000	305.00
Temporary lodging facility	30,000	210.00
Unaccompanied officers quarters	44,000	222.00

Size Cost Adjustment

Military Construction Cost Indices

State	Index
Alabama	**0.83**
Mobile	0.84
Montgomery	0.83
Anniston AD	0.83
Fort Rucker	0.81
Maxwell AFB	0.83
Mobile	0.84
Redstone Arsenal	0.85
Alaska	**1.84**
Anchorage	1.67
Clear AFB	2.13
EarecksonAFB	3.44
Eielson AFB	2.02
Elmendorf AFB	1.67
Fairbanks	2.00
Fort Greeley	2.14
Fort Richardson	1.67
Ft Wainwright	2.00
Arizona	**0.99**
Flagstaff	0.97
Tucson	1.01
Davis Monthan AFB	1.01
Fort Huachuca	1.14
Luke AFB	0.98
Yuma MCAS	1.15
Yuma PG	1.15
Arkansas	**0.87**
Fort Smith	0.85
Pine Bluff	0.89
Fort Chaffee	0.85
Little Rock AFB	0.85
Pine Bluff Arsenal	0.89
California	**1.19**
29 Palms MCB	1.35
San Diego	1.19
San Francisco	1.20
Beale AFB	1.22
Camp Pendleton MC	1.19
Centerville Beach	1.10
China Lake NWC	1.29
Concord	1.20
Edwards AFB	1.29
El Centro NAF	1.24
Ft Hunter Liggett	1.25
Fort Irwin	1.29
Los Angeles	1.12
March AFB	1.05
Monterey	1.16
Oakland AB	1.37
Point Magu	1.12
Port Sur	1.16
Port Hueneme	1.12
Riverbank AAP	1.14
San Bruno	1.20
San Clemente Island	1.90
Seal Beach	1.12
Sharpe AD	1.17
Sierra AD	1.27
Stockton	1.14
Travis AFB	1.24
Vandenberg AFB	1.22
Colorado	**1.05**
Buckley AFB	1.02
Colorado Springs	1.09
Denver	1.02
Air Force Academy	1.09
Cheyenne Mountain	1.16
Fort Carson	1.09
Peterson AFB	1.09
Pueblo AD	0.94
Rock Mountain ARS	1.02
Schriever AFS	1.16
Connecticut	**1.08**
Bridgeport	1.05
New London	1.10
New London area	1.10
Delaware	**0.98**
Dover	1.00
Wilmington	0.97
Dover AFB	1.00
Florida	**0.85**
Miami	0.90
Panama City	0.80
Cape Canaveral	0.97
Eglin AFB	0.82
Homestead AFB	0.90
Jacksonville area	0.93
Key West NAS	1.09
Mayport	0.93
McDill AFB	0.88
Orlando	0.84
Panama City area	0.80
Patrick AFB	0.98
Pensacola area	0.83
Tyndall AFB	0.80
Georgia	**0.85**
Albany	0.78
Albany area	0.82
Athens	0.84
Atlanta	0.91
Fort Benning	0.80
Fort Gillem	0.91
Fort Gordon	0.84
Fort McPherson	0.91
Fort Stewart	0.82
Robins AFB	0.82
Kings Bay	0.99
Moody AFB	0.85
Hawaii	**1.71**
Honolulu	1.67
Kaneohe Bay NAS	1.75
Barking Sand	1.74
Fort DeRussy	1.55
Fort Shafter	1.57
Hickam AFB	1.55
Kaneohe MCAS	1.75
Pearl Harbor	1.67
Pohakuloa	1.94
Schofield Barracks	1.66
Tripler AMC	1.68
Wheeler AFB	1.66
Ford Island	1.67
Idaho	**1.07**
Boise	1.00
Mtn Home	1.14
Mtn Home AFB	1.14
Illinois	**1.17**
Belleville	1.11
Chicago	1.22
Great Lakes NTC	1.26
Rock Island Arsenal	1.05
Scott AFB	1.19
Forest Park	1.22
Indiana	**0.97**
Indianapolis	0.99
Logansport	0.96
Crane NWSC	1.06
Fort Ben Harrison	1.04
Grissom AFB	1.02
Iowa	**1.05**
Burlington	1.11
Des Moines	1.00
Iowa AAP	1.16
Kansas	**0.93**
Manhattan	0.96
Wichita	0.91
Fort Leavenworth	1.05
Fort Riley	1.01
Kansas AAP	0.97
McConnell AFB	0.91
Kentucky	**0.94**
Lexington	0.91
Louisville	0.97
Fort Campbell	1.05
Fort Knox	1.07
Louisville NAS	0.97
Louisiana	**0.92**
New Orleans	0.94
Shreveport	0.89
Barksdal AFB	0.89
Fort Polk	0.89
Louisiana AAP	0.89
New Orleans AB	0.94
Maine	**1.06**
Bangor	1.07
Portland	1.05
Brunswick	1.05
Cutler Winter Harbor	1.01
Kittery/Portsmouth	1.06
Maryland	**0.98**
Baltimore	0.89
Lexington Park	1.08
Aberdeen PG	0.89
Andrews AFB	0.98
Fort Detrick	0.98
Fort Meade	0.98
Fort Ritchie	0.92
Harry Diamond Lab	0.98
Indian Head	0.96
Patuxent River	1.08
Annapolis	0.98
Bethesda	0.98
Cheltonham	0.98
Chesapeake Beach	0.90
Thurmont	1.08
Massachusetts	**1.11**
Boston	1.15
Fitchburg	1.08
Army M & M Lab	1.13
Fort Devens	1.15
Hanscomb AFB	1.21
Michigan	**1.16**
Detroit	1.18
Marquette	1.15
Detroit Arsenal	1.18
Minnesota	**1.07**
Duluth	1.10
Minneapolis	1.04
Mississippi	**0.86**
Biloxi	0.92
Columbus	0.81
Columbus AFB	0.81
Gulfport area	0.92
Keesler AFB	0.92
Meridian	0.95
Missouri	**0.98**
Kansas City	1.00
Sedalia	0.95
Fort Leonard Wood	1.09
Lake City AAP	1.04
St. Louis AAP	1.04
Whiteman AFB	1.01
Montana	**1.16**
Billings	1.16
Great Falls	1.15
Malmstrom AFB	1.15
Nebraska	**0.94**
Grand Island	0.88
Omaha	1.00
Cornhusker AAP	0.88
Offutt AFB	1.00
Nevada	**1.18**
Hawthorne	1.15
Las Vegas	1.21
Fallon	1.19
Hawthorne AAP	1.15
Nellis AFB	1.25
New Hampshire	**1.04**
Concord	1.05
Portsmouth	1.04
Portsmouth area	1.04
New Jersey	**1.18**
Newark	1.19
Trenton	1.17
Bayonne	1.21
Earle	1.21
Fort Dix	1.17
Fort Monmouth	1.16
Lakehurst	1.21
McGuire AFB	1.17
Picatinny Arsenal	1.23
New Mexico	**0.98**
Alamagordo	0.98
Albuquerque	0.99
Cannon AFB	1.06
Holloman AFB	0.98
Kirtland AFB	0.99
White Sands MR	1.03
New York	**1.08**
Albany	1.02
Buffalo	1.14
New York City	1.51
Fort Drum	1.15
Long Island	1.11
Scotia	1.02
USMA	1.40
Watervliet AFS	1.02
Niagara	1.14
North Carolina	**0.86**
Fayetteville	0.88
Greensboro	0.84
Camp Lejeune	0.94
Cherry Point	0.94
Fort Bragg	0.88
New River	0.94
Pope AFB	0.88
Seymour AFB	0.82
Sunny Point	0.91
North Dakota	**1.05**
Grand Forks	1.01
Minot	1.10
Ohio	**0.99**
Dayton	0.97
Youngstown	1.00
Ravenna AAP	1.03
Wright-Patterson	0.97
Oklahoma	**0.90**
Lawton	0.91
Oklahoma City	0.89
Altus AFB	0.98
Fort Sill	0.91
McAlester AAP	0.84
Tinker AFB	0.89
Vance AFB	0.91
Oregon	**1.10**
Pendleton	1.11
Portland	1.08
Umatilla AD	1.24
Pennsylvania	**1.03**
Philadelphia	1.08
Pittsburgh	0.98
Carlisle Barracks	0.93
Indiantown Gap MR	1.00
Letterkenny AD	0.99
Mechanicsburg	0.93
New Cumberland	0.93
Philadelphia area	1.08
Tobyhanna AD	1.05
Warminster	1.06
Willow Grove	1.06
Rhode Island	**1.06**
Newport	1.09
Providence	1.03
South Carolina	**0.86**
Charleston	0.88
Columbia	0.84
Beaufort	1.04
Charleston AFB	0.88
Fort Jackson	0.84
Shaw AFB	0.82
South Dakota	**0.93**
Rapid City	0.91
Sioux Falls	0.95
Ellsworth AFB	0.91
Tennessee	**0.87**
Chattanooga	0.83
Memphis	0.91
Volunteer AAP	0.90
Arnold AFS	0.87
Memphis NAS	0.99
Texas	**0.82**
San Angelo	0.81
San Antonio	0.83
Brooks AFB	0.83
Camp Bullis	0.83
Corpus Christi	0.90
Dallas	0.88
Dyess AFB	0.97
Fort Bliss	0.91
Fort Hood	0.85
Fort Sam Houston	0.83
Fort Worth	0.88
Goodfellow AFB	0.81
Ingleside NS	0.94
Kingville area	0.91
Lackland AFB	0.83
Laughlin AFB	0.88
Lone Star AAP	0.89
Longhorn AAP	0.80
Randolph AFB	0.83
Red River AD	0.89
Sheppard AFB	0.94
Utah	**1.03**
Ogden	1.04
Salt Lake City	1.02
Dugway PG	1.05
Fort Douglas	1.02
Hill AFB	1.04
Tooele AD	1.05
Vermont	**0.91**
Burlington	0.90
Montpelier	0.92
Virginia	**0.92**
Norfolk	0.94
Richmond	0.92
Camp Peary	0.94
Chesapeake	0.94
Dahlgren	0.98
Fort A.P. Hill	0.90
Fort Belvoir	0.98
Fort Eustis	0.94
Fort Lee	0.94
Fort Monroe	0.94
Fort Myer	0.98
Fort Pickett	0.94
Fort Story	0.94
Quantico	0.98
Radford AAP	0.94
Vint Hill Farms	0.90
Wallops Island	1.12
Langley AFB	0.94
Washington	**1.06**
Bangor	1.16
Everett	1.11
Spokane	1.06
Tacoma	1.06
Bremerton	1.16
Fairchild AFB	1.06
Fort Lewis	1.06
Indian Head	1.16
McChord AFB	1.06
Silverdale	1.16
Whidbey Island	1.27
Yakima Firing Range	1.07
West Virginia	**0.95**
Bluefield	0.93
Charleston	0.97
Sugar Grove	1.43
Wisconsin	**1.13**
Madison	1.14
Milwaukee	1.12
Badger AAP	1.22
Fort McCoy	1.18
Wyoming	**1.01**
Casper	0.98
Cheyenne	1.04
F.E.Warren AFB	1.04
Washington DC	**0.98**
Fort McNair	0.98
Walter Reed AMC	0.98
Bolling AFB	0.98

Index

Practical References for Builders

National Construction Estimator

Current building costs for residential, commercial, and industrial construction. Estimated prices for every common building material. Provides manhours, recommended crew, and gives the labor cost for installation. Includes a CD-ROM with an electronic version of the book with *National Estimator*, a stand-alone *Windows*™ estimating program, plus an interactive multimedia video that shows how to use the disk to compile construction cost estimates.
672 pages, 8½ x 11, $72.50. Revised annually

Getting Financing & Developing Land

Developing land is a major leap for most builders — yet that's where the big money is made. This book gives you the practical knowledge you need to make that leap. Learn how to prepare a market study, select a building site, obtain financing, guide your plans through approval, and then control your building costs so you can ensure yourself a good profit. Includes a CD-ROM with forms, checklists, and a sample business plan you can customize and use to help you sell your idea to lenders and investors.
232 pages, 8½ x 11, $39.00

Construction Forms for Contractors

This practical guide contains 78 useful forms, letters and checklists, guaranteed to help you streamline your office, organize your jobsites, gather and manage records and documents, keep a handle on your subs, reduce estimating errors, administer change orders and lien issues, monitor crew productivity, track your equipment use, and more. Includes accounting forms, change order forms, forms for customers, estimating forms, field work forms, HR forms, lien forms, office forms, bids and proposals, subcontracts, and more. All are also on the CD-ROM included, in *Excel* spreadsheets, as formatted Rich Text that you can fill out on your computer, and as PDFs.
360 pages, 8½ x 11, $48.50

Contractor's Guide to Change Orders

This book gives you the ammunition you need to keep contract disputes from robbing you of your profit. You'll learn how to identify trouble spots in your contract, plans, specifications and site; negotiate and resolve change order disputes, and collect facts for evidence to support your claims. You'll also find detailed checklists to organize your procedures, field-tested sample forms and worksheets ready for duplication, and various professional letters for almost any situation.
382 pages, 8½ x 11, $79.00

Drafting House Plans

Here you'll find step-by-step instructions for drawing a complete set of house plans for a one-story house, an addition to an existing house, or a remodeling project. This book shows how to visualize spatial relationships, use architectural scales and symbols, sketch preliminary drawings, develop detailed floor plans and exterior elevations, and prepare a final plot plan. It even includes code-approved joist and rafter spans and how to make sure that drawings meet code requirements. **192 pages, 8½ x 11, $34.95**

Journeyman Electrician's Preparation & Study Guide

This is not only a great study guide filled with sample electrician's exam questions — it teaches you how to quickly turn to the code section that answers the questions. Most electrician's exams give you about 2 minutes per question — not enough time to browse through 800 pages of fine print looking for each answer. This manual, based on the 2008 and 2011 *NEC* editions, explains how the Code is organized, so you understand where the information you need is located. Then it shows how to rearrange and tab your copy of the Code to streamline your search efforts. Next, you learn a step-by-step search procedure, in which you're shown how to analyze the question to determine its subject, know where to look in the index, find the exact article, then turn right to the Code section that answers your question. **96 pages, 8½ x 11, $34.00**

CD Estimator

If your computer has *Windows*™ and a CD-ROM drive, CD Estimator puts at your fingertips over 150,000 construction costs for new construction, remodeling, renovation & insurance repair, home improvement, framing & finish carpentry, electrical, concrete & masonry, painting, earthwork and heavy equipment, and plumbing & HVAC. Quarterly cost updates are available at no charge on the Internet. You'll also have the *National Estimator* program — a stand-alone estimating program for *Windows*™ that *Remodeling* magazine called a "computer wiz," and *Job Cost Wizard*, a program that lets you export your estimates to QuickBooks Pro for actual job costing. A 60-minute interactive video teaches you how to use this CD-ROM to estimate construction costs. And to top it off, to help you create professional-looking estimates, the disk includes over 40 construction estimating and bidding forms in a format that's perfect for nearly any *Windows*™ word processing or spreadsheet program. **CD Estimator is $108.50**

Residential Property Inspection Reports on CD-ROM

This CD-ROM contains 50 pages of property inspection forms in both Rich Text and PDF formats. You can easily customize each form with your logo and address, and use them for your home inspections. Use the CD-ROM to write your inspections with your word processor, print them, and save copies for your records. Includes inspection forms for grounds and exterior, foundations, garages and carports, roofs and attics, pools and spas, electrical, plumbing, and HVAC, living rooms, family rooms, dens, studies, kitchens, breakfast rooms, dining rooms, hallways, stairways, entries, laundry rooms. **$79.95**

Insurance Restoration Contracting: Startup to Success

Insurance restoration — the repair of buildings damaged by water, fire, smoke, storms, vandalism and other disasters — is an exciting field of construction that provides lucrative work that's immune to economic downturns. And, with insurance companies funding the repairs, your payment is virtually guaranteed. But this type of work requires special knowledge and equipment, and that's what you'll learn about in this book. It covers fire repairs and smoke damage, water losses and specialized drying methods, mold remediation, content restoration, even damage to mobile and manufactured homes. You'll also find information on equipment needs, training classes, estimating books and software, and how restoration leads to lucrative remodeling jobs. It covers all you need to know to start and succeed as the restoration contractor that both homeowners and insurance companies call on first for the best jobs. **640 pages, 8½ x 11, $69.00**

Stained Concrete Interior Floors

Turn concrete slabs into works of art. This book shows you concrete design options, how to estimate costs, and even how to sell your services and write contracts for floor staining. Large color photos show how to correct problem floors, test your stain before beginning, apply dyes, grouts and sealers, and maintain stained concrete floors. In addition, you'll find information on specialty techniques and the tools you'll need for the job. Includes resources and websites for tools, supplies, equipment and training to help you become a concrete floor staining "pro." Full of charts, helpful hints and step-by-step instructions that should help you make extra income as a concrete floor staining expert. **100 pages, 8½ x 11, $35.00**

Guide to Stamped Concrete

Become a concrete stamping expert with the practical tips in this book. Here you'll find hundreds of ideas and sources for stamping designs. You'll learn of site conditions affecting stamped concrete and how to avoid problems. Shows everything from preparing the subgrade to erecting forms, installing reinforcement, and placing the concrete. Gives different methods of stamping concrete, coloring stamped concrete, applying color hardener and release agents, installing expansion joints, and special techniques for finishing and sealing the concrete. Shows how to improve the durability of stamped concrete, and how to fix minor flaws. Explains how to write a fair contract for the work you perform and how to determine what to charge your customers for the finished job. **142 pages, 8½ x 11, $45.00**

Craftsman's Construction Installation Encyclopedia

Step-by-step installation instructions for just about any residential construction, remodeling or repair task, arranged alphabetically, from *Acoustic tile* to *Wood flooring*. Includes hundreds of illustrations that show how to build, install, or remodel each part of the job, as well as manhour tables for each work item so you can estimate and bid with confidence. Also includes a CD-ROM with all the material in the book, handy look-up features, and the ability to capture and print out for your crew the instructions and diagrams for any job. **792 pages, 8½ x 11, $65.00**

Contractor's Plain-English Legal Guide

For today's contractors, legal problems are like snakes in the swamp — you might not see them, but you know they're there. This book tells you where the snakes are hiding and directs you to the safe path. With the directions in this easy-to-read handbook you're less likely to need a $200-an-hour lawyer. Includes simple directions for starting your business, writing contracts that cover just about any eventuality, collecting what's owed you, filing liens, protecting yourself from unethical subcontractors, and more. For about the price of 15 minutes in a lawyer's office, you'll have a guide that will make many of those visits unnecessary. Includes a CD-ROM with blank copies of all the forms and contracts in the book. **272 pages, 8½ x 11, $49.50**

Contractor's State License Guide — Law & Business Exam

Here you'll find all the information required for the law and business examination for the State of California: how to answer questions on employee issues, contracts, job management, safety, insurance, bookkeeping, estimating, bid procedures, licensing, mechanic's liens, and building codes. Includes sample exams to help you find the areas you need more work on. Designed for the California Contractor Exam, but should help raise your score on any state's contractor exam. **462 pages, 8½ x 11, $99.95**

Estimating Home Building Costs, Revised

Estimate every phase of residential construction from site costs to the profit margin you include in your bid. Shows how to keep track of manhours and make accurate labor cost estimates for site clearing and excavation, footings, foundations, framing and sheathing finishes, electrical, plumbing, and more. Provides and explains sample cost estimate worksheets with complete instructions for each job phase. This practical guide to estimating home construction costs has been updated with digital Excel estimating forms and worksheets that ensure accurate and complete estimates for your residential projects. Enter your project information on the worksheets and Excel automatically totals each material and labor cost from every stage of construction to a final cost estimate worksheet. Load the enclosed CD-ROM into your computer and create your own estimate as you follow along with the step-by-step techniques in this book. **336 pages, 8½ x 11, $38.00**

Residential Construction Performance Guidelines, 4ᵗʰ Ed.

Created and reviewed by more than 300 builders and remodelers, this guide gives cut-and-dried construction standards that apply to new construction and remodeling. It defines corrective action necessary to bring all construction up to standards. Standards are listed for sitework, foundations, interior concrete slabs, basement and crawl spaces for block walls and poured walls, wood-floor framing, beams, columns and posts, plywood and joists, walls, wall insulation, windows, doors, exterior finishes and trim, roofs, roof sheathing, roof installation and leaks, plumbing, sanitary and sewer systems, electrical, interior climate control, HVAC systems, cabinets and countertops, floor finishes and more. **120 pages, 6½ x 8½, $44.95**

Estimating & Bidding for Builders & Remodelers

This 5th edition has all the information you need for estimating and bidding new construction and home improvement projects. It shows how to select jobs that will be profitable, do a labor and materials take-off from the plans, calculate overhead and figure your markup, and schedule the work. Includes a CD with an easy-to-use construction estimating program and a database of 50,000 current labor and material cost estimates for new construction and home improvement work, with area modifiers for every zip code. Price updates on the Web are free and automatic. **272 pages, 8½ x 11, $89.50**

Construction Contract Writer

Relying on a "one-size-fits-all" boilerplate construction contract to fit your jobs can be dangerous — almost as dangerous as a handshake agreement. *Construction Contract Writer* lets you draft a contract in minutes that precisely fits your needs and the particular job, and meets both state and federal requirements. You just answer a series of questions — like an interview — to construct a legal contract for each project you take on. Anticipate where disputes could arise and settle them in the contract before they happen. Include the warranty protection you intend, the payment schedule, and create subcontracts from the prime contract by just clicking a box. Includes a feedback button to an attorney on the Craftsman staff to help should you get stumped — *No extra charge*. **$99.95**. Download *Construction Contract Writer* at http://www.constructioncontractwriter.com

Estimating With Microsoft *Excel*, 3ʳᵈ Ed.

Most builders estimate with *Excel* because it's easy to learn, quick to use, and can be customized to your style of estimating. Here you'll find step-by-step instructions on how to create your own customized automated spreadsheet estimating program for use with *Excel*. You'll learn how to use the magic of *Excel* to create detail sheets, cost breakdown summaries, and links. You'll put this all to use in estimating concrete, rebar, permit fees, and roofing. You can even create your own macros. Includes a CD-ROM that illustrates examples in the book and provides you with templates you can use to set up your own estimating system. **148 pages, 7 x 9, $44.95**

Construction Estimating Reference Data

Provides the 300 most useful manhour tables for practically every item of construction. Labor requirements are listed for sitework, concrete work, masonry, steel, carpentry, thermal and moisture protection, doors and windows, finishes, mechanical and electrical. Each section details the work being estimated and gives appropriate crew size and equipment needed. Includes a CD-ROM with an electronic version of the book with *National Estimator*, a stand-alone *Windows*™ estimating program, plus an interactive multimedia video that shows how to use the disk to compile construction cost estimates.
432 pages, 11 x 8½, $39.50

Masonry & Concrete Construction Revised

Shows on-site preplanning and layout through the construction of footings, foundations, walls, fireplaces and chimneys. An added appendix on safety regulations, with a condensed OSHA reference. Improved bid-winning estimating techniques. The emphasis is on integrating new techniques and materials with tried-and-true methods. Includes information on cement and mortar types, mixes, coloring agents and additives, and suggestions on when, where and how to use them; calculating footing and foundation loads, with reference tables and formulas; forming materials and systems; pouring and reinforcing concrete slabs and flatwork; block and brick wall construction, with seismic requirements; crack control, masonry veneer construction, brick floors and pavements, design considerations and materials; cleaning, painting and repairing all types of masonry. **304 pages, 8½ x 11, $37.75**

Standard Estimating Practice

Estimating isn't always an easy job. Sometimes snap decisions can produce negative long-term effects. This book was designed by the American Society of Professional Estimators as a set of standards to guide professional estimators. It's intended to help every estimator develop estimates that are uniform and verifiable. Every step that should be included in the estimate is listed, as well as aspects in the plans to consider when you're estimating a job, and what you should look for that may not be included. The result should help you produce more consistently accurate estimates.
506 pages, 8½ x 11, $89.00

Construction Estimating

This extremely well-organized book shows the best and easiest way to estimate materials for room additions or residential structures. It gives estimating tables and procedures needed to make a fast, accurate, and complete material list of the structural members found in wood- and steel-framed buildings. This book is divided into 72 units, each of them covering a separate element in the estimating procedure. Covers estimating foundations, floor framing, wall framing, ceiling framing, roof framing, roofing materials, exterior and interior finish materials, hardware, steel joist floor framing, steel stud framing, and steel ceiling joist and rafter framing. **496 pages, 8½ x 11, $49.50**

Residential Wiring to the 2008 *NEC*

This completely revised manual explains in simple terms how to install rough and finish wiring in new construction, alterations, and additions. It takes you from basic electrical theory to current wiring methods that comply with the 2008 *National Electrical Code*. You'll find complete instructions on troubleshooting and repairs of existing wiring, and how to extend service into additions and remodels. Hundreds of drawings and photos show you the tools and gauges you need, and how to plan and install the wiring. Includes demand factors, circuit loads, the formulas you need, and over 20 pages of the most-needed 2008 *NEC* tables to help your wiring pass inspection the first time. Includes a CD-ROM with an Interactive Study Center that helps you retain what you've learned, and study for the electrician's exam. Also on the CD is the entire book in PDF format, with easy search features so you can quickly find answers to your residential wiring questions.
304 pages, 8½ x 11, $42.00

Building Contractor's Exam Preparation Guide

Passing today's contractor's exams can be a major task. This book shows you how to study, how questions are likely to be worded, and the kinds of choices usually given for answers. Includes sample questions from actual state, county, and city examinations, plus a sample exam to practice on. This book isn't a substitute for the study material that your testing board recommends, but it will help prepare you for the types of questions — and their correct answers — that are likely to appear on the actual exam. Knowing how to answer these questions, as well as what to expect from the exam, can greatly increase your chances of passing.
320 pages, 8½ x 11, $35.00

Contractor's State License Guide – 'B' General Building Exam

Everything you need to pass the General Building License exam for the State of California. You'll find hundreds of multiple choice questions and answers to help you pass the state exam. Originally written for the State of California, this exam guide can be used to help you raise your score on any state's licensing exam. Includes two books: a study guide and a sample test.
350 pages, 8½ x 11, $99.00

2011 *National Electrical Code*

This new electrical code incorporates sweeping improvements to make the code more functional and user-friendly. Here you'll find the essential foundation for electrical code requirements for the 21st century. With hundreds of significant and widespread changes, this 2011 *NEC* contains all the latest electrical technologies, recently-developed techniques, and enhanced safety standards for electrical work. This is the standard all electricians are required to know, even if it hasn't yet been adopted by their local or state jurisdictions. **880 pages, 8½ x 11, $85.00**

Also available: **2008 *National Electrical Code*, $75.00**

2011 Ugly's Electrical Reference

The most popular pocket-sized electrical book in America. Ugly's is used by electricians, engineers, designers and maintenance workers, instructors and the military. This unique book explains bending conduit, National Electrical Code tables, wiring configurations, complex electrical formulas, and much more. This 2011 edition contains all the electrical material that has made this reference famous, but also reflects 2011 *NEC* changes and new color-coded wiring diagrams. Also includes updated coverage of Alternative Energy, Combination Circuits, Conductor Properties, Conduit Bending, Conversion Tables, Insulation Charts, Metric System, Ohm's Law, and a General First Aid Section.
198 pages, 4 x 6, $18.95

Also available: **2008 Ugly's Electrical Reference, $16.95**

Builder's Guide to Accounting Revised

Step-by-step, easy-to-follow guidelines for setting up and maintaining records for your building business. This practical guide to all accounting methods shows how to meet state and federal accounting requirements, explains the new depreciation rules, and describes how the Tax Reform Act can affect the way you keep records. Full of charts, diagrams, simple directions and examples to help you keep track of where your money is going. Recommended reading for many state contractor's exams. Each chapter ends with a set of test questions, and a CD-ROM included FREE has all the questions in interactive self-test software. Use the Study Mode to make studying for the exam much easier, and Exam Mode to practice your skills.
360 pages, 8½ x 11, $35.50

Home Builders' Jobsite Codes 2009

A spiral-bound, quick reference to the 2009 *International Residential Code* that's filled with easy-to-read and understand code requirements for every aspect of residential construction. This user-friendly guide through the morass of the code is packed with illustrations, tables, and figures, to illuminate your path to inspection and approval. **281 pages, 5½ x 8½, $28.95**

Pipe & Excavation Contracting Revised

This popular manual has been updated and improved to bring it more current with modern earthmoving and trenching equipment, refined excavation techniques, stricter safety rules, and improved materials. Shows how to read plans and compute quantities for both trench and surface excavation, figure crew and equipment productivity rates, estimate unit costs, bid the work, and get the bonds you need. Learn how to choose the right equipment for each job, use GPS, how to lay all types of water and sewer pipe, work on steep slopes or in high groundwater, efficiently remove asphalt and rock, and the various pipe, joints and fittings now available. Explains how to switch your business to excavation work when you don't have pipe contracts, and how to avoid the pitfalls that can wipe out your profits on any job. **328 pages, 8½ x 11, $35.00**

Basic Engineering for Builders

This book is for you if you've ever been stumped by an engineering problem on the job, yet wanted to avoid the expense of hiring a qualified engineer. Here you'll find engineering principles explained in non-technical language and practical methods for applying them on the job. With the help of this book you'll be able to understand engineering functions in the plans and how to meet the requirements, how to get permits issued without the help of an engineer, and anticipate requirements for concrete, steel, wood and masonry. See why you sometimes have to hire an engineer and what you can undertake yourself: surveying, concrete, lumber loads and stresses, steel, masonry, plumbing, and HVAC systems. This book is designed to help you, the builder, save money by understanding engineering principles that you can incorporate into the jobs you bid. **400 pages, 8½ x 11, $39.50**

Basic Lumber Engineering for Builders

Beam and lumber requirements for many jobs aren't always clear, especially with changing building codes and lumber products. Most of the time you rely on your own "rules of thumb" when figuring spans or lumber engineering. This book can help you fill the gap between what you can find in the building code span tables and what you need to pay a certified engineer to do. With its large, clear illustrations and examples, this book shows you how to figure stresses for pre-engineered wood or wood structural members, how to calculate loads, and how to design your own girders, joists and beams. Included FREE with the book — an easy-to-use limited version of NorthBridge Software's *Wood Beam Sizing* program. **272 pages, 8½ x 11, $38.00**

Commercial Metal Stud Framing

Framing commercial jobs can be more lucrative than residential work. But most commercial jobs require some form of metal stud framing. This book teaches step-by-step, with hundreds of job site photos, high-speed metal stud framing that works in both residential and commercial construction. It describes the special tools you'll need, how to use them effectively, and the material and equipment you'll be working with. You'll find the shortcuts, tips and tricks-of-the-trade that take most steel framers years on the job to discover. Shows how to set up a crew to maintain a rhythm that will speed progress faster than any wood framing job. If you've framed with wood, this book will teach you how to be one of the few top-notch metal stud framers in both commercial and residential construction. **208 pages, 8½ x 11, $45.00**

Easy Scheduling

Easy Scheduling presents you with a complete set of "real world" scheduling tools that are specifically tailored to meet the needs of small- to medium-sized construction businesses. Step by step, it shows you how to use *Microsoft Project* to build a schedule that will synchronize everyone's efforts into an organized system that becomes the foundation of all planning and communication for all your jobs. You'll see how to establish realistic project goals, set checkpoints, activities, relationships and time estimates for each task, as well as establish priorities. You'll learn how to create a project flowchart to keep everyone focused and on track, and see how to use CSI (Construction Specification Institute) coding to organize and sort tasks, methods, and materials across multiple projects. If you want an easy way to schedule your jobs, *Microsoft Project* and *Easy Scheduling* is the answer for you. (Does not include *Microsoft Project*.) Published by BNI. **316 pages, 8½ x 11, $59.95**

Steel-Frame House Construction

Framing with steel has obvious advantages over wood, yet building with steel requires new skills that can present challenges to the wood builder. This book explains the secrets of steel framing techniques for building homes, whether pre-engineered or built stick by stick. It shows you the techniques, the tools, the materials, and how you can make it happen. Includes hundreds of photos and illustrations, plus a FREE download with steel framing details and a database of steel materials and manhours, with an estimating program. **320 pages, 8½ x 11, $39.75**

Code Check Complete

Every essential building, electrical and mechanical code requirement you're likely to encounter when building or remodeling residential and light commercial structures. Comes spiral-bound, with over 400 drawings that answer your code questions with up-to-date answers. Includes quick-glance summaries to alert you to important code changes. Compiled by code-certified building/home inspectors, this new book is like having four guides in one, big, easy-to-understand guide. **240 pages, 6½ x 8½, $40.00**

Concrete Construction

Just when you think you know all there is about concrete, many new innovations create faster, more efficient ways to do the work. This comprehensive concrete manual has both the tried-and-tested methods and materials, and more recent innovations. It covers everything you need to know about concrete, along with Styrofoam forming systems, fiber reinforcing adjuncts, and some architectural innovations, like architectural foam elements, that can help you offer more in the jobs you bid on. Every chapter provides detailed, step-by-step instructions for each task, with hundreds of photographs and drawings that show exactly how the work is done. To keep your jobs organized, there are checklists for each stage of the concrete work, from planning, to finishing and protecting your pours. Whether you're doing residential or commercial work, this manual has the instructions, illustrations, charts, estimating data, rules of thumb and examples every contractor can apply on their concrete jobs. **288 pages, 8½ x 11, $28.75**

Planning Drain, Waste & Vent Systems

How to design plumbing systems in residential, commercial, and industrial buildings. Covers designing systems that meet code requirements for homes, commercial buildings, private sewage disposal systems, and even mobile home parks. Includes relevant code sections and many illustrations to guide you through what the code requires in designing drainage, waste, and vent systems. **202 pages, 8½ x 11, $29.95**

Standard Plans For Public Works Construction, 2009 Ed.

This visual reference, also updated and revised to comply with the Federal regulations for metric documentation, is the graphic companion to the "Greenbook." Hundreds of detailed drawings, cross sections, design criteria, and dimensions graphically depict all aspects of public works construction. Every dimension is listed in both feet/inches and metric equivalents. This book, along with the "Greenbook," sets the standard for quality and uniformity in public works construction. **375 pages, 8½ x 11, $87.95**

Business Letters for the Construction Industry

Here you'll find over 100 professionally-written model letters for virtually every situation. Put your business in the best possible light with a well-written letter — especially when you can use that letter to improve a bad situation. Use these letters over and over again to resolve disputes, win new clients, clarify proposals, coordinate with architects, subcontractors, owners, and insurers, schedule meetings and inspections, and to respond to complaints or difficult situations. Included are letters responding to threats of legal action, of commendation to workers, of job performance, apology for defective or delayed work; letters for justification of change orders and price increases; letters explaining your insurance liability, drug testing, injury at work, overtime, equipment use, and more. Practically every letter you'll have to write is in this book, already written, and available on *MS-Word* on the CD-ROM enclosed. Just load the letter you need, change a few phrases, print out and send, or e-mail, and you're free to spend your time on more productive endeavors. **376 pages, 8½ x 11, $59.95**

Sweets Green Building Square Foot Costbook 2012

If your customers are demanding their buildings meet LEED® green building standards, estimating construction costs can represent quite a challenge — especially if you've never built a green building before. This new book contains square foot prices for over 50 different types of green buildings, broken down by construction division. It includes articles on the cost of LEED® certification, green roof design, and the goals of other LEED® certified builders throughout the U.S. All of the costs in the book have been carefully adjusted for 2012. Included are government projects, residential and commercial buildings, schools and libraries, and medical and recreational facilities, reflecting the vast array of "green" materials and technologies used in construction today. If the unknown costs of building green have kept you from bidding on jobs you could have had, you'll recover the cost of this book many times over in the future job bids you're sure to win. **198 pages, 8½ x 11, $53.95. Published by Building News Inc.**

Estimating Excavation

How to calculate the amount of dirt you'll have to move and the cost of owning and operating the machines you'll do it with. Detailed, step-by-step instructions on how to assign bid prices to each part of the job, including labor and equipment costs. Also, the best ways to set up an organized and logical estimating system, take off from contour maps, estimate quantities in irregular areas, and figure your overhead. **448 pages, 8½ x 11, $39.50**

Architects, Contractors, Engineers, Guide to Construction Costs, 2012 Edition

Since 1969, architects, contractors and engineers alike have looked to the ACE (Architects, Contractors, Engineers) Guide to Construction Costs as a practical resource for all their construction needs. Whether the job is for general construction, remodeling, building maintenance, or repair, the ACE Guide to Construction Costs provides the most accurate and up-to-date data for material and installation costs, labor and equipment rates, and even adjusted allowances for overhead and profit. The Guide also breaks down all unit and summary costs for every type of structure ... all organized into construction divisions. It also includes prevailing wage rates for the 75 largest U.S. Metropolitan areas, square foot costs, Americans With Disabilities costs (ADA), production and demolition rates, energy factors, purchasing costs, equipment rental rates, and much more! **176 pages, 8½ x 11, $60.95**

Moving to Commercial Construction

In commercial work, a single job can keep you and your crews busy for a year or more. The profit percentages are higher, but so is the risk involved. This book takes you step-by-step through the process of setting up a successful commercial business: finding work, estimating and bidding, value engineering, getting through the submittal and shop drawing process, keeping a stable work force, controlling costs, and promoting your business. Explains the design/build and partnering business concepts and their advantage over the competitive bid process. Includes sample letters, contracts, checklists and forms that you can use in your business, plus a CD-ROM with blank copies in several word-processing formats for both Mac™ and PC computers. **256 pages, 8½ x 11, $42.00**

2009 Greenbook: Standard Specifications for Public Works Construction

The Greenbook gives approved standards for all types of public works construction — from the depth of paving on roads to the adhesive used on pavement markers. It standardizes public works plans and specs to provide guidelines for both cities and contractors so they can agree on construction practices used in public works. The book has been adopted by over 200 cities, counties, and agencies throughout the U.S. The 2009 edition is the 15th edition of this complete reference, providing uniform standards of quality and sound construction practice easily understood and used by engineers, public works officials, and contractors across the U.S. Includes hundreds of charts and tables. **450 pages, 8½ x 11, $76.50**

Contractor's Guide to *QuickBooks Pro* 2010

This user-friendly manual walks you through *QuickBooks Pro*'s detailed setup procedure and explains step-by-step how to create a first-rate accounting system. You'll learn in days, rather than weeks, how to use *QuickBooks Pro* to get your contracting business organized, with simple, fast accounting procedures. On the CD included with the book you'll find a *QuickBooks Pro* file for a construction company. Open it, enter your own company's data, and add info on your suppliers and subs. You also get a complete estimating program, including a database, and a job costing program that lets you export your estimates to *QuickBooks Pro*. It even includes many useful construction forms to use in your business. **344 pages, 8½ x 11, $57.00**

See checklist for other available editions.

Excavation & Grading Handbook Revised

The foreman's, superintendent's and operator's guide to highway, subdivision and pipeline jobs: how to read plans and survey stake markings, set grade, excavate, compact, pave and lay pipe on nearly any job. Includes hundreds of informative, on-the-job photos and diagrams that even experienced pros will find invaluable. This new edition has been completely revised to be current with state-of-the-art equipment usage and the most efficient excavating and grading techniques. You'll learn how to read topo maps, use a laser level, set crows feet, cut drainage channels, lay or remove asphaltic concrete, and use GPS and sonar for absolute precision. For those in training, each chapter has a set of self-test questions, and a Study Center CD-ROM included has all 250 questions in a simple interactive format to make learning easy and fun. **512 pages, 8½ x 11, $42.00**

Construction Surveying & Layout

A practical guide to simplified construction surveying. How to divide land, use a transit and tape to find a known point, draw an accurate survey map from your field notes, use topographic surveys, and the right way to level and set grade. You'll learn how to make a survey for any residential or commercial lot, driveway, road, or bridge — including how to figure cuts and fills and calculate excavation quantities. Use this guide to make your own surveys, or just read and verify the accuracy of surveys made by others. **256 pages, 8½ x 11, $51.95**

National Renovation & Insurance Repair Estimator

Current prices in dollars and cents for hard-to-find items needed on most insurance, repair, remodeling, and renovation jobs. All price items include labor, material, and equipment breakouts, plus special charts that tell you exactly how these costs are calculated. Includes a CD-ROM with an electronic version of the book with *National Estimator*, a stand-alone *Windows*™ estimating program, plus an interactive multimedia video that shows how to use the disk to compile construction cost estimates. **488 pages, 8½ x 11, $74.50. Revised annually**

The Contractor's Legal Kit

Stop "eating" the costs of bad designs, hidden conditions, and job surprises. Set ground rules that assign those costs to the rightful party ahead of time. And it's all in plain English, not "legalese." For less than the cost of an hour with a lawyer, you'll learn the exclusions to put in your agreements, why your insurance company may pay for your legal defense, and how to avoid liability for injuries to your sub and his employees. It also includes a FREE CD-ROM with contracts and forms you can customize for your own use. **352 pages, 8½ x 11, $69.95**

Building Code Compliance for Contractors & Inspectors

An answer book for both contractors and building inspectors, this manual explains what it takes to pass inspections under the 2009 *International Residential Code*. It includes a checklist for every trade, covering some of the most common reasons why inspectors reject residential work: footings, foundations, slabs, framing, sheathing, plumbing, electrical, HVAC, energy conservation and final inspection. The requirement for each item is explained, and the code section cited. Knowing in advance what the inspector wants to see gives you an (almost unfair) advantage. To pass inspection, do your own pre-inspection before the inspector arrives. If you're considering a career in code enforcement, this can be your guidebook. **8½ x 11, 232 pages, $32.50**
